129694

D1576504

ST. HELENS COMMUNITY LIBRARIES

3 8055 01077 0931

25.00

333.7

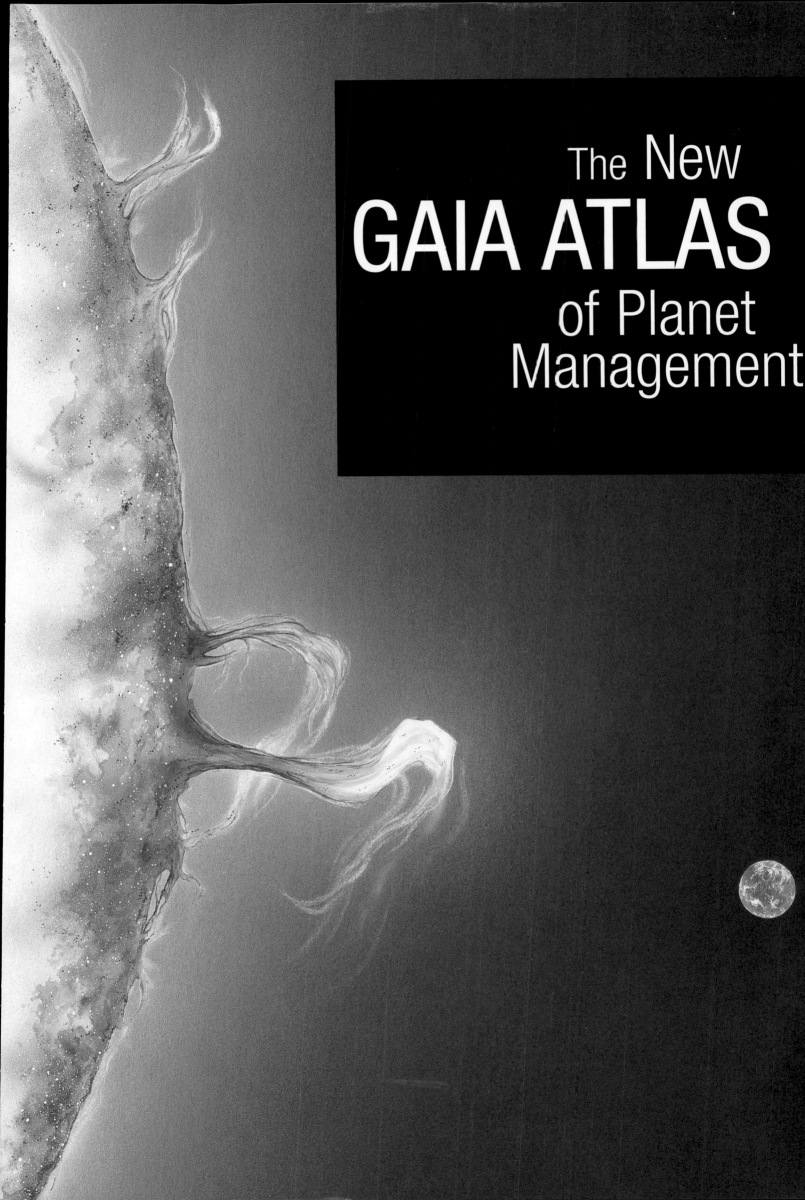

The New
GAIA ATLAS
of Planet
Management

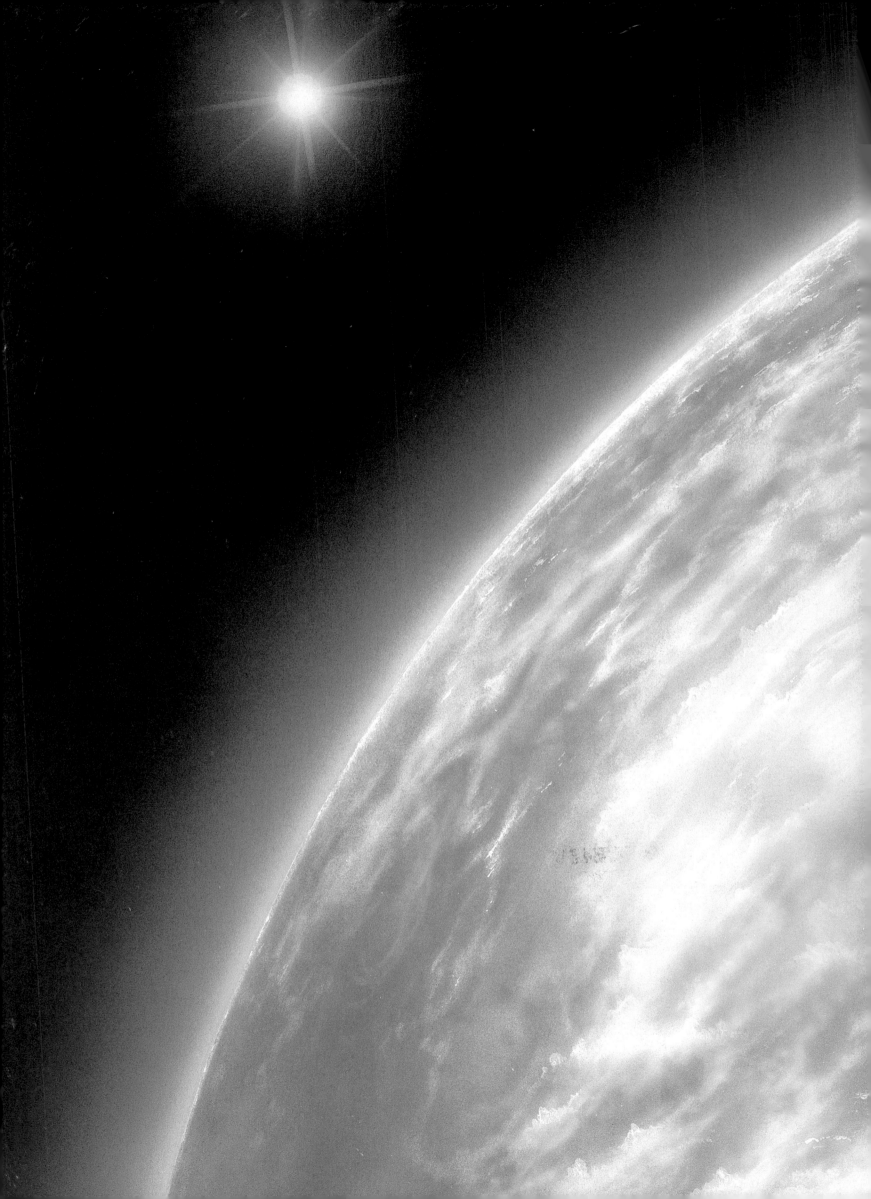

The New GAIA ATLAS of Planet Management

general editors

Norman Myers & Jennifer Kent

foreword by

Edward O. Wilson

NEWTON-LE-WILLOWS
LIBRARY
TEL: 01744 677886
01744 677887

Gaia Books

A GAIA ORIGINAL

Books from Gaia celebrate the vision of Gaia,
the self-sustaining living Earth, and seek to help
readers live in greater personal and planetary harmony.

Editorial	Pip Morgan
Design	Lucy Guenot
Illustrations for revised edition	Bill Donohoe
Production	Louise Hall
Picture research	Aruna Mathur
Text preparation,	
proofreading and index	Aardvark Editorial
	and Kelly Thompson
Direction	Patrick Nugent

 ® This is a Registered Trade Mark of Gaia Books

Copyright © 1984, 1993, 2005
Gaia Books is an imprint of Octopus Publishing Group
2–4 Heron Quays, London, E14 4JP

The right of Norman Myers and Jennifer Kent to be identified as
the authors of this work has been asserted in accordance
with Sections 77 and 78 of the Copyright, Designs
and Patents Act 1988, United Kingdom.

All rights reserved including the right of reproduction
in whole or in part in any form.

First published in the United Kingdom in 1985
by Pan Books Ltd, and in 1991and 1996 by Gaia Books Ltd.

ISBN 1-85675-209-7
EAN 9 781856 752091

This edition first published in 2005.
A catalogue record of this book is
available from the British Library.

Printed and bound in China

10 9 8 7 6 5 4 3 2 1

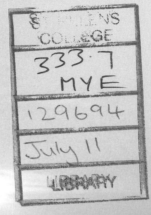
ST PHILLEN'S
COLLEGE
333.7
MYE
129694
July 11
LIBRARY

About this book

This is no ordinary atlas. It maps and analyses a living planet at a critical point in its history – as one species, our own, threatens to disrupt and exhaust its life-support systems. It charts the growing divisions in the human family. And it proposes that we have the chance to redirect our course, and become caretakers of our future.

The New Gaia Atlas of Planet Management is a first approach to this challenging task. It organizes the mass of available environmental data, statistical predictions, and often conflicting opinions and solutions into a simple, coherent structure. It is divided into seven sections: Land, Oceans, Elements, Evolution, Humankind, Civilization, and Management; each of these is considered from three perspectives: Potential resources, Crises, and Management alternatives.

This structure enables us to examine any critical area of concern and to weigh up: first, what it has to offer; second, where, how, and why things are obviously going wrong; and third, how we might set about putting things right, by applying a range of alternative strategies.

More than a structure for a book, this analytical formula offers one possible approach to planet management. We hope it will spur the rising global debate on our future prospects.

To those hundreds of people
whose work we have admired:
thank you for enabling us to join up all the pieces
that make the big picture.

To those hundreds of thousands of people
who chose to buy earlier editions of this book:
thank you for inspiring us to do it all again.

To those hundreds of millions of people
who endure life on a divided planet:
may you soon experience one-world living.

To those hundreds of billions of people of the future:
may this book help today's generation to leave a
better Gaian home for you all.

Norman Myers and Jennifer Kent

CONTENTS

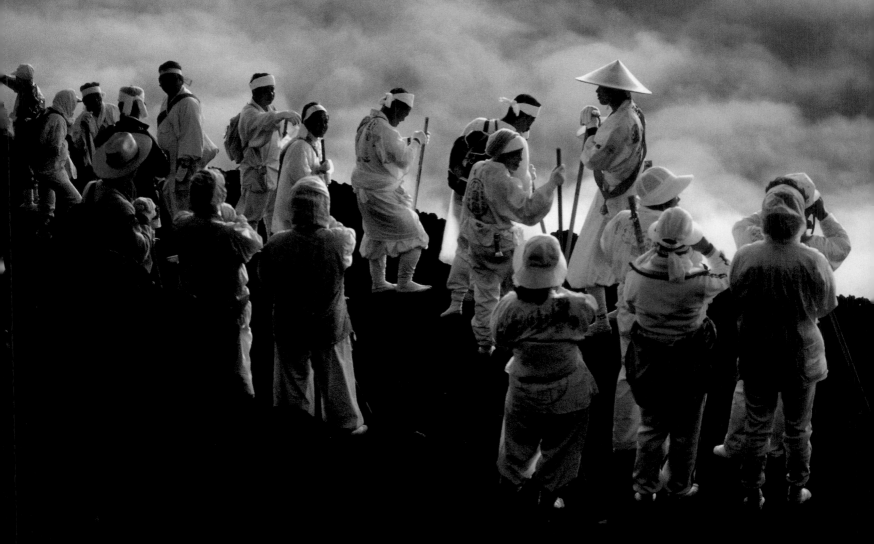

NEWTON-LE-WILLOWS
LIBRARY
TEL: 01744 677886
01744 677887

Foreword

by Edward O. Wilson
Professor at Harvard University, who ranks as a doyen of environmentalists in academia, as witness his many inspirational books, two of which have been awarded the Pulitzer Prize.

This atlas is a major contribution to an all-important subject. To understand both of these claims, consider what might be called the First Principle of Human Ecology: *Homo sapiens* is a species limited to a very small niche. Our minds may soar outwards to the edge of the universe and inwards to subatomic particles, but our bodies are locked inside a tiny envelope of physical and biological constraints. True, we have learned how to endure some of Earth's least hospitable environments, but only when enclosed within bubbles containing manufactured environments. Even there, slight malfunctions can be fatal and extended residences psychologically unbearable.

Fortunately, Earth provides a self-regulating bubble that sustains us indefinitely without any thought or contrivance of our own. Within this sheath exists the biosphere, the totality of all of life, a fragile membrane clinging to the face of the planet, and upon which we are absolutely dependent.

This perspective follows from what deserves to be called the First Principle of Human Evolution: we are a biological species in a biological world. Our physical and mental natures exhibit, to use Darwin's striking phrase, the indelible stamp of our origin. We belong in this biosphere, we were born here, we are closely suited to its exacting conditions, and not all of it either, but just parts of the more productive terrestrial sectors and climatic regions.

It follows inexorably that our self-interest is best served by not overly perturbing Earth's environment. This, the message of the *Gaia Atlas*, can be put another way by redefining environmental damage as that which alters our surroundings in any direction contrary to humanity's hereditary needs. We are not evolving into something new, as science fiction writers sometimes like to dream, and are highly unlikely to do so in the foreseeable future. Scientific knowledge knows no bounds, but human biology and emotion stay the same. As complex eukaryotic organisms we cannot, like bacteria, mutate to fit a spoiled environment. The human genome will attempt invasive genetic modification only at great risk.

The human genome is the code of human identity, and exquisitely well adapted to Earth's unspoiled environment. The disparity between our genetic and cultural evolution is the root of the problems of civilization. It has made modern humankind a potentially self-destructive chimera, a creature of hard-wired paleolithic emotions and medieval political systems, that are empowered by godlike science and technology.

It seems best, therefore, to be very conservative about the environment, at least until we get our own lives straightened out. And best to try to understand right now what we are doing to our planet and hence to ourselves. We are the first species to become a geophysical force, single-handedly altering Earth's atmosphere and climate. We have initiated the sixth great extinction spasm of geological history by the massive destruction of ecosystems and the loss of plant and animal species.

There is nothing inevitable about this mindless destruction. It can be slowed, halted, then (except for the extinction of biodiversity) reversed. The effort will not be unbearably expensive for the world economy. The amount needed as a single outlay, for example, to protect 25 of the most critically endangered ecosystems, plus core tropical forest wilderness areas in the Amazon and Congo Basins and New Guinea, has been estimated to be about $30 billion, which is one-thousandth of the annual World Domestic Product and also happens to be one-thousandth of the value of ecosystems services provided free each year by Earth's surviving natural ecosystems.

Such investments and other moves to create a green economy would result in immediate advances of energy and material conservation. That, when combined with the payout of the new technologies and products required, would more than cover the costs of stabilizing Earth's environment. Grateful generations to come would say that we were the ones who finally figured things out. We were the ones who settled our species down before we wrecked the planet.

Introduction

The fragile miracle

The sphere of rock which is our home originally coalesced from the dust of ancient stars. Orbiting the huge hydrogen furnace of the sun, bathed by radiant energy and the solar wind, the globe is white hot and molten beneath the crust: continents ride in a slow dance across its face, ocean floors spread. And between its dynamic surface and the vacuum of space, in a film that is thin beyond imagining, lies the fragile miracle we call the biosphere.

When the first astronauts circled the Earth, millions of listeners heard them describe the beauty of the planet, "like a blue pearl in space", and were caught up in a moment of unprecedented human revelation. Since then, much has been written about "Spaceship Earth" on whose finite resources we all depend. And the more we explore the solar system, the more singular we understand our world to be. The atmospheric mix of gases, for instance, is entirely different not only from that of nearby planets but from what would be predicted by Earth's own chemistry. This extremely unlikely state of affairs appears to have arisen alongside the evolution of life, and persisted, despite all possible accidental perturbations of cosmic travel, for perhaps two billion years. Life, by its very presence, is apparently creating and even maintaining the special conditions necessary for its own survival.

It was a group of space scientists devising life-detection experiments for other planets who first stumbled on this phenomenon of the self-sustaining biosphere – and named it Gaia, the living planet. Since then, we have begun to learn much more about the planetary life-support systems which rule our lives – sadly, mainly by disturbing them.

Within this life realm, every organism is linked, however tenuously, to every other. Microbe, plant, and animal, soil dweller and ocean swimmer, all are caught up in the cycling of energy and nutrients from sun, water, air, and earth. This global exchange system flows through various transport mechanisms, from ocean currents to climate patterns and winds; from animal travel to the processes of feeding, growth, and decay. Information, too, flows through the biosphere – reproduction transfers the store of genetic coding to new generations and creates new experiments as learning and communication occur between individuals. And throughout the life zone, change and diversity, specialization and intricate interdependence are found at every level.

It is with this remarkable planet, and what we are doing to it, and to ourselves, that this book is concerned. UFOs apart, we are unlikely to find another Gaia.

The protective atmosphere
Like the feathers of a bird, the layers of the atmosphere provide equable surface temperatures, shield life from the "rain" of cosmic particles, and block lethal ultraviolet radiation.

Exosphere

Ionosphere

Stratosphere
Troposphere

O_2

Photosynthesis

3,000°C
100 km down

Planetary life-support systems
The living world, or biosphere, stretches around our planet in a film much thinner than the dew on an apple. A hundred kilometres down beneath our feet, the globe is already white hot, at 3,000°C. Thirty kilometres up above our heads, the air is too thin and cold for survival. In between, the green world flowers, richest around the tropical zones where the ice age glaciations have never reached. Here, in the tropical forests and the shallow sunlit seas and reefs, much of Earth's living wealth of species is concentrated.

The Earth's green cover is a prerequisite for the rest of life. Plants alone, through the chemistry of photosynthesis, can use sunlight energy and convert it to the chemical energy animals need for survival. It was the emergence of photosynthesizing algae in the oceans which first released free oxygen into the atmosphere – a cataclysmic event for existing life-forms, but a pre-condition for present-day existence. The ocean microflora still supply 70% of our oxygen, and this in turn maintains the protective ozone layer in the upper atmosphere. The oceans act as a "sink" for carbon dioxide from the air.

Plant cover provides the basis of all food chains, mediates water cycles, stabilizes microclimate, and protects the living soil – the foundation of the biosphere. Soil micro-organisms and anaerobic microbes in the shallow muds of swamp and sea floor ceaselessly work to recycle decaying matter back into the nutrient system.

Temperature feedback

Earth's life-support systems are still little understood. Surface temperatures have remained suitable for life for many aeons, despite changes in solar flux. Feedback systems for temperature control are the levels of carbon dioxide and water vapour in the air – both affected by plant cover. Carbon dioxide acts as an insulator in the "greenhouse" effect (pp. 124–25). Another is Earth's "albedo" – its shininess. High albedo from light-covered areas cools the Earth. Most of Gaia's albedo value comes from cloud cover (influenced by vegetation), and from ice caps and oceans. Microflora in the oceans and plants on the land can darken or lighten these areas, thus altering their albedo. Atmospheric pollution raises carbon dioxide levels, while forest clearance and desertification raise albedo.

Ozone layer

Albedo effect

"Greenhouse" effect CO_2

N

O_2

CO_2

Earth without life

Water cycle

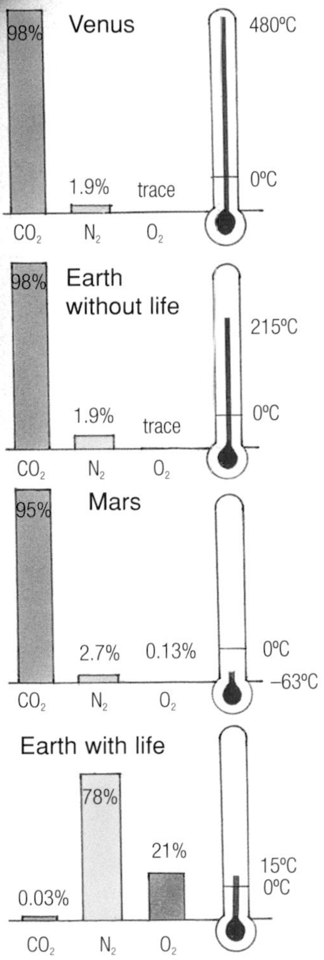

Venus

98%			480°C
	1.9%	trace	0°C
CO_2	N_2	O_2	

Earth without life

98%			215°C
	1.9%	trace	0°C
CO_2	N_2	O_2	

Mars

95%			
	2.7%	0.13%	0°C
CO_2	N_2	O_2	−63°C

Earth with life

	78%		
		21%	15°C
0.03%			0°C
CO_2	N_2	O_2	

The unique planet

The most remarkable characteristic of living matter is that it is self-organizing. In contrast with the overall trend towards disorder or "entropy" evident in the universe, life creates order from the materials around it, exporting waste in the process. Thus life is capable of influencing its environment.

When space scientists began devising life-detection experiments, one group suggested that a life-bearing planet might show an unexpected mix of gases in its atmosphere if life's chemistry were at work. Looking at Earth in this light, their predictions were borne out with a vengeance. Earth's mix of gases, and temperature, were hugely different from what they predicted for a "non-living" Earth, as well as from neighbouring planets (above). The fact that these conditions appeared to have arisen and persisted alongside life led to the Gaia hypothesis – the proposal that the biosphere, as a living organism, operates its own "life-support" systems through natural feedback mechanisms for its own long term benefit.

Accelerating evolution

Though we live in a largely humanized world of suburbs and cities, governments and wars, each of us carries within us the birth and death of stars, and the long flowering of Gaia.

Evolution is usually dated from the emergence of life, that "almost utterly improbable event with infinite opportunities of happening" (Jim Lovelock). But this event itself was a stage in a process that has continued since time, as we know it, began – when, some 15 billion years ago, the Big Bang sent pure energy flooding out into a waking universe.

As this energy dispersed and the universe cooled, a patterning set in, and stable "energy structures" emerged in a new order known as matter. Over billions of years, the particles, atoms, and elements of matter formed and were processed and reprocessed in the heart of stars, until a higher order emerged – life itself.

Our probes into space have found life's chemical precursors widely distributed. Indeed, space seems to be littered with the "spare parts of life" awaiting the right conditions for assembly. On our primeval planet, these conditions were found: the fierce energies of radioactivity and ultraviolet radiation, and the abundant presence of hydrogen, methane, ammonia, and water. In Earth's oceans, the first strands of DNA, and then the self-replicating double helix, could well have formed and broken countless times. But once the seed was set, the birth of the biosphere had begun.

Over nearly four billion years, the experiments, the increasing diversity, and complexity continued until, as the life-support systems of our planet stabilized, a still higher order of complexity emerged – intelligence and conscious awareness.

Throughout its 15 billion years, the pace of the universe's development has been accelerating, each new wave of innovation building up to trigger the next, in a series of "leaps" to further levels of change and diversification. Compress this unimaginable timescale into a single 24-hour day, and the Big Bang is over in less than a ten-billionth of a second. Stable atoms form in about four seconds; but not for several hours, until early dawn, do stars and galaxies form. Our own solar system must wait for early evening, around 6 p.m. Life on Earth begins around 8 p.m., the first vertebrates crawl on to land at about 10.30 at night. Dinosaurs roam from 11.35 p.m. until four minutes before midnight. Our ancestors first walk upright with 10 seconds to go. The Industrial Revolution, together with all our modern age, occupies less than the last thousandth of a second. Yet in this fraction of time, the face of this planet has changed almost as much as at any but the most tumultuous times in the prehistoric past.

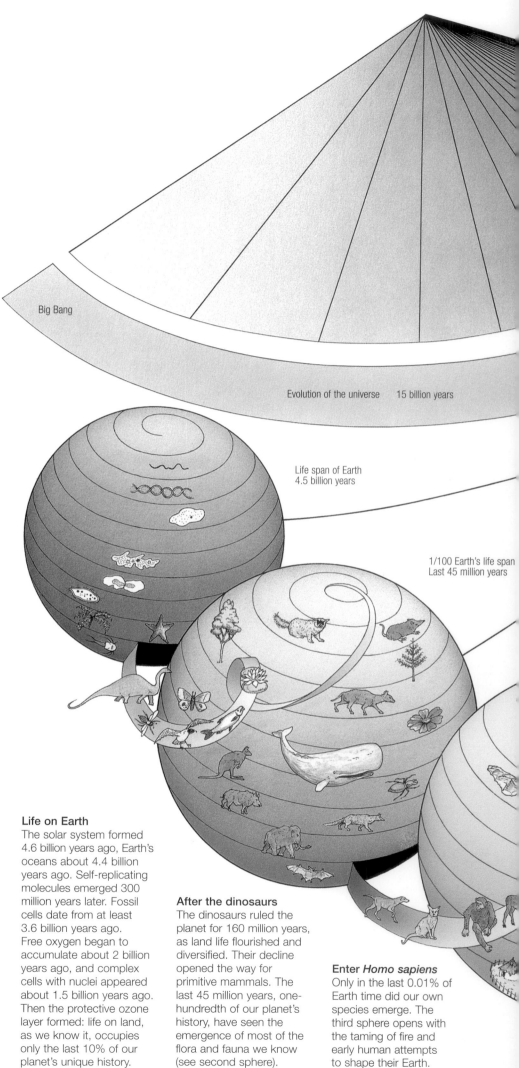

Big Bang

Evolution of the universe   15 billion years

Life span of Earth
4.5 billion years

1/100 Earth's life span
Last 45 million years

Life on Earth
The solar system formed 4.6 billion years ago, Earth's oceans about 4.4 billion years ago. Self-replicating molecules emerged 300 million years later. Fossil cells date from at least 3.6 billion years ago. Free oxygen began to accumulate about 2 billion years ago, and complex cells with nuclei appeared about 1.5 billion years ago. Then the protective ozone layer formed: life on land, as we know it, occupies only the last 10% of our planet's unique history.

After the dinosaurs
The dinosaurs ruled the planet for 160 million years, as land life flourished and diversified. Their decline opened the way for primitive mammals. The last 45 million years, one-hundredth of our planet's history, have seen the emergence of most of the flora and fauna we know (see second sphere).

Enter *Homo sapiens*
Only in the last 0.01% of Earth time did our own species emerge. The third sphere opens with the taming of fire and early human attempts to shape their Earth.

The momentum of evolution

The fantastic acceleration in the process of evolution is illustrated by these five spheres with "time" winding spirally down them. The first represents the last 4.5 billion years, the entire history of our planet. It traces the evolution of DNA, of the first cells, and, much later, of nucleated cells and sexual reproduction. The birth of our oxygen-rich atmosphere due to photosynthesizing algae is indicated by the deepening blue tinge. Each successive sphere represents an enlargement of just the last one-hundredth of the timescale illustrated in the previous one. The second sphere represents the last 45 million years, the third the last 450,000 years, the fourth the last 4,500 years, and the fifth only the last 45 years. Emerging in the third sphere, humankind has triggered a further acceleration in evolution.

The atomic age

Propelled by the Industrial Revolution and boosted by human technological evolution we have harnessed the atom, cracked the genetic code, broken out into space, and changed the face of our planet.

1/100,000,000 Earth's life span
Last 45 years

The major civilizations

The world's civilizations emerged in the last 1% of human existence (4,500 years), following the domestication of species and important technological inventions.

1/10 000 Earth's life span
Last 450,000 years

1/1,000,000 Earth's life span
Last 4,500 years

Latecomers to evolution

Gaia went its creative way for several billion years, becoming steadily more diverse, complex, and fruitful. Then, in the last few seconds of life's "evolutionary day", *Homo sapiens* appeared – a creature that has wrought changes as great as several glaciations and other geological upheavals together, and has done it all within a flicker of the evolutionary eye. The evolution of *Homo sapiens* has produced a being that can think: a being that is aware, that can speculate about tomorrow, and can even plan for it.

Evolution has also equipped us to create our own form of planetary ecosystem. Whereas natural selection works through a trial-and-error process, undirected and unhurried, we can choose preferred forms of evolution, creating changes that might otherwise have taken millions of years to occur.

The greatest natural development through evolution in terms of energy conversion was the emergence of photosynthesis, two billion years ago. A mere 50,000 years ago we learned to harness fire, and thus to use the stored energy of plants in the form of wood. A few hundred years ago we moved on to exploit coal, then oil. Now, however, we are on the verge of widespread exploitation of the sun's energy through solar cells – potentially as marked an advance for Earth's course as that of photosynthesis itself. Similar breakthroughs include domestication of wild species and genetic engineering: quantum leaps to match the evolution of sexual reproduction.

Among the greatest advances of all is our ability to control disease and thus to increase our numbers. Within the last 150 years, the human population has grown from around one billion in the 1830s, to two billion in the 1930s, to four billion in 1975, to five billion in 1987, and to well over six billion in 2003. Herein we witness the phenomenon of exponential growth, a process that marks not only our increasing numbers, but also our consumption of energy and resources, our accumulating knowledge, and our expanding communications network.

Exponential growth is one of the most important concepts we shall encounter in this book. It is growth that is not simply additive (two plus two equals four and another two makes six) but is self-compounding (two multiplied by two equals four, multiplied by two equals eight). Very few people realize its implications for our future existence on Earth. For example, if Africa maintains its 2.4 percent growth rate of 2003 until 2050, its population of 860 million people will triple to 2.6 billion.

The advance beyond our entrenched expectation for exponential growth in consumption will probably represent the greatest evolutionary leap of all.

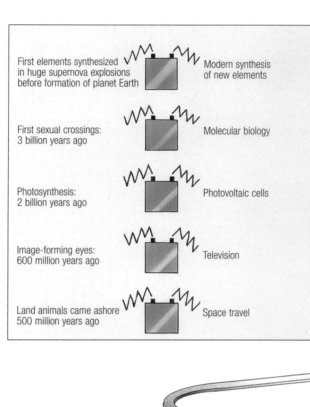

First elements synthesized in huge supernova explosions before formation of planet Earth — Modern synthesis of new elements

First sexual crossings: 3 billion years ago — Molecular biology

Photosynthesis: 2 billion years ago — Photovoltaic cells

Image-forming eyes: 600 million years ago — Television

Land animals came ashore 500 million years ago — Space travel

Evolution: revolution
We stand at a unique point in evolution, when planet-wide changes are proceeding faster than ever. The illustration (right) shows four examples of accelerated growth. With the invention of the rocket, our species can leave the biosphere and travel into space – a development as revolutionary as the step from water on to land 500 million years ago. Similar breakthroughs are shown in the box (left).

1500

2000

Population   Energy consumption   Information   Mobility

The long shadow

Today, the rise of human numbers casts a shadow over planet Earth. In 2003 we reached a total of 6.3 billion people, and we are plainly failing to feed, house, educate, and employ many of these in basically acceptable fashion. Worse, the human community is projected to reach at least 9.2 billion before the population explosion comes to an end late this century.

The problem does not lie only in a sheer outburst of numbers but also in an outburst of consumerism. More than one billion people in developed countries enjoy lifestyles that impose a grossly disproportionate pressure on our planetary ecosystem. A billion people in developing and transition countries have recently attained middle-class status and are consuming as fast as they can make it to the shopping mall. This consumerism is powered by a sudden expansion in technological know-how – we can use and misuse ever-greater stocks of natural resources, even use them up. In fact, rather than a "population crisis" or a "resource crisis", we should speak of a single over-arching crisis: the crisis of humankind. The shadow stems from all of us, and it will darken all our lives.

On land, we plough up virgin areas, even though most are marginal at best. Soil, one of the most precious of all resources, is washed or blown away in tens of billions of tonnes every year. To compound this tragedy, we pave over or otherwise "develop" large tracts of productive cropland each year. Deserts expand, or rather degraded lands are tacked on to them, at a rate threatening almost one-third of the Earth's land surface. Forests in the tropics are giving way to the small-scale agriculture of millions of slash-and-burn cultivators, at a rate that will leave little forest by mid-century. As the forests fall, species in their millions will lose their habitats, almost all forever.

In the oceans, we ravage one fishery after another. We cause dolphins, seals, and other marine mammals to follow the sad track of the great whales. We pollute the seas, just as we poison lakes and rivers in almost every part of the world. We desecrate our landscapes with growing piles of refuse, some of it toxic. In the atmosphere, we disrupt the carbon dioxide balance, triggering climatic dislocations that will upset every part of the human habitat and its enterprise worldwide.

Not surprisingly, this overtaxing of ecosystems leads to other sorts of breakdown. As more people seek greater shares of declining resources, conflicts erupt. Military conflagrations have killed more people since 1945 than all the soldiers in World War II. In fact, it is the breakdown in our social systems, our economic structures, and our political mechanisms that generates the greatest threat of all. The shadow over planet Earth will never be deeper and darker than when it is lengthened by a mushroom cloud.

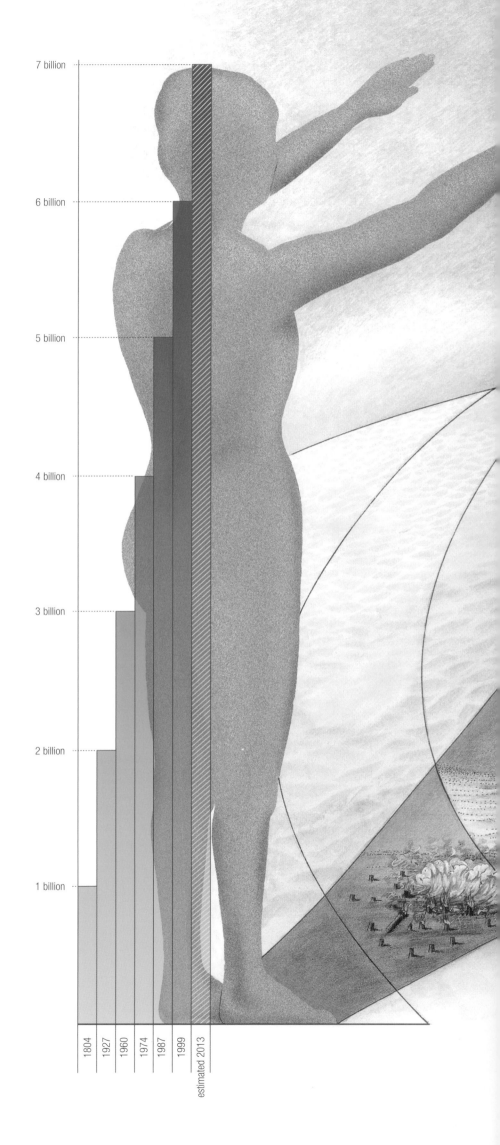

Deforestation

Desertification

Human suffering

Atmospheric pollution

Ocean pollution

Elemental depletion

Climatic dislocation

Evolution in crisis

Global breaking points

Bang or whimper?

NEWTON-LE-WILLOWS
LIBRARY
TEL: 01744 677886
01744 677887

The final test

Humanity, this sudden new evolutionary development which has had such a high impact upon the planet, now threatens not only its own survival but that of many parts of the biosphere itself. The rapidly manifesting global crises, the long shadow cast by the fast-growing figure of humankind, is stretching into the very heart of our biosphere. Since wandering early tribes began to fire the forests, this shadow has spread across land and ocean, through air, water, and soil, into space, and deep into the life-blood of evolution itself.

We might look upon our global crises as a challenge as well as a threat — we are sitting our final evolutionary examination for our viability as a species. But the time limit is rapidly approaching.

The changes in change

We live in a time of change. Well, we all know that: change on every side, change without parallel in history, change that will leave our futures unrecognizable. However, our capacity to recognize change does not seem to have changed much. For instance, we cannot sense that the atmosphere is changing more now than in the last 100,000 years, nor that the world's population increased by a quarter of a million people yesterday. If at least 50 species were effectively lost yesterday, how would we know? We could not see, smell, or taste the change.

Our incapacity to recognize change may cost us dearly. We seem to be programmed to dismiss it, to tune it out. "I've smoked for 30 years, so what harm will another year do?" – even though we know that sooner or later that extra year could mark a terminal change. Recall the man who fell out of a 20th-storey window and said as he passed the 10th floor, "Nothing new so far". Our evolutionary equipment has taught us to deal with the bear that suddenly turns up at our prehistoric cave, but we are less able to figure the notion of five bears turning up some day next week. Techno-wizards we may be, yet we don't really sense what we're doing – how we are changing our planet, our lifestyles, our aspirations to an extent that should leave us gasping with the sheer onrush of change.

The changes since 1950 (right) have brought costs. Humans have drastically altered almost half of all ice-free land, ruined a third of croplands, and appropriated over half of the available fresh water. They have doubled the fixation rate of nitrogen over natural sources, bringing on massive pollution, and have destroyed half of tropical forests. They have effectively extinguished hundreds of thousands of species. They have increased carbon dioxide in the atmosphere by almost a third, eventually causing severe dislocations in global climate. These changes have levied costs of trillions of dollars per year.

Rising to meet the supersize challenges ahead may perhaps be the biggest change in civilization. Be assured, we can certainly find ways to live in accord with our Earth, our world, and hence with each other. Whether we will actually devise the eco-technologies, backed by the right policies, political leadership, and public opinion is another matter. We may find that the most valuable resource, and the one in shortest supply, is our willingness to change our understanding of how best to live on our limited planet.

Those daunted by this extreme prospect should remember that the choice is not between change and no change. Rather it is between change that we choose for our future and change that we suffer as a result of our past. Shall we choose to choose?

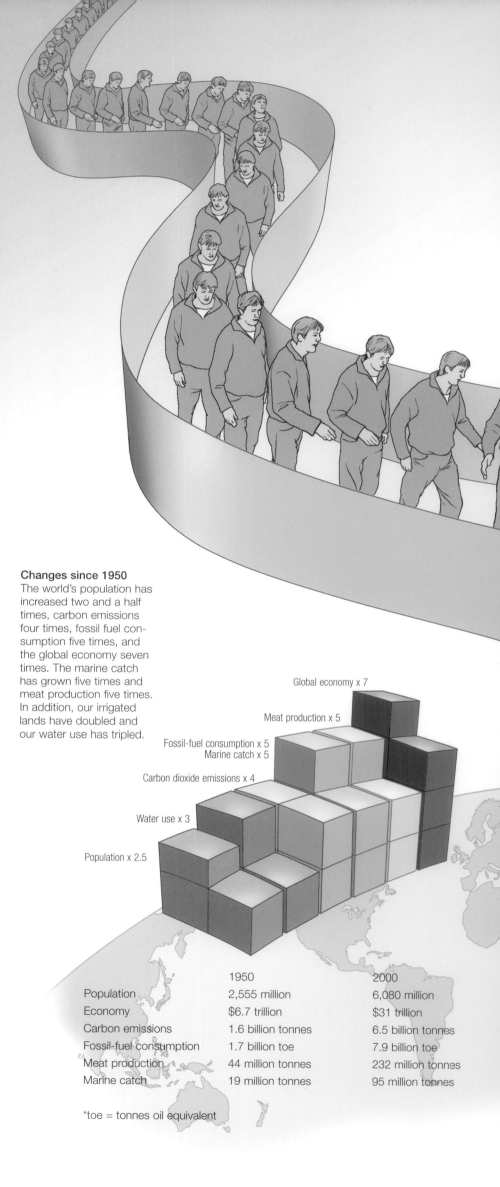

Changes since 1950
The world's population has increased two and a half times, carbon emissions four times, fossil fuel consumption five times, and the global economy seven times. The marine catch has grown five times and meat production five times. In addition, our irrigated lands have doubled and our water use has tripled.

Global economy x 7

Meat production x 5

Fossil-fuel consumption x 5
Marine catch x 5

Carbon dioxide emissions x 4

Water use x 3

Population x 2.5

	1950	2000
Population	2,555 million	6,080 million
Economy	$6.7 trillion	$31 trillion
Carbon emissions	1.6 billion tonnes	6.5 billion tonnes
Fossil-fuel consumption	1.7 billion toe	7.9 billion toe
Meat production	44 million tonnes	232 million tonnes
Marine catch	19 million tonnes	95 million tonnes

*toe = tonnes oil equivalent

Doing more with less

If we are to achieve sustainable economies and societies, we must learn to do a far better job of doing more with less. In fact, the world must aim to cut its use of natural resources by 50% by the year 2050. The developing countries probably will not have the capability, let alone the inclination, to do this by 2050. This means that developed countries should plan on a 90% cut, feasible through the Factor Ten strategy. If this sounds like an impossible prospect, bear in mind that since 1973 we have slashed energy use in many "best practice" instances by three-quarters. In certain sectors, developed countries will find themselves learning (to cite the futurist Amory Lovins) to do just about everything with just about nothing.

Making choices

How will we make choices about our future now that we are at a moment of realization and decision?

The acceleration in change

The table shows that we now adopt new technologies at a rate beyond the imaginations of people just a century ago.

Technology timescales

The column on the right shows the years taken for new technologies to reach one-quarter of the US population:

1873 electricity discovered	46
1876 telephone	35
1886 petrol car	55
1906 radio	22
1926 television	26
1953 microwave oven	30
1975 personal computer	16
1983 mobile phone	13
1991 the worldwide web	7

The rise in our ecological footprint

Humans' "ecological footprint" – the amount of environmental goods and services that each of us consumes – has been rising steadily as our economic activities expand and as our numbers keep growing. In 1961 humankind's total footprint was only 70%, but by 1999 it had topped 120%. For the first time in human history, we are solidly into "overshoot" – a huge transition, and of entirely the wrong sort.

Humanity's ecological demand and capacity 1960–1999

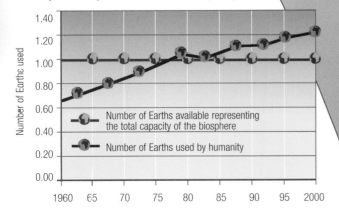

Number of Earths used

1.40
1.20
1.00
0.80
0.60
0.40
0.20
0.00

Number of Earths available representing the total capacity of the biosphere

Number of Earths used by humanity

1960   65   70   75   80   85   90   95   2000

Increase in material flows

Consider the amount of materials we now use or waste in support of our lifestyles. Citizens of industrialized countries need huge volumes of bricks, cement, iron, oil, chemicals, paper, and many other materials. They also generate vast quantities of pollutants and other waste, plus they cause similarly large quantities of materials to be excavated or moved around in their pursuit of valuable minerals ("hidden flows").

To produce a kilogram of gold, for instance, requires moving 350 tonnes of materials – and hence the gold ring on your finger effectively weighs 3 tonnes. In the US the physical displacement of materials is about 80 tonnes per person per year, or over 1,000 times a typical American's weight. US outflows from economic activity amount to 25 tonnes per American per year, well over twice as much as in Japan. This rises to 80 tonnes when "hidden flows" are taken into account. Of all material outflows, carbon dioxide accounts for an average of more than 80% by weight.

Crisis or challenge?

Humankind can be seen as either the climax of evolution's course, or as its greatest error. No other creature is a fraction so precocious. No other can think about the world, plan to make it better, and dream of the best possible. Yet no other reveals such capacity for perverse behaviour – for gross misuse of its habitat and for reckless proliferation of numbers, without thought for the consequences.

In certain senses, humanity is becoming a super-malignancy on the face of the planet, spreading with insidious effect and fomenting ultimate crisis in covert fashion. A cancer cell is unusually vital, since it replicates itself with remarkable vigour; it is also exceptionally stupid, since it ends by killing the host upon which it depends for its own survival. But unlike the cancer cell, we are coming to realize the nature of what we are doing. Can we learn fast enough, act soon enough?

This is not the first time the Earth's community has encountered crisis. Gaia has even benefited from periodic upheavals. Were it not for the dramatic demise of the dinosaurs, there would have been scant opportunity for mammals to become pre-eminent – with all that has meant for the supreme mammal, *Homo sapiens*. Out of crisis can come advance, provided the impetus of change does not "overshoot" into catastrophe. On past occasions, there have been thousands of years, even millions, for the corrective workings of the biosphere to adapt and adjust to new stresses. This time, there are just a few decades, far too short a period for Gaia to work its restorative course, unless it is done with the symbiotic support of humankind.

If we can match up to the crisis, Gaia may well move forwards into an unprecedented period of development – development in its proper broad sense, embracing development of Earth's resources and of humanity's capacity to live well. If we fail, *Homo sapiens* could eventually be discarded as an evolutionary blind alley.

To achieve a breakthrough, we must learn a tough lesson. While it is often all right to adapt through small steps, improving an established course through "fine tuning", there are times when we must do an "about turn", and take more drastic corrective action. The tale of the French schoolchildren and their experimental frog is salutary. They took the frog and dropped it into a saucepan of boiling water, whereupon the frog skipped right out – instant rejection of an environment that proved distinctly unsuitable. But when the schoolchildren dropped the frog into a saucepan of cold water, and slowly heated it up, the frog swam round and round, adapting itself to the rising heat … until it quietly boiled to death.

Crises have both positive and negative characteristics. They can represent a threat to the status quo, but at the same time can be seen as a symptom that something is wrong. They thus represent an opportunity to correct an imbalance and move on to a new level of organization. This is reflected in the Chinese character "ji" (here painted by a classical Chinese calligraphist) indicating both a crucial point and an opportunity.

"Once a photograph of the Earth, taken from the outside, is available ... a new idea as powerful as any other in history will be let loose."
Fred Hoyle, 1948

LAND

Introduced by David Pimentel
Professor of Insect Ecology & Agricultural Sciences,
Cornell University, Ithaca, NY, USA

The world population, expanding by a quarter of a million people each day, is experiencing severe problems with food supplies. Already there are critical shortages of cropland, fresh water and fossil energy. All of these natural resources are essential for the production of food as well as for the support of the many other activities of humans.

Agriculture faces enormous challenges ahead if future generations are to enjoy a sustainable food supply. The World Health Organization indicates that more than three billion people are malnourished, roughly half of them lacking micro-nutrients and the other half simply short of food. The Food and Agricultural Organization reports that per-person food availability of basic cereal grains has been steadily decreasing for the past 20 years despite advances in biotechnology and agro-strategies. Cereals are the mainstay of human diets, comprising about 80 percent of food supply. Although cereal grain harvests per hectare have increased slowly since 1985, harvests are being shared among ever more people, thereby decreasing the amount per person.

More than 99.8 percent of our food supply, in terms of calories, comes from our land; just 0.2 percent comes from the oceans and other aquatic ecosystems. This emphasizes the importance of cropland in productive food systems.

At a time when food production must increase to meet the needs of a rapidly expanding world population, per-person cropland has declined as much as 20 percent during just the past decade. Ideally, there should be 0.5 hectares of cropland per person to provide nutritious food. Unfortunately, and because of population growth and cropland degradation, less than half of this is available per person worldwide.

Moreover, soil productivity is reduced by exposure of soil to both wind and rain erosion, especially when soils are not adequately protected with vegetation. This is a major problem in developing countries where the rural poor remove soil-protecting crop residues for cooking fuel. Erosion not only robs the soil of water but also of soil nutrients. Yearly, more than 10 million hectares of world cropland are degraded and lost because of soil erosion. In addition, each year about 10 million more hectares of irrigated cropland are destroyed by salinization. At the same time, the world's forests are being cleared to replace cropland lost to erosion and salinization.

As well as fertile soil, crop production needs fresh water. Rainfall of 1,000 mm per year provides the minimum water needs for most crops (1,000 litres of water are required to produce one kilogram of grain and other crops). Conservation of both soil and water depend on retaining vegetation cover to protect the soil from erosion. Already there are major water shortages in many parts of the world. About 70 percent of the fresh water consumed worldwide is used for irrigation.

Modern agriculture depends on large inputs of fossil energy for fertilizers, irrigation, machinery, and pesticides. Around 1,000 litres of oil equivalents are required to produce one hectare of corn or rice. Oil and natural gas are finite resources that are being rapidly depleted worldwide, and the increasing prices are having major impacts, especially for poor families.

Looking to the future, agriculturists must conserve soil, water, energy, and biological resources.

The Land Potential

Marvellous stuff, soil. Sterile and boring as it may appear, often mucky too, this thin layer covering the planet's land surface is the biosphere's foundation, our primary resource.

Soil is as lively as an army of migrating wildebeest and as beautiful as a flock of flamingos. Teeming with life of myriad forms, it deserves to be classified as an ecosystem in itself – or rather, as many ecosystems. One hectare of good quality soil in a temperate zone may contain at least 300 million small invertebrates – mites, millipedes, insects, worms, and other mini-creatures. As for micro-organisms, a mere 30 grams of soil may contain one million bacteria of just one type, as well as 100,000 yeast cells and 50,000 bits of fungus mycelium. Without these micro-organisms, the soil could not convert nitrogen, phosphorus, and sulphur into forms available to plants.

According to Harvard's Professor Edward O. Wilson, there is far more biological complexity in a handful of soil in Virginia than on the entire surface of Jupiter. Yet we invest more money in exploring the planets than in finding out how our basic life-support systems work here on Earth.

So next time you tread on earth (as opposed to concrete or asphalt), take a look at what lies at your feet. It is likely to be a fairly loose material, half made up of masses of tiny particles, the other half of water and air. This curious assembly of inorganic constituents derives originally from rock which, being weathered by rainwater, atmospheric gases, ice, and roots, has slowly broken down into a form in which it can support multitudes of life-forms. These in turn enable it to support plants. Through a constantly self-reinforcing process, the soil becomes enriched with dead organic matter, some of which is called humus – the stuff that helps to make soil fertile.

The process of soil formation is slow. At best, even when sediments build up quickly, formation of 30 centimetres may take 50 years. More usually, when new soil is formed from parent rocks, one centimetre may need from 100 to 1,000 years. So to form soil to the depth of this page could take as long as 10,000 years. Unfortunately, reversing the process by human or natural disturbance is all too quick. Soils can be degraded in a fraction of the time they take to form (see p. 39).

Our green planet

In the end, or rather in the beginning, we are all plants. Without the green mantle for our planet supplied by a third of a million plant species, animal

The fertile soil

Not all the soil which covers the Earth's ice-free land surface is suitable for growing crops. In fact, of the total area of 13.5 billion ha, about one-quarter of the globe, little over one-tenth presents no serious limitations to agriculture. The rest is either too dry, too wet, too poor in nutrients ('mineral-stressed'), too steep, too shallow, or too cold.

Around 30% of the Earth's land surface suffers from drought (not surprising, when the Sahara occupies nearly 1 billion ha). Mineral-stressed soils account for a further 23%. Soils that are too thin to be much use cover 22%, while waterlogged soils account for 10%. Permafrost soils, i.e. ground that is permanently frozen, cover 6%. Then there are the huge ice lands of Antarctica and Greenland.

The illustration shows how the world's soil resources are shared out, each segment of the "globe" showing the percentage of total land area and proportions of soil types for the continent it represents. Notice how the fertile soil is far from evenly distributed, with Europe claiming the largest portion relative to its land area. The pie-charts on the continents show how the land is being used for forest, grazing, cultivation, or "other" (wild, urban, etc.) purposes.

North and Central America
Soil suited to growing crops accounts for 25% of the land, yet less than half of this is used as such. Millions of hectares of arable land in the US have been paved over or covered by urban sprawl.

South America
The major limiting factor is mineral stress (41%), the affected areas generally being vast tracts of forest. Tropical forest soils are typically low in nutrients.

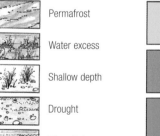

Permafrost	Arable/ permanent cropland
Water excess	
Shallow depth	Permanent pastureland
Drought	
Mineral stress (poor in nutrients)	Forest/wood land
No serious limitations for agriculture	Other land

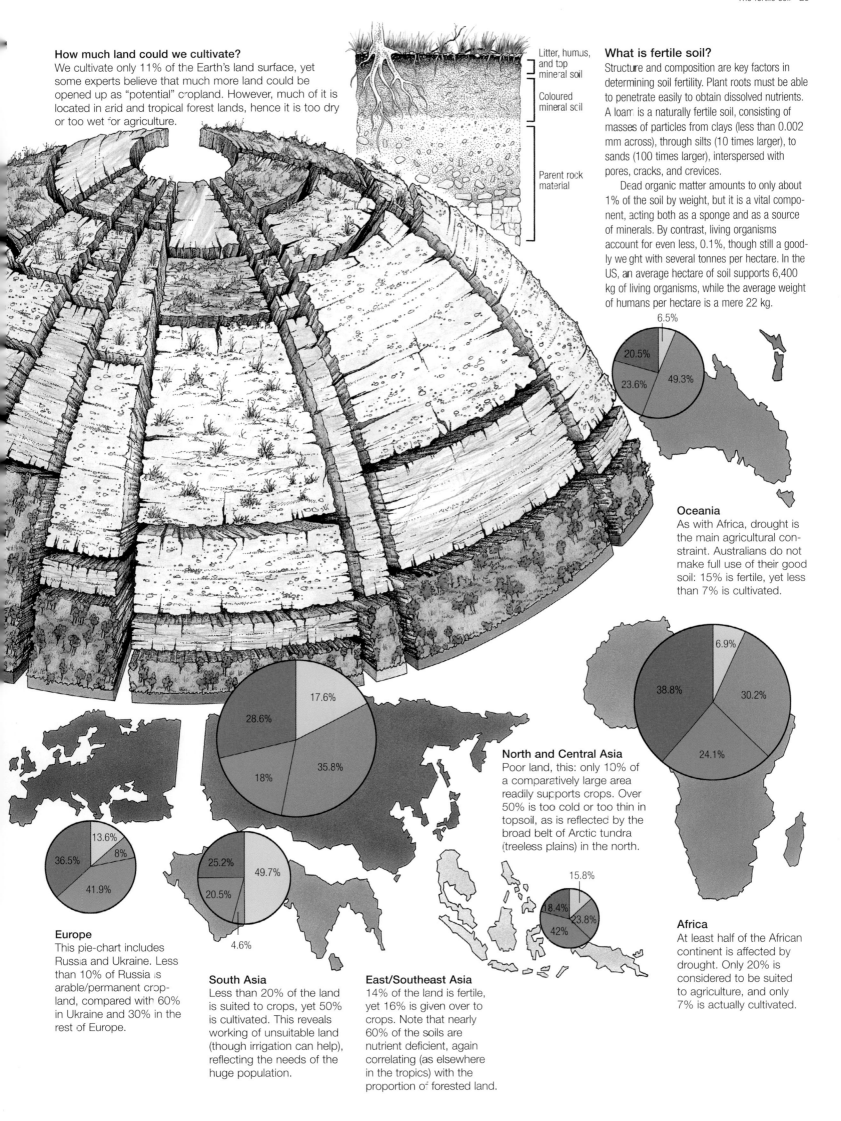

How much land could we cultivate?

We cultivate only 11% of the Earth's land surface, yet some experts believe that much more land could be opened up as "potential" cropland. However, much of it is located in arid and tropical forest lands, hence it is too dry or too wet for agriculture.

Litter, humus, and top mineral soil

Coloured mineral soil

Parent rock material

What is fertile soil?

Structure and composition are key factors in determining soil fertility. Plant roots must be able to penetrate easily to obtain dissolved nutrients. A loam is a naturally fertile soil, consisting of masses of particles from clays (less than 0.002 mm across), through silts (10 times larger), to sands (100 times larger), interspersed with pores, cracks, and crevices.

Dead organic matter amounts to only about 1% of the soil by weight, but it is a vital component, acting both as a sponge and as a source of minerals. By contrast, living organisms account for even less, 0.1%, though still a goodly weight with several tonnes per hectare. In the US, an average hectare of soil supports 6,400 kg of living organisms, while the average weight of humans per hectare is a mere 22 kg.

Oceania

As with Africa, drought is the main agricultural constraint. Australians do not make full use of their good soil: 15% is fertile, yet less than 7% is cultivated.

North and Central Asia

Poor land, this: only 10% of a comparatively large area readily supports crops. Over 50% is too cold or too thin in topsoil, as is reflected by the broad belt of Arctic tundra (treeless plains) in the north.

Africa

At least half of the African continent is affected by drought. Only 20% is considered to be suited to agriculture, and only 7% is actually cultivated.

Europe

This pie-chart includes Russia and Ukraine. Less than 10% of Russia is arable/permanent cropland, compared with 60% in Ukraine and 30% in the rest of Europe.

South Asia

Less than 20% of the land is suited to crops, yet 50% is cultivated. This reveals working of unsuitable land (though irrigation can help), reflecting the needs of the huge population.

East/Southeast Asia

14% of the land is fertile, yet 16% is given over to crops. Note that nearly 60% of the soils are nutrient deficient, again correlating (as elsewhere in the tropics) with the proportion of forested land.

life as we know it (including *Homo sapiens*) would never have evolved. Millions of years ago it was the rise of plant life that boosted the stock of oxygen in the atmosphere from a trace gas to the one-fifth proportion that fostered the outburst of animal life.

Plants convert sunlight into the stored chemical energy on which all animal life depends for food (and humans for fuel, too). Some biologists believe that the demise of a single plant species may eventually lead to the extinction of 20–40 animal species as the ecological consequences reverberate up food chains.

The enormous diversity of plants offers adaptations to every conceivable environment from desert to tundra, with the tropics having the richest speciation. We depend on this green wealth at every turn,

from indirect benefits for soil and climate to direct supplies for our tables, factories, and hospitals.

How much plant life is there on the planet, and where does it grow most abundantly? Answers suggest where we might look to increase our growing of crops or our production of fibre. "Phytomass" is the scientific term to measure an amount of dry plant material (undried plant matter is three or four times heavier), and it is expressed in tonnes per hectare. When we speak of dry animal matter, we use the term "zoomass"; phytomass and zoomass together comprise biomass. Of all biomass (terrestrial and aquatic), 99 percent is plants.

Not surprisingly, we find that forests and woodlands contain the great bulk of all terrestrial phytomass, around 1,000 billion tonnes. Of this

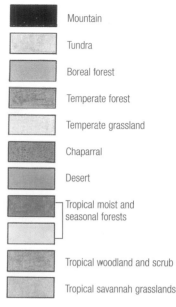

■	Mountain
▫	Tundra
▨	Boreal forest
▨	Temperate forest
▫	Temperate grassland
▨	Chaparral
▨	Desert
▨	Tropical moist and seasonal forests
▫	
▨	Tropical woodland and scrub
▨	Tropical savannah grasslands

The green potential

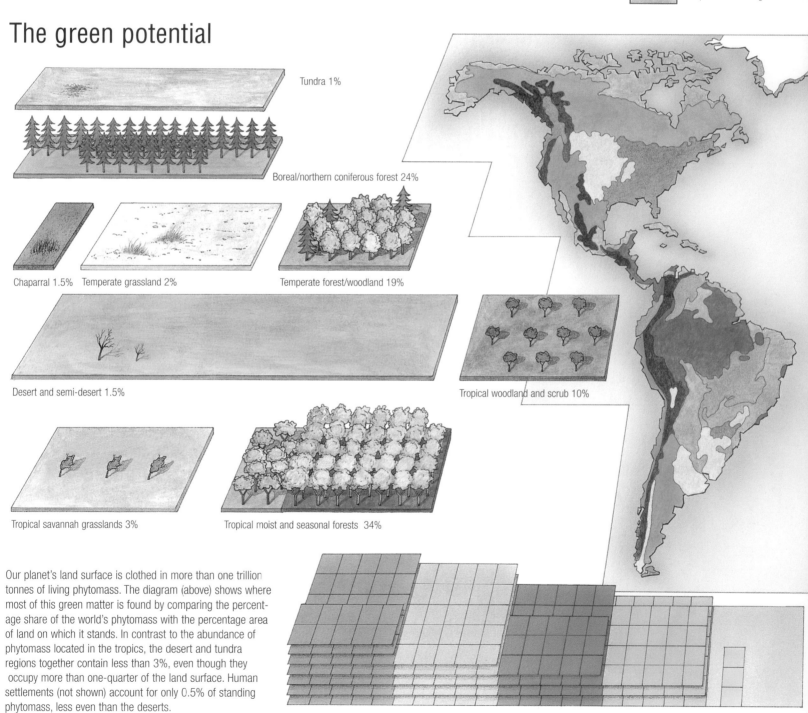

Tundra 1%

Boreal/northern coniferous forest 24%

Chaparral 1.5%   Temperate grassland 2%   Temperate forest/woodland 19%

Desert and semi-desert 1.5%   Tropical woodland and scrub 10%

Tropical savannah grasslands 3%   Tropical moist and seasonal forests 34%

Our planet's land surface is clothed in more than one trillion tonnes of living phytomass. The diagram (above) shows where most of this green matter is found by comparing the percentage share of the world's phytomass with the percentage area of land on which it stands. In contrast to the abundance of phytomass located in the tropics, the desert and tundra regions together contain less than 3%, even though they occupy more than one-quarter of the land surface. Human settlements (not shown) account for only 0.5% of standing phytomass, less even than the deserts.

| Irrigated sugarcane 120–160 tonnes | Papyrus swamp 50–125 tonnes | Tropical forest 90 tonnes | Well-watered lawn 70 tonnes | Desert 3 tonnes |

amount, two-fifths is in tropical forests, even though they now cover less than eight percent of the land surface. Curiously enough, our cultivated crops amount to less than seven billion tonnes of standing phytomass, a trifling 0.5 percent, even though they cover more of the land surface than tropical forests.

Comparing the amounts of total living phytomass is only one way of estimating the "green potential" of different ecosystems and regions. Another way is to consider the amount of new plant material generated each year. Again, forests are in the forefront: they account for almost half of Earth's annual terrestrial production of well over 100 billion tonnes.

With year-round growth, tropical forests can produce as much as 90 tonnes of plant material per hectare per year, or almost twice as much phytomass as is generated by temperate forests – and a higher level of productivity than for any other vegetation type except for a few forestry plantations, water weeds such as water hyacinth, ultra-moist savannahs, and high-yielding crops, such as sugarcane. Because organic matter is speedily decomposed, however, annual net increment in virgin tropical forest is usually nil.

Thanks to intensive agriculture, our crops produce 15 billion tonnes of phytomass each year (11 percent of the world's total). A good corn crop in the US can generate 15–20 tonnes of plant material per hectare per year, while white potatoes can yield almost 30 tonnes.

In general, the amount of new phytomass produced each year in moist parts of the world

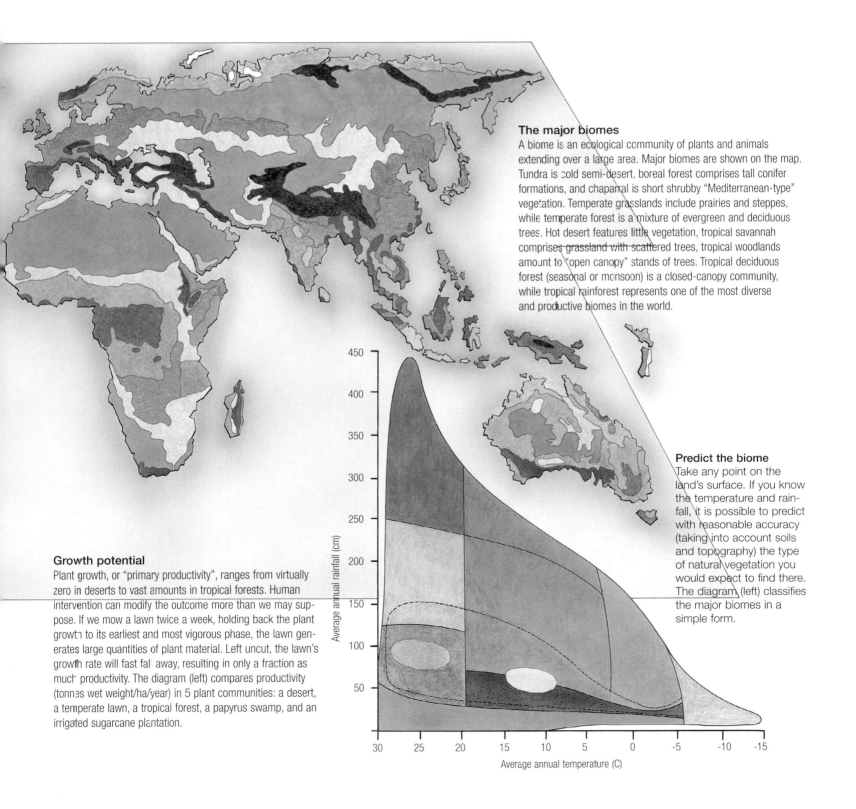

The major biomes
A biome is an ecological community of plants and animals extending over a large area. Major biomes are shown on the map. Tundra is cold semi-desert, boreal forest comprises tall conifer formations, and chaparral is short shrubby "Mediterranean-type" vegetation. Temperate grasslands include prairies and steppes, while temperate forest is a mixture of evergreen and deciduous trees. Hot desert features little vegetation, tropical savannah comprises grassland with scattered trees, tropical woodlands amount to "open canopy" stands of trees. Tropical deciduous forest (seasonal or monsoon) is a closed-canopy community, while tropical rainforest represents one of the most diverse and productive biomes in the world.

Predict the biome
Take any point on the land's surface. If you know the temperature and rainfall, it is possible to predict with reasonable accuracy (taking into account soils and topography) the type of natural vegetation you would expect to find there. The diagram (left) classifies the major biomes in a simple form.

Growth potential
Plant growth, or "primary productivity", ranges from virtually zero in deserts to vast amounts in tropical forests. Human intervention can modify the outcome more than we may suppose. If we mow a lawn twice a week, holding back the plant growth to its earliest and most vigorous phase, the lawn generates large quantities of plant material. Left uncut, the lawn's growth rate will fast fall away, resulting in only a fraction as much productivity. The diagram (left) compares productivity (tonnes wet weight/ha/year) in 5 plant communities: a desert, a temperate lawn, a tropical forest, a papyrus swamp, and an irrigated sugarcane plantation.

Average annual rainfall (cm)

450
400
350
300
250
200
150
100
50

30   25   20   15   10   5   0   -5   -10   -15

Average annual temperature (C)

doubles as we move from boreal to the temperate zones, and more than doubles as we move from the temperate zones to the tropics. Similarly, ecological complexity increases towards the tropics, from "simple" communities with few species in the polar regions to communities with great abundance and diversity at the Equator.

Forests and the biosphere

The world's forests represent the most exuberant expressions of nature ever to grace the planet. Whether among the giant Douglas firs of Oregon, the aged oaks of Sherwood Forest in Britain, the vast fir forests of Siberia, or the rainforests of Amazonia and Borneo, we feel small and insignificant by comparison. Ranging across a quarter of the planet's land surface, the forests generally support greater stocks of biomass, produce new biomass faster, and harbour greater abundance of species (both plant and animal) than any other ecological zone.

Not only are forests the powerhouses of obvious biospheric processes – notably photosynthesis and biological growth, creation of fertile humus, and transfer of energy. Their exceptional contribution to the biosphere goes much further. Forests play major roles in the planetary recycling of carbon, nitrogen, and oxygen. They help to determine temperature, rainfall, and other climatic conditions. They are often the fountainheads of rivers. They constitute the major gene reservoirs of our planet, and they are the main sites for the emergence of new species. Indeed, forests contribute as much to evolution as several other biomes put together.

Among many goods supplied by forests, the principal one is wood, which serves many purposes. It is among the first raw materials that we use, and it is likely to be our last. It plays a part in more activities of a modern economy than virtually any other commodity, and almost every major industry depends on forest products in at least one of its processes. Wood also serves many purposes as plywood, veneer, hardboard, particle-board, and chipboard. It is competitive, too, since substitutes such as steel, aluminium, cement, and plastics need more energy in their production. Furthermore, we use much wood in the form of paper, that key medium of civilization. Having expanded by 40 percent since 1965, the world's industrial wood harvest now amounts to 1.5 billion cubic metres per year.

From a human standpoint, we can look upon forests as the great providers and protectors. They maintain ecological diversity, they safeguard water-sheds, they protect soil from erosion, they supply fuel for around one-third of the world's people, they provide wood for paperpulp and industrial timber, and they are pleasing to the eye. Without them, our planetary home would be much poorer, yet in certain parts of the tropics especially, we are losing this heritage at an alarming rate (see pp. 40–41).

The global forest

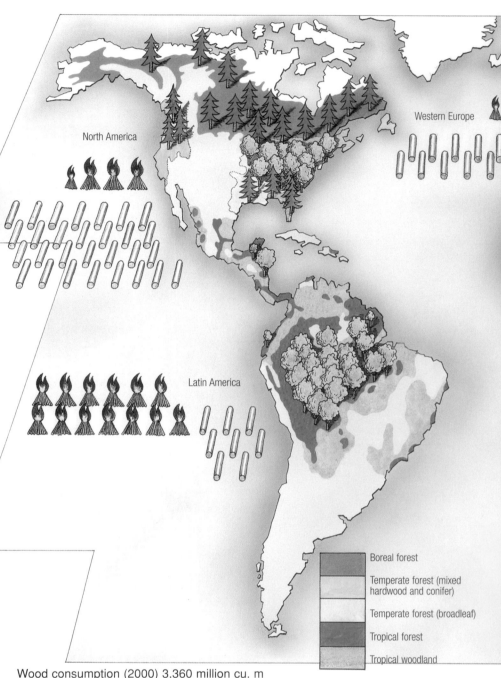

North America

Western Europe

Latin America

Boreal forest

Temperate forest (mixed hardwood and conifer)

Temperate forest (broadleaf)

Tropical forest

Tropical woodland

Wood consumption (2000) 3,360 million cu. m

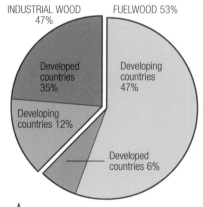

INDUSTRIAL WOOD 47%

FUELWOOD 53%

Developed countries 35%

Developing countries 47%

Developing countries 12%

Developed countries 6%

 Coniferous forest 20 million ha

Broadleaved forest 20 million ha

 Fuelwood 20 million cu. m

Industrial wood 20 million cu. m

Land where tree crowns cover more than 30% of the area is known as closed forest. More than half the world's closed forests comprise broadleaved trees. Of coniferous forests, three-fifths are located in the former Soviet Union and over one-quarter in North America.

The two kinds of tree symbol on the map (above), represent a fixed area of closed forest. The firewood and log symbols indicate how much wood is produced for fuel and industrial purposes; combined, they give the annual woodcut for each region.

World wood consumption

We now consume around 3.4 billion cubic metres of wood a year, enough to cover a city the size of UK's Birmingham to the height of a 10-storey building. About 64% of this wood comes from non-coniferous forests (generally hardwoods), and 36% from conifers (soft-woods). The pie-chart (left) highlights the disparity in usage between the developed and developing worlds.

Eastern Europe/former Soviet Union

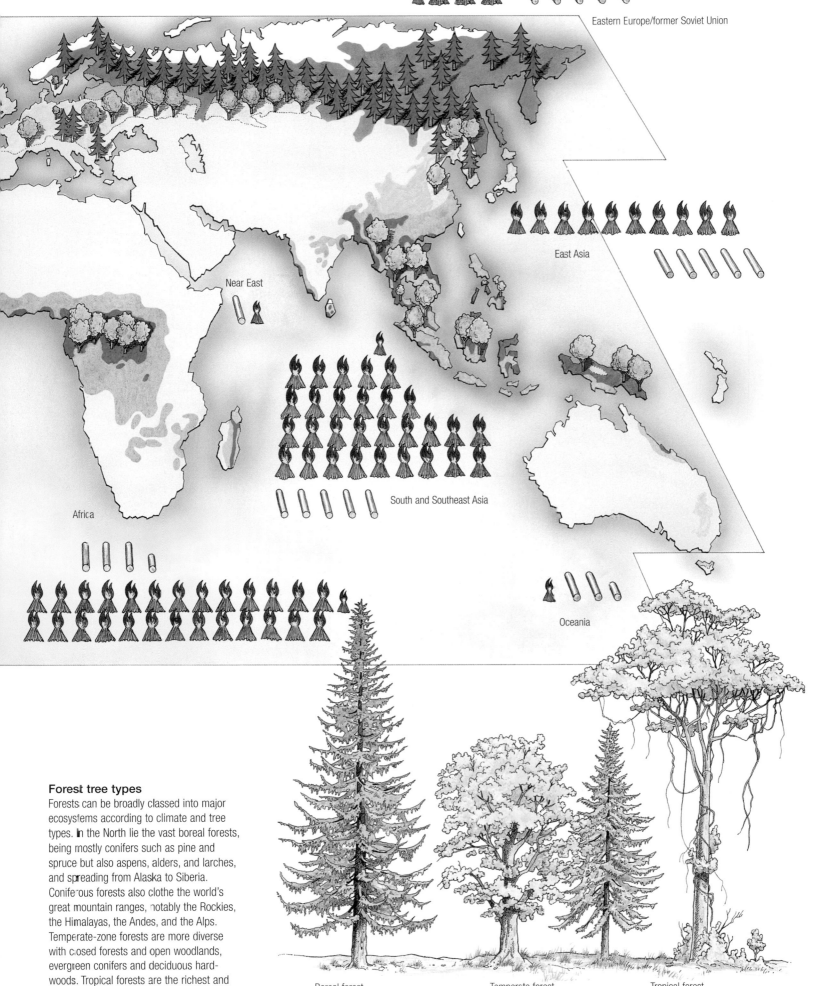

East Asia

Near East

South and Southeast Asia

Africa

Oceania

Boreal forest

Temperate forest

Tropical forest

Forest tree types

Forests can be broadly classed into major ecosystems according to climate and tree types. In the North lie the vast boreal forests, being mostly conifers such as pine and spruce but also aspens, alders, and larches, and spreading from Alaska to Siberia. Coniferous forests also clothe the world's great mountain ranges, notably the Rockies, the Himalayas, the Andes, and the Alps. Temperate-zone forests are more diverse with closed forests and open woodlands, evergreen conifers and deciduous hardwoods. Tropical forests are the richest and densest of all, with luxuriant growth and great diversity of species.

Powerhouses of the tropics

Tropical forests form a green band around the Equator, extending roughly 10 degrees north and south. This means that they account for only a small proportion, less than eight percent, possibly a lot less, of the Earth's land surface. Yet they comprise roughly half of all growing wood on the planet, and the rainforests harbour at least 60 percent, perhaps even 80 percent, of all species – a genetic resource that increasingly serves our daily welfare via agriculture, medicine, and industry. They also comprise the most complex and diverse ecosystems on Earth.

A 1.5 hectare patch of forest may hold over 200 tree species alone. They grow in multi-layered profusion: tall "emergents" piercing the canopy; lianas, stranglers, and climbers with aerial roots festooning the topmost branches and their buttressed trunks; lichens, mosses, and algae adorning every surface; an array of fungi colonizing the forest floor. Almost every branch is hung with epiphytic ferns, orchids, or bromeliads, while smaller trees and shrubs compete for light and space below. This intricate plant life supports an even greater diversity of insect and animal life, much of it with specialized life cycles.

Yet for all their intrinsic interest, these forests are almost unknown to us. Science has identified less than one in five, perhaps only one in 50, of their species. If you go into a tract of forest with a net, you would need only a few hours to catch an insect not yet known to science (and to be named after you). We know more about certain sectors of the moon's surface than about the Amazonian heartlands – and the moon will be around for a long while to come, whereas tropical forests are being disrupted and destroyed with every tick of the clock. Each time a tract of forest is cleared, several species, perhaps potentially valuable to humans, may be lost forever.

Most people (developers included) are surprised to learn that the soils that support the most luxuriant tropical forests are generally of low quality and unsuited to agriculture. Receiving very little of their nutrient supplies from the shallow, impoverished soil, tropical forests have built up stocks of key minerals above the ground, within the vegetation. When leaves fall or a tree crashes to the ground, decomposer organisms recycle most of the nutrients within a few weeks, in contrast with the many months required in a temperate forest. Thus, tropical forests have an almost leak-proof system to retain nutrients within their living structures. They flourish despite the soils, not because of them.

Insofar as tropical forests constitute a kind of benchmark for life processes, we shall not understand life properly until we understand tropical forests. They are revealing more about evolution than all other natural environments put together.

The growth of agriculture

The first great developments in agriculture took place 10,000 years ago in a series of river basins, notably the Nile, the Euphrates/Tigris, the Yangtse,

Tropical forests

"The gloom and a solemn silence combine to produce a sense of the past, the primeval – almost of the infinite. The tropical forest is a world in which man seems an intruder, and where he feels overwhelmed by the contemplation of the ever-acting forces, which, from the simple elements of the atmosphere, build up a great mass of vegetation which overshadows, and almost seems to oppress the earth."
Alfred Russell Wallace, naturalist and explorer, on his trip to Amazonia, 1890

Tropical forest
There are three main types of tropical forest: moist forest, deciduous forest, and dry woodland. The first two types have been grouped on the map as moist forest, distinct from open, dry woodland.

Patterns of forest regeneration

When large gaps in the forest canopy occur (such as those caused by slash-and-burn agriculture, landslides, and typhoons), the microclimate of the mature forest disappears. The forest floor becomes exposed to direct sunlight; the air and soil become dry; and temperatures fluctuate widely between day and night. Certain pioneer species are adapted to take advantage of these conditions, and for them growth is fast and life is short. Most die within 15 years, and their timber is light and soft. Second-wave pioneers also demand plenty of light and grow rapidly, but live longer, perhaps a century or more. These trees fix large amounts of nitrogen, playing a strategic role in restoring the nutrient bank and thereby setting the stage for the return of the mature-phase species. Bulldozing of all vegetation has severe repercussions. The soils are likely to become irreversibly impacted and otherwise impoverished. In the end, all that may replace what was once spectacular forest is scrappy, low-grade scrub.

Low-grade scrub   Total forest destruction   Uncut forest

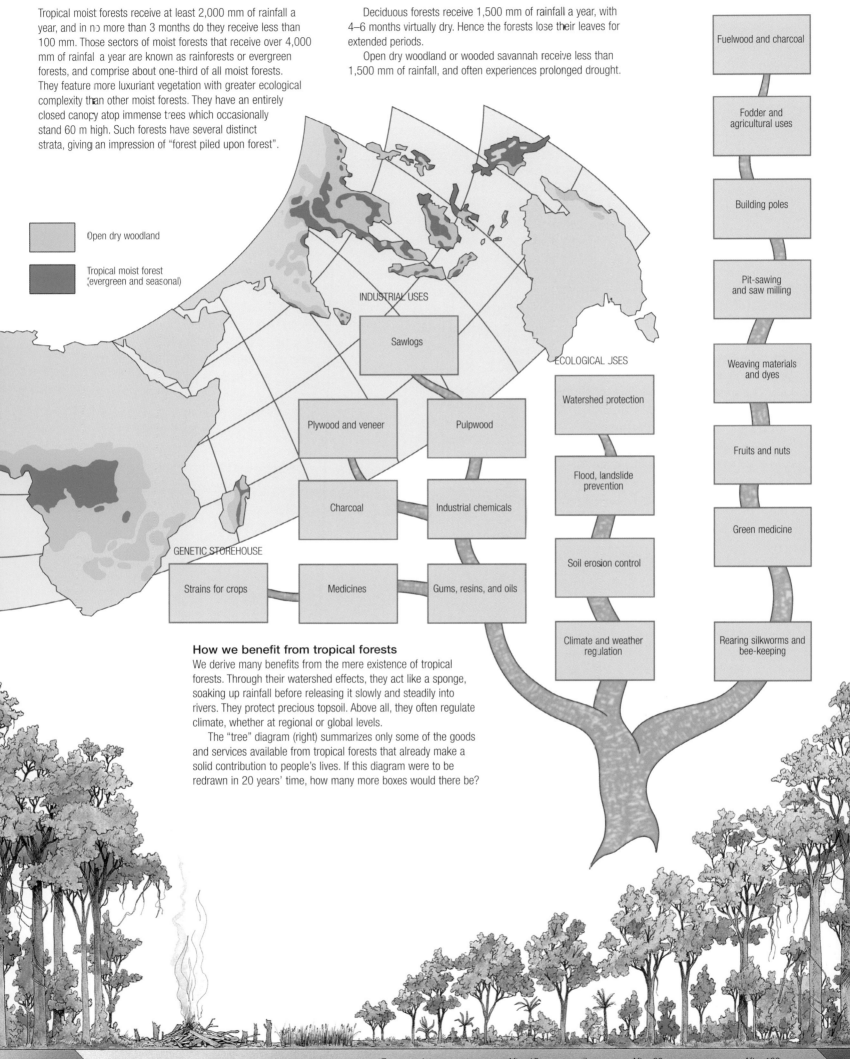

SUBSISTENCE NEEDS

Tropical moist forests receive at least 2,000 mm of rainfall a year, and in no more than 3 months do they receive less than 100 mm. Those sectors of moist forests that receive over 4,000 mm of rainfall a year are known as rainforests or evergreen forests, and comprise about one-third of all moist forests. They feature more luxuriant vegetation with greater ecological complexity than other moist forests. They have an entirely closed canopy atop immense trees which occasionally stand 60 m high. Such forests have several distinct strata, giving an impression of "forest piled upon forest".

Deciduous forests receive 1,500 mm of rainfall a year, with 4–6 months virtually dry. Hence the forests lose their leaves for extended periods.
Open dry woodland or wooded savannah receive less than 1,500 mm of rainfall, and often experiences prolonged drought.

Open dry woodland

Tropical moist forest (evergreen and seasonal)

INDUSTRIAL USES

Sawlogs

ECOLOGICAL USES

Plywood and veneer

Pulpwood

Watershed protection

Charcoal

Industrial chemicals

Flood, landslide prevention

GENETIC STOREHOUSE

Soil erosion control

Strains for crops

Medicines

Gums, resins, and oils

Climate and weather regulation

Fuelwood and charcoal

Fodder and agricultural uses

Building poles

Pit-sawing and saw milling

Weaving materials and dyes

Fruits and nuts

Green medicine

Rearing silkworms and bee-keeping

How we benefit from tropical forests

We derive many benefits from the mere existence of tropical forests. Through their watershed effects, they act like a sponge, soaking up rainfall before releasing it slowly and steadily into rivers. They protect precious topsoil. Above all, they often regulate climate, whether at regional or global levels.

The "tree" diagram (right) summarizes only some of the goods and services available from tropical forests that already make a solid contribution to people's lives. If this diagram were to be redrawn in 20 years' time, how many more boxes would there be?

Uncut forest | Forest cut and burned | Farm in use (2–3 years) | Two years later: pioneers established | After 15 years, small primaries emerge | After 60 years, primaries dominate | After 100 years, as intact forest

and the Ganges/Brahmaputra (see pp. 162–63). In these tropical areas with their year-round warmth and river-supplied water, people exploited the fertile floodplains to embark on an enterprise that ranks as a human advance to match mastery of fire and the art of writing – and much more important in terms of basic human survival.

Since this first exercise in agriculture, we have dug up a sizeable sector of our planet, 15 million square kilometres in all (the US covers just under 10 million square kilometres). The most productive areas to date have often been the temperate-zone lands, so called because of their supposedly clement climates. The year-round warmth of the tropics is fine for crop plants, but it is also fine for weeds, pests, and diseases: the tropics lack that great pesticide of temperate zones known as winter. Moreover, many temperate-zone lands feature naturally fertile soils, whereas many tropical soils have lost their nutrients through millennia of tropical downpours that wash out crucial minerals. An area of just one hectare of naturally rich soil in UK's East Anglia or the US's Iowa can yield as much harvest in a year as 10 hectares of naturally impoverished soil in Bolivia or Zambia.

At the same time, temperate-zone farmers, being members of the affluent world, can afford to maintain their soils' fertility by means of ever-growing inputs of synthetic fertilizer, plus capital-intensive machinery and other costly investments. In other words, temperate-land farmers can now engage in "industrialized agriculture", an option not generally available in the developing world.

On a global scale, our croplands generated an adequate harvest, more or less, until about the middle of the last century. Since that time, we have witnessed the growth of human numbers and of human aspirations, twin pressures that have caused us to concentrate on a handful of high-yielding crop varieties – especially wheat, rice, maize, and potato – to supply us with the bulk of our dietary needs.

New territories to grow these crops were opened up during 1950–1980: grain-growing areas expanded by one-quarter, but since 1981 they have steadily declined. The potential for expansion in the near future is limited as gains are offset by losses, due primarily to erosion. So much for the hopes of the Food and Agricultural Organization (FAO) for us to have expanded our global croplands by a further one-seventh during the final two decades of the last century. Growth in food output must therefore come from efforts to protect soil, improve irrigation and restore the productivity of degraded land, along with the high-yielding varieties of crops and fertilizers which have powered the increase in food output since the 1950s – all at a price.

Animals for food

Humans began to domesticate animals around the same time as they began to cultivate plants. They probably started with dogs, using them for hunting

The world croplands

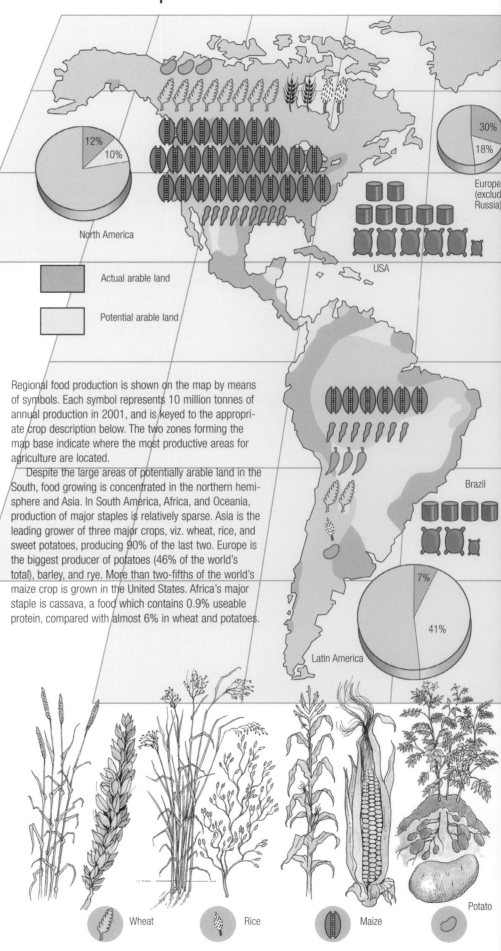

Regional food production is shown on the map by means of symbols. Each symbol represents 10 million tonnes of annual production in 2001, and is keyed to the appropriate crop description below. The two zones forming the map base indicate where the most productive areas for agriculture are located.

Despite the large areas of potentially arable land in the South, food growing is concentrated in the northern hemisphere and Asia. In South America, Africa, and Oceania, production of major staples is relatively sparse. Asia is the leading grower of three major crops, viz. wheat, rice, and sweet potatoes, producing 90% of the last two. Europe is the biggest producer of potatoes (46% of the world's total), barley, and rye. More than two-fifths of the world's maize crop is grown in the United States. Africa's major staple is cassava, a food which contains 0.9% useable protein, compared with almost 6% in wheat and potatoes.

Wheat is the most important grain in terms of world food production, providing a staple food for over one-third of the world's population. It is grown principally in temperate climates and in some sub-tropical regions, too. The protein content varies between 8% and 15%.

Rice is the leading tropical crop in Asia. Wet-rice cultivation allows for continuous cropping, so it supports high densities of population. Nutritionally it is an excellent food, with a protein content of 8–9%.

Maize In the US, the largest producer of maize, the bulk of the crop is fed to livestock. As food for people, maize is a staple crop in South America and Africa. The average protein content is 10%.

Potato Potatoes grow successfully

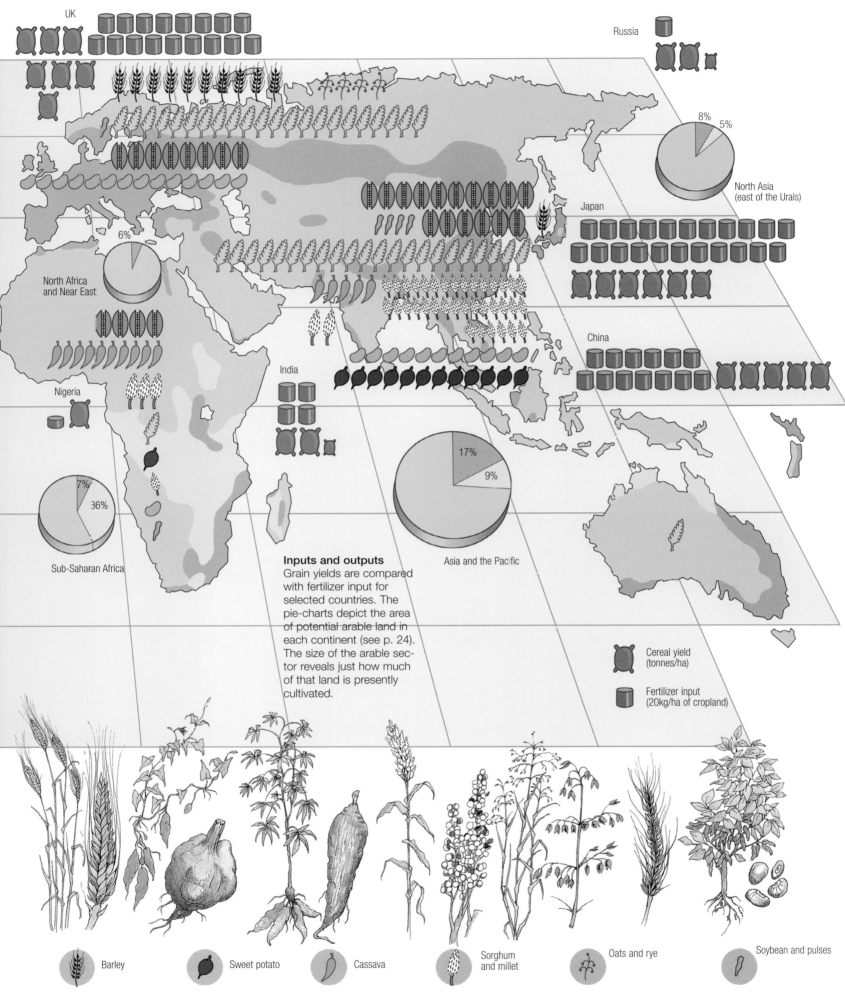

UK

Russia

North Asia
(east of the Urals)

8% 5%

Japan

North Africa
and Near East

6%

China

Nigeria

India

Sub-Saharan Africa

7%
36%

17%
9%

Asia and the Pacific

Inputs and outputs
Grain yields are compared
with fertilizer input for
selected countries. The
pie-charts depict the area
of potential arable land in
each continent (see p. 24).
The size of the arable sector reveals just how much
of that land is presently
cultivated.

Cereal yield
(tonnes/ha)

Fertilizer input
(20kg/ha of cropland)

Barley   Sweet potato   Cassava   Sorghum
and millet   Oats and rye   Soybean and pulses

in cool, moist, temperate regions,
and are a staple carbohydrate in
many developed countries.
Barley is used mainly for animal
feed and as malting for beer and
whisky. In parts of Asia and Ethiopia
it is still an important food crop.

Sweet potato Commonly grown in
wetter tropical regions, sweet potatoes are generally used as a secondary rather than a staple food.
Their chief food value is starch.
Cassava is a very important food
crop in Africa, being extremely

resistant to drought. It has a very
low protein content and should
be supplemented with other high-
protein foods.
Sorghum and millet These tropical
grains are staple foods in drier parts
of Africa and Asia. The grains lack

gluten and cannot be used for
bread making.
Oats and rye Both these crops
prefer cool, damp climates. Oats
are grown mainly for feeding livestock, while rye's chief use is for
bread flour.

Soybean and pulses In poorer
regions, pulses may form the
principal source of dietary protein.
Soybeans may contain between
30% and 50% protein.

in return for a dependable food supply. Then, as humans learned the arts of crop husbandry, they found it more convenient to herd wild herbivores and pen them close to settlements. From that early stage, growing crops and raising livestock advanced side by side.

Today, we enjoy a range of domesticated animals that includes cattle, sheep, goats, pigs, buffalo, chickens, ducks, geese, and turkeys. These creatures supply us with high-quality protein in the form of meat, milk, and eggs. They also supply us with hides, wool, and other material items. Also important is draught power. Large numbers of people in developing countries still depend upon oxen and buffalo. In India alone there are almost 100 million buffalo. Among certain pastoralist peoples such as the Masai of East Africa, livestock represents on-the-hoof wealth and hence a source of social status.

Despite our appetite for meat and milk, the number of animal species we have domesticated is a good deal less than that of plants. The nine types of animal represented on the map account for almost all our animal protein from livestock. This protein demands a grazing area of 3.5 billion hectares (an expanse equivalent to three and a half times the size of the US), a much greater area than that for crops (1.5 billion hectares). Note, however, that not all animals graze all of the time since camels, and particularly goats, consume much foliage from woody plants. Factory farming is becoming wide-spread in many parts of the developing world and the world's meat economy is being further distorted by the "new consumers" (see pp. 234–35).

In 2000, humans consumed 230 million tonnes of meat or about 38 kilograms per person. Yet only one in three of the world's people eats a meat-centred diet, and it is the developed world that consumes the lion's share. In the world's premier meat-eating nation, the US, per capita consumption is 122 kilograms a year, compared with 85 kilograms in Germany, 77 in the UK and Brazil, and 50 in China. In India, meat consumption per person per year is a mere five kilograms, what the average US citizen consumes in less than two weeks.

With 81 percent of the world's population and 74 percent of the world's livestock, developing nations enjoy only around 56 percent of all meat and 45 percent of all milk produced. This maldistribution is all the more unfortunate in that domestic animals represent a sound way for developing-world people to broaden their food supply. Livestock eats not only grass, foliage, and other plant material indigestible by humans; certain types, notably chickens, pigs, and fish consume all manner of detritous material, such as farmyard garbage and kitchen refuse.

Domestic livestock levies sizeable environmental problems. Its ever-growing demand for new pastures can serve to take over forests and wildlife habitats. Ruminants generate methane amounting to a sixth of global emissions, a share that is likely to climb in

The world's grazing herd

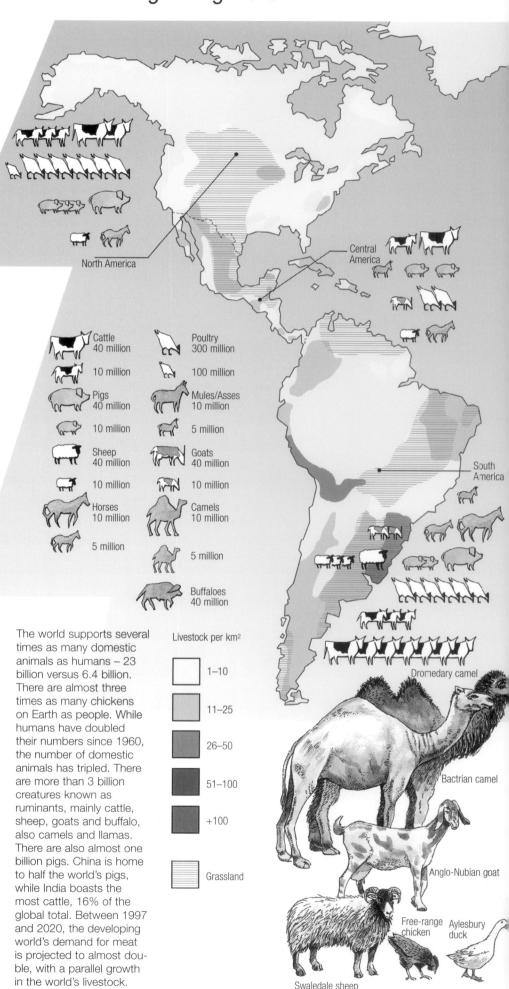

Cattle 40 million	Poultry 300 million
10 million	100 million
Pigs 40 million	Mules/Asses 10 million
10 million	5 million
Sheep 40 million	Goats 40 million
10 million	10 million
Horses 10 million	Camels 10 million
5 million	5 million
Buffaloes 40 million	

Livestock per km²
1–10
11–25
26–50
51–100
+100
Grassland

The world supports several times as many domestic animals as humans – 23 billion versus 6.4 billion. There are almost three times as many chickens on Earth as people. While humans have doubled their numbers since 1960, the number of domestic animals has tripled. There are more than 3 billion creatures known as ruminants, mainly cattle, sheep, goats and buffalo, also camels and llamas. There are also almost one billion pigs. China is home to half the world's pigs, while India boasts the most cattle, 16% of the global total. Between 1997 and 2020, the developing world's demand for meat is projected to almost double, with a parallel growth in the world's livestock.

Dromedary camel
Bactrian camel
Anglo-Nubian goat
Free-range chicken
Aylesbury duck
Swaledale sheep

Low-grade grazers
Marginal land grazers, browsers, and foragers efficiently convert otherwise unusable energy.

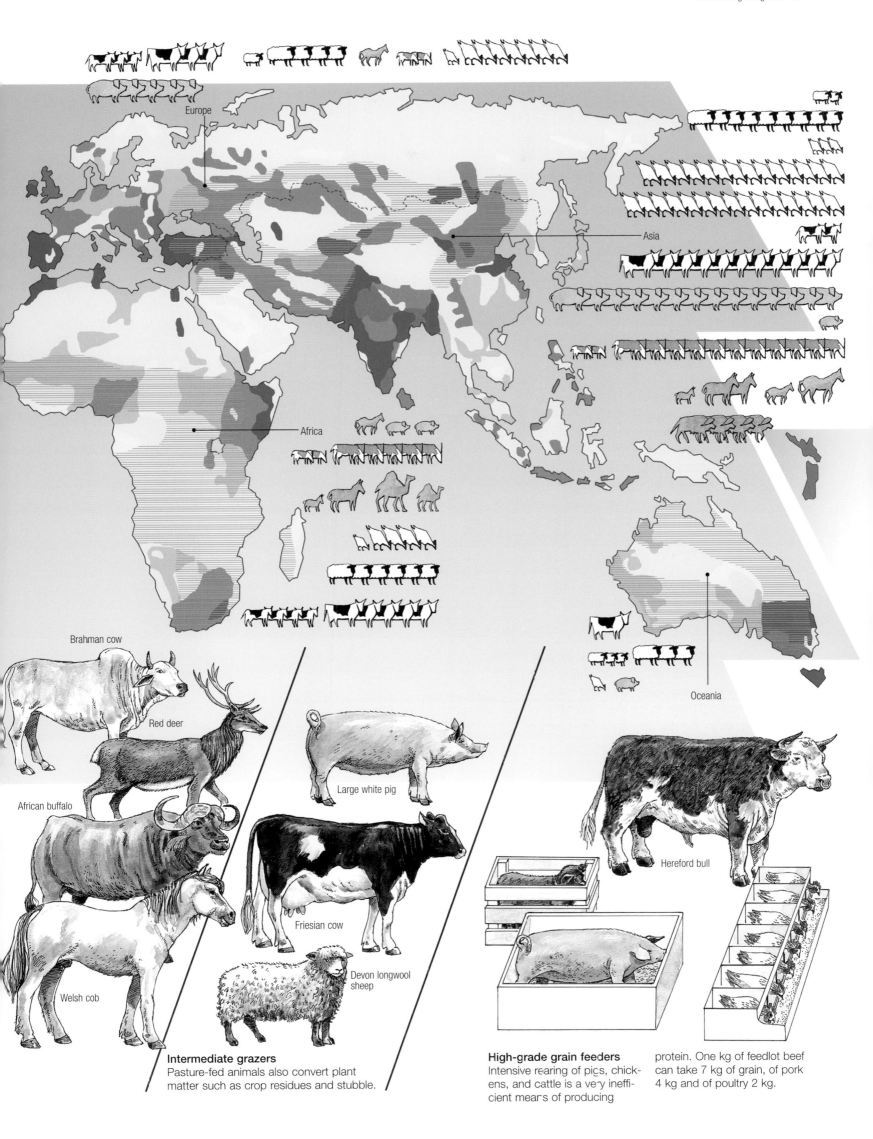

Europe

Asia

Africa

Oceania

Brahman cow

Red deer

African buffalo

Large white pig

Friesian cow

Welsh cob

Devon longwool
sheep

Hereford bull

Intermediate grazers
Pasture-fed animals also convert plant
matter such as crop residues and stubble.

High-grade grain feeders
Intensive rearing of pigs, chickens, and cattle is a very inefficient means of producing

protein. One kg of feedlot beef
can take 7 kg of grain, of pork
4 kg and of poultry 2 kg.

response to expanding appetites for meat. Livestock wastes are widely implicated in waterway pollution, toxic algal blooms, and extensive fish kills.

The ability to feed ourselves

There is no doubt that we produce enough food to send everybody to bed with a full stomach. Yet tens of millions starve, and 800 million developing-world citizens are undernourished (see pp. 46–47). The problem is that the Earth is less than "fair" in allocating its land resources. Some sectors are much better endowed with fertile soils than others; some are much more vulnerable to natural injury; and some respond much better to human manipulation. At the same time, we must recognize that we, in return, have been less than fair to the Earth. We have abused it by over-working its soils, prodigally felling its forests, over-grazing its grasslands, and mistreating its other gifts.

The global larder

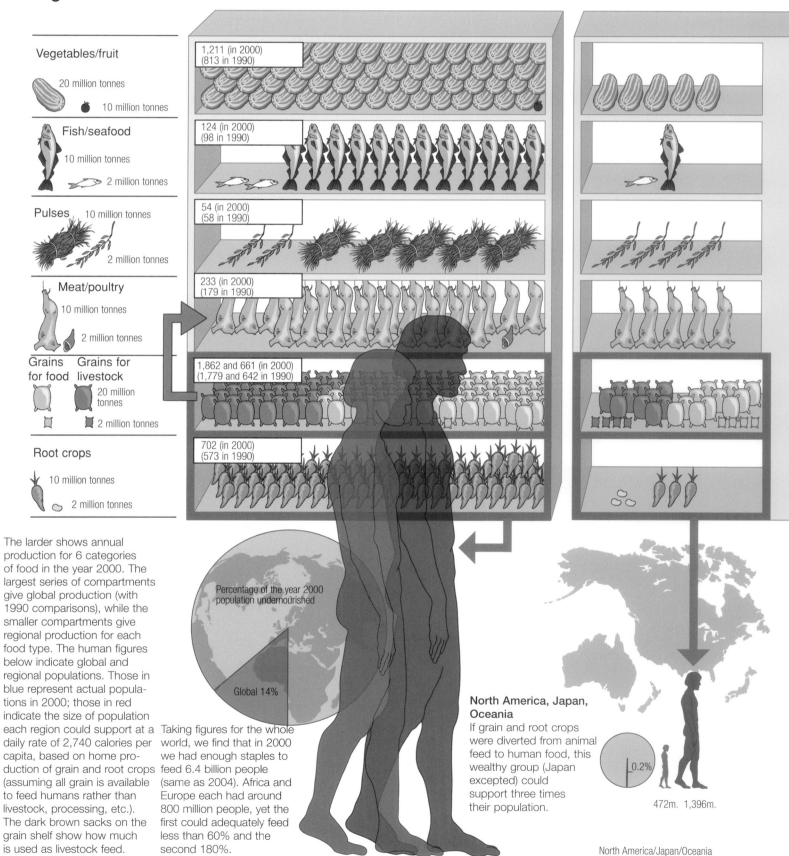

Vegetables/fruit
20 million tonnes
10 million tonnes

1,211 (in 2000)
(813 in 1990)

Fish/seafood
10 million tonnes
2 million tonnes

124 (in 2000)
(98 in 1990)

Pulses   10 million tonnes
2 million tonnes

54 (in 2000)
(58 in 1990)

Meat/poultry
10 million tonnes
2 million tonnes

233 (in 2000)
(179 in 1990)

Grains   Grains for
for food   livestock
20 million tonnes
2 million tonnes

1,862 and 661 (in 2000)
(1,779 and 642 in 1990)

Root crops
10 million tonnes
2 million tonnes

702 (in 2000)
(573 in 1990)

The larder shows annual production for 6 categories of food in the year 2000. The largest series of compartments give global production (with 1990 comparisons), while the smaller compartments give regional production for each food type. The human figures below indicate global and regional populations. Those in blue represent actual populations in 2000; those in red indicate the size of population each region could support at a daily rate of 2,740 calories per capita, based on home production of grain and root crops (assuming all grain is available to feed humans rather than livestock, processing, etc.). The dark brown sacks on the grain shelf show how much is used as livestock feed.

Taking figures for the whole world, we find that in 2000 we had enough staples to feed 6.4 billion people (same as 2004). Africa and Europe each had around 800 million people, yet the first could adequately feed less than 60% and the second 180%.

Percentage of the year 2000 population undernourished

Global 14%

North America, Japan, Oceania

If grain and root crops were diverted from animal feed to human food, this wealthy group (Japan excepted) could support three times their population.

0.2%

472m. 1,396m.

North America/Japan/Oceania

World 6,434 million
(cf. year 2000 population 6,057 million)

Our meagre sense of husbandry has brought us to a point where, when many more mouths are clamouring to be fed, the resource base itself is falling into critical disrepair. Yet we certainly possess the technological skills and economic capacity to supply a rightful place for the entire human family at Earth's feast table. All we appear to lack is the ultimate commitment to say "Yes, let's do it".

But "Let's do it" entails far more than simply ploughing up more land, or applying more sensitive agricultura skills. The basic problems are political and economic rather than technical and scientific. Poor people are generally hungry because they lack the financial means to grow enough food or to buy it. While a transfer of relief food (especially using grain as human food instead of livestock feed) from the developed world would help to relieve immediate hunger, it would tackle symptoms not problems. Poor people need to be able to feed themselves, and to do that their entire lifestyles need to be upgraded.

Latin America

Much of the arable land is under-used. Half the grain production goes to feed livestock, yet almost 50 million people are undernourished.

481m. 446m.

10%

Europe

Enough food here to feed almost twice as many people but still almost 30 million undernourished in the eastern sector (transition countries).

Europe
Europe (Eastern) 2%

794m. .1,436m

Africa

A region with 13% of the world's population is trying to survive on 6% of its staple crop production. 200 million are undernourished.

Africa
25%

794m. 474m.

Asia

Despite high food production, the sheer size of population stretches the land beyond its limits. 540 million are undernourished.

Asia
16%

3,479m. 2,679m.

The Land Crisis

As human numbers and expectations rise, we demand still more from our natural resource base. Yet we continue to degrade forests, overgraze grasslands, lose land to urban development, and erode topsoil at alarming rates. Indeed, few resource problems are so important, while so little publicized, as this last problem – the disappearance of our soil. Each year, many billions of tonnes are washed away by rainfall and blown away by the wind.

Human activity has caused erosion rates to increase many times over natural rates. We cultivate steep slopes without adequate terracing, practise inexpert flatland cultivation, and allow livestock to overgraze grasslands. We overwork the soil until its robust structure turns to dust. Worst of all, we eliminate tree cover, whether forests, shelterbelts, or hedgerows, and thus the soil washed and blown off our farmlands eventually makes its way into rivers, lakes, and oceans. In effect, it is funnelled into a vast "sump", never to return. The process erodes away a crucial basis of our civilization.

There is no known way to replace our soil. If we wait upon natural processes, we shall wait for centuries if not millennia. The disappearance of our soil threatens to undermine our very means of feeding ourselves. Yet because erosion is such a cryptic and "silent" problem, few leaders give it a fraction of the attention it deserves. It is hard to whip up public opinion about the issue. In the US, a supposedly "advanced" country, soil on cultivated lands is eroding many times faster than it can reform. A similar sad tale can be told around the world, especially in the humid tropics with their thunderstorms. Violent downpours rip the topsoil from hillsides, carving great gulleys in the landscape, while windstorms ravage semi-arid zones planted to crops.

Half of all arable lands are suffering the problem at unacceptable levels: the cropland base is shrinking as our gains in bringing new land under the plough are offset through soil erosion. As the population continues to rise, so the global decline in grain area per person from 0.16 hectares in 1980 to 0.11 hectares in 1999 seems set to continue. Today, already more than 400 million people live in countries with less than the minimum 0.7 hectares of land required to supply a vegetarian diet for one person without the use of artificial chemicals and with loss of soil and nutrients. Even with low projections of population growth this total could soar to 600 million by 2025. It is the double pressure of growth in human numbers and need to nourish people better that chiefly drives soil erosion. Farmers everywhere

The disappearing soil

Echoes of the Dust Bowl

Soil erosion has been exceeding soil formation on one-third of US cropland (see map). Despite memories of the devastating Dust Bowl of the 1930s, when 40 million hectares of arable land on the Great Plains were severely damaged, overproduction was encouraged at the expense of soil cover. So great was public concern at the effects of soil loss, plus resentment of farm subsidy schemes, that in 1986 Congress ushered in the Conservation Reserve Program to give farmers an economic incentive to conserve the soil on their most erodible land. In return for an annual payment of about $120 per ha, farmers converted cropland to grassland or woodland for ten years to enable it to recover. At the end of the first stage of the scheme in 1990, around 14 million ha had entered the programme, yet this represented only one-quarter of the highly erosion-prone land. The CRP, together with the expansion of "conservation tillage" agriculture, is reducing erosion rates, but croplands are still losing around 2 billion tonnes a year. Annual costs to the US are estimated at $44 billion. The map (below) shows the cumulative effects of erosion in the US.

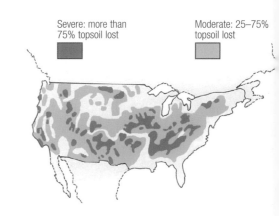

Severe: more than 75% topsoil lost

Moderate: 25–75% topsoil lost

Global land loss

Humans have severely degraded 35 million sq. km, an area almost four times that of the US. More than one-third of this is due to agricultural activities (see table below). Each year more than 100,000 sq. km of croplands are lost through erosion, waterlogging, salinization, etc. A further 200,000 sq. km become severely degraded.

Human-induced land degradation

	Land area (000s sq. km)	Total affected by severe/very severe land degradation (000s sq. km)	Amount of severe/very severe land degradation due to agricultural activities (000s sq. km)
Sub-Saharan Africa	23,772	5,931	1,996
North Africa and Near East	12,379	4,260	759
North Asia, east of Urals	21,033	4,421	1,180
Asia and Pacific	28,989	8,407	3,506
South and Central America	20,498	5,552	1,795
North America	19,237	3,158	2,427
Europe	6,843	3,274	727
World	134,907	35,003	12,390

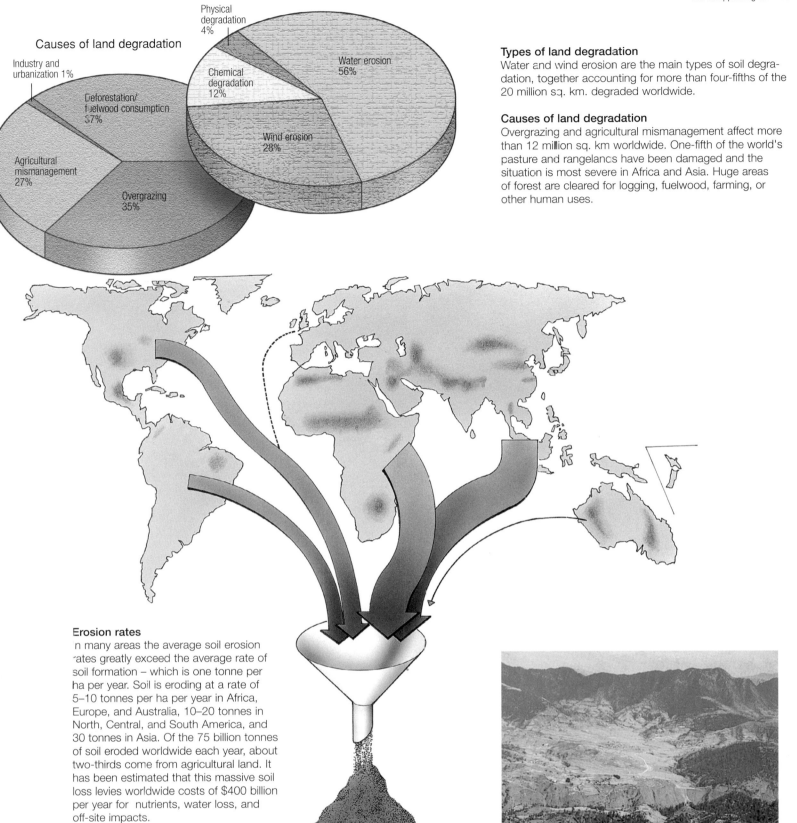

Causes of land degradation

Industry and urbanization 1%

Deforestation/fuelwood consumption 37%

Agricultural mismanagement 27%

Overgrazing 35%

Physical degradation 4%

Chemical degradation 12%

Water erosion 56%

Wind erosion 28%

Types of land degradation

Water and wind erosion are the main types of soil degradation, together accounting for more than four-fifths of the 20 million sq. km. degraded worldwide.

Causes of land degradation

Overgrazing and agricultural mismanagement affect more than 12 million sq. km worldwide. One-fifth of the world's pasture and rangelands have been damaged and the situation is most severe in Africa and Asia. Huge areas of forest are cleared for logging, fuelwood, farming, or other human uses.

Erosion rates

n many areas the average soil erosion rates greatly exceed the average rate of soil formation – which is one tonne per ha per year. Soil is eroding at a rate of 5–10 tonnes per ha per year in Africa, Europe, and Australia, 10–20 tonnes in North, Central, and South America, and 30 tonnes in Asia. Of the 75 billion tonnes of soil eroded worldwide each year, about two-thirds come from agricultural land. It has been estimated that this massive soil loss levies worldwide costs of $400 billion per year for nutrients, water loss, and off-site impacts.

Annual soil loss: 75 billion tonnes – worldwide costs $400 billion.

Soil timescales

Formation of 2.5 cm of topsoil can take anything from 100 to 2,500 years, depending on the soil type. Reversing this process is all too quick: we can destroy 2.5 cm of soil in as little as 10 years.

5mm of topsoil

Loss through erosion

Years   10   20   30   40   50   60   70   80   90   100

New island in the Bay of Bengal

Around one quarter of a million tonnes of topsoil are washed off the deforested mountain slopes of Nepal each year, and a further sizeable amount from the Himalayan foothills in India's sector of the Ganges catchment zone. As a result, in the early 1970s an offshore island emerged in the Bay of Bengal, covering some 2,500 sq. m. By the late 1990s it had expanded to 10,000 sq. m and could reach 25 or even 30 sq. km within the next one to two decades. The island has been claimed by India as New Moore Island, and by Bangladesh as South Talpatti. Nepal, the country which contributes most to the phenomenon, has not been consulted.

are over-exploiting their lands. In 50 years we look likely to run out of oil and out of much of our food-producing lands. We shall find substitutes for oil, but nobody has yet come up with a substitute for topsoil.

The decline of the tropical forest

Every year, 170,000–180,000 square kilometres of tropical forests and woodlands – about the size of Washington State – are eliminated. We are also witnessing the degradation of further thousands of square kilometres of forest a year. (A degraded forest is one that has been so grossly disrupted that it is no more than an impoverished travesty of true forest.)

So pervasive and rapid is the loss of tropical forests that most remaining tracts of these superb exemplars of nature may disappear within 25 years – except for sizeable isolated blocs in western Brazilian Amazonia, the Guyana Shield, the Congo

basin, and Papua New Guinea, plus a few relics in the form of parks and reserves.

Part of the problem is that people everywhere want more wood, and thus the commercial logger looks increasingly to tropical forests. Logging in the tropics degrades at least 35,000 square kilometres of forest annually. Selective logging is the usual commercial principle, but in practice this heavily degrades the residual forest because many unharvested trees are damaged beyond recovery.

After many decades, a heavily logged forest ecosystem can sometimes regenerate. It generally does not get the chance. The main damage done by loggers is unwitting. They lay down a network of timber-haulage tracks, allowing land-hungry farmers to penetrate deep into the forest heartlands. Slash-and-burn agriculture, which, with its previously low

200 million cu. m of fuel-wood consumption

200 million cu. m of indus-trial consumption of wood

Shrinking forests

The demand for agricultural land, whether planned or unplanned, is the chief cause of the depletion of tropical forests. Unplanned agriculture, i.e. "spontaneous settlement" by slash-and-burn cultivators, is much more difficult to quantify than planned agriculture for cash-crop plantations, cattle ranches, and organized smallholder cultivation. The bottom graph demonstrates the demand for agricultural land in the tropics.

The rate at which the world's tropical moist forests are disap-pearing is shown in the central graph. Between 1950 and 1975, at least 1.2 million sq. km were destroyed. Both the 1980s and the 1990s saw a further loss of more than 1.5 million sq. km.

Consumption: industrial vs. fuelwood

In 1955, consumption of industrial wood exceeded that of fuel-wood, but by 1975 the balance had tipped in favour of fuelwood, reflecting the demands of a growing developing-world population. By 1975 there was a severe deficit in supply of fuelwood. The shortfall in supply had serious repercussions: burning dung and crop residues instead, rather than returning them to the crop fields, robs the soil of fertilizers and so reduces food output. In Africa and Asia, at least 400 million tonnes of animal dung were burned each year. If this natural fertilizer were used on croplands it could pro-duce an extra 20 million tonnes of grain, enough to make up the diets of 500 million malnourished people. Between the year 2000 and 2015 the demand for fuelwood is projected to increase by almost one-third (see pp. 122–23).

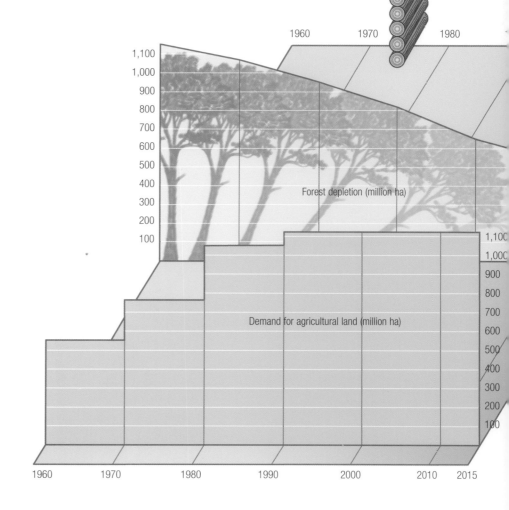

Forest depletion (million ha)

Demand for agricultural land (million ha)

Loss of green cover

Some 8,000 years ago, almost half of the land was covered by forest. By the year 2000, the area covered by tropical forest and woodland had declined substantially and, by 2015, a further large decline is projected. This contrasts markedly with temperate forests and woodland, whose area remains fairly constant thanks to reforestation.

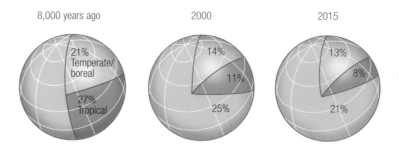

population densities, represented a sustainable use of the forest, now poses by far the biggest threat. Between 200 and 500 million of these cultivators account for more than half of all deforestation and gross degradation. Squeezed out of traditional farmlands for reasons ranging from maldistribution of land to inadequate rural development, these displaced or "shifted" cultivators see little alternative to their lifestyle.

A similar sentiment applies to fuelwood gatherers, who, unless supplied with "tree farms" and village woodlots, see little option but to continue with their present over-harvesting. Fuelwood gathering depletes at least 8,000 square kilometres of tropical forest each year, and at least twice as much open woodland and scrub forest.

Not so hard placed is the cattle rancher, who torches at least 8,000 square kilometres of forest each year, mainly to raise beef for lucrative export markets in the developed world. Ranchers could double their output on existing pastures if they were to run their operations more efficiently, but government inducements have encouraged them to ranch extensively rather than intensively. When pastureland soils lose their residual fertility within half a dozen years and weeds overrun the holding, the rancher simply moves on to another patch of forest and repeats the process. Fortunately, the Brazilian government has ended the subsidies that have long fostered ranchers' deforestation in Amazonia.

In several senses, we all play a part in the decline of tropical forests. We seek specialist hardwoods at unrealistically low prices. We demand cheap beef from formerly forested pasturelands. But hardly anyone can claim that his or her hand is not, in some indirect way, on the chainsaw and machete at work in tropical forests. We shall all eventually suffer if tropical forests continue to disappear.

Consumer demand levies a heavy cost for Amazonia
European demand for Brazilian beef in the wake of BSE and Foot and Mouth Disease, and increasing soybean production, were surely major, if indirect, factors in the increased deforestation of 2002 and 2003, when a further 50,000 sq. km of Amazonia forest were lost (almost twice the size of Belgium). Amazonia's cattle population more than doubled to 57 million during 1990–2002, a period when Europe's share of processed meat imports from Brazil rose from 40% to 74%. Similarly, soybean production is increasing rapidly: the State of Mato Grosso has more hectares devoted to soybeans than Illinois or Iowa, the largest soybean states in the US.

8,000 years ago | Today

Temperate and boreal forests

Tropical forests

The effects of forest clearance

"Man has gone to the Moon but he does not know yet how to make a flame tree or a birdsong. Let us keep our dear countries free from irreversible mistakes which would lead us in the future to long for those same birds and trees."

Former president Houphouet-Boiny of Côte D'Ivoire, a country which has lost well over 90% of its original forests and woodlands.

When the forest cover in a watershed is removed, the repercussions are far-reaching. The forests' sponge effect is lost, and the release of rainfall becomes erratic. Farmers in the valleylands of southern Asia are particularly vulnerable: rivers such as the Ganges, Brahmaputra, Irrawaddy, Salween, and the Mekong no longer supply regular amounts of irrigation water – which causes the Green Revolution (see pp. 62–63) to be less revolutionary than anticipated.

City-dwellers suffer, too. In the hinterland of Manila and Panama City, deforestation has caused so much injury to watershed functions that urban water supplies are threatened, bringing on a risk of contaminated water and pandemics. In Ecuador, Kenya, and Thailand, cities experience "brownouts" caused by loss of hill forest: washed-off sediment leads to silting up of hydroelectric dams.

Clearance of tropical forests could also severely affect the world's climate. In Amazonia, more than half of all moisture circulating through the region's ecosystem remains within the forest: rainwater is absorbed by plants, before being "breathed out" into the atmosphere. Were a large part of the forest to disappear, the remainder would become less able (however well protected) to retain so much moisture – and the effects could extend further, even drying out the climate for crops in southern Brazil.

More importantly, tropical forests help to stabilize the world's climate by absorbing solar radiation: they simply "soak up" the sunshine. When forests are cleared, the "shininess" of the planet's land surface increases, radiating more of the sun's energy back into space (the "albedo" effect). An increase in albedo can disrupt convection patterns, wind currents, and rainfall in lands far beyond the tropics.

Tropical forests do not significantly affect Earth's oxygen balance, but they play an important part in the carbon dioxide budget. Burning forests release considerable quantities of carbon into the skies, causing a build-up of carbon dioxide that is surely triggering a "greenhouse" effect, bringing on drier climates for some, especially Americans. What if the great grain belt of North America starts to unbuckle, with less food not only for North Americans but for dozens of countries that import their grain?

The advancing deserts

In several drier parts of the world, deserts are increasing at an alarming rate. In those few areas where the process is natural, we call it desertization,

Destroying the protector

As long as forest cover remains intact, rivers run clear and clean, and they run regularly throughout the year. When the forest disappears, the downstream effect is a regime of floods followed by droughts. Washed-off sediment not only causes riverbeds to silt up, but it also chokes hydropower dams and suffocates coastal fisheries.

Flooding in the Ganges Plain, as in Bangladesh above, provides a graphic example of the effects of deforestation. As the Himalayan foothill forests are cleared for agriculture, 500 million people in the valley grow ever-more vulnerable to flooding. Something similar applies in the Yangtse Valley in China. In 1998, heavy flooding of the Yangtse river destroyed 50,000 sq. km of farmland crops, claimed 3,600 lives, affected 240 million people, and caused economic losses of $36 billion. The Chinese government views trees as being worth three times as much when left standing as when cut, because of their water storage and flood control capacities.

Forest watershed removed

Topsoil washed down

Flood plain

Silted-up river

Displaced forest peoples

Several million people still follow traditional lifestyles within tropical
forests. Generally disregarded by the outside world, the first that
we often hear about these peoples is when they shoot arrows at
bulldozers. As recently as the early 1970s, the Tasaday tribe was
discovered in a Philippines forest cut off by a 15-km strip from the
outside world and pursuing a Neolithic lifestyle in isolation.

So fast are these groups being squeezed out of existence that
in Brazilian Amazonia, which recently featured 230 native groups
with an estimated 2 million people, there are now only half as many
such groups with a total below 50,000 persons. For example, the
Kayapos have been massacred in their thousands by illegal settlers, and have been forcibly transferred from their homelands. The
photograph above shows the Megkronotis Indians (of the Kayapos)
trudging through the ashes of a forest they refuse to abandon.

Scouring the land for fuel

Many rural families now find it as hard to heat the evening supper
bowl as to fill it. As fallen wood becomes scarce, villagers lop
branches, fell trees, even uproot stumps. Removing residues robs
soil of nutrients, while clearing shrubs hastens erosion, leaving a
barren landscape. More than 2 billion people in developing
countries rely on wood, charcoal, or dung for fuel.

but where the desert encroaches through human hand, we term it desertification – an ugly word for an ugly process. In fact, it is less than accurate to assert that the desert is advancing or encroaching. Rather a strip of additional desert is being "tacked on" to the original. In certain areas far away from true deserts, lands are being degraded to a desert-like condition.

Desertification affects more than one-third of the Earth's land surface and the people hardest hit are the poor who depend on the soil for their livelihoods. More than 250 million people are directly affected by desertification and one billion are at risk in 110 countries. This latter figure could almost double by 2025. Every year $42 billion (1990 $s) in income and 150,000 square kilometres of productive land are being lost because of desertification, land degradation, and declining agricultural productivity. To reiterate: desertification is caused by human misuse or overuse of the land, mainly by overgrazing by livestock and deforestation for fuelwood.

It has been estimated that a 20-year global effort to halt and even reverse the process would cost only $10–22 billion per year. With the benefits far outweighing the costs, why don't governments invest the funds to combat desertification? A main reason lies with the status of the people affected. They are "marginalized" people in two senses: they live in marginal lands and they are marginal to the politico-economic structures of their countries. National leaders know they represent no threat to the system if their needs are ignored.

Governments frequently funnel sizeable sums of money into drylands when trouble of a different sort erupts. For instance, in the war between Ethiopia and Somalia in the 1970s, the superpowers poured in vast funds in the form of military hardware on the grounds that the region was close to oil-tanker shipping lanes from the Persian Gulf. These funds would have been enough to rehabilitate degraded lands in the two countries – also to halt desertification along much of the entire Saharan frontier.

Our hungry world

There are two forms of malnutrition in our world. While millions of people in the developing countries starve to death each year, developed countries are making themselves ill by overeating. An average developing-world person enjoys only about four-fifths as many calories as an average developed-world person, little over two-thirds as much protein, and one-third as much animal protein. Given the grain fed to livestock, many a developed-world citizen accounts for several times as much food as his or her counterpart in the developing world. Most absurd of all is the recent news that whereas there are 840 million undernourished people on the planet, there are 1.2 billion over-nourished people. Thus the scandal of the waistline: expanding excessively among the rich and shrinking excessively among

The encroaching desert

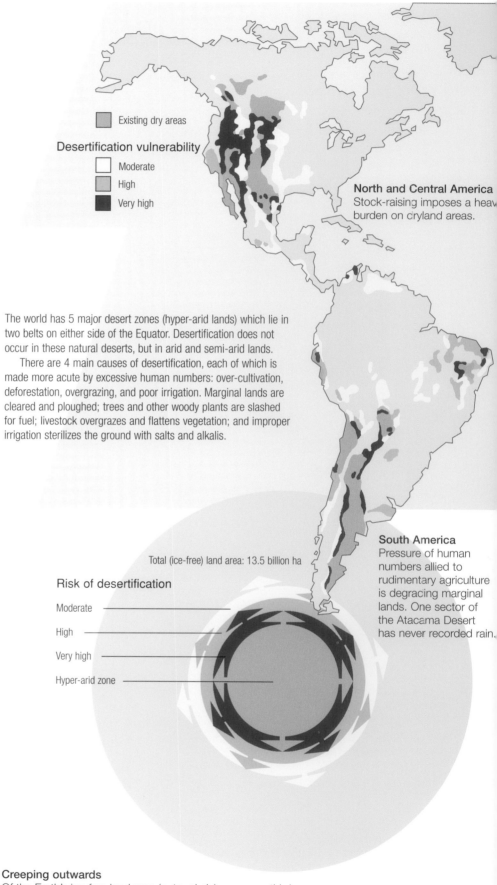

Existing dry areas

Desertification vulnerability
Moderate
High
Very high

North and Central America
Stock-raising imposes a heavy burden on dryland areas.

The world has 5 major desert zones (hyper-arid lands) which lie in two belts on either side of the Equator. Desertification does not occur in these natural deserts, but in arid and semi-arid lands.

There are 4 main causes of desertification, each of which is made more acute by excessive human numbers: over-cultivation, deforestation, overgrazing, and poor irrigation. Marginal lands are cleared and ploughed; trees and other woody plants are slashed for fuel; livestock overgrazes and flattens vegetation; and improper irrigation sterilizes the ground with salts and alkalis.

Total (ice-free) land area: 13.5 billion ha

Risk of desertification
Moderate
High
Very high
Hyper-arid zone

South America
Pressure of human numbers allied to rudimentary agriculture is degrading marginal lands. One sector of the Atacama Desert has never recorded rain.

Creeping outwards
Of the Earth's ice-free land area (outer circle), over one-third is already affected or likely to be affected by desertification. The inner core represents extreme desert (hyper-arid zone). Spreading out from this are the areas of our land base at very high, high, and moderate risk respectively.

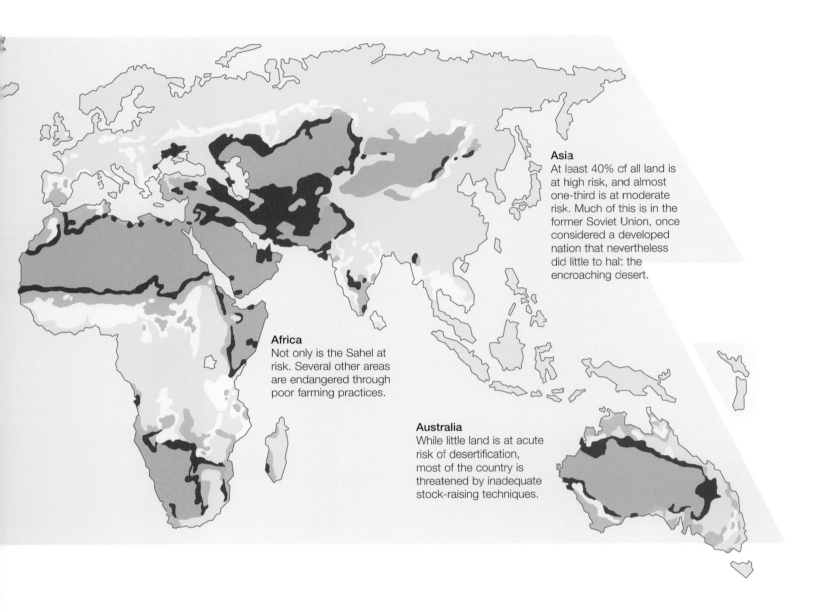

Asia
At least 40% of all land is at high risk, and almost one-third is at moderate risk. Much of this is in the former Soviet Union, once considered a developed nation that nevertheless did little to halt the encroaching desert.

Africa
Not only is the Sahel at risk. Several other areas are endangered through poor farming practices.

Australia
While little land is at acute risk of desertification, most of the country is threatened by inadequate stock-raising techniques.

The Sahel disaster

Desertification was brought to the world's attention by the Sahel disaster of the early 1970s. The ostensible cause of the debacle lay with the drought that overtook the semi-arid zone dwellers of the Sahel, but the main problem lay further in the past. For the previous two decades, the region enjoyed better-than-average rainfall. Consequently, when cash-crop cultivation in lands further south started to expand along with their human populations, throngs of pastoralists and cultivators moved north towards the fringe of the Sahara. Lands that had not been dug for centuries were cultivated, and livestock was crowded on to smaller areas of pasture. (The photograph (right) shows the effects of over-grazing in Niger.) Sadly, these migrant peoples knew, from their tribal traditions, that the moister phase would probably be transitory, which made the drought all the more terrible when it finally struck – more than 100,000 people and 3.5 million head of livestock perished in the early 1970s. Disaster hit the region again in the early-to-mid 1980s.

The crisis still persists right along the Sahel region. Human activities continue to reduce the productivity of the lands that speedily degrade under stress.

the poor. Even a domestic cat in Europe or North America receives more meat each day than many a person in the developing world.

The great majority of the world's hungry live in the developing world where, at the start of the new millennium, there were 800 million people, a sixth of the population, who did not eat enough for an active working life. Whilst there had been a decline of 100 million between 1980 and 1990, the next decade saw a reduction of only 20 million. Sub-Saharan Africa suffered a huge increase, from 125 million in 1980 to 166 million in 1990 and 200 million in 2000. Today, Asia features prominently, too, with 540 million undernourished. This includes 120 million in China and 230 million in India, both of which countries have a rising class of "new consumers" (see pp. 234–35) whose appetites for meat mean that more and more grain is fed to livestock rather than hungry people. In 2003 there was a global grain shortfall of 105 million tonnes – the largest on record and knocking a sizeable hole in the world's consumption of 1,930 million tonnes. On top of that was the need to feed the additional 80 million people added to the world population. At the start of 2003, global grain reserves totalled only 59 days of consumption, whereas the minimum needed for food security is reckoned to be 70 days.

"If we were to keep a minute of silence for every person who died in 1982 because of hunger, we would not be able to celebrate the coming of the 21st century because we would still have to remain silent."

Fidel Castro, March 1983

Hunger and glut

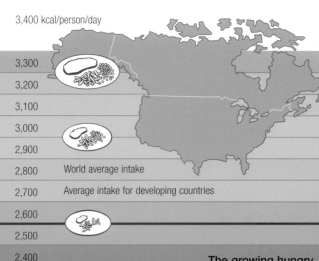

3,400 kcal/person/day

3,300 — Average intake for developed countries
3,200
3,100
3,000
2,900
2,800 — World average intake
2,700 — Average intake for developing countries
2,600
2,500
2,400
2,300 — Average intake for well-being
2,200
2,100 — Minimum for basic nutrition
2,000
1,900
1,800
1,700
1,600
1,500 — Intake below which severe malnutrition can be expected

The growing hungry
A minimum daily calorie intake of 2,100 calories should provide enough for basic nutrition, but much depends on a person's activity. A subsistence farmer with heavy labour may need 3,500 calories per day. Conversely, a woman with her smaller body size needs fewer calories – though a pregnant woman needs an additional 300 calories a day and her lactation will require an extra 500 calories a day. A child may get by on 1,000 calories. An adult intake below 1,500 calories a day is likely to result in severe malnutrition, or even starvation.

Headline news
There are 150 million underweight babies and young children in the developing world, and each year 6 million die from hunger and hunger-related diseases. This figure is equivalent to 40 jumbo jet crashes a day with no survivors. A similar number of adults succumb.

The geography of hunger is one of the starkest indicators of the North–South divide. As the world map, above, confirms, the average diet in the North provides a good deal more than the essential average daily intake of calories. The average diet in many countries of the developing world (particularly in Sub-Saharan Africa) by contrast, not only falls below the world average calorific intake, but often also falls below the minimum intake required for survival, let alone health. Malnutrition is the concealed cause of many diseases, particularly among children. With their pot bellies and sunken eyes, they quickly become vulnerable to infection. Perhaps worst of all, diarrhoeal diseases drain from a child's stomach much of the nutriment it has ingested, thus reinforcing basic malnutrition.

Undernutrition is associated with around three-fifths of the 11 million deaths of babies and young children each year – a statistic that would be shocking if it were only a tenth as much. We could save many of them for an outlay of just a few dollars each through programmes promoting breastfeeding, rehydration therapy (to counteract diarrhoea), immunization, and improved care generally.

In developed countries, malnutrition takes the form of overconsumption of sugars and fats resulting in obesity, heart disease, and diabetes. The US with its "supersize" and "value" meals has become a country of fast-fat and junk-food junkies. Obesity-related illnesses – ranging from heart disease and strokes to diabetes and cancer, and often brought on in part by gorging on grain-fed meats – cost around $120 billion annually (two and a half times more than smoking-related costs), plus another $33 billion spent on weight-loss schemes and dietary drugs. The combined total is far more than the country's fast-food industry's annual revenues of $110 billion. Every year these obesity-related illnesses kill 300,000 Americans, compared with 400,000 killed by cigarettes, the latter figure being on the decline. The problem is becoming acute in many developing countries, too, with their rising incomes and rising aspirations for meat-based diets (see pp. 234–35). In China there are now over 1,000 foreign-based fast-food outlets, and the swiftly spreading fad of fatty meats threatens to bring on an epidemic of heart disease. During the period 2000–2020 China is expected to suffer an increase in heart attacks of 21%, followed by Russia 26%, Indonesia 33%, India 45%, Mexico 95%, and Saudi Arabia 101%, many such attacks being due in part to obesity.

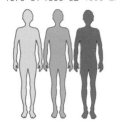

Each figure = 5 million undernourished.
Outlined figures indicate declines in
undernourishment.

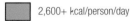

1979–81 1990–92 1998–2000

2,600+ kcal/person/day

2,100–2 600

less than 2,100

The hunger gap
The average daily require-
ment for well-being is estimated to be 2,350 calo-
ries, yet developed-world
citizens receive 40% above
this. While the average for
developing-world citizens is
2,700 calories, many sub-
sist on far less. In Ethiopia,
the average is less than
1,900; in the Democratic
Republic of Congo, less
than 1,600.

Bear in mind that not all grain goes directly into
people's stomachs. Far from it; only about half in
many developed countries. The rest reaches
them via the stomachs of cattle pigs, poultry,
and other domestic animals. In 2001, this
diverted grain amounted to 685 million
tonnes – just five percent of this would have
been enough to make up the diets of the
world's 840 million malnourished people.

The sharp disparity of hunger and glut
occurs not only among, but within, many
countries of the developing world, where the top
fifth of the population may be 10–20 times more
affluent than the bottom fifth. In Brazil and the
Philippines, average diets may suggest that things
are not so bad, yet each country has around 17 million undernourished people. In Sub-Saharan Africa,
at least 100 million are so severely undernourished
they can be considered on the verge of starvation.
In Somalia and Mozambique, the poor suffer an
average deficit of 400–500 calories per day, as
compared with the 2,100 calories they should ingest
as an absolute minimum. We should bear all this in
mind when we hear the protests of those who eat
less in one day than a typical British person consumes by midday – and tries to do many hours of
hard labour off it.

At a global food conference you will see that
many political leaders from developing countries (like
their colleagues from the rich world) are, frankly, fat.
Their lives will be shortened just as surely as those of
the hungry multitudes whom they earnestly discuss.
Perhaps attendance at such a conference should be
made conditional upon a suitably trim figure?

Hunger extends beyond physical suffering and
misery. It reduces capacity to work and increases
susceptibility to disease. Among children, insufficient
protein can retard physical and mental development.

Some observers urge that poor countries should
grow more food for themselves. So they should, and
they would feel encouraged to do so if they did not
allocate so much land to cash crops for export. As
a first look at some solutions – how we can manage
our affairs to the advantage of all – it is fitting to
examine the cash-crop factor (see pp. 52–53).

Global warming
Global warming will prove to be bad news for
many major crops. When summer temperatures
rise above 34°C, photosynthesis slows down, and
when it reaches 37°C, it exceeds the tolerance of
many crops altogether. Roughly speaking, each one
degree C rise above the optimum during the growing season can reduce grain yields by 10 percent.

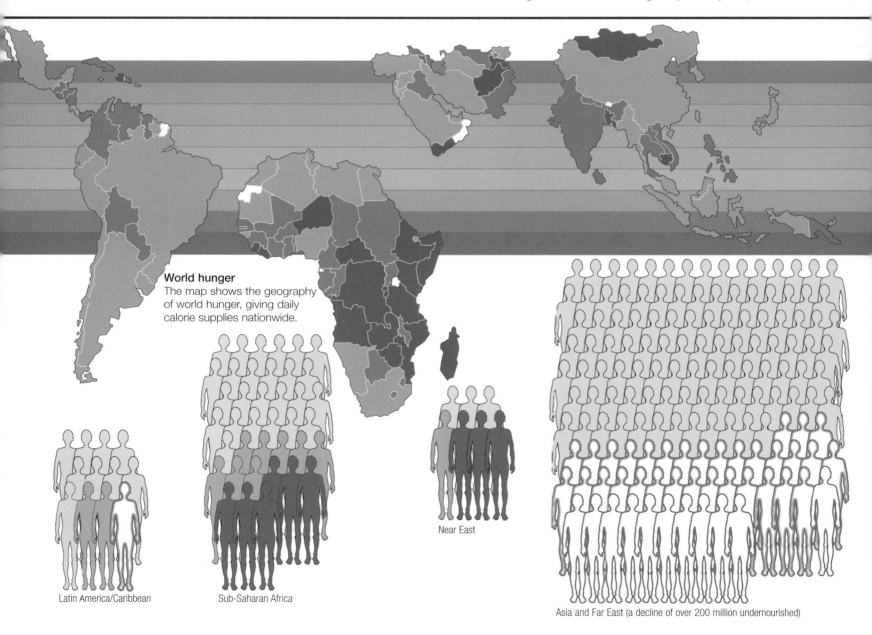

World hunger
The map shows the geography
of world hunger, giving daily
calorie supplies nationwide.

Latin America/Caribbean

Sub-Saharan Africa

Near East

Asia and Far East (a decline of over 200 million undernourished)

There are problems for crop fertilization, too. Rice, for instance, enjoys total fertilization at 34°C, but loses almost its entire capacity at 40°C.

Moreover, global warming will lead to outbreaks of pests and diseases that will further reduce our food supplies. Thus far, less than one percent of insects flourish in such large numbers to become pests; only a few hundred are a persistent problem. Only a few percent of insect species are prevented from being pests because they are kept in control by predators such as wasps and spiders. In the future, some of these predators may become unduly vulnerable to extinction, with the result that potential pests become actual pests. Much the same applies to weedy plants.

Also at undue risk are those many insect species that pollinate crop plants. If we were to lose half of all mammals – elephants, tigers, whales, and the like – that would be an appalling tragedy, but in most respects we would get by. If, conversely, we were to lose half of all insect species, much of our agriculture would soon be in dire trouble.

Finally, note that global warming will knock out extensive wildlife habitats, some of them critical to species' survival. Scientists have identified 25 areas that feature exceptional concentrations of endemic species (found nowhere else) and that face exceptional threat of habitat destruction. These "biodiversity hotspots" contain the last homelands of 44 percent of plant species and 35 percent of vertebrate species (except fishes) on land. They open the way for "silver bullet" responses on the part of conservation planners. Suppose the hotspots could be safeguarded at a cost of, say, $2 billion per year. This is no great sum; conservationists spend $10 billion a year already on largely "scattergun" activities, and in any case $2 billion equates to less than one day of military spending. The outlay would go far to knocking a huge dent in the whole mass-extinction problem. But several of the hotspots, such as the Cape Floristic Province at the tip of South Africa, would, like all vegetation communities, seek to escape global warming by migrating away from the Equator and towards the poles. Plant species in areas, such as Florida, would have plenty of land in which to seek refuge by migrating northwards, whereas many of the Cape Floristic Province plants would need to migrate southwards and end up in the sea.

In many localities apart from the hotspots, species will find global warming bringing on conditions that overwhelm their survival capacities. Huge numbers will become extinct, whether at once or, more likely, in the long run. A recent cautious assessment by an international team of scientists indicates that at least a million species and possibly several million species could be doomed through this factor alone.

New threats to society?
Enviromental security is a new phenomenon that reflects those environmental factors that ultimately underpin all our economies and hence our societies

The deadly greenhouse

Global warming and human health
In Asia in 2003, heatwaves in India, Bangladesh, and Pakistan took temperatures to 50°C. In India's state of Andhra Pradesh alone, 1,200 people died from the heat. In China, flooding along the Huai and Yangtze rivers swept through 650,000 homes. In Europe, a record heatwave claimed 35,000 lives. In a globally warmed world we can expect that vector-borne infections, such as malaria (see below) and dengue fever, plus food-borne infections, such as salmonellosis, all of which proliferate in warmer weather, will flourish like never before. Moreover, human populations living at the present margins of malaria and dengue fever will be all the more susceptible if these diseases expand their geographic range, due to their having little if any in-built immunity. In addition, there has been a surge in many infectious diseases, including such new ones as HIV/AIDS, hantavirus, hepatitis C, and SARS. Even more importantly, gross disruption of agricultural systems is likely to lead to a decline in food supplies, especially in those regions that already suffer widespread malnutrition – whereupon malnutrition and disease will reinforce one another. Indeed, it is not going too far to say that there could be unprecedented pandemics ahead, thanks to global warming.

Temperature "migrations"
For each 1°C rise in temperature, climate belts in mid-latitudes will shift polewards by 100–150 km (in mountainous areas, a few will shift upwards by 150 m). Vegetation communities will try to keep up with the climatic habitats to which they are suited, by likewise migrating, though they will have to attempt the move by heading through "development deserts" of farmlands and cities. They will also have to accomplish their treks at a speed ten times faster than when they have had to migrate following glaciations. A likely result is that many crops, forests, and wildlife species will find the challenge too great.

Withering of wheat
During the heatwaves that swept Europe from Britain to Ukraine in 2003, world wheat harvests fell by an amount equal to half the US crop. Eastern Europe recorded the smallest crop in three decades. Ukraine, a one-time "breadbasket", harvested only 5 million tonnes, a drop of 75% over the previous year. Result, climbing prices for wheat-based products (bread, pasta, etc.) worldwide.

Spread of malaria
The map compares the present extent of malaria with the projected extent in 2055 if temperatures continue to rise at current rates.

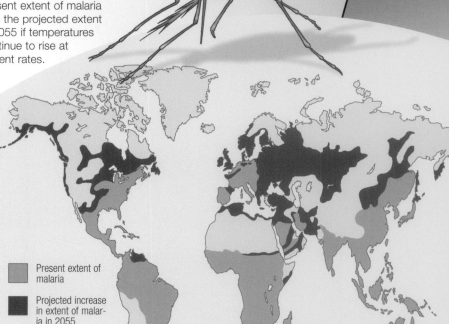

Present extent of malaria

Projected increase in extent of malaria in 2055

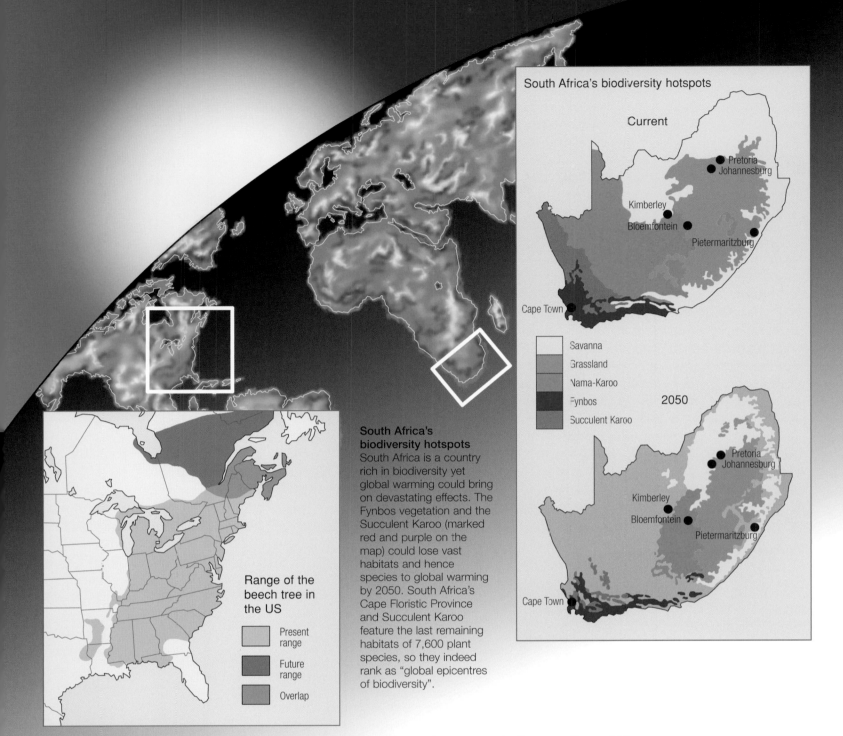

South Africa's biodiversity hotspots

Current

Cape Town
Kimberley
Bloemfontein
Pretoria
Johannesburg
Pietermaritzburg

- Savanna
- Grassland
- Nama-Karoo
- Fynbos
- Succulent Karoo

2050

Pretoria
Johannesburg
Kimberley
Bloemfontein
Pietermaritzburg
Cape Town

South Africa's biodiversity hotspots

South Africa is a country rich in biodiversity yet global warming could bring on devastating effects. The Fynbos vegetation and the Succulent Karoo (marked red and purple on the map) could lose vast habitats and hence species to global warming by 2050. South Africa's Cape Floristic Province and Succulent Karoo feature the last remaining habitats of 7,600 plant species, so they indeed rank as "global epicentres of biodiversity".

Range of the beech tree in the US

- Present range
- Future range
- Overlap

Beech's bleak future

The beech tree, now common throughout the eastern US, may find that in a globally warmed world it will be restricted to a distant and much smaller range. The map (above) shows what could happen with just a doubling of CO_2 emissions between 1990 and 2050.

Goodbye to major tourist attractions?

Global warming will mean that the temperatures of New England in the Fall become too warm for the sugar maples with their brilliant red colours. Other vacation spectacles could be in dire trouble. The Everglades could be flooded out of existence, and Rocky Mountain ski resorts could lose much of their snow cover.

Potential effects of climate change on agriculture over the next 50 years
(Overall, global warming will prove severely damaging to our agriculture)

Climatic element	Expected changes by 2050s	Confidence in prediction	Effects on agriculture
CO_2	Increase from 360 ppm to 450–600 ppm	Very high	Good for crops; increased photosynthesis; reduced water use
Sea-level rise	Rise by 10–15cm Increased in South and offset in North by natural subsidence/rebound	Very high	Loss of land; coastal erosion; flooding; salination of ground water
Temperature	Rise by 1–2°C. Winters warming more than summers. Increased frequency of heatwaves	High	Faster shorter, earlier growing seasons; range moving north and to higher altitudes; heat stress; increased evapotranspiration
Precipitation	Seasonal changes by plus or minus 10%	Low	Impacts on drought risk, soil workability, waterlogging, irrigation supply, transpiration
Storminess	Increased wind speeds, especially in the North	Very low	Waterlogging; soil erosion; reduced infiltration of rainfall
Variability	Increases across most climatic variables. Predictions uncertain	Very low	Changing risk of damaging events (heatwaves, frost, droughts, floods) which affect crops and timing of farm operations

and our political stability. When these environmental resources (water, soil, vegetation, climate, and whatever others are the prime components of a nation's environmental foundations) are degraded, our security declines, too. While the problem may not always trigger outright conflict, it helps to destabilize societies in an already unstable world – a world in which we can expect the destabilizing process to become more common as growing numbers of people seek to sustain themselves from declining environments.

For instance: water is a strategic resource that may well prompt future tensions, conflicts, and violence in many parts of the world. Other resources – topsoil, fuelwood, hardwood timber, and fish – are under rising demand and are in increasingly short supply. The biggest threat of all will surely prove to be climate dislocations as global warming imposes shifts in weather patterns, undermines agriculture and health, and generally disrupts the world we know.

Consider deforestation. The watershed services supplied by forests were graphically illustrated in 1998 in China. Weeks of near-record flooding in the Yangtse river basin affected 240 million people and caused $36 billion worth of damage. The Chinese government acknowledged that the disaster was severely exacerbated if not caused outright by deforestation in the upper reaches of the watershed (see p. 42). The government ordained a halt to tree cutting in the areas at issue, as well as converting a good many logging firms into tree-planting firms.

Or consider desertification. In the Sahel zone of Africa, not a single government survived the droughts of the 1970s and 1980s, several fell twice over, and a few have been moving towards still further collapse. Over the next two decades tens of millions of people could be on the move from the Sahel region if desertification is not contained, with the prospect for tension in receiver areas.

All in all, then, national security is no longer about fighting forces and weaponry alone. Increasingly it relates to watersheds, croplands, forests, genetic resources, climate, and other factors rarely considered by military experts and political leaders. Taken together they deserve to be viewed just as crucial to a nation's security as military prowess. The situation is epitomized by the leader who refuses to permit one square metre of national territory to be ceded to a foreign invader, while allowing hundreds of square kilometres of topsoil to be eroded away each year.

All this highlights the need for collective security. Climate change is a problem to which all nations contribute; by which all will be affected; from which no nation can remotely hope to insulate itself; and against which no nation can deploy worthwhile measures on its own. So environmental security lies beyond the scope of established diplomacy and international relations. It emphasizes cooperation rather than confrontation within the international arena. Indeed, it postulates the biggest change for the nation-state since it emerged 500 years ago.

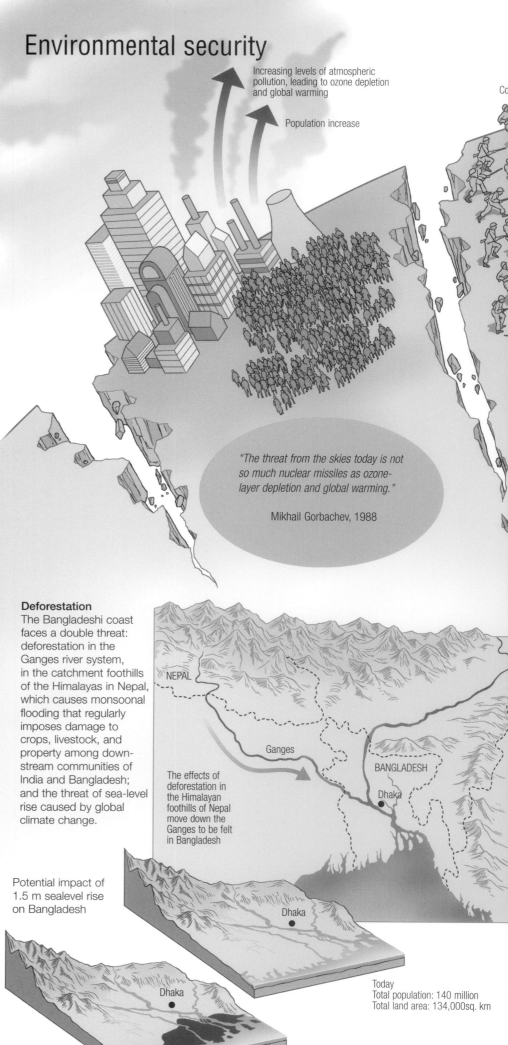

Environmental security

Increasing levels of atmospheric pollution, leading to ozone depletion and global warming

Population increase

"The threat from the skies today is not so much nuclear missiles as ozone-layer depletion and global warming."

Mikhail Gorbachev, 1988

Deforestation
The Bangladeshi coast faces a double threat: deforestation in the Ganges river system, in the catchment foothills of the Himalayas in Nepal, which causes monsoonal flooding that regularly imposes damage to crops, livestock, and property among downstream communities of India and Bangladesh; and the threat of sea-level rise caused by global climate change.

The effects of deforestation in the Himalayan foothills of Nepal move down the Ganges to be felt in Bangladesh

NEPAL

Ganges

BANGLADESH

Dhaka

Potential impact of 1.5 m sealevel rise on Bangladesh

Dhaka

Dhaka

Today
Total population: 140 million
Total land area: 134,000sq. km

1.5 m sea-level rise
Total population affected: 26 million (19%)
Total land area affected: 22,000sq. km (16%)

Shrinking forests

Cracking under the strain
The environmental pressures caused by human activities are putting the Earth under enormous strain, bringing stress, conflict, and even war as more and more people try to survive on reduced natural resources or become environmental refugees.

Increased desertification

Erosion of topsoil

"The environmental problems of the poor will affect the rich as well in the not too distant future, transmitted through political instability and turmoil."

Gro Harlem Brundtland,
Chair, World Commission on
Environment and Development, 1986

"War is often thought of in terms of military conflict, or even annihilation. But there is a growing awareness that an equal danger might be chaos as a result of environmental catastrophes and mass hunger."

Willy Brandt, former
Chancellor of Germany

Environmental refugees

Of the nearly one billion additional people added to the global population during the 1990s, a good proportion will have been among communities with a cash income of $1 per day or less. They will have included the people most likely to be subsisting, or rather struggling to survive, in environments too wet, too dry, or too steep for sustainable agriculture. In Sub-Saharan Africa, these environments will have needed to support an extra 150 million people during the 1990s, and in India 165 million. Many of them will join the throngs of environmental refugees, estimated to total 25 million in the mid-1990s – or a total greater than all other forms of refugees put together, viz. people fleeing political oppression, religious persecution, and ethnic troubles (see pp. 200–201). This, however, is a cautious and conservative figure. Scattered throughout the developing world in the mid-1990s were 135 million people threatened by severe desertification and 650 million suffering water shortages. While some of these people would have been included in the 25 million figure, many could well have been driven to migrate without being counted as environmental refugees. The eventual total of environmental refugees could soar to a whopping 250 million in a globally warmed world. Extensive communities will be overtaken by sea-level rise and coastal flooding, by disruptions of monsoon systems and other rainfall regimes, and by droughts of unprecedented severity and duration. Among regions affected would be the low-lying coastal plains of China and India, and delta areas such as the mouth of the Nile and the whole of Bangladesh, plus drought-prone Sub-Saharan Africa. Certain island nations of the Pacific and Indian Oceans, while featuring only small populations, would be entirely eliminated.

In short, large numbers of destitute people could soon start to pose entirely new threats to international stability. This would be especially the case if the refugees were to feel they can best find sanctuary by heading for the developed nations. They would do this partly because developed nations offer most prospect of support (in principle at least), and partly because these nations could rightly be seen as the principal source of global warming.

Indirect linkages

In many instances, the environment/conflict linkages are readily apparent. In other cases, the impact is more deferred and diffuse, as in the case of species extinctions and gene depletion, with all that means for genetic contributions to agriculture, medicine, and industry. Probably the most deferred and diffuse impact of all, although the most consequential all round, will prove to be that of climatic change. Build-up of carbon dioxide and other greenhouse gases in the global atmosphere will, if continued as projected, engender far-reaching disruptions for temperature and rainfall patterns. As a result of possibly warmer and drier weather in its grainlands, leading to severe and persistent droughts, the USA's great grain belt could become unbuckled. Conversely, Russia and Ukraine, possibly enjoying better rainfall in part of their territories, could become major suppliers of surplus food. India could conceivably find itself better off in rainfall terms, Pakistan worse off – in turn, affecting the relations between these two traditional adversaries. There will be many other "winners" and "losers" in a greenhouse-affected world, with all manner of destabilizing repercussions for a world already experiencing other kinds of environmental turmoil. It will be a world in which many of us will end up as direct losers and in which all of us will be indirect losers.

Managing the Land

We live in a hungry world, faced with a deepening land crisis. The costly "escape" strategy of bringing ever-more land under the plough will only worsen this crisis, and still barely feed our growing numbers if we carry on as today. The solution lies not in how much land we have but how we use it.

Cash-crops trade: bonds or bondage?

Cash crops can be either boon or bane for developing countries. In some instances they supply much impetus to the development process by bringing crucial foreign exchange earnings which lubricate emergent economies. But all too often, because the land could be better employed in growing food for hungry local people rather than non-essential commodities for foreigners, they slow down the development process.

It is difficult for developing economies to break free from the cash-crop bind. For most developing nations, "going it alone" would be impossible: their domestic market is too small, their resource base too narrow. Unless they can trade in the world marketplace, they cannot purchase the tools and technology they need for development. And those countries that have no mineral resources must find the means to earn foreign exchange as best they can. Even if they prefer not to follow a Western model of development, those developing countries that suffer increasing poverty and a deteriorating resource base need hard cash simply to purchase a more critical export from the developed world – grain.

Where does the answer lie? Firstly, the developing countries must get their priorities right. In many such countries, agriculture is subordinated to urban development and industrialization. Were a cash-crop strategy to be made more selective, it could avoid heavy dependence on a single export commodity, and place more emphasis on efficient food production, a more efficient share-out of farmlands, and fairer distribution of income.

Secondly, international agencies could change their approach to aid and development within the agricultural sector. Although some developing countries have inherited colonial cash-crop links, and others have entered the vicious cash-crop circle by accident, all too many have been led there, even pushed there, by misconceived aid programmes. Not enough of these countries' leaders have the inclination, let alone the means, to reject aid that deflects their development strategies from their most urgent priority of feeding their people.

Cash-crop factor

The major grain exporters
Grain produced in the North is distributed worldwide. More than 100 countries depend on these grain shipments. In the past four decades the value of the international food trade has tripled and the weight of food shipped between countries has quadrupled.

Imports/Exports over 1 million tonnes
- Wheat
- Coarse grains
- Sugar
- Soybeans
- Coffee
- Rice
- Cotton lint
- Cocoa
- Tobacco leaf

Barrels of oil (x10) bought by one tonne of commodity

Commodity	1980	1990	2003
Coffee			
Sugar			

What commodities can buy
In 1980, one tonne of coffee bought around 95 barrels of oil, yet in 1990 it could purchase 67 and in 2003 only 39. Similarly sugar, a less valuable commodity, has declined in purchasing power by three-fifths since 1990.

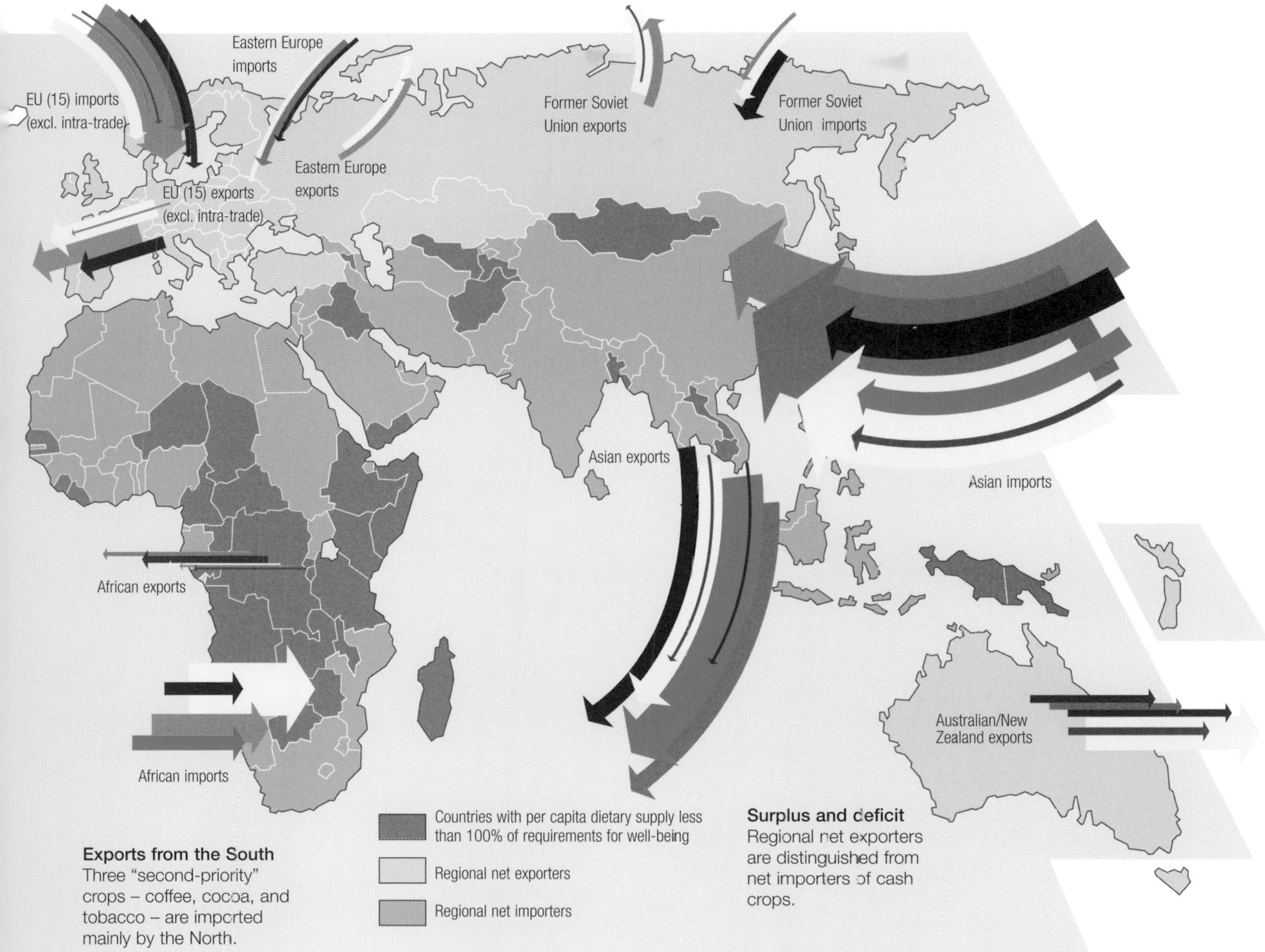

Eastern Europe
imports

EU (15) imports
(excl. intra-trade)

Former Soviet
Union exports

Former Soviet
Union imports

Eastern Europe
exports

EU (15) exports
(excl. intra-trade)

Asian exports

Asian imports

African exports

African imports

Australian/New
Zealand exports

Exports from the South
Three "second-priority"
crops – coffee, cocoa, and
tobacco – are imported
mainly by the North.

Countries with per capita dietary supply less
than 100% of requirements for well-being

Regional net exporters

Regional net importers

Surplus and deficit
Regional net exporters
are distinguished from
net importers of cash
crops.

The spread of cash crops

Huge expanses of developing countries have been given over
to cash crops for export, notably bananas in the Caribbean and
Central America, coffee in Brazil and Colombia, cocoa along the
West African coast, rubber in Southeast Asia, and cotton and
peanuts in the Sahel sector of West Africa.

Morocco, Ivory Coast, Zimbabwe, Ecuador, and Chile have
become prime sources of out-of-season fruits and vegetables for
North America and Europe, simply so that rich-world citizens can
enjoy flowers and strawberries throughout their winter. The exports
earn much money for a few business leaders, often foreigners;
over half of Chile's trade, for example, is controlled by just 5
multinational corporations. Worse, the cash-crops business leaves
hundreds of millions of developing-world peasants without land
on which to grow food for local consumption. At the height of
the 1984 famine in Ethiopia, prime farmland was being taken to
grow cottonseed, linseed, and rapeseed for export to Europe, and
during the mid-1980s famine in the Sahel, several countries were
producing record harvests for export.

Cash crop categories

Cash crops generate funds for the producer countries through their
export value in the world marketplace. They fall into two main categories: essential food crops such as grains and legumes, mainly
produced in the North and traded worldwide; and less essential
crops such as coffee, cotton, and tobacco, predominantly produced
in the South for export to the North (often reflecting colonial trading
links). The map shows trade flows of 10 major cash crops in 2001.

Some of the less essential crops command relatively high
prices on world markets and generate more money than the land
could produce through growing staple foods – for much of the
time. But the catch lies in the phrase "for much of the time".
Commodity prices are fickle: when consumer demand soars, prices
are good, whereupon many farmers are persuaded to go into cash
crops, switching from growing food to non-essential items. When
the global economy turns down again, prices crash and the farmer
is left caught between a rock and a hard place.

In just the past four decades the value of the international
food trade has tripled and the weight of food shipped between
countries has quadrupled.

NEWTON-LE-WILLOWS
LIBRARY
TEL: 01744 677886
01744 677887

A streamlined food supply

As international trade expands and the world's economy grows more integrated, so the food of rich-world citizens tends to reach their meal tables from a "global farm" via a "global supermarket". At most major food stores in the North, consumers purchase products from all over the world. Similarly, millions of developing world people, together with large numbers of former Soviet Union citizens, consume grain from North America, Australia, and Argentina. Only a tenth of all food grown enters international trade, but a similar integrative pattern occurs within individual countries as agriculture gives way to "agribusiness".

There is much to be said for a commercial system that enables us to enjoy abundant and diversified products from remote croplands and to benefit from those farmers who produce most food cheapest.

We now produce sufficient food to feed the whole of Earth's human population (albeit 840 million people are not getting adequate supplies, pp. 46–47), a feat that would have been impossible 100 years ago.

That we manage to feed such multitudes is due in part to giant enterprises that dominate our food system – they not only handle the sale of food, but often control the growing, processing, and distribution, too. It all makes for a streamlined operation with more, better, and cheaper food. But there is a snag. We face a situation in which mega-corporations are coming to wield virtual monopoly power over key sectors of the food trade. Since 1970 a few giant petro-corporations have taken over hundreds of small seed businesses that hitherto produced seeds in a vast variety to suit diverse environments, tastes, and price ranges. By controlling the production of

The global supermarket

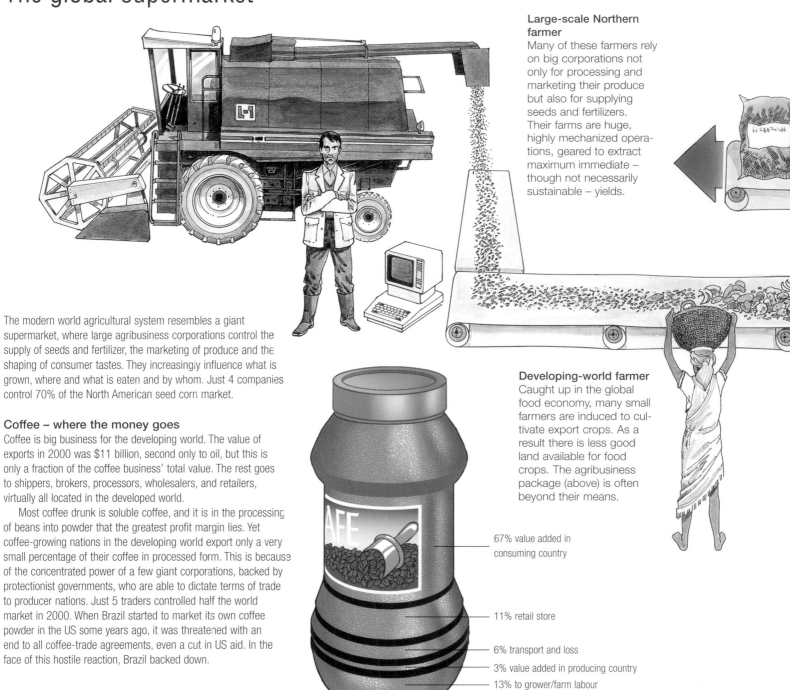

Large-scale Northern farmer
Many of these farmers rely on big corporations not only for processing and marketing their produce but also for supplying seeds and fertilizers. Their farms are huge, highly mechanized operations, geared to extract maximum immediate – though not necessarily sustainable – yields.

The modern world agricultural system resembles a giant supermarket, where large agribusiness corporations control the supply of seeds and fertilizer, the marketing of produce and the shaping of consumer tastes. They increasingly influence what is grown, where and what is eaten and by whom. Just 4 companies control 70% of the North American seed corn market.

Coffee – where the money goes

Coffee is big business for the developing world. The value of exports in 2000 was $11 billion, second only to oil, but this is only a fraction of the coffee business' total value. The rest goes to shippers, brokers, processors, wholesalers, and retailers, virtually all located in the developed world.

Most coffee drunk is soluble coffee, and it is in the processing of beans into powder that the greatest profit margin lies. Yet coffee-growing nations in the developing world export only a very small percentage of their coffee in processed form. This is because of the concentrated power of a few giant corporations, backed by protectionist governments, who are able to dictate terms of trade to producer nations. Just 5 traders controlled half the world market in 2000. When Brazil started to market its own coffee powder in the US some years ago, it was threatened with an end to all coffee-trade agreements, even a cut in US aid. In the face of this hostile reaction, Brazil backed down.

Developing-world farmer
Caught up in the global food economy, many small farmers are induced to cultivate export crops. As a result there is less good land available for food crops. The agribusiness package (above) is often beyond their means.

67% value added in consuming country

11% retail store

6% transport and loss

3% value added in producing country

13% to grower/farm labour

seeds, a petro-corporation can breed crops that need extra-large dollops of synthetic fertilizer, pesticides, and other petroleum-based additives, regardless of more desirable trends for future agriculture (e.g. away from reliance on fossil-fuel inputs). What happens when the oil wells run dry? The corporation answers that it will tackle this at the time, but meanwhile it is a private profit-making concern, not a public charity.

Even more insidious in its ultimately detrimental impact on agriculture is the support given by giant corporations to the "farmers' lobby" in developed nations. The Common Agricultural Policy (CAP) of 15 EU nations cost $50 billion in 2003, encouraging farmers to produce surpluses, such as the famous butter mountains and milk lakes. Agricultural subsidies in all OECD nations totalled almost $350 billion in 2003. These subsidies help depress the prices of produce from the developing world by undercutting competition. At the same time, the overproduction of food by the US and Western Europe leads to the dumping of subsidised, low-priced produce on poor countries, putting local small farmers at a grave commercial disadvantage.

The global supermarket, dominated in part by giant corporations, is potentially a powerful medium that could serve us all. But much refinement on the part of governments, consumer organizations, and the like is required if it is to serve the best needs of customer and stockholder alike. A seven-year international boycott, led mainly by citizen activists, succeeded in persuading Nestlé to agree to market its powdered milk as an alternative rather than a substitute for mother's milk. There is now an international code of practice on the marketing

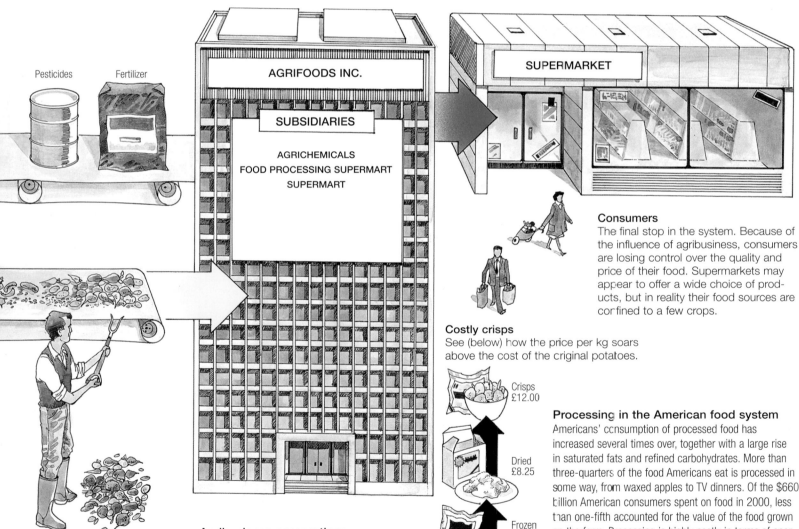

Small-scale Northern farmer
Due to limited economies of scale, many small farmers find it hard to keep going. In the US, the number of farms has declined from 6 million in the 1950s to 2 million today – 7% of farms accounted for 76% of agricultural sales in 2002.

Agribusiness corporations
Large corporations exercise much control over the supply of pesticides, fertilizers, seed, and machinery to farmers. Six companies led by Syngenta, Bayer and Monsanto supply three-quarters of the $30 billion global pesticides market. These three also control a major share of the $35 billion global seed market. Similarly, just a couple of dozen corporations dominate the processing, manufacture, and marketing of food. From their position of commercial power, giant corporations exert undue influence over prices for farmer and consumer alike.

Consumers
The final stop in the system. Because of the influence of agribusiness, consumers are losing control over the quality and price of their food. Supermarkets may appear to offer a wide choice of products, but in reality their food sources are confined to a few crops.

Costly crisps
See (below) how the price per kg soars above the cost of the original potatoes.

Crisps £12.00
Dried £8.25
Frozen £1.50
Canned £0.95
Fresh £0.88

Processing in the American food system
Americans' consumption of processed food has increased several times over, together with a large rise in saturated fats and refined carbohydrates. More than three-quarters of the food Americans eat is processed in some way, from waxed apples to TV dinners. Of the $660 billion American consumers spent on food in 2000, less than one-fifth accounted for the value of the food grown on the farm. Processing is highly costly in terms of energy, then there are the costs of getting the food from the cropland to the table. Not only is this extremely wasteful, it is also unhealthy. One-fifth of the vegetables Americans eat are French fries and potato chips. Food companies spend more on advertising ($30 billion a year) than any other industry. The same applies in Austria, Belgium and France. Fewer than 50 US corporations account for the great bulk of the $500 billion food-processing industry. When incomes rise consumers often seek greater variety of high-value food imports. Processed and semi-processed products account for two-thirds of all agricultural trade.

of breast-milk substitutes. This success story shows that progress can be made if enough citizens insist that their voices are heard.

The forest cash crop

More people everywhere want more wood. Today, we consume 3.4 billion cubic metres per year, half of it as fuel. By 2015, consumption could increase by almost 30 percent (see pp. 122–23).

In Europe and North America a large amount of wood is consumed in the form of pulp for paper: the two regions account for two-thirds of the world total. Developing countries have powerful incentives to develop their own sources of pulp. As literacy increases, so does the demand for paper.

As for industrial timber, Northerners increasingly seek specialist hardwoods, notably those from the tropics, for construction and semi-luxury purposes (see right). By contrast, timber in the South is used mostly for essential purposes. Yet because prices for wood are determined internationally, and thus tend to be set by consumption in the richer North, Southerners find themselves squeezed out of the marketplace. When Northerners have to pay a little more for stylish veneer, they may complain about inflation, but the upshot does not generally affect their living standards. For a person in the South, an increase in price often means doing without.

These imbalances are aggravated by the forestry policies of several developed nations. For example, Japan fears for its economic security in world wood markets and so adopts a "siege strategy". It builds up its own forest stocks and grows more wood than it cuts, while depending heavily on foreign sources of timber. Within the context of Japan's needs, this approach makes sense, but within a global setting it illustrates the "tragedy of the commons" – and will ultimately paint Japan itself into an ever-tighter corner.

What can we do to improve the global wood situation? Plenty. But we need to act as a community of nations for the benefit of all humankind. Adequate funding should be provided for the establishment of commercial fuelwood plantations in the tropics, where the year-round steamy-warm climates are ideal for generating wood – thus relieving fuelwood-gathering pressure on virgin forest. In addition, developed countries should examine their forestry policies with a view to producing more home-grown timber and encouraging greater recycling of paper. The Earth can certainly supply us with sufficient wood. Can we shift to forestry strategies that are sustainable?

Planting tomorrow's trees

In the North we claim to know a good deal about how to manage forests. Virtually all of Europe's original forests have been replaced by intensively managed tree stands. In the South, ironically, much of the deforestation problem lies with the clear-cut logging pioneered in the North. Mechanized operations in the tropics are often wasteful, with as much

Harvesting the forest

Forest products represent one of our most valuable categories of cash crops. As such, they are widely traded around the world, albeit with unequal patterns between the developed and developing worlds (83% of the $145 billion world exports in 2000 were accounted for by developed countries). This trade is likely to expand, especially insofar as two of the main consuming regions – Japan and Western Europe (outside Scandinavia) – intend to continue to import huge volumes, even though they could grow more wood at home. Britain, for example, which imports the great bulk of its wood needs, could reduce its demand by planting more trees on under-utilized land.

The world's leading producers (and consumers) of paper are the US, Japan, and China. All industrial nations together account for three-quarters of paper use – not so surprising when the world's computers alone account for 115 billion sheets of paper each year. In 1998 the average consumer in developed countries used 160 kg of paper a year (335 kg in the US), compared with the average person in a developing country, less than 20 kg. Only 10% of the paper produced is for long-lasting products – 90% is used once and discarded. Much more use of recycled paper is required.

The developed world also demands specialist hardwoods for numerous construction purposes, as well as for luxury items such as parquet floors, fine furniture, decorative panelling, and weekend yachts. In Switzerland, whose forests are extensive and under-utilized, abachi wood is imported from the Ivory Coast to make super-fine coffins.

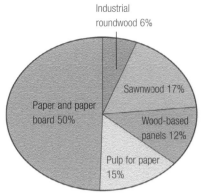

Trade in forest products
Industrial roundwood and sawn-wood accounts for almost a quarter of the value of world trade ($138 billion). Pulp, paper, and paperboard make up almost two-thirds.

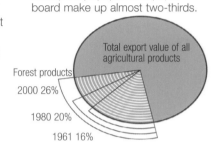

A valuable export
In 1961 forest products accounted for 16% of all agricultural exports. By 2000 the share had increased to 26%.

Product demand in the North …
Northerners use huge amounts of wood for constructing houses, office buildings, railway sleepers, pit props, and the like. They also consume a great deal of paper products (notably packaging materials), as well as luxury hardwood items.

… and South
Southerners likewise consume much wood, but mostly for fuel. Almost all houses in the Third World use wood, but not as high-grade construction material, rather as simple building poles. As for paper products, the average Southerner consumes all too little – to the detriment of education and communications.

World trade flows
Most softwood trade arises
and remains within the North.
By contrast, most hardwood trade
stems from the developing world.

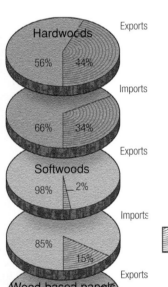

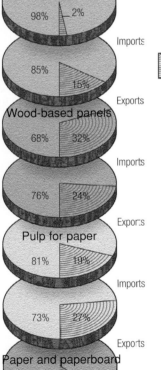

Hardwoods
Exports
56%   44%
Imports
66%   34%

Softwoods
Exports
98%   2%
Imports
85%   15%

Wood-based panels
Exports
68%   32%
Imports
76%   24%

Pulp for paper
Exports
81%   19%
Imports
73%   27%

Paper and paperboard
Exports
88%   12%
Imports
74%   26%

Proportion of trade by
developing countries

Wood production
Since 1996, the developing
world's share of roundwood
production has remained
fairly constant at 2 billion
cu. m (60% of the total).

A source of revenue
When large numbers of
huge logs are taken from a
Southeast Asia forest (top
right), at least half of the
remaining trees are injured
beyond recovery. Yet the
logger does not care.
Governments could be
much tougher in enforcing
less harmful harvesting
techniques, but the urgent
need for hard cash often
means that they fail to see
their forests as sources of
future revenue. Fortunately,
a partial breakthrough is
in the form of increased
wood processing: the
veneer sheet (bottom right)
earns several times more
foreign exchange than
a raw log, thus relieving
pressure to exploit every
forest tract.

as three-quarters of the residual canopy damaged from the extraction of a few commercially valuable species. Unlike temperate forests, tropical forests can hardly withstand such disruption because of their ecological complexity.

The major Northern advance in recent years has been in genetic engineering. Trees grown from tissue culture can quickly reforest large areas of denuded land, and can be further engineered with useful commercial qualities. At the same time, industrial plantations, generally consisting of genetically uniform stands, are more vulnerable to pathogens and other pests. Widespread disease and pest outbreaks are common throughout conifer plantations in the United States and Central Europe.

In the South and because of the critical environmental roles played by tropical forests, it is better to establish "tree farms" on already deforested lands rather than to harvest natural forests. Establishing such plantations on just five percent of already deforested lands could provide almost twice as much commercial wood as is currently harvested from all natural tropical forests.

In addition, there is a need to establish fuelwood plantations in order to relieve pressure on natural forests. We should aim to increase fivefold the number of fuelwood trees planted each year, especially around farms and in village woodlots, at an annual cost of perhaps $1 billion. Note, too, that a sound way to establish such plantations – community forestry – relies on the involvement of local people. If everybody's ideas are sought from the start, there is more chance that all villagers will want to plant trees and care for them, and to harvest them sustainably. Similar community efforts are needed to stabilize degraded watersheds, as witness the successful coordination of foresters and villagers in parts of China and India.

We are slowly starting to appreciate the manifold benefits offered by tropical forests, by contrast with temperate forests. These benefits will become available only when we manage forests selectively and with ecological insights. We are also now recognizing the vital ecological roles of tropical forests, especially in conserving soil, regulating water flows, generating rainfall, and moderating climates both local and global.

Preventing erosion and desertification

The loss of soil and the spread of deserts are by no means confined to the developing world. A large share of the nearly three million square kilometres of arable land lost in the final quarter of last century was in the developed world.

There are many ways to tackle the problem. We can establish shelterbelts of trees, practise better livestock husbandry, and plant resilient grass cover. We can use a more caring agriculture, in good lands as well as poor ones. But the single best approach is to halt the migration of too many farmers into unsuitable

Forests of the future

Tropical and temperate forests are so different in their biological make-up, that two fundamentally different approaches to their management are needed. Temperate forests are expanding slightly, thanks to reforestation. Even in densely settled zones such as southwest Germany, a quarter of the landscape is given over to forests.

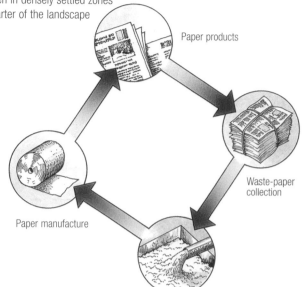

Paper products

Waste-paper collection

Pulping factory

Paper manufacture

Recycling paper
Through greater recycling, developed countries could reduce their demand for paper pulp by at least a quarter – which would be only half as much as they achieved during World War II.

Forest management in the South
In most developing countries, forestry departments are understaffed and underfunded. Foresters see their main duty as keeping people out of forests, rather than helping them to establish woodlots, fuelwood plantations, and other village forestry projects. International agencies now direct much emphasis to the sustainable development of tropical forests, and they promote forestry as a pivotal aspect of rural advancement. Under the World Bank is the Global Environment Facility (GEF) supporting activities in developing and transition countries in six areas – biodiversity, climate change, international waters, land degradation, the ozone layer, and persistent organic pollutants (POPs).

Replanting watersheds
Governments are realizing the value of restoring tree cover on upland watersheds, thus bringing benefits to virtually everyone in the local community.

Community forestry
With the support of international agencies, many countries are encouraging their citizens to become actively involved in fuelwood plantations. In Gujarat, India, for instance, schoolchildren have been raising as many tree seedlings as government officials.

Forest certification

Widely seen as important for better forest management, only 2% of the global forest area is certified as yet. This includes just 18,000 sq. km in the tropical forests of Bolivia, Brazil, Guatemala, and Mexico.

Sustainable land use

A strategy with much potential is agroforestry (below), which amounts to growing trees and food crops alongside each other. Both forest lands and marginal lands, normally unsuitable for crops, can be used for food production. Certain tree species, notably leguminous species, fix atmospheric nitrogen in the soil thus restoring soil fertility.

Extractive reserves

Brazil's rubber tappers (above) have a vision of development centred around "extractive reserves" – areas managed by local communities for uses compatible with forest survival, e.g. tapping trees and gathering fruits and nuts. Since 1990 the Brazilian government has recognized 30 reserves covering 50,000 sq. km.

The Chipko movement

In 1974, the women of Reni in northern India took simple but effective action to stop tree felling. They hugged trees that lumberjacks wanted to fell. This protest saved 12,000 sq. km of watershed forests. The photograph (below) exemplifies the fierce concerns felt by many local people for their forests.

Forest management in the North

Destructive logging is by no means confined to the tropics. Old-growth forests in Canada and the western US are being logged at unsustainable rates. The challenge is to halt the rapid mining of these forests and to intensify efforts to exploit secondary forests and plantations on a sustainable basis. In recent years, foresters in countries of the former Soviet Union have planted one million ha per year, and stimulated natural forest growth on a similar-size area. Also important is to make more efficient use of wood. Timber mills can reduce manufacturing waste through a variety of technologies such as using thinner saw blades and computerized scanners to detect defects in logs. In the US, for example, enhanced efficiency that matches Japanese levels would save enough wood to reduce the number of trees cut by a quarter.

areas. In essence, the problem lies with the people who have been rendered landless, are pushed to the fringes of their national societies, and head for ecologically vulnerable territories. In short, we must keep marginal people out of marginal lands. The key lies in the enhanced use of our more productive agricultural lands. We must try to produce three-quarters of the extra food needed in the future from existing farmlands rather than from new territories.

There is no doubt that we can do it, as shown by some notable instances. If more farmers in Java prac-tised the intensive and sustainable agriculture that has been standard in neighbouring Bali (which features as many people per unit area as Java, often more), much of Java's devastated land could be rejuvenated into a garden isle like Bali. Other parts of Southeast Asia could be more productive if people were encouraged to follow similarly sustainable agricultural systems. If newcomers to Amazonia adopted the traditional crop-growing strategies of long-established peasants in humid Latin America and the fertile floodplains of

Amazonia with their yearly enrichment of alluvial silt, the newly opened up areas could support millions of small-scale farmers in perpetuity. Only a very small fraction of tropical forests need to be used to produce a flourishing agricultural civilization rivalling those of historic times in the Ganges and Mekong floodplains.

For established croplands to produce twice as much food will often mean a basic shift in agricultural strategies. The Green Revolution (see pp. 62–63) should be complemented by an Evergreen Revolution, in which we make much better use of scarce water through technologies such as trickle-drip irrigation (see p. 69). We should also give priority to growing food for local communities rather than diverting crop-lands for cash crops for export (see pp. 52–53). Of course, this will not appeal to people with a stake in the cash-crop status quo, notably the local elites who profit from the export trade. These are people who, during the Sahel disaster in the 1970s, were respon-sible for maldistribution of $6 billion of foreign aid. Only one percent went to forest programmes, such

Terracing
Especially susceptible to erosion are hilly areas with fertile soils, notably volcanic zones with their intensively cultivated hill slopes. The answer is to construct terraces as exemplified by the 2,000-year-old rice terraces of the northern Philippines.

Managing the soil

The landscape above has been compressed in terms of scale to show the changes in land use as one moves from good agricultural land (left) to desert (right). The techniques suited to each category include soil-conserving practices and intensive use of high-potential lands; reduction of overload on arable lands to prevent topsoil loss; a sustainable mix of crops and livestock on intermediate farmlands; protection of vulnerable drylands and montane areas; and efforts to halt desertification and to rehabilitate already degraded lands.

Good land: intensified use
The best way to safeguard poor land is to make full use of the good land. The principal strategies include multiple land use, growing crops in rapid rotation, and interplanting several crops at a time. The process can generally be enhanced by irrigation. Organic farming uses crop residues and other forms of mulch as "green manure". A few "garden farm" agro-ecosystems employ several dozen crops on just a couple of hectares, fostering renewable use of croplands.

Medium-value land
Moderately dry lands can be cultivated for crops that withstand long rainless spells, e.g. millet, sorghum, amaranth, certain beans, and fast-maturing maize. But to safeguard against erosion, the farmer should employ a series of additional crops that restore soil fertility, such as cowpea and groundnut, and allow for regular fallow periods.

as desert-halting shelterbelts, and only three or four percent went to traditional grain-growing agriculture.

Many other lands need a basic switch in development planning to make more efficient use of existing croplands. For instance, we need a redirection of emphasis from industry and manufacturing to agriculture for local purposes; and from favouring the top 10 percent (entrepreneurs who will be the "locomotives" of economic growth) to favouring the bottom 40 percent (the poorest of the poor). While this runs counter to much conventional wisdom concerning development, it runs parallel to the fortunately re-oriented policies of the World Bank since the late 1970s.

A costly revolution

The Green Revolution is one of the most remarkable advances ever seen in agriculture. In the developed world it started to work its wonders during the 1940s, leading to record crops in Western Europe and North America from the 1950s onwards. In the developing world there was a time lag, but from the early 1960s

Hardy animals
Best suited to the marginal lands are disease-resistant varieties of cattle and sheep that can survive droughts and subsist on little forage. While such animals do not generate large amounts of meat and milk, they cause less harm to their environment than do more exotic breeds.

Trees for Africa
One sound way for Sub-Saharan Africa to meet its food needs lies not with planting more grain but with planting more trees. Windbreaks made of trees can enhance soil moisture by 15–25% and increase crop productivity by 5–10%. Trees can rehabilitate denuded upland catchments and stabilize river flows for the 40% of farmers in the developing world who depend upon upstream watersheds for their water supplies. As a very preliminary and conservative estimate, the amount of extra grain provided thereby can average 5–10%. Water supplies of sufficient quantity and quality for domestic household use can help to reduce disease, since 90% of disease cases in the developing world are related to contaminated water. When a person is sick with diarrhoea, malaria or some other major disease due to inadequate water supply, 5–20% of the person's food intake is needed simply to offset the disease. In these various ways, planting trees rather than grain crops can help provide 15–45% of food requirements, yet this aspect of the food challenge is scarcely heeded anywhere.

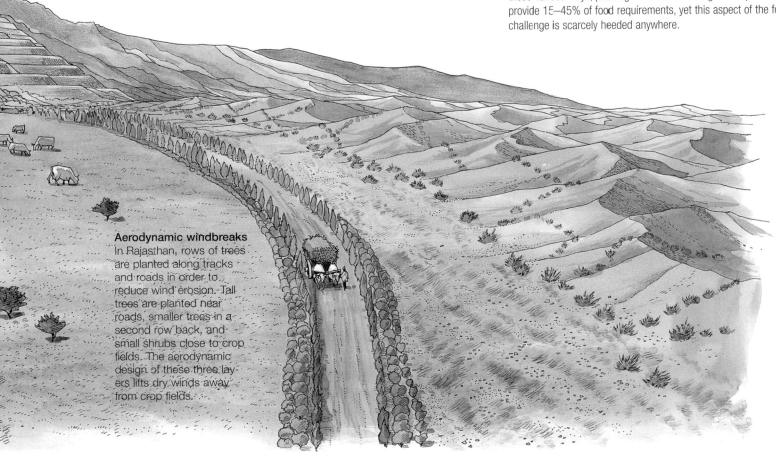

Aerodynamic windbreaks
In Rajasthan, rows of trees are planted along tracks and roads in order to reduce wind erosion. Tall trees are planted near roads, smaller trees in a second row back, and small shrubs close to crop fields. The aerodynamic design of these three layers lifts dry winds away from crop fields.

Favoured trees
Many wild trees and shrubs are available to help resist desertification. *Prosopis* species, for instance, are not only highly resistant to drought but their pods are rich in protein and make good livestock fodder. *Casuarina* trees grow fast in sand and, being tall and upright, make first-rate windbreaks. *Leucaena* trees grow swiftly, too. They make fine fuelwood and, because they fix their own nitrogen, restore soil fertility.

Livestock lands
Dry savannahs and grasslands readily suffer through over-large herds of cattle, sheep, and goats. The aim must be to reduce excess numbers, though in many areas it is difficult to persuade herdsmen to sell off parts of their holdings (livestock is often viewed as the chief means of "storing wealth"). A back-up strategy lies in rotational grazing which offers recovery periods for over-worked pastures. Devegetated lands can be improved with leguminous grasses such as clover and alfalfa in order to restore soil fertility.

Established desert
Natural desert is irreversible. It is in the borderlands of deserts that we need to apply caring agricultural techniques to stop lands which have been rendered agriculturally worthless from being "tacked on" to natural desert. Shrubs and bushes serve as barriers to hold back dunes; while certain woody plants, such as guayule and jojoba, produce rubber and liquid wax. Other anti-desert plants include various types of brushwood and hardy trees.

exceptional productivity became the norm in several parts of tropical Asia and Latin America. India, for example, produced only around 50 million tonnes of grains and related food crops per year in the early 1950s, but after the Green Revolution took off the total soared from 120 million tonnes in 1960 to 365 million tonnes in 2001, and annual food production per person increased from 240 to 310 kilograms, while food imports were dramatically cut. Between 1997 and 2020, however, India's grain demand is projected to rise by 80 million tonnes (40 percent).

There is a price to this success story. The Green Revolution consists principally of "high yield" varieties of rice, wheat, and maize, varieties which produce bumper harvests and in some cases mature faster so that the farmer can grow two or even three crops in a year. But they are not so much high-yield as high-response varieties. They do their job only when they receive stacks of fertilizer, pesticides, irrigation water and other additives, together with sound farming techniques. Fertilizer from fossil

fuels, a key component of the package, was cheap during the Revolution's early years, but after OPEC imposed its first price hike in 1973, costs soared. The situation was aggravated as crops demanded ever-greater inputs of fertilizer. High-yield varieties need 70–90 kilograms of nitrogen per hectare, whereas the average amount available in most developing countries was only about 25 kilograms. If India's farmers were to apply fertilizer at the same rate as Dutch farmers, they would need almost as much as the world's total fertilizer use.

Equally to the point, there has been a levelling off of increases in the yield of global grain. The problem lies with the "fertilizer response ratio", i.e. the return in increased yields produced by using additional fertilizer. Worldwide, this response ratio is decreasing as farmers reach the biological limits of the new hybrid strains.

There have also been adverse economic and social repercussions. The high-yield varieties tend to be planted by those farmers who can afford the

Cornucopia

The performance of high-yield crops depends on climate and technology. The best average yield for wheat is two and a half times the world average, but three-quarters that of the highest achieved and just over a third of the theoretical maximum. The Green Revolution has a good way to go yet.

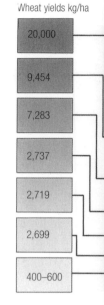

Wheat yields kg/ha

20,000

9,454

7,283

2,737

2,719

2,699

400–600

Green revolution?

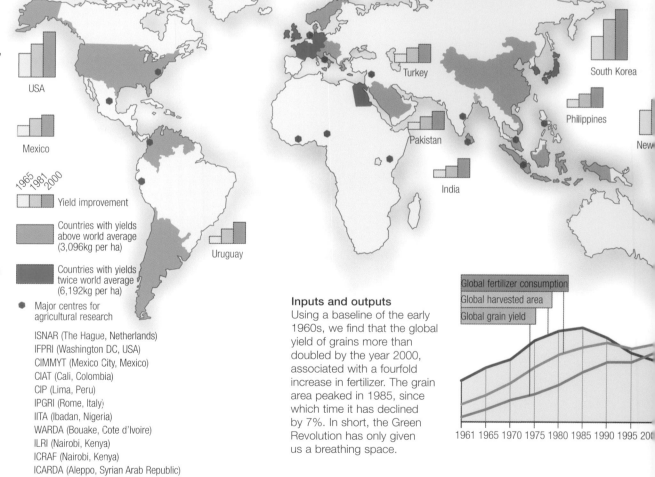

As a result of the Green Revolution, a good number of countries have expanded their output of grain crops in exceptional fashion – notably of rice, wheat, and maize, the three leading grains. If we take a global average grain yield of 3,100 kg/ha (year 2000), we find that substantial numbers of countries now achieve harvests well over this level, some of them double. In the developed world, which had a head start, we find that UK, France, the Netherlands, and Japan are among those nations which have yields twice the global average. Only Egypt and South Korea have so far managed it from developing countries. But average grain yields conceal the most dramatic success stories of the Green Revolution. During the two decades 1961–1981, India doubled its wheat yield and the Philippines its rice yield. More than half of all wheat lands in India and Pakistan now feature Green Revolution varieties, and in the Philippines half of ricelands. Meanwhile, researchers continue to develop new crops and agro-technologies. The map (above) shows the location of some of the major international centres for agricultural research.

USA

Mexico

1965 1981 2000

Yield improvement

Countries with yields above world average (3,096kg per ha)

Countries with yields twice world average (6,192kg per ha)

● Major centres for agricultural research

ISNAR (The Hague, Netherlands)
IFPRI (Washington DC, USA)
CIMMYT (Mexico City, Mexico)
CIAT (Cali, Colombia)
CIP (Lima, Peru)
IPGRI (Rome, Italy)
IITA (Ibadan, Nigeria)
WARDA (Bouake, Cote d'Ivoire)
ILRI (Nairobi, Kenya)
ICRAF (Nairobi, Kenya)
ICARDA (Aleppo, Syrian Arab Republic)
ICRISAT (Ratancheru, India)
IWMI (Colombo, Sri Lanka)
ICLARM (Penang, Malaysia)
IRRI (Los Banos, Philippines)
CIFOR (Bogor, Indonesia)

Turkey

South Korea

Philippines

Pakistan

New

India

Uruguay

Inputs and outputs

Using a baseline of the early 1960s, we find that the global yield of grains more than doubled by the year 2000, associated with a fourfold increase in fertilizer. The grain area peaked in 1985, since which time it has declined by 7%. In short, the Green Revolution has only given us a breathing space.

Global fertilizer consumption
Global harvested area
Global grain yield

1961 1965 1970 1975 1980 1985 1990 1995 200

expensive additives. The bigger harvests generate greater incomes, which can then be invested in extra land. Slowly but steadily, the rich farmers broaden the gap between themselves and the poor farmers.

In short, the Green Revolution has achieved some remarkable breakthroughs, but it has many drawbacks and it is plainly running out of steam. The challenges are enormous. After more than doubling our grain supplies between 1950 and 1980, the following decade saw an increase of less than one-quarter. Grain production per person peaked in the mid-1980s at 342 kilograms, and actually declined by 2002 to less than 300 kilograms. Yet we must increase grain harvests by at least 40 percent by 2025 just to maintain current levels for a projected population of 7.9 billion. We are largely squandering the time the Green Revolution bought us to sort out larger problems, notably the runaway growth of population and the grossly inequitable distribution of land and food.

In short, we need a new agriculture based on an Evergreen Revolution. Fortunately, we possess the essentials of just such an advance in the Gene Revolution (see pp 70–71).

The North's agricultural model

American farmers seem to be remarkably successful. Less than one percent of the US populace, they feed their fellow citizens and provide a large share of all grain on international markets – around one-third in 2001. They produce 11 percent of the world's wheat, 18 percent of its sorghum, and 40 percent of its maize on only 11 percent of the world's croplands. For decades, the world has benefited from US food surpluses, but the prospect of further success is illusory. While "industrial agriculture" is very productive, it can also be extraordinarily destructive – in a slow, quiet manner, which means that the situation can become critical before it appears serious.

What are the costs of this "advanced" agriculture? The first and heaviest toll must surely be in soil loss.

Theoretical maximum
Highest achieved (year 2000)
Highest average (major wheat producers)
Developed-country average
Global average
Developing-country average
Traditional-varieties average

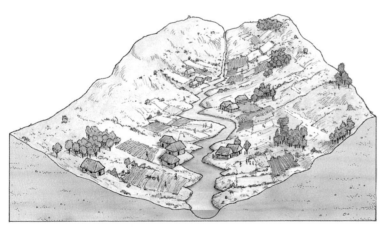

Before and after in Muda
A multi-faceted landscape with a pluralist society (above) has been transformed into a homogenized landscape dominated by larger holdings (below). The landless resort to slash-and-burn farming in Malaysia's forests.

What the Green Revolution promised Muda
1. To increase Malaysia's self-sufficiency in rice.
2. To increase farmers' incomes, with fair shares for all.

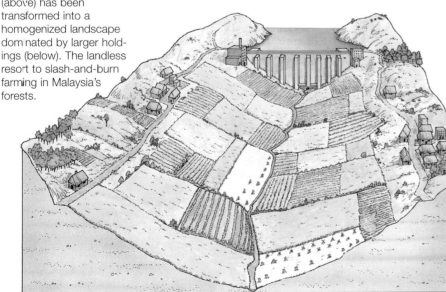

Promise and reality: Muda River
However productive the Green Revolution in agronomic terms, its economic and social success has been mixed at best. In northern Malaysia, the Muda river area reveals what can go wrong. A $90-million dam enabled irrigated paddies to produce two crops of high-yield rice a year, and by the early 1970s, output had almost tripled. The area, which accounted for 30% of Malaysia's rice-growing land, formerly supplied 30% of the country's rice, a share that rapidly rose to 50%. Malaysia had been only half self-sufficient in rice, but by 1974 it was 90%. Whereas average incomes for all categories of farmers increased, however, the wealthier categories enjoyed a boost of 150% while poorer farmers experienced only a 50% advance. Worse still, the harvests failed to expand after 1974, due to the "plateauing" effect. The more fertilizer farmers applied to their crops, the more their per-unit returns diminished and total yields finally levelled off. In this second stage, real incomes fell for all farmers, but especially for the poor who, by 1979, dropped below pre-Revolution levels. Moreover, the richer farmers, finding themselves with more disposable income, started to buy up land from the poorer farmers, causing the bottom sector of the community to take up tenant farming or to be pressurized off the land altogether.

"To those that have shall be given …": the gap between the well-to-do and the absolutely impoverished increases within the developing world, as well as between the developing world and the developed world. This regrettable pattern has been repeated in virtually all countries of the Green Revolution, with the exception of egalitarian societies.

The nation has lost at least one-third of its best soil. Whilst there has been some relief by the retirement of highly erodible farmland under the Conservation Reserve Program (CRP) and the expansion of "conservation tillage", there are still extensive areas of high erosion in the western plains of Texas and Colorado and in the upper Mississippi and Missouri river basins in Iowa and Minnesota. Secondly, the prodigal application of synthetic fertilizers and pesticides causes much water pollution. Thirdly, the spread of irrigation, which accounts for more than 80 percent consumptive water use, is steadily depleting the country's groundwater stocks. Finally, transport costs of food distribution amount to many billions of dollars a year when food can travel 2,400–4,000 kilometres from the farm to dinner plate.

Not surprisingly, the industrialization of agriculture in the US has turned many farms into sizeable commercial enterprises. Since 1950 there has been a steady trend towards large holdings, until now there are little over a third as many farmers. Due to the escalating costs of fertilizer, pesticides, fuel, and land itself, many farmers have run themselves deeply into debt, with interest payments rising to hundreds of billions of dollars in the 1980s and 1990s. Hence, farmers have felt obliged to reap ever-larger harvests each year in indifference to environmental costs. Fortunately, the country's Farm Service Agency set up the voluntary Conservation Reserve Program to help farmers safeguard environmentally sensitive land. In return for rental payments and cost-share assistance, farmers plant long-term, resource-conserving crops, thus, improving water quality, controlling erosion, and enhancing wildlife habitats.

In short, US agriculture of the past half century epitomizes the successes and the failures of industrial farming worldwide. This agricultural model has been widely copied and adapted in Green Revolution regions. The success is self-evident in terms of food grown, but the adverse impacts of industrial agriculture are all too apparent. In recent times, US farmers, together with many farmers in other nations, have begun to pull back from the unsustainable marginal lands they have been farming, and slowing the massive growth in fertilizer and pesticide use. Both these trends have contributed to a general levelling off of grain output.

Subsidizing food production

Food in rich countries costs less in real terms, allowing for inflation, than it has ever done. Yet it is certainly not cheap because of the many hidden costs, mainly environmental costs, that are not reflected at the checkout counter. The problem lies primarily with huge subsidies worldwide, totalling $635 billion per year, of which $510 billion are reckoned to be "perverse" in that they are harmful to the economy as well as the environment (see pp. 232–33). Such subsidies promote pesticides and chemical fertilizers

Agriculture in the balance

Each year there are more mouths to feed – at least 80 million more. That we have largely managed to feed them so far is an extraordinary tribute to the success of agriculture. Grain production rose from 624 million tonnes in 1950 to 1,862 million in 2000. Much of this massive increase arises from Western-type "high tech" solutions, using oil-based fertilizers and new hybrids planted in huge monocultures. But the 50-year success story conceals a major loss of momentum: the growth in global grain production since 1984 has averaged less than 1% while that of global population has averaged 1.7%. The result is that the global peak of 342 kg per person in 1984 declined to 302 kg by 2000. In 2002 and 2003 the global grain harvest fell short of consumption by over 90 million tonnes. Are the scales tipping towards failure?

Each sack represents 50 million tonnes of grain

Eating oil
Since 1950, population growth and environmental degradation have halved grain lands per head, but per capita fertilizer use has increased fourfold. Grain production per person peaked in 1984, since when it has fallen by 14%.

Population

5kg fertilizer per capita

Area of harvested land per capita

Food grain per capita

Feed grain per capita

			6.1 billion
		5.3 billion	110kg
	4.8 billion	155kg	
2.5 billion	159kg	123kg	
89kg 135kg	28kg 129kg 160kg	27kg	23kg
5.5kg			
0.23ha 1950	0.15ha 1984	0.13ha 1990	0.11ha 2000

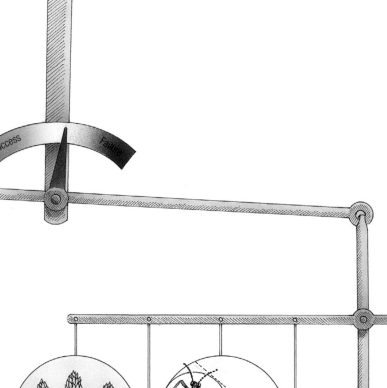

The costs of advanced agriculture

Many of today's farmers practise a form of "deficit financing". To meet urgent needs such as interest on loans, they are depleting our future land base, destroying our genetic heritage both wild and cultivated, using up fossil energy and groundwater supplies, and applying toxic chemicals to croplands. We lose nearly half our crops to resistant pests and bad storage, produce "milk lakes" we cannot dispose of, and use vital land to grow feed for livestock that fosters unduly meat-rich diets. Meanwhile, poorer countries experience falling food sufficiency, plus inadequate research facilities.

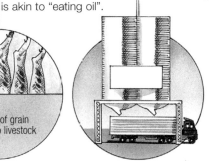

Spreading monocultures
Vast areas are planted with identical crop strains, all vulnerable to the same pathogens and all helping to erode genetic diversity (see pp. 172–73).

Race against nature
Intensive spraying often fails to eradicate the pests that thrive on monocultures and take over one-third of our harvests. Resistant and mutant forms often stay one jump ahead.

The oil farmers
Industrialized agriculture depends on so much oil for fertilizers, pesticides, irrigation, and machinery that modern agriculture is akin to "eating oil".

Lost genes
Traditional crop varieties are swept away by the bulldozer and replaced by the new hybrids, yet these old forms hold vital genetic material.

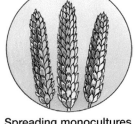

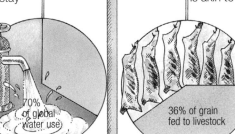

The new dust bowls
Deforestation, overploughing, or overgrazing of dry lands destroy the soil.

Thirsty crops
Irrigation is vital to the miracle grains and now takes more than 70% of global freshwater consumption.

Wasteful diets
36% of the world's grain is fed to livestock for the meat-rich diet of the long-rich countries and the new consumers (see pp. 234–35).

Surplus and waste
Rich-government subsidies induce farmers to overproduce, leading to vast surpluses of grain and meat, plus wine and milk lakes.

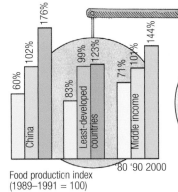

Food production index
(1989–1991 = 100)

1950s
self-sufficient
2000
34% grain imported

Leaving the poor behind
Even before world grain production per capita peaked, many low-income countries experienced a decline in food production per person, despite total production increasing.

Relying on grain imports
Egypt, with its fertile floodplain in the Nile, used to be self-sufficient in grain. Sadly, it is now heavily dependent on imported food.

Land concentration
Wealth breeds wealth: large holdings increasingly crowd out smallholders (who are generally more productive), as in Latin America (above).

Biased research and development
Green Revolution research has tended to ignore crops, such as cassava, sorghum, and millet, grown by small farmers in Latin America and Africa.

that severely contaminate both the atmosphere and water supplies. They foster short-rotation cropping and reduced fallows that exacerbate soil erosion. They encourage high-yielding monocultures that cause genetic wipe-out among old varieties of food plants. They aggravate land clearing for agriculture that is the largest single cause of deforestation, especially in the tropics. They underpin many agricultural activities that release greenhouse gases.

A European Union cow earns more in subsidies each day than the cash income of 1.3 billion people in the developing world. Moreover, 90 percent of subsidies in the European Union go to the largest one-quarter of farmers, the ones who need help the least – a case of "To him that hath shall be given". Still more absurd, many rich-nation subsidies allow food exports to be sold at prices 20–50 percent below the cost of production, thus undermining farmers and their struggling agriculture in the developing world. The United Nations Development Programme estimates that US farm subsidies alone cost poor countries about $50 billion a year in lost agricultural exports. Clearly, subsidies should be switched from production to sustainable agriculture. They would then support sound landscapes and amenities, clean water, recreation, sport, flood protection, and carbon sinks. The countryside does much more than grow food.

Despite their huge payments, farmers do not always produce food that is fit to eat. In 2001, there was an outbreak of foot-and-mouth disease in the UK, an epidemic that caused more than five million animals to be slaughtered at a cost to the nation (including tourism losses) of $16 billion. But it was not nearly so threatening to human health as BSE ("mad cow" disease), with as many as a million UK cattle infected. BSE was caused by recycling livestock remains (meat, bones, even feathers) into animal feed. Who would have thought of turning cows into carnivores? Exposure to BSE in humans via contaminated meat has been strongly linked to Creutzfeldt-Jakob Disease (vCJD) – which led to 139 deaths in the UK by early 2004.

Not just beef but other forms of meat are hazardous to health. According to Britain's consumer magazine "Which?", 30 percent of chickens sold in supermarkets should be declared "Unfit for human consumption". In Europe 130 million people are affected by food-borne diseases each year, while in the US 76 million people fall ill annually. In the northeastern US 23,000 chickens, turkeys, and other poultry are sold daily, 40 percent of them harbouring avian influenza viruses. The sheer number of animals reared, transported, slaughtered, and processed creates first-rate conditions for dangerous pathogens.

The new agricultural revolution
We need a new revolution in agriculture, both political and scientific. Fortunately, the germ of the scientific one already exists. But the political will and

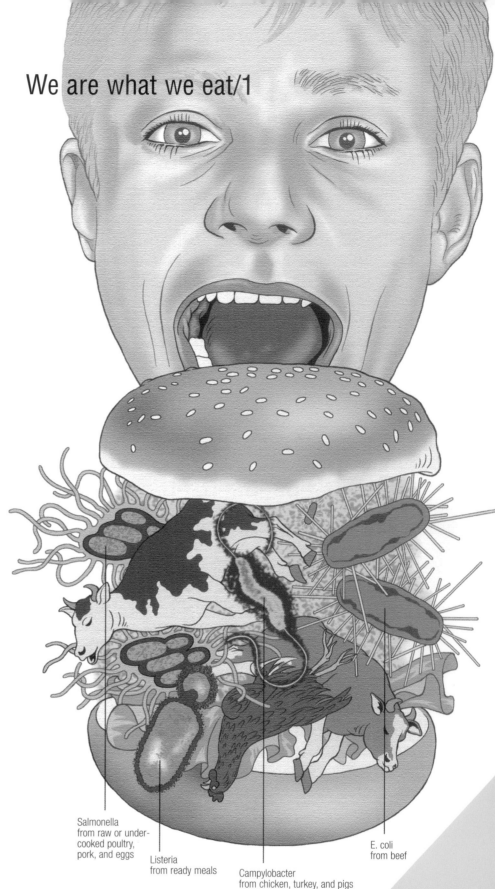

We are what we eat/1

Salmonella from raw or under-cooked poultry, pork, and eggs

Listeria from ready meals

Campylobacter from chicken, turkey, and pigs

E. coli from beef

Food-borne Illnesses
The WHO estimates that almost a third of people in rich countries suffer from food-borne diseases. The financial burden in medical costs and lost work productivity is somewhere between $34 billion and $110 billion per year. In the UK, food poisoning cases have increased by 600% in the last 15 years, to 5 million.

Fast food, quick death
Meat consumption extends beyond steaks. The fast-food industry – hamburgers, frankfurters, and the like – is a bedrock of American cuisine. Every day a quarter of all American adults visit a fast-food outlet. The industry is spreading its tentacles far and wide, and a good part of the McDonald's advertising budget is directed at the vast potential markets of developing countries. Big Food has used lobbying, educational materials, and contracts with schools food services to influence youngsters' eating habits. Advertising and sales campaigns are quick to equate grain-fed beef with a developing country's prestige. The carnivore culture has many eager customers insofar as climbing the "animal protein ladder" becomes a hallmark of material success. To cite an advert, "Enjoy our hamburger and join the Western world". Thus, a twist on the title of this spread: We are what we eat.

The real price of food
Consumers pay three times for their food: first, over the counter; second, through their taxes to fund subsidies; and third, through bills to clean up the mess created by intensive farming.

SARS
Civets cats, a delicacy in wild-game restaurants in southern China, have been linked to the SARS (severe acute respiratory syndrome) epidemic, which affected 8,000 people and killed almost 800 worldwide.

GM crops
Concern over GM contamination in food is widespread (see pp. 70–71). Soybeans accounted for 62% of the area of GM crops planted worldwide in 2002. Much of it was used as a major protein ingredient for livestock feed.

The meat/grain connection
Reducing meat consumption by eating one less meat dish a week saves 30 kg of grain and 40,000 gallons of water a year. If each American took this step it would save 9 million tonnes of grain, enough to feed 30 million people. Yet, since 1990, Americans' meat consumption has risen by almost a tenth. In Europe, by contrast, there has already been a decline of one meat dish a week, consumption being down from 1990 by a seventh.

Over the counter
The EU Common Agricultural Policy (CAP) imposes higher food costs on consumers: around 48 billion euros in 2000.

Subsidies
Subsidies allow food exports to be sold at prices 20–50% below the cost of production. Farm incomes are propped up by subsidies: 40 billion euros for EU farmers in 2000.

Clean-up costs
The external costs of UK's agriculture (pollution, damage to natural capital, health costs of, etc.) exceed £2 billion a year.

Obesity
The world now features more overweight than underweight people (see pp. 46–47) This absurd situation is led by the US, where over half its citizens are clinically overweight. It possesses more people on diets than ever before, yet ever-more overweight people, too. Obesity-related illnesses and deaths, often brought on in major measure by gorging on oversized fast foods and drinks, are a major drag on the nation's economy. In certain countries, fatty foods could eventually cause as many additional premature deaths as from AIDS. The UK has proposed a "fat tax" targeting obesity-related foods such as burgers.

More meat more methane
Livestock emit 16% of the world's methane, the second most powerful greenhouse gas after carbon dioxide.

BSE worldwide
Map shows the geographical distribution of countries that reported at least one confined case of BSE between1989 and January 2004. The bar chart shows the number of reported cases of BSE worldwide between 2001 and 2003. The figures for each bar are the total for these three years.

Reported confirmed cases of BSE

AUSTRIA 1
FINLAND 1
GREECE 1
ISRAEL 1
LUXEMBOURG 1
CANADA 2
SLOVENIA 3
CZECH REPUBLIC 8
POLAND 9
JAPAN 9
DENMARK 11
SLOVAKIA 13
NETHERLANDS 63
SWITZERLAND 87
BELGIUM 99
ITALY 115
GERMANY 285
PORTUGAL 329
SPAIN 376
FRANCE 650
EIRE 762
UNITED KINGDOM 2,958

means to apply it are yet half-formed. Hitherto, our approach has been to "bend" the environment to suit our crops. Now, thanks to plant breeders and genetic engineers, we can bend the plants instead – manipulating crops to flourish in harmony with their environments rather than in spite of them. Instead of pouring in fertilizer, water, weedkillers, and pesticides, we can grow plants that fend for themselves – desert-dwellers, such as jojoba, new arid-land staples, such as the morama bean or buffalo gourd, crops tolerant of extreme temperatures, and even strains of wheat, barley, and tomatoes that permit seawater irrigation.

We already make use of legumes which produce their own fertilizer via the symbiotic nitrogen-fixing bacteria in their roots. We may soon manage to transfer this capacity to other plants, whereupon farmers need not fear the rising cost of synthetic nitrogen. Crop breeders are also exploiting disease resistance in wild species to develop crops with built-in defences against viruses and pests.

These breakthroughs are the centrepieces of the forthcoming Gene Revolution, which promises to dramatically improve the production of our major crop species. To succeed, it will require greater emphasis on research than ever before, and a

More research
Increased funding and new research centres are badly needed, especially in low-income areas, to develop locally adapted strains and cultivation techniques relevant to small and large-scale farmers.

Towards a new agriculture

Ecology has shaped integrated pest management, water-conserving irrigation methods, new organic fertilizers, and new uses of crop residues and green mulches to protect land and improve energy efficiency. Conservation tillage prevents soil loss; it is now employed on 44 million hectares in the US. Future crops will be more self-sufficient and high-yielding, tailored to their setting. But research support is slim. The farms of the future will need more research and greater protection of the genetic resources which provide the raw material for the Gene Revolution.

Managing pests
Integrated pest control has been enormously successful. It aims not to wipe out pests but to keep them at tolerable levels, by applying a range of "natural" restraints – mixed planting; clearing pest reservoirs such as stagnant pools; introducing natural predators; releasing sterile pest males; and even using hormones to interfere with maturation.

Conservation tillage
Minimum-till farming is energy-efficient and protects the soil. Crop residues and stubble left on the land retain nutrients and prevent erosion. Next year's crop is sown in shallow, restricted furrows, or drilled in without turning the soil.

Plants with a future
Food plants adapted to harsh lands are offering us new solutions.

The Somalian yeheb bush
This arid-land native has nutritious peanut-sized seeds, and could be a staple crop of the deserts.

The hairy wild potato
To keep aphids at bay, this wild plant mimics the alarm scent of aphids. These pest-deterrent traits could one day be bred into crops.

Hairy potato

Yeheb

Smallholdings

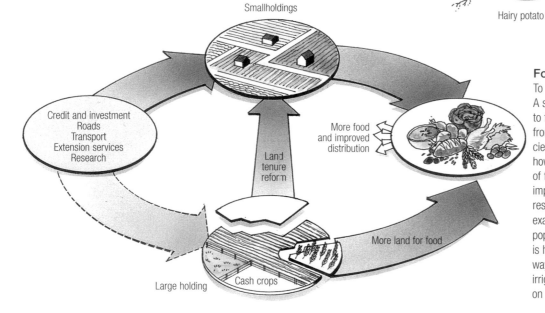

Credit and investment
Roads
Transport
Extension services
Research

More food and improved distribution

Land tenure reform

More land for food

Large holding   Cash crops

Food first in the South
To feed the South, the new agriculture must be truly revolutionary. A sharp turnaround is called for, from over-emphasis on industry to farming, from export cash crops to domestic supply of food, and from commercial landholder to small farmer. To achieve food sufficiency, small farmers must be backed by regional cooperation, for however willing and productive they may be, they need a package of facilities to succeed. These include: credit and better prices; improved marketing, transport and advisory services; appropriate research; and security of tenure and access to good land. The best example of "food first" has been China, feeding 20% of the world's population on 7% of the world's arable land. But China's agriculture is heading into deep trouble. Its croplands are shrinking to make way for cities, towns, factories, roads, etc.; and water for crop irrigation is in ever-shorter supply. At the same time, China takes on an extra 8 million people each year through population growth.

Mixed cropping
Interplanting and crop rotation maintain soil balance, reduce pest invasions, and, by providing green cover below row plants, prevent evaporation and erosion. Legumes, which fix nitrogen, restore fertility if planted between maize or permanent crops.

new set of economic strategies to take agriculture out of its "Cinderella" status. However, unlike Green Revolution technologies, Gene Revolution research and marketing are being undertaken mainly by the private sector. This may have implications for the speed at which the Gene Revolution spreads.

Most of all, the revolution requires political changes – a revolution so profound that each individual will be affected. For as long as rich-world citizens, by their high-meat diets, continue to support the inequitable meat/grain connection, land will be over-worked, and people will go hungry. And as long as certain developing nations emphasize industry, urbanization,

and cash crops at the expense of food sufficiency and the small farmer, the same applies.

Given proper back-up, the small farmers (who today make up over half of the world's poor) can feed themselves. Given the right advice, rich citizens can improve their diets. Given our new scientific understanding, the land can supply a sustainable harvest to feed us. It is merely a matter of getting our priorities right.

GM foods
Genetically modified (GM) foods have raised a political furore in both Europe and North America,

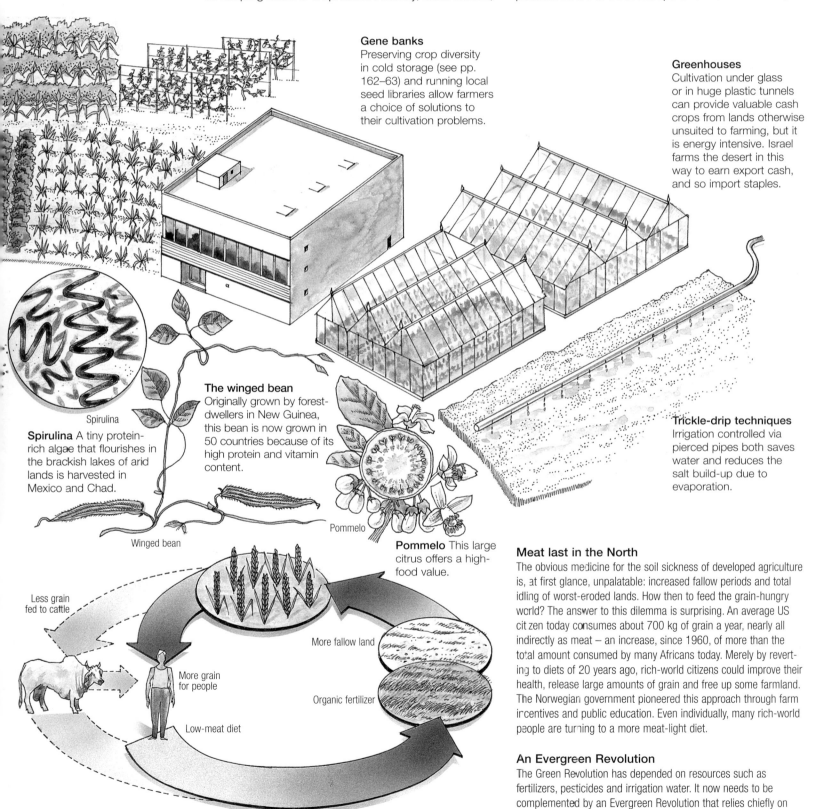

Gene banks
Preserving crop diversity in cold storage (see pp. 162–63) and running local seed libraries allow farmers a choice of solutions to their cultivation problems.

Greenhouses
Cultivation under glass or in huge plastic tunnels can provide valuable cash crops from lands otherwise unsuited to farming, but it is energy intensive. Israel farms the desert in this way to earn export cash, and so import staples.

Spirulina
Spirulina A tiny protein-rich algae that flourishes in the brackish lakes of arid lands is harvested in Mexico and Chad.

The winged bean
Originally grown by forest-dwellers in New Guinea, this bean is now grown in 50 countries because of its high protein and vitamin content.

Winged bean

Pommelo

Pommelo This large citrus offers a high-food value.

Trickle-drip techniques
Irrigation controlled via pierced pipes both saves water and reduces the salt build-up due to evaporation.

Less grain fed to cattle

More grain for people

Low-meat diet

More fallow land

Organic fertilizer

Meat last in the North
The obvious medicine for the soil sickness of developed agriculture is, at first glance, unpalatable: increased fallow periods and total idling of worst-eroded lands. How then to feed the grain-hungry world? The answer to this dilemma is surprising. An average US citizen today consumes about 700 kg of grain a year, nearly all indirectly as meat – an increase, since 1960, of more than the total amount consumed by many Africans today. Merely by reverting to diets of 20 years ago, rich-world citizens could improve their health, release large amounts of grain and free up some farmland. The Norwegian government pioneered this approach through farm incentives and public education. Even individually, many rich-world people are turning to a more meat-light diet.

An Evergreen Revolution
The Green Revolution has depended on resources such as fertilizers, pesticides and irrigation water. It now needs to be complemented by an Evergreen Revolution that relies chiefly on science in the form of the latest plant breeding.

and still further afield. They could signal one of the biggest advances ever achieved in farming – or they could trigger all manner of ecological backlashes and health problems. The scientific evidence one way or the other is far from complete, and may not become so without field trials extending over several crop seasons. Public opinion is deeply divided, sometimes bitterly so. Extremism flourishes. The stakes are high with huge sums invested by giant agro-businesses. It all adds up to a combustible mix of fact and fiction, opinion and prejudice, and governments pitted against each other in one of the most acrimonious policy debates for decades.

The main proponents of GM foods are Americans, the main sceptics are Europeans. American farmers have long planted GM crops, such as corn, canola, soybeans, squash, papaya, and cotton, and they are by far the world's largest exporters of GM foods. Europe, by contrast, features only small amounts of GM crops but has become the site of grand-scale resistance. All in all, tens of millions of farmers grow GM crops on 700,000 square kilometres in 18 countries led by Brazil, South Africa, the US, Argentina, Canada, and China. The expanse increased by 15 percent in 2003 alone.

Why do GM foods generate such strident reactions? GM crops will resist pests, grow in salty soils, and produce food that is more nutritious and more stable in storage. Nor is there any doubt about the urgent need for more bountiful farming when our numbers are likely to increase by over 1.5 billion people within another two decades. Unfortunately, the hungriest people are the poorest people who generally cannot afford the new biotechnologies.

Why are many Europeans so severely alarmed about what they sometimes term "Frankenfoods"? Scientists for the most part are guardedly in favour of GM farming, or at least neutral. But they register a strong proviso: that there should be sufficiently comprehensive field trials, over however long a period of time, to demonstrate that GM crops are safe in terms of both the environment and public health. Conclusive results may not become available for several seasons.

Whatever the arguments, there are deep-seated concerns among the European public, concerns that mostly have little to do with strict science. Many European consumers are still wary about science in the food arena after the "mad cow" fiasco in Britain, even though the problem had nothing to do with genetic engineering. Conversely, Americans insist that their country has the highest food safety standards in the world, and they point out that for the past several years they have been eating large quantities of genetically modified foods without apparent ill-effects.

In response to these challenges, GM advocates need to improve their communications if ever public opinion is to be persuaded that the advantages outweigh the risks. There is a premium on listening to, as well as speaking to, the public. Certain of the

The gene revolution

Decaf coffee
Every tenth cup of coffee consumed worldwide is a decaf, and the version you can order in your local coffee shop is artificially decaffeinated, meaning that it is somewhat de-flavoured as well. Decaf coffee is in big demand because caffeine can raise blood pressure, trigger palpitations, and make sleep difficult. Now the Brazilians have discovered a coffee berry strain in their plantations that is naturally almost caffeine-free while retaining full flavour. It occurs in just three bushes that feature 15 times less stimulant than commercial strains. But who shall be said to "own" the genes and hence garner the profits from a breeding breakthrough? The original coffee plants were long ago taken from Ethiopia to Brazil, and today the two countries are arguing over who should benefit from the vital genetic material. Much is at stake: retail sales of coffee worldwide are worth $70 billion per year.

DNA cloning
Reproductive cloning could be used to generate animals with special features. For instance, certain animals could be genetically modified and then mass-produced to serve as models for study of human diseases. Therapeutic cloning could eventually be used in humans to produce organs from single cells or even healthy cells to replace diseased cells in degenerative diseases, such as Parkinson's and Alzheimer's. Cloning technology can be further applied in support of threatened species. In 2001 Italian scientists cloned a healthy baby mouflon, an endangered wild sheep. Among species that might lend themselves to this "test-tube" technique are such severely imperilled and charismatic species as the giant panda and the Sumatran tiger, both on the verge of extinction.

Terminator genes
These prevent plants from producing fertile seeds for use when sowing next year's crop. They allow a seed company to protect its investment in new varieties by requiring farmers to buy new seeds each year – an approach that is at odds with the long-standing tradition of farmers holding back some of their grain to plant the following year. Thus, the terminator is not about improving agriculture, it is about sterilizing seeds and wresting control of seeds and plant breeding from farmers. Fortunately, the bioscience industry giant, Monsanto, has agreed to stop developing terminator genes.

Monarch butterfly
The monarch butterflies of North America are notable not only for their beauty but for their pollinating services. They are becoming notable, too, for their susceptibility to pollen from Bt corn blown on to close-by milkweeds which form feeding grounds for the butterflies. Huge numbers of monarchs fly through the North American corn belt on their spring and summer migrations from Canadian to Mexican forests.

Genetic pollution
Although Mexico allows the import of GM crops, in 1998 the country banned new planting of GM corn in a bid to protect its traditional varieties. By 2001 there were reports of contamination in Oaxaca, the centre of origin and diversity for the staple crop.

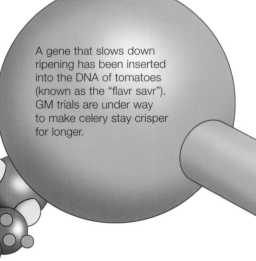

A gene that slows down ripening has been inserted into the DNA of tomatoes (known as the "flavr savr"). GM trials are under way to make celery stay crisper for longer.

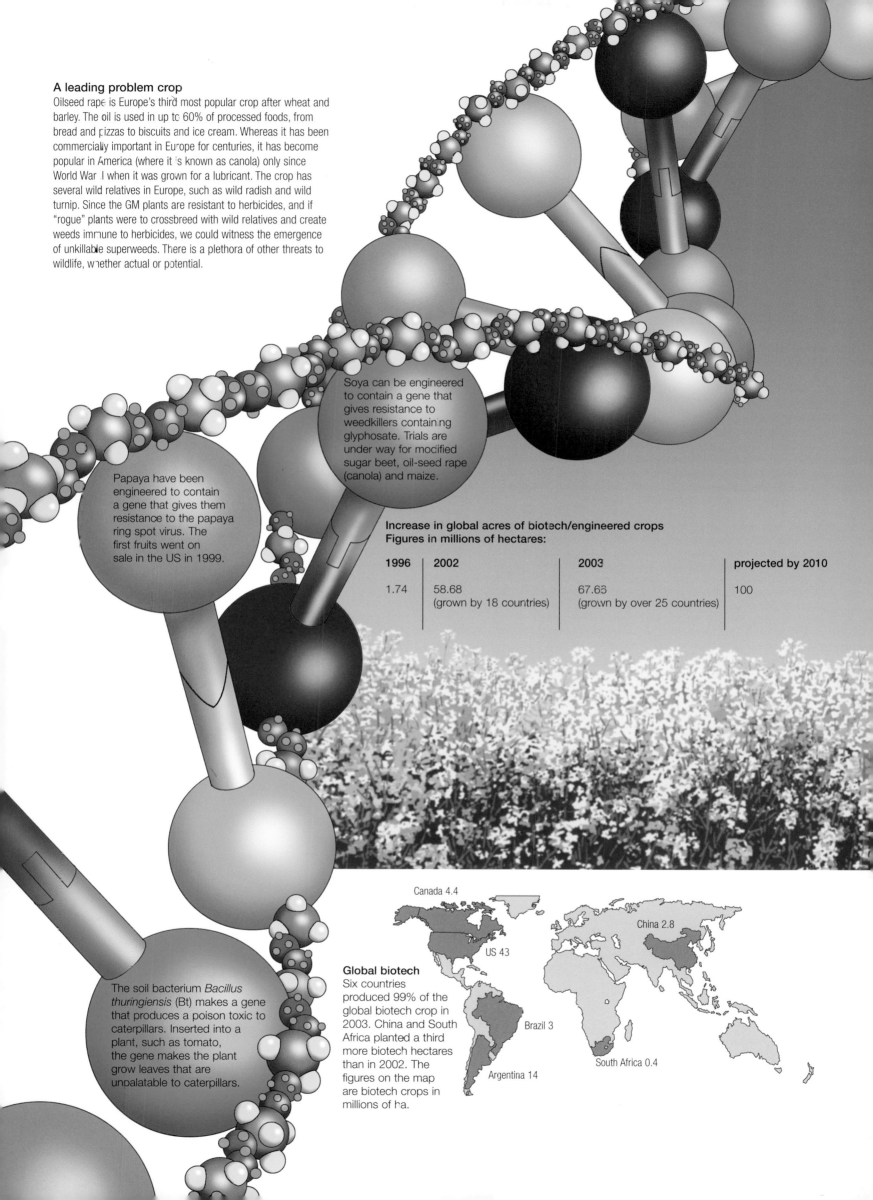

A leading problem crop

Oilseed rape is Europe's third most popular crop after wheat and barley. The oil is used in up to 60% of processed foods, from bread and pizzas to biscuits and ice cream. Whereas it has been commercially important in Europe for centuries, it has become popular in America (where it is known as canola) only since World War I when it was grown for a lubricant. The crop has several wild relatives in Europe, such as wild radish and wild turnip. Since the GM plants are resistant to herbicides, and if "rogue" plants were to crossbreed with wild relatives and create weeds immune to herbicides, we could witness the emergence of unkillable superweeds. There is a plethora of other threats to wildlife, whether actual or potential.

Soya can be engineered to contain a gene that gives resistance to weedkillers containing glyphosate. Trials are under way for modified sugar beet, oil-seed rape (canola) and maize.

Papaya have been engineered to contain a gene that gives them resistance to the papaya ring spot virus. The first fruits went on sale in the US in 1999.

Increase in global acres of biotech/engineered crops
Figures in millions of hectares:

1996	2002	2003	projected by 2010
1.74	58.68 (grown by 18 countries)	67.66 (grown by over 25 countries)	100

The soil bacterium *Bacillus thuringiensis* (Bt) makes a gene that produces a poison toxic to caterpillars. Inserted into a plant, such as tomato, the gene makes the plant grow leaves that are unpalatable to caterpillars.

Canada 4.4

China 2.8

US 43

Brazil 3

South Africa 0.4

Argentina 14

Global biotech

Six countries produced 99% of the global biotech crop in 2003. China and South Africa planted a third more biotech hectares than in 2002. The figures on the map are biotech crops in millions of ha.

public's fears are not without some foundation, especially as concerns the political leverage of giant corporations. It is not only a case of the public's understanding of science but of scientists' understanding of the public.

The rise of the organic movement

Conventional agriculture is largely a case of eating oil, given that oil is a basic factor in fertilizers and pesticides as well as fuel for machinery. We need to adapt to a less damaging and sustainable form of agriculture. How about organic agriculture?

As the Worldwatch Institute describes it, organic farming is a "system that prohibits synthetic pesticides and artificial fertilizers, and instead relies on ecological interactions to raise yields, reduce pests, and rebuild soil fertility". Farmers rotate crop varieties and compost to return nutrients to the soil, and they attract beneficial insects to reduce pest outbreaks and disease. Even though harvests may be a bit less than from "industrial" agriculture, there are lots of health benefits. Foods grown without pesticides contain much higher concentrations of antioxidants and other health-promoting compounds that are associated with reduced risk of cancer, stroke, heart disease, and other major illnesses.

Moreover, organic farming generally disallows growth hormones and antibiotics in livestock, and it rejects all GM crops. Hence, it reduces groundwater pollution, emits fewer greenhouse gases, increases carbon storage, improves soil health, and enhances biodiversity. Organic farms in Europe can feature five times as many wild plants, including rare and threatened species, at least a quarter more birds, three times as many butterflies, and remarkable increases in soil biotas, including earthworms.

The world market for organic produce swelled to $23 billion by 2002, with 51 percent or $12 billion accounted for by the US and 46 percent ($10 billion) by Western Europe. There has also been rapid growth in export markets for developing countries. Tesco, the UK's largest supermarket chain, aims to offer over 700 organic items, including fresh produce, meat, frozen and prepared foods, dairy items, bakery goods, alcohol, baby foods, and pet foods. Organic cotton is sold by such garment giants as The Gap, Levi's, and Patagonia.

As the Worldwatch Institute emphasizes, public enthusiasm for organic foods not only reflects a backlash against conventional foods, notably the "mad cow" scare in the UK, but it supports the holistic approach to farming. In addition, the very term "organic" implies meal tables that not only feature foods grown without carcinogenic pesticides and other toxins, but also a lifestyle that highlights fresh wholefoods, and home cooking rather than fast food. In short, organic foods are no longer a counter-culture item. They are rapidly becoming mainstream. Because of their lifestyle attributes, they could go far to help with the overeating epidemic.

We are what we eat/2

Farmers' markets

In the US, farmers' markets grew from nearly 300 in the mid-1970s to more than 3,100 in 2002. Roughly 3 million people visit these markets every week and spend over $1 billion each year. Farmers within a radius of 56 kilometres bring their goods to an urban market area and sell them directly to customers, thus eliminating hosts of middle men. There is next to no transportation involved, whereas a typical mealtime item in America travels over 1,600 kilometres. In 2003 the UK had 450 farmers' markets with 15 million visits and $300 million in annual sales. At a typical Saturday market there are 40 sellers and 4,000 customers.

In both the US and the UK, these markets represent an outlet for organic growers and the first "fully organic produce" market opened in the UK in 2003. In Japan, farmers sell about 60% of their produce directly to consumers through a network of 1,000 clubs with sales of $15 billion a year.

"Organic farming delivers the highest quality, best tasting food, produced without artificial chemicals or genetic modification, and with respect for animal welfare and the environment, while helping to maintain the landscape and rural communities."
HRH the Prince of Wales,
Patron, the UK Soil Association

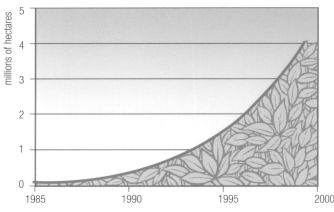

Certified organic area in the European Union, 1985–1999

Organic farming in the European Union

In 1999, almost 4 million hectares – 3% of the total agricultural land – was devoted to organic farming in the EU. Since 1985, organic farming has been spreading at an average annual growth rate of 30% – more than any other region in the world.

The UK experience

Only 4% of Britain's farmlands are organic, by contrast with more than 10% in Germany and Sweden. The country devotes a mere 4% of its $5.4 billion in farm subsidies to organic and environmentally friendly farming. The rest goes on "industrial" farming, yet the price of clean-ups and other costs for government and business (damage to wildlife and its habitats, greenhouse gases among other pollutants, soil erosion, animal diseases such as "mad cow", and food poisoning) amount to over $4 billion per year. Switching half of the country's farming to organic could cut these costs by as much as two-thirds. Moreover, moving to organic methods would create thousands of jobs at a time when agriculture faces its worst employment crisis in 70 years. If the number of organic farms increased by just 10%, at least 17,000 jobs could be created, or almost as many as the number of farmers leaving the sector each year.

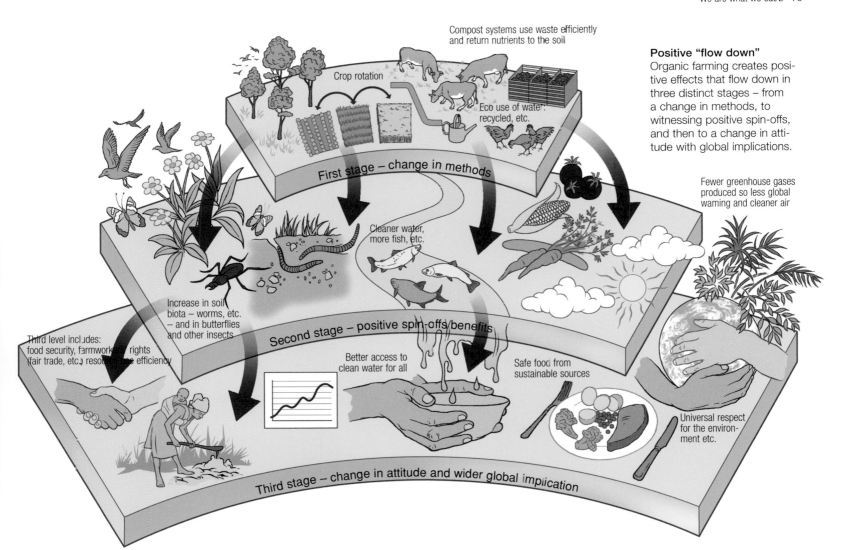

Positive "flow down"
Organic farming creates positive effects that flow down in three distinct stages – from a change in methods, to witnessing positive spin-offs, and then to a change in attitude with global implications.

Compost systems use waste efficiently and return nutrients to the soil

Crop rotation

Eco use of water: recycled, etc.

First stage – change in methods

Fewer greenhouse gases produced so less global warming and cleaner air

Increase in soil biota – worms, etc. – and in butterflies and other insects

Cleaner water, more fish, etc.

Second stage – positive spin-offs/benefits

Third level includes: food security, farmworkers' rights (fair trade, etc.) resource efficiency

Better access to clean water for all

Safe food from sustainable sources

Universal respect for the environment etc.

Third stage – change in attitude and wider global implication

Food safety
Organic farmers rely on developing a healthy, fertile soil and growing a mixture of crops. They do not feed their animals regular doses of antibiotics and other drugs that are common in factory farming. They do not rely on artificial chemical fertilizers and pesticides.

In addition, organic food standards ban the use of additives linked to asthma and heart disease. They also ban GM soya, maize, and other products in animal feed as well as in human food products.

Environmental benefits
350 chemicals are routinely used in conventional farming in the UK, but £120 million a year is spent removing them from water supplies. Organic agriculture permits only 4 pesticides, resulting in a greater diversity of birds, butterflies, and plants on organic farms.

Poor farmers' benefits
Farmers in India, Kenya, Brazil, Guatemala, and Honduras have doubled or sometimes tripled their yields by switching to organic or semi-organic techniques. Many African countries grow organic fruit, vegetables, oil crops, herbs, spices, tea, and coffee.

The spread of organic agriculture
In 2004, organic agriculture covered more than 240,000 sq. km in 88 countries – an expanse almost equivalent to that of the UK. The leader was Australia with 10 million ha, followed by Argentina with almost 3 million ha. Since 1996, the UK's organic area has surged from 50,000 to 724,523 ha. Almost 80% of UK households buy organic food, spending around £1 billion – more than any other European country apart from Germany. The UK aims for 70% of its organic food sales to be home-produced by 2010. In total, Europe has 170,000 farms covering 55,000 sq. km. In several nations, including Italy, Sweden, Finland, and Switzerland, 5–10% of agricultural lands are now organic, while Austria has reached 13%.

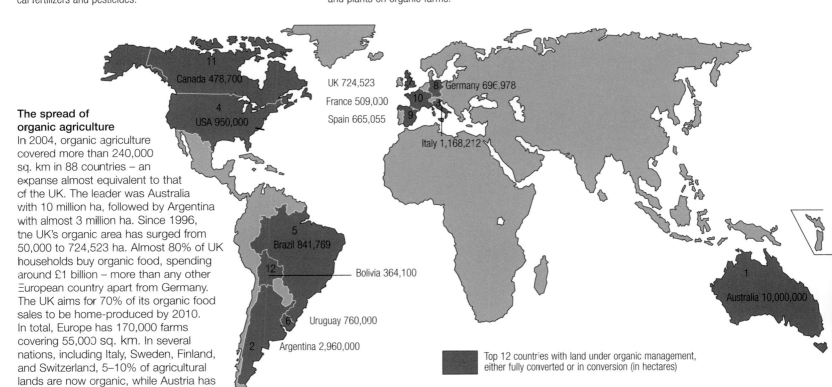

11 Canada 478,700
UK 724,523
France 509,000
8 Germany 696,978
Spain 665,055
4 USA 950,000
Italy 1,168,212
5 Brazil 841,769
12 Bolivia 364,100
6 Uruguay 760,000
2 Argentina 2,960,000
1 Australia 10,000,000

Top 12 countries with land under organic management, either fully converted or in conversion (in hectares)

OCEAN

Introduced by Carl Safina
President of the Blue Ocean Institute and author
of *Song for the Blue Ocean*.

The sea's eternally changing surface creates an ironic illusion of changelessness – yet of all things that can be said of the ocean, the simplest and truest is that it has indeed changed. For most, the change lies hidden. The eternal motion of water transports contaminants and aids the global smear of alien species. This same fluidity instantly closes the ocean's skin to hide the tracks of vessels and scars inflicted upon the sea floor, and the silent, empty spaces where formerly so many fishes teemed. Because that fluid surface defies fences, it fosters the greatest human commons anywhere, wherein we execute the largest-scale commercial hunting of wildlife ever. The collective weight of humanity may lie on land, but we levy heavy pressure upon the sea, too.

Until recently, whenever the question arose of how to feed our population-bombed future, thoughts turned seaward. As land frontiers evaporated, the ocean presented a final frontier for a lawless "gold-rush" for riches. Governments sped subsidized fleets to the hunt carrying the most sophisticated high-tech detection devices the oceans had ever seen. Foreign boats and then foreign overfishing replaced by increased fishing power proved no less destructive just because they were home-grown. Those boats took our cod, our tuna, our sharks, our youth, and our innocence.

In the 1970s, countries began declaring "exclusive economic zones" of the waters out to 200 nautical miles from their coasts, defending them against for-eign exploiters. It took another 20 years for the full realization to sink in: that an ocean could be depleted by mere nets and hooks, no matter who put them in the water. Now the doubt is gone. Waves of new ocean studies are reporting the extent of overfishing, failures of ocean management, fish-farm contamination, invading species and new diseases, ocean dead zones, coastal crowding and pollution, dying coral reefs – and what could be done to ease such problems.

The bad news can seem overwhelming. But take heart; some solutions have been logged. Turtle drownings have been reduced by putting escape doors in trawl nets or using large "circle" hooks. Seabirds can be protected with devices designed to scare them from industrial fishing lines, by fishing at night or setting nets deeper. The United Nations successfully eliminated the 40-mile-long "curtains-of-death" drift-nets in the 1990s. Some whales have recovered enough to support whale-watching ventures. Even certain fish are recovering due to stricter regulations. These real improvements to serious problems should inspire hope and a new ethic of ocean stewardship, spurring more vigorous, widespread application of potential solutions – because they can work.

We have a long way to go. The frontier mentality must yield to the public trust, the needs of future generations, and our ethical responsibilities to other creatures. Some of the answers to ocean recovery lie in fishing more slowly than fish can breed, farming seafood less destructively, reducing incidental kill of marine life, zoning human activities, and closing the ocean frontier within the rule of law. Where these things have been attempted, the results are affirming; animals recover, habitats improve. While we have seen much depletion and diminishment, we have also seen the rise of conservation awareness and an ethic that forever binds the restorers with the takers, all of us one and the same, differing merely in degree.

So, yes, there is hope, if we work for it.

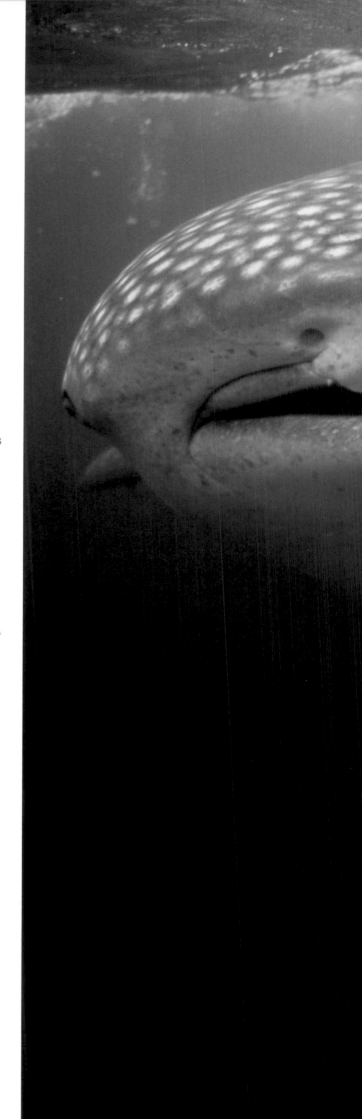

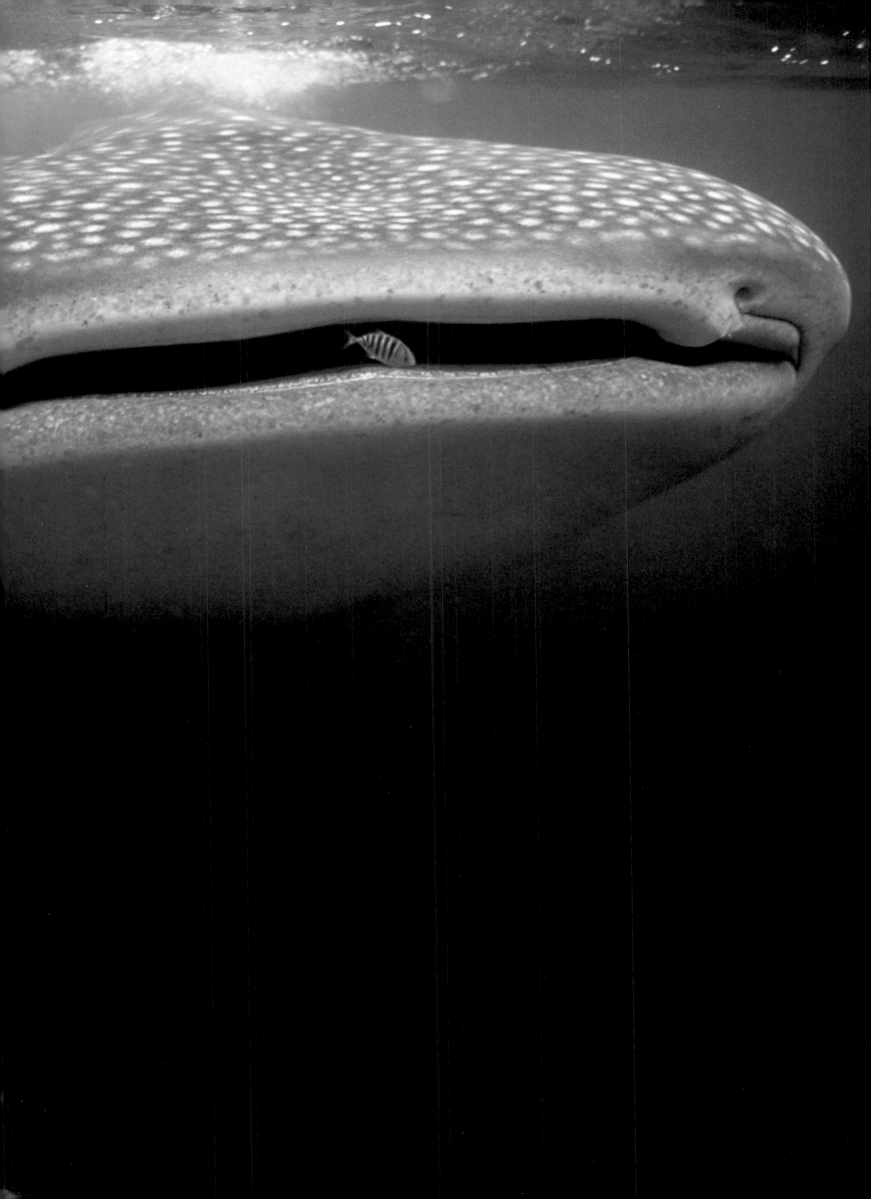

The Ocean Potential

Our planet should not be called Earth but Ocean, since at least seven-tenths is covered with seas.

We know little about this water planet. Although the oceans are just as diverse as the land, and interwoven with human history, we tend to see them as barriers, as alien spaces. In reality, ocean ecosystems are continuous – or rather, the single ecosystem of a world ocean with land masses as the true barriers, though gradients of temperature and salinity separate the oceans into a series of discrete regions.

It takes a leap of the imagination to perceive the integral role of the ocean in our planet's workings. The interdependent circulatory systems of ocean and atmosphere determine climatic flows right around the globe. At the same time, the great accumulations of seawater, almost entirely placid beneath the surface, exert a major stabilizing influence on climate: their very bulk produces a "flywheel" effect, a powerful buffer for what would otherwise be drastic fluctuations in our weather. The oceans also serve as a great reservoir of dissolved gases which helps to regulate the composition of the air we breathe.

The oceans give no more of a liquid covering to the globe than a film of moisture on a football, yet their depth and grandeur are remarkable – Mount Everest could readily be lost in the Mariana Trench. Underwater landscapes are extraordinarily varied, with spectacular geologic features. Along the edges of land masses are barely sloping continental shelves, accounting for about eight percent of the ocean's expanse. Fed by sediments washed off the land, the shelves are often very fertile, and support abundant fisheries. Twice as extensive are the continental slopes with gradients 4–10 times steeper, reaching down as far as 500 metres. Eventually, these drop away to 3,000 metres or more, until they meet the "foothills" of the abyssal floor. This vast plain, sometimes with barely a pimple in thousands of kilometres, elsewhere scarred and rugged like terrestrial "badlands", is broken at the centre by mighty ridges, stretching the length and breadth of the four great oceans. Matching them in scale are giant canyons and long, narrow trenches, located along continental margins and associated with island arcs, the deepest plunging 11,000 metres below the surface.

Little known and apparently remote, the ocean is a remarkably rich "resource realm". With better understanding, we might learn to draw sustainable benefit from its fisheries, minerals, and energy, and from its services as a gigantic weather machine. The ocean ecosphere constitutes a magnificent frontier

The world ocean

The ocean is a single dynamic medium, its waters constantly on the move under the influence of the sun's heat (which provides the initial thrust), the Earth's rotation and solar and lunar tides. The major currents, great "travelators" of the ocean, deliver huge masses of water over long distances, providing a continuous interchange between warm equatorial water and cold water from the poles. The consequences for climate, marine ecosystems, and fisheries are vital. The warm Gulf Stream, for instance, surging along faster than any ship, transports 55 million cu. m per second – 50 times more water than all the world's rivers. Without it, the "temperate" lands of northwestern Europe would be more like the sub-Arctic. The Peru current and the Benguela current of southwest Africa produce marine bonanzas as they bring in nutrient-rich waters dragged to the surface by offshore winds – a superabundance of plankton, fish, and seabirds. The map shows the major warm and cold surface currents, and the densities of human populations, a great proportion of them living in the coastal zones.

The water planet
The unconventional hemispheres (below) reveal the ocean's true extent: the "sea" hemisphere is almost all water – over 90%. Even the "land" hemisphere is still 50% water.

Land hemisphere

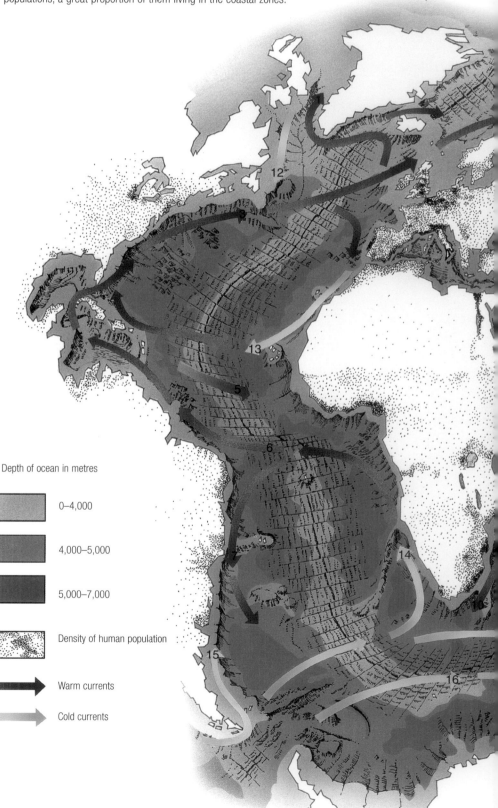

Depth of ocean in metres

0–4,000

4,000–5,000

5,000–7,000

Density of human population

Warm currents

Cold currents

The sea floor's wealth

The dramatic ridges and trenches of the ocean abyss express
its history, for the sea floor has long been in motion. Just as the
continental "plates" drift on a hot, partially molten underlayer, so
the ocean bed is made up of moving plates. The great mid-oceanic
ridges mark where plates are separating: the molten underlayer
pushes up through the rift to form ridge material, while the sea
floor spreads steadily away from the ridge axis. At the ocean margins, deep trenches occur as the oceanic and continental plates
collide and one is drawn down under the other. Understanding
sea-floor plate interactions helps scientists predict the locations
of valuable minerals for future exploitation.

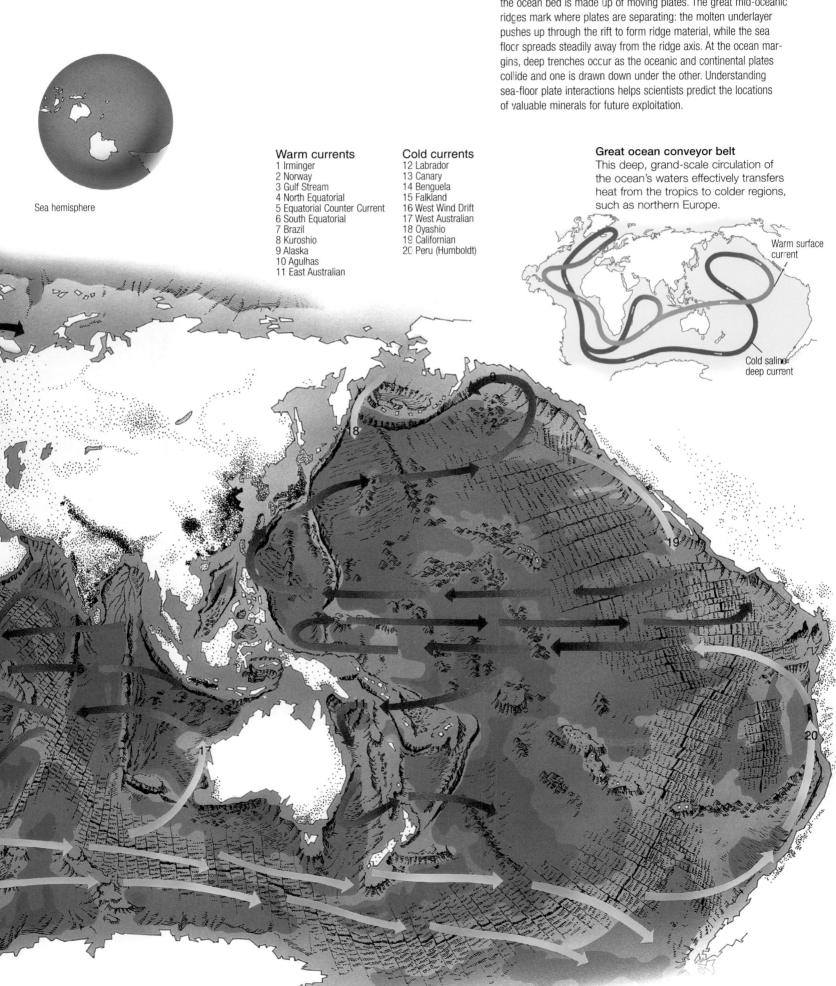

Sea hemisphere

Warm currents
1 Irminger
2 Norway
3 Gulf Stream
4 North Equatorial
5 Equatorial Counter Current
6 South Equatorial
7 Brazil
8 Kuroshio
9 Alaska
10 Agulhas
11 East Australian

Cold currents
12 Labrador
13 Canary
14 Benguela
15 Falkland
16 West Wind Drift
17 West Australian
18 Oyashio
19 Californian
20 Peru (Humboldt)

Great ocean conveyor belt
This deep, grand-scale circulation of
the ocean's waters effectively transfers
heat from the tropics to colder regions,
such as northern Europe.

Warm surface
current

Cold saline
deep current

of scientific research – as exciting to many scientists as our exploration of the Sea of Storms on the waterless surface of the Moon.

The living ocean

The ocean is where life began. Almost four billion years ago there evolved simple single-celled algae and bacteria very similar to those that form the basis of life in today's oceans. Collectively known as phytoplankton (from the Greek, meaning "drifting plants"), these microflora exploit the energy of the sun and nutrients in water to manufacture complex molecules of living tissue and form the cornerstone of the marine food chain (see right).

Just as on land, life is unevenly distributed in the oceans. In certain sectors the sea floor is covered with extensive sand stretches, which, while no more lifeless than the Sahara, are distinctly impoverished compared with the rest of the ocean. At the other extreme, "rainforests" flourish, particularly in coastal wetlands, estuaries, and reefs in upwelling zones. The Great Barrier Reef of northeastern Australia harbours 400 types of coral, 1,500 species of fish and 4,000 species of mollusc.

Finally, there is the deep ocean: pitch-dark, near freezing, yet far from lifeless. Our preliminary probings of this remote realm reveal more than 2,000 species of fish, and at least as many invertebrates, many of them grotesque and primitive in form, being the result of adaptations to an unpromising environment. But plainly they are altogether unprimitive, in that they subsist, indeed flourish, in such conditions.

The ocean is three dimensional. Its plant wealth is not "fixed" insofar as phytoplankton drift far and wide and are estimated to produce 20 billion tonnes of new growth each year. Here, then, is an ecosphere fundamentally different from that on land, yet one so fertile that it supports huge quantities of biomass.

Phytoplankton represent a tiny fraction of the biomass of terrestrial plants, yet they may account for around half of net photosynthesis in the biosphere. Individually insignificant, they amount together to some of the most important organisms on Earth. As "primary producers" they make up the base of the marine food chain. When they die, absorbed carbon falls with them to the bottom of the sea and remains there as marine sediment. Moreover, phytoplankton absorb large amounts of CO_2 from the atmosphere. Of the eight billion tonnes (gigatons) of carbon that humans emit into the atmosphere each year, at least three billion tonnes is taken up by phytoplankton, and roughly the same by terrestrial ecosystems. Thus, phytoplankton play a vital role in slowing global warming. But note two connected factors. It may be that phytoplankton are already, or could soon become, semi-saturated with CO_2, in which case they would absorb less of the growing amounts of atmospheric CO_2, and thereby indirectly increase global warming. Secondly, our depletion of the ozone layer serves to reduce the phytoplankton's

Living oceans

0m
100m

2,500m

5,000m

Offshore wind

The euphotic layer is a biosphere that extends down to 100 m at most and is the uppermost zone of the sea where there is sufficient light penetration for photosynthesis.

Light

Upwelling

Phytoplank

Phytoplank

1 Where offshore winds blow, nutrient-rich water is dragged up to the surface. Minute marine plants (phytoplankton) flourish by exploiting the sun's energy in conjunction with mineral salts and carbon dioxide. A cubic metre of seawater may contain 200,000 such plants, notably diatoms.

The simplified biocycle (above) illustrates how the primary energy converters, marine plants, provide the basis for all other marine life, just as land plants do for land ecosystems. At each stage in the food chain there is a 90% energy loss.

Areas of abundance

Biologically productive areas of ocean occur primarily in coastal zones, where nutrients are washed down from the land and where surface winds and ocean currents work together in dredging up nutrient-rich sediments from the sea floor. One example of an upwelling occurs at the Great Newfoundland Banks, where a meeting of warm and cold currents creates a maelstrom of seawater over a 150,000-sq. km submerged plateau, generating phytoplankton in exceptional abundance. Flourishing off the plants are huge shoals of sardine-like fish, capelin, which in turn support many millions of cod, plus gannets, kittiwakes, and razorbills, also seals and humpbacked whales. Regrettably, this fishery has been grossly over-harvested by the ultimate predator, humans (pp. 82–83). The fish biomass, i.e. the amount of fish remaining in intensively exploited fisheries, is about one-tenth that of 50 years ago.

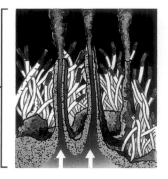

Sulphur-based life-forms

In 1977 a new deep-sea ecosystem was discovered. Like land animals around a waterhole, strange-looking worms, clams, and blind white crabs cluster around hot vents in the ocean floor, dependent on bacteria which have the unique capacity to metabolize hydrogen sulphide.

2 Of the diverse communities of zooplankton, some feed off phytoplankton and some prey on each other. Especially numerous are radiolarians, arrow worms, sea gooseberries, and copepods. Added to these are free-swimming larvae of shore- and bottom-dwellers, such as worms, crabs, and echinoderms.

3 The "small fry" zooplankton in turn are consumed by squid, jellyfish and shoaling fish, such as herring and anchovies. Baleen whales, too, exist on a zooplankton diet, mainly copepods and krill. The basking shark, one of the world's largest fishes, also sustains itself on a largely plankton diet.

4 Next in the chain, feeding on the smaller shoaling fish, are medium-sized predators, such as tuna. These bulky, fast-swimming fish are in turn eaten by marlin and sharks. Similarly, most seal species feed on small fish, while themselves serving as prey to larger creatures, such as leopard seals and sharks.

Antarctic Convergence

The band of the Southern Ocean between 50° and 60°S is known as the Antarctic Convergence. Counter-rotating currents of cold and sub-Antarctic water travelling northwards (the East and West Wind Drifts) here pass under and interact with sub-tropical water moving south. The resulting turbulence drives nutrient-rich water to the surface, making the area highly productive, with great swarms of a crustacean known as krill forming the staple food for penguins, seals, squid, and whales.

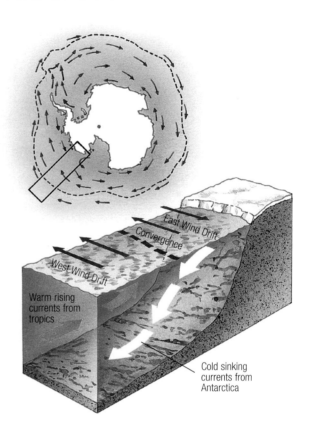

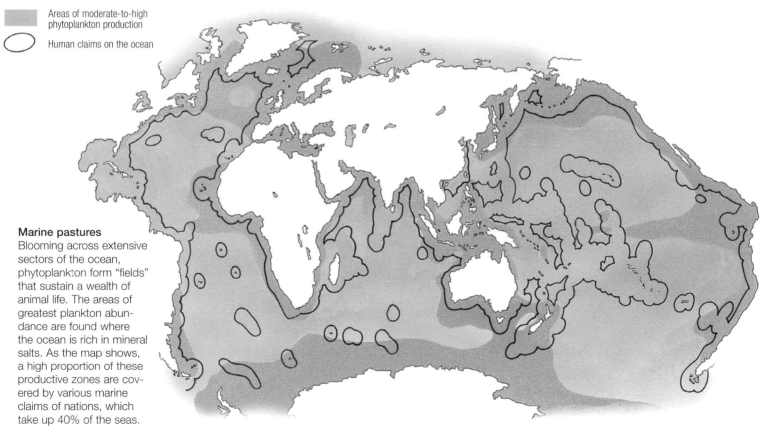

Marine pastures

Blooming across extensive sectors of the ocean, phytoplankton form "fields" that sustain a wealth of animal life. The areas of greatest plankton abundance are found where the ocean is rich in mineral salts. As the map shows, a high proportion of these productive zones are covered by various marine claims of nations, which take up 40% of the seas.

capacity to absorb CO_2. In these several ways, then, the insignificant-looking plant swarms of the oceans are a pivotal factor in our very climate.

Shores, reefs, and islands

The narrow coastal fringes of the world's ocean are at once its most productive and most vulnerable zones. Their shallow waters, saturated with sunlight and richly supplied with nutrients, provide the basis of most of our fisheries. Coastal and island ecosystems also serve as a great meeting ground between land and sea. Large numbers of people live here, whether in traditional fishing communities or in cities, and exploit the wealth of these ocean borderlands.

The vital margins

Coastal ecosystems represent an extremely valuable resource, one that is increasingly threatened by human activities (pp. 92–93). Their rich life depends on high levels of primary production, or generation of the vegetable matter which provides the "base energy" of all food chains. Phytoplankton and sea plants are the primary producers of the oceans, their abundance and growth rates varying among ecological zones. The pie chart below shows the proportional areas of open ocean, continental shelves, and coastal sectors, while the columns compare their primary productivity per unit area, illustrating dramatically the concentration of marine wealth in the ocean margins. Algal beds, reefs, and estuaries are more than 16 times as productive as the open ocean, while mangroves are well over 20 times.

The four vital ecosystems for humankind and for marine life-forms are saltmarshes, mangroves, estuaries, and coral reefs. Saltmarshes are tidal wetlands of temperate zones, mangroves the tropical equivalent, and their predominant offshore plants are seagrasses, being flowering plants that bloom beneath the sea. Seagrass meadows of the tropics are grazed by sea turtles, dugongs, and manatees, and in the temperate zones they form rich winter food reserves for ducks and geese. In both zones the vegetation acts as a nutrient trap for shellfish, such as shrimps, and for many finfish. In addition, the plants serve to filter out pollution, to mitigate the

57   **162**

Open ocean

Continental shelf

1,215

900

810

300

225

Estuary

Algal bed and coral reef

Upwelling

Mangrove

Saltmarsh

Productive ecosystems

The pie chart (above) shows the small ocean area, less than 1%, occupied by coastal ecosystems. The columns show the "mean net primary productivity" of upwelling areas and coastal ecosystems in grams of carbon/sq. m/year.

Mangrove wealth

Mangroves fringe more than half of all tropical shores, and harbour huge quantities of fish and shellfish, notably prawns and oysters. In Indonesia, mangrove fish have been farmed since the 15th century. The simplest form of prawn culture involves netting mature prawns (right) as they leave mangroves for offshore spawning grounds. Between mangroves and dry land we sometimes find useful wetlands. Along the Malay Peninsula, for instance, grows the Nypa swamp palm, which supplies local people with fruit, sugar, vinegar, alcohol, and fibre.

beating of storm waves and powerful currents, and to prevent erosion of coastlines. Estuaries, plentifully supplied with fertile silt washed down from rivers, cover twice the area of saltmarshes and mangroves. These river embayments or "tidal ponds" where seawater and freshwater communities intermingle, are very productive and feature vast numbers of annelid worms, crustaceans, and molluscs. Whenever we sit down to a dish of crabs, oysters, mussels, or prawns, we can thank the extreme productivity of estuaries. Further, they serve as nurseries for ocean fish, such as silverside, anchovy, and catfish. In one of the finest fishing areas in the world, the continental shelf of the eastern US, at least three-quarters of fished species spend part of their life cycles in estuaries.

Most diverse of all – and among the world's oldest ecosystems, first emerging 200 million years ago – are coral reefs. They feature more plant and animal phyla (major categories of life) than any other ecosystem: 90,000 species have been described but the total could be 1–2 million. They also reveal more mutual-benefit relationships, or symbioses, between organisms than any other community.

Other coastal ecosystems supply us with a host of products for our material welfare. Rocky shores feature algae of many shapes and sizes. Seaweeds alone supply alginate compounds that contribute to hundreds of end products, such as plastics, waxes, polishes, deodorants, soaps, detergents, shampoos, cosmetics, paints, dyes, and food stabilizers.

	Saltmarsh
	Mangrove
	Coral reef
	Continental shelf
	Upwelling zone
	Open ocean

Saltmarshes
Saltmarshes provide many ecological functions. They supply valuable coastal protection. Saltmarsh grasses and other estuarine plants help control erosion and pollution: as upland water flows down through fresh and salt marshes, much of the sediments and pollutants it carries are filtered out. In some areas they are grazed by livestock, and they are an important habitat for wading birds. Fishes, crabs, and shrimps live in saltmarshes where they find shelter from predators.

Estuaries
An estuary is a partially enclosed body of water which forms when fresh water from rivers and streams flows into the sea and mixes with the salty water. US examples include San Francisco Bay, Chesapeake Bay, and Tampa Bay. There are many different habitats in and around estuaries: shallow open waters, freshwater and salt marshes, mud and sand flats, oyster reefs, mangrove forests, river deltas, tidal pools, seagrass and kelp beds. Shore and sea birds, fish, crabs and lobsters, clams, marine mammals, and reptiles all depend on estuaries to live, feed, breed or to rest during migration. Coastal wetlands in the Gulf of Mexico are essential to three-quarters of US migrating waterfowl. In addition, three-quarters of the US commercial fish catch and at least four-fifths of recreational fish catch make their habitat in estuaries.

Coral pharmacopoeias
A coral reef is an arena of intense competition for food and space – as this swarming Red Sea community demonstrates. To safeguard their space, reef organisms generate chemicals useful to humans, e.g. histamines, hormones, and antibiotics.

Filling our nets

People have fished rich offshore waters since the very earliest times, as upwelling currents and seasonal migrations of shoals have brought the wealth of the seas to our nets. This marine catch represents more than 70 percent of the world's total fishery. Even today, despite territorial limits and deep-sea fleets, the global shoal remains a renewable resource which nations share, because neither the fish nor the ecosystems of the oceans on which our marine catch depends recognize human boundaries.

In 1950, the global marine harvest was around 20 million tonnes. During the following three decades we regularly expanded our catch at extraordinary rates, rising to 67 million tonnes by 1980. This dramatic gain was due to the increased exploitation of existing stocks, the discovery of new stocks, and the development of improved fishing technology. But it was not to last. During the 1980s and 1990s, the increase averaged little over one percent as more and more stocks became depleted. In 2001, the global marine catch was 92 million tonnes, down from 95 million tonnes in 2000.

Having quintupled the marine harvest in five decades, we have now reached the limit of sustainable yields of "wild" fish. Fortunately, aquaculture is increasing rapidly to make up the shortfall (pp. 96–97). A "sustainable yield" refers to the optimum annual catch that can be derived indefinitely from harvested species without causing a failure in the stock.

Fishery biologists tell us that when we start to exploit a virgin stock, the fish respond by reproducing more abundantly. Yet the same biologists tell us that often they do not know how many fish were there in the first place. Our lack of knowledge is made worse by our highly efficient fishing methods and the demands of money markets, which call upon the exploiters to recoup their investments within just a few years, regardless of how long the fishery resource may take to recover. Result: our view of what might be a sustainable yield can be far different from Nature's.

We harvest five main groups of marine species. Northerners' preferences are largely made up of demersal fish (primarily bottom-dwellers) that include cod, haddock, sole, skate, hake, and plaice. Pelagic fish (surface-dwellers) include herring, mackerel, anchovy, and tuna. These two groups account for 40 million tonnes of the annual marine catch. Crustaceans, such as lobsters, crabs, shrimps, krill, and other shellfish, provide more than 7 million tonnes (1.5 million from aquaculture). Cephalopods, including the octopus and squid families, yield around 3.4 million tonnes.

As for marine mammals, notably whales, their potential has been squandered, and is now tailing away to the merest fraction of what it might have been with rational management.

The global shoal

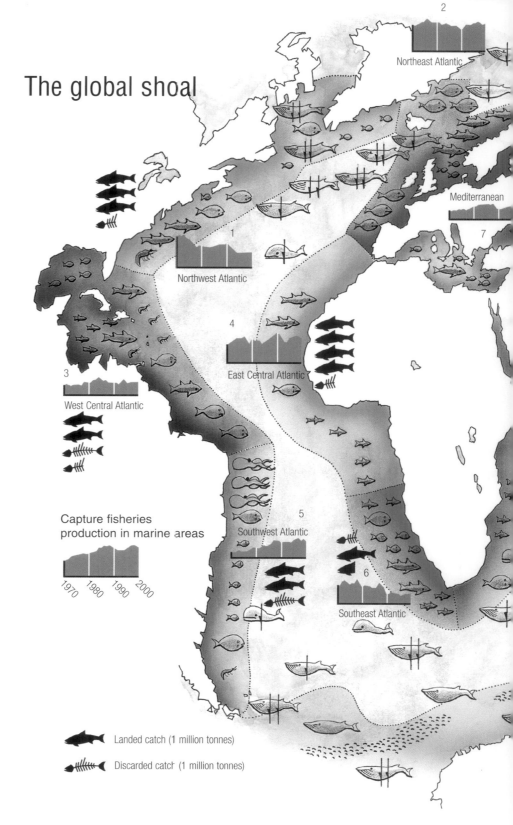

Capture fisheries production in marine areas

1970   1980   1990   2000

Northeast Atlantic

Mediterranean

Northwest Atlantic

East Central Atlantic

West Central Atlantic

Southwest Atlantic

Southeast Atlantic

Landed catch (1 million tonnes)

Discarded catch (1 million tonnes)

The map shows the marine fisheries catch and discards of the late 1990s by fishing region, together with trends for 1970–2000. Several areas are already fished to the limit of their sustainable potential or even beyond it. Symbols on the map (above) also show the distribution and exploitation of whale stocks, plus the vast swarms of tiny shrimp-like krill in the Southern Ocean, with a biomass of 500–600 million tonnes. At present, we catch 125,000 tonnes a year, but with superior management and a better understanding of their vital role in the ocean ecosystem, Antarctic krill could become an important source of protein as long as they remain within the catch limits set by the Convention on the Conservation of Antarctic Marine Living Resources. While seafood amounts to less than 1% of our diets by calories, it is much more important in terms of animal protein, a crucial element in our food. In the case of developed-world citizens, the seas also provide a good deal more as fishmeal fed to aquaculture species and to livestock and as fertilizer.

Bycatch

Each year, 20 million tonnes of "unwanted" marine species are discarded, thrown back into the sea. These can be too young, or "non-target" species, or simply "over quota". Some become food for other species, many are dead or dying. Discards not only affect current populations, they also influence future populations by denying the species' opportunity to replenish.

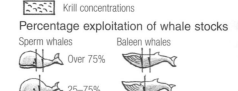

Krill concentrations

Percentage exploitation of whale stocks

Sperm whales	Baleen whales
Over 75%	
25–75%	
less than 25%	

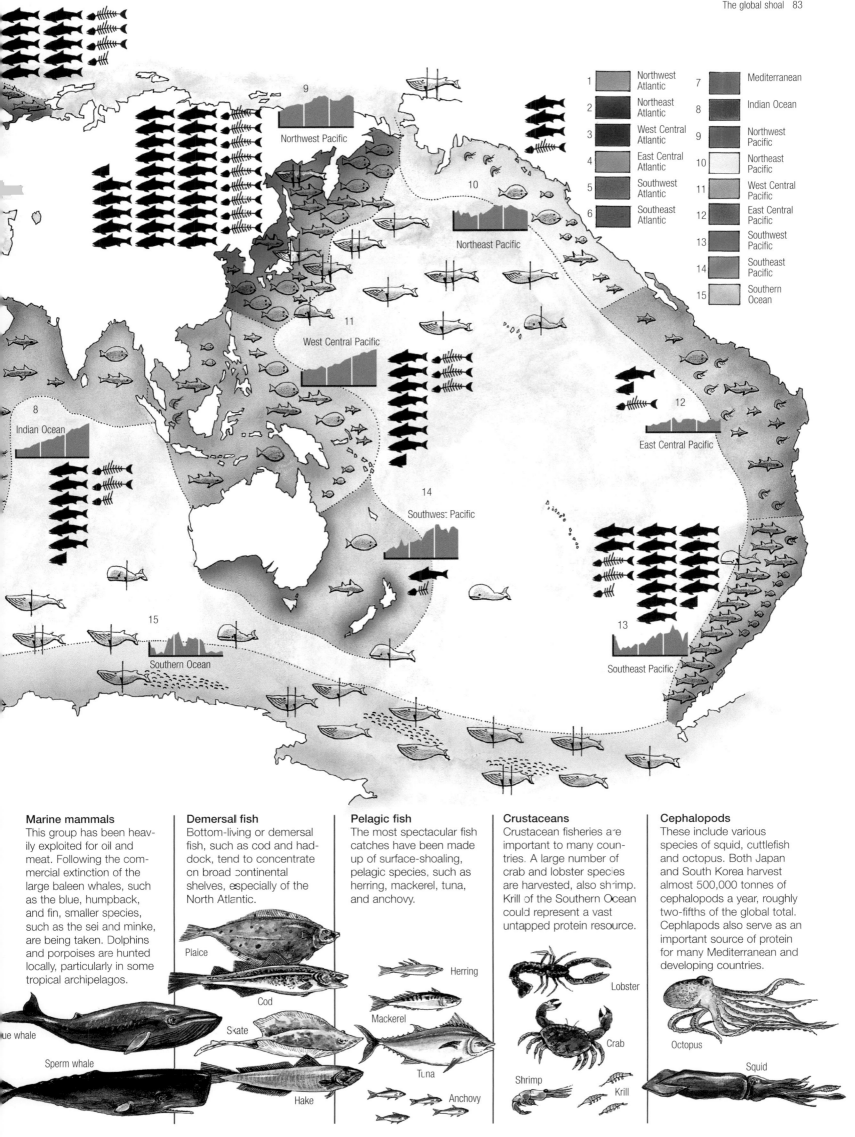

Legend:
1 Northwest Atlantic
2 Northeast Atlantic
3 West Central Atlantic
4 East Central Atlantic
5 Southwest Atlantic
6 Southeast Atlantic
7 Mediterranean
8 Indian Ocean
9 Northwest Pacific
10 Northeast Pacific
11 West Central Pacific
12 East Central Pacific
13 Southwest Pacific
14 Southeast Pacific
15 Southern Ocean

9 Northwest Pacific

10 Northeast Pacific

11 West Central Pacific

8 Indian Ocean

14 Southwest Pacific

12 East Central Pacific

15 Southern Ocean

13 Southeast Pacific

Marine mammals

This group has been heavily exploited for oil and meat. Following the commercial extinction of the large baleen whales, such as the blue, humpback, and fin, smaller species, such as the sei and minke, are being taken. Dolphins and porpoises are hunted locally, particularly in some tropical archipelagos.

Blue whale

Sperm whale

Demersal fish

Bottom-living or demersal fish, such as cod and haddock, tend to concentrate on broad continental shelves, especially of the North Atlantic.

Plaice

Cod

Skate

Hake

Pelagic fish

The most spectacular fish catches have been made up of surface-shoaling, pelagic species, such as herring, mackerel, tuna, and anchovy.

Herring

Mackerel

Tuna

Anchovy

Crustaceans

Crustacean fisheries are important to many countries. A large number of crab and lobster species are harvested, also shrimp. Krill of the Southern Ocean could represent a vast untapped protein resource.

Lobster

Crab

Shrimp

Krill

Cephalopods

These include various species of squid, cuttlefish and octopus. Both Japan and South Korea harvest almost 500,000 tonnes of cephalopods a year, roughly two-fifths of the global total. Cephlapods also serve as an important source of protein for many Mediterranean and developing countries.

Octopus

Squid

The new technological revolution

Though ocean technology is an infant phenomenon as yet, it could supply us with sizeable flows of critical minerals and energy. The "us", however, probably comprises very few nations – those with the funds and expertise to gain a head start in the nascent industry. The wealth of the oceans is beyond doubt. Continental shelves harbour nearly half of the Earth's oil and gas resources, while seawater itself contains over 70 elements, some very important. One cubic kilometre of seawater holds about 230 million tonnes of salt, one million tonnes of magnesium, and 65,000 tonnes of bromine. We have extracted salt by evaporation for more than 4,000 years, and today we extract magnesium and bromine by chemical processes.

Not yet exploited but much more important are manganese nodules on the sea floor. These potato-shaped objects have a high metal content, primarily manganese (25–30 percent), plus nickel (1.3 percent), copper (1.1 percent), cobalt (0.25 percent), molybdenum, and vanadium, all of which are valuable in steel alloys. Although most manganese deposits are spread thinly over large areas, often at great depths, certain concentrations could, in the future, support commercial operations. The richest and most extensive deposits occur in large areas of the northeastern, central, and southern Pacific.

Most accessible are deposits of silver, copper, and zinc in Red Sea muds. Still more readily available is uranium in seawater – much more than on land. Japan, with a strong commitment to nuclear energy and no domestic stocks of uranium, could one day meet its domestic needs – currently 6,000 tonnes of uranium a year – from the Black Current off its coast, which carries more than five million tonnes a year.

As for generating energy from the oceans, tidal, wave, and thermal projects all have potential, and are beginning to be exploited.

Much of the ocean's mineral wealth lies beyond national jurisdictions of any sort, and should count as part of the common heritage of humankind (pp. 102–103). The global community already shares certain technologies, both between nations and through international consort a (the oil industry is an obvious example). Yet there will still be winners and losers in the race for ocean wealth, with most nations simply lacking the technology.

Ocean technology

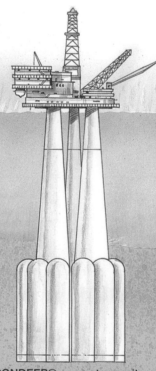

Dredging
Used to mine many materials, from sand and gravel to diamonds, dredgers also help to keep shipping lanes open. Technology has increased the depth of operation and positioning systems aid monitoring and accuracy, enabling their use for a range of environmentally sensitive projects. Dredging can, however, degrade water quality by lifting harmful pollutants from the ocean floor. It can also alter, disrupt or destroy fish habitats, affecting the way they feed and reproduce.

Wave energy
Wave energy has vast potential. Early efforts faced too many technical challenges to become viable but there has been a resurgence since the mid-1990s and several projects are underway worldwide. There are now two decades of experience with offshore oil and gas platforms, and corresponding scope for technology transfer. The global potential for wave energy is an estimated 2 terawatts (TW).

Spiral wave power
The Dam Atoll was a conceptual design from the US, with potential applications from cleaning up oil spills and reducing wave erosion to desalination and power generation.

CONDEEP® concrete gravity platform
These massive structures store thousands of tonnes of crude oil in enclosed submarine concrete tanks. The Stratford B platform in the North Sea had a displacement weight of 900,000 tonnes and could operate at the edge of the continental shelf at depths of over 140 m. The Brent B platform consists of 19 interconnected 61m-high cylinders, three of which extend upwards supporting the deck which is 170 m above the sea floor.

The frontier of the marine technology revolution is steadily being pushed deeper into the oceans in the search for critical resources, despite the challenges of safety, cost-effectiveness, and territorial rights. The illustration demonstrates a range of ocean technology from inshore to deep water, the coastal and continental shelf operations being the most established. Dredging, for instance, is a big-business operation, mining sand, gravel, and shell deposits for cement for the construction industry. An estimated 500 billion tonnes of gravel alone lie on the Atlantic shelf of North America. The oil and gas industries were pioneers in exploiting coastal mineral deposits, beginning off California in 1891. They moved into deep-water oil technology in the 1960s, boosting development in the 1970s as the cost of land-based crude oil and natural gas soared. The guyed (deep-ocean) tower shown here could operate down to 300 m; another rig system, known as the "tension leg platform", could operate down to 500 m. Deposits of manganese nodules are mostly found at great depths, hence they are not being developed as yet due to high costs and common-property resource issues. While recovery areas at depths of 4,000–5,000 m can be explored with underwater TV systems and other techniques, commercial exploitation of the nodules is not expected to be economically and technically viable until well into the 21st century.

Ocean wealth and investment

The map indicates major reserves of mineral-rich nodules and sediments, active seawater extraction plants and areas with OTEC potential. In many countries, investment slowed due to soaring costs and uncertain profits, but Japan increased its expenditures, concentrating on uranium extraction, nodule mining, and OTEC. Seabed investigations by other countries include a US survey of polymetallic sulphides along the rift zone off Oregon (the only known large deposit lying within the proposed US exclusive economic zone), and the French exploration of manganese nodule deposits lying in their economic zone off Tahiti. Many nations that might not have considered OTEC/DOWA activities in the past may now look to the technologies again in view of the potential to extend their borders under UNCLOS Article 76 relating to the definition of continental shelf. Higher oil prices and huge downside environmental implications are changing the economics of fossil-fuel energy supplies in relation to OTEC/DOWA and other renewables, although more research and development investment is needed.

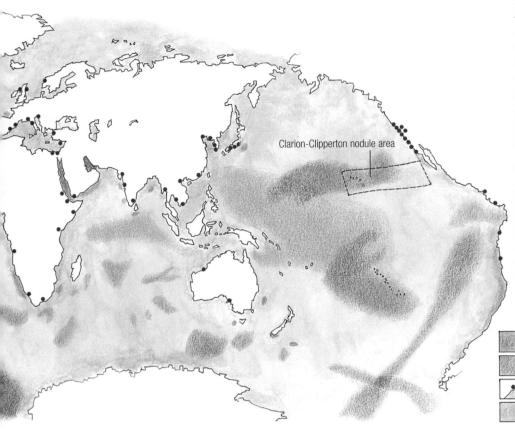

Clarion-Clipperton nodule area

Main areas of manganese nodules

Metal-rich sediments

Mineral extraction plants from seawater

Offshore phosphorite deposits

OTEC potential (areas with temperature gradients of 22°C or more)

Tension Leg Platform (TLP)

The first US tension-leg platform was in 1760 ft of water, and the latest – in the Gulf of Mexico Magnolia field – is in nearly 4,700 ft of water, a record depth for this type of floating structure.

Ocean Thermal Energy Conversion (OTEC)

OTEC exploits the temperature difference between the warm surface and cool bottom layers in tropical and sub-tropical seas to provide power. The process works like a giant refrigerator in reverse, evaporating and condensing a working fluid to drive a turbine that produces electricity. For OTEC, a temperature difference of 20°C is adequate, favouring islands and many developing countries. There is major market potential.

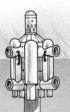

Manganese nodule mining

The recovery of mineral-rich nodules from depths as great as 5,000 m has proved feasible in pilot tests, but it is extremely costly. It is also dependent on seabed ownership issues (p. 103). The borders of 80 countries have the potential to be expanded under Article 76 of the United Nations Convention on the Law of the Sea (UNCLOS) which states "By definition, borders can be expanded based on a complex set of criteria that define the water depth, including the 2,500-m contour, sea-floor geology and sediment thickness, as well as distance from the coastline".

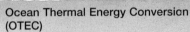

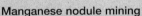

Guyed tower

This anchored structure was one of a new generation of deep-water oil platforms in the 1980s. Block 480 platform, for example, in the Gulf of Mexico was placed at a depth of 300 m and pinned to the sea floor by a spoke-like array of cables, each more than 900 m long.

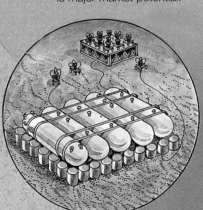

Deep-sea oil production

Designed to extract oil at depths where platform recovery is uneconomic, these structures would be gas- or nuclear-powered.

The ends of the Earth

Remote and ice-bound, the polar environments used to be among the least disturbed on Earth. But things are changing: a tug-of-war between protection of unique ecosystems and exploitation of critical assets dominates their future.

We tend to think of the polar zones as being similar, yet they are quite different. The Arctic is essentially an enclosed sea, the smallest of the oceans and the only one to be almost entirely landlocked. By contrast, the Antarctic comprises a vast open ocean surrounding an ice-covered land mass: Antarctica covers 14 million square kilometres – larger than the US and Mexico combined – and with 95 percent of its surface covered by ice, it is the coldest climate on Earth. A third of the Arctic is underlaid with continental shelves from surrounding territories; it supports some of our richest fishing grounds. In Antarctica, by contrast, much of the sea is overlain with ice shelves. The region contains nine-tenths of all ice on the planet; the ice cap averaging 2,200 metres deep compared with a few dozen metres at the North Pole.

The polar zones are not the lifeless deserts we might expect. Each summer, the Arctic fringes break out into spectacular blooms. There are 3,000 species of flowering plant, plus large numbers of herbivores, from lemmings to reindeer and caribou. The Arctic also has four million inhabitants, including 50 distinct indigenous peoples. The Antarctic has only two flowering plant species (plus a number of mosses and lichens), no native vertebrates, and (alone among continents) no long-standing human settlements. Scientific research stations bring thousands of scientists and support staff. Many stay only during the summer, leaving about 900 to brave months of extreme cold and permanent darkness in winter. Yet the surrounding ocean, one of the most productive zones on Earth, generates massive summer outbursts of marine phytoplankton, fostered by exceptionally rich, nutrient-bearing upwellings. These support vast populations of krill which provide the food base for eight species of whale and the main support of 40 bird species, from penguins (90 percent of the bird biomass) to albatrosses.

The Arctic's mineral resources are known to be vast and already reserves are being exploited. As for Antarctica, there are great oil deposits lying under the narrow continental shelf. In 1998, the Antarctic Treaty Environmental Protection Protocol became legally effective, banning "any activity relating to mineral resources, other than scientific research" and the continent's mineral resources may be considered as "frozen stakes" for the next half century.

While the ocean offers abundant resources, ignorance and misunderstanding are placing this wealth in jeopardy, causing gross impoverishment of many fisheries, near extinction for most large whales, widespread pollution of fish-rich waters, and degradation of many coastal habitats and fish nursery grounds.

Polar zones

Main areas of distribution of:

Cod	
Alaska pollock	
Capelin	
Fur seal	
Harp/hooded seals	
Coal field	
Mining	
Oil and gas	
Major ice drifts	

Arctic resources

Fish Pollock in the Bering Sea is the largest single-species fishery in the world, providing a substantial proportion of the US' annual fish catch. The Barents Sea has the world's largest remaining cod stock, accounting for half the global cod catch, and is highly threatened by overfishing, illegal fishing, and industrial development. High quotas for 2004 are unsustainable, according to the WWF, and illegal catches totalling an estimated 100,000 tonnes a year further deplete stocks. The fishery could suffer the same fate as the Canadian cod stock, which collapsed in the 1990s and has still not recovered. Expanded shipping and oil exploration plans present further threats.

Seals Every spring, thousands of harp and hooded seals haul out of the ice in the North Atlantic and Arctic oceans to give birth. For centuries, the pups have been clubbed for their valuable fur coats. In 1983, the EC banned sealskin imports, which led to the end of the large-scale hunt. According to IFAW, in 1995 the Canadian government announced its intention to revitalize the Atlantic sealing industry; since then, over a million seals have been killed. Other threats lie with polar bears, which feed on seal blubber, and declining fish populations.

Minerals Two-thirds of the former USSR's gas reserves lie north of the Arctic Circle and Alaska supplies a quarter of US' oil. Recoverable Alaskan oil reserves are estimated at 2–12 billion barrels and there is great pressure for its development. The Arctic holds some of the world's largest deposits of coal, iron, copper, lead, and uranium. Alaska's mining industry, including gold, zinc, and diamonds, was worth $1 billion a year during 1995–2000.

Environment According to a report by the Worldwatch Institute, the Arctic environment is being exposed to Persistent Organic Pollutants (POPs), including pesticides, industrial chemicals, and waste products. The average loss of Arctic sea ice between 1979 and 2002 was 360,000 sq. km per decade. Large areas of frozen tundra could disappear in the next 50–100 years.

Antarctic resources

Wildlife protection The Convention on the Conservation of Antarctic Marine Living Resources (CCAMLR) was designed to protect the Antarctic ecosystem from the consequences of a rapidly expanding krill fishery and to aid recovery of the great whales and other species dependent on krill for food, plus other over-exploited species of fish.

Fish The seas around Antarctica include 100 fish species, though only a few, such as the Antarctic cod and Patagonian toothfish have been extensively trawled. Between 1970 and 1998, almost 9 million tonnes of krill and fish were taken from the Southern Ocean. Illegal fishing of Patagonian toothfish (estimated at two to five times the legal catch) kills hundreds of thousands of seabirds in longlines – at least 144,000 albatrosses and 400,000 petrels since 1996, according to CCAMLR estimates. Patagonian toothfish catches have already reached unsustainable levels: it is a slow-maturing species and does not breed until 10 years old.

Whales Large areas of the Southern Ocean have been designated a whale sanctuary. Blue and humpback whales were fully protected in the 1960s; this was extended to fin and sei whales in the 1970s. By 1986, the International Whaling Commission suspended all commercial whaling, but some nations, e.g. Japan, Norway, and Iceland, have exploited a loophole in IWC regulations allowing whales to be taken for "scientific purposes".

Seals There are six seal species (two-thirds of the world's total). Strict international agreements govern the harvesting of Antarctic seals (the Convention for the Conservation of Antarctic Seals – CCAS). Limited numbers are culled for scientific purposes.

Minerals Geologists believe there may be over 900 major mineral deposits, but few in ice-free areas. The world's largest coalfield may lie in the Transantarctic Mountains, while US researchers believe there is oil in the continental shelf. Under the terms of the Environment Protocol (1991), however, "any activity relating to mineral resources, other than scientific research, shall be prohibited" for at least 50 years.

Environment Antarctica's pure environment holds vital interest for scientists studying the Earth's evolution, atmosphere and climate. Cores drilled out of the ice yield data on temperature and carbon dioxide changes over centuries, even millennia, as well as radioactive and toxic pollution increases since 1945.

Main areas of distribution of:

- Antarctic cod
- Toothfish
- Krill concentration
- Krill distribution
- Coal-bearing area
- Potential oil and gas areas
- Mineral occurrences

Antarctic Convergence

Maximum ice

Antarctic Circle

Weddell Sea

West Antarctic Ice Shelf

Cobalt Copper Nickel

Copper

South America

Gold Manganese Molybdenum Silver

Copper

Gold

Iron Titanium

Iron Copper

Uranium

Cobalt Chromium Copper Iron Nickel Platinum

Ronne Ice Shelf

• SOUTH POLE

Transantarctic Mountains

Ross Ice Shelf

Iron Lead Zinc

Ross Sea

Prince Charles Mountains

Amery Ice Shelf

Iron

Molybdenum

Molybdenum Iron

Manganese

Molybdenum Tin

Minimum ice

Krill

Krill

Krill are estimated to have a total biomass greater than any multicellular animal on Earth, including man. They are the staple diet of Antarctic whales (whose migration is linked to their life cycle), seals, squid, penguins, and other seabirds. They are also hunted by humans for consumption, farmed fish food, and bait for recreational fishing. Harvesting the massive swarms of krill in the Southern Ocean began in 1976 and reached more than 500,000 tonnes by 1981. Subsequent catch limits were set at 2.7 million tonnes under CCAMLR. The current catch by countries such as Japan, US, Korea, Poland, and the Ukraine is around 120,000 tonnes per year, well within sustainable levels. This may change with the expansion of aquaculture, or fish farming, with a doubling of production in the 1990s to 45 million tonnes in 2000 (compared to capture fisheries of 96 million tonnes). The aquaculture industry worldwide consumes 70% of fish oil and 34% of fishmeal. The latter may rise to 50% by 2010, with fish-feed producers looking at Antarctic krill to meet future demand – and also to colour salmon naturally. The biotechnology industry could place similar pressures on krill.

The Ocean Crisis

Declining fish stocks

Large investments in fishing fleets during the 1970s and 1980s, together with government subsidies (pp. 96–97 and 232–233), helped boost the marine catch. Too many fishermen and boats chasing too few fish severely stretched many fisheries. Some collapsed. Among the casualties were haddock, capelin, Atlantic cod, Atlantic herring, and Southern African pilchard. To compensate for these declines, landings of other species increased. In many fishing regions, the harvest either reaches or exceeds the estimated sustainable yield.

Part of the problem has been our ignorance of marine ecosystems. Another part has been the technology employed by large, long-distance fleets, such as purse-seining or using fine nets to "vacuum" the sea. Technological advance in fishing has brought its problems – most evident in the waters off developing countries. Indiscriminate fishing by long-distance foreign fleets has declined, but misuse of aid offered to establish national fisheries, intended to help local communities, resulted in the same over-exploitation – depleting the fish stocks and depriving the poorer coastal peoples of their livelihood. The confrontation between capital-intensive fisheries and coastal fishing communities affects many millions of people. Today's commercial fishers use satellite positioning equipment, sonar, huge nets, spotter planes and factory ships capable of freezing the catch at sea.

The main cause, however, has been the expanding demand for fish and fish products. Also, as people eat more meat, they create a booming demand for animal-feed supplements, including fishmeal. Almost a quarter of the global fish catch goes into non-food uses, such as meal and oil. Others simply want more fish. Japan, for instance, relies on fish and seafood for 45 percent of its animal-protein supply (the global average is 15 percent).

The global harvest has reached the limit of sustainable yields estimated by the Food and Agriculture Organisation (FAO) as 100 million tonnes annually. In 2002, the marine catch totalled only 70 million tonnes and aquaculture is increasingly filling the gap – though not without penalties for wild fish used as feed. Environmental pressures, such as chemical pollution and the destruction of nursery grounds, then have an increased effect on the resource productivity. Climate change will also seriously affect fisheries because the warming of surface waters will disrupt ocean currents and plankton populations.

Empty nets

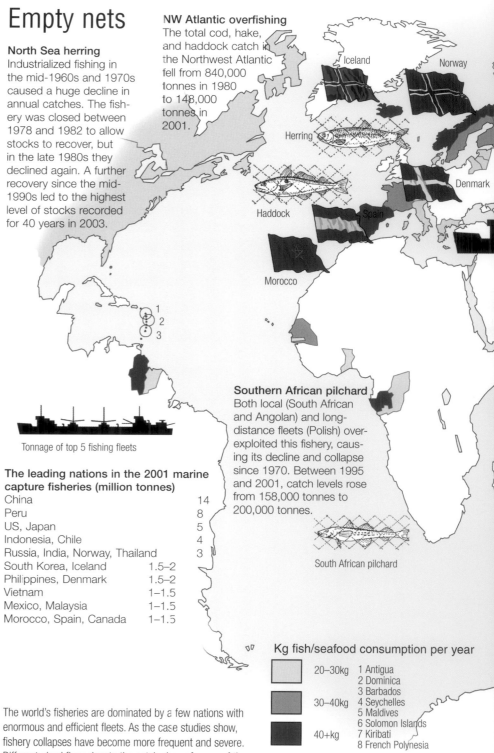

North Sea herring
Industrialized fishing in the mid-1960s and 1970s caused a huge decline in annual catches. The fishery was closed between 1978 and 1982 to allow stocks to recover, but in the late 1980s they declined again. A further recovery since the mid-1990s led to the highest level of stocks recorded for 40 years in 2003.

NW Atlantic overfishing
The total cod, hake, and haddock catch in the Northwest Atlantic fell from 840,000 tonnes in 1980 to 148,000 tonnes in 2001.

Tonnage of top 5 fishing fleets

The leading nations in the 2001 marine capture fisheries (million tonnes)

China	14
Peru	8
US, Japan	5
Indonesia, Chile	4
Russia, India, Norway, Thailand	3
South Korea, Iceland	1.5–2
Philippines, Denmark	1.5–2
Vietnam	1–1.5
Mexico, Malaysia	1–1.5
Morocco, Spain, Canada	1–1.5

Southern African pilchard
Both local (South African and Angolan) and long-distance fleets (Polish) over-exploited this fishery, causing its decline and collapse since 1970. Between 1995 and 2001, catch levels rose from 158,000 tonnes to 200,000 tonnes.

South African pilchard

Kg fish/seafood consumption per year

20–30kg	1 Antigua
	2 Dominica
	3 Barbados
30–40kg	4 Seychelles
	5 Maldives
	6 Solomon Islands
40+kg	7 Kiribati
	8 French Polynesia

The world's fisheries are dominated by a few nations with enormous and efficient fleets. As the case studies show, fishery collapses have become more frequent and severe. Different-sized flags denote the catch sizes of some of the top fishing countries for 2001: these 20 nations account for 80% of the total marine catch, with China heading the list at 14 million tonnes, followed by Peru with 8 million tonnes. A further 8 countries took more than 3 million tonnes. The size of the flags on the map reflect this.

Ship symbols denote the national tonnage of the top five fishing fleets. The global fishing fleet comprises 4 million decked and undecked vessels, many unpowered.

Disappearing cod
According to the World Wide Fund for Nature, the world's cod fisheries are disappearing fast, declining from 3.4 million tonnes in 1970 to a million tonnes in 2000. Particularly threatened is the world's largest remaining stock in the Barents Sea. North America's catch has declined by 90% since the early 1980s, while in European waters, the North Sea cod catch is now just a quarter of what it was two decades ago. Over- and illegal fishing together with oil exploration could "wipe out cod by 2020".

Fishing quotas
Quotas have exacerbated the problem of "illegal, unreported and unregulated (IUU) fishing" which, according to the FAO, is "growing both in scope and intensity" – in some localities the catch of commercially valuable species may exceed permitted levels by over 300%.

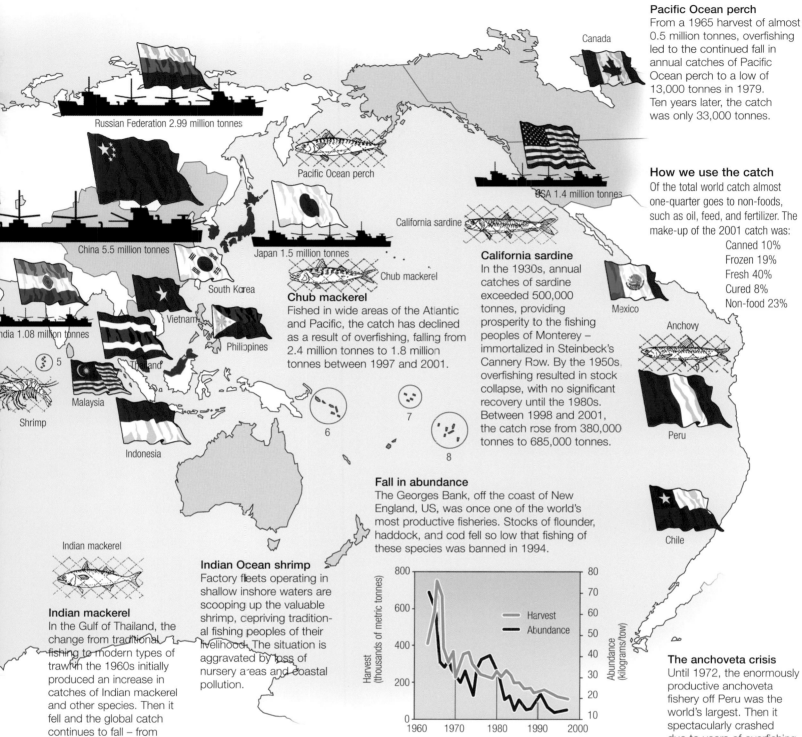

Pacific Ocean perch
From a 1965 harvest of almost 0.5 million tonnes, overfishing led to the continued fall in annual catches of Pacific Ocean perch to a low of 13,000 tonnes in 1979. Ten years later, the catch was only 33,000 tonnes.

How we use the catch
Of the total world catch almost one-quarter goes to non-foods, such as oil, feed, and fertilizer. The make-up of the 2001 catch was:

Canned 10%
Frozen 19%
Fresh 40%
Cured 8%
Non-food 23%

Russian Federation 2.99 million tonnes

Canada

USA 1.4 million tonnes

China 5.5 million tonnes

Japan 1.5 million tonnes

South Korea

Pacific Ocean perch

California sardine

Mexico

Anchovy

Vietnam

India 1.08 million tonnes

Philippines

Thailand

Malaysia

Shrimp

Indonesia

Peru

Chile

Chub mackerel

Chub mackerel
Fished in wide areas of the Atlantic and Pacific, the catch has declined as a result of overfishing, falling from 2.4 million tonnes to 1.8 million tonnes between 1997 and 2001.

California sardine
In the 1930s, annual catches of sardine exceeded 500,000 tonnes, providing prosperity to the fishing peoples of Monterey – immortalized in Steinbeck's Cannery Row. By the 1950s, overfishing resulted in stock collapse, with no significant recovery until the 1980s. Between 1998 and 2001, the catch rose from 380,000 tonnes to 685,000 tonnes.

Fall in abundance
The Georges Bank, off the coast of New England, US, was once one of the world's most productive fisheries. Stocks of flounder, haddock, and cod fell so low that fishing of these species was banned in 1994.

Indian mackerel

Indian mackerel
In the Gulf of Thailand, the change from traditional fishing to modern types of trawl in the 1960s initially produced an increase in catches of Indian mackerel and other species. Then it fell and the global catch continues to fall – from 304,000 tonnes in 1997 to 184,000 tonnes in 2001.

Indian Ocean shrimp
Factory fleets operating in shallow inshore waters are scooping up the valuable shrimp, depriving traditional fishing peoples of their livelihood. The situation is aggravated by loss of nursery areas and coastal pollution.

The anchoveta crisis
Until 1972, the enormously productive anchoveta fishery off Peru was the world's largest. Then it spectacularly crashed due to years of overfishing combined with that year's strong El Niño current, when a mass of warm water intruded upon the cool and nutrient-rich Peru current underpinning the fishery. The catch continues to fluctuate: in 1997, it reached 7.7 million tonnes, then in 1998 only 1.7 million tonnes before rising to 8.7 million tonnes in 1999 and 11.3 million tonnes in 2000. By 2001, it was down again to 7.2 million tonnes.

Factory fishing off West Africa
Africa's coasts feature some prolific fisheries. Industrial fishing fleets have exploited this zone with sophisticated catching gear and cold-storage facilities – long-distance equipment characteristic of advanced nations rather than of local African enterprises. In the mid-1960s, West Africans watched half their catch being taken away by developed nations. By the mid-1970s, the 22 African nations concerned had increased their catch substantially – but witnessed their share decline to one-third of all fish taken, the bulk being accounted for by the former USSR, Spain, France, Poland, Japan, and 14 other developed nations. One tonne of fishmeal fed to livestock in Europe produced less than half a tonne of pork or poultry, far less again if used as fertilizer to grow animal-feed grains. Had the West African fish resources been used for direct human consumption by the people of West Africa, they would have represented an additional 12 kg of animal protein per person per year – a 50% increase for many people.

Aquaculture
With increasing pressure on marine resources, aquaculture production, both marine and inland, has also been increasing. Whilst it helps meet our appetites for fish and seafood, the fish-feed requirements of this form of farming put pressure on wild fisheries. More than two pounds of wild fish is needed to produce one pound of farmed salmon (salmon food comprises ground sardines, anchovies, mackerel, herring, and other fish). By 2010, aquaculture worldwide could be demanding half of the fishmeal produced worldwide (up from one-third in 2001).

The bulk of world marine aquaculture production is in China – with 10 million tonnes of the total 18 million tonnes in 2001. Other major marine producers include Japan (0.7 million), Chile and Norway (0.5 million), Spain and South Korea (almost 0.3 million). Inland aquaculture totalled 22 million tonnes, again dominated by China with 16 million tonnes

Aquaculture is causing problems for coastal ecosystems, particularly mangroves (pp. 92–93).

Sources of marine pollution

The seas are a sump. They continuously absorb vast quantities of silt and minerals washed down from the land. Now, however, we are asking them to accept growing amounts of human-generated materials as well, notably sewage sludge, industrial effluent (including radioactive wastes), and agricultural runoff, all with their chemical contaminants.

The oceans can do a good job for us as a huge "waste treatment works". The key question is, how much waste can they safely handle? That is to say, what sorts of waste are they fitted to absorb, where can they best accommodate it, how long will it take to degrade via natural means – and what level of adverse consequences are we prepared to accept?

These critical factors are not receiving nearly enough attention. Each year, we dump hundreds of new chemicals into the seas, to go with the thousands already there, and with next to no idea of their potential impact. Human-made toxic substances are being detected in deep ocean trenches, even as far as Antarctica. This phenomenon is the result of global circulatory systems, processes that we hardly understand.

Chemical runoff caused by humans into the oceans is much greater than Nature's contribution:

Pollutants from human activities entering the sea

Maritime transportation 12%
Atmosphere 33%
Dumping 10%
Runoff and land-based discharge 44%
Offshore production 1%

Polluting the oceans

At least 75% of all marine pollution derives from land-based activities. The illustration below shows a major conveyor of these pollutants, a river flanked by both agricultural land and industry, a scene that reflects much of the industrialized North. As the river becomes polluted, a high percentage of waste is flushed downstream and deposited in the biologically productive estuarine waters and coastal zones. Here, the poisons enter marine food chains, building up their concentrations in higher species. This process of bioamplification was sharply illustrated in Japan in the early 1950s by Minamata disease – methyl mercury poisoning due to eating tuna with heavy concentrations of mercury in their tissues (the wastes originated from a coastal factory). By 1975, there were 3,500 known victims.

Rubbish in the sea

Until it became illegal in the late 1980s, ships were discarding 6 million tonnes of rubbish into the sea each year. Other garbage comes from the shores. Whilst many items can be degraded by the seas, the process can take months or years: woollen cloth one year, a tin can 100 years, and a plastic bottle 450 years! This debris can be extremely harmful to marine life. For instance, the plastic rings from beverage "six packs" can become caught around the snouts of seals and sealions, preventing feeding and even breathing.

Agricultural runoff

Pesticides and herbicides, not readily biodegradable, are persistent pollutants. As they pass through marine food chains, their effect is concentrated. Nitrates from fertilizers over-enrich water, causing algal growth and eventual deoxygenation.

Urban centres

Municipal drainage systems pour out domestic and industrial sewage, contaminated with toxic chemicals, heavy metals, oil, and organic nutrients. Construction sites release enormous amounts of sediment into rivers.

Industry

Much of the complex mix that goes into industrial waste ends up in the sea. Included in this mélange are partially biodegradable food wastes, persistent pesticides, and heavy metals. It often takes a human casualty to alert us to the source of the pollution.

Nuclear facilities

Whilst there is a global ban on dumping low-level nuclear waste at sea, radioactive effluent still reaches coastal waters from nuclear-fuel reprocessing plants.

Oil refineries

In the early 1980s, accidental oil loss and seepage from coastal oil refineries contributed some 100,000 tonnes of oil annually to ocean pollution. According to the US National Academy of Sciences, more than 200 million gallons of petroleum enter the world's seas each year. An additional 180 million gallons seep into the ocean naturally from the seafloor.

stal "dead zones"

ophication occurs in aquatic
ystems whereby high nutrient
entrations stimulate algal blooms.
e blooms cloud water and block
ght. When the algae die and decom-
e, they create a feast for bacteria,
h in turn causes oxygen levels to fall,
the marine species must leave or die.
sed almost exclusively by human
ities, these coastal "dead zones" are
oming increasingly common and are
ated to number 150 worldwide. The
of Mexico has a periodic dead zone
to 22,000 sq. km which fortunately
ppears each winter, but the eastern
c Sea has a permanent dead zone
ering up to 100,000 sq. km.

mercury 2.5 times the natural rate, manganese 4 times, zinc, copper, and lead 12 times, antimony 30 times, and phosphorus 80 times. As for oil, human-caused pollution – often by wanton carelessness and even deliberate discharge – accounts for four-fifths or more of the total volume entering the sea. We hear much about oil-killed birds and other marine life, though they generally recover their numbers within a few years. Much worse damage is caused by insidious pollutants: certain components of oil are toxic, others are carcinogenic, and they tend to persist for long periods. In addition, there are heavy metals such as mercury, lead, cadmium

and arsenic, plus chemicals such as DDT and PCBs, all of which must rank high on the list of harmful pollutants. We have learned to our cost of the effects of mercury through the Minamata episode in Japan (p. 90) and more recent deaths in Indonesia; and we have discovered too late the impact of DDT and PCBs, through reproductive failures among birds of prey and other wildlife.

The most significant factor of all is that at least 75 percent of ocean pollution arises from human activities on land rather than at sea, and that 90 percent of these pollutants remain in coastal waters, by far the most biologically productive sector of the

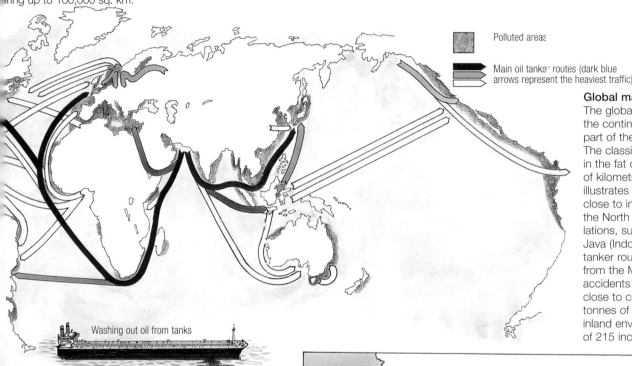

■ Polluted areas

⮕ Main oil tanker routes (dark blue
arrows represent the heaviest traffic)

Global marine pollution

The global circulation of ocean currents and the continuum of marine life mean that no part of the ocean is exempt from pollution. The classic example is the discovery of DDT in the fat of Antarctic penguins, thousands of kilometres from source. The map (left) illustrates pollution hotspots – coastal areas close to industrial conurbations, such as the North Sea, and regions with high popu-lations, such as Rio de Janeiro (Brazil) and Java (Indonesia). The map also shows oil tanker routes, the heaviest traffic being from the Middle East to Europe. Most tanker accidents occur along congested routes, close to coasts. In 1998, more than 100,000 tonnes of oil were spilled into marine and inland environments worldwide as a result of 215 incidents.

Washing out oil from tanks

Sewage dumping

Nuclear dumping

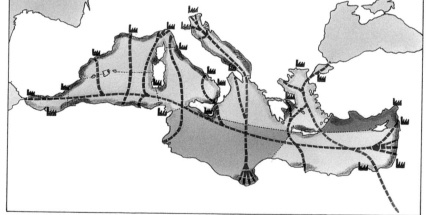

Seaborne pollution

Oil tankers transport more than 100 million tonnes of oil on an average day. Collisions are rare but they do occur – with disastrous consequences. The *Exxon Valdez* spill of 1989 caused much harm to wildlife, killing 300 harbour seals, 3,000 sea otters, 250,000 sea birds. In 1999, the *Erika* shed 14,000 tonnes of oil polluting more than 100 miles of Atlantic coastline. In 2002, the *Prestige* shed 60,000 tonnes off the coast of Spain. Oil spread to the south coast of England, and to the Canary Islands, and 300,000 seabirds died. More than 900 km of coastline were closed to fishing. Clean-up costs and lost fishing revenues in the imme-diate aftermath amounted to $6 billion. Incidents such as these will lead to a gradual phase-out of single-hull tankers between 2003 and 2015.

The polluted Mediterranean

The Mediterranean is a notorious pollution black spot. The 160 million people along its coasts and a similar number of yearly tourists contribute a heavy sewage load – more than 500 million tonnes – into a sea that is not easily flushed clean. Other pollutants include 120,000 tonnes of mineral oils, 60,000 tonnes of detergents, 100 tonnes of mercury, 3,800 tonnes of lead, and 3,600 tonnes of phosphates. Oil tankers regularly cross the Mediterranean, and a third of the world's oil spills have been in its waters. According to the WWF, over 2,500 tonnes of oil is spilled from ships into the Mediterranean every day – almost one million tonnes a year, 15 times worse than the Prestige disaster of 2002.

- - - Oil tanker routes

▨ High sewage pollution

🏭 Industrial centres

▨ Industrial pollution

▨ Areas of heavy oil pollution from
land-based sources

oceans. The wanton destruction that is occurring in these vital zones will have serious consequences, not only for the marine realm but for human welfare.

Our vulnerable coastline

The destruction of marine habitats is most serious in coastal zones where saltmarshes, estuaries, mangroves, and coral reefs – all areas of great ecological complexity and vital to our welfare – are especially vulnerable to human degradation (pp. 80–81). Oil terminals, for example, tend to be sited along coasts, often built on valuable saltmarsh or near estuaries.

Coastal cities often look to nearby wetlands as a cheap way to dispose of rubbish, such as industrial refuse and household garbage. Equally damaging is the dredging of offshore sand and gravel that destroys fish-spawning grounds. In the US, many important coastal wetlands have been lost: California, Florida, and Louisiana are all coastal states that have lost a large proportion of their wetlands (California over 90 percent).

Especially susceptible are estuaries, "crossroads" between land and ocean ecosystems, and hence locations of much human activity. Estuaries are extremely productive in terms of fish life. The US is rich in estuaries. Those along the Atlantic and Gulf coasts are very important as fishery and shellfish resources. As many as 95–98 percent of commercial fishery species of these regions spend their early life feeding in the rich, warm, and sheltered estuarine waters. But for how long can they sustain their productivity, in the face of a proliferation of industrial complexes which are not only sited on wetlands, but spill their wastes into the fertile waters? Many of these prime habitats are being degraded at a rate that eliminates entire communities of fish as in the Chesapeake Bay (right).

In the tropics, similar pressures are contributing to the destruction of both mangroves and coral reefs. In the Philippines, for example, more than 90 percent of the 25,000 square kilometres of coral reefs are threatened, mainly from destructive fishing practices, sedimentation caused by deforestation, and bleaching. Similarly, Philippine mangroves are in decline due to severe habitat degradation, having been reduced from 5,000 square kilometres in the 1920s to only 1,500 square kilometres today. Much of this loss is due to clearing for culture ponds to rear fish and prawns.

Eutrophication (p. 91) brought on by sewage and fertilizer runoff is another cause of habitat loss. The added phosphates and nitrates cause a "bloom" of algae; as they decompose they use up much oxygen, choking out other life.

Despite the designation of "Wetlands of International Importance" under RAMSAR (an international convention, signed at Ramsar, Iran, in 1971), the pressure of rising human numbers and the demand for resources are eradicating wholesale these irreplaceable ecosystems.

Destruction of habitat

Well over half of the human population lives within 100 km of the coasts. Some of the largest metropolitan areas border estuarine regions – Tokyo, São Paulo, New York, Shanghai, Calcutta, Buenos Aires, Seoul, Bombay, and Rio de Janeiro. In several cases these conurbations have all but obliterated coastal wetlands, being biologically productive areas which are also important as pollution filters and as natural buffers between land and sea.

Just as harmful, if often less dramatic than pollution, are the effects of dredging and other forms of land mismanagement. For example, the sludge dredged from the waterways of south Louisiana forms a "levee" or continuous raised spoil bank, which effectively impounds many marshes. Natural drainage channels are either interrupted or cut, leading to widespread habitat destruction.

Chesapeake Bay
Chesapeake Bay on the US Atlantic coast is one of the world's most productive ecosystems and has long provided oysters, crabs, and fish in abundance. The bay has become depleted due to industrial pollution and agricultural fertilizers. While it once supplied a catch of more than 100 million tonnes a year, in 2001 it provided only 1.5 million tonnes.

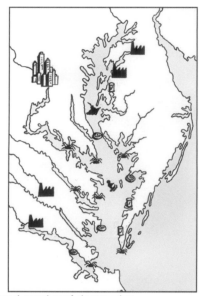

Causes of mangrove and coral reef destruction

- Coastal areas prone to habitat destruction
- Clear felling
- Agriculture
- Coastal development
- Salt ponds
- Mining
- Waste
- Coral reef destruction

The Mississippi Delta
The discovery of oil in 1901 led to construction of a vast network of waterways (below); this activity, together with land drainage, adversely affected the wetlands, notably the shrimp nursery areas and menhaden fisheries of the Gulf of Mexico.

PACIFIC OCEAN
4–9% coral reef destroyed

CARIBBEAN SEA AND ATLANTIC OCEAN
22% of coral reef destroyed

MEXICO, PANAMA
65–70% mangrove loss

Seagrasses threatened
On top of urban pollution is the threat from invasive alien species. Tropical algae have caused problems to seagrasses in areas of the Mediterranean along the French and Italian Rivieras.

Conversion to agriculture and aquaculture

In Asia and Africa, shortage of arable land has led to clearance of mangroves for agriculture, e.g. rice cultivation in West Africa. The more traditional activity of impounding mangroves for aquaculture ignores the natural value of mangroves as well as the environmental effects of the chemicals and waste products from aquaculture, which pollute and destroy adjacent waters and habitats. Aquaculture production grew from 7 million tonnes in 1984 to 38 million in 2001 (worth $56 billion), about 60% in inland waters.

Oil pollution

Oil spills are a threat to vegetation and wildlife, as in the mangroves (above). Saltmarshes are oil traps and recovery times can range from one or two years to decades.

Salt pond construction

A classic example of conflicting resource needs in coastal zones lies with the clearance of mangroves for salt/brine evaporation ponds as in N.W. India, West Africa, and Malaysia.

SOUTHEAST AND EAST ASIA
34% coral reef destroyed

PHILIPPINES
70% mangrove loss

PAKISTAN, MALAYSIA, MYANMAR, THAILAND
75–85% mangrove loss

MIDDLE EAST
35% coral reef destroyed

INDIAN OCEAN
59% coral reef destroyed

TANZANIA, INDONESIA, GABON, COTE D'IVOIRE, ANGOLA, GUINEA-BISSAU
50–70% mangrove loss

Waste disposal

Garbage and solid waste are often dumped in mangroves, while sewage effluents and hazardous chemicals contribute to their poisoning.

Mining

Mine waste can smother mangrove roots. In northern Puerto Rico, for example, mining for sand and an airport development led to the destruction of a large tract of mangrove.

Coastal development

Mangrove clearance for domestic and industrial development is a major problem, particularly in high-income countries. In southern Queensland, Australia, large mangrove tracts have been destroyed. Over half of original saltmarshes in the US have been destroyed, mostly to create land for homes, industry, and agriculture.

The threat from storms

Storm surges, flooding, and hurricane damage to coastlines have become all too familiar on our TV screens. The economic costs of such weather-related disasters have soared, with an average of more than $40 billion per year during the 1990s. Wetland plants and soils act as a natural buffer between land and sea, absorbing flood waters and dissipating storm surges. In the Indian state of Orissa, mangroves were cleared from the coast to make way for prawn farming. In 1999, a cyclone caused mass mortality.

Mangrove forest destruction

Since 1950, extensive losses of mangrove have occurred and now only 180,000 sq. km remain worldwide. Up to half the original extent may have been destroyed. Thailand has lost four-fifths of its mangrove cover – much of the losses occurring since 1975 – and Panama lost two-thirds just during the 1980s. Plantation forestry helps some areas but the net trend is negative. The map (left) pinpoints areas of widespread mangrove loss and coral reef destruction. Large tracts of mangrove have been cut to provide timber, pulp, or fuel, or they have been cleared for agriculture, and for coastal development. In Asia, over 400,000 ha of mangroves have been converted into brackish-water aquaculture for shrimp farming – a large source of foreign exchange for developing countries.

The assault on coral reefs and lagoons

At least 10% of the world's coral reefs have been degraded beyond recovery, 30% are critical and could be lost in one or two decades, another 30% are threatened and could disappear in two to four decades. Less than a third are stable. Scientists estimate that if we lose 30% of the world's reef area in the next 10–20 years, almost 10% of coral reef species could become extinct. The following are factors in their decline: dredging and removal of coral for construction; terrestrial erosion; pollution from sewage, industrial waste, thermal and desalination effluents, and oil; tourism; coastal development; mining and blasting; oil and gas production; overfishing; climate change (both sea-level rise and increased ocean temperatures).

The tragedy of the commons

"Whales have become newly symbolic of real values in a world environment of which man is newly aware. Whales live in families, they play in the moonlight, they talk to one another, and they care for one another in distress. They are awesome and mysterious. In their cold, wet, and forbidding world they are complete and successful. They deserve to be saved, not as potential meatballs, but as a source of encouragement to mankind."

Victor Scheffer, American Whale Expert

The ocean has given rise to all manner of conflicts, from disputes over resources to the depletion of marine species. This is not so much due to the aggressive nature of fishing peoples and others "who go down to the seas in ships". Rather the problem lies with the nature of the marine realm as a "commons environment".

Apart from coastal zones, all people enjoy open access to the ocean for them to exploit as they see fit. Each individual or nation has viewed the resources as free for the taking; each has sought to outdo the rest. This self-defeating process is compounded as the competition for a diminishing resource grows more severe, until all too often the exploiters drive the resource to the verge of extinction.

The tragic futility of this outcome is symbolized by the record of the great whales. A whale swimming in the ocean belongs to nobody. When it is killed, it becomes the private property of the whaler and the profit accrues to the whaler alone. As the hunting intensifies, whalers have to spend extra effort in finding their target, but it is commercially worth their while. Worse still, all people, including the whalers, face an aggravated risk of a whale species becoming extinct.

After 1900 whaling focused primarily on the Antarctic, where the whales congregated in summer to feed. The first Antarctic whale to be hunted commercially was the humpback, with a total of around 7,000 a year. Once humpback stocks dropped, the blue whale, the largest living mammal, became the target, with about 7,000 a year being harvested in the 1930s. Next in line was the fin whale. More efficient catcher boats steadily produced a massive rise in exploitation levels, with 26,000 fin whales taken in 1940, the peak catch for this species. After the fin, the sei whale became the main quarry, with a peak catch of 20,000 in 1965. Finally, the whaling industry switched to the smaller minke whale.

Whose ocean?

Conflict is the theme song of the oceans – a commons environment where largely uncontrolled exploitation and competition for resources make the original inhabitants the inevitable losers. Of these, none has suffered more heavily than the great whales.

A non-sustainable harvest

The first species to attract unwanted human attention was the right whale, so dubbed because it was the "right" one to pursue, being easy to catch and a rich source of oil and whalebone. The Victorian women's desire to cut a fine figure led to a huge demand for whalebone corsets, and the right whale was ultimately driven almost to extinction. Another early victim was the Western grey whale, hunted for oil, meat, and blubber. These disasters were only the beginning of the story. In the last century with improved technology, soaring demand for whale products, and with no common management strategy, we over-hunted species after species. As each stock fails, we turn our attention to the next. CITES listed the minke to ban international trade in its products but Japan, Norway, and Iceland are exempt from this ban.

The great whales: killing or watching

Several populations of the great whales are endangered, numbering 500 or less. Other whale stocks have improved a bit and there has been pressure for whaling to begin again, particularly by Japan, which kills about 440 minke whales a year under its "scientific whaling programme". In 2000, Norway killed almost 500 whales. Whale meat supplies a $50 million market in Japan. Each whale can be worth up to $30,000 wholesale so it is little wonder that Japan calls for a sustainable quota of up to 3,000 minke. Being left alone, whales can contribute vast sums to local economies. By 1998 whale watching earned $1 billion in revenues worldwide from 9 million tourists in 87 countries. South Africa's earnings reached $90 million a year by the late 1990s.

Sei whale
Length: 12–16 metres
Weight: 20–30 tonnes

Humpback whale
Length: 12–15 metres
Weight: 25–40 tonnes

400,000

200,000

100,000

150,000

25,000

1900 1920 1940 1960 1980 2000

Defeat of the giants

Hunting the great whales is no longer viable. It will take many years for their populations to recover, if at all. The population curves (below) are based on baleen whale populations for the last century. Seven of the 13 great whale species are still considered to be vulnerable or outright endangered; only a few populations have recovered to pre-exploitation levels.

In 1946, the International Whaling Commission was established to regulate the industry, but it was an abject failure as quotas lacked a scientific base and were often ignored. By the late 1970s, and as world concern for whales mounted with more non-whaling countries joining the IWC, stricter limits were applied and finally a moratorium on commercial whaling was achieved in 1986. But the IWC can only make rules; it cannot enforce them. Regrettably, certain countries continue to hunt, though any return to full-scale whaling is not on the cards. When a "management procedure", or workable harvesting quota, was unveiled by the IWC in 1991, Iceland stated it would not accept any procedure that did not meet the wants of its whalers and resigned from the Commission in 1992. Norway resumed whaling in 1993, albeit on a very limited scale. More than 22,000 whales were killed between 1986 and 2001. Japan, Norway and Iceland have exploited

a loophole in IWC regulations allowing whales to be taken for "scientific purposes". In 2003, Iceland announced plans to resume "scientific" whaling of 250 whales per year – 100 fin and 50 sei whales, both considered endangered species, plus 100 minke whales.

The present-day ocean crisis can be likened to the parable of the "grazing commons" in medieval England. Traditionally, herdsmen grazed their cattle on common pasture. One pasture area would support, say, 10 herdsmen, each with one cow. If one keeper brought along an extra cow, this would result in slightly less grazing per cow, although for the enterprising individual the loss would be more than offset by his receiving two shares of the grazing. If all the other herdsmen followed suit, they would all find themselves poorer through the overgrazing. While each user worked out a personal plan, the collective result was that the commons was wrecked.

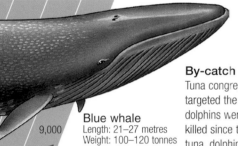

123,000

Fin whale
Length: 18–22 metres
Weight: 30–80 tonnes

9,000

Blue whale
Length: 21–27 metres
Weight: 100–120 tonnes

5,000

Fishing to extinction

How soon shall we find we have all but extinguished cod, tuna, halibut, mackerel, marlin, and other big fish? The collapse of the Grand Banks cod fishery in 1992 led to a boom in shrimp and sea urchins, the cod's prey. The urchins, in turn, have devoured the kelp forests, leaving vast stretches of the sea floor as "urchin barrens".

By-catch

Tuna congregate under schools of dolphin, and fishermen have targeted the dolphin in order to catch the tuna. Many captured dolphins were discarded dead or dying – up to 7 million dolphins killed since the late 1950s. Due to pressure from consumers of tuna, dolphin mortality in the Eastern Pacific tuna fishery has fallen by 93%.

The troubled oceans

Conflict between humans and marine mammals has always been intense. The huge 50-km driftnets of the 1970s and 1980s, intended for tuna and squid, killed hundreds of thousands of non-target species including whales, dolphins, sea turtles, and sharks. These "walls of death" were banned in the early 1990s outside 200-mile EEZ limits, but smaller nets up to 2 km long are still a serious threat. In Mexico's Gulf of California, the vaquitas – the world's smallest porpoise – is down to only 500 individuals. New Zealand's Maui dolphins number fewer than 100, and the Philippines' Irrawaddy dolphins only 70. Around 300,000 cetaceans still die each year as by-catch and large numbers of whales suffer injury from net entanglement.

A rather different confrontation arises when a marine resource serves several needs. In the North Atlantic, capelin is taken for fishmeal, but is also eaten by cod – itself a valuable food fish.

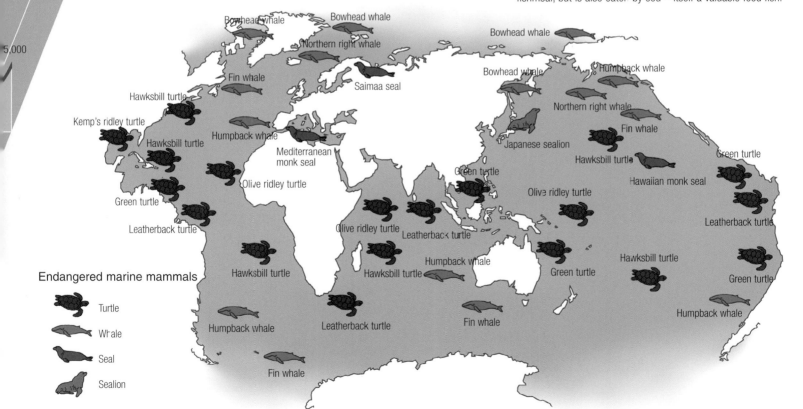

Endangered marine mammals

Turtle
Whale
Seal
Sealion

Managing the Ocean

Despite much research, we lack the understanding to exploit marine resources in a sustainable manner. The ocean is beset with crises, both ecological and political, and attempts at management have a long history. Fortunately, there are signs of hope. Fisheries planning has become more precise, and there are over 70 conventions and agreements directly concerned with protecting the marine environment.

A new fishing strategy

Thus far we have made an appalling hash of fishing the oceans. As much as three-fifths of major marine fisheries are at or over maximum sustainable yield. One-fifth has been severely depleted, or are recovering from depletion, and remain far less productive than they once were. The other one-fifth is only moderately exploited.

How shall we do a better job of taking a sustainable harvest from the sea? Hitherto we have employed an approach resembling that of hunter-gatherers towards agriculture; we have exploited wild creatures in a wild manner, with predictable results. We can take a huge step forwards right away by applying measures we have long known to be valid and yet persistently ignored to our cost. We can agree on realistic catch quotas based on a true understanding of the population dynamics of fisheries, and enforce them strictly. We can impose moratoria on fishing stocks before they crash, rather than too late as with the Peruvian anchovy and North Sea herring. We can abolish those perverse subsidies, $25 billion per year, that grossly encourage overfishing, and hence are harmful both to national economies and marine environments. Probably the two most important measures we

Harvesting the sea

With ever-rising demand for the ocean's living protein and increasing depletion of fisheries and marine mammals, we can no longer afford to ignore ecosystem interactions in our fishing policies. Despite a welter of fishery bodies, quotas for both fish and mammals have generally been too high, reflecting political compromise rather than scientific advice, and protection has been ineffectual. In the future, we shall need more realistic quotas and tougher enforcement, while fishery management will increasingly involve choices – where to tap a food chain, which species to harvest and how much, and which to protect.

The 1983 Common Fisheries Policy (CFP) brought together several fishing agreements developed in the 1970s, linking biological, social and economic aspects of the fishing industry. Subsequent reforms focus on a longer-term, sustainable approach to encourage rebuilding of fisheries from dangerously low levels. Also targeted is overcapacity of fishing fleets.

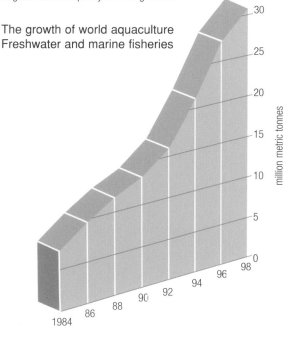

The growth of world aquaculture
Freshwater and marine fisheries

Fishery management

Since the 1930s there has been a proliferation of fishery commissions and advisory bodies dealing with fishing areas and quotas of fish and mammal species. Some work in a consultative capacity, others set quotas and have their own back-up research programmes. The North Pacific Fur Seal Commission was the first of these bodies to be established in 1911. Within the Exclusive Economic Zones (EEZs), coastal states rather than fishery commissions have had more direct control over quotas and catches.

Aquaculture

Aquaculture from both marine and inland fishing areas provides almost one-third of the world's fish supply. Production has increased from 7 million tonnes in 1984 to 38 million tonnes in 2001, when China was the world's largest producer with 26 million tonnes.

Fishery commissions and advisory bodies

Management
1 CCAMLR Commission for the Conservation of Antarctic Marine Living Resources
2 CEPTFA Council of the Eastern Pacific Tuna Fishing Agreement
3 CCSBT Commission for the Conservation of Southern Bluefin Tuna
4 GFCM General Fisheries Commission for the Mediterranean
5 IATTC Inter-American Tropical Tuna Commission
6 IBSFC International Baltic Sea Fishery Commission
7 ICCAT International Commission for the Conservation of Atlantic Tunas
8 IPHC International Pacific Halibut Commission
9 IWC International Whaling Commission
10 NAFO NW Atlantic Fishery Organization
11 NASCO North Atlantic Salmon Conservation Organization
12 NEAFC North East Atlantic Fisheries Commission
13 NPAFC North Pacific Anadromous Fish Commission
14 PSC Pacific Salmon Commission
15 SEAFO South East Atlantic Fisheries Organization

Otter vs. clam

Protection of the Californian sea otter in 1972 was welcomed by conservationists, but had some unforeseen consequences. An increase in sea otters was matched by a decrease in clams and sea urchins on which the otter feeds. Reduction of sea urchins resulted in vigorous growth of kelp (seaweed), which in turn provided shelter for fish. Traditional clam-gathering and harvesting of sea urchins once provided income for coastal towns but these were subsequently partially replaced by tourism. The upper diagram shows the pre-protection ratio of the sea otter to other coastal species, the lower one the situation a decade or so later.

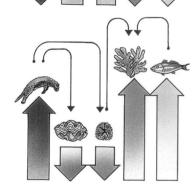

Scientific bodies
16 ICES International Council for the Exploration of the Sea
17 PICES North Pacific Marine Science Organization

Advisory bodies
18 APFIC Asia-Pacific Fisheries Commission
19 CECAF Fishery Committee for the EC Atlantic
20 COREP Regional Fisheries Committee for the Gulf of Guinea
21 CPPS South Pacific Permanent Commission on Marine Resources
22 COFREMAR Joint Permanent Commission for the Argentina/Uruguay Maritime Front
23 NAMMCO North Atlantic Marine Mammal Commission
24 WECAFC Western Central Atlantic Fishery Commission
25 WIOTO Western Indian Ocean Tuna Organization

can take, however, are to reduce our pressure on ocean resources overall, and adopt a fundamentally modified strategy for fishing. Thus far we have tended to concentrate on individual fish species, invoking a concept of maximum sustainable yield. For the future, we must take account of ecological interactions within an entire ocean community and apply a multi-species management strategy.

In the Antarctic Ocean, for example, we find many species of whale and seal, together with vast colonies of seabirds, all supported by abundant stocks of krill. The blue whale's numbers have declined by more than 95 percent, and all other krill-feeding whale species, with the exception of the minke, have been grossly depleted. As a result, the consumption of krill has been reduced from about 150 million tonnes a year to only about 35–45 million tonnes. So far as we can tell, this has released

a large amount of krill for the seabirds and seals. These feeding links have major significance for our plans to harvest krill. Would the deficit, if we create one, hit the seabirds and seals – or would it fall on the whale species, many of which are struggling to move away from the brink of extinction?

Human hunters have long posed a threat to marine mammals. Whales, dolphins, manatees, dugongs, turtles, Californian sea otters, sealions, certain seals, and polar bears have suffered wide-spread loss. Most of the 100-plus major species need protection. But safeguard measures are not enough unless we also take account of prey stocks, many of which are increasingly harvested for human consumption. An ecosystem-level approach will not only help the disappearing mammals. It will support the long-term welfare of the whole ocean community, including humankind.

Krill – the vital link
Antarctic waters are among the most productive in the world, the main link in the food chain being shrimp-like krill (p. 87). During the summer, they feed on phyto- and zoo-plankton, and grow from about 45 mm to 140 mm. Summer swarms of krill have been estimated at 500–600 million tonnes, a huge amount of living matter for only one species.

Changing demands on krill
Prior to their exploitation, the great whales consumed a large proportion of the annual crop of krill, which also supported abundant seabird and seal colonies. Since the great whales' decline, seals and seabirds have become the major krill consumers. Human fisheries take only 0.06% of the total krill stock, but future demand needs to be taken into account if ever the baleen whales are to recover. Fish-feed producers could also turn to Antarctic krill as a way to overcome consumer concerns over canthaxanthin, an artificial colouring added to the feed of farmed salmon and trout to enhance flesh colour.

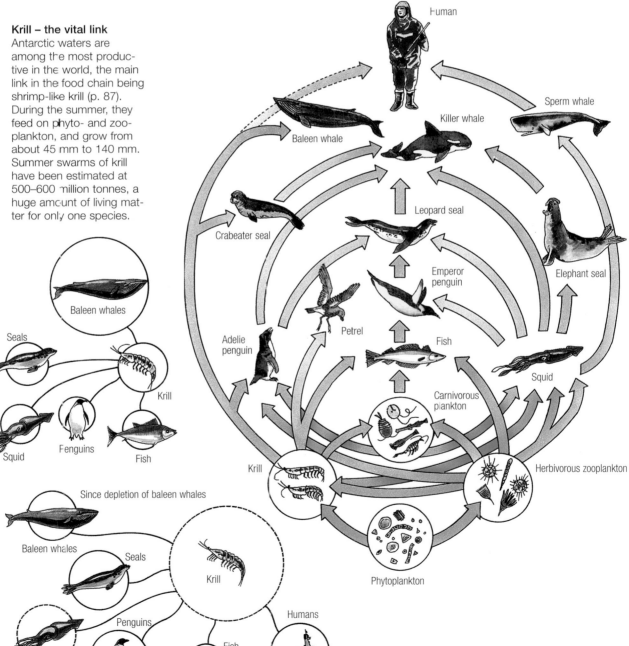

Human

Sperm whale

Killer whale

Baleen whale

Leopard seal

Crabeater seal

Elephant seal

Emperor penguin

Adelie penguin

Petrel

Fish

Squid

Carnivorous plankton

Krill

Herbivorous zooplankton

Phytoplankton

Baleen whales

Seals

Krill

Squid

Fenguins

Fish

Since depletion of baleen whales

Baleen whales

Seals

Krill

Penguins

Humans

Fish

Squid

Pollution control

The ocean offers scope for us to dispose of waste, but it requires vast care. Common sense demands that we should reduce pollution at source, and clean up its past legacy. In dealing with pollution problems which cross regional boundaries, the international convention is a useful tool. Under the International Convention for the Prevention of Pollution from Ships (known as MARPOL), limits are set on the amounts of oil, noxious substances, sewage, and garbage that ships can discharge. In certain sensitive zones, such as the Baltic and Mediterranean Seas, oil discharge is prohibited altogether. What is more, oil cargoes can be "fingerprinted" through additives and culprits of pollution identified. As a result, the amount of oil released at sea has been considerably reduced even though oil tanker traffic has increased. Also important is the London Dumping Convention of 1972 which banned the dumping of radioactive waste at sea.

Among other actions, international conventions have established legally binding agreements and rules for dumping, with a grey list of substances permitted to be dumped in trace amounts, and a black list for those requiring special authorization.

Matching the international approach are important conventions dealing with specific areas. The Bonn Agreement of 1969 focused on the control of oil pollution in the North Sea – a heavily polluted and congested shipping area. The agreement safeguards vulnerable coastal areas from spillage, with member countries agreeing to cooperate in any clean-up operations.

The Helsinki Convention (1974) was the first to cover not only marine pollution but also the more serious issue of land-based pollution. This convention highlights the need for an overall strategy at regional level, and has served as a prototype for United Nations Environment Programme (UNEP) initiatives. To its credit, UNEP has picked up the environmental football and has run far with it. Its Regional Seas Programme involves 140 states and territories working together to improve the marine environment and make better use of its resources. In some regions, hostile nations sit down at the same table to resolve common problems through common solutions. This strategy represents a quantum leap in "environmental diplomacy".

The problems of ocean pollution have seemed intractable precisely because they have been international problems, but the Regional Seas Programme demonstrates that the community of nations can prove itself equal to some unusually difficult challenges. In addition, the 1995 Global Programme of Action for the Protection of the Marine Environment from Land-based Activities (GPA) addresses problems at regional, sub-regional, and national levels, helping guide the efforts of the individual Regional Seas programmes to deal with land-based pollution.

Clean-up for the ocean

Spearheading the clean-up of the oceans is the regional approach exemplified in UNEP's Regional Seas Programme, backed by international conventions and improved technology. There have been many regional advances (see map) and international conventions to tackle the issue, such as the International Convention for the Prevention of Pollution from Ships (MARPOL) (1973, 1978); Convention on the Prevention of Marine Pollution by Dumping of Wastes and Other Matter (London Convention, 1972); the International Convention on the Control of Harmful Anti-fouling Systems on Ships (AFS, 2001); International Convention on Civil Liability for Bunker Oil Pollution Damage (Bunkers Convention, 2001).

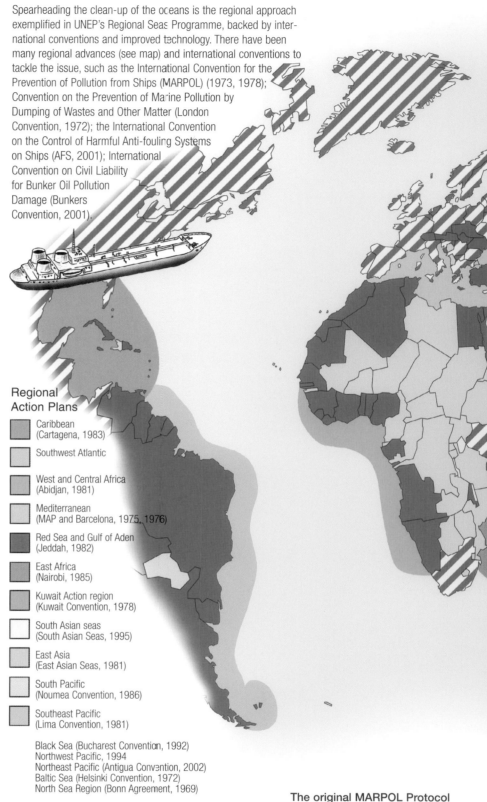

Regional Action Plans

- Caribbean (Cartagena, 1983)
- Southwest Atlantic
- West and Central Africa (Abidjan, 1981)
- Mediterranean (MAP and Barcelona, 1975, 1976)
- Red Sea and Gulf of Aden (Jeddah, 1982)
- East Africa (Nairobi, 1985)
- Kuwait Action region (Kuwait Convention, 1978)
- South Asian seas (South Asian Seas, 1995)
- East Asia (East Asian Seas, 1981)
- South Pacific (Noumea Convention, 1986)
- Southeast Pacific (Lima Convention, 1981)

Black Sea (Bucharest Convention, 1992)
Northwest Pacific, 1994
Northeast Pacific (Antigua Convention, 2002)
Baltic Sea (Helsinki Convention, 1972)
North Sea Region (Bonn Agreement, 1969)

The original MARPOL Protocol
This set minimum distances from land for the discharge of treated and untreated sewage, garbage, and toxic waste.

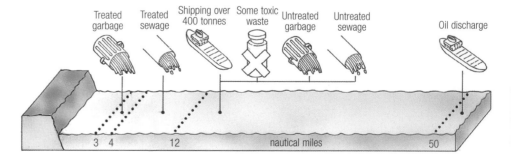

Treated garbage | Treated sewage | Shipping over 400 tonnes | Some toxic waste | Untreated garbage | Untreated sewage | Oil discharge

3 4   12   nautical miles   50

Crude oil washing

This technology replaces the washing-out of crude-oil tanks at sea, a serious cause of pollution. The waxy and asphaltic tank sediments are dispersed by "washing" with high-pressure jets of crude oil, diverted from the ship's cargo during discharge.

The precautionary principle

Applying the precautionary principle means giving the environment the benefit of the doubt if there is scientific uncertainty about the effect that any action may have on it. The decision to apply the principle to the protection of the North Sea (agreed by North Sea states in 1987) came in the wake of the problems caused by the previous "permissive principle", which allowed chemicals to be dumped in the sea regardless of whether they were damaging. Under the precautionary principle, lack of full scientific certainty should not be used as a reason for postponing measures to prevent environmental damage. The principle has since been adopted by the United Nations Environment Programme, the Barcelona Convention for the Mediterranean, and the Nordic Council.

MARPOL (1973)

In 1967, the *Torrey Canyon* ran aground entering the English Channel, spilling 120,000 tonnes as to the potential for massive pollution resulting from maritime accidents and led to many of the conventions in place today, particularly MARPOL. In 1989, the *Exxon Valdez* spilled 250,000 barrels of oil into Alaska's Prince William Sound. The clean-up costs alone were $3 billion and the incident led to calls for the introduction of double-hulled tankers and a gradual phase-out of single-hulled vessels. The 1978 Protocol to MARPOL introduced new methods for washing oil cargo tanks; other protocols limit the size of cargo tanks, and make the use of inert gas compulsory, cutting the threat of explosions. In 1997, an extra annexe was added to deal with air pollution. The International Maritime Organization (IMO) is considering a further annexe, relating to toxic marine life in ballast water. There are more than 100 parties to MARPOL.

Incineration at sea

In the 1980s, purpose-built incineration ships destroyed about 100,000 tonnes of liquid wastes a year, mostly in the North Sea. Uncertainties about this disposal alternative to direct dumping include the risk of creating toxic materials in flue gases, and the effect emissions may have on sensitive marine life. This practice was subsequently banned in the North Sea.

■ Countries that have ratified, accepted, approved, or acceded MARPOL

□ Countries with oil-disposal facilities

The Mediterranean Action Plan (MAP)

This plan was adopted in 1975 by 16 Mediterranean States and the EC, under the auspices of the United Nations Environment Programme (UNEP). Traditional national rivalries were set aside in favour of concerted action to clean up the Mediterranean. Its legal framework comprises the Barcelona Convention adopted in 1976 and revised in 1995, and 6 protocols covering such areas as land-based pollution (e.g. sewage, industrial waste, and agricultural pesticides); dumping from ships and aircraft; transboundary movements and disposal of hazardous wastes; and environmental protection for biodiversity. In 1995, the Mediterranean Commission for Sustainable Development began to facilitate the participation of all stakeholders in the region.

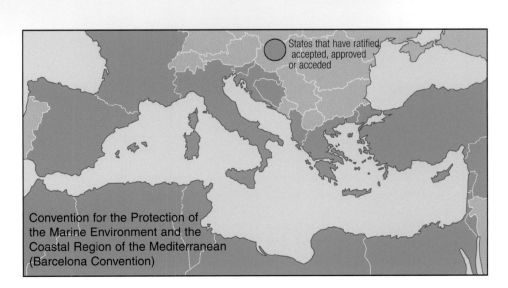

States that have ratified, accepted, approved or acceded

Convention for the Protection of the Marine Environment and the Coastal Region of the Mediterranean (Barcelona Convention)

The Antarctic heritage

Antarctica, a common heritage of all humanity if ever there was one, remains under the aegis of the Antarctic Treaty of 1961. Some 27 nations, seven of which have established territorial stakes in the continent, hold the sole decision-making rights over all activities in the region. There are a further 18 acceding nations who agree to abide by the Treaty but may attend consultative meetings only as observers. These 45 nations represent about two-thirds of the world's population.

True, the Treaty has proved a successful experiment in international cooperation insofar as nations as different as the US, the former USSR, the UK, and Argentina have agreed to keep one-tenth of the Earth's land surface demilitarized, nuclear-free, and devoted to research. But membership is small and until recently it was absurdly difficult for another nation to accede. Hence, the charge that it has been an "exclusive" club dominated by developed nations, an association of the world's largest real-estate operators, and a last stand of colonialism.

Even before the Treaty, developing countries were pressing for a global regime for Antarctica. A proposal in the 1950s by India was withdrawn after opposition from future Treaty nations but the matter has been repeatedly raised. In 1982–1983, Malaysia asked the General Assembly to put Antarctica on the agenda. To counter criticism, the Treaty powers responded by inviting acceding states to observe

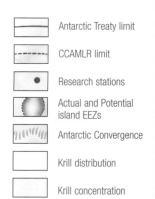

— Antarctic Treaty limit

- - - CCAMLR limit

• Research stations

Actual and Potential island EEZs

Antarctic Convergence

Krill distribution

Krill concentration

Managing Antarctica

Explorers laid the first claims to Antarctica in the early part of last century, and by 1943 the continent was staked out by 7 nations: Argentina, Australia, Chile, France, New Zealand, Norway, and UK. It was another 30 years before an approach to international management was formulated in the Antarctic Treaty, signed by the claimants and 5 additional nations. Despite territorial disputes, since 1959 the Treaty powers have managed the Antarctic as an area devoted to peaceful purposes. Research is coordinated by the Scientific Committee on Antarctic Research. The map shows the scope of the Treaty and CCAMLR.

Parties to the Antarctic Treaty have adopted over 200 recommendations and negotiated 5 separate international agreements, collectively known as the Antarctic Treaty System (ATS). These five are the Agreed Measures for the Conservation of Antarctic Fauna and Flora (1964); Convention for the Conservation of Antarctic Seals (1972); Convention on the Conservation of Antarctic Marine Living Resources (1980); Convention on the Regulation of Antarctic Mineral Resource Activities (1988); and Protocol on Environmental Protection to the Antarctic Treaty (1991 ratified 1997). There are now calls for greater protection for the area's fauna and flora by scientists who fear they will be exploited for their complex survival strategies in such cold temperatures.

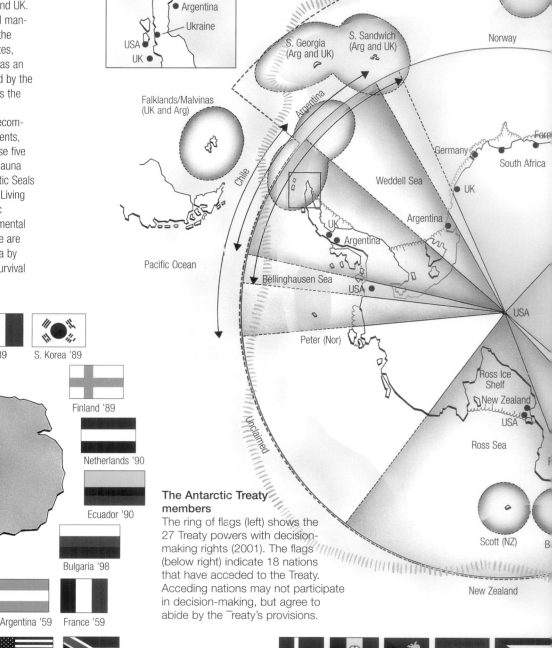

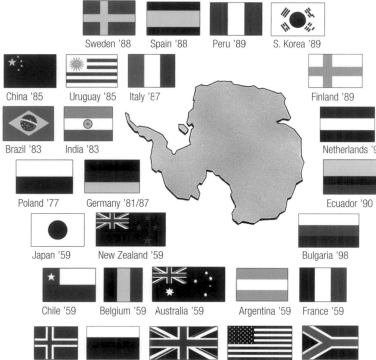

Sweden '88   Spain '88   Peru '89   S. Korea '89

China '85   Uruguay '85   Italy '87   Finland '89

Brazil '83   India '83   Netherlands '90

Poland '77   Germany '81/87   Ecuador '90

Japan '59   New Zealand '59   Bulgaria '98

Chile '59   Belgium '59   Australia '59   Argentina '59   France '59

Norway '59   Russia '59   UK '59   USA '59   South Africa '59

The Antarctic Treaty members

The ring of flags (left) shows the 27 Treaty powers with decision-making rights (2001). The flags (below right) indicate 18 nations that have acceded to the Treaty. Acceding nations may not participate in decision-making, but agree to abide by the Treaty's provisions.

Denmark '65   Romania '71   PNG '81   Hungary '84   Cuba '84

CCAMLR

The Convention on the Conservation of Antarctic Marine Living Resources is primarily concerned with controlling Antarctic fisheries, particularly krill, to ensure that catch levels neither jeopardize krill populations nor impede the recovery of the great whales and other species. Despite this new "ecosystem" approach, conservationists maintain that CCAMLR's powers are inadequate and pressures on krill are increasing (p. 87 and p. 97).

their meetings, and by agreeing to release more of their internal documents.

When the first major world oil crisis in the early 1970s coincided with the first scientific research findings that Antarctica was very likely to contain oil, attitudes to the continent changed, and the claims of Treaty parties took on greater economic significance. Conservationists became concerned about the fate of Antarctica in the 1970s and 1980s and pressed for the establishment of the continent as a World Park, dedicated to both science and the preservation of wilderness. Mining, however well monitored and controlled, they argued, would inevitably harm the continent.

Between 1982 and 1988, the Treaty nations debated whether to adopt a Minerals Convention to permit mining of fossil fuels and other resources.

Supporters of controlled mining argued that there was a "duty to develop": with ever-increasing pressures on the Earth's natural resources it would not be in humanity's interest to deny access to Antarctica's mineral resources.

As the Minerals Convention moved towards adoption, domestic political expediency moved Australia and France to refuse to sign. They were followed by several other Treaty nations until the hardline pro-mining US, Japan, and UK changed their minds with the signing of the Madrid Protocol in October 1991. This landmark Environmental Protection Protocol, finally ratified in 1997, bans mining for a minimum of 50 years and designates the whole continent and its dependent marine ecosystems a "natural reserve devoted to peace and science". The protocol may be reviewed and

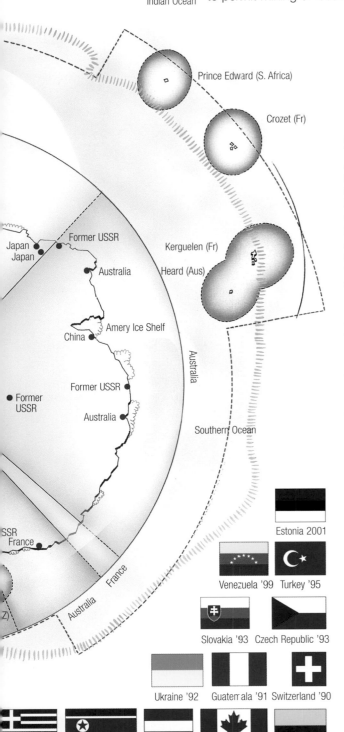

Indian Ocean

Prince Edward (S. Africa)

Crozet (Fr)

Japan
Japan
Former USSR

Kerguelen (Fr)

Australia
Heard (Aus)

Amery Ice Shelf
China

Former USSR

Australia

Former
USSR

Australia

Southern Ocean

SSR
France

France

Australia

Estonia 2001

Venezuela '99   Turkey '95

Slovakia '93   Czech Republic '93

Ukraine '92   Guatemala '91   Switzerland '90

Greece '87   N. Korea '87   Austria '87   Canada '88   Colombia '89

Antarctica's hidden wealth

The first direct evidence of Antarctica's huge oil potential came in 1973, when drilling on the continental shelf of the Ross Sea discovered traces of gaseous hydrocarbons, an initial indicator of oil and gas. A secretly commissioned US government report estimated that the combined potential of the Ross, Weddell, and Bellinghausen Seas was 45 billion barrels of oil (15 billion exploitable barrels) and 30 trillion cu. m of natural gas. Compared to proven oil reserves elsewhere, such as the 8 billion barrels of the North Slope oilfield of Alaska, this is a considerable stock. Despite the half-century mining ban, the continent will still be looked upon by some as a source of future minerals.

Antarctic science

Scientists from all over the globe brave the harsh conditions of Antarctica for the chance to work in a unique, pristine environment. Antarctic ice contains the history of the atmosphere, essential for improving our knowledge of global climate. British Antarctic scientist Joe Farman was the first to detect a "hole" in the ozone layer (pp. 128–129) in 1984 covering an area as big as the US. There are about 60 research bases where scientists study the environment and the effects of pollution reaching the area from the rest of the world.

Threats to Antarctica

Global warming: not only affects the distribution and composition of Antarctica's species, it could one day cause catastrophic rises in global sea level. The loss of Antarctic ice would also have major implications because of the role it plays in influencing the world's climate and weather (pp. 102–107).

Ozone layer depletion: increases in ultraviolet B (UVB) radiation are harmful to krill and thus affect the marine food chains of the Southern Ocean.

Commercial tourism: more than 13,000 visited in the 2002–03 Antarctic summer, taking two-week trips on ships and yachts.

Overfishing: Both legal and illegal fishing threatens sustainable yields.

Bioprospecting: there are calls for laws for it to be undertaken on a sustainable basis, perhaps along the guidelines of the UN Convention on Biological Diversity.

Invaders: freezing temperatures mean few species have invaded Antarctica in the last 25 million years. Many species are endemic (they occur nowhere else). A predicted 2°C rise in temperature over the next 100 years would weaken this natural barrier.

Pollution: DDT has been found in seals, the eggs and bodies of penguins, and in the snow.

overturned if 75 percent of the nations with voting rights change their minds. The agreement made a firm foundation for the continent's future, but further measures are vital. The Antarctic Treaty system has demonstrated an ability to survive and contribute to change, and may be a useful model for international cooperation in a wider context.

From high seas to managed seas

Nations used to exercise exclusive control only over their "territorial sea", being a narrow coastal zone about three nautical miles wide (roughly the sector that could be covered by cannon fire from land). All the rest were subject to the doctrine of the "freedom of the high seas". This tradition persisted, with minor amendments such as an extension of the territorial sea to 12 nautical miles (and occasionally to 200 nautical miles), until the 1960s, when it became plain that advancing technology was allowing certain nations to take an undue share of the ocean's wealth.

In the 1960s, a philosophy was enunciated that the ocean (or at the very least its deep seabeds) should become a common heritage of humankind, to be managed by an international body such as the United Nations. This "universalist" spirit stimulated the convening of the Third Law of the Sea Conference (UNCLOS), which eventually ran from 1973 to 1982. The aim was to develop a single all-embracing treaty, covering all issues, including fisheries, navigation, continental shelves, the deep seabed, scientific research, and pollution of the marine environment. The result was to be a "package deal" that would establish a world order for whatever uses were to be made of the oceans.

UNCLOS has enabled us to progress a long way beyond the hopelessly confused situation of the 1960s. Moreover, it is inspiring us to draw upon a large body of customary laws and established treaties. It serves to reinforce many existing conventions and organizations. Finally, it provides a starting point from which we can develop new rules, regulations, and practices. We also have a large number of international treaties dealing with separate marine issues, e.g. the International Maritime Organisation (IMO) for navigation and the control of pollution from ships, and UNEP's Regional Seas Programme (p. 98) with regard to the clean-up of specific areas.

In 1994, the UNCLOS treaty finally entered into force, one year after the required 60th country ratified – Guyana. UNCLOS III places more than 40 percent of the ocean under the jurisdiction of coastal states, divided into four zones (right). The traditional "freedom of the seas" remains for 60 percent of the ocean, but two-fifths of this, the deep seabeds area, is designated the "common heritage of mankind", and will be controlled by an International Seabed Authority (ISA).

The convention addresses six main sources of ocean pollution: land-based and coastal activities;

The laws of the sea

Our view of the legal status of the ocean is turning full circle. Once it was a boundless two-dimensional expanse, belonging to no one. Now we perceive it as a finite, three-dimensional resource, which should belong to all. Over the centuries, this traditional "freedom of the seas" has been gradually encroached on by national claims, fishing agreements, and a growing body of customary and international laws.

In the last 50 years, however, a new principle emerged to dominate the conference tables. Like a beacon, the idea of "common heritage" steered the long deliberations of UNCLOS III. Since coming into force in 1994 it has gained near-universal acceptance as the basis for all actions dealing with the oceans and the law of the sea.

Mare Liberum 1609
The Dutchman Grotius first proclaimed the "freedom of the seas" in keeping with the exploratory spirit of the age. Territorial waters were limited to about 3 nautical miles from land.

19th-century agreements
In 1839, Belgium ignored an Anglo-French Oyster Beds treaty, demonstrating the need for multilateral support. The first international convention on the Policing of the North Sea Fisheries beyond Territorial Waters was signed in 1882.

Regulating exploitation
In 1893, the US tried to control exploitation of fur seals, but an international tribunal ruled this illegal. The Convention on North Pacific Fur Seals (1911) was the first international agreement on stock regulation.

The League of Nations Conference 1930
The first major international conference on the law of the sea raised two issues destined to dominate conferences for 50 years: territorial sea limits and "common heritage". An enlightened delegate, Snr Suarez, proposed that living ocean resources should be viewed as a common patrimony.

Fishery commissions 1930s and 1940s
Commissions set up to regulate fisheries proved politically ineffective and unable to implement scientific advice. The NE and NW Atlantic Commissions, for example, did not cover all states fishing the area, and most such bodies were slow to appreciate the importance of quotas.

UNCLOS I–III

With just four conventions, the First and Second UN Conferences on the Law of the Sea (UNCLOS I and II) tried to provide a comprehensive formula for managing the world ocean. But the conferences fell far short of their aim. In a promising start towards rationalized ocean management, UNCLOS III (1973–1982) united the Laws of the Sea into one "written constitution".

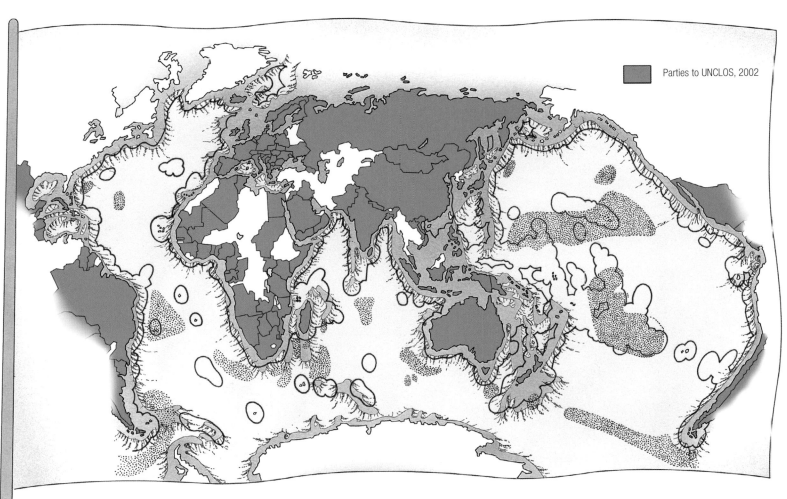

Continental shelf
Open ocean
EEZ (Exclusive Economic Zones)
Extensive manganese nodule deposits

Parties to UNCLOS, 2002

President Truman's Unilateral Proclamation 1945

The discovery of oil and gas in the continental shelves sparked off a race between coastal states to extend their territorial limits. The front-runner was the US, led by President Truman. Chile and Peru followed in 1947, each claiming over 200 nautical miles.

The Agreement on Straddling and Highly Migratory Fish Stocks

The agreement regulates the catch of deep-water and migratory species such as tuna, swordfish, and cod, offering a precautionary approach to the preservation and management of rapidly dwindling fisheries.

Exclusive Economic Zone (EEZ)

EEZs have a profound impact on the management and conservation of ocean resources since they recognize the right of coastal states to jurisdiction over 38 million square nautical miles of ocean space. Coastal states are free to "exploit, develop, manage and conserve all resources – fish or oil, gas or gravel, nodules or sulphur – to be found in the waters, on the ocean floor and in the subsoil of an area extending 200 nautical miles from its shore." Almost 90% of known and estimated hydrocarbon reserves under the sea fall under some national jurisdiction. So, too, do the rich phytoplankton pastures lying within 200 miles of the coast. Almost 90 coastal states have economic jurisdiction up to the 200-nautical mile limit and 98% of the world's fisheries fall under some nation's jurisdiction. Also, a large percentage of world oil and gas production is offshore.

UNCLOS III

UNCLOS III placed more than 40% of the ocean under the jurisdiction of coastal states, defined in 4 zones of increasing sizes: (1) Territorial Sea (12 nautical miles from land) guarantees sovereign rights; (2) Contiguous Zone (24 miles) guarantees control for limited purposes; (3) Exclusive Economic Zone (200 nautical miles) guarantees functional rights over economic activity, scientific research, and environmental preservation; (4) Continental Shelf, where states may explore and exploit without infringing the legal status of water and air above.

Common heritage

In 1967, Ambassador Pardo, the Maltese representative to the UN, declared the resources of the deep seabeds to be the "common heritage of mankind". This echoed the 1930 proposal by Snr Suarez, except that it was now backed with political muscle. Between UNCLOS I and 1973, the number of UN member states had doubled to over 140. Most of the new voters were developing nations.

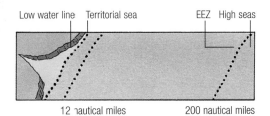

Low water line   Territorial sea   EEZ   High seas

12 nautical miles   200 nautical miles

continental-shelf drilling; potential seabed mining; ocean dumping; vessel-source pollution; and pollution from or through the atmosphere.

A testing ground for planet management

The state of the world's ocean is a litmus test of our emergent skills in planet management. Focus almost anywhere in the 360 million square kilometres of the world ocean and you will find some sign of humanity's impacts, however slight. Move in close to the major centres of population and the symptoms are all too apparent.

Year by year, our influence becomes more pervasive. New technologies enable us to reach ever further into the ocean, while industrial pollutants highlight its complexity as an ecosystem by turning up thousands of kilometres from human habitation. As we come to grips with the multiple dimensions of ocean ecosystems, it is increasingly clear that, while they may sometimes prove as robust as ecosystems on land, our errors in ocean management can be even harder to remedy.

An agreed strategy for managing our ocean resources is essential. The UN Convention on the Law of the Sea (UNCLOS) reserves 60 percent of the ocean as a common resource, where the traditional freedoms of the seas still apply. It also recognizes the wealth of the ocean floor as a common planetary inheritance of all humankind.

Simultaneously, it places 40 percent of the ocean under the control of individual nations in the form of 200-nautical mile Exclusive Economic Zones (EEZs), together with the relevant seabed resources. This may fly in the face of common-heritage values, but national ownership rights can sometimes promote a sense of responsibility.

There are also dangers inherent in this approach. The ocean cannot readily be sliced up like some gigantic pie. It is a continuous ecosystem and many of its components, especially the major currents, flow to the horizons with indifference to human politics. That is to say the ocean is an indivisible resource, whereas the nation state tends to be a divisive force at a global level. However well it performs as a management tool to serve national needs, the nation state, virtually by definition, is incapable of matching up to the collective needs of the community of nations. The world ocean will be a critical proving ground if we are to achieve our new role as planet caretakers.

Climate change

The world's climate is warming up – just as the debate about climate change is heating up, too. During the past 10 years a United Nations agency, the Intergovernmental Panel on Climate Change (IPCC), has produced one set of reports after another, each more forceful than before, and all reflecting the views of over 2,000 of the best experts worldwide. The agency tells us that "Most of the observed

Future oceans

The migratory routes of the Arctic tern, humpback whale, and the Pacific and Atlantic salmon highlight the way marine life links far-flung corners of the world ocean. The map (right) also shows some early building blocks for ocean management. Intense shipping activity in the English Channel, for example, has resulted in traffic-management schemes designed to cut shipping losses and pollution. Nation states which are at odds ideologically have come together to work on management schemes for the Caribbean and for vulnerable enclosed seas, such as the Baltic and Mediterranean.

Pressures on the world ocean will grow as we seek to harness both its renewable and non-renewable resources, from mackerel to manganese nodules. Some marine ecosystems can be designated as conservation areas, such as Australia's Great Barrier Reef Marine Park and Hawaii's Northwestern Hawaiian Islands Coral Reef Ecosystem Reserve. Others, such as the Antarctic Ocean, demand multi-species management strategies if they are to produce a sustainable yield.

Cleaning up the Caribbean

The Caribbean may not yet be as polluted as some other semi-enclosed seas, but the prevailing east-to-west currents trap pollutants against the coasts. Pesticide residues wash down from island banana, cotton, and sugar plantations and industry often discharges effluent direct into the sea. Only 2–16% of the region's sewage is treated. In the US, the Mississippi River injects pollutants from industries, cities, and farms. Cruise ships dump their unwanted "waste" – something the recently established Ocean Conservation and Tourism Alliance is trying to address (70% of cruise destinations are in the world's "biodiversity hotspots", including the Caribbean). There are clear implications for tourism and fisheries.

While the Caribbean Action Plan was slow to take off, the threat to the region induced 28 nations, many with divergent political views, to adopt new treaties to protect and develop the marine environment in the Wider Caribbean Region. Such treaties included the 1990 Protocol Concerning Specially Protected Areas and Wildlife and the 1999 Protocol Concerning Pollution from Land-based Sources and Activities.

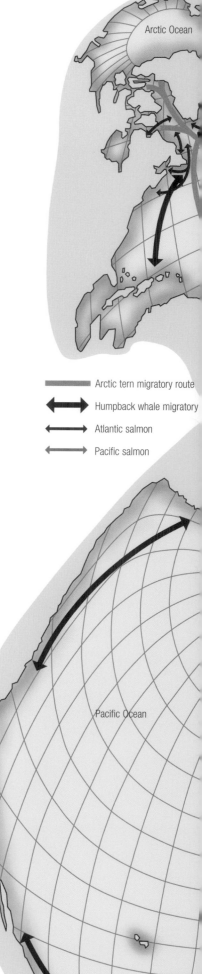

Arctic Ocean

▬▬ Arctic tern migratory route

◀▬▶ Humpback whale migratory

◀▬▶ Atlantic salmon

◀▬▶ Pacific salmon

Pacific Ocean

Warm surface water

Cold bottom water

Ocean energy
The world ocean could be a major source of renewable energy, whether in the form of algal biomass, currents, tides, waves, or the thermal energy exploited by OTEC technology (left). With all these activities, as with the exploitation of manganese nodules (in the Pacific) and metalliferous muds (in the Red Sea), or with offshore oil production, environmental impact assessment will be a key management tool.

Multi-species management

The sustainable development of the world ocean's living resources depends on enormous inputs of scientific information, as in the case of the Antarctic fisheries (p. 87). The productivity of Antarctic waters is extraordinary, with the standing stock of the shrimp-like krill estimated at up to 500–600 million tonnes. "Super swarms" of krill may be several kilometres across and contain several million tonnes. But many other species also depend on this resource (p. 97), necessitating multi-species management. Over-exploiting krill could push some protected whale stocks towards "incidental" extinction. Elsewhere, and as a sign of shifting societal priorities, whale watching is a $1 billion a year industry. In Iceland, the number of whale watchers rose from 100 in 1991 to 44,000 in 2000, with benefits to the Icelandic economy exceeding that which would be gained by a return to commercial whaling.

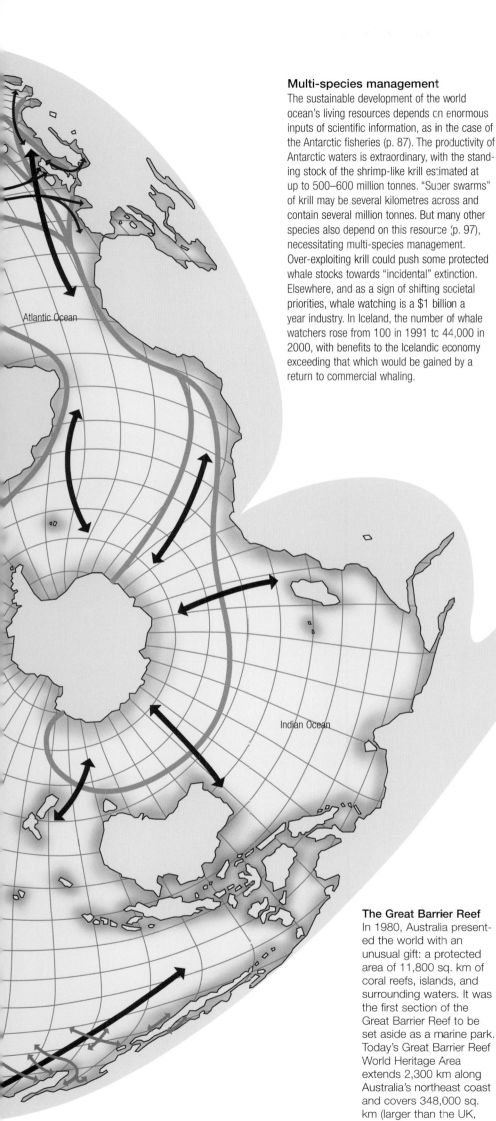

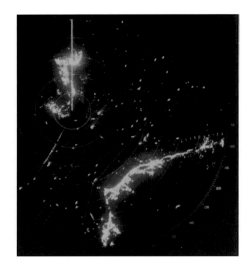

Policing the sea lanes

In 1990, more than 60 ships were involved in collisions in UK waters alone. Worldwide, 175 ships were lost that year. Traffic management schemes have been introduced in accident-prone spots, such as the English Channel (see radar picture, above), but accidents still happen. Oil spillages at sea are a chronic problem, but EC satellite experts have developed methods of detecting slicks from the air before the offending tankers have time to sail away. Similarly, satellite data help to show which countries are to blame for the toxic chemicals, radioactive pollution, and untreated sewage along with oil slicks in the North Sea and other polluted regions. As well as policing, satellite research is yielding data essential to better understanding of the marine environment. Europe's ERS-1 satellite, launched in 1991, surveys the oceans and sea ice, providing data for climate modelling and to help answer questions about ocean–atmosphere interactions, such as El Niño, and ocean circulation.

The Great Barrier Reef

In 1980, Australia presented the world with an unusual gift: a protected area of 11,800 sq. km of coral reefs, islands, and surrounding waters. It was the first section of the Great Barrier Reef to be set aside as a marine park. Today's Great Barrier Reef World Heritage Area extends 2,300 km along Australia's northeast coast and covers 348,000 sq. km (larger than the UK, Holland, and Switzerland combined). The Reef comprises the world's largest network of "marine highly protected areas" with strict protection for 110,000 sq. km. While tourism can continue in the new, scientifically based network of marine protected areas, commercial and recreational fishing is not permitted. The reef is one of Australia's most valuable tourism assets. It supports 400 species of coral and 1,500 fish species. Major threats include agricultural runoff (e.g. from sugar cane) and eutrophication (p. 91); urban development, affecting water quality; pollution from shipping, mining; industry, oil drilling, and tourism. One of the greatest threats to the future of all the planet's tropical coral reefs is climate change (p. 93).

Atlantic Ocean

Indian Ocean

warming of the last 50 years is attributable to human activities [and] further human-induced changes are inevitable. Global warming will have adverse consequences undermining the very foundations of sustainable development".

Scientific uncertainty exists about some aspects of global warming. But overall, the science is akin to that of smoking and cancer: highly compelling while less than finally (or terminally?) certain. If we were to wait until climatologists reach wall-to-wall agreement, it will be too late to do anything much about global warming because there will be momentum built into the warming processes.

Since record keeping began in 1880, the 16 warmest years have occurred since 1980 – and 2003 was the second hottest year on record, beaten only by 1998. As an ostensible result, we are witnessing all-time highs for droughts, wild fires, floods, and hurricanes among other "natural" disasters. Ice around the world is melting at ever-faster rates. These phenomena are surely a portent of climate change knocking on the door.

The worst impacts may well occur in the form of sea-level rise as a result of thermal expansion of the oceans, plus ice melting. Sea level is expected to rise during the present century by anywhere between 0.09 and 0.88 metres, and a rise approaching the latter level would inundate half of Bangladesh's ricelands – this in a country of almost 150 million people and one of the most densely populated countries on Earth. Other countries with low-lying river floodplains and rice-growing territories would likewise be swamped, notably those of India, Thailand, Vietnam, Indonesia, and China.

In many localities, shorelines would retreat by an average of 1,500 metres or nearly one mile. This is all the more serious in that half of humanity lives within 100 kilometres of a coastline. Not all these billions of people would see their homes disappear beneath the waves, but storm surges would penetrate a good way inland, pushing huge coastal communities into zones already densely populated (pp. 206–207). Dozens of small islands are set to disappear completely, eliminating entire nations. Human rights, anyone?

No doubt about it, we are the first generation in history with the capacity to alter the planet's climate. Key question: does this capacity gives us the right to do it? Some sceptics assert that humans are smart and will find ways to adapt to these gross disruptions. They even propose that if the US were to lose all its agriculture as a result of global warming, that would be no big deal since agriculture accounts for only two percent of the US economy. That's like saying that the heart makes up only two percent of the human body.

To cite the environmental leader Lester Brown, and with respect to the negotiation stalemate on the Kyoto Protocol: Could the speed at which the world is melting break the diplomatic ice?

Global fever

Melting ice
Glaciers in the Alps, Andes, Himalayas, and Greenland are now smaller than at any time in the past 5,000 years. The global icemelt rate has doubled since 1988. Most ice is held at the poles, and Antarctica is 'calving' icebergs the size of Delaware, while still bigger breakaways are anticipated within just another few years. The icecap covering much of the Arctic Ocean has already lost almost one fifth of its expanse in just the past 20 years; the region's sea ice has thinned by well over two-fifths, and its mass by half.

Antarctica's ice sheet matches the US in size. It averages 2.6 km thick, making it a giant reservoir for over nine-tenths of the world's fresh water. Specially vulnerable are the ice shelves that reach out from the continent into surrounding seas, and they are breaking up faster than ever. In 2000, an iceberg almost the size of Connecticut broke away to melt into the sea.

The number of glaciers in Montana's Glacier National Park has fallen from 150 to under 50 since 1850.

The Gulf Stream
Several thousand years ago, a warming phase caused the North Atlantic Conveyor (a deep-ocean "river") to alter course, whereupon the Gulf Stream turned southwards in mid-ocean, leaving north-western Europe with a climate like that of Iceland today and hence with scant agriculture of any sort. It all happened in just a few decades, leaving no time for human communities to adjust. Scientists believe the overnight shift was due to a decline in the North Atlantic's salinity. They point out, too, that today the Greenland glaciers are melting fast, and Siberia's great rivers are also pouring great amounts of fresh water into the Arctic Ocean.

Coral bleaching
Since the early 1980s, there has been a series of bleaching episodes, notably in the Caribbean, but also around Taiwan, the Maldives, Australia, and Hawaii – indeed, in virtually all tropical waters that feature coral reefs. The bleaching causes extensive morbidity and mortality throughout coral communities. The causes lie with either global warming or white-band disease, or the two working in synergizing unison. Well over one-tenth of all corals have been destroyed (p. 93 and p. 103).

Feedback loops
As sunlight reaches ice and snow, around four-fifths of the light is reflected back into space and only one-fifth is absorbed as heat. Conversely, when sunlight reaches land or open water, only one-fifth is bounced back into space and four-fifths is converted into heat. The result is a still greater increase in temperatures, making for a "positive feedback loop" whereby a trend feeds on itself. As a result, both the poles could lose their ice cover even more quickly than scientists suppose thus far.

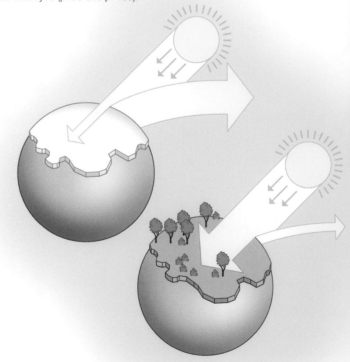

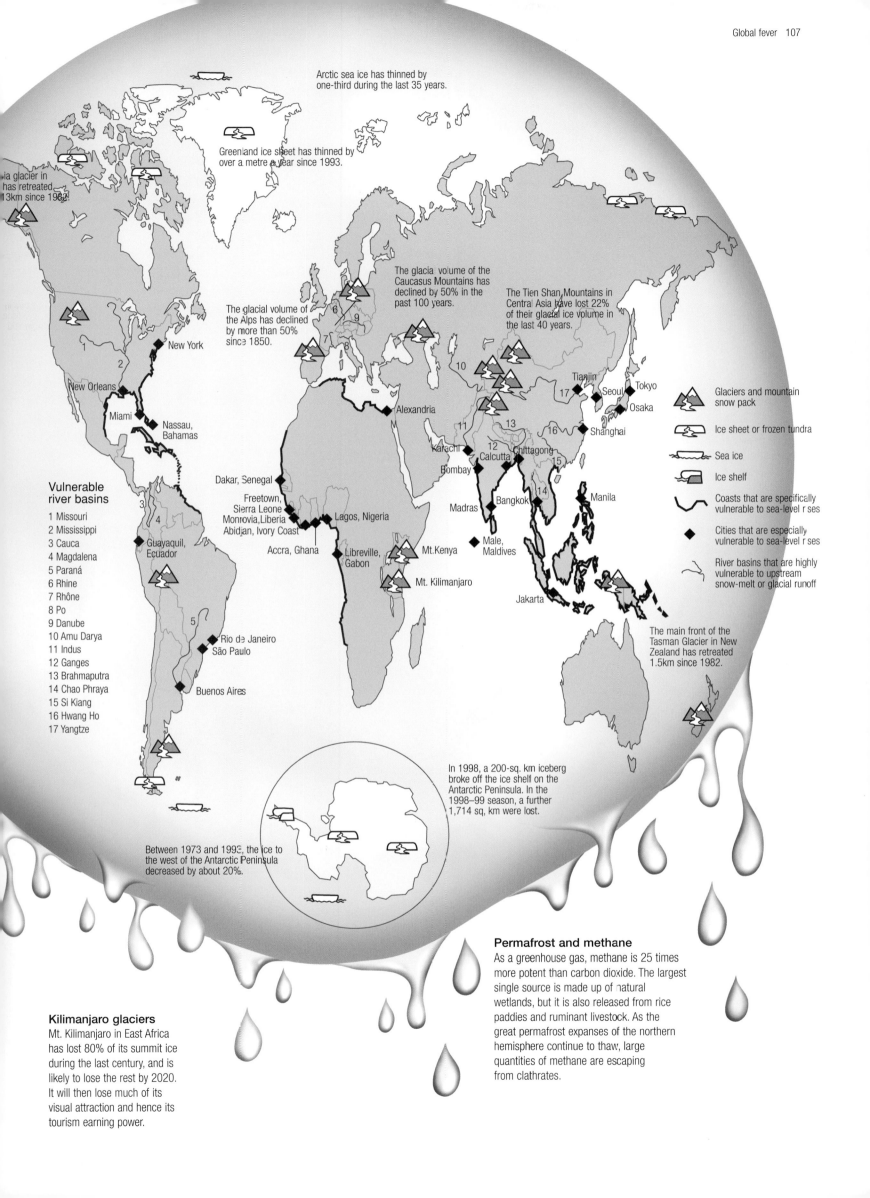

Arctic sea ice has thinned by one-third during the last 35 years.

Greenland ice sheet has thinned by over a metre a year since 1993.

...ia glacier in ...has retreated ...3km since 198...

The glacial volume of the Alps has declined by more than 50% since 1850.

The glacia volume of the Caucasus Mountains has declined by 50% in the past 100 years.

The Tien Shan Mountains in Central Asia have lost 22% of their glacial ice volume in the last 40 years.

New York

New Orleans

Miami

Nassau, Bahamas

Alexandria

Tianjin

Seoul   Tokyo

Osaka

Shanghai

Karachi   Calcutta   Chittagong

Bombay

Madras

Bangkok

Manila

Male, Maldives

Jakarta

Vulnerable river basins

1 Missouri
2 Mississippi
3 Cauca
4 Magdalena
5 Paraná
6 Rhine
7 Rhône
8 Po
9 Danube
10 Amu Darya
11 Indus
12 Ganges
13 Brahmaputra
14 Chao Phraya
15 Si Kiang
16 Hwang Ho
17 Yangtze

Dakar, Senegal

Freetown, Sierra Leone
Monrovia, Liberia
Abidjan, Ivory Coast

Lagos, Nigeria

Accra, Ghana

Libreville, Gabon

Mt.Kenya

Mt. Kilimanjaro

Guayaquil, Ecuador

Rio de Janeiro
São Paulo

Buenos Aires

Glaciers and mountain snow pack

Ice sheet or frozen tundra

Sea ice

Ice shelf

Coasts that are specifically vulnerable to sea-level r ses

Cities that are especially vulnerable to sea-level r ses

River basins that are highly vulnerable to upstream snow-melt or glacial runoff

The main front of the Tasman Glacier in New Zealand has retreated 1.5km since 1982.

In 1998, a 200-sq. km iceberg broke off the ice shelf on the Antarctic Peninsula. In the 1998–99 season, a further 1,714 sq. km were lost.

Between 1973 and 1993, the ice to the west of the Antarctic Peninsula decreased by about 20%.

Permafrost and methane

As a greenhouse gas, methane is 25 times more potent than carbon dioxide. The largest single source is made up of natural wetlands, but it is also released from rice paddies and ruminant livestock. As the great permafrost expanses of the northern hemisphere continue to thaw, large quantities of methane are escaping from clathrates.

Kilimanjaro glaciers

Mt. Kilimanjaro in East Africa has lost 80% of its summit ice during the last century, and is likely to lose the rest by 2020. It will then lose much of its visual attraction and hence its tourism earning power.

ELEMENTS

Introduced by James E. Lovelock, originator of the Gaia hypothesis

To my mind, the outstanding spin-off from space research is not new technology, but that for the first time we have been able to look at Earth from the outside – and have been stimulated to ask new questions.

Having worked on the Martian atmosphere, looking for signs of life, I later switched back to Earth and concentrated on the nature of our own atmosphere. This work resulted in the Gaia hypothesis, which suggests that the planet is, in a real sense, alive – a superorganism comprising all life on Earth and its environment, and one capable of manipulating conditions to suit its own needs.

It was a long way from devising plausible life-detection experiments to the hypothesis that Earth's atmosphere, and the cycling of elements within it, is actively maintained and regulated by the biosphere. But we found that the chemistry of the atmosphere violates the rules of steady state chemistry. Disequilibria of the scale that we observed (p. 11) suggest that the atmosphere is not merely a biological product, as oxygen often is, but more probably a biological construction – like a cat's fur, or a bird's feathers; an extension of a living system, designed to maintain a chosen environment.

We defined Gaia as a complex entity involving the Earth's biosphere, atmosphere, oceans, and soil, the totality constituting a "feedback" or "cybernetic" system which seeks an optimal physical and chemical environment for life on this planet. Gaia remains a hypothesis, but much evidence suggests that many elements of this system act as the hypothesis predicts.

Meanwhile, the human species, aided by the industries at its command, has significantly altered some of the planet's major chemical cycles. We have increased the carbon cycle by 20 percent, the nitrogen cycle by 50 percent, and the sulphur cycle by over 100 percent. We have increased the flow of toxins into air, water, and food chains. We have reduced the planet's green cover, while our factory outpourings reach the upper atmosphere, and far into the oceans. And as our numbers grow, so will these perturbations.

If the biosphere does control the atmosphere, the control system is unlikely to be easily disturbed. Nevertheless, we shall have to tread warily to avoid the cybernetic disasters of runaway positive feedback or of sustained oscillation between two or more undesirable states. We could wake one morning to find that we have landed ourselves with the lifelong task of planetary maintenance engineering. Then, at last, we should be riding in that strange contraption, "Spaceship Earth".

I hope and believe that we shall achieve a sensible and economic technology which is more in harmony with Gaia. We are more likely to achieve this goal by retaining and modifying technology than by a reactionary "back to nature" campaign. A high level of technology is by no means always energy-dependent. Think of the bicycle, the hang glider, modern sailing craft, or a mini-computer performing in minutes human-years of calculation, yet using less electricity than a light bulb. The elemental resources of Gaia – energy, water, air, and climate – are so abundant and self-renewing as to make us potential millionaires. And potentially, at least, we have the intelligence to learn how to work with Gaia, rather than undermining her.

These words were written in 1984 and I am glad to find nothing that needs changing, except perhaps in emphasis. I wish that I had known in 1984 how little time was left for us to change our polluting ways for then I would have stressed that it is sheer hubris to imagine that we could be the stewards of the Earth. Sadly, we may soon discover that caring for the Earth is even more important than caring for humanity.

The Elemental Potential

We all know that energy supplies us with heat and light. It carries us about. It makes our machines function. Indeed, it sustains our entire economic system. So much is obvious. But energy also fuels our lifestyles in less apparent ways. It not only cooks our food, it grows it. Without massive energy subsidies in the form of fertilizers and pesticides, our agriculture would be much less productive. At mealtimes, we are in effect, eating oil and coal.

By exploiting the planet's fossil fuels, which represent the biologically stored solar energy of millennia, we have been able to build up and power an industrial civilization which is radically different, both in nature and scale, from earlier civilizations. A single tonne of oil generates energy equivalent to the output of 660 horses over 24 hours.

But this new energy wealth is not shared equitably. An average American consumes, both directly and indirectly, more than 300 times as much energy as the average Ethiopian. Without sufficient affordable energy, the world's developing nations will find that basic development programmes are stillborn. Given the constraints on fossil fuels and the problems associated with nuclear power (pp. 136–37), there has been growing interest in harnessing the largest nuclear reactor in our solar system: the sun.

The sun radiates more energy into space than 200 million billion of our largest existing commercial nuclear reactors – although the Earth receives only one part in a billion of this vast output. Even so, our annual solar energy budget is roughly equivalent to 500,000 billion barrels of oil, or 440 times the world's proven oil reserves in 2002. Incoming solar energy striking the Earth's atmosphere is equivalent to 10,000 times all the energy we currently consume. In the year 2001, the capacity of all the world's photovoltaic (PV) cells was little more than the largest coal-fired power plant and accounted for less than 1 percent of global electricity – but 2002 was the fifth consecutive year of more than 30 percent growth in the industry. Exploitation of the energy trapped by plants (biomass energy) supplies at least 11 percent of the world's energy budget, and many possibilities exist for its future exploitation (pp. 144–45).

For a while, the non-renewable energy sources, predominantly fossil fuels, together with nuclear power, will continue to make a solid contribution to our energy needs. But we shall need to develop many of the more promising renewable energy options shown here, especially in view of the contribution of fossil fuels to CO_2 buildup and climate change (pp. 124–25). By far the best option is energy efficiency.

The global powerhouse

The sun's energy is the mainspring of all life on Earth. Without it the oceans would freeze as temperatures on the planet's surface drop almost to absolute zero (−273°C). Solar energy drives the great geophysical and geochemical cycles that sustain life, among them the water cycle, the oxygen cycle, the carbon cycle, and the climate. The sun provides our food by photosynthesis, and most of our fuel. Fossil fuels are simply stored solar energy, the product of photosynthesis millions of years in the past. Over 99% of the energy flow in and out of the Earth's surface results from solar radiation. Heat from the Earth's core and the gravitational forces of sun and moon supply the rest. Solar radiation striking the Earth is equivalent to all the energy from 173 million large power stations going full blast all day, every day, but 30% of this energy is reflected back into space. Most of the rest either warms the air, sea, and land (47%) – or fuels evaporation and the water cycle (23%).

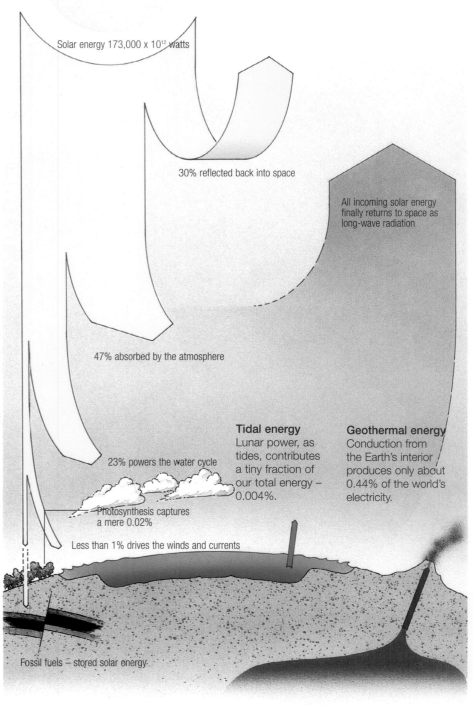

Solar energy 173,000 x 10^{12} watts

30% reflected back into space

All incoming solar energy finally returns to space as long-wave radiation

47% absorbed by the atmosphere

23% powers the water cycle

Tidal energy
Lunar power, as tides, contributes a tiny fraction of our total energy – 0.004%.

Geothermal energy
Conduction from the Earth's interior produces only about 0.44% of the world's electricity.

Photosynthesis captures a mere 0.02%

Less than 1% drives the winds and currents

Fossil fuels = stored solar energy

The human energy budget

Prior to the Industrial Revolution, the sun was the only source of energy widely available to humankind. It provided food for muscles – a fit person generates in a day's work the equivalent of a single-bar electric fire for an hour. Wood has been used since prehistory. Sails to use sun-created wind were first raised 5,000 years ago, windmills 2,000 years later, and water-wheels 2,000 years after that. Coal came into general use just 300 years ago, and oil and gas only in the last 150 years. Not until the 20th century did non-solar energy arrive in the forms of geothermal and nuclear power. The natural flows of energy that have been used for millennia are known as renewable sources. The amount of energy that fossil fuels can supply is ultimately limited by geology, and they are known as non-renewable sources. The pie chart below shows the current contribution of each energy source and how this might change by the year 2030. As global energy demand grows and non-renewable sources begin to run out, attention is focusing more and more on renewables.

Oil

Oil is the world's largest energy source, supplying 35% of our energy. With oil costing over $50 a barrel in 2004 and continued political instability in the Middle East, this share is not likely to alter much by 2030.

Coal

Coal is the most plentiful fossil fuel and just 3 countries (China, Russia, and the US) own 53% of the world's reserves. Coal's share of the world energy supply is just 23% and falling. Concerns about acid rain and greenhouse gas emissions restrict its growth.

Natural gas

Natural gas accounts for 21% of the world's current energy supply. It is expected to increase to 26% by 2030, as many countries plan to use it to reduce dependence on oil and to lessen the environmental problems associated with other fossil fuels. Combustion of natural gas emits only about half the CO_2 of an equivalent amount of coal.

Biomass

Biomass is plant or animal matter that can be converted into fuel. It currently provides about 11% of the world's energy, and it is the main fuel for 3 billion people, mostly in the form of wood. In some poor countries it accounts for 90% of all fuel burned.

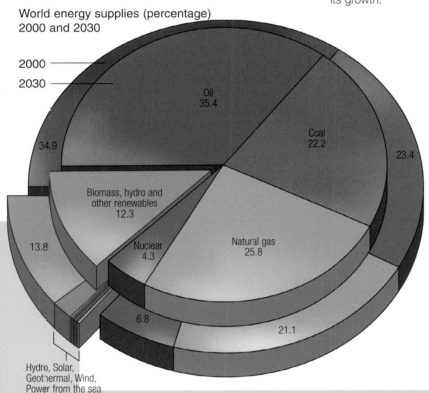

World energy supplies (percentage) 2000 and 2030

2000
2030

Oil
35.4
34.9

Coal
22.2
23.4

Biomass, hydro and other renewables
12.3
13.8

Nuclear
4.3

Natural gas
25.8
21.1

6.8

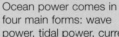

Hydro, Solar, Geothermal, Wind, Power from the sea

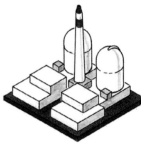

Nuclear power

Nuclear power, once hailed as the answer to all the world's energy problems, contributes less than 7% to the world's energy supply. In 2003, there were 440 reactors operating in 31 countries and 30 under construction. Sharply rising costs and the loss of public confidence have resulted in few new reactors being ordered, though developing countries, such as China and India, are increasingly looking towards nuclear to reduce their dependence on coal.

Hydropower

Falling water generates 17% of the world's electricity but just 2% of the world's energy supply. It is still greatly under-exploited, especially in the developing world, where large dams often carry heavy environmental and social costs.

Solar

The sun already contributes significantly to the energy needs of buildings through windows and walls. Photovoltaic (PV) cells to convert sunlight to electricity are increasingly viable as an energy source as manufacturing becomes cheaper. Between 1998 and 2003, world production of PV cells jumped by almost 400% from 153 megawatts to 742 megawatts. If this growth continues PVs could soon become a significant source of energy.

Power from the sea

Ocean power comes in four main forms: wave power, tidal power, current power, and ocean thermal energy conversion (which exploits temperature differences between the surface and depths). The ultimate energy potential is massive, but only a small fraction is likely to be harnessed.

Geothermal

The Earth's temperature rises 1°C every 30 m down, and more in geologically active areas. Geothermal power makes use of this heat, either directly as hot water or to produce electricity. There are geothermal plants in 22 countries, currently producing 1% of the world's electricity.

Wind

Windmills can be used to generate electricity or to do mechanical work. Wind energy is the fastest growing energy source and capacity tripled between 1998 and 2002. Nearly three-quarters of global wind capacity is in Europe, but there is much potential for the developing countries, especially India and China.

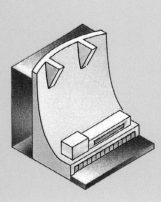

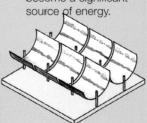

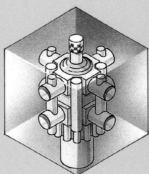

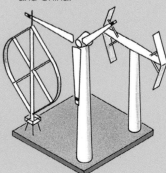

Energy-rich, energy-poor

The grossly unequal endowments of non-renewable and renewable energy, inherited by the world's countries by virtue of geology, biological history, or geographical location, mean that there can be no single energy solution for the problems which have emerged since the first oil shock engineered by the Organization of Petroleum Exporting Countries (OPEC). For instance, coal cannot be the single best alternative to oil, any more than nuclear fission can.

Many of the glib energy formulas which surfaced after the OPEC breakthrough simply do not work. Big may not always be best, and small is not uniformly beautiful. There is growing recognition that the only way forwards is to consider all potential sources of energy, together with all the component needs which go to make up the overall energy picture, while highlighting the absolute priority of moving beyond fossil fuels. This has led some countries to focus more on

Energy units key

Energy is measured in joules and tonnes of oil equivalent (toe). Power (measured in watts) is the rate of energy delivered. I watt = I joule/second. 1 kilowatt-hour (kWh) = 1,000 watts for 1 hour. 1 mtoe (million tonnes of oil equivalent) is roughly equal to 12 billion kWh, or 1.5 million tonnes of coal.

The energy store

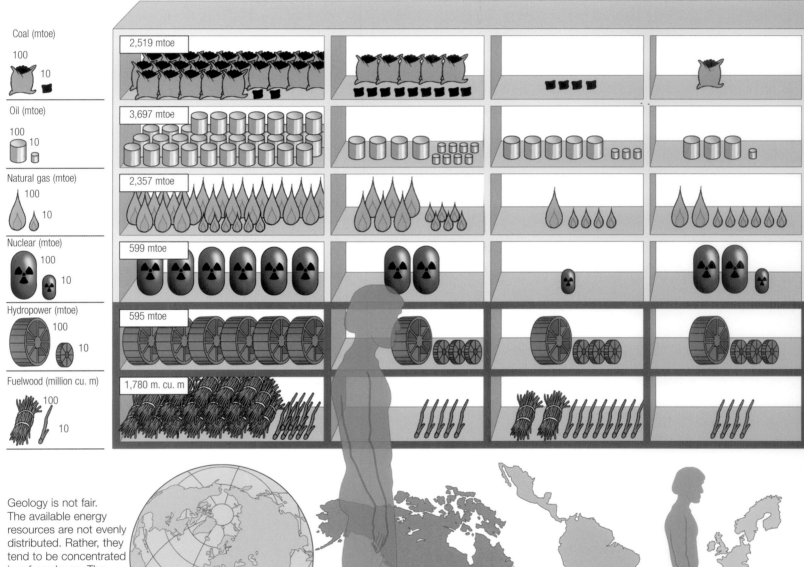

Coal (mtoe)
100
10

Oil (mtoe)
100
10

Natural gas (mtoe)
100
10

Nuclear (mtoe)
100
10

Hydropower (mtoe)
100
10

Fuelwood (million cu. m)
100
10

2,519 mtoe

3,697 mtoe

2,357 mtoe

599 mtoe

595 mtoe

1,780 m. cu. m

Geology is not fair. The available energy resources are not evenly distributed. Rather, they tend to be concentrated in a few places. The OECD countries account for 15% of the world's population, 7.5% of the world's proven oil reserves, 45% of coal, and 9% of natural gas. Russia accounts for 6% of oil reserves, 16% of coal, and 27% of natural gas. The 2003 production of coal, oil, and natural gas in 7 regions (plus China) is shown on the top three shelves; three renewables (nuclear, hydropower, and fuelwood) are shown in terms of consumption only. Regions such as Africa and Latin America with few fossil fuel reserves must rely on fuelwood and expensive oil imports. The height of each human figure (right) reflects regional per-capita energy consumption.

Energy consumption per-capita toe, 1999

Global energy consumption 1.6

8.1

1.2

4.5

North America
The US has large oil reserves and, with less than 5% of the world's population, uses almost a quarter of all primary (oil, coal, natural gas, hydroelectricity, and nuclear) energy produced.

Latin America
Although it has few reserves, Latin America is a net energy exporter, thanks to Mexican and Venezuelan oilfields, and consumes only 6% of the world's primary energy. Fuelwood shortages are acute in some countries.

Western Europe
Oil is still the main source of energy in Western Europe. Natural gas and nuclear supply 26% and 21% respectively, and coal 10%. In 2001, Europe had 70% of the world's wind power capacity.

how much energy they are likely to need, and then on the whole range of sources which might help meet that need.

Energy efficiency will help close the gap between supply and demand, but many countries will continue to show striking mismatches between the energy they consume (let alone need) and the energy they produce or can potentially produce. Many developed nations owe their prosperity to domestic stocks of fossil fuels which they are close to exhausting (if they have not already done so). Thanks to world trade, however, OECD nations continue to consume more than half of global primary energy. Energy demand in the emerging economies of developing Asia is projected to more than double by 2025.

The leading fossil fuel is still oil. It accounts for 35 percent of total energy supply worldwide, although its contribution could fall in face of rising prices and political instability. Its future contribution could tail away as it is used more as a chemical feedstock. Natural gas could last more than half as long again as oil. Coal, by contrast, is available in abundance; total reserves are estimated to be 200 times the amount we consume each year. But fossil fuels are all "dirty".

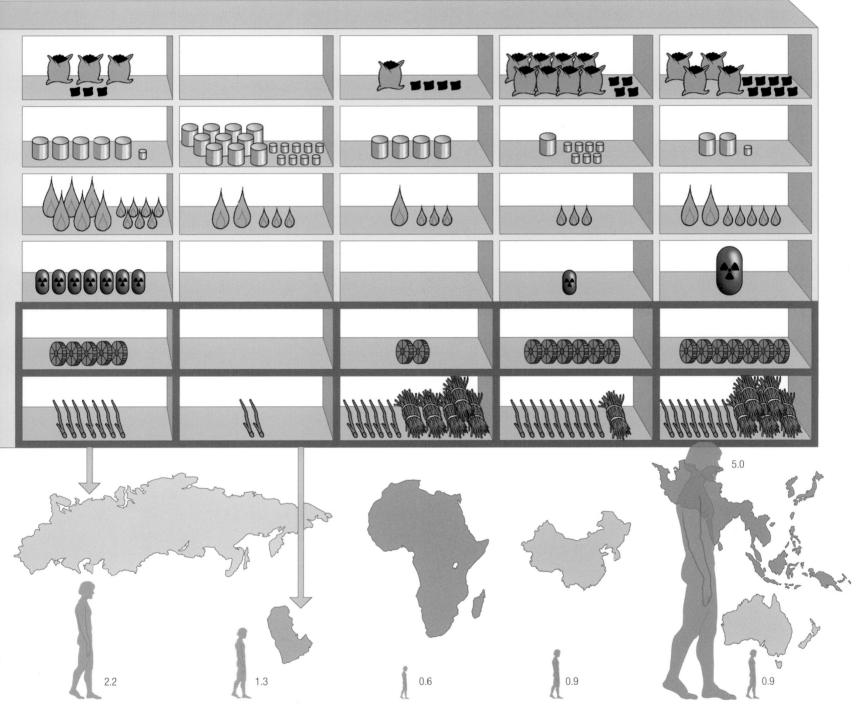

Eastern Europe
The former USSR in Eastern Europe is rich in energy resources. Russia was the second largest oil producer in 2003 and has by far the largest reserves of coal (more than 25% of the global total).

Middle East
Over 60% of the world's known oil reserves are in the Middle East (23% in Saudi Arabia, 11% in Iran, 10% in Iraq). Producing 14% of the world's primary energy, the region consumes only 4% as yet.

Africa
Apart from Libyan, Algerian, and Nigerian oil, and South African coal, Africa is ill-supplied with fossil fuels. Biomass provides 80% of the energy needs of an African villager. Wood is often burned inefficiently.

China
China is the world's largest producer of coal (with more than a third share in 2003). Coal provides 80% of primary energy and nuclear, while less than 1% as yet, is projected to quadruple by 2020.

Far East/Oceania
The Far East is energy-poor apart from China (left) and Indian coal. Australia has 8% of the world's coal reserves. Japan, which produces only a small amount of coal, has to import almost all its energy needs.

Our changing climate

Climate is an expression of the great interacting realms of atmosphere, land, and ocean. A region may enjoy a climate of hot dry summers and cold dry winters, with intervening seasons of warm, moist conditions. Or it may experience a climate of warm, damp summers and mild, wet winters, with nothing much better – as viewed by some people at least – in between. By contrast to climate, weather is what we experience day by day, in the form of cloudy or blue skies, rain and humidity, wind, etc. Whereas weather can change from hour to hour and week to week, climate represents an average pattern over years, decades, and centuries.

Over lengthy periods climate can change. A long-term shift of only 1°C is enough to trigger profound changes, as witness the Little Ice Age in Western Europe, with its peak in the late 17th century. A drop of 4°C is enough to bring on a full ice age, with swift impacts on the planet's habitats. At the onset of the last glaciation almost 11,000 years ago, advancing ice sheets eliminated huge forests of the northern hemisphere in just a couple of centuries. As for more recent change, what we now assume is "normal" is actually one of the warmest phases of the past 1,000 years. This warm phase should be regarded as approaching an

The maritime effect
Winds, the Earth's rotation, and the placement of the continents cause the great ocean currents. Because they move huge masses of water, sometimes cold and sometimes warm, from region to region, they also influence climate. Thus, the UK, warmed by the North Atlantic Drift originating off Florida, has a milder climate than Labrador, which is on the same latitude but is cooled by a current from the Arctic Ocean.

The climate asset

Five major factors shape climate: the sun's energy, the atmosphere, the Earth's shape and position in space, its rotation, and the oceans. Because the Earth is a sphere, air is warmed more at the Equator than at the poles. As the warm, moist air rises, it flows polewards, cooling and drying as it goes. On reaching latitude 30° or so, it begins to sink, warm up, and flow back towards the Equator. These vertical flows of air on either side of the Equator, called "Hadley cells", are responsible for the belts of desert and arid land found around the Tropics of Cancer and Capricorn. Air, as wind, flows from areas of high pressure associated with higher temperatures, towards areas of low pressure. The energy of the Earth's rotation, the "Coriolis force", bends the winds to give the characteristic patterns shown on the map (right). The diagram (below) illustrates the vegetational impact of rainfall and temperature. Where cold polar winds meet the warm westerlies of the mid-latitudes, we find the changeable weather typical of temperate regions. The movement of large masses of ocean water also influences climate since small differences in temperature absorb or release enormous quantities of heat. The map shows the seven main climatic types, the size of the circles indicating mean annual precipitation.

Latitude and temperature
The subsolar point, where the sun appears directly overhead, varies with the seasons between 23°N and 23°S. Here the sun's rays are perpendicular to the Earth's surface. With increasing latitudes, less sunshine is intercepted and average temperatures fall.

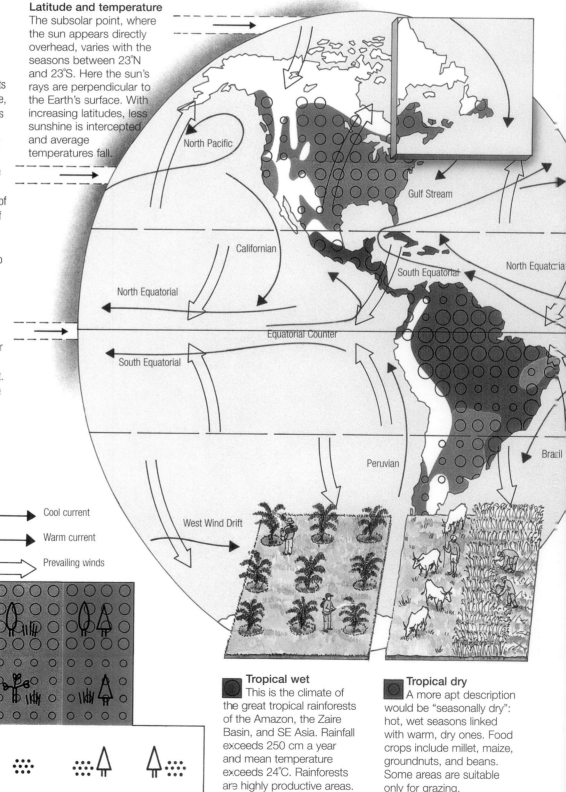

North Pacific

Gulf Stream

Californian

South Equatorial

North Equatorial

North Equatorial

Equatorial Counter

South Equatorial

Brazil

Peruvian

West Wind Drift

Rainfall

- Tropical rainforest
- Thorn forest
- Temperate forest
- Boreal forest
- Chapparal
- Grassland
- Tropical scrub
- Desert or tundra

→ Cool current
→ Warm current
⇒ Prevailing winds

Heavy

Moderate

Light

Negligible

Hot   Warm   Cool   Cold

Tropical wet
This is the climate of the great tropical rainforests of the Amazon, the Zaire Basin, and SE Asia. Rainfall exceeds 250 cm a year and mean temperature exceeds 24°C. Rainforests are highly productive areas.

Tropical dry
A more apt description would be "seasonally dry": hot, wet seasons linked with warm, dry ones. Food crops include millet, maize, groundnuts, and beans. Some areas are suitable only for grazing.

extreme for sustained "good weather". The nine warmest years on record have occurred since 1990.

Climate change has major implications for our capacity to keep producing food. Throughout the world, climate is a critical factor in agriculture. During the late 1960s, the Sahel drought brought disaster to entire nations. In 1972, another drought inflicted such damage on the Soviet wheat crop that it helped to quadruple world prices within two years. In 1974, a delayed monsoon in India wrought havoc for millions of people. In 1975, pulses of cold air ravaged Brazil's coffee crop, causing inflationary upheavals in coffee prices around the world.

In 2002 and 2003, record or near-record heat waves hit the world grain harvest, particularly affecting India and the US. In 2003, Eastern Europe harvested its smallest wheat crop in 30 years (Ukraine's fell from 21 million tonnes in 2002 to five million tonnes, compelling this leading exporter to import wheat). China's grain harvest fell by 20 million tonnes. Then, 2004 was the fifth straight year of grain harvest shortfalls.

Conversely, a stable climate with slow and predictable changes can be a tremendous asset. Just as much as energy or water, climate represents an "elemental" dimension to our Earth that can enrich our lives.

How land shapes climate
The rain-shadow effect of coastal mountains is well known. As warm, moist winds rise on the windward side they expand and cool, causing their water vapour to condense and fall as rain. As the dry, cool air descends on the other side of the mountains, it is compressed and warmed – whereupon the dry, warm winds create a markedly different climate and vegetation, as in California's Sierra Nevada.

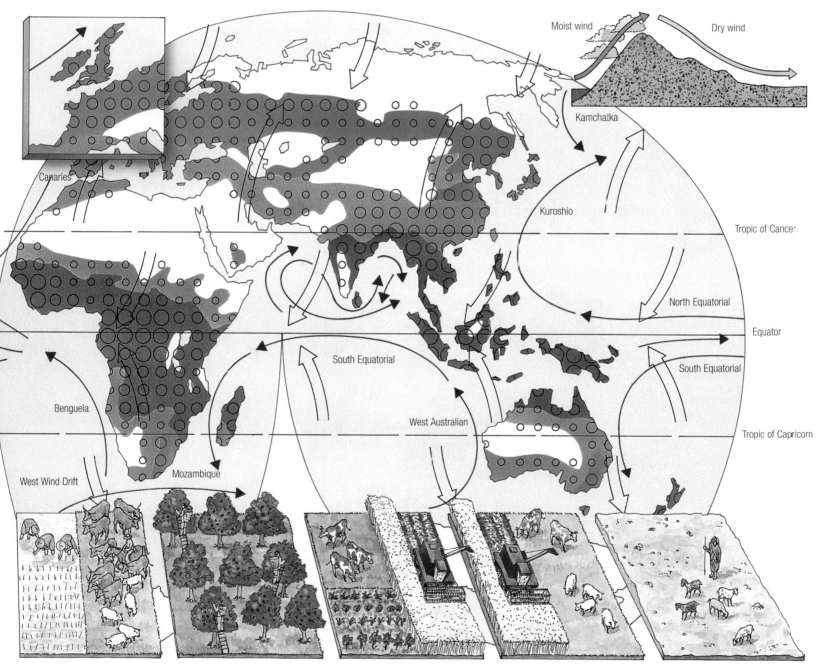

Warm humid	**Warm dry**	**Cool humid**	**Cool dry**	**Mountains**
The climate of southeastern US and much of China is warm and humid. It is ideally suited to multiple cropping since the warm temperatures and regular rainfall enable crops to be grown all year round.	The long, dry summers and mild, wet winters of the Mediterranean once fostered early civilization. With irrigation, many crops can be grown, but this can be an unforgiving climate if badly managed.	The dominant role of northern Europe has had its foundations in its cool, humid climate. The constraints on agriculture are the low levels of sunlight, cold winters, and short-term summer dryness.	The great grasslands (Russian steppes, North American plains/prairies, South American pampas) are cool and dry. These are the lands of wheat, corn, and cattle. Rainfall is low and irregular in summer.	Mountainous regions, with poor soil cover and low temperatures, are unsuited for most crops.

The liquid of life

Water, water everywhere – but it is astonishing how little of it is directly usable. We survive on such a small amount thanks to natural recycling (below right), which both replaces the water once is has been used and also cleans it.

While the "usable hydrosphere" contains more water than we are likely to need in the foreseeable future, the problem – as is so often the case with natural resources – is that water is not evenly distributed around the globe. Many people spend their time fighting floods, others go thirsty.

Although the sun evaporates half a million cubic kilometres of water from the oceans each year, the usable water is that proportion of evaporated water which ends up on land and runs off into rivers and lakes. Here we are talking of 47,000 cubic kilometres of water, less than a tenth of the total originally evaporated from the seas. This figure, furthermore, is only an average, taking no account of seasonal and other fluctuations. The "stable runoff" available for use, while much lower, is still a phenomenal amount of water. Of course, as we become more "advanced", so we use ever-increasing amounts of water.

Certain sectors of our economies are particularly thirsty, with agricultural irrigation accounting for almost 70 percent of annual water consumption worldwide (not so surprising when we consider it takes 1,000 tonnes of water to produce just one tonne of grain), industry 23 percent, and domestic needs 8 percent. In Africa, agriculture accounts for 87 percent, industry 5 percent, and households 7 percent. In Europe, industry accounts for 54 percent, agriculture 33 percent, and households 13 percent.

Perhaps more than we recognize, our lifestyles depend on the availability of fresh water. In 1900, the average global runoff was around 30,000 cubic metres per person, falling to 17,000 cubic metres per person in 1950 and only 7,000 cubic metres per person in 2000 – reflecting the fact that the global population grew from 1.65 billion to 6.07 billion. By 2025, there could be 8 billion people and only 5,000 cubic metres per person. If, for whatever reason, our taps were to run half dry, our household routines would collapse, our health would be at risk, factories would grind to a halt, and agriculture would be in dire straits.

We should remember, too, that we are not the only species dependent on fresh water: four-fifths of the world's 734 endangered fish species live in freshwater environments. The entire fabric of our societies could begin to unravel. We may take fresh water for granted, but we do so at our peril. Improving water catchment, storage, supply, and use, tackling supply leakages and perverse subsidies (which encourage misuse and overuse), together with recycling techniques should enable us to stretch our global water resource almost indefinitely (pp. 148–49).

The freshwater reservoir

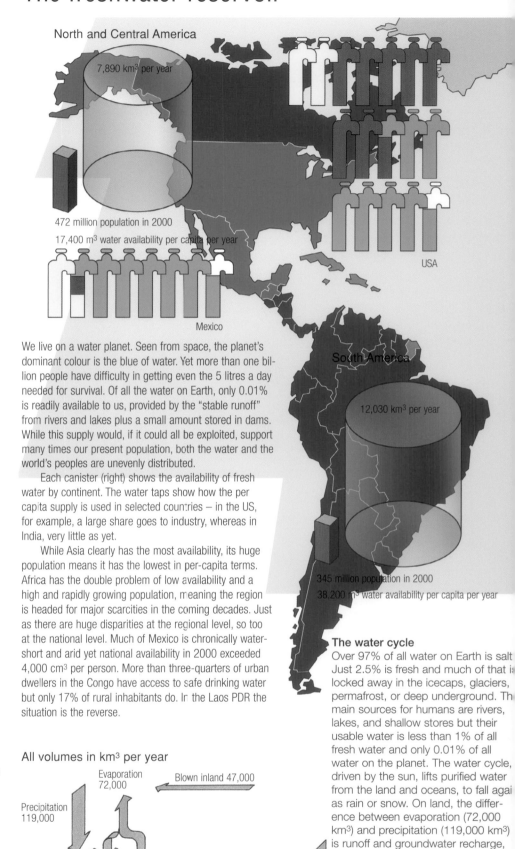

North and Central America

7,890 km³ per year

472 million population in 2000

17,400 m³ water availability per capita per year

Mexico

USA

South America

12,030 km³ per year

345 million population in 2000

38,200 m³ water availability per capita per year

We live on a water planet. Seen from space, the planet's dominant colour is the blue of water. Yet more than one billion people have difficulty in getting even the 5 litres a day needed for survival. Of all the water on Earth, only 0.01% is readily available to us, provided by the "stable runoff" from rivers and lakes plus a small amount stored in dams. While this supply would, if it could all be exploited, support many times our present population, both the water and the world's peoples are unevenly distributed.

Each canister (right) shows the availability of fresh water by continent. The water taps show how the per capita supply is used in selected countries – in the US, for example, a large share goes to industry, whereas in India, very little as yet.

While Asia clearly has the most availability, its huge population means it has the lowest in per-capita terms. Africa has the double problem of low availability and a high and rapidly growing population, meaning the region is headed for major scarcities in the coming decades. Just as there are huge disparities at the regional level, so too at the national level. Much of Mexico is chronically water-short and arid yet national availability in 2000 exceeded 4,000 cm³ per person. More than three-quarters of urban dwellers in the Congo have access to safe drinking water but only 17% of rural inhabitants do. In the Laos PDR the situation is the reverse.

The water cycle

Over 97% of all water on Earth is salt. Just 2.5% is fresh and much of that is locked away in the icecaps, glaciers, permafrost, or deep underground. The main sources for humans are rivers, lakes, and shallow stores but their usable water is less than 1% of all fresh water and only 0.01% of all water on the planet. The water cycle, driven by the sun, lifts purified water from the land and oceans, to fall again as rain or snow. On land, the difference between evaporation (72,000 km³) and precipitation (119,000 km³) is runoff and groundwater recharge, viz. 47,000 km³. This is the water "income" on which we mainly depend. Our groundwater "capital" may be greater, but is costly to extract and slow to replenish itself.

All volumes in km³ per year

Evaporation 72,000

Blown inland 47,000

Precipitation 119,000

Fresh water in glaciers/ permanent snow cover 24,064,000

Freshwater lakes/rivers 93,120

Evaporation 505,000

Precipitation 458,000

Fresh ground water 10,530,000

Runoff 47,000

Oceans 1,338,000,000

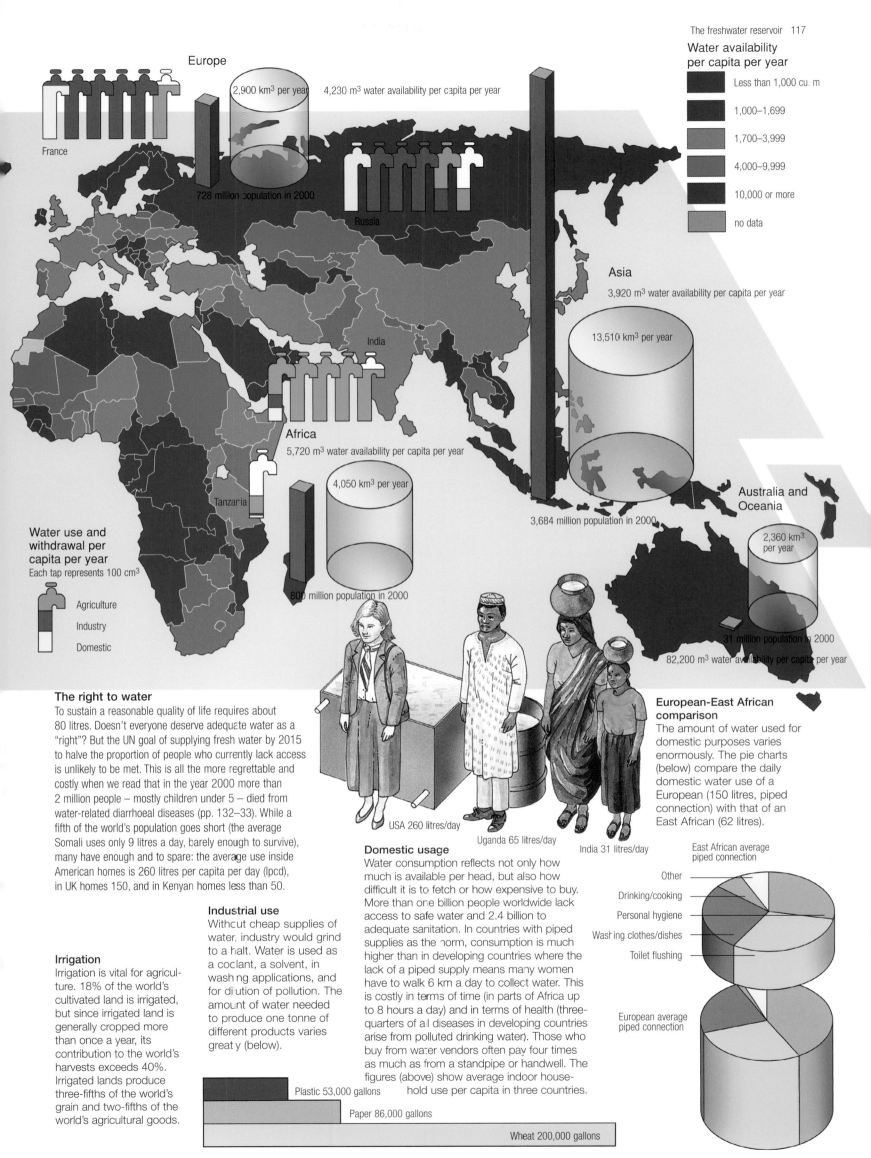

Water availability per capita per year

- Less than 1,000 cu. m
- 1,000–1,699
- 1,700–3,999
- 4,000–9,999
- 10,000 or more
- no data

France

Europe

2,900 km³ per year 4,230 m³ water availability per capita per year

728 million population in 2000

Russia

Asia

3,920 m³ water availability per capita per year

13,510 km³ per year

India

Africa

5,720 m³ water availability per capita per year

4,050 km³ per year

3,684 million population in 2000

Tanzania

800 million population in 2000

Australia and Oceania

2,360 km³ per year

31 million population in 2000

82,200 m³ water availability per capita per year

Water use and withdrawal per capita per year

Each tap represents 100 cm³

- Agriculture
- Industry
- Domestic

USA 260 litres/day

Uganda 65 litres/day

India 31 litres/day

The right to water

To sustain a reasonable quality of life requires about 80 litres. Doesn't everyone deserve adequate water as a "right"? But the UN goal of supplying fresh water by 2015 to halve the proportion of people who currently lack access is unlikely to be met. This is all the more regrettable and costly when we read that in the year 2000 more than 2 million people – mostly children under 5 – died from water-related diarrhoeal diseases (pp. 132–33). While a fifth of the world's population goes short (the average Somali uses only 9 litres a day, barely enough to survive), many have enough and to spare: the average use inside American homes is 260 litres per capita per day (lpcd), in UK homes 150, and in Kenyan homes less than 50.

Irrigation

Irrigation is vital for agriculture. 18% of the world's cultivated land is irrigated, but since irrigated land is generally cropped more than once a year, its contribution to the world's harvests exceeds 40%. Irrigated lands produce three-fifths of the world's grain and two-fifths of the world's agricultural goods.

Industrial use

Without cheap supplies of water, industry would grind to a halt. Water is used as a coolant, a solvent, in washing applications, and for dilution of pollution. The amount of water needed to produce one tonne of different products varies greatly (below).

Domestic usage

Water consumption reflects not only how much is available per head, but also how difficult it is to fetch or how expensive to buy. More than one billion people worldwide lack access to safe water and 2.4 billion to adequate sanitation. In countries with piped supplies as the norm, consumption is much higher than in developing countries where the lack of a piped supply means many women have to walk 6 km a day to collect water. This is costly in terms of time (in parts of Africa up to 8 hours a day) and in terms of health (three-quarters of all diseases in developing countries arise from polluted drinking water). Those who buy from water vendors often pay four times as much as from a standpipe or handwell. The figures (above) show average indoor house-hold use per capita in three countries.

Plastic 53,000 gallons

Paper 86,000 gallons

Wheat 200,000 gallons

European-East African comparison

The amount of water used for domestic purposes varies enormously. The pie charts (below) compare the daily domestic water use of a European (150 litres, piped connection) with that of an East African (62 litres).

East African average piped connection

- Other
- Drinking/cooking
- Personal hygiene
- Washing clothes/dishes
- Toilet flushing

European average piped connection

Mining our mineral wealth

The planet's mineral wealth has been tapped since prehistory, its surface dotted with the workings and spoil-heaps of earlier mining activities. Where once we picked shallow excavations with antlers and other crude tools, today we use dynamite and massive machines to extract the minerals which underpin almost every aspect of our lives.

Fortunately, we still have sufficient stocks of most minerals, and the "showdowns" which were predicted in the wake of the first OPEC oil crisis now seem a rather more distant prospect – although the potential for such showdowns undoubtedly exists.

Industry depends heavily on some 80 minerals, including a number which, like aluminium, are in relatively plentiful supply. True, a few countries will soon exhaust their domestic supplies of such materials, but there is enough elsewhere to go round. A small number of minerals (chromium, manganese, platinum, cobalt), however, qualify as strategic commodities. That is, they are critically important to industry, while being in relatively short supply.

Americans use 600 kilograms of metals per person a year. Vehicle manufacturing in the country accounts for 20 percent of aluminium consumption, 14 percent of steel, and 10 percent of copper. In industrial countries as a whole transport accounts for 70 percent of lead, 37 percent of steel, 33 percent of aluminium, and 27 percent of copper, while the construction industry accounts for 34 percent of steel, 30 percent of copper, 17 percent of lead, and 19 percent of aluminium.

A large proportion of the 80 minerals are abundant enough to meet all our anticipated needs, or, where they are not, ready substitutes exist. But some represent a rather thornier problem, even when greater recovery and recycling are taken into account: for example, lead, sulphur, tin, tungsten, and zinc.

An average of almost 140 kilograms of metals were produced per person in 2000. Finished steel totalled 763 million tonnes with a value of $229 billion – way ahead of aluminium with 24 million tonnes and $36 billion. Platinum was the most expensive at $17 billion a tonne, and gold at $9 million with aluminium less than $1,500 a tonne and coal only $40.

China has become a leading steel producer and consumer. The country accounted for one third of the total global growth in copper and two-fifths of aluminium in the 1990s – a reflection of its rapid industrialization and growing number of new consumers (pp. 234–35). The US, the EU, and Japan are heavily dependent upon imports of several minerals and will inevitably face rising prices for some key materials. Supply restrictions are less likely, however, since producer countries in the developing world are generally dependent on steady exports for foreign exchange. In Zambia, for example, minerals make up more than two-thirds of the value of merchandized exports. Meanwhile, countries like the US have stockpiles of the more critical minerals (opposite page).

The mineral reserve

No essential mineral resource will run out, although some key reserves may well become much depleted. This apparent contradiction is resolved by grasping the distinction between reserves and resources. The total amount of a mineral in the Earth's crust is the resource, an amount that is determined by geology, and fixed. Our reserves are that amount of a mineral which can be economically recovered for use. Some reserves have been identified, others remain undiscovered. Thus the size of our reserves is variable, dependent not only on absolute availability, but also on changing factors such as extraction cost, market price or exploration effort.

The map and pie charts show the major consumers of 5 key minerals, their percentage share of year 2000 consumption, and, where available, life expectancy at 0% and 5% growth over 1999 levels.

Mining exploration

In 2001, more than $2 billion was invested in mining exploration, though this was less than half of the 1997 peak of $5.2 billion. Latin America accounted for 28% and Africa 14%, while Australia and Canada each attracted 17% (the US only 8%).

Aluminium
3.7% 2.4%
1.2%
16.6% 24.5%
14.6% 23.3%
13.8%

Copper
6.6% 1.7%
0.8%
14.1% 19.7%
18% 27.2%
11.9%

Aluminium (202–48 years):
In the US, consumption averages 22 kg per person, while in Africa it is less than one kg. Globally, 29% of aluminium comes from recycled sources.

Copper (28–18 years):
Chile is the world's largest producer, where it accounts for 40% of exports by value. Taiwan's consumption averages 29 kg per person and Australia's is 9 kg.

Recycling

In the iron and steel industry, more than a third of production now comes from scrap (more than half in industrialized nations). North America and Western Europe consume around a third of aluminium. Recycling can bring major energy savings. For example, it requires 95% less energy to produce one tonne of secondary aluminium from scrap, copper 7 times less and steel 3.5 times less. Scrap is now a vital source of supply for metals.

Substitution

Metals that are easy to substitute include antimony, cadmium, selenium, tellurium, and tin. Tin has been losing out to glass, plastics, steel, and aluminium in the can-making and packaging industries. But substitution is no panacea: platinum is an unrivalled catalyst and stainless steel depends on chromium.

Reserve base
(million tonnes/carats)

Aluminium ore (Bauxite)	33,000	Tin	11
Copper	940	Uranium	3.1
Diamond	1,250	Zinc	460
Gold	0.09	Antimony	3.9
Iron ore	150,000	Cadmium	1.8
Lead	140	Chromium	1,800
Manganese	5,000	Cobalt	13
Nickel	140	Mercury	0.24
Platinum group	0.08	Molybdenum	0.02
Silver	0.6	Tantalum	0.15

Consumption of metals

- USA
- Western Europe
- Other industrial countries
- Transition countries
- China and India
- Africa
- Latin America
- Others

Lead

26.6%
26.2%
7.3%
17.7%
11.5%
1.9%
6.5%
2.3%

Lead (21–14 years):
More than a quarter of the world's lead is from China. Together, the US and Western Europe account for 53% of total consumption, with China and India 11.5%.

Steel

16.2%
20.2%
12.4%
19.4%
21.5%
2.1%
5.3%
2.9%

Steel:
Canadian consumption of 600 kg per person is dwarfed by Taiwan with over 1,000 kg! Together, the US and Western Europe account for 36% of total consumption, with China and India 21.5%.

Gold

7.3%
22.2%
5.7%
21.7%
23.4%
12%
3.2%
4.5%

Gold:
Western Europe accounts for 22% of total consumption, and China combined with India 23%.

American stockpiles

As one of the world's largest consumers of strategic minerals, the US is particularly vulnerable to interruptions to its supplies, importing 100% of its manganese and over 70% of its chromium in 2003, largely from developing countries.

Stockpiling

Minerals are an integral part of diplomacy. Each country tries to ensure access to those minerals which affect its vital national interests, especially defence. Strategically important minerals are vulnerable to interruptions of supply, often for political reasons. Lacking indigenous supplies, many Western countries have been building up stockpiles of such minerals as manganese, chromium, cobalt, and platinum. An unintended effect of stockpiles is to even out sharp fluctuations in mineral prices.

American stockpiles 2003/4

- Chromium 800,000 tonnes
- Aluminium and bauxite 42,000 tonnes
- Manganese 1,250,000 tonnes
- Tin 35,000 tonnes
- Cobalt 2,700 tonnes
- Tantalum 580 tonnes
- Palladium 1,820 kg
- Platinum 650 kg

The Elements Crisis

Over the past 30 years the world has encountered a new crisis: the elements crisis. Some elements are seen to be in increasingly short supply, while others, in the form of pollution, are turning up in the wrong places – and causing havoc in the process. Nothing alerted people to the new realities more than the first oil shock of 1973–1974.

Until 1973, the world's consumers forgot – if, indeed, they ever knew – that they were spending energy capital accumulated over many millions of years. They forgot that they were exploiting Nature's literally "unrepeatable offer". OPEC had its own reasons for shocking its clients out of their complacency, but in doing so it did the world a long-term service.

The most pronounced effects of the energy crisis were in the developing countries, where commodity exports bought ever-less oil. In 1975, for example, a tonne of copper bought 115 barrels of oil; six years later it bought half as much. Furthermore, the poorer nations have been less successful in reducing their oil dependence, leaving them acutely vulnerable to further oil shocks. During the 1991 Gulf crisis their economies were particularly hard hit by the unprecedented daily oil price fluctuations that rocked the global economy. The problem was compounded by the declining oil output from the former USSR, US, and the North Sea. The Middle East's share of the oil market increased from 27 percent in 1990 to nearly 30 percent in 2003 and oil is no longer the stable, cheap resource it once was.

If we continue consuming oil at present rates, known reserves will be depleted in 40 years. New extraction techniques will squeeze more oil from production wells. But the more we spend on winning the oil, the higher its eventual price in a market containing many substitute energy sources. Oil, in short, may run out faster in terms of what we can afford than of what is physically available.

New major players are affecting demand and world markets, too. In the early 1990s, China's oil production was fairly level with consumption, but by 1993 the country was reliant on imports. Ten years later, China's consumption of 5.9 million barrels a day far exceeded production of 3.4 million barrels a day. With huge increases projected elsewhere in the developing world, the global demand for oil could reach 120 million barrels per day by 2025 (cf. 78 million in 2003). If the average Chinese used as much oil as the average American, China would require a sixth more oil than the entire world produced each day in 2003. Oil (like grain) will be high on China's import agenda in the coming decades and the US could find itself up against stiff competition.

The oil crisis

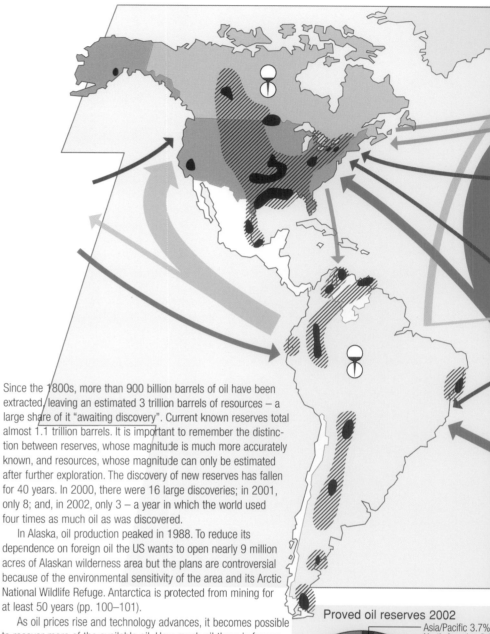

Since the 1800s, more than 900 billion barrels of oil have been extracted, leaving an estimated 3 trillion barrels of resources – a large share of it "awaiting discovery". Current known reserves total almost 1.1 trillion barrels. It is important to remember the distinction between reserves, whose magnitude is much more accurately known, and resources, whose magnitude can only be estimated after further exploration. The discovery of new reserves has fallen for 40 years. In 2000, there were 16 large discoveries; in 2001, only 8; and, in 2002, only 3 – a year in which the world used four times as much oil as was discovered.

In Alaska, oil production peaked in 1988. To reduce its dependence on foreign oil the US wants to open nearly 9 million acres of Alaskan wilderness area but the plans are controversial because of the environmental sensitivity of the area and its Arctic National Wildlife Refuge. Antarctica is protected from mining for at least 50 years (pp. 100–101).

As oil prices rise and technology advances, it becomes possible to recover more of the available oil. How much oil there is for use is thus a function not only of the absolute amount present, but also of its price and the level of technology. The availability of oil is also a function of politics since the resources are very unevenly distributed (pie charts, right). The map (above) shows regional oil consumption per capita in 2002, location of proven reserves, the lifetime of those reserves at current consumption levels, and prospective areas for oil and gas. The arrows plot the trade in oil between nations, not detailed shipping movements.

The fossil-fuel era

In 2003, fossil fuels (oil, coal, and natural gas) accounted for 83% of the world's primary energy consumption. By the end of this century, only coal will still be abundant, even though we have used as much coal since World War II as had previously been used in the whole of human history. Production of oil has peaked in many oil-producing nations, including the US (in the 1970s) and UK (late 1990s). The oil depletion curve covers only conventional sources. Oil sand and shale could more than double the total amount of oil available, though with additional production costs. Some oil firms are investing heavily in solar and wind energy.

Proved oil reserves 2002

Middle East 65.4%
Asia/Pacific 3.7%
North America 3.6%
Africa 7.4%
Europe/Eurasia 9.3%
Latin America 10.6%

Oil production 2002

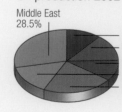

Middle East 28.5%
Asia/Pacific 10.7%
North America 13.7%
Africa 10.6%
Latin America 14.4%
Europe/Eurasia 22.0%

Oil consumption 2002

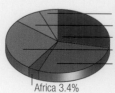

Middle East 5.9%
Latin America 8.4%
North America 27.9%
Asia/Pacific 28.1%
Europe/Eurasia 26.3%
Africa 3.4%

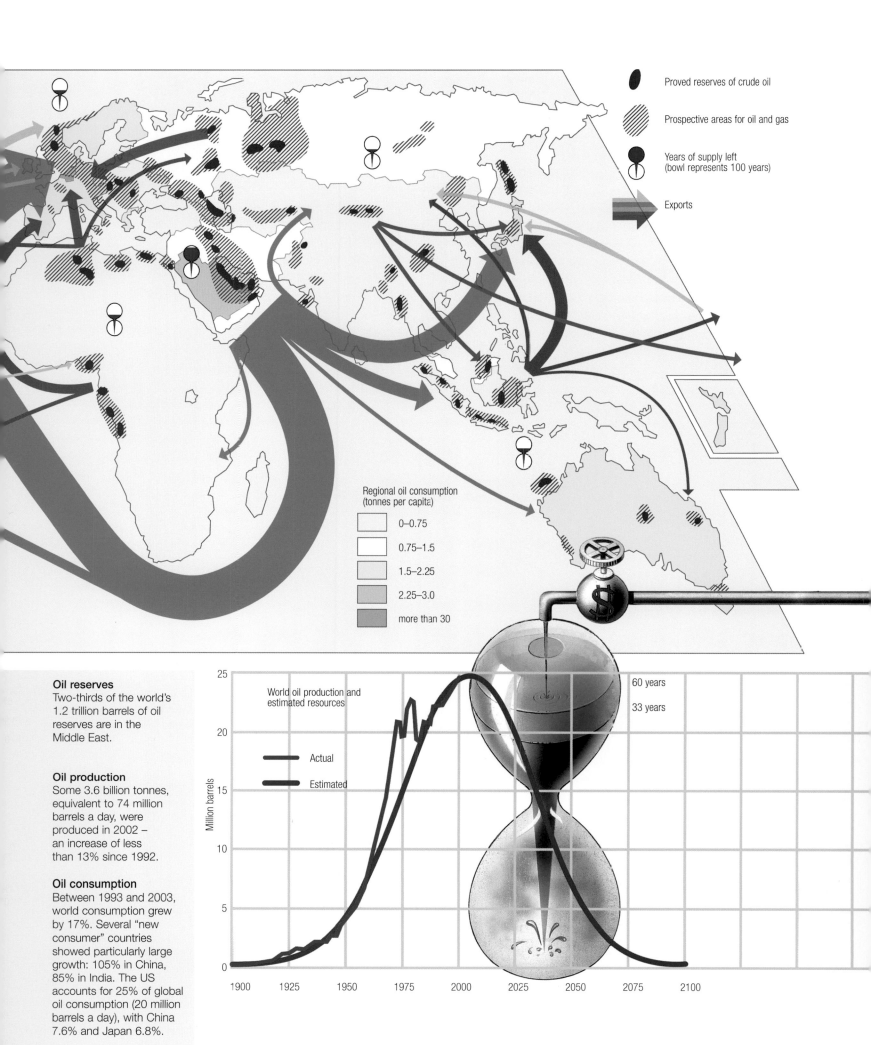

Proved reserves of crude oil

Prospective areas for oil and gas

Years of supply left
(bowl represents 100 years)

Exports

Regional oil consumption
(tonnes per capita)

0–0.75

0.75–1.5

1.5–2.25

2.25–3.0

more than 30

Oil reserves
Two-thirds of the world's
1.2 trillion barrels of oil
reserves are in the
Middle East.

Oil production
Some 3.6 billion tonnes,
equivalent to 74 million
barrels a day, were
produced in 2002 –
an increase of less
than 13% since 1992.

Oil consumption
Between 1993 and 2003,
world consumption grew
by 17%. Several "new
consumer" countries
showed particularly large
growth: 105% in China,
85% in India. The US
accounts for 25% of global
oil consumption (20 million
barrels a day), with China
7.6% and Japan 6.8%.

World oil production and
estimated resources

Actual

Estimated

60 years

33 years

Million barrels

25

20

15

10

5

0

1900   1925   1950   1975   2000   2025   2050   2075   2100

The other energy crisis

Almost three billion people worldwide rely for energy on wood, charcoal, or other biomass (dung, crop residues). In many developing countries, especially where the poorest third of humankind live, fuelwood dominates daily life, as increasing amounts of time and labour are spent in finding it and carrying it home. People often cut trees faster than the timber stock replenishes itself. Moreover, their growing numbers and the increasing human densities spread the problem further afield. As a result, a potentially sustainable wood-gathering activity becomes destructive and, ultimately, unsustainable.

The fuelwood issue, in fact, is a classic instance of how impoverished people in the developing world can find themselves obliged to destroy tomorrow's livelihood in order to secure today's essentials. They do it not out of ignorance. They do it out of tragic compulsion. If it has to be bought, the price can account for a large share of a family's cash income. For many families, it now costs as much to heat the supper bowl as to fill it.

More than half of all wood cut worldwide each year is used as fuel for cooking and heating, around 90 percent of it in the developing world. Fuelwood and charcoal production accounts for over 90 percent of the wood harvested in Africa, 80 percent in Asia, and 70 percent in Latin America. The effects of fuelwood shortages are most severe in impoverished areas, where alternatives are inaccessible or unaffordable. More than 2 billion people worldwide are still without access to electricity (pp. 144–45).

Shortages of fuelwood and charcoal are especially severe in Central America, Sub-Saharan Africa, and parts of Asia. For many in the developing world, then, the energy crisis does not devolve into a debate on how to limit the electricity consumed in a gadget – orientated home. It strikes directly at the struggle to keep body and soul together.

We have already seen (p. 42) how deforestation brings a tide of troubles in its wake. Unless we devise a response to this great and growing energy problem, we can expect that the number of people overcutting an already thin resource will increase pressures on forests. In the case of fuelwood deficits, there are some added woes. An estimated 800 million poor seek substitutes in materials such as dung – a case of diverting from fields (in the form of natural fertilizer) to hearth (in the form of fuel), reducing crop production. Or they utilize crop wastes which could otherwise be used as natural fertilizers or livestock fodder.

The implications of fuelwood shortages are tremendous, and the longer the damage continues, the harder it will be to find long-term solutions.

In the hothouse

The Earth is naturally protected by gases, notably CO_2 and water vapour, that absorb radiation. They serve to retain some of the sun's warmth through what is commonly referred to as the "greenhouse

The fuelwood crisis

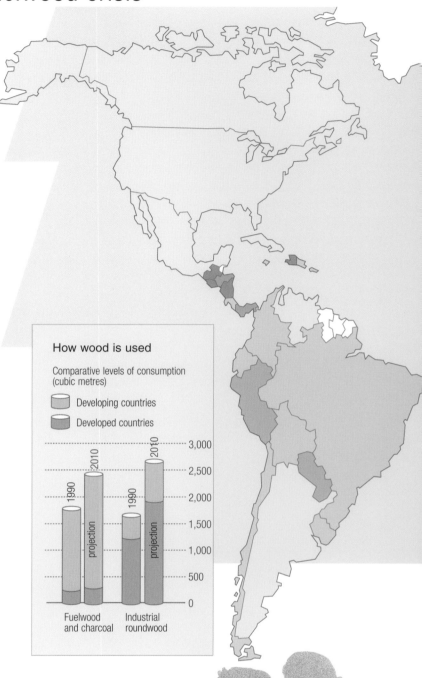

How wood is used

Comparative levels of consumption (cubic metres)

Developing countries

Developed countries

Fuelwood and charcoal — 1990, 2010 projection

Industrial roundwood — 1990, 2010 projection

Need, availability and the impact on women, health, and education

Shortages are acute in the arid and semi-arid areas of Africa. In Sub-Saharan Africa many women and children have to trek long distances in search of fuelwood, then carry their heavy loads (sometimes up to 20 kg) back to burn the wood in an inefficient cookstove. Poor ventilation leads to smoke inhalation which causes respiratory diseases and 2.5 million premature deaths worldwide each year. Heavy loads expose women to spinal and uterine problems. Girls are often kept away from school in order to assist with fuelwood gathering, depriving them of literacy and job opportunities.

A vicious spiral

Virtually all the trees within a radius of 70 km of Ouagadougou (capital city of Burkina Faso in the Sahel) have been consumed for fuelwood. Scarcity is worst in the ecologically fragile drylands and highlands where loss of tree cover leads to flooding, soil erosion, and the silting up of riverbeds or dams. The search for alternative fuels leads to the burning of dung that would otherwise return fertility to the soil. This reduces crop yields, forcing farmers to clear more forest to maintain food supplies. This, in turn, reduces the availability of fuelwood and results in another twist down the vicious spiral (right).

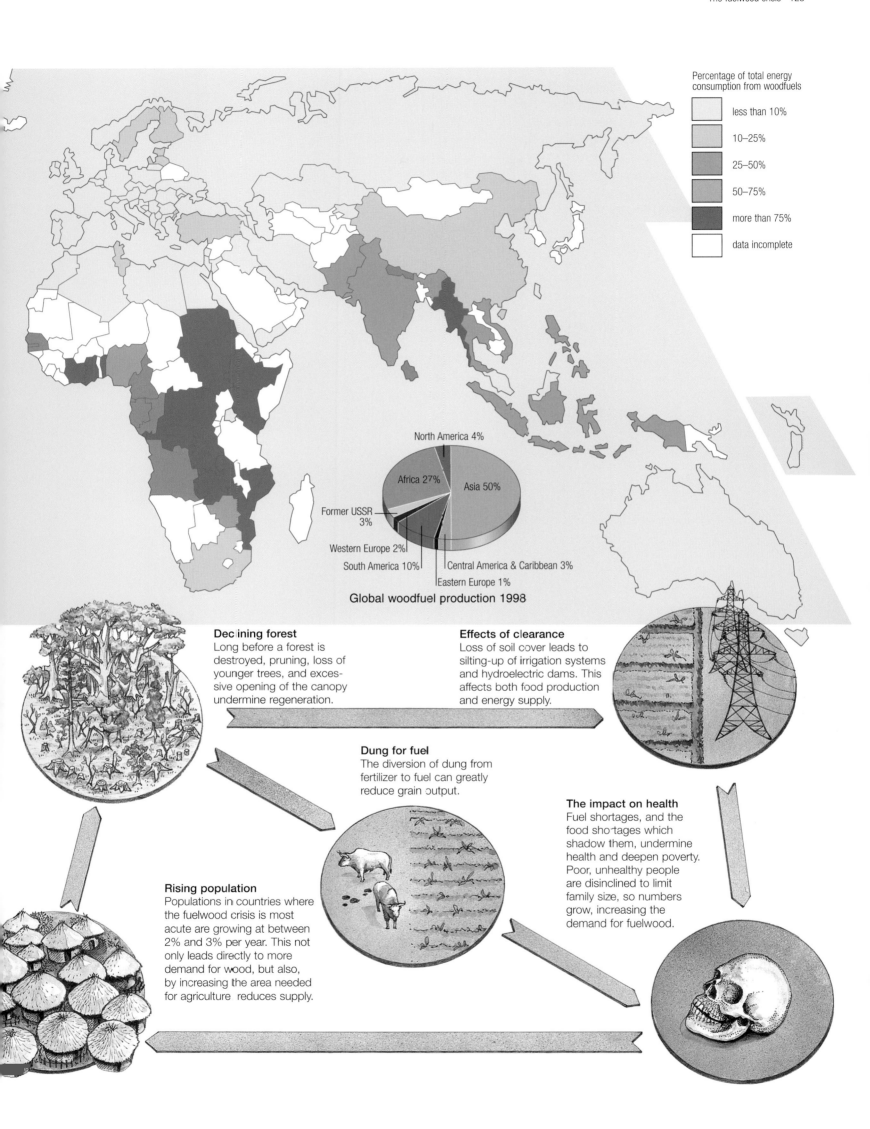

Percentage of total energy consumption from woodfuels

less than 10%

10–25%

25–50%

50–75%

more than 75%

data incomplete

North America 4%

Africa 27%

Asia 50%

Former USSR 3%

Western Europe 2%

South America 10%

Eastern Europe 1%

Central America & Caribbean 3%

Global woodfuel production 1998

Declining forest
Long before a forest is destroyed, pruning, loss of younger trees, and excessive opening of the canopy undermine regeneration.

Effects of clearance
Loss of soil cover leads to silting-up of irrigation systems and hydroelectric dams. This affects both food production and energy supply.

Dung for fuel
The diversion of dung from fertilizer to fuel can greatly reduce grain output.

The impact on health
Fuel shortages, and the food shortages which shadow them, undermine health and deepen poverty. Poor, unhealthy people are disinclined to limit family size, so numbers grow, increasing the demand for fuelwood.

Rising population
Populations in countries where the fuelwood crisis is most acute are growing at between 2% and 3% per year. This not only leads directly to more demand for wood, but also, by increasing the area needed for agriculture reduces supply.

effect". Without these gases, the Earth's surface temperature would be far cooler and hostile to life.

In the early Earth, carbon dioxide accounted for over 70 percent of the atmosphere. In addition, the sun was about one-quarter less powerful. So it was carbon dioxide and other "greenhouse gases" that kept the temperature warm enough for life. Over many aeons, the sun has grown warmer, but temperatures have remained acceptable because carbon dioxide concentrations have steadily declined. So the human-induced increase in atmospheric carbon dioxide since the onset of the Industrial Revolution is essentially the reversal of a natural trend. In 1750, the carbon dioxide concen-

tration was about 280 parts per million by volume (ppmv), whereas today it is around 375 ppmv, and is projected to be somewhere between 450 ppmv and 550 ppmv by 2050. This points to a steady warming of the planet's climate, with the potential of large-scale disruptions for the world's biotas, agriculture, and sea levels (pp. 126–27).

About 6.4 billion tonnes of carbon are added to the global atmosphere each year due to fossil-fuel burning. A further 1.6 billion tonnes is due to deforestation and other land-use changes, and fuelwood burning. The main carbon emitters are industrial countries dependent on fossil fuels. China and India, among other countries, are also becoming major

The greenhouse effect

Incoming radiation
Of the incoming short-wave solar radiation, only 24% hits the Earth's surface directly, 3% of which is promptly reflected back into space. The rest gets caught up in the Earth's atmosphere, where it is scattered back to space (25%), deflected to the surface (26%), or simply absorbed (25%).

2001 373 ppmv
1960 317 ppmv
1750 280 ppmv

CO$_2$ levels in the atmosphere have increased by 31% from 1750 to 2002. Before the last century, CO$_2$ levels had not risen above 300 ppmv at any time in the past 100,000 years. Between 1960 and 2002, they rose by 18% from 317 ppmv to 373 ppmv.

Total outflow of energy
3+25+67+5=100

Incoming solar radiation

25%

100%

3%

Outgoing terrestrial radiation

67%

5%

Energy absorbed by atmosphere
25+109+29=163

Energy re-radiated from atmosphere
96+67=163

CO$_2$ plays a key role in determining the Earth's climate. It lets through most of the incoming short-wave radiation from the sun, but traps and retains much of the long-wave radiation that the Earth radiates out into space. The net effect is to keep the Earth's surface at a higher temperature than if CO$_2$ were not present in the atmosphere. This is the "greenhouse effect".

The Earth has remained at a relatively stable temperature, and one suitable for life to flourish, for billions of years. Gaian scientists argue that life on Earth has moulded the environment, just as the changing environment influenced the evolution of life in a manner that actively promotes life. The carbon cycle is one of the most important aspects of this interaction. Carbon is released to the atmosphere by volcanic activity, respiration, and decay, and now by human activity. Plant life removes carbon from the air and "fixes" it in living cells. Burial of dead organisms removes carbon from the system. Two major CO$_2$ "sinks" are the oceans and certain forests. The latter can fix 1–2 tonnes of carbon per sq. km of land area per year. Hence, there is a further reason to reduce deforestation and accelerate reforestation.

24%

26%

Outgoing radiation
The Earth, being cooler than the sun, emits its energy in longer wavelengths (infrared). Because the atmosphere is largely opaque to these wavelengths, they bounce back and forth between the surface and atmosphere. So the equivalent of 109% of incoming solar radiation is absorbed, and 67% is re-radiated into space.

96%

109%

29%

114%

Absorbed at surface
24+26-3=47

Lost from surface
114+29-96=47

Latent and sensible heat

Latent heat (24%) and sensible heat (5%) are two significant energy flows which are absorbed by the atmosphere.

emitters. Of these eight billion tonnes, roughly three billion tonnes are taken up by the oceans and the same by terrestrial ecosystems. This leaves an annual net addition to the atmosphere of two billion tonnes of carbon a year.

Carbon dioxide is singled out as the main problem pollutant because it is so ubiquitous and the largest single contributor to greenhouse-related warming (64%). It is also the least susceptible to major reduction in a politically and economically acceptable manner. Other human-influenced "greenhouse gases" include methane, accounting for around 19% of global warming, CFCs (6%), other halocarbons (5%), and nitrous oxide (6%). Although carbon dioxide is regard-

ed as the most potent source, methane absorbs radiation 23 times more effectively, and CFCs do so 15–16,000 times more. (CFCs were banned in industrial countries in 1996 and developing countries must follow suit by 2010.)

Between 2001 and 2025, global carbon emissions are projected to rise by more than half, with much of the increase expected in the developing world where emerging economies portend large increases in fossil-fuel consumption. Hence, there will still be substantial increases in global carbon, despite increased efforts on the part of industrialized countries to lower their own emissions and undertake carbon trading.

Global emissions

The distribution of greenhouse gas emissions by country is a matter of sharp controversy. The US is clearly the biggest polluter, accounting for nearly 25% of all CO_2 emissions, followed by China with 13.5% and Russia with 6.2%. More difficult is the analysis of deforestation sources, and of rice production where methane is the major pollutant. The Earth has a capacity to absorb greenhouse gases, and many in the developing world are questioning how this capacity should be shared between countries. Their view is that the rich North has usurped this capacity through its industralization, and that the countries of the South are emitting gases well within their "share" – and need to continue to emit before they get their development paths on to a sustainable track.

The greenhouse gases (GHGs)

CO_2's main sources are fossil-fuel combustion, wood burning, deforestation, and land-use change generally. Methane is very difficult to control because it is associated with emissions from cattle and other ruminants, from rice paddies and other wetlands, and from leaks in the gas and coal industries. The CFCs and other halogenated compounds are mostly linked to refrigerants, foam production, and fire retardants (now being supplanted by hydrofluorocarbons due to the destructive effect CFCs and hydrochlorofluorocarbons (HCFCs) have on the ozone layer). Nitrous oxides are associated with fossil-fuel combustion, the use of fertilizers, and land-use change (especially forest destruction). Low-altitude ozone is created by the action of sunlight on aerial pollutants, notably from car exhausts and industry. The pie chart (right) gives the relative contributions to the warming.

Contribution of different gases to global warming, 1997

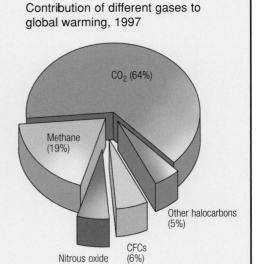

CO₂ (64%)
Methane (19%)
Other halocarbons (5%)
CFCs (6%)
Nitrous oxide (6%)

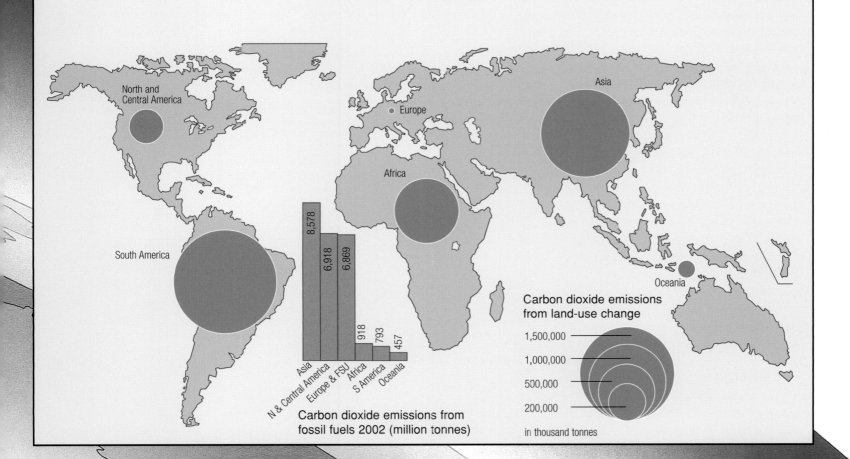

North and Central America

Asia

Europe

Africa

South America

Oceania

8,578
6,918
6,869
918
793
457

Asia
N & Central America
Europe & FSU
Africa
S America
Oceania

Carbon dioxide emissions from fossil fuels 2002 (million tonnes)

Carbon dioxide emissions from land-use change

1,500,000
1,000,000
500,000
200,000

in thousand tonnes

The effects of global warming

Since 1950, temperatures have shown a global increase of 0.65°C. Since records began in the 1800s, ten of the 16 hottest years have occurred since 1990, with 2003 the second hottest. Scientific estimates from the Intergovernmental Panel on Climate Change (IPCC) suggest a range of global warming from 1.4°C–5.8°C by 2100, with a best guess of around 2.5°C. Over the last 100,000 years of glacial advance and retreat, the global temperature does not appear to have fluctuated by more than 3° or 4°C.

For sea-level rise, the best estimate is a global increase of 0.09–0.88 metres by 2100. This will affect densely populated coastal areas, and in time lead to the inundation of whole islands, such as the Maldives (where two-thirds of the land is less than one metre above sea level) and Pacific atolls. Particularly vulnerable are large coastal cities and crowded agricultural regions, such as river deltas in the South. At least 26 million people in Bangladesh and over 70 million in coastal China will be at risk.

In the agriculture field, there will be gainers and losers. Because average temperatures are expected to increase more near the poles than near the equator, the shift in climate and agricultural zones will be more pronounced in high latitudes. The geography of migrating food production will result in very different trading patterns and possible territorial conflicts. More northerly and southerly regions, rather poor in agricultural output, could become more productive. Higher yields in some areas may compensate for decreases in others – but then again they may not, particularly if today's major food exporters, such as the US, suffer serious losses.

Human health may prove to be equally significant. Global warming will enable malaria and other tropical scourges to spread beyond their usual haunts, and when they attack human communities in, say, southern Europe, they will encounter "targets" that have long lost any residual resistance. The costs of health care will rise and impoverished countries with poorly developed health provision will suffer greatly.

Scientists agree that human activities are changing the climate, though it is difficult to put a "price tag" on either climate change or on policies to prevent it. If the Earth's surface warms as predicted, however, billions of people are likely to become more vulnerable to more drought, famine, and flooding. The money spent on taking action now could be viewed as an insurance premium for protection against a hard-to-measure but potentially devastating risk.

Ozone layer depletion

Climatic change and ozone depletion are chemically connected. Both are global in extent: there is no hiding place from their effects. One of the main greenhouse gases of the past few decades has been the chlorofluorocarbon (CFC) group, and the formulations CFC 11 and CFC 12 – used in

Climate chaos

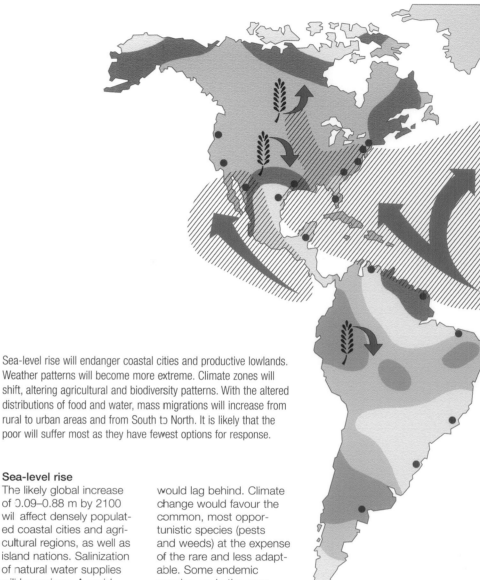

Sea-level rise will endanger coastal cities and productive lowlands. Weather patterns will become more extreme. Climate zones will shift, altering agricultural and biodiversity patterns. With the altered distributions of food and water, mass migrations will increase from rural to urban areas and from South to North. It is likely that the poor will suffer most as they have fewest options for response.

Sea-level rise

The likely global increase of 0.09–0.88 m by 2100 will affect densely populated coastal cities and agricultural regions, as well as island nations. Salinization of natural water supplies will be serious. A rapid melting of the West Antarctic ice sheet, the release of vast stores of frozen methane (a potent greenhouse gas) in the tundra of the North, and reversal of the Gulf Stream represent devastating scenarios.

Refugees

The impact will be most noticeable in regions already vulnerable to variations in rainfall and temperature, and will create a new burst of refugees amongst the most destitute, thus adding to social burdens in recipient nations. In a globally warmed world there could be 250 million "environmental refugees" (pp. 200–201).

Biodiversity

Climatic zones could shift several hundred kilometres towards the poles, whereupon flora and fauna would lag behind. Climate change would favour the common, most opportunistic species (pests and weeds) at the expense of the rare and less adaptable. Some endemic species, as in the case of South Africa's Cape Floristic Province hotspot, would have little alternative but to migrate into the sea.

Unpredictable weather

Direct association between atmospheric warming and greater extremes of weather is difficult to prove, but we should surely plan for more extreme weather patterns. What chance, for instance, that during the hurricane season in the Caribbean, a storm will not bypass Miami (one has come close already) but will actually strike the city? In Europe, two days of flooding in 2002 forced 450,000 people to evacuate, and a heat wave in 2003 killed 35,000 people, ten times as many as perished during the 9/11 attack. Since 1980 there have been almost 11,000 weather-related disasters leading to 575,000 deaths and costs of $1 trillion.

Agricultural changes

The impact on agriculture depends crucially on the speed of the onset of climate change, and the scope for adaptation in crop and livestock genetics and water management. There may be severe effects in some regions, especially those least able to adjust. Grain could become almost as valuable a commodity as oil in terms of national security.

Reducing the impact

The Kyoto Protocol set specific reduction targets for the highest GHG-emitter (Annexe 1) nations to be accomplished between 2008 and 2012. The US, which emits a quarter of the world's CO_2, has so far refused to ratify.

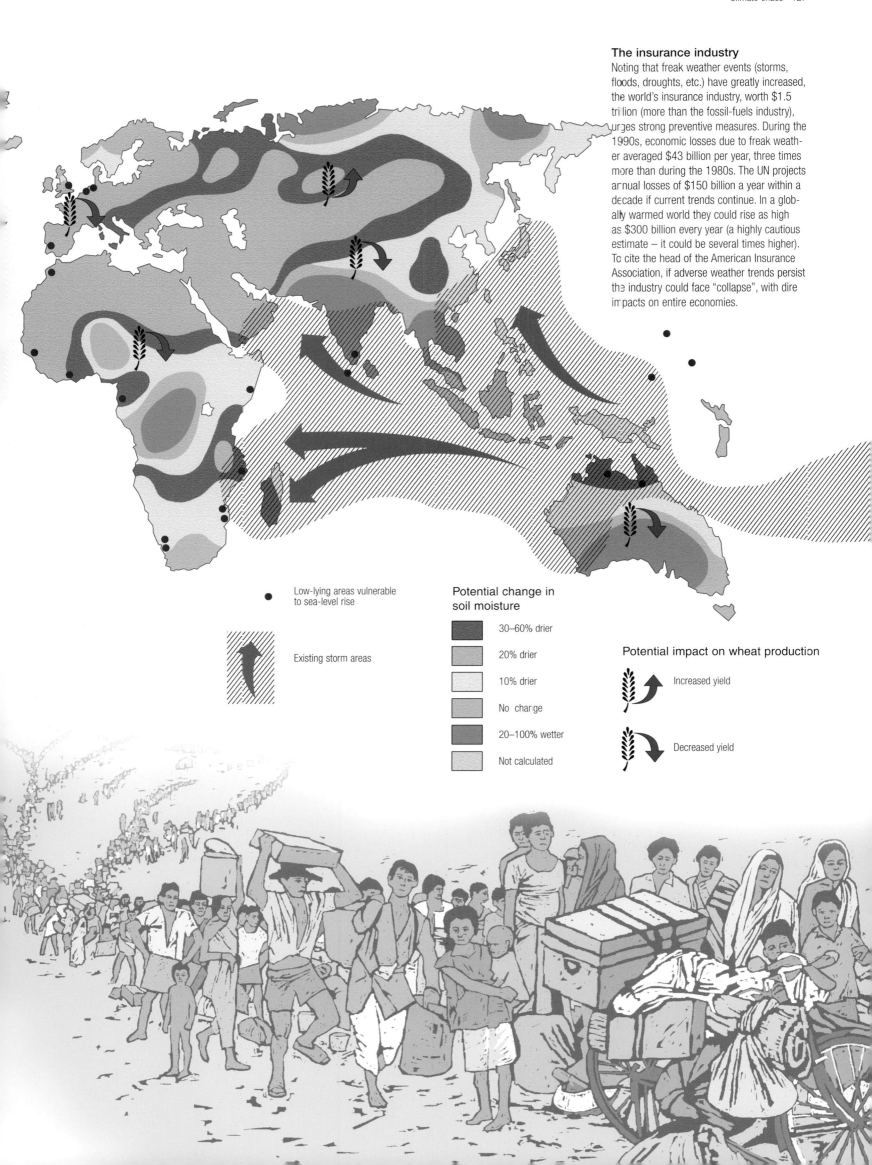

The insurance industry
Noting that freak weather events (storms, floods, droughts, etc.) have greatly increased, the world's insurance industry, worth $1.5 trillion (more than the fossil-fuels industry), urges strong preventive measures. During the 1990s, economic losses due to freak weather averaged $43 billion per year, three times more than during the 1980s. The UN projects annual losses of $150 billion a year within a decade if current trends continue. In a globally warmed world they could rise as high as $300 billion every year (a highly cautious estimate – it could be several times higher). To cite the head of the American Insurance Association, if adverse weather trends persist the industry could face "collapse", with dire impacts on entire economies.

- Low-lying areas vulnerable to sea-level rise

Existing storm areas

Potential change in soil moisture
- 30–60% drier
- 20% drier
- 10% drier
- No change
- 20–100% wetter
- Not calculated

Potential impact on wheat production
- Increased yield
- Decreased yield

refrigerants and air-conditioning – are also the most active ozone destroyers.

The ozone layer is found in the stratosphere 15–50 kilometres above the Earth's surface. It acts as a shield, absorbing high-energy ultraviolet (UVB) radiation which is hazardous to life.

In the early 1970s, James Lovelock first identified the build-up of CFCs in the atmosphere, these being manmade chemicals whose active life is over 70 years. Concern for the effect of CFCs on stratospheric ozone mounted until the first clear evidence of ozone depletion emerged in 1984 when British scientists in Antarctica found an area as big as the US contained next to no ozone. This is the notorious "ozone hole", the result of complex chemical reactions in a slow-moving, circumpolar vortex where the interaction of the chemicals, spring sunshine, and ice crystals become very effective ozone destroyers.

In September 2003, the Antarctic ozone hole measured 28 million square kilometres, almost matching the record set in September 2000, and its thinnest level (i.e. 50 percent below the pre-ozone hole period of 1964–1976) peaked near 18 million square kilometres, two-thirds the size of the ozone hole. The hole extends to southern South America, a southern sector of Australia, and the tip of South Africa. While there are signs that CFCs have levelled off in the stratosphere and are decreasing in the lower atmosphere, scientists predict it will take several decades for the ozone hole to stop forming.

The relative warmth of the Arctic is the main reason why a similar ozone hole does not form over the North Pole, though some scientists suggest that the after-effects of large volcanic eruptions could lead to ozone loss over the Arctic within just a few decades.

Ironically, because ozone heats the outer atmosphere, its loss should contribute to a reduction in the global warming effects of CFCs. The relationship is by no means a cancelling out of opposing effects, however, and the loss of stratospheric ozone as an ultraviolet shield is altogether seen as a more serious threat than its contribution to atmospheric cooling. Increased exposure to UV-B radiation will give rise to increased numbers of human skin diseases and cataracts. It may also damage agriculture and aquatic ecosystems, and even accelerate climate change.

Atmospheric pollution

In both developed and developing countries, air pollution is a common hazard. Concerns over acid rain first arose in the 1960s with the emergence of dying lakes and forest damage in parts of the northern hemisphere – including Sweden, Norway, parts of central Europe, and the eastern part of North America. Thousands of lakes are now lifeless and numerous species of plants, birds, and insects have declined in acidified non-aquatic areas such as forests. Defoliation was worst in Byelorussia,

Holes in the ozone map

A thin veil of ozone high in the Earth's atmosphere protects life below from the portion of the sun's ultraviolet radiation that would otherwise stress many forms of life. The consequences of increased exposure to radiation represent threats to human health, as well as to animals, plants, and the environment. This ozone veil has been damaged by the release of CFCs and other ozone-destroying chemicals once popular in aerosol sprays, plastic foams, refrigerants, and fire-fighting equipment. In 1987, and following scientific agreement on ozone-layer cepletion, the world's governments moved at instant speed (just 9 months) to conclude a treaty to eliminate these ozone-destroying chemicals. Under the resulting Montreal Protocol, more than 180 nations have committed to phasing out the use of nearly 100 ozone-damaging substances. By 2000, the consumption of such substances had been reduced by 85% and the Protocol's Multilateral Fund had disbursed more than $1 billion in 114 developing countries to assist them with their phase-out process. The phase-out is complete in developed countries and developing countries have until 2010. Meantime, and as the three-stage phase-out period began in developing countries, a black market for these chemicals has sprung up in southern Asia and certain other developing countries.

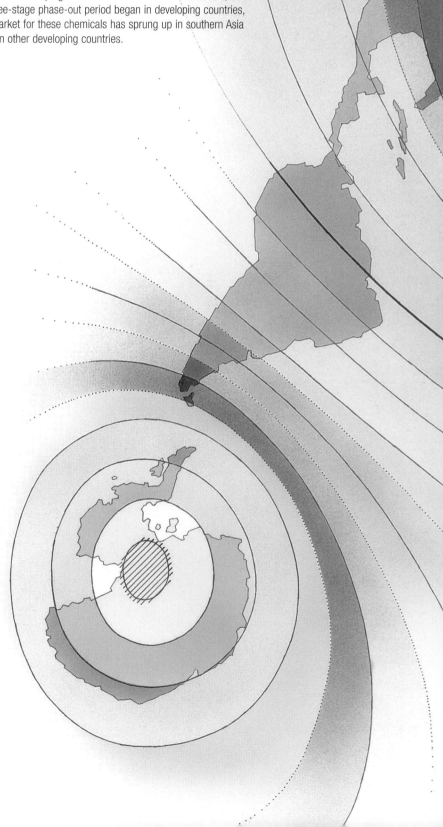

Possible consequences of ozone depletion
Human health: skin cancer (melanoma and nonmelanoma); premature ageing of the skin; cataracts and other eye damage; immune system suppression.

Wildlife: the effect of increased UV-B on wildlife and single-celled organisms in shallow water is potentially severe. Worst-case increases affect crop production and kill marine phytoplankton, which plays a vital role in absorbing excess CO_2, meaning that their loss adds to global warming.

Climate: effects on terrestrial and aquatic biogeochemical cycles could alter both sources and sinks of greenhouse and chemically important trace gases.

The ozone "hole"
Not a "hole" as such, but a thinning of the protective layer of gas high in the earth's atmosphere. It forms in August and can last for several months until increasing temperatures cause a weakening of winds surrounding the South Pole and a mixing of ozone-poor air inside the vortex with ozone-rich air outside. This coloured satellite image (below), taken on September 11th 2003, shows the ozone hole (dark blue) above Antarctica. It is 28.2 million sq. km in size. The yellow parts of the image show where the ozone levels are highest.

Percentage change in ozone per decade

0%	− 9%
− 1%	− 10%
− 2%	− 20%
− 3%	− 30%
− 4%	− 35%
− 6%	Localized total depletion of up to 95%
− 8%	

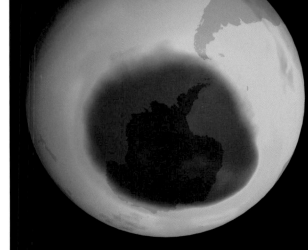

Czechoslovakia, and the UK, while the economic loss of European forests as a whole was estimated at around $30 billion annually. If other impacts were added, such as the effects on human health and buildings, the cost could have been almost ten times as much.

Acid rain comes from millions of tonnes of sulphur dioxide (SO_2) and nitrogen oxides (NOx) released into the atmosphere by industry and vehicles. These gases react with water in the air to form acid rain, mist, and snow, which fall to the ground in areas far removed from the point of origin, often in another country. The phenomenon has hit worst in parts of Canada and the US, and central and northern Europe – though today sectors of China, Japan, Russia, Nigeria, and Venezuela are all under attack from this silent scourge.

Acid rain has become something of an umbrella term and other air pollutants are included under its heading. Some of the most important are volatile organic compounds (VOCs), associated with vehicle emissions and the chemical industry, ammonia, and ozone near the Earth's surface, formed by the action of sunlight on NOx and VOCs. Ozone pollution can increase human susceptibility to infection and respiratory disease, reduce certain crops and damage natural vegetation. In large urban areas, ozone mixes with other pollutants to create smog, which afflicts cities worldwide.

Various international measures have been introduced to tackle air pollution, the first being the Convention on Long-Range Transboundary Air Pollution (CLRTAP) in 1979, ratified by 49 European and North American countries (pp. 146–47). There have been eight subsequent protocols covering sulphur dioxide emissions, NCx, VOCs, international cost-sharing for the monitoring of air pollutants, heavy metals, and persistent organic pollutants (POPs). All but one – the 1999 Protocol to Abate Acidification, Eutrophication, and Ground-level Ozone – have entered into force. Other initiatives in Europe include the Restrictions on Hazardous Substances (RoHS) under which manufacturers wishing to do business in Europe are required to produce lead-free products.

Between 1990 and 1998, European emissions of sulphur dioxide fell by 44 percent, NOx by 21 percent, and ammonia by 15 percent, but the problems associated with air pollution in the past are not going to disappear any time soon. Even in developed countries, forest recovery is likely to take decades, and water bodies will continue to be affected, if not by acid rain, then by a host of other contaminants. This applies in developed and developing countries alike.

Death from polluted water
Water is a supposed fount of life, yet each year around five million people (13,700 a day) die from diseases caused by unsafe drinking water, lack of

The invisible threat

Acid rain, including sleet and snow, is produced primarily by the release of SO_2 and NOx into the atmosphere. The chief sources of such emissions tend to be electrical generating plants, industrial boilers, and large smelters. Gases that are vented into the air by tall smokestacks get caught up in prevailing winds where, in the course of transport over land, they are transformed into cilute solutions of sulphuric and nitric acids. Their deposition as acid rain can have dire effects on ecosystems. Acidified water leaches important plant nutrients out of the ground and activates heavy metals, such as cadmium and mercury, contaminating water supplies.

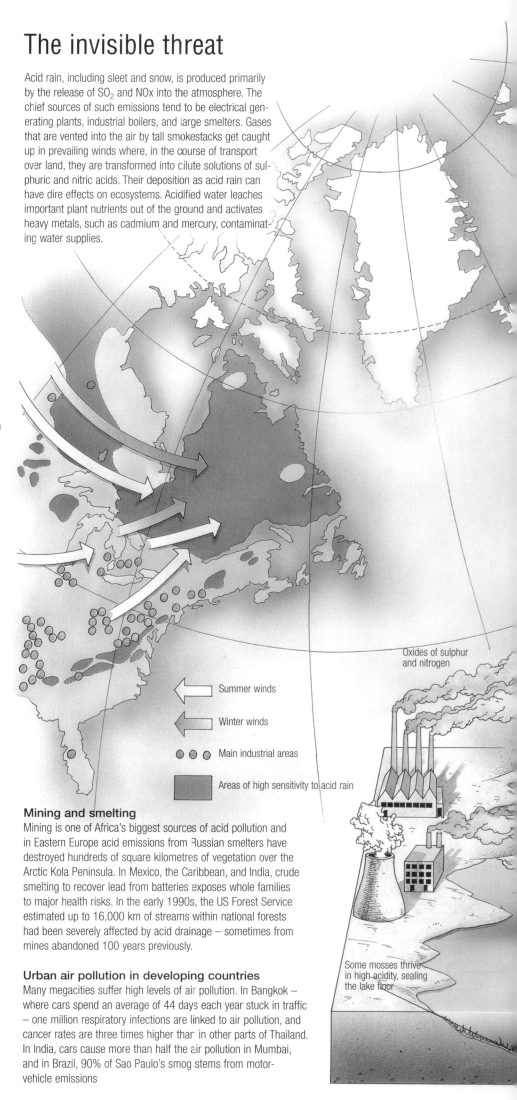

Oxides of sulphur and nitrogen

Summer winds

Winter winds

Main industrial areas

Areas of high sensitivity to acid rain

Some mosses thrive in high acidity, sealing the lake floor

Mining and smelting
Mining is one of Africa's biggest sources of acid pollution and in Eastern Europe acid emissions from Russian smelters have destroyed hundreds of square kilometres of vegetation over the Arctic Kola Peninsula. In Mexico, the Caribbean, and India, crude smelting to recover lead from batteries exposes whole families to major health risks. In the early 1990s, the US Forest Service estimated up to 16,000 km of streams within national forests had been severely affected by acid drainage – sometimes from mines abandoned 100 years previously.

Urban air pollution in developing countries
Many megacities suffer high levels of air pollution. In Bangkok – where cars spend an average of 44 days each year stuck in traffic – one million respiratory infections are linked to air pollution, and cancer rates are three times higher than in other parts of Thailand. In India, cars cause more than half the air pollution in Mumbai, and in Brazil, 90% of Sao Paulo's smog stems from motor-vehicle emissions

Acid rain

Acidification once ranked among the most serious threats to the environment in the northern hemisphere. Although there has been much progress in controlling acid emissions in certain developed countries, the threat is still very real in many other countries of the world, notably in Asia, where SO_2 emissions are projected to triple between 1990 and 2010.

The map shows areas of North America and Europe that are particularly sensitive to acid rain, typically with thin, rocky topsoils. Acid deposition travels from e.g. the Ohio Valley in the US to southeastern Canada, and from e.g. the UK, Germany and Poland in industrialized Europe to Scandinavia, Switzerland, Austria and the Netherlands.. Of Sweden's 85,000 lakes, 10,000 are so acidified that sensitive organisms no longer survive in them, and 7000 have to be kept alive by liming. Large expanses of forest soils in the south-west of the country are acidified. This is of major concern to a country almost two thirds forested, and the eventual recovery will be slow. Acidification once ranked among the most serious threats to the environment in the northern hemisphere. Although there has been much progress in controlling acid emissions in certain developed countries, the threat is still very real in many other countries of the world, notably in Asia, where SO2 emissions are projected to triple between 1990 and 2010 (see China below).

...and in China

In the 1980s, acid rain occurred in regions covering 1.7 million sq. km. By the 1990s, its effects were felt over 3 million sq. km. South and southwest China has become the third largest acid rain-prone region in the world after northern Europe and North America. Today, one-third of China is affected, with economic losses of at least $13 billion a year.

Oxides combine with water to become acid rain

Acid snow at high altitudes

Snows melt damaging soil, where trees grow

Fish die

Developing world worst

Pressure groups in the North successfully campaigned for the reduction of lead in petrol. Following the phase-out, lead emissions decreased sharply during the 1980s and early 1990s. By 2002 they were 93% lower than in 1982. Many developing-world countries, however, still have intolerably high levels of lead in the atmosphere. In Bangkok, Mexico City, and Jakarta, exposure has stemmed largely from car exhausts. In India, while new passenger cars with catalytic converters can use unleaded gasoline, many of the country's cars are old, and the two/three-wheeled vehicles (mostly powered by two-stroke engines) run on leaded gasoline. According to the World Bank the costs of converting to unleaded gasoline are outweighed 5–10 times by health and economic benefits.

Smog in Los Angeles

The geographical features of Los Angeles serve to promote the formation of smogs. Wind patterns and the surrounding mountains create conditions for the formation of temperature. inversions, which occur when a layer of warm air overlies a layer of cooler air, preventing air pollution from escaping. The smog in Los Angeles is seen as a brownish orange haze between May and October. Smog is composed of a number of chemicals, notably ozone and peroxyacetyl nitrate (PAN), both of which are extremely harmful to plants – the impact on southern California ecosystems has been dramatic . Smog can also cause respiratory problems.

Sunlight

Inversion

City of Los Angeles

San Gabriel mountains

Lead emissions and lead poisoning

Lead is added to petrol to improve its combustion, then released to the air as fine particles. It has also been used in the manufacture of water pipes, computer monitors, paint, certain PVC products, and lead-acid batteries. While lead emissions from gasoline additives have now declined to zero in many industrial countries, one fifth of the petrol sold today is leaded. In many countries of Africa and western and southern Asia, unleaded gasoline is still scarce. As of February 2005 only 36 countries were signatories to the 1998 Aarhus Protocol relating to the phase-out of leaded petrol, and only 24 have ratified. The maximum lead intake for an average 70 kg human is about 6 µg/kg body weight/day. Children absorb lead more easily, so a maximum for them is 1.2 µg/kg/day. There is, however, no safe level for children, and 130-200 million worldwide may suffer the harmful effects of lead poisoning.

Ground-level ozone

According to the American Lung Association, more than half of the US population (160 million people) are threatened by air heavily polluted with ozone or tiny particles of soot. Most of the top 10 worst-polluted counties are in California, and Los Angeles continues to top the list for ozone pollution, which occurs when hydrocarbons and nitrogen oxides combine with heat and sunlight. This is referred to as ground-level ozone, or smog.

sanitation, and insufficient water for hygiene – many of these diseases are preventable. Diarrhoeal diseases alone take the lives of more than two million children each year and leave many more underweight, mentally and physically stunted, a prime target for deadly diseases, and unable to take part in everyday activities such as school. According to water expert Peter Gleick of the Pacific Institute in Oakland, California, "if no action is taken to address unmet basic human needs for water, as many as 135 million people will die from these diseases by 2020". Even if (now looking unlikely) the Millennium Development Goal of "halving the proportion of people without sustainable access to safe drinking water and improved sanitation" by 2015 is met, then "34–76 million people will perish". These are the awful statistics we should bear in mind while we brush our teeth and shower each morning, using as much water in that short time as someone thousands of miles away has to make out on for all purposes all day.

The 1980s was declared the "Water Supply and Sanitation Decade" when unprecedented efforts brought improved water sources to 1.3 billion people and sanitation to 750 million. Yet the efforts had to fight against population growth. In 1980, 1.8 billion people lacked access to safe drinking water and 1.7 billion to adequate sanitation. By 1990, these figures were 1.1 billion and 2.4 billion and remained much the same by 2000.

All too often, there is not enough water in developing-world communities for basic domestic needs, so it tends to be used time and again. It ends up as thoroughly dirty water, an ideal habitat for pathogens, including carriers of disease.

The health costs of inadequate sanitation in developing countries is enormous. In one way or another, water is implicated in diseases (right), including trachoma, schistosomiasis, malaria, elephantiasis, typhoid, cholera, infectious hepatitis, leprosy, yellow fever, guinea worm disease, poliomyelitis, trypanosomiasis, and probably worst of all, diarrhoea. Every hour, 230 children die from diarrhoeal diseases: if this scourge could be eliminated, we would see an end to much of the malnutrition that is associated with more than half of child deaths in the developing world, and that fosters many other diseases.

In addition to water-related deaths, many times more sufferers are left grossly debilitated, hardly able to do a decent day's work. There are still further costs. If inadequate or unsafe water causes child deaths on a vast scale, such deaths stimulate birth rates, which in turn perpetuate population growth.

Hazardous chemicals: a growing problem

We have fostered an insidious spread of toxic chemicals and metals in quantities that are very hard to detect. DDT, dieldrin, and other pesticides

Water that kills

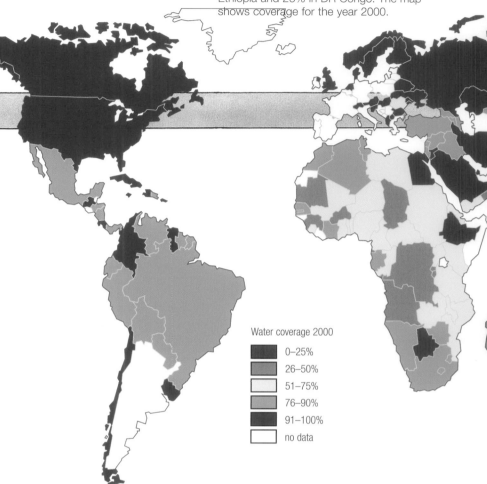

Between 1980 and 2000, 2.4 billion people gained access to safe water and 600 million to improved sanitation. Despite this huge effort, Sub-Saharan Africa still lags way behind with safe water rates as low as 12% in rural Ethiopia and 26% in DR Congo. The map shows coverage for the year 2000.

Water coverage 2000
- 0–25%
- 26–50%
- 51–75%
- 76–90%
- 91–100%
- no data

The provision of clean, adequate supplies of water and the safe disposal of human waste represent one of the most urgent problems facing the developing world today. In the absence of such facilties, rivers, lakes, and ponds serve both as a source of "clean" water for human settlements and as a sink for all their wastes.

In practical terms, lack of drinking water means no supply with n several hundred metres; lack of sanitation means no bucket latrine or pit privy, let alone sewerage system. So ponds and rivers are the main sources of drinking water – and the main sites for impromptu toilets.

Three-quarters of all diseases in developing countries arise from polluted drinking water. Of these, diarrhoea is the most serious since it increases the risk of death for severely malnourished children. Malnutrition is associated with more than half of child deaths and two-thirds of deaths from diarrhoea are associated with malnutrition. Water contaminated with arsenic or fluoride is also a problem in some countries.

There are several types of water-related disease: they either breed in or are spread by water. The main types of water-related diseases are classified (right), with specific examples alongside.

Dangerous waterholes

The rural poor, who lack access to standpipes, have little choice but to collect their water from rivers, streams, ponds, mud holes or wells. Millions of women and children often spend 6–8 hours a day walking long distances to bring home a few litres of dirty water.

Chemical contamination of drinking water

Some contaminants arise from natural processes, others from human activities, such as industry and mining. In Bangladesh, 97% of the population depend on 2.5 million tubewells for drinking water, many of which contain dangerous levels of arsenic. In 2004, Bangladesh topped a list of 23 countries exposed to arsenic, with 85 million people at risk from skin cancers, kidney and liver failure, respiratory problems – even death. 24 million have suffered levels of arsenic poisoning. In India in 2003, pesticides were found in 17 brands of bottled water. In 1996, one billion litres of bottled water were sold in Asia, projected to reach 5 billion by 2006.

At low levels, fluoride in drinking water can aid dental health but in excessive amounts it can be toxic, causing mottling of teeth enamel. In China alone, 30 million people suffer from chronic fluorosis and in England, 750,000.

In the 1990s, diarrhoea "killed more children than all the people lost to armed conflict since the Second World War". Human Development Report, 2003, UN Development Programme

Safe water and sanitation – for whom?

In developed countries, most people have ample, clean, piped water and mains sanitation. In developing countries, 1 in 4 people does not have easy access to water, and half lack proper sanitation. During the 1980s "Drinking Water Supply and Sanitation Decade" the supply of drinking water and sanitation facilities increased noticeably, but today (2004) the situation is still dire with 1.2 billion lacking access to safe water and 2.4 billion to adequate sanitation.

Global sanitation coverage

	1990	2000
Urban	81%	86%
Rural	28%	38%

Global water coverage

	1990	2000
Urban	94%	94%
Rural	64%	71%

"The number of water taps per 1,000 persons is a better indication of health than the number of hospital beds."
World Health Organization

"Half the world's hospital beds are occupied by people suffering from water-borne diseases."
UN Environment Programme

Deaths
thousands per year   1,000   100

Infections
100 millions per year

100 thousands per year

Water-breeding insects such as mosquitoes, carry malaria, filariasis, and yellow fever. Blackflies transmit river blindness.

Malaria carried by mosquitoes, affects 300 million people and kills more than 1 million each year. Sub-Saharan Africa suffers 90% of all deaths – mostly children under 5. Two-fifths of the world's population are at risk. More than 40 million workdays are lost each year, with an economic cost exceeding $120 billion.

Water-washed diseases such as trachoma, leprosy, and conjunctivitis, are spread by insufficient water for personal hygiene.

Trachoma is a contagious inflammation of the inner lining of the eyelids, often causing blindness. 150 million cases (6 million already blind); 500 million at risk. Improved water and sanitation could reduce the infection rate by one quarter.

Water-based diseases are carried by invertebrates – schistosomiasis by snails, guinea worm by a crustacean waterflea.

Schistosomiasis has been linked to the spread of irrigation canals and dams, a prime habitat for snails. 200 million affected in 70 countries, 20 million severely so. At least 500 million at risk. Improved water and sanitation could reduce the infection rate by three-quarters.

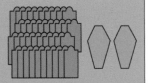

Waterborne diseases are spread by drinking/washing in contaminated water and include typhoid, dysentery, and cholera.

Diarrhoea 4 billion cases each year. Leads to dehydration, causing over 2 million deaths (mostly children under 5). Repeated attacks exacerbate malnutrition, reducing food intake and absorption. Correct management, e.g. oral rehydration therapy (ORT) could save 1.8 million lives per year.

Defective sanitation aids the spread of intestinal worms. Eggs are excreted in human faeces. The infection cycle begins on swallowing the eggs.

Hookworm larvae usually enter humans by burrowing through the soles of the feet. Heavy infestations cause death in children. Intestinal helminths affect 1.5 billion people and can lead to malnutrition, anaemia, and poor growth.

are suspected of causing cancer and birth defects, among other problems. Polychlorinated biphenyls (PCBs), used in plastics and electrical insulators, are unusually toxic and persistent, and affect the vital organs, as do heavy metals. Commercially, we use up to 100,000 synthetic chemicals and each year we introduce another 1,000. While most are likely to pose little risk for the environment or human health, some are toxic even in minute quantities.

Certain pollutants, especially pesticides and PCBs, accumulate in fatty tissues of organisms. As they pass up food chains – from, say, microscopic creatures in water bodies, to plants, and finally to

eaters of plant-eaters such as humans – they become concentrated. This bio-amplification can magnify their effective dosage by 10–100 times at each stage. These persistent organic pollutants (POPs) occur in traces in every one of us. Released in one part of the world they can, through evaporation or deposit, travel with the atmosphere to locations far away from their source.

Pesticides are particularly prominent. Without some measure of pesticidal protection (could be by natural, organic, or other "safe" chemicals), many crops could decline by as much as half due to insect

Widening circle of poison

Our planetary environment is a closed system. Persistent materials pumped into the air, dumped in rivers and seas, or hidden from view in landfills do not simply disappear. The waste by-products of our industrial processes are a growing threat, sometimes an international threat. Until recently, the developed world has regularly shipped to the developing world chemicals classified as too dangerous for use in their country of origin. The irony is that the same chemicals (especially pesticides) can return to the developed world on imported bananas, coffee beans, tomatoes, and other foods.

After several decades of use (or abuse?), there is increasing concern about the cumulative effects of exposure to toxic chemicals. Irreversible health effects can occur at levels below those currently considered "safe". Pesticides and dioxins can affect immune and reproductive systems, while heavy metals, such as lead and mercury, can affect cognitive and physical development. While leaded petrol has been phased out in many developed countries, lead is still a major environmental health problem (pp. 130–31). According to the Worldwatch Institute, the costs of childhood lead poisoning in the US are estimated at $43 billion per year.

These toxic chemicals affect everyone everywhere. Even in the cold Arctic, the Inuit people have been found to have the highest human concentrations of industrial chemicals and pesticides on Earth. Children are particularly susceptible to toxins in the environment since they eat more, breathe more and drink more per pound of body weight than do adults – all while their brains and nervous systems are still developing.

Heavy metals and the body
Arsenic, beryllium, cadmium, cobalt, chromium, iron, lead, nickel, selenium, titanium, and zinc are carcinogenic. Mercury and lead attack the central nervous system, nickel and beryllium damage the lungs, antimony can lead to heart disease, and cadmium causes kidney damage.

Polyvinyl chloride (PVC)
Up to 30 million tonnes of PVC is made a year, involving ethylene dichloride and vinyl chlorine monomer. Both chemicals are highly carcinogenic, with links to organ damage.

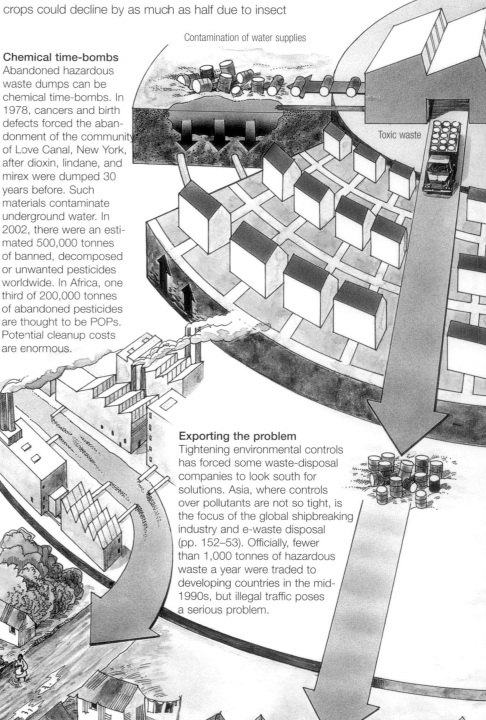

Contamination of water supplies

Toxic waste

Chemical time-bombs
Abandoned hazardous waste dumps can be chemical time-bombs. In 1978, cancers and birth defects forced the abandonment of the community of Love Canal, New York, after dioxin, lindane, and mirex were dumped 30 years before. Such materials contaminate underground water. In 2002, there were an estimated 500,000 tonnes of banned, decomposed or unwanted pesticides worldwide. In Africa, one third of 200,000 tonnes of abandoned pesticides are thought to be POPs. Potential cleanup costs are enormous.

Exporting the problem
Tightening environmental controls has forced some waste-disposal companies to look south for solutions. Asia, where controls over pollutants are not so tight, is the focus of the global shipbreaking industry and e-waste disposal (pp. 152–53). Officially, fewer than 1,000 tonnes of hazardous waste a year were traded to developing countries in the mid-1990s, but illegal traffic poses a serious problem.

Toxic landfills

People living near toxic waste dumps are increasingly vulnerable to certain cancers, birth defects, and low birth weights. Mothers who have lived within 3 km of a landfill are said to have one-third higher risk of giving birth to a baby with congenital defects than those living 3–7 km away.

and disease damages. Worldwide, over two million tonnes of pesticides are used each year – one-fifth in the US. Between 1997 and 2000, the US exported 30,000 tonnes of banned, severely restricted, or never registered pesticides, more than half directly to the developing world and much of the rest routed through European ports – possibly finally ending up in developing countries. Since 2000, however, exports have been limited by two treaties governing trade.

During the 1990s, as much as 300–500 million tonnes of hazardous waste were generated worldwide each year – at least fourth-fifths of it in the industrial countries. In South and Southeast Asia, hazardous waste dumping from industrialized countries has caused significant problems. Now, however, thanks to the Base Convention, only about 10 percent of all hazardous waste crosses international borders, mostly between the industrial nations themselves, though Canada's less restrictive laws meant that in 1999 the country took in twice as much hazardous waste from the US as did Mexico.

More than 150 nations have negotiated a treaty to phase out a "dirty dozen" – nine pesticides, PCBs, dioxins, and furans. In 2004, the Stockholm

DDT

Wholesale use of DDT pollutes rivers and accumulates in the fatty tissues of living organisms. As small fish are eaten by big fish, which, in turn, are eaten by birds (and people), so the ratio of DDT to body weight increases through bio-amplification. For example, Arctic cod and turbot have DDT concentrations 1,000 times higher per gram of fat than the zooplankton on which they feed. DDT is still one of the most commonly detected pesticides in mothers' milk. While banned in more than 60 countries, many tropical countries still depend on DDT to control malaria.

Perfect produce?
Northerners attach great importance to the appearance of imported food. A large share of all agrochemicals serve to improve the look of vegetables and fruit.

Polychlorinated biphenyls (PCBs)

PCBs are synthetic chemicals present in industrial materials, such as inks, paint additives, coolants, and lubricants. Once PCBs enter the environment, bio-amplification occurs. Samples taken in the North Sea, for example, indicated a PCB concentration of 0.000002 parts per million (ppm) in seawater, but 160 ppm in marine mammals. In the late 1970s, North America placed a ban on PCB manufacture and import following concerns about its impacts on health and environment. Tests on animals revealed a link to cancer, and adverse effects on the immune, reproductive, nervous, and endocrine systems.

Developing-world toxics
The riskiest chemicals are often exported to developing countries. Those designed to control insect pests, weeds, rodents, fungi, and other organisms, can, if incorrectly applied or stored, be extremely harmful to humans. Associated risks are cancer, birth defects, damage to the nervous system, and the functioning of the endocrine system.

Endocrine disrupting chemicals (EDCs)

In the 1980s and 1990s, fish and beluga whales in the Great Lakes showed cancers, ulcers, and other deformities. Florida alligators developed mis-shapen reproductive organs. Similar problems in gulls, mink, eagles, and other animals have been blamed on chemicals that mimic hormones and disrupt the endocrine system. EDCs are found in insecticides, herbicides, fumigants, fungicides, detergents, paints, resins, and certain plasticizers. Between 1997 and 2000 the US exported 165,000 tonnes of pesticides associated with endocrine disruption.

Chemical-resistant pests
Some 500 insect and mite species, 270 weed species, and 150 plant diseases have become resistant to one or more pesticides, requiring higher quantities or more toxic chemicals to restrict them: more toxic to humans as well as pests.

Pesticides
Global production of pesticides (insecticides, herbicides, fungicides, rodenticides) has grown 42-fold since 1945 – more than $30 billion worth are now applied to crop fields, household lawns, in buildings and in treatment of insect-borne diseases, such as malaria. Birds, in particular, are affected: one-tenth of 670 million birds exposed to pesticides on US farmlands each year are killed.

Convention on persistent organic pollutants (POPs) finally entered into force. The treaty also focuses on measures to clean up decades-worth of hazardous waste now decaying and leaching chemicals into the environment. The Rotterdam Convention entered into force in 2004, too, requiring exporters trading in hazardous substances to first obtain the "Prior Informed Consent" (PIC) of importers before proceeding.

Nuclear energy – a failed promise?

The vision of cheap nuclear electricity may have evaporated, but many protagonists still believe that nuclear power provides the main hope for the abundant energy they see as critical for future social and environmental stability, notwithstanding the 1986 disaster at Chernobyl. An expanding nuclear industry, they argue, will reduce reliance on fossil-fuel burning and hence reduce the "greenhouse effect" (pp. 124–25). There are risks, they admit, but these must be traded off against potential benefits. During the 1960s and 1970s, energy utilities in the US, UK, Japan, France, the former USSR, and other countries committed huge financial and scientific resources to their nuclear development programmes.

Early predictions to the effect that nuclear power would provide 50 percent of the world's electricity by the end of the last century proved way off the mark. By 2002, 440 reactors in 31 countries supplied just 16 percent (and 11 percent of primary energy). By 2015, this share could fall to 13 percent

The nuclear dilemma

Far from providing a cheap and plentiful supply of energy that would satisfy demand for the foreseeable future, nuclear energy has provided us with an expensive energy source fraught with intractable technical problems and unacceptable environmental and health risks. Long-lived radioactive wastes cast a shadow which reaches across the generations. But although the nuclear industry is down, it certainly is not out (map, right). Some countries, including China (which wishes to reduce its dependence on polluting coal and plans to quadruple nuclear capacity by 2020), India, Russia, and South Korea still want to press ahead with nuclear power. In 2004, 30 reactors were under construction in 12 countries worldwide, including 4 in China (with another 4 planned), 9 in India, 6 in Russia, and one in South Korea (another 8 planned). Japan, lacking sufficient natural resources of its own, wants to provide 40% of its energy from nuclear by 2010. The country has 3 reactors under construction and another 13 planned, but recent public trust issues surrounding safety inspections may threaten them. Other countries including the US, Belgium, Sweden, Finland, Spain, and Germany are upgrading existing plants. In the US no new nuclear reactors have been ordered since 1978 and there are none under construction in Western Europe. Planned reactors in Iran and North Korea have raised concerns over nuclear weapons proliferation. The nuclear industry is not going to disappear, but is seen as a particularly high-risk option – not as the energy panacea originally promised.

A nuclear dead-end?

In 1974, the International Atomic Energy Authority estimated there would be 4,450 gigawatts (gw) of nuclear capacity worldwide in 2000. This was cut ninefold by 1986 and Chernobyl. Actual capacity in 2001 was 350 gw. Projections for 2015 and 2025 are 400 gw and 385 gw. Electricity companies are discovering it is cheaper and easier to encourage energy efficiency, and so reduce demand, than to build new capacity to meet growing demand. A dollar invested in energy efficient technology frees up several times more energy than a dollar spent on nuclear power: compact fluorescent light bulbs, for example, use less than one quarter as much electricity as traditional incandescents. The nuclear era may turn out to be unexpectedly short-lived.

Canada

USA

Mexico

31–75% of electricity generated by nuclear power

11–30%

0–10%

Brazil

Argentina

Terrorism

Warheads

Waste

Escalating plant costs

Citizens' movements

Risk of accidents

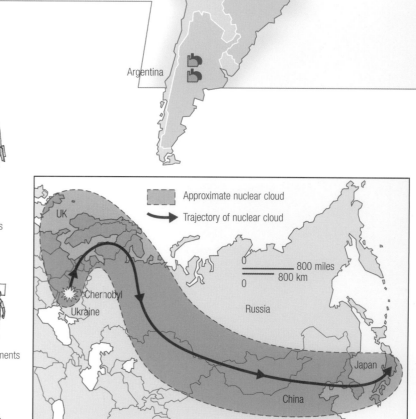

Approximate nuclear cloud

Trajectory of nuclear cloud

UK

Chernobyl
Ukraine

Russia

Japan

China

800 miles
800 km
0

(10.6 percent), though developing countries are expected to see annual four percent growth of nuclear-powered electricity between 2001 and 2025, with developing Asia likely to account for 95 percent of the total increase in the developing world.

Nuclear power is at a crossroads. Its portents are not propitious. It has fallen into its present doldrums through a number of factors: the environmental and health risks inherent in nuclear power stations, as revealed by a lamentable list of accidents; the problems of radioactive emissions and waste disposal, so far unresolved in convincing fashion; tighter government safety; the need for lengthy planning horizons and the large-scale investments required; the over-selling of its cause by the nuclear industry;

the proliferation of nuclear weaponry and terrorism; and the severe and pervasive reservations on the part of the public, inadequately addressed or even discounted by the industry.

A final problem, not one of the industry's making, is the challenge from clean and renewable energy sources, plus efficiency and conservation. Yet the debate about nuclear's future takes place against a background of two vital counterbalancing factors: the world's fast-growing need for more energy, especially electricity (two billion people worldwide still without access); and the imperative of reducing carbon dioxide emissions. Which of these two sets of determinants will predominate – will nuclear power fade or flourish?

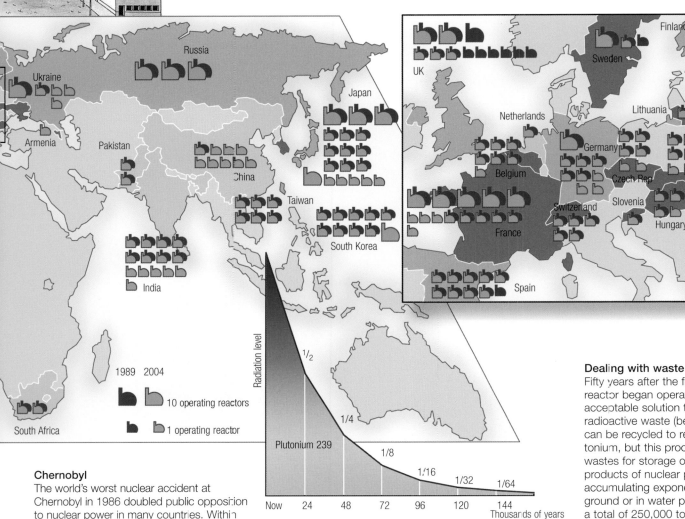

1989   2004

🏭 10 operating reactors

🏭 1 operating reactor

Chernobyl
The world's worst nuclear accident at Chernobyl in 1986 doubled public opposition to nuclear power in many countries. Within two days, radioactive clouds were carried by winds to the UK and Scandinavia, then moved eastwards across Siberia, China and Japan (map, left). Eastern Europe and Scandinavia were hit the hardest. The official death toll was put at almost 3,600, but the true total could have been more than 30,000. 400,000 people were forced to abandon their homes and 160,000 sq. km remain contaminated by radioactivity. Three-quarters of the radiation fell on Belarus, where thyroid cancer rates among children are 100 times higher than pre-accident levels. More than 3 million of Ukraine's population are still affected. Costs of the accident are estimated at more than $350 billion – possibly way more than the value of nuclear electricity ever generated in the former Soviet Union.

How long does radiation last?
Every radioactive substance has a "half-life" – the length of time it takes for half its radioactivity to die away. Some radioactive materials become safe relatively quickly: iodine 131, for example, has an 8-day half-life. After 50 days, its activity has dropped by over 90%. Nuclear reactors produce toxic wastes, including plutonium 239 with its half-life of 24,000 years (above). Even after 50,000 years, it will have lost only three-quarters of its radioactivity and still be lethal. But if plutonium 239's half-life seems long, consider uranium 238 with a half-life of 4.5 billion years.

Dealing with waste
Fifty years after the first commercial nuclear reactor began operating, there is still no acceptable solution to the problem of radioactive waste (below). Used fuel rods can be recycled to recover uranium and plutonium, but this process creates more wastes for storage or disposal. The by-products of nuclear power production are accumulating exponentially, stored underground or in water pools at nuclear plants – a total of 250,000 tonnes in 2001. Other radioactive waste problems include the tailings from uranium mining, and the emerging question of how to shut down old stations.

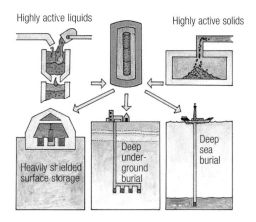

Highly active liquids

Highly active solids

Heavily shielded surface storage

Deep underground burial

Deep sea burial

Environmental conflicts

Run-down of environmental resources can lead to violence. In about a quarter of the 50-plus wars and other armed conflicts of recent times, environmental resources have figured prominently. More than five million people died in such resource-related conflicts during the 1990s, another six million fled to neighbouring countries, and as many as 15 million became displaced within their own countries.

The most important resource in this context is water, provided it is available in sufficient quality and quantity for all daily purposes. Everyone should enjoy it virtually as a human right, on the grounds that it is essential to many fundamental life processes.

The total of 1.2 billion people who do not have enough water is rising. By 2025, it could soar to three billion. Consider the challenge for India. Already several regions of this "wet" country are short of water. India is obliged by international treaties to send parts of the Ganges' flows to Bangladesh and parts of the Indus flows' to Pakistan. So serious is the situation that fully one quarter of India's grain harvest could eventually be put at risk through water shortages in its main breadbasket areas. Water wars ahead?

Worldwide, at least 180 million tonnes of grain, one-tenth of the global harvest, are produced by depleting water supplies. Since the average world grain consumption is a third of a tonne per person per year, this means that half a billion people are being fed by grain produced through unsustainable use of water. This applies especially to Asia, which supports roughly three-fifths of the world's people but has little over one-third of the world's renewable water.

In a still wider context, most of the 80 million people (2004) added to the world's population each year are in countries already short of water. At the same time, global grain demand has been growing steadily, and the 100-plus countries that import a good part of their grain are effectively importing water.

Many other environmental problems could cause resource conflicts: topsoil loss, spreading deserts, shrinking forests, grand-scale pollution, and global warming. We cannot respond to these new security threats through old-fashioned measures. We cannot resist an advancing desert by sending tanks against it. We cannot halt soil erosion by bombing it. We cannot stop acid rain with infantry. We cannot drive back global warming by launching missiles at it.

Yet however much interdependence is a built-in facet of our new world, we have yet to mobilize the political collaboration to reflect it. We simply do not recognize it as a strict fact of life. Regrettably, the changed outlook is not coming easily. The two most important features of our new world have nothing to do with conventional politics or economics, least of all with military strategies. First, no territory can support an indefinite increase either in its population or in its consumption of resources, let alone both; and second, that all mainstream policies of all governments assume that, on the contrary, it can.

Resource wars

Of more than 1,800 international water-related disputes during the last 50 years, fully one quarter were outright hostile, with 37 occasions when rival countries resorted to military violence. At least 51 countries within 17 international river basins are at risk of water disputes during the current decade. They include, notably, Israel and Palestine, who view water supplies as central to their negotiations: there is simply not enough water to satisfy all needs of both sides. Israelis receive 350 litres of water per person per day, compared to just 70 litres for the Palestinians. The WHO recommends a minimum of 100 litres per day.

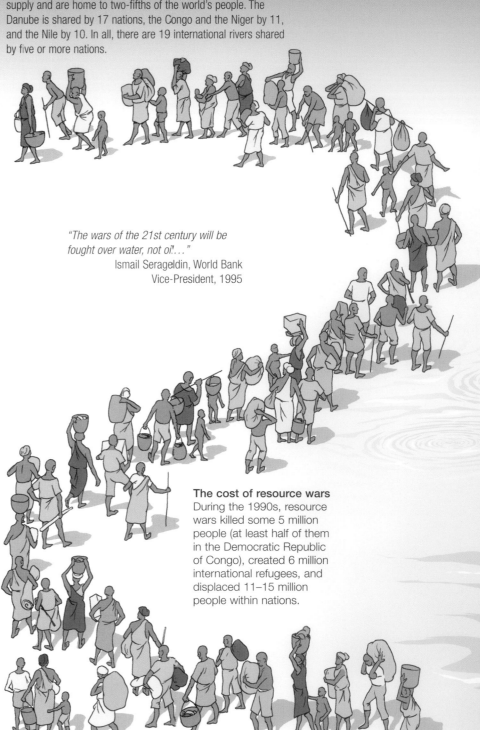

Water conflicts

Some 261 international rivers are shared by two or more countries. Their watersheds account for two-fifths of the world's freshwater supply and are home to two-fifths of the world's people. The Danube is shared by 17 nations, the Congo and the Niger by 11, and the Nile by 10. In all, there are 19 international rivers shared by five or more nations.

"The wars of the 21st century will be fought over water, not oil..."
Ismail Serageldin, World Bank
Vice-President, 1995

The cost of resource wars
During the 1990s, resource wars killed some 5 million people (at least half of them in the Democratic Republic of Congo), created 6 million international refugees, and displaced 11–15 million people within nations.

High-value resources stimulate conflict

Many developing countries highly dependent on resource royalties suffer corruption and/or unrest. In Angola, there have been long-running battles for control of the country's rich oil and diamond deposits, with a 1992–2001 bounty worth $4 billion. Angola is the world's fifth largest producer of non-industrial diamonds and the second largest producer of oil in Sub-Saharan Africa. Other conflicts have occurred in Sierra Leone and Liberia (diamonds), Congo (copper and uranium), Borneo and Cambodia (timber). Iraq has the world's third largest proven oil reserves.

The Aral Sea

The Amu Darya in Central Asia is being drained dry by upstream cotton farmers in Uzbekistan and Turkmenistan. Since the late 1960s, the Aral Sea has lost half its area and three-quarters of its volume – only the diminished flow of the Syr Darya keeps it from disappearing. Also gone are 20 of 24 fish species and a fish catch once totaling 44,000 tonnes a year and supporting 60,000 jobs.

Not enough water

One person in 5 lacks enough water for drinking, cooking, washing, and sanitation and uses no more water each day than a rich-world person uses with every toilet flush.

The Nile River

During colonial times two treaties gave extensive water rights to Egypt and Sudan. Egypt has the right to three-quarters of the 74 billion cu. m (bcm) available, and Sudan a quarter. However, the Nile tributaries, including the Blue Nile and the White Nile, flow through 8 other countries, none of which were included in treaty negotiations: Kenya, Uganda, Tanzania, Burundi, Rwanda, the Democratic Republic of Congo, Ethiopia, and Eritrea. Since 1959, all 10 countries have massively increased their human numbers, thus massively decreasing their per-capita water supply. Egypt's 72 million people of 2003 will likely exceed 100 million by 2025, by which time the population within the Nile Basin as a whole is expected to double. Egypt will have to cater for the needs of its additional people with increased withdrawals from the Nile – at the same time as the other countries in the basin will be looking for increased and secure supplies upstream. It will be hard to see how they can do it without breaching the 1959 treaty. Tanzania has already announced plans for a 168-km pipeline drawing water from Lake Victoria, yet Egypt can veto any plans that might threaten its Nile flows. In the 1980s, Boutros Boutros-Ghali declared "The next war in our region will be over the water of the Nile, not politics". According to the UN, other "flashpoints" in Africa include the Niger, Volta, and Zambezi basins.

Water disputes

Already there have been disputes between India and Bangladesh over the Ganges, and Brazil and Argentina over La Plata. Water conflicts – either between or within countries – increased from 5 per year in the 1980s to 22 in 2000. Conflicts relating to agricultural water in 23 countries incurred costs of $55 billion between 1990 and 1997. We can expect there will be many more instances, unless we can rise to the challenge in a cooperative spirit.

Sharing water sources

Many countries also share groundwater aquifers which supply half of global drinking water, two-fifths of industrial and one-fifth of agricultural water. China's Yellow River has dried up as far as 600 km inland due to heavy demand for industry and households. this leaves farmers without irrigation water and fishermen without a catch.

Potential for violence

Water disputes with marked potential for violence (map) include the Nile's flows through countries such as Uganda, Sudan, Ethiopia, and Egypt; the Tigris' and Euphrates' flows from Turkey to Syria and Iraq; the Mekong River's flows through Laos, Vietnam and Cambodia; and the Rio Plata's flows between Brazil and Argentina.

Turkey, Syria, Iraq
TIGRIS & EUPHRATES RIVERS

Israel, Syria, Jordan
FIVE JORDAN & SEA OF GALILEE

China, Laos, Cambodia, Vietnam
MEKONG RIVER

Egypt, Sudan, Ethiopia, Uganda
THE NILE

Brazil & Argentina
RIO PLATA

Area of conflict over access to water

Managing the Elements

When Thomas Edison founded the first electric utility, his intention was to sell illumination rather than electricity. People do not want electricity, oil, and gas, but the services they provide, such as heating, lighting, transport, and cooking. The challenge of the new energy path is to meet the demand for energy services as efficiently and as cleanly as possible. The way we manage energy needs to change from increasing energy supply to meeting energy demand. The sheer scale of our energy use makes the path of ever-more gas and oil fields and ever-more consumption of resources and pollution increasingly dangerous. Our ability to respond to the threat of global warming will depend on how quickly we are prepared to follow a different energy path of, first and foremost, the "clean and renewables", and above all, energy efficiency.

Harnessing renewable energy is not a new idea. The Greeks and Persians developed the principles of passive solar design 2,500 years ago. Modern technologies can vastly increase the efficiency with which renewable energy is harnessed. Solar collectors have special coatings to enable them to produce high temperatures even when the sun is hidden by cloud. Small hydropower plants have electronic governors to maintain stable output and operate under remote control. Modern wind turbines use the latest composite materials and computer-aided design, and can anticipate changing wind behaviour.

Renewables create more jobs than conventional energy industries because their capital requirements are more modest and their labour needs are greater. A renewable energy strategy would therefore be logical for developing countries with more spare labour than capital. This is all good news for pioneering economies. Although non-biomass renewables currently meet less than three percent of global energy demand, the technical potential of these inexhaustible and clean energy sources far exceeds total energy use.

Our energy-thirsty economies are demanding ever-greater amounts. Fortunately, this need not lead to one crisis after another. There are lots of ways for us to find the path forwards – and far from burdening our economies, it will often save us money. But the most productive way for us to meet our energy needs is by making better use of what we have. There is little point in going to all the expense and trouble of tapping renewable energy with low-impact technologies only to find it leaking from buildings and inefficiently used in appliances and vehicles. A determined drive to introduce energy efficient technology and behaviour in all sectors of the economy is the most vital component of the new energy path.

The new energy path

The hydrogen economy
The hydrogen fuel cell heralds the arrival of hydrogen-based economies. Hydrogen powers the fuel cell via an electrochemical process to convert hydrogen into electricity and heat. The fuel cell is twice as efficient as the internal combustion engine, and it emits nothing but water vapour. Hydrogen can come from many sources, including the electrolysis of water, using electricity from any source (such as wind power, solar energy, or hydroelectricity) to electrolyse the water. Already hydrogen is the fuel of choice for the new fuel-cell engines being developed by car makers around the world. Both Honda and Toyota manufactured the first fuel-cell cars in late 2002, followed in 2003 by Daimler-Chrysler and Ford. California now has several hydrogen stations. At Munich Airport, a hydrogen station fuels 15 airport buses with hydrogen-burning engines. Most ambitious of all, the Iceland government plans to convert its entire energy economy to hydrogen.

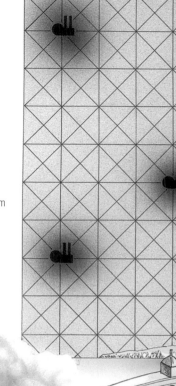

"Grid" system

The shape of the new system
In contrast to the massive, centrally controlled coal and nuclear plants which can take upwards of 10 years to plan and build, renewable sources can be small, local, and quick to develop, allowing cost-effective and flexible planning. Using diverse and decentralized renewable sources can minimize transmission and distribution losses, while strengthening the overall electricity grid. Reliability goes up and dependence on fossil fuel goes down.

The nuclear no-no
Nuclear power is eminently renewable but it is potentially one of the dirtiest of all energy sources due to its long-term (thousands of years) radioactivity. It is accident prone, and it is vulnerable to terrorists. It is simply uncompetitive: in the US, where the industry is no longer propped up with huge subsidies, no new plants have been commissioned for a whole quarter century.

High-energy/supply-side landscape
Today's dominant energy policy is tipped in favour of supply, justifying the building of new power stations, drilling of new gas fields, or opening of new oil pipelines. It bears no regard to people's actual needs, and meets what it considers to be an ever-increasing demand for energy through a complex, centralized distribution system, with highly polluting technologies.

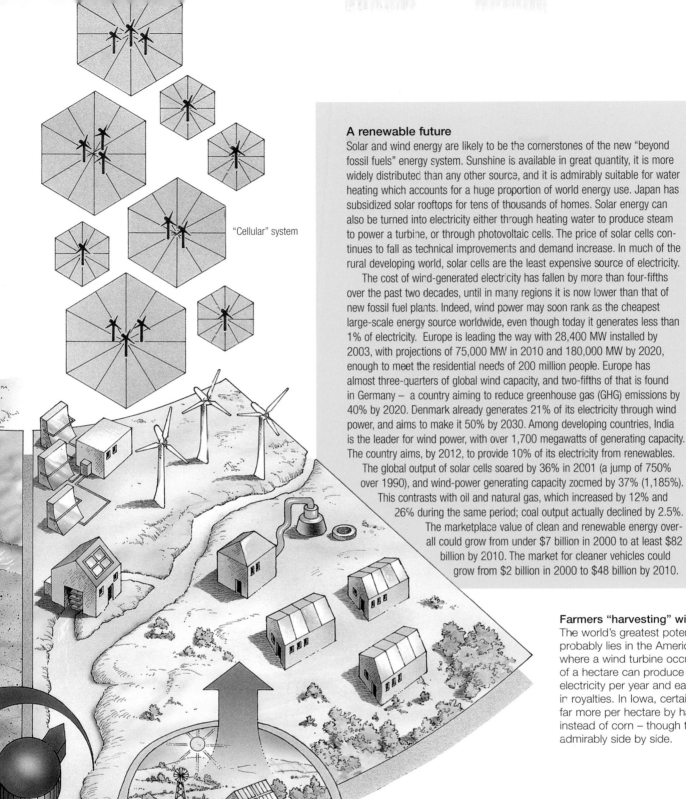

"Cellular" system

A renewable future

Solar and wind energy are likely to be the cornerstones of the new "beyond fossil fuels" energy system. Sunshine is available in great quantity, it is more widely distributed than any other source, and it is admirably suitable for water heating which accounts for a huge proportion of world energy use. Japan has subsidized solar rooftops for tens of thousands of homes. Solar energy can also be turned into electricity either through heating water to produce steam to power a turbine, or through photovoltaic cells. The price of solar cells continues to fall as technical improvements and demand increase. In much of the rural developing world, solar cells are the least expensive source of electricity.

The cost of wind-generated electricity has fallen by more than four-fifths over the past two decades, until in many regions it is now lower than that of new fossil fuel plants. Indeed, wind power may soon rank as the cheapest large-scale energy source worldwide, even though today it generates less than 1% of electricity. Europe is leading the way with 28,400 MW installed by 2003, with projections of 75,000 MW in 2010 and 180,000 MW by 2020, enough to meet the residential needs of 200 million people. Europe has almost three-quarters of global wind capacity, and two-fifths of that is found in Germany – a country aiming to reduce greenhouse gas (GHG) emissions by 40% by 2020. Denmark already generates 21% of its electricity through wind power, and aims to make it 50% by 2030. Among developing countries, India is the leader for wind power, with over 1,700 megawatts of generating capacity. The country aims, by 2012, to provide 10% of its electricity from renewables.

The global output of solar cells soared by 36% in 2001 (a jump of 750% over 1990), and wind-power generating capacity zoomed by 37% (1,185%). This contrasts with oil and natural gas, which increased by 12% and 26% during the same period; coal output actually declined by 2.5%. The marketplace value of clean and renewable energy overall could grow from under $7 billion in 2000 to at least $82 billion by 2010. The market for cleaner vehicles could grow from $2 billion in 2000 to $48 billion by 2010.

Farmers "harvesting" wind

The world's greatest potential for wind power probably lies in the American Great Plains, where a wind turbine occupying one-tenth of a hectare can produce $100,000 worth of electricity per year and earn the farmer $2,000 in royalties. In Iowa, certain farmers now earn far more per hectare by harvesting wind power instead of corn – though the two can operate admirably side by side.

Low-energy/demand-side landscape

The demand for electricity reflects the demand for the services it can provide – hot showers, clean clothes, data storage and retrieval, etc. Such a services-oriented perpective tips the energy demand–supply balance in favour of demand. Elecricity consumers are then better placed to make suppliers recognize their needs, and meet them in the most appropriate ways.

Cleaner fossil fuels

The transition to a renewable energy future will take time, so there remains the need to use fossil fuels for the foreseeable future. Acid emissions from coal-fired plants have been somewhat reduced by the fitting of flue gas desulphurization equipment, although the price paid for this is a reduced efficiency entailing the burning of more coal for the same amount of energy released. New power stations can use cleaner, more efficient technologies to reduce the amount of coal needed. Only about 40% of the energy released from burning fossil fuels provides useful service. The rest is lost as waste heat. By tapping this "waste" and piping it direct to homes and industry, the efficiency of modern plants can be raised to 80% as combined heat and power (CHP) schemes reduce the amount of fossil fuel needed (and hence carbon emissions). CHP is well established in many countries, ranging from small systems for single factories and hospitals to large power stations heating extensive residential districts in cities.

The fifth fuel

The shift to renewable energy technologies will take time, but our second energy option, energy efficiency, could be implemented quickly. Energy efficiency means producing the same final energy services – light, heat, transport, etc. – while using less energy to do so. In turn, this means less economic cost, less conflict over the siting of power plants, and, for many countries, less military or political cost to maintain access to foreign energy resources. Furthermore, energy efficiency offers the most direct, cost-effective method to counter global warming and air pollution.

Consider the humble compact fluorescent light bulb, much more efficient than conventional incandescents, since using less than a quarter as much electricity. Production soared 13-fold between 1988 and 2001, when the 1.8 billion bulbs in use lowered electricity needs by the output of 40 coal-fired power plants. Americans could save almost $2 billion per year if each household were to replace just three traditional bulbs with compact fluorescents.

The well-being of society is not inexorably tied to its level of energy consumption. True, for the 30 years following World War II, energy consumption seemed proportional to economic growth, but since we learned something about the real price of oil in 1973 and 1979, we have "gained more energy" through increased efficiency of use than through all new sources brought on stream.

The US has been saving $200 billion worth of energy per year compared with 1973 and its oil price hike, yet it is still wasting upwards of $300 billion a year, a total that is climbing steadily. Both Presidents Bush objected that the Kyoto Protocol would harm the American economy, ostensibly because it would mean a cutback on the fossil fuels that underpin many economic activities such as electricity generation and the car culture. Yet the best way for the US to meet its energy needs is through greater efficiency. Fortunately, the US is starting to wise up on energy. Its Energy Star programme sets an energy efficiency standard met by two-thirds of computers and monitors and by all laser printers. Meantime, Japan is two or even three times (depending on the sector) as energy efficient as the US, yet it could still do far better and thus save mountains of money for its economy.

Today's technologies could improve the efficiency of appliances by at least a third, and avoid more than half of projected consumption growth in the industrial world by 2030. In developing countries, people could save as much as three-quarters of their energy through a range of improvements in building insulation, cooking, heating, lighting, and electrical appliances.

Supplying energy to the South

Developing countries have begun to face up to the fuelwood crisis, but if they are to meet the entire challenge, they must plant trees several times faster as a whole, and in the worst-off areas between 15

An energy-efficient future

Energy efficiency vs. more energy

According to the USA's Alliance to Save Energy, the need for 800 new power plants between 2002 and 2020 could be reduced to less than 200. Adopting the household appliance efficiency standards agreed to by both the first Bush and the Clinton administrations would eliminate the need for 127 power plants. More stringent air-conditioner efficiency standards would eliminate the need for another 43, while stronger standards for commercial air conditioning would take care of another 50. Increasing the energy efficiency of new buildings over the next 20 years would save a further 170, and improving the energy efficiency of existing buildings, including air conditioners, commercial lighting, and commercial cooling, would save 210 plants. Total: 600 power plants.

IBM reduced its energy use by 25% between 1991 and 2000 simply through energy conservation, saving the equivalent of a year's power for 1.5 million homes for a year. This was not only good for IBM – it saved $530 million – but it was good for the environment. IBM avoided almost 5.6 million tonnes of CO_2, the equivalent of 1.4 million cars driving 16,000 km. The British government encourages energy efficiency in businesses through reduced taxes for energy-efficient equipment, exemptions for certain processes, and fuels and emissions trading schemes.

Domestic efficiency

A programme of draught proofing, insulating walls, roofs, floors, and windows, and improved electronic controls for heating systems could cut in half the energy needed to keep a conventional building warm in winter. For new buildings, design and construction techniques exist which can virtually do away with the need for space heating or cooling. For instance, specially coated glazing can cut heat loss from a building sevenfold compared even with double glazing. The most efficient, mass-produced fridges and freezers use 75% less electricity than previously available models, while compact fluorescent light-bulbs use 70–80% less electricity than standard filament bulbs for the same light output.

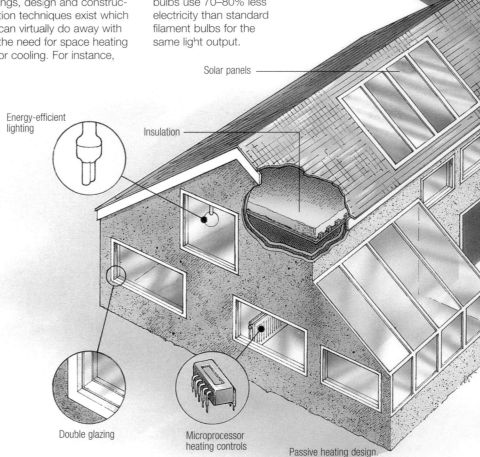

Domestic

Energy-efficient lighting

Insulation

Solar panels

Double glazing

Microprocessor heating controls

Passive heating design.

Industry

Businesses are a major contributor to greenhouse gas (GHG) emissions, thus their conservation, energy efficiency, recycling, and waste management policies are fundamental to the health of the planet. For years, energy-intensive industries have seen efficiency as a way of reducing costs. Some have developed ways to recycle products and to use wastes as fuel. Significant energy savings can come, too, from using more efficient electric motors, new sensors and control devices, and advanced heat-recovery systems such as Combined Heat and Power. Cleaner, more efficient process technologies can yield large energy savings, even through extra capital expenditure.

Energy efficiency and energy savings

If every fifth American consumer was persuaded to purchase one of the most efficient refrigerators available, the electricity savings would eliminate the need for at least 4 large coal-fired power plants. By 2020, the higher energy efficiency standard for central air-conditioning systems is expected to cut consumer electricity bills by $1.1 billion a year.

Standby power wasted

Appliances left in "standby" – computers, TVs, videos, microwaves, etc. – cost American consumers more than $1 billion per year. New efficiency standards on these household products reduce the energy demand of standby by 75%.

Energy efficiency in buildings

Amory Lovins of the Rocky Mountain Institute lives at 6,500 feet in the Colorado Rockies where the winter temperature often remains below freezing for weeks if not months. Thanks to exceptional energy-efficiency installations, his annual heating bill is less than $50. In Sweden, architects now design office blocks so well insulated that they keep warm through workers' body heat alone. The air stays fresh through regular recycling.

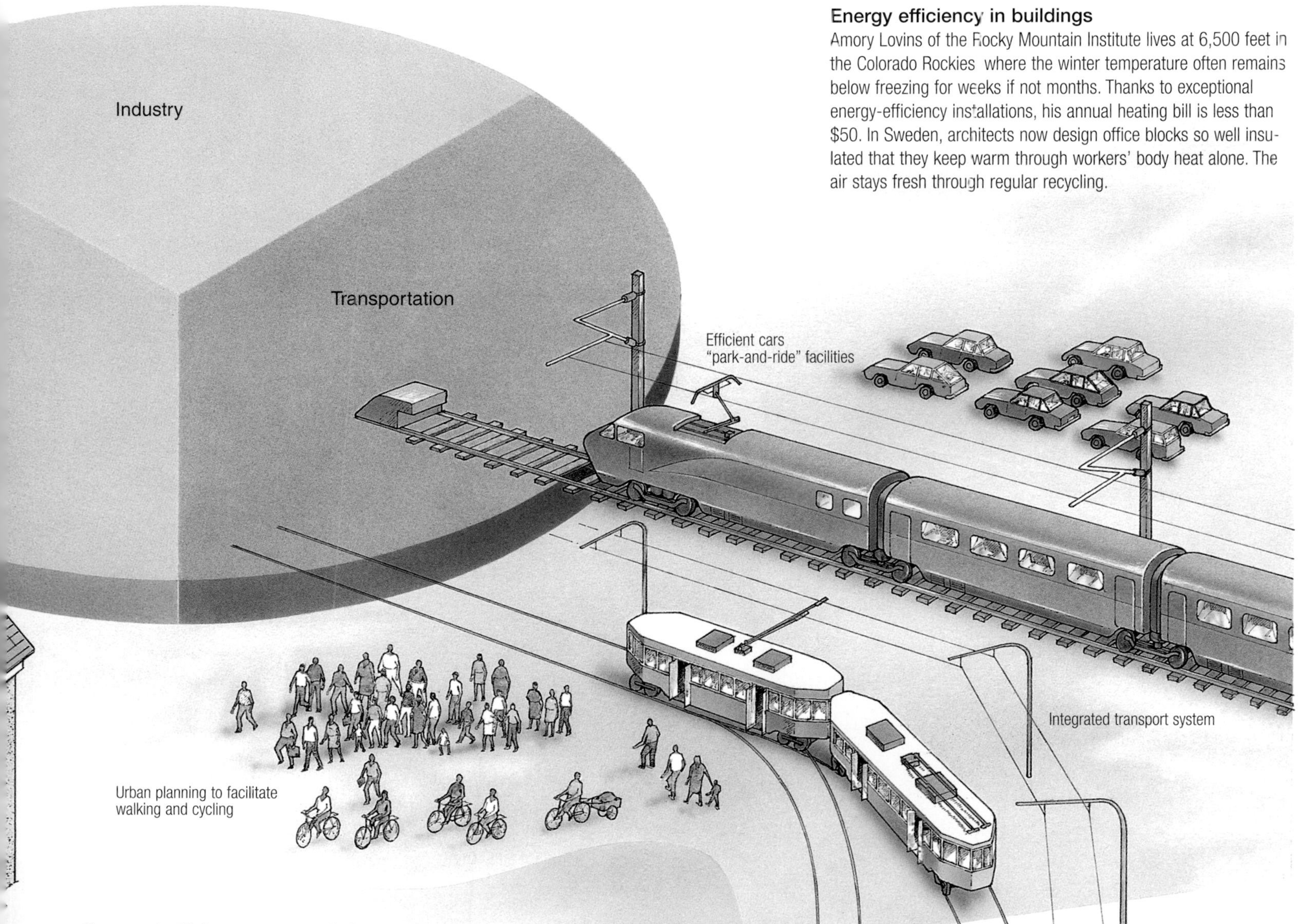

Industry

Transportation

Efficient cars "park-and-ride" facilities

Integrated transport system

Urban planning to facilitate walking and cycling

Transport efficiency

A rapidly growing energy user, the transport sector is responsible for more than one-fifth of all energy consumption in industrial countries and it is rising rapidly in developing and transition countries due to the increasing demand for cars (pp. 234–45). We can turn to the more efficient and less-polluting hybrid or twin-fuel cars that gain 100 km per gallon of gasoline while emitting 40% less CO_2 than a similar-sized gasoline car. But mass-transport systems, such as buses, trams, and trains, are far more energy efficient. Integrated transport systems provide transport links tailored to need, such as "park-and-ride" facilities at rail and bus stations. Such services, together with land-use planning to reduce home-to-work distances and transport demand, are vital to a new energy path. Already there are bus-based rapid transit systems in Ottawa, Pittsburg, Bogota, Nagoya, and Curitiba. Shanghai has invested $10 billion in a rapid-transit system, and has followed Singapore's example of adopting strong disincentives for car ownership, including registration limits and high taxes on large vehicles. Car sharing is a trend growing rapidly in Europe, North America, and Asia. Each shared car can eliminate four cars from the road.

and 50 times as fast. The task is not as simple as raising money. Local people need to be helped to confront challenge in ways they think are relevant. Too often the approach has been a "top down" affair, with urban bureaucrats trying to impose their plans on rural communities. Result: the planted trees are not cared for – or are poached. At least as important as money is a "grassroots" spirit that mobilizes the initiative of local people. An expansive strategy along these lines is underway, known as "community forestry", which looks at village wood-lots not only as sources of fuelwood but as safe-guards for topsoil, as windbreaks to protect crops, and as sources of food. At the same time, we could do much through the simple expedient of improved

cooking stoves that generate more heat while burning less wood.

Other forms of biomass, notably crop plants, are available besides wood. Most developing nations are in the tropics, where plants generally thrive. Sugar cane, cassava, and maize contain enough sugar or starch to generate the fuel ethanol through fermentation, while fast-growing waterweeds and algae produce methane. Brazil already obtains much liquid fuel from biomass – producing 27 million tonnes of sugar a year, and 15 billion litres of ethanol. A "petroleum plantation" need never run dry.

Of course, the sun's energy can be tapped through other means, such as photovoltaic cells and solar pumps. Alternative technologies range from

Good news
The 10-year Global Village Energy Partnership (GVEP) initiative is one of three pro-grammes under The Clean Energy Initiative launched at the 2002 World Summit on Sustainable Development. It aims to provide better energy services in developing coun-tries whilst enhancing econom-ic and social development and reducing poverty. As of 2004, more than 300 organizations had enlisted.

Managing energy in the South

Managing energy policy in developing countries is often much more complex than in industrialized countries where energy strate-gies are chiefly determined by price competition between the three main fuels (oil, coal, and gas) supplied by large, often monopolistic, public or private suppliers. An extensive infrastructure provides each consumer with a range of options for meeting their energy needs. In developing countries, biomass (dung, wood, and char-coal) joins the fuel mix, especially in poorer countries, playing a far larger role than fossil fuels. The penetration of electricity is typically small and confined to major cities. Two billion people worldwide lack access to electricity and all the benefits that service provides, such as light, mechanization, and communication. More than 600 million of these people are in Africa. Fossil fuels are rarely cheap enough for anything but the most essential uses.

Reforestation

Since wood is the primary fuel in the South, successful reforesta-tion programmes are key to future energy security. South Korea was almost totally deforested due to overlogging and fuelwood extraction during the Japanese occupation of 1910–1945 and the Korean War (1950–1953). National reforestation and conservation programmes since the 1970s have ensured tree planting on mountains and hillsides throughout the country, with the added benefit of the environmental services tree planting provides, e.g. flood control and the forests' capacity to store water and thus recharge aquifers. South Korea's approach to reforestation was to combine strong government support – it paid 65% of the costs – with intensive local participation. Village committees with locally elected leaders selected the best sites for planting and offered villagers a chance to share in the profits. Grassroots involvement is an essential condition for reforestation. Now three-quarters of South Korea is forested. And the country's few remaining old-growth forests are protected in nature reserves. Kenya's highly successful Greenbelt Movement had planted 10 million trees by 2000, and there are similar programmes in 30 other African countries.

Fuel from sugar cane

Brazil produces ethanol from sugar cane, and the cost price is half that of gasoline. Brazil's ethanol-fuel programme was a big, albeit brief, success in the mid-1980s, when the majority of new cars sold ran on pure ethanol. By the late 1990s, the share had plunged and the gov-ernment introduced lower sales tax on flex-fuel vehi-cles powered by ethanol or gasoline or a combination of the two. Soaring gaso-line prices and air pollution could make these vehicles attractive in other parts of the world, especially in sugar cane-producing countries. An arrangement under the CDM (right) will lower the sale prices of Brazilian ethanol-powered vehicles and German firms can earn carbon credits towards their country's Kyoto targets.

Fuelwood plantations

A plantation of fast-growing trees, such as *Leucaena*, can yield up to 50 tonnes of wood per ha each year. They are especially useful for meeting urban fuelwood needs but can be expensive to set up. In Indonesia, over 30,000 ha of fuelwood plantations have been established on Java alone. In the mid-1990s, around a third of plantations in developing countries were primarily for fuelwood.

Village woodlots

Village woodlots are part of a new approach to reforestation known as "social" or "community" forestry. Trees planted on village or private land produce wood and other products for village use, rather than commercial, use. Foresters educate and advise, the villagers manage.

established items, such as hydropower and geothermal energy, to innovative devices, such as high-tech windmills and tidal power. There are plenty of options to help developing countries through their energy squeeze, provided the technology and investment can be made available. In an interdependent world, it makes economic and political sense for the North – which uses and wastes most energy – to ensure that the South has the resources needed to harness its energy resources on a sustainable basis.

The potential for renewables is vast, especially for those countries dependent on increasingly costly imports of fossil fuels or those countries, like China, needing to make the switch from environmentally damaging coal. Developing-country energy demand will continue to rise rapidly, especially as the tide of "new consumers" comes in stronger and faster (pp. 234–35). Global electricity demand is projected to double by 2030 and energy consumption overall by two-thirds. This will have major implications for global climate unless alternatives to fossil fuels are quickly brought on stream. Fortunately, we now have laws and mechanisms to promote this.

Global laws of the air

The global nature of problems such as climate change has resulted in a new kind of cooperation between governments, especially as concerns agreements. We are witnessing the birth of global "laws of the air", some bringing more birth pains than others.

The Clean Development Mechanism (CDM)
Under the Kyoto Protocol's "Clean Development Mechanism" an industrialized country investing in a renewable-energy project in a developing country can claim credit for avoided GHG emissions. It is a win–win situation because the developing country can switch from CO_2-emitting, coal-generated electricity, and the industrialized country can use "credits" to meet its Kyoto target (see p. 147).

Hydropower schemes
Small-scale hydro projects (< 10 MW) are relatively cheap and simpler to construct than larger systems which rely on a dam, penstock, turbine, and generator. Since electricity is generated close to the point of use, they do not require massive extra investment in a grid to distribute the energy produced. They are ideal for powering rural industries and supplying schools and hospitals. China alone has an estimated 60,000 small hydropower schemes, while the country's enormous Three Gorges Dam is expected to provide around 10% of the country's electricity demand.

Wind power
Small, efficient windmills provide energy for pumping water to irrigate cropland and supply livestock. Even with moderate winds, wind power can pump water more cheaply than diesel or bullock power. On a large scale, wind farms can provide the non-fossil-fuel electricity the developing world badly needs. India is already the world's fifth largest windpower-producing nation and China is investing heavily.

Biogas
The fermentation of animal dung or crop residues in an airtight container (below) yields a methane-rich gas (biogas), which can be used to heat stoves, light lamps, run machinery, or produce electricity. The residue left by biogas production can be used as a fertilizer for food or trees, or as a component in animal feed. Sewage systems built to collect human wastes for biogas production also help to improve hygiene. Biogas digesters such as the 6 million in China, can be built for as little as $50.

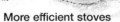

Biogas chamber

Pig sty

Outlet pit

Inlet

Gas storage chamber

Gas outlet

Fermentation chamber

More efficient stoves
Almost 3 billion people worldwide rely on wood, charcoal, or other biomass (dung, crop residues) for energy. People often cook over open "three-stone" fires that are dirty and dangerous – they are linked to 1.6 million deaths in developing countries each year.

India has one of the world's largest improved cookstove programmes, with 30 million set up since 1985. The All-India Women's Conference (AIWC) enlist women to promote improved "chulhas" made of dung, mud, and hay, with a metal "chimney". The Indian government pays a third of the $5 cost. They are fuel efficient (saving trees and the long treks to find fuelwood) and smokeless (saving lives). They also reduce the need for agricultural biomass and cattle dung to be diverted away from fertilizing crop fields.

Photovoltaics (PVs)
Solar cells offer an affordable way to get modern renewable energy services to developing countries, aiding education (light), health (refrigeration for vaccines), income (powering water pumps), and communications (computers). China plans to invest $1.2 billion in photovoltaics over 5 years and South Africa plans solar electrification for 350,000 homes and 1.5 million people in rural areas.

The ozone layer treaty is widely hailed as a landmark in environmental diplomacy. A first international agreement in 1985 created a mechanism for cooperation on research. After alarming scientific evidence had been gathered, the Montreal Protocol on Substances that Deplete the Ozone Layer was signed in 1987, committing signatory nations to a timetable of cuts in emissions of ozone-depleting CFCs and halons (right).

International diplomacy is famous for moving at a glacial pace. Yet faced with a serious global problem, the world community moved quickly from a commitment-free convention to a binding treaty affecting powerful commercial interests and everyday products. What was the secret of the protocol's success? Public concern, backed by the international scientific community, while UNEP and NGOs, such as Friends of the Earth and Greenpeace, formed a powerful consensus for action. The US already had strict ozone-protection legislation, and urged the more reluctant Europeans, Russians, and Japanese to act. Perhaps the single most vital factor in the treaty's success was the creation of a fund to help developing countries, including China, make the transition to CFC substitutes. These countries argued that it was unfair for the North to expect the South to incur the cost of switching to substitutes to solve a problem the South had no role in creating. Without the South's participation, growing CFC use in the developing world would have overwhelmed the treaty's reductions.

Far less successful has been the 1992 UN Framework Convention on Climate Change, where intransigence on the part of the US (with only 5 percent of the world's population but responsible for 25 percent of the world's carbon dioxide output) prevented any binding targets to stabilize carbon emissions at 1990 levels by 2000. This was despite calculations from scientists of the IPCC that stabilizing global climate would require a carbon dioxide slashing of at least 60 percent. Rejection of the subsequent Kyoto Protocol by two of the biggest emitters of greenhouse gases (the US and Russia), together with Australia, prevented the required "parties accounting for 55 percent of 1990 carbon dioxide emissions" for it to enter into force. However, in late 2004, the Russian Parliament voted in favour and subsequent ratification by President Putin meant Russia became the 36th industrialized country to agree to cut six GHGs (including carbon dioxide) by at least five percent below 1990 levels between 2008 and 2012. During 1992–2002, the US increased its carbon dioxide emissions by almost 14 percent, with a total increase almost twice that of India, a nation with almost four times as many people.

Our growing demand for water
Water shortages are one of the greatest challenges we face in the coming decades – alongside climate change. While an infinitely renewable resource, too

Managing the atmosphere

The laws of the air
The atmosphere, like the oceans, recognizes no boundaries. Problems caused in one country or region can readily spread to others. Issues, such as acid rain, ozone layer depletion, and climate change, can be addressed only by international agreement. New conventions and protocols regarding the atmosphere and climate provide some hope and positive models for international diplomacy. The 1979 Convention on Long-Range Transboundary Air Pollution (CLRTAP) was the first to recognize the principle that one state should not damage another with its air pollution. It has evolved to handle issues, such as transboundary flows of persistent organic pollutants (POPs) and heavy metals, though it was originally a mechanism to manage "regional" transboundary air pollutants, such as sulphur, nitrogen oxides (NOx), and volatile organic compounds (VOCs), together with acid rain and ground-level ozone. The "Montreal Protocol on Substances that Deplete the Ozone Layer" shows that cooperation can head off global environmental problems.

The 30% Club
The 1985 CLRTAP (Helsinki) Protocol on Sulphur Emissions committed nations to reduce sulphur emissions from 1980 levels by 30% by 1993. Many nations achieved the goal and went further – 21 parties reduced their emissions by more than 50% by 1993, and 11 achieved at least 60%. Others, notably the US and UK, refused to join the club.

CLRTAP, 1979
The Convention on Long-Range Transboundary Air Pollution was the first international agreement on air pollution, signed by all European and North American countries. Its subsequent protocols cover sulphur emissions (Helsinki, 1985, and Oslo, 1994), nitrogen oxides (1988) and volatile organic compounds (VOC/Geneva, 1991), international cost-sharing for the monitoring of air pollutants (EMEP/Geneva, 1984), and heavy metals plus persistent organic pollutants (POPs) (1998, both entered into force 2003). The latest is the 1999 Protocol to Abate Acidification, Eutrophication, and Ground-level Ozone, with 31 signatories and 11 ratifications, but it had not entered into force as of mid-2004.

Montreal Protocol, 1989
Under the 1985 Vienna Convention for the Protection of the Ozone Layer, the Montreal Protocol has been ratified by 183 nations, and has been revised as more data on the perilous state of the ozone layer has come to light. Production and consumption of ozone-depleting chlorofluorocarbons (CFCs), carbon tetrachloride, methyl chloroform, and halons have been banned in developed countries since 1996. Developing countries have until 2010. Worldwide CFC use fell by 86% between 1980 and 1998.

Global air circulation
The Equator receives more of the sun's energy than the poles because the sun is directly overhead. The air at the Equator heats up, expands, and rises to high altitudes. This air cools and descends in the sub-tropics on either side of the Equator. Winds at low altitudes return air towards the Equator to replace the rising air, completing a circulation pattern. Further polewards, the pattern of circulation is more complex. As warm air is transferred polewards it is replaced by cold air moving towards the Equator. Because the planet is spinning, the circulating air is dragged with it in great spirals. The air system carries water vapour and heat around the globe, also pollutants.

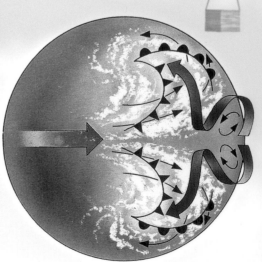

NOx and VOCs

Under CLRTAP, the 1988 (Sofia) protocol called for a freeze on nitrogen oxide (NOx) emissions at 1987 values by 1995. 17 parties acceded. The 1991 VOC protocol called for 21 nations to cut their emissions of smog-causing VOCs by 30% by 1999.

North America (incl. Mexico)
15.76 16.62 16.83

Western Europe
9.07 8.83 9.01

Eastern Europe and the former Soviet Union
11.9 7.53 8.45

World
4.1 3.88 4.06

Middle East (incl. Turkey)
4.38 3.21 5.33

Developing Asia
1.43 1.79 2.09

Industrialized Asia (incl. Australia, Japan
8.89 10.17 11.07

Africa
1.05 1.02 0.99

Central and South America
1.96 2.28 2.48

Signatories to the Kyoto Protocol

30 Annexe 1 countries, accounting for 61.6% of 1990 emissions have ratified the protocol

3 Annexe 1 and 95 non-Annexe 1 countries have ratified, accepted, acceded or approved the protocol

5 Annexe 1 countries failed to ratify the protocol and 5 non-Annexe 1 countries failed to take it further than the signature stage

Per capita global carbon emissions

1990 2000 2010

Figures are in tonnes of CO_2 per capita

UNFCCC, 1992

The UN Framework Convention on Climate Change was approved at the Rio Earth Summit in 1992, with industrialized countries agreeing to the non-binding "guideline" of stabilizing their CO_2 emissions at 1990 levels by the year 2000. Most countries did not achieve this goal. The treaty introduced procedures, such as emissions trading and the Clean Development Mechanism (CDM).

For those developing and transition nations with low CO_2 emissions as yet, emissions trading could open up the way to finance development of clean and renewables. Russia's emissions have fallen way below those of 1990 and the country could earn up to $20 billion a year in carbon trading.

The CDM provides for implementation of projects that reduce GHG emissions in mainly developing nations in return for certified emission reductions (CERs) for developed nations, and in doing so assists the cause of sustainable development in host countries.

Bilateral agreements

The international dimension of air pollution is well illustrated by Germany's decision to pay for sulphur dioxide scrubbers on Czech power plants contaminating German airspace, and Sweden similarly assisting Poland. The money invested reaps cleaner air in these West European countries than by spending it on their own industries.

Carbon dioxide emissions

North America is by far the largest emitter of CO_2, with 6.7 million tonnes in 2000, for an average of 16.6 tonnes per capita (see bars on map). Compare Eastern Europe 7.5 tonnes, Western Europe 8.8 tonnes, developing Asia 1.8 tonnes, and Africa one tonne.

The Kyoto Protocol, 1997

The Kyoto Protocol of 1997 called for industrial countries to undertake cuts in GHG emissions averaging 5.2% (from 1990 levels) between 2008 and 2012. Developing countries were not included in the first phase to allow for economic expansion. Ratification of the protocol required parties accounting for 55% of 1990 emissions for the treaty to enter into force. By July 2004, only 44% had been attained, outsiders including Australia, Russia, and the US. Russia finally ratified in November 2004, but the US has kept itself firmly out of the picture in order to protect its fossil fuels (the country accounts for one-quarter of the world's CO_2 emissions). The Protocol, which entered into force on 16th February 2005, created two flexibility "mechanisms" in the form of GHG emissions trading and the Clean Development Mechanism (CDM) which aim to assist countries attain sustainable development and meet the goals of the UNFCCC.

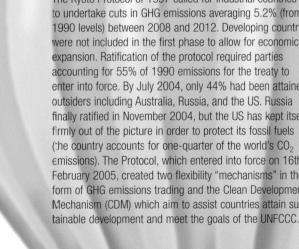

much of it is in the wrong place. Just six countries (Brazil, Russia, Canada, Indonesia, China, and Colombia) account for half of all renewable fresh water. Shortages can occur within as well as between countries: China has seven percent of renewable fresh water but most is in the southern part of the country. In 2003, 12 million Ethiopians faced famine, yet four-fifths of the flow of the Nile originates within the country's territory. (See also pp. 138–39.)

Global freshwater consumption rose more than sixfold last century. Water tables are falling due to over-pumping of ground water – for example, withdrawals from the Ogallala aquifer in the US are three times the recharge rate. Many rivers, such as Amu Dar'ya, Colorado, Ganges, Indus, Rio Grande, and Yellow, run dry for parts of the year. Wetlands, while crucially important for ecosystem services estimated to be worth $15 trillion (water storage and purification, aquifer recharge, flood and shore erosion controls, regulation of local climate, and support for many species) have been drastically reduced worldwide.

If we carry on with "business as usual" there can only be deep trouble ahead. Fortunately, we have plenty of options. The thirstiest sector, irrigation agriculture, accounts for 70 percent of water use, producing as much as 40 percent of global agricultural goods and 60 percent of global grain on 18 percent of our croplands. Global irrigation efficiency averages only 43 percent, but in Texas's High Plains low-pressure and low-energy precision sprinkler systems reach 80–95 percent efficiency and at the same time produce water savings of up to 37 percent. Drip irrigation, invented in the 1960s in water-short Israel, applies small amounts of water direct to the parts of the plant that need it most, resulting in much more food being grown with only half as much water, and with reduced risk of salinization. Only about 280,000 square kilometres of cropland (one percent of all irrigated lands) now receive the benefits of this Blue Revolution. Plainly, there is much scope for the future.

By 2025, around three billion people will be living in countries classified as suffering water stress or water scarcity. By that time, too, agriculture will still consume the largest (though a somewhat reduced) share of the world's water. Domestic water demand is projected to increase from 9.4 percent (in 1995) to 13.9 percent (an increase of 71 percent), livestock from 2.1–3.1 percent (71 percent), and industry from 8.7–11.3 percent (50 percent) – although we should remember that industry does not generally "consume" water in the exorbitant way that agriculture does.

Part of the problem lies with water subsidies in agricultural, industrial, and domestic sectors, that encourage misuse and overuse of scarce water resources. Even water-short countries such as Egypt, the cost of water as a share of supply is often as low as 20 percent. Government subsidies alone (e.g. apart from externality costs) total almost $70 billion a year worldwide and three-quarters of these can be called "perverse" in that they are harmful to both

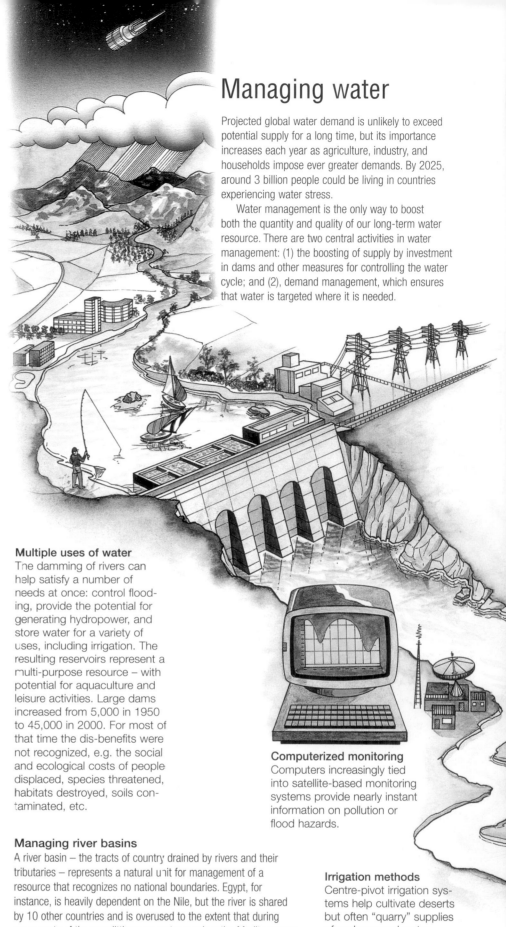

Managing water

Projected global water demand is unlikely to exceed potential supply for a long time, but its importance increases each year as agriculture, industry, and households impose ever greater demands. By 2025, around 3 billion people could be living in countries experiencing water stress.

Water management is the only way to boost both the quantity and quality of our long-term water resource. There are two central activities in water management: (1) the boosting of supply by investment in dams and other measures for controlling the water cycle; and (2), demand management, which ensures that water is targeted where it is needed.

Multiple uses of water

The damming of rivers can help satisfy a number of needs at once: control flooding, provide the potential for generating hydropower, and store water for a variety of uses, including irrigation. The resulting reservoirs represent a multi-purpose resource – with potential for aquaculture and leisure activities. Large dams increased from 5,000 in 1950 to 45,000 in 2000. For most of that time the dis-benefits were not recognized, e.g. the social and ecological costs of people displaced, species threatened, habitats destroyed, soils contaminated, etc.

Computerized monitoring

Computers increasingly tied into satellite-based monitoring systems provide nearly instant information on pollution or flood hazards.

Managing river basins

A river basin – the tracts of country drained by rivers and their tributaries – represents a natural unit for management of a resource that recognizes no national boundaries. Egypt, for instance, is heavily dependent on the Nile, but the river is shared by 10 other countries and is overused to the extent that during some parts of the year little or no water reaches the Mediterranean. Similarly, Mexico and six US states rely on water from the Colorado River, with little reaching Mexico or the Gulf of California. Water tables are falling right around the world as more and more people demand more and more water. These pressures will aggravate disputes over river basins and other resources. Activities in one part of a basin can have far-reaching impacts, thus it is vital that developers are fully aware of the repercussions of a particular project or activity. The river basin, like most natural resources, must be managed as a shared concern, even though this can be problematic when they cross political boundaries. One third of 263 international river basins are shared by more than two countries, thus the potential for conflict is enormous. On the other hand, the potential for collaboration is also there.

Irrigation methods

Centre-pivot irrigation systems help cultivate deserts but often "quarry" supplies of underground water. Drip-feed irrigation systems help conserve scarce water resources, remove the threat of parasitic disease spread by irrigation canals, and reduce soil salinization (which has reduced yields on one-fifth of our irrigated croplands).

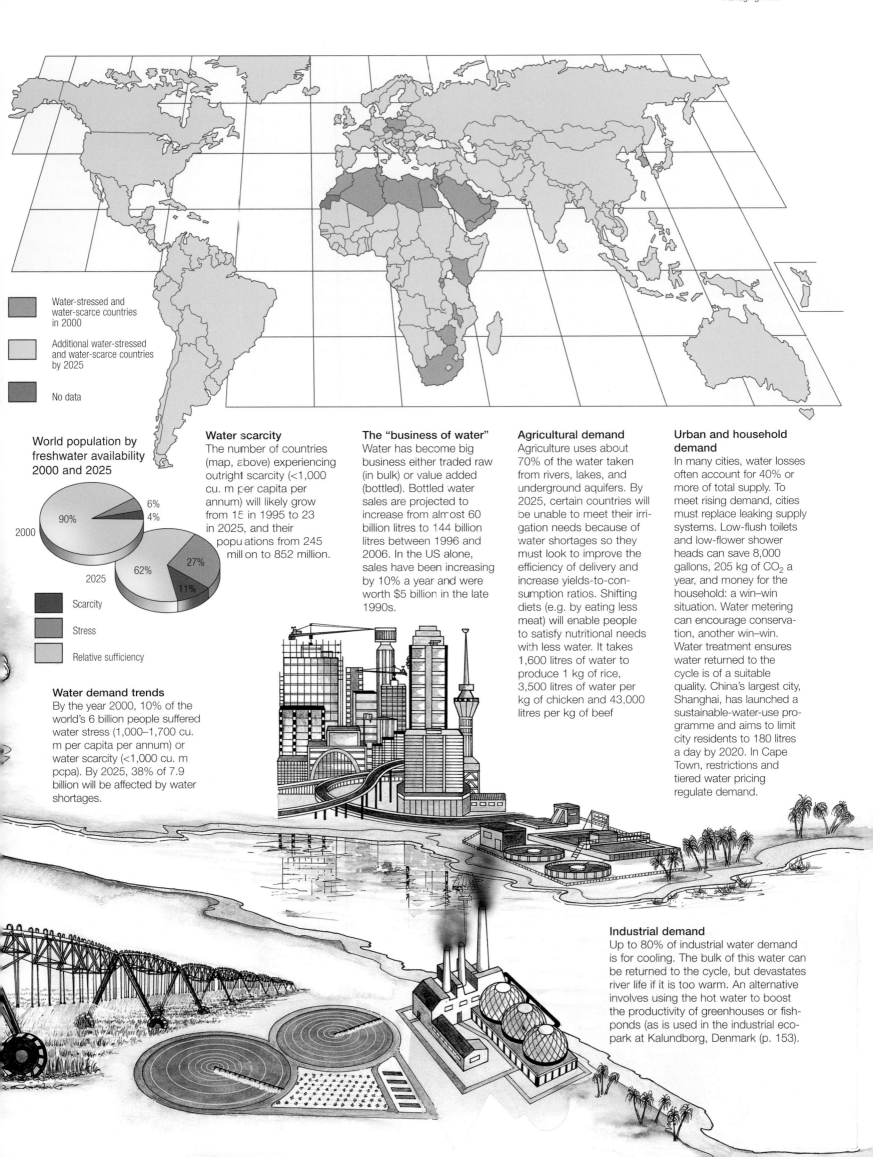

Water-stressed and water-scarce countries in 2000

Additional water-stressed and water-scarce countries by 2025

No data

World population by freshwater availability 2000 and 2025

2000: 90%, 6%, 4%

2025: 62%, 27%, 11%

Scarcity

Stress

Relative sufficiency

Water demand trends

By the year 2000, 10% of the world's 6 billion people suffered water stress (1,000–1,700 cu. m per capita per annum) or water scarcity (<1,000 cu. m pcpa). By 2025, 38% of 7.9 billion will be affected by water shortages.

Water scarcity

The number of countries (map, above) experiencing outright scarcity (<1,000 cu. m per capita per annum) will likely grow from 15 in 1995 to 23 in 2025, and their populations from 245 million to 852 million.

The "business of water"

Water has become big business either traded raw (in bulk) or value added (bottled). Bottled water sales are projected to increase from almost 60 billion litres to 144 billion litres between 1996 and 2006. In the US alone, sales have been increasing by 10% a year and were worth $5 billion in the late 1990s.

Agricultural demand

Agriculture uses about 70% of the water taken from rivers, lakes, and underground aquifers. By 2025, certain countries will be unable to meet their irrigation needs because of water shortages so they must look to improve the efficiency of delivery and increase yields-to-consumption ratios. Shifting diets (e.g. by eating less meat) will enable people to satisfy nutritional needs with less water. It takes 1,600 litres of water to produce 1 kg of rice, 3,500 litres of water per kg of chicken and 43,000 litres per kg of beef

Urban and household demand

In many cities, water losses often account for 40% or more of total supply. To meet rising demand, cities must replace leaking supply systems. Low-flush toilets and low-flower shower heads can save 8,000 gallons, 205 kg of CO_2 a year, and money for the household: a win–win situation. Water metering can encourage conservation, another win–win. Water treatment ensures water returned to the cycle is of a suitable quality. China's largest city, Shanghai, has launched a sustainable-water-use programme and aims to limit city residents to 180 litres a day by 2020. In Cape Town, restrictions and tiered water pricing regulate demand.

Industrial demand

Up to 80% of industrial water demand is for cooling. The bulk of this water can be returned to the cycle, but devastates river life if it is too warm. An alternative involves using the hot water to boost the productivity of greenhouses or fish-ponds (as is used in the industrial eco-park at Kalundborg, Denmark (p. 153).

economies and environments (pp. 232–233). Until these subsidies are phased out, water will continue to literally "run down the drain".

Water supply and sanitation

The International Drinking Water Supply and Sanitation Decade 1981–1990 encapsulated an impulse that we should all take pride in – for the first time in history a concerted effort to supply some of the most basic facilities to more than one billion people in the developing world. It was an ambitious aim, not simply because of its grandiose scope but because few political leaders bothered with the issue. Yet the community of nations got together in 1978 to talk about taps and latrines, and to devise a plan to supply them on a grand scale. Alas, that it became, in the UN's

"Amount of water it would take, per day, to support 4.7 billion people at the UN daily minimum, 2.5 billion gallons. Amount of water used, per day, to irrigate the world's golf courses, 2.5 billion gallons."
Worldwatch Institute, 2004

words, the "lost decade of development". The downturn in the world economy, the doubling of long-term debts, and population growth all conspired to prevent the Decade from achieving its objective of universal access to water and sanitation. And yet 1,200 million people received a water supply, and 770 million received sanitation facilities, for the very first time.

One of the greatest impacts of the Decade was the higher priority given to water supply and sanitation issues at both national and international levels. Many developing country governments learned that health programmes based on glossy new hospitals in cities only divert attention from real priorities such as clean water in rural areas – the zone where there is most need. Instead, they can get a better return on each "health dollar" if they invest it in preventive medicine, primarily in the form of plentiful supplies of clean water. Ironically, it was the lack of financial and human resources that eventually forced governments and external agencies to adopt new approaches to

Clean water for all

The scope of the UN's Water and Sanitation Decade objective was massive. Launched at the UN General Assembly with the aim of "providing water and sanitation for all" by 1990, it was soon clear that full implementation would be a remote possibility. Rapid population growth, migrations of people from rural areas to cities, war, famine, and drought were added to the problems of debt and the global economic downturn which thwarted the Decade's objective. The Decade achieved remarkable results, however, especially in rural water supplies, where the number of people with access to facilities increased by 240%; the number with new sanitation facilities increased by 150%.

At the Year 2000 Millennium Summit, world leaders pledged "to halve, by 2015, the proportion of people without sustainable access to safe drinking water and basic sanitation". Then, in late 2003, the UN proposed that World Water Day on 22 March 2005 should mark the beginning of the 2005–2015 International Decade on "Water for Life", during which time there would be a "step up focus on water-related issues, promoting women managers and international cooperation among all stakeholders to achieve the water-related goals of the Millennium Declaration ... (and) coordinate a response to make it a "decade for action".

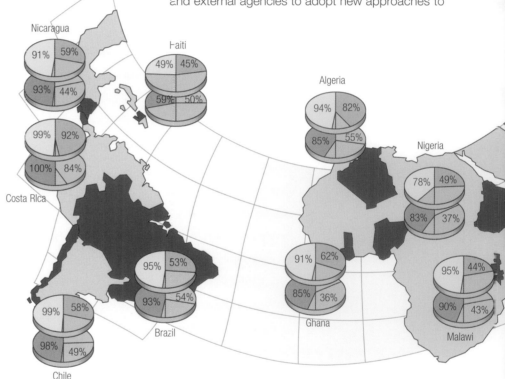

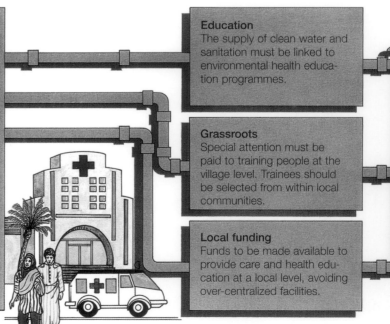

Funds
Secure and reliable funding is vital for the huge investments required. This means a combination of local funds and those derived from central governments, overseas donors, and banks. The cost of providing safe water and sanitation for all by 2025 would be $23 billion a year.

Policy
To provide universal access to 50 litres per person per day by 2015, policy should: "foster complementary water supply and sanitation projects; focus on underserved populations; generate replicable and self-sustaining programmes; develop socially relevant and affordable systems; link supply and sanitation with other improvements".

Education
The supply of clean water and sanitation must be linked to environmental health education programmes.

Grassroots
Special attention must be paid to training people at the village level. Trainees should be selected from within local communities.

Local funding
Funds to be made available to provide care and health education at a local level, avoiding over-centralized facilities.

promoting safe water and sanitation. Many more facilities could be built with existing resources, and their use and maintenance improved, if the beneficiaries were involved at all stages of development and operation. The agencies began to be sensitive to the key roles that could be played by women, community leaders, and others. The Decade also brought about some remarkable improvements in drilling, water treatment, and sanitation technologies. As a result, the new technological solutions were cheaper and more efficient than those installed when the Decade began.

At the start of the 1980s, there were 1.8 billion people without safe drinking water and 1.7 billion without adequate sanitation. By 1990, and the call from the World Summit for Children for universal access to safe water and sanitation by the year 2000, the figures were 1.1 billion and 2.4 billion. By 2000, and the UN Millennium Development Goal (MDG) of halving of the numbers of people without improved access to water and sanitation, the numbers unserved remained much the same as in 1990.

As for the future: to achieve the MDG targets for Africa, Asia, Latin America, and the Caribbean, an additional 1.6 billion people will need improved access to water (292,000 a day) and 2.2 billion to sanitation (400,000 a day) between 2000 and 2015. At the global level, even if the targets for water and

Bangladesh
99% | 97%

Myanmar
99% | 93%

89% | 66%

43% | 29%

Indonesia
90% | 69%

92% | 62%

95% | 79%

Ethiopia
% | 12%

88% | 61%

% | 17%

India

Sri Lanka
98% | 70%

91% | 62%

Population with sustainable access to an improved water source

Urban | Rural — 2000

Urban | Rural — 1990

Rural services still lag behind
In Africa, rural water and sanitation supplies reached less than half the population in 2000, while in urban areas they reached 85%. Of course, there are variations within regions, and some countries, such as Malawi, Ethiopia, and Nigeria, saw little progress in the 1990s (map, left). 40 billion work hours are lost each year in Africa due to the need to fetch drinking water. Many children, particularly girls, are prevented from going to school for want of latrines, squandering their intellectual and economic potential. In rural Asia, less than a third of the population had access to sanitation – meaning 1.6 billion did not.

What does "improved" water and sanitation mean?
In practical terms, lack of drinking water means no supply within several hundred metres; lack of sanitation means no bucket latrine or pit privy, let alone sewerage system. Ponds and rivers are the main sources of drinking water – and the main sites for impromptu toilets. According to the WHO:
Water supply: household connection; public standpipe; borehole; protected dug well; protected spring; rainwater collection.
Sanitation: connection to a public sewer or to septic system; pour-flush latrine; simple pit latrine; ventilated improved pit latrine.

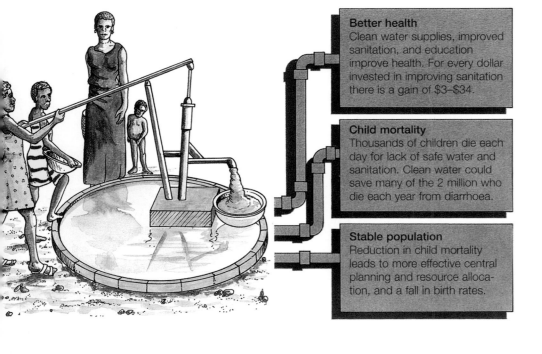

Better health
Clean water supplies, improved sanitation, and education improve health. For every dollar invested in improving sanitation there is a gain of $3–$34.

Child mortality
Thousands of children die each day for lack of safe water and sanitation. Clean water could save many of the 2 million who die each year from diarrhoea.

Stable population
Reduction in child mortality leads to more effective central planning and resource allocation, and a fall in birth rates.

South Africa – getting on with it
South Africa is a thirsty country tackling rising water demand head on. The country not only has 44 million people, but a vast richness of biological diversity (pp. 152–53) – all competing for scarce water. Around 160 introduced land species have become "invasive", mostly water-guzzling plants. The South African government's "Working For Water" programme has cleared invasive alien plants from about a million ha of land at more than 300 sites and created employment for at least 30,000 workers, thus relieving poverty at the same time. Each household enjoys a certain amount of water free, after which various tiered pricing comes into effect.

Clean water for rural South Africans
In South Africa's karoo, a small community with no electricity and undrinkable borehole water is benefiting from a solar still funded by the government. Using heat from the sun to distill the brackish borehole water the Kerkplaas community can now provide its own drinking water instead of having it transported to them by truck. The technology has significant implications for water provision in South Africa's rural towns relying on boreholes. The system is simple to operate, inexpensive, and provides drinking water for 40 people.

sanitation coverage are met, there will still be at least 600 million without water and 1.3 billion without sanitation.

Recall that while water is an infinitely renewable resource, water shortages are one of the greatest challenges we face in the coming decades – and we should act now to prevent its misuse and overuse.

Towards a conserver society

While reviewing energy, water, and other elements, we have seen how we need to make better use of our resources. We have enough and to spare, provided we are less profligate in our ways, and fortunately there is massive scope for us to improve. The challenge lies not so much with "technical fixes", but with our approach to our world around us. Hitherto, we have engaged in something of a Wild West economy, supposing that there are always pastures new beyond the horizon. Now we know there are no new horizons to explore and exploit: our planet is a closed ecosystem, and we are running up against the boundaries of our biosphere.

So, a more appropriate image is Earth as a spaceship, where most materials have to be recycled. For us, "moving on" will be a case of leaving behind the throwaway society, and advancing to a conserver society where, to qualify as citizens, we must shift entrenched attitudes and thinking. We need to recognize that there is rarely such a thing as "waste": rather, there are materials that end up in the wrong place.

The transition has already begun, assisted by various laws and legislation, such as the European Union Directives on Packaging and Waste, Waste Electrical and Electronic Equipment (WEEE) and End-of-Life Vehicles (ELV). By 2001, 30 nations had implemented "Take Back" laws making industry financially or physically responsible for the end-of-life management of their products and packaging.

Major new businesses are emerging (extra jobs, too!) to exploit waste products. Forward-looking manufacturers are designing products from tea-pots to cars with final disassembly and recycling in mind. Waste-sharing "cities" can match suppliers of waste material with those who need it.

In the main, the conserver society depends on the commitment of individuals, and of industry and other commercial interests. But they can be inspired by government incentives and penalties. Governments can foster the anti-waste campaign by initiatives to eliminate "concealed waste", even by helping to make planned obsolescence obsolete. Increasing product lifetime through better design, repair, and re-use is more effective than recycling, since it does not require processing recycled materials. Waste's role as a renewable energy source is also attracting attention. In the US, there were 103 facilities operating in 2003, but less than one percent of the country's total energy demand is met through such schemes.

Waste into wealth

Every living organism uses energy to process raw materials, and in doing so it often produces waste. In natural systems, such wastes are soon exploited by other organisms, in a perpetual cycle of re-use. Human communities process materials on a grand scale, using enormous quantities of energy and other resources. We produce mountains of waste (today, the average American generates more than a tonne of waste each year, two-thirds of it buried in landfills), the bulk of which passes through the system just once. Some developing countries are trying to work out ways in which they can improve the working conditions of their recyclers. As for the developed countries, although the 'throwaway society' still flourishes, new recycling industries are emerging, generating employment and boosting energy efficiency.

A world of waste
We produce about 2 billion tonnes of municipal solid waste (MSW) a year world-wide – a figure projected to increase by a third between 2004 and 2008. In many countries, waste is seen as a problem, not a resource; as something to be dumped rather than converted into useful products. As the flow diagram (below) shows, we are beginning to close the circle by recycling a growing number of materials.

Recycling plastic
Fleece fabrics that are warm, durable, weather resistant, lightweight, and comfortable are made from recycled plastic soda bottles. The fibre is mostly used for jackets, vests, pants, blanket throws, and accessories; it is also used in carpets, home furnishings, and fibrefill. In the UK, less than 6% of plastic bottles sold in 2003 were recycled. Plastic bags can take 10–20 years to decompose yet UK citizens used 8 billion in 2000. Ireland has introduced a tax on these bags and some UK supermarkets offer incentives for their re-use. Plastic cups can be turned into pencils, rulers, and other stationery items. Remarkable Pencils Ltd in the UK produces over 20,000 pencils per day, saving 20,000 plastic cups from landfills. Each year, Americans throw away 25 billion styrofoam cups – but as yet there is no readily recycled product for styrofoam.

Jobs from junk
An international e-business has sprung up out of one of Nairobi's poorest and most troubled neighbourhoods. Eco-sandals is a non-profit, community-based, dot-com business with the sole aim of supporting the local community. Local people from the Korogocho (meaning "without hope") shantytown work in the design, manufacture, and marketing of sandals made from recycled tyre treads.

Sorting waste for re-use
The key to material recovery and recycling is separation, whether performed by "rubbish sifters", such as Cairo's 60,000 zabbaleen, or by the latest automatic sorting equipment.

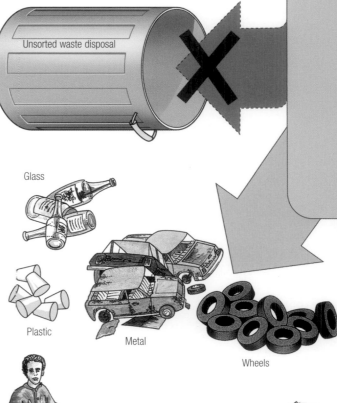

Unsorted waste disposal

Glass

Plastic

Metal

Wheels

Compostable

Recovered materials

"Cradle-to-cradle" products

Washing machines, PCs, VCRs, fridges – in fact, almost every other durable that people now buy, use up, and ultimately throw away – could be leased, with products returned to the manufacturer for continuous repair, re-use, and re-manufacture, rather than selling more and more products that are more and more likely to be scrapped prematurely. Already, there is a boom in re-manufacturing. 1996 revenues were worth $53 billion.

Recycling steel: The most recycled metal in the world. More than a third of global production comes from scrap. The US recycling rate was around 70% in 2002, where recycled iron and steel saves enough electricity to power a fifth of households for a year. In the UK, only two-fifths of steel packaging was recycled in 2002, well below the 60% European average. Each tonne of recycled steel saves 1.3 tonnes of mining waste, 1.5 tonnes of iron ore, 0.5 tonnes of coking coal, plus 75% of the energy (and resultant emissions) and 40% of the water required to produce virgin steel.

Recycling aluminium: Anything made of aluminium can be recycled again and again – not just cans but foil, window frames, furniture, and automotive parts. With regular collection/recycling schemes, used drinks cans can appear back on supermarket shelves within 6–8 weeks. Recycling cans eliminates waste, saves a lot of energy, conserves natural resources, cuts down on the amount sent to landfills, and provides revenue for recyclers and collection agents, such as charities and local government.

Recycling mobile phones: They can be recycled for reconditioning then re-use in developing and transition countries. Charities, such as Oxfam and ActionAid, can raise funds by acting as recycling agents. In the UK, 15 million mobiles are discarded each year – together with batteries and chargers this would amount to 1,500 tonnes of potentially hazardous landfill. Similar schemes operate for printer cartridges, yet an estimated 700 million were thrown away worldwide in 2003.

Recycling household waste: In the UK, each person produces half a tonne of household waste per year but only 12% is recycled or composted, with 78% going to landfill and 9% incinerated. The US generates twice as much per capita, but recycles 19%, while 66% goes to landfill. Denmark recycles 19%, Japan over 40%.

Recycling carpets: Every year, 2 million tonnes of carpet becomes waste in the US. In landfills, it lasts for 20,000 years; if burned, it releases toxic chemicals from PVC backing. Interface Inc. leases floor covering, taking back only worn sections for replacement – reducing consumption of new material by 80%. Re-manufacturing creates almost zero waste and saves money, materials, and energy.

Recycling e-waste: Every year, businesses replace 60 million computers and, by 2010, this could reach 250 million. Specialist resellers, often in partnership with corporations, software companies, and non-profit organizations, put unwanted PCs to productive use around the world. TVs, VCRs, stereos, copiers, and fax machines can also be re-used, refurbished, or recycled. But recycling e-waste is not without its hazards (pp. 130–31).

Recycling paper: In 1999, paper consumption averaged 350 kg per person in the US, 200 kg in the UK, 33 kg in China, and less than 5 kg in India. Most of the paper we use is discarded and in some industrial countries paper makes up 40% of MSW. The US recovery rate of 46% still means 44 million tonnes are discarded each year (more than all the paper used in China). While 43% of the world's paper is currently recycled, there is no good technical or economic reason why this should not be doubled. Fibre-rich countries, such as Canada and Sweden, are not in the front rank of paper recyclers. Germany recycles 72%, S. Korea 66%, Canada 47% and Sweden 55%.

Recycling glass: The average UK family uses 500 glass bottles and jars a year. Many are recycled at one of the 50,000 bottle banks, but glass still makes up 8% of MSW. Benefits include energy savings, lower emissions, reduced landfill, and less quarrying – for each tonne of recycled glass, 1.2 tonnes of raw materials are preserved.

Industrial eco-parks: waste as a resource

Kalundborg, Denmark, is a blueprint for "industrial ecosystems" with its materials- and energy-exchange projects. An oil refinery employs waste heat from a power plant, and provides sulphur to a wallboard producer. At the same time, the power plant supplies steam to heat water for aquaculture and warms greenhouses and homes. The complex has greatly reduced its use of oil, coal, and water, also emissions of CO_2 and SO_2. In China's Tianjin Economic and Technological Development Area (TEDA), wastes produced by one business become raw materials for another. Circulation and interdependence among enterprises means no waste discharge. Similar industrial parks are underway in Sweden, Canada, and the US.

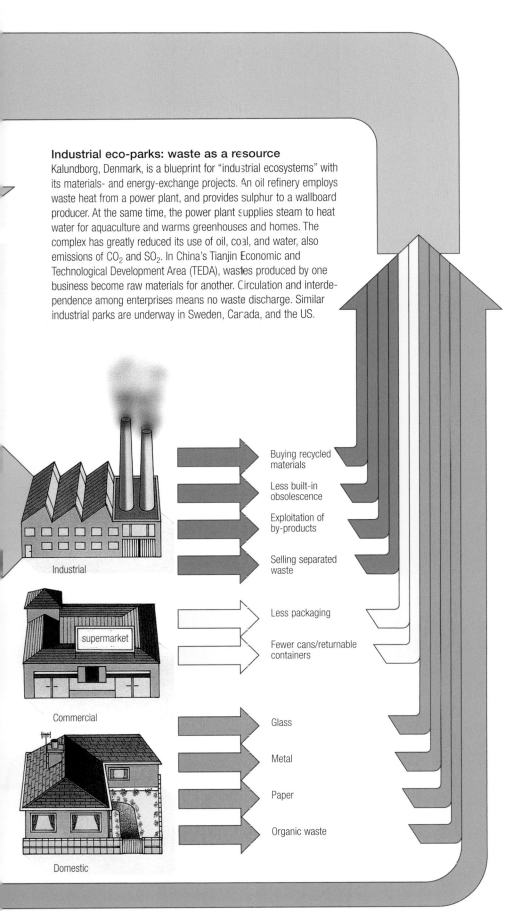

Industrial

Buying recycled materials

Less built-in obsolescence

Exploitation of by-products

Selling separated waste

supermarket

Commercial

Less packaging

Fewer cans/returnable containers

Glass

Metal

Paper

Domestic

Organic waste

EVOLUTION

Introduced by Paul Ehrlich
Professor of Population Studies, Stanford University, USA

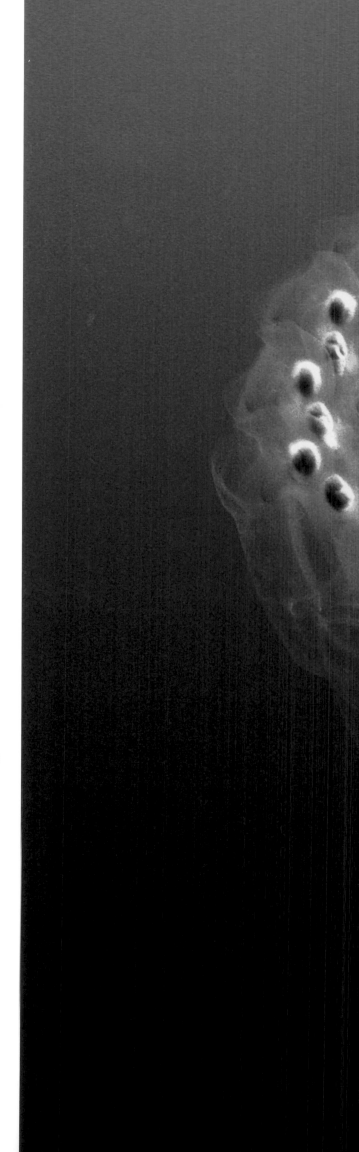

The human population has reached over six billion people by, in essence, "burning its capital" – destroying and dispersing a one-time bonanza of fossil fuels, minerals, deep soils, water, and the vast biological diversity generated by the process of evolution. It is the loss of biological diversity that may prove the most serious; certainly it is the most irreversible. *Homo sapiens* depends on the genetic variety present in the many millions of species and billions of their populations for an impressive range of services, many of them absolutely essential to the support of civilization.

We are causing some loss of biodiversity directly, by wiping out or severely over-harvesting certain species and populations, from rhinoceroses, elephants, spotted cats, and whales to orchids and cacti. But the major danger comes indirectly, from habitat destruction. Humanity is paving over, ploughing under, chopping down, damming, poisoning, and otherwise ruining habitats at a truly horrifying rate. It is primarily this that threatens the mountain gorilla, the California condor, and a host of lesser known organisms. The destruction of tropical forests alone could easily reduce the organic diversity of our planet by 50 percent in the next few decades.

Attempts are being made to arrest the decay of Earth's organic diversity: the Convention on International Trade in Endangered Species has delayed the extermination of some prominent species; at least on paper, a world system of "Biosphere Reserves" is being organized; and scientists working in the new discipline of countryside biogeography are struggling to find ways to make already seriously disturbed areas more hospitable to populations of organisms vitally important to us. But our efforts may be too little and too late. It is one thing to draw lines on maps around areas of tropical forest and declare them protected, quite another to find the will and resources to preserve them in perpetuity.

Even today, too much attention is focused on the preservation of species, whereas the loss of populations and the genetic diversity within species are probably more immediate and vital issues. The biochemical make-up of plants, for instance, is notoriously variable geographically – and plant chemicals have provided a great many of society's medicines and industrial products. By the time species are recognized as endangered, their utility to human beings is often greatly compromised: populations have been exterminated or are too small to be significant in delivering vital ecosystem services, gene pools are too depleted to permit successful domestication, and characteristics useful to us are lost.

What should be done is clear. In developed nations, disturbance of more land should be forbidden, and creation of additional exotic monocultures (golf courses, wheat fields, tree plantations) restrained. Priority should be given to enhancing habitats in the huge areas transformed by humanity, establishing more reserves on relatively undisturbed land and in the sea, and arresting the steady flux of poisons into the air and water, especially greenhouse gases and compounds that mimic natural hormones and may disrupt the development of many organisms. Programmes to protect and re-establish relatively natural ecosystems are doomed to failure if climates change rapidly and poisoning proceeds unchecked.

The problem is vastly more serious in the less developed nations, where raw population pressure and poverty make the continued destruction of natural systems seem inevitable and funds to ameliorate the impacts of climate change and toxification are unavailable. Poor nations, like poor people, must look always to their immediate needs. It is only by finding ways to help them provide for those needs that the rich nations can support conservation in the poor nations, and thus (in the long run) save themselves – for human survival is intertwined with the survival of biodiversity and thus with the fate of every natural system.

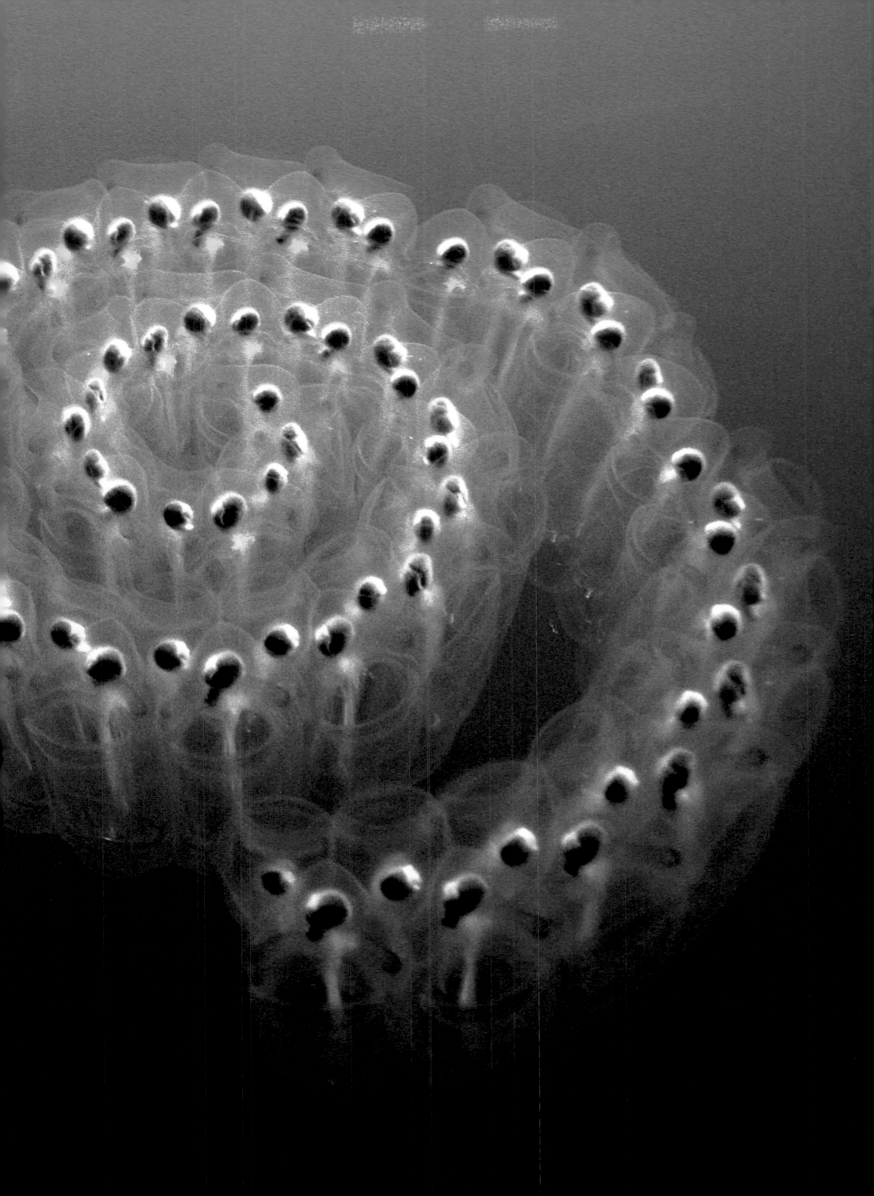

The Evolutionary Potential

The first flickerings of life emerged almost four billion years ago, shortly after the planet coalesced from a swirling mass of gases into solid state. From a primeval impulse of DNA, the "building block" of life, there has evolved a steadily expanding stream of life-forms, swelling to a flood as species have become ever-more numerous and diverse. The creative flow has been far from constant, however. It got off to a slow start, and as recently as the late Permian stage 225 million years ago, there were probably no more than 350,000 species, mostly marine creatures. But thereafter the spread of life on to land led to an outburst of evolution that has ultimately produced many millions of species.

Not that the prehistoric parade has merely grown larger. Certain categories of life have emerged to dominate from time to time, and have then been relegated to the sidelines. Our modern world is sometimes considered primarily a world of mammals and birds. But mammals and birds, which constitute only one in 700 at most of today's community, are relative newcomers. They did not reach prominence until towards the end of a reptilian era that had lasted for 160 million years.

The evolutionary process has culminated in today's array of life, a vast resource of material on which natural selection can work to generate still more abundant and complex manifestations of life. Our present life pool represents but a small part of the potential panoply of life that will steadily develop if *Homo sapiens*, a newly dominant species, allows the process to persist with the evolutionary capacity that has been at work since the beginning of life.

Peering into the dim past, then, we can discern a procession of ever-changing life-forms, with new ones appearing as old ones fade from the scene. The average duration of a species has been only a few million years, which means that of the half billion or so species that have ever lived, virtually all have disappeared.

As you gaze on the life pool of today, reflect that it does not amount to a mere conglomeration of species that go their separate ways. They depend on each other for multiple purposes. Plants, for example, supply more than food for plant eaters. They also help to maintain the mix of gases in our atmosphere, notably oxygen, nitrogen, and carbon dioxide, which support virtually every last form of life. Even the lowliest manifestations of life, bacteria, serve to

The life pool

All life is one. This is not a cliché but a biological fact. Over almost 4 billion years, a teeming variety of life-forms has evolved, yet in every living cell there are common features of nucleic acids that encode inheritance, and adenosine triphosphate that provides energy. In every living organism, hormones and similar compounds carry vital chemical messages. In turn, organisms are linked together in intricate ecosystems. What happens to one can affect all: our present biosphere has evolved only after photosynthesis in early algae and plants began to release essential oxygen into the atmosphere. Evolution produces vast diversity, yet it links all living forms in a single process.

We, as members of the species *Homo sapiens*, are the first life-forms to modify evolutionary processes, yet we do so largely in ignorance and by accident. We take small account of the intricate food chains that maintain both species and ecological harmony, or of the rich store of genetic information that species represent. Indeed, scientists have identified only one in four, possibly one in eight, of the planet's organisms (see below).

The biosystem is a library of survival strategies. It makes up an entire literature, a language and a tradition, every unique part of which may bear upon any other. Built up over billions of years of selection and extinction, it is as fragile as it is fecund.

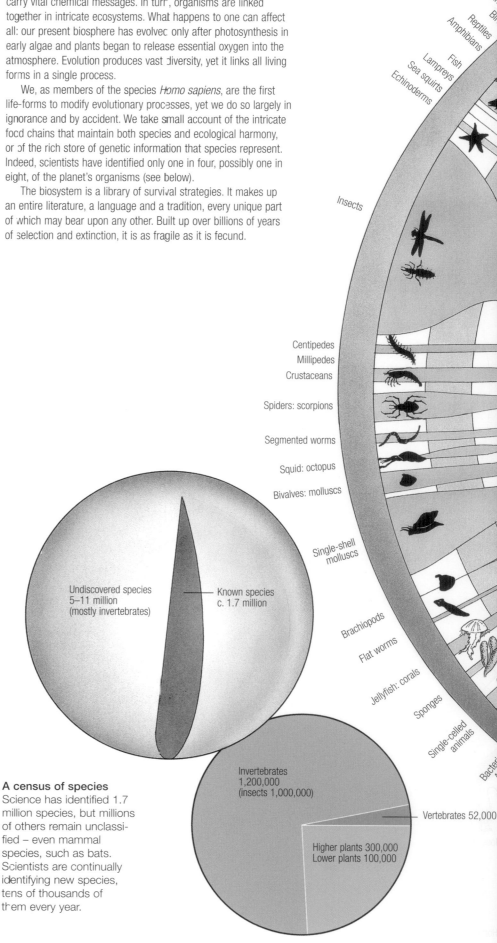

Undiscovered species 5–11 million (mostly invertebrates) — Known species c. 1.7 million

Invertebrates 1,200,000 (insects 1,000,000)

Vertebrates 52,000

Higher plants 300,000
Lower plants 100,000

A census of species
Science has identified 1.7 million species, but millions of others remain unclassified – even mammal species, such as bats. Scientists are continually identifying new species, tens of thousands of them every year.

Insects

Centipedes
Millipedes
Crustaceans

Spiders: scorpions

Segmented worms

Squid: octopus

Bivalves: molluscs

Single-shell molluscs

Brachiopods

Flat worms

Jellyfish: corals

Sponges

Single-celled animals

Bacteria

Reptiles
Amphibians
Fish
Lampreys
Sea squirts
Echinoderms

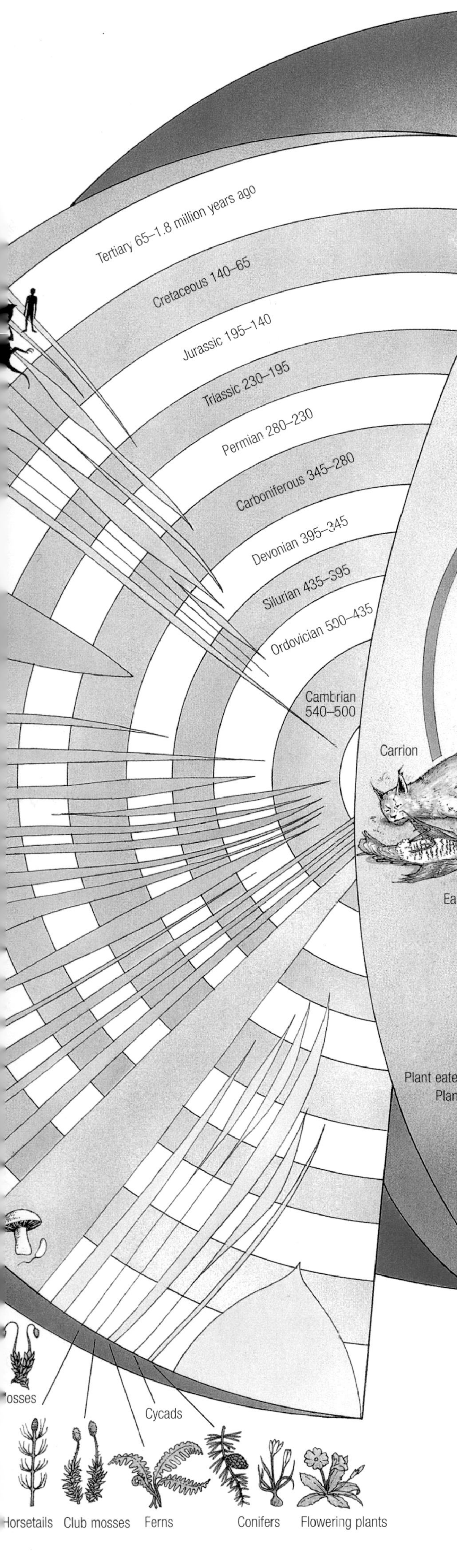

Food chains, food webs

Plants draw their resources from sunlight and soils. Photosynthesis and nutrients sustain them. In turn, plants sustain herbivores large and small, which may themselves succumb to predators. When predators and survivors die, they become food for carrion eaters, then insect larvae. Bacteria finally break them down into inorganic substances. These, drawn from the soil by plants, help to maintain the cycle. Similar systems, plankton-based, exist in the oceans. All are susceptible to disruption by human activities.

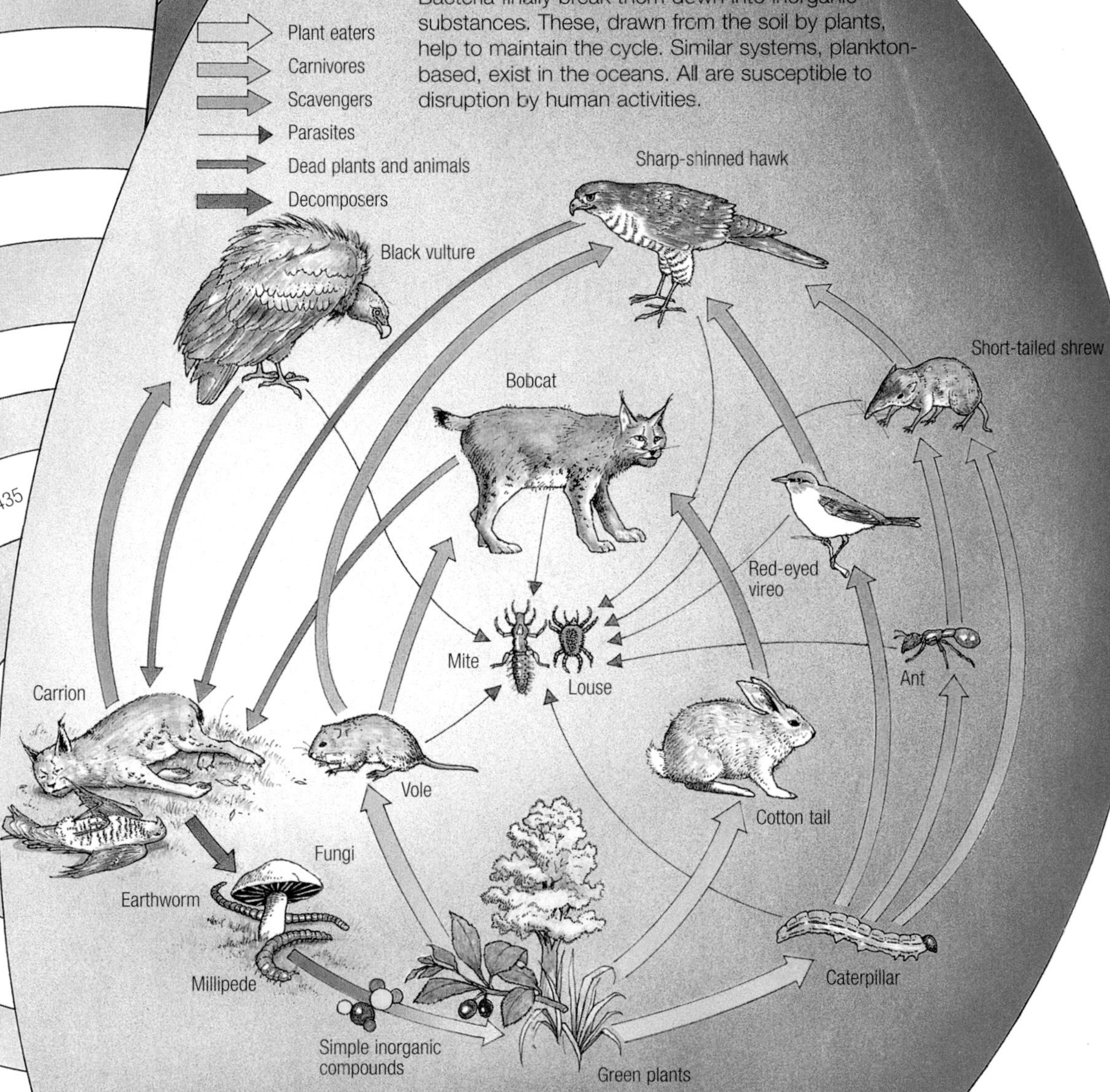

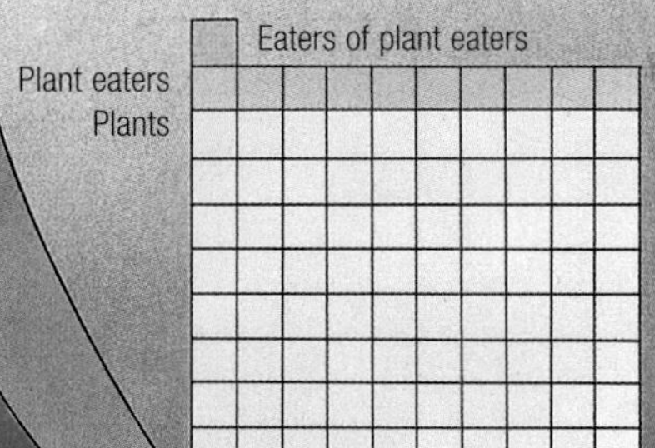

Plant eaters
Carnivores
Scavengers
Parasites
Dead plants and animals
Decomposers

Tertiary 65–1.8 million years ago
Cretaceous 140–65
Jurassic 195–140
Triassic 230–195
Permian 280–230
Carboniferous 345–280
Devonian 395–345
Silurian 435–395
Ordovician 500–435
Cambrian 540–500

Sharp-shinned hawk
Black vulture
Bobcat
Short-tailed shrew
Red-eyed vireo
Ant
Mite
Louse
Carrion
Vole
Cotton tail
Fungi
Earthworm
Millipede
Simple inorganic compounds
Green plants
Caterpillar

osses
Cycads
Horsetails   Club mosses   Ferns   Conifers   Flowering plants

Eaters of plant eaters
Plant eaters
Plants

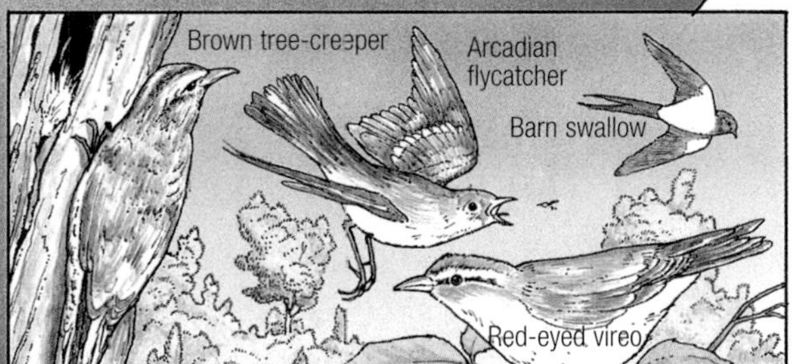

Brown tree-creeper
Arcadian flycatcher
Barn swallow
Red-eyed vireo

The edible pyramid

Plants use solar energy to synthesize glucose, a task beyond any animal. Plants provide 10 of the amino acids essential to animal survival. Without plants' photosynthesis, the life we know could not exist. All over the planet, on land and sea, plants act as the base of virtually every food chain.

Finding a niche

An organism exists in an environmental context, or ecological niche, which reflects its particular adaptations. Modified over time, these adaptations confirm it in its niche: new species are formed by divergence from previous norms. Many individuals, all pursuing their own survival strategy, can then inhabit the same general environment. Thus birds in one tree may not seek the same food; or – by catching insects on the leaves, under the bark, or on the wing – they may seek the same food but in different ways.

recycle nutrients that keep plants flourishing. In short, the life pool is much more than the sum of its parts. It is a single unifying phenomenon of our planet Earth, making it the only planet known to feature the genetic code of life, DNA.

Cooperative evolution

The life pool is the product of billions of years of evolution. We humans think of ourselves as the pinnacle of this process – more advanced, more important, and, above all, more powerful than lower forms of life, especially microbial life, which seems to us hardly alive at all.

But recent science has overturned these views to give a startling picture of our true place in nature. In the words of US scientist Lynn Margulis: "Far from leaving micro-organisms behind on an evolutionary ladder, we are both surrounded by them and composed of them." Microbes are everywhere: in soil; in every living structure; the foundation and stuff of all ecosystems. They are the rulers of our cells and bodies. This is certainly a "bug-driven" world.

The familiar division of life-forms into plants and animals is far less significant than the fundamental division of microbial life into two types, dauntingly named the prokaryotes (bacteria) and the eukaryotes (modern complex cells). The evolution of microbial life stretches back at least 3.7 billion years to the origins of life on Earth. For the first two billion years, the only life-forms were bacteria, yet these lowly creatures invented all the chemistry of life, such as photosynthesis to tap the sun's energy, fermentation to release the energy of dead matter, and oxygen breathing. In so doing they transformed the Earth, atmosphere, and oceans. Microbes have created the world we know.

Science is also making remarkable discoveries about evolution. To the classic mechanisms of random genetic mutation and survival of the fittest, must now be added gene swapping, the habit of bacteria of borrowing bits of genetic material floating in the medium around them. By this means bacteria have conducted a "fast-track" evolutionary process for almost four billion years.

Moreover, the Darwinian view of competition as the single driving force of evolution – nature red in tooth and claw – is now seen as naive. Cooperation to mutual advantage has often proved an equally successful evolutionary strategy – and one pioneered by microbes again. Long ago, bacterial cells once foreign and hostile to each other began entering into partnerships, sharing functions and genes through a process termed endosymbiosis. And so arose the modern eukaryotic cells and hence the evolution of plant and animal life, as the eukaryotes, with their complex cell structure and ability to specialize, formed new associations in multi-celled communities and organisms. We, *Homo sapiens*, are the product of microbial interaction and cooperation, a process of symbiotic evolution that continues today.

The web of Gaia

Far from being "lords of creation", we humans are a part of nature, beings woven from the web of Gaia. Our bodies are microbial collectives, communities of cooperative cells. The library of life's history is written within each one of us. As Charles Darwin said, "Each living creature must be looked at as a microcosmos, a little universe". We are accustomed to think of the geological history of the Earth, and the history of life, as separate strands. But we are learning that this is not so. Rather, the evolution of life and the environment have progressed hand in hand, each changing the other. Cells are the fundamental units of life, and they need a narrow range of conditions – temperature, moisture, chemistry – to survive. By exchanging energy and materials with the environment, cells not only sustain their internal state, but alter neighbouring conditions. Over aeons, the whole environment is thus shaped and sustained by cell activity. The gases of the air, the chemistry of soil and water, the very rocks beneath our feet are a product of this long interaction. The evolution of cellular life is mapped, right, from the beginnings almost 4 billion years ago, through the long age of bacteria, to the symbiotic origins of modern cells, and thence to multi-cellular plant and animal life and the biosphere of Gaia we know today.

Bacteria's long reign

The history of Earth's environment is written in the bacteria, which alone shaped it for the first 2 billion years. Ancient archebacteria reflect the conditions in the early Earth. There are salt-loving types, forms that thrive in sulphur springs or hot deep-sea vents, and fermenters that live without oxygen, breaking down dead matter in sediments. The younger "true" bacteria reveal the dramas that followed: blue-green algae with their great invention, photosynthesis, and its by-product, oxygen, that profoundly changed the world; and oxygen-breathing aerobic bacteria, the first consumers.

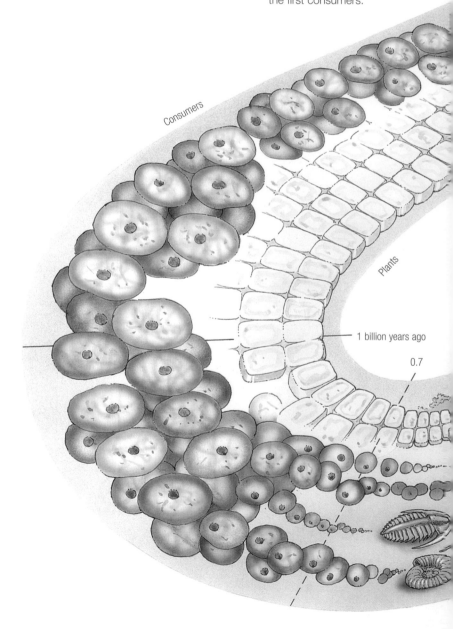

Consumers

Plants

1 billion years ago

0.7

Endosymbiosis

Cooperation and community have been central to life's evolutionary strategy. All the larger organisms are communities of cells. It now seems that the cells themselves are a product of ancient experiments in communal living. Evidence is increasingly accepted that certain key organelles in eukaryotic cells are the descendants of once free-living bacteria, that long ago took up residence inside other bacteria, known as urkaryotes, in a symbiotic relationship. According to this endosymbiosis idea, the first such resident was an aerobic bacterium, ancestor of the mitochondrion present in all modern cells. Later this host/mitochondrion partnership was joined by another resident, probably a photosynthesizing cyanobacterium – an ancestor of the chloroplast. From this new partnership all plants have evolved, and the process of symbiotic evolution continues today.

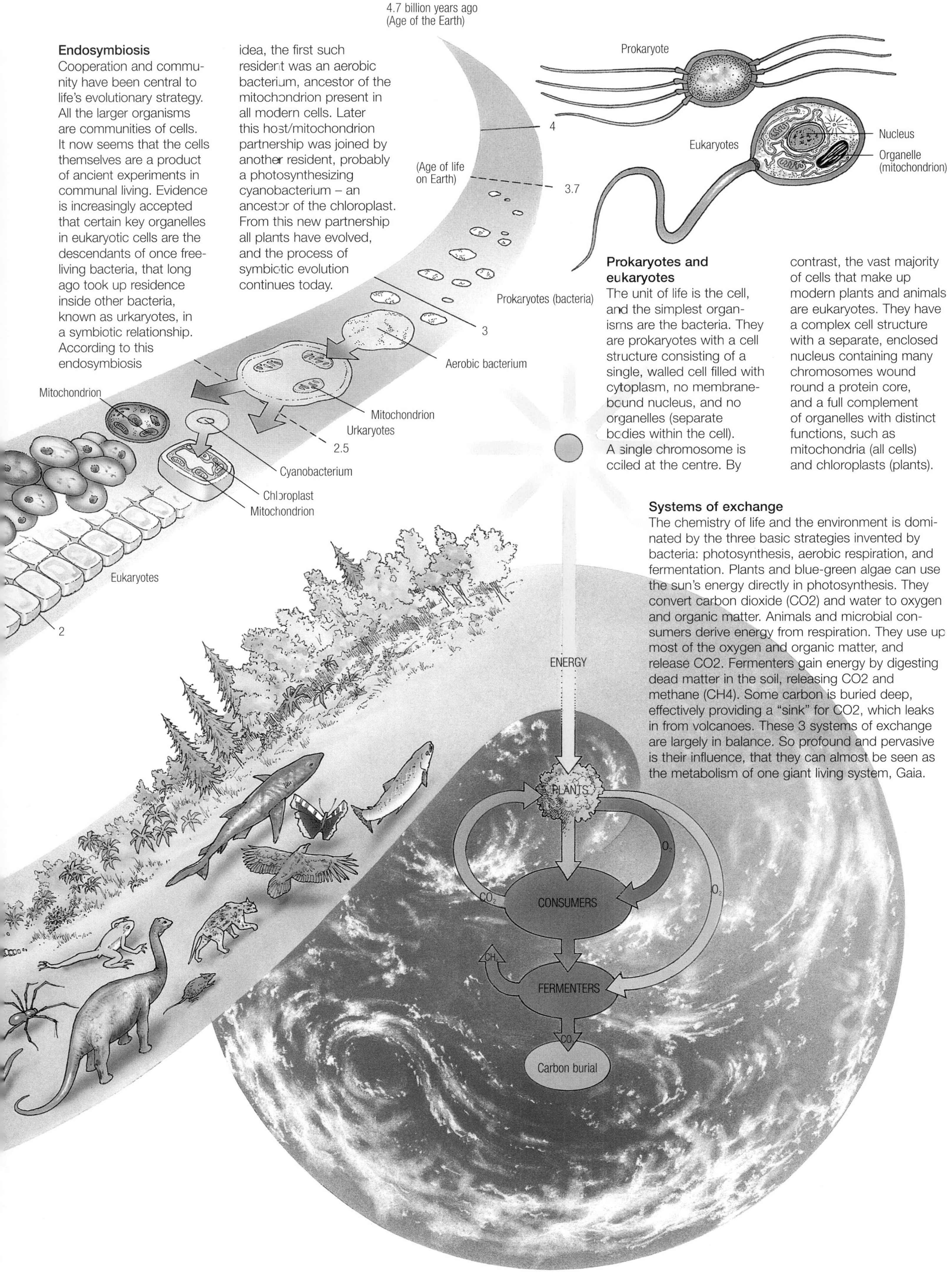

4.7 billion years ago
(Age of the Earth)

Prokaryote

4

(Age of life on Earth)

3.7

Eukaryotes

Nucleus

Organelle
(mitochondrion)

Prokaryotes (bacteria)

3

Aerobic bacterium

Mitochondrion

Mitochondrion

Urkaryotes

2.5

Cyanobacterium

Chloroplast
Mitochondrion

Eukaryotes

2

Prokaryotes and eukaryotes

The unit of life is the cell, and the simplest organisms are the bacteria. They are prokaryotes with a cell structure consisting of a single, walled cell filled with cytoplasm, no membrane-bound nucleus, and no organelles (separate bodies within the cell). A single chromosome is coiled at the centre. By contrast, the vast majority of cells that make up modern plants and animals are eukaryotes. They have a complex cell structure with a separate, enclosed nucleus containing many chromosomes wound round a protein core, and a full complement of organelles with distinct functions, such as mitochondria (all cells) and chloroplasts (plants).

Systems of exchange

The chemistry of life and the environment is dominated by the three basic strategies invented by bacteria: photosynthesis, aerobic respiration, and fermentation. Plants and blue-green algae can use the sun's energy directly in photosynthesis. They convert carbon dioxide (CO_2) and water to oxygen and organic matter. Animals and microbial consumers derive energy from respiration. They use up most of the oxygen and organic matter, and release CO_2. Fermenters gain energy by digesting dead matter in the soil, releasing CO_2 and methane (CH_4). Some carbon is buried deep, effectively providing a "sink" for CO_2, which leaks in from volcanoes. These 3 systems of exchange are largely in balance. So profound and pervasive is their influence, that they can almost be seen as the metabolism of one giant living system, Gaia.

ENERGY

PLANTS

O_2

CO_2

CONSUMERS

O_2

CH_4

FERMENTERS

CO_2

Carbon burial

Most challenging of all is the new view of the evolution of the Earth itself. Far from seeing its changing geology and evolving biota as two separate strands, science now begins to describe them as forming one integral process, which over the aeons has woven the seamless web of Gaia.

The natural habitat

Our blue planet, the only planet known to support any spark of life, supports it in extraordinary abundance and variety. From the tallest mountain peak to the deepest ocean trench, from rainless desert to dripping rainforest, there is scarcely a corner of the Earth's surface which does not reveal some variation on life's theme. Indeed, the diversity of our evolutionary resource defies imagination.

This evolutionary resource is anything but uniform. Life's most basic impulses send it racing down endlessly branching paths. Wherever we go, we encounter environmental variety. Each woodland, each stretch of open savannah, each wetland or montane ecosystem, has its own distinctive communities of plants and animals. But life has evolved clear strategies to meet such environmental challenges – and we see the results in recognizable associations such as the "spruce–moose" biome of North America's boreal forests.

Moreover, just as environments change, so life strategies are themselves in constant flux, developing ever-new variations on the vital theme. The key factors which help shape the patterns of life, and particularly vegetation patterns, include temperature and rainfall, together with two closely connected factors – latitude and altitude.

Once we know how hot or wet an environment is, or how cold and dry, and provided we know its location, we can make a fair guess about what forms of plant life are likely to predominate. Of course, other factors, such as soil type and topography, can also have an important influence. But, as a general rule, we know that at the Equator we shall find year-round warmth and moisture, and we shall expect to encounter evergreen rainforest.

As we move towards the tropics, rainfall becomes more seasonal, and we expect to see deciduous trees able to counter periodic drought. As the average rainfall decreases, we encounter increasingly open woodland, giving way to bush and then grassy plains. Finally, after moving through various forms of scrub, we find continental deserts. Other kinds of desert are found in seemingly unlikely places. The coastal deserts of Chile and Namibia, for example, are formed where cold offshore currents cool the air and prevent it rising high enough to produce rain.

Moving the tropics towards the poles, we find these vegetation patterns echoed by different forest formations and different types of grassland. The conditions are colder and winter becomes a force to be reckoned with. We encounter communities which are less fecund and varied than their tropical

Life strategies

Combinations of warmth and rainfall generate diverse life strategies. To portray these life strategies, biologists use an idealized or super-continent (right). It balloons to the north, reflecting the great land masses of Eurasia and North America. It tapers towards the Equator, and extends like a teardrop into the southern hemisphere to represent the shape of southern Africa and South America.

Compare this super-continent with a real-world map. We can see that if Mexico were to bulge out along the Tropic of Cancer, instead of almost dwindling away, we would have another vast desert corresponding to the Sahara; and if Africa bulged out along the Equator, we could expect a rainforest of Amazonian proportions.

Life strategies are broadly classified into large domains, known as biomes. These biomes reflect basic bio-communities which have evolved mainly in response to local variations in climate and topography.

Freshwater ecosystems

From river to sea, we encounter many kinds of life strategies. When the river is narrow and its current fast, plants cannot survive and most fish cannot thrive. When the river bed is less steep, plants root in the mud which lies in sheltered spots near the river banks. The current is still fast, but fish, such as trout or minnow can breed here. Further downstream, where the banks slope more gently, the water is turbid and the bed is full of sand and gravel, bream flourish. Finally, in the more salty and muddy estuarine region, flounder and smelt predominate, while salmon pass through on their spawning and feeding migrations.

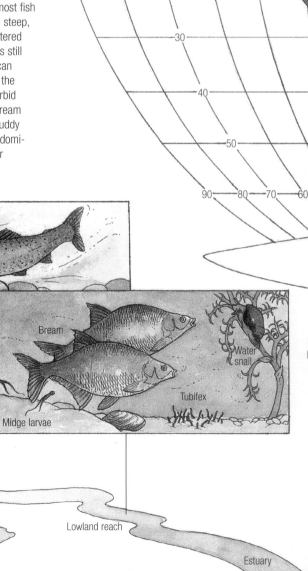

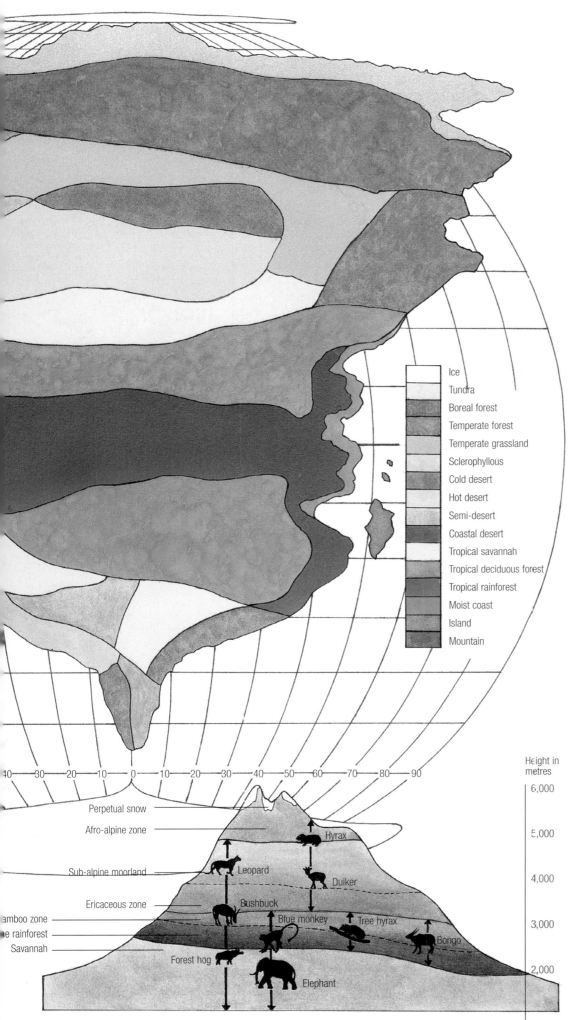

Ice
Tundra
Boreal forest
Temperate forest
Temperate grassland
Sclerophyllous
Cold desert
Hot desert
Semi-desert
Coastal desert
Tropical savannah
Tropical deciduous forest
Tropical rainforest
Moist coast
Island
Mountain

Height in metres

6,000
5,000
4,000
3,000
2,000

Perpetual snow
Afro-alpine zone
Sub-alpine moorland
Ericaceous zone
amboo zone
e rainforest
Savannah

Hyrax
Leopard
Duiker
Bushbuck
Blue monkey
Tree hyrax
Bongo
Forest hog
Elephant

40 30 20 10 0 10 20 30 40 50 60 70 80 90

Montane ecosystem
In the montane ecosystems of Africa, there is a complex succession of vegetation zones between the savannah at the lowest level, and the icefields which hitherto capped such mountains as Mount Kenya, Kilimanjaro, and the Mountains of the Moon. Moving up through the haunts of the elephant, forest hog, blue monkey, and bushbuck, we find far fewer animals as the ice comes closer.

Boreal forest
The boreal forest, accounting for 10% of the super-continent, fringes the northern sub-polar regions. Moose browse on spruce and birch, falling prey in turn to the timber wolf.

Temperate forest
Sometimes growing as tall as their boreal counterparts, the trees of the temperate forest cover 7% of the super-continent. They are a mixture of deciduous and coniferous trees, and shelter a bewildering array of insects, birds, and animals.

Savannah
Herbivores, such as the wildebeest and zebra, are found in their millions on open savannah, which covers 12% of the super-continent. Their predators include the lion, leopard, and cheetah.

Desert
Deserts cover almost one-quarter of the Earth's land surface (warm and semi-deserts, 18%, and cool-winter deserts, 7%). The cacti, roadrunner, and chuckwalla lizard (above) are found in the hot deserts of North America.

Tropical forest
Less than 10% of the supercontinent is covered by tropical forests. The rainforests (less than a third of tropical moist forests) are exceptionally rich in species; less so are tropical deciduous forests.

counterparts. Here, life strategies branch out from distinctive adaptations in response to seasonal change: caribou migrate to less harsh areas, birds head for distant horizons, while bears and squirrels go underground. In some areas of the world we can move through a bewildering succession of life strategies within a surprisingly short distance – for example, as we climb through a montane ecosystem.

Shaping our food base

Until 10,000 years ago our ancestors had little effect on the plants and animals around them. Then came a quantum leap with more profound implications for biodiversity than any during the previous million years, both for humankind and for a growing spectrum of once wild species. Often accidentally, our ancestors domesticated a few animals and plants, entering into an evolutionary partnership with selected species. No other living creature has accomplished this much control over the evolutionary process, and it has been an advance to alter the face of the Earth.

The first essential step occurred when our ancestors concentrated on those forms of wild grasses – grains – that promised to yield most food. They planted varieties with larger individual grains, with shorter growing seasons, and with other attributes that would serve their needs. They began to apply selection pressures that hitherto had remained the domain of "natural" evolution. Before long, they had developed types of wheat, for example, whose seed heads did not "shatter" and drop their seeds to the ground when ripe: these early breeders preferred to keep the seeds for their own use. This meant that without human help, wheat plants could no longer propagate themselves.

A similar pattern was repeated with animals, such as sheep and cattle. Selected for their docility among other traits, domesticated strains must soon have lost their capacity to survive on their own. Not only tamed by humans, but weighed down with flesh or milk, today's cattle breeds would be hard put to survive in the wild.

As one domestication followed another, our ancestors assembled a group of species that supplied them with a growing range of benefits. From these early successes, there evolved the phenomenon of full-scale agriculture. Today, a considerable proportion of the Earth's surface is devoted to staple crops or to huge herds of livestock. As a result of this "globalization" of basic food sources, a growing proportion of the world's population feeds from a common bowl.

Curiously enough, our ancestors contented themselves with just a handful of domesticates. Although hunter-gatherers had exploited hundreds of plants and dozens of animals, these early agriculturalists confined their attentions mainly to a total of less than 50 species. These basic food sources still meet our needs today. Just 30 crops supply 95 percent of our nutrition, and a mere eight, led by wheat,

Partners in evolution

Homo sapiens has derived great benefit from a special partnership with Earth's plant and animal species. Intensive farming of a minority of species has released a large proportion of humankind for work other than food growing, and enabling thousand-fold increases in human population.

Purposeful crossbreeding to produce improved varieties is a modern development. Previously, agriculturalists would select the more productive species and leave evolution to work its own advances by natural crossbreeding. As a result, the earliest domestications occurred in the areas of greatest diversity shown on the world map, right, where the probability of "crosses" leading to improved varieties was greatest. The areas are not rigidly defined; some species were being domesticated at the same time in different places.

Animal farm

As with crop plants, humankind has evolved a special partnership with animals: a small number of highly efficient animals provide all our needs. For example, dairy cows can yield up to 6,000 litres per lactation with current farming methods. They are fed high-energy concentrates by computer-controlled feeders. The price of this efficient production is the near-total dependence of such animals on their keepers.

NORTH AMERICA
Turkey

MESO AMERICA
Maize
Tomato
Cassava
Sweet potato
Turkey

HIGHLAND SOUTH
AMERICA
Potato
Peanut

 Areas of origin: domestic plants and animals

 Maize: dispersal

Travelling partners
Our most valued and adaptable crops have travelled with us in early migrations, invasions, explorations, and to colonial settlements. Some have spread to the far corners of the Earth. Others, such as coffee, now dominate lands far from their point of origin. The map shows the peregrinations of corn.

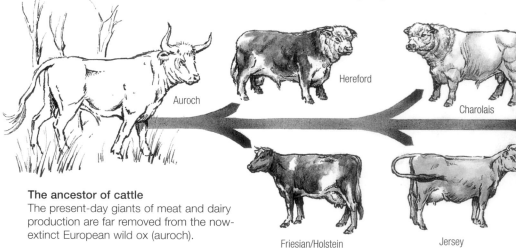

Auroch

Hereford

Charolais

Friesian/Holstein

Jersey

The ancestor of cattle
The present-day giants of meat and dairy production are far removed from the now-extinct European wild ox (auroch).

The corn story

Originally allowed to grow in fields of primitive corn because it enhanced the yield, the wild Mexican grass Teosinte became the ancestor of modern corn (also known as maize). The diagrams (right) which are based on modern breeding experiments, reveal how the hard outer casing of the Teosinte "spike" is gradually made softer. Eventually, we arrive at the giant modern variety (far right), drawn to scale – its kernel fruit totally exposed. Without human intervention to remove and plant its kernels, modern corn would become extinct in a few generations. The seedlings would be so densely clustered that they would compete among themselves for water, soil, and nutrients, and fail to reach reproductive size.

Teosinte

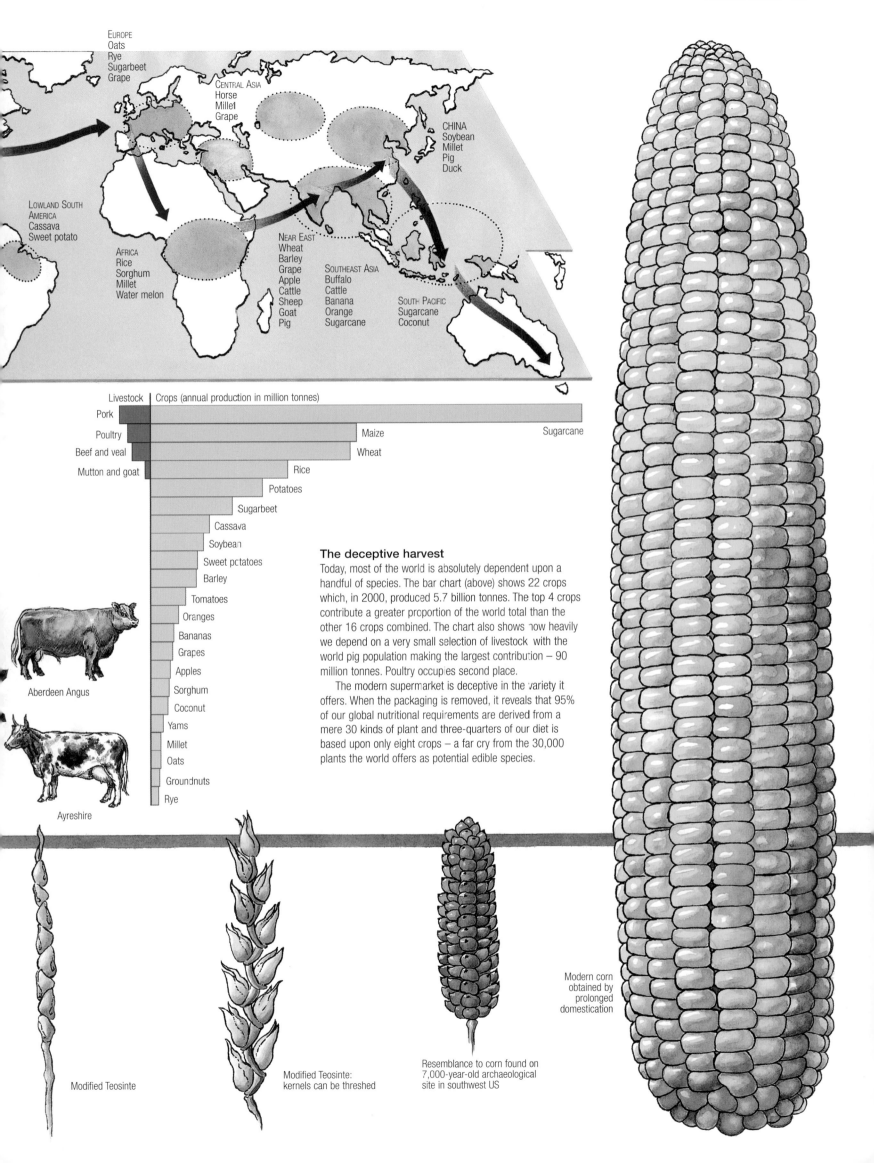

EUROPE
Oats
Rye
Sugarbeet
Grape

CENTRAL ASIA
Horse
Millet
Grape

CHINA
Soybean
Millet
Pig
Duck

LOWLAND SOUTH
AMERICA
Cassava
Sweet potato

AFRICA
Rice
Sorghum
Millet
Water melon

NEAR EAST
Wheat
Barley
Grape
Apple
Cattle
Sheep
Goat
Pig

SOUTHEAST ASIA
Buffalo
Cattle
Banana
Orange
Sugarcane

SOUTH PACIFIC
Sugarcane
Coconut

Livestock | Crops (annual production in million tonnes)

Pork
Poultry
Beef and veal
Mutton and goat

Sugarcane
Maize
Wheat
Rice
Potatoes
Sugarbeet
Cassava
Soybean
Sweet potatoes
Barley
Tomatoes
Oranges
Bananas
Grapes
Apples
Sorghum
Coconut
Yams
Millet
Oats
Groundnuts
Rye

Aberdeen Angus

Ayreshire

The deceptive harvest

Today, most of the world is absolutely dependent upon a handful of species. The bar chart (above) shows 22 crops which, in 2000, produced 5.7 billion tonnes. The top 4 crops contribute a greater proportion of the world total than the other 16 crops combined. The chart also shows how heavily we depend on a very small selection of livestock with the world pig population making the largest contribution – 90 million tonnes. Poultry occupies second place.

The modern supermarket is deceptive in the variety it offers. When the packaging is removed, it reveals that 95% of our global nutritional requirements are derived from a mere 30 kinds of plant and three-quarters of our diet is based upon only eight crops – a far cry from the 30,000 plants the world offers as potential edible species.

Modified Teosinte

Modified Teosinte:
kernels can be threshed

Resemblance to corn found on
7,000-year-old archaeological
site in southwest US

Modern corn
obtained by
prolonged
domestication

maize and rice, provide three-quarters of our diets. Our meat and milk come from a still smaller range of species. Thus, we practise an agriculture that is, in terms of its array of sources, not much more than a Neolithic agriculture. What prospects could lie ahead for us if we were to develop more of these evolutionary partnerships, realizing more of the potential of the genetic resources around us?

Tapping diversity

Diversity is the hallmark of life on Earth, manifested through species, races, and populations within a species, or individuals within a population. Just as the millions of species that make up the life stream are bewilderingly diverse to the eye, so outwardly

identical organisms prove to be astonishingly diverse if we concentrate our gaze on the level of the gene.

One individual organism may have thousands of genes, each gene influencing an inherited trait such as height, weight, growth rate, or disease resistance. Even if the individuals within a species are counted in millions or billions, such statistics shrink in scale when compared with the number of potential genetic permutations the individuals could produce. And it is this diversity, passed on by genes, which holds the key to a species' ability to adapt to environmental pressures. Naturally, only a tiny fraction of the genetic potential is ever expressed, since most organisms die before they can reproduce. Even so, this genetic potential is one of our world's most valuable resources.

The genetic resource

Our genetic resources represent an extraordinarily stocked library. Each species can be seen as a single book on one of an unknown number of shelves, each page a slice of its gene pool.

So far, we have made surprisingly little use of this library, concentrating on a few volumes of immediate interest. Yet even these few volumes have provided us with uncounted benefits, some of which are described here.

Tragically, this vast, valuable, and irreplaceable gene library is being vandalized. Complete volumes, indeed entire shelves, are being lost in bouts of habitat destruction, and key sections of the library are now in danger of being gutted. We are losing genetic information and materials whose value we can only guess at. Once the value of the library is fully recognized, its beneficiaries will be more likely to secure its future.

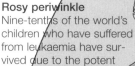

Jojoba
Long considered a desert curiosity, jojoba produces a wax which is a good substitute for sperm whale oil, and is used widely in cosmetics and lubricants. Jojoba oil sells for $22–44 per kg.

Rosy periwinkle
Nine-tenths of the world's children who have suffered from leukaemia have survived due to the potent therapies of the rosy periwinkle.

Tilapia
The East African tilapia fish converts food to flesh faster than most other fish and is increasingly used in aquaculture.

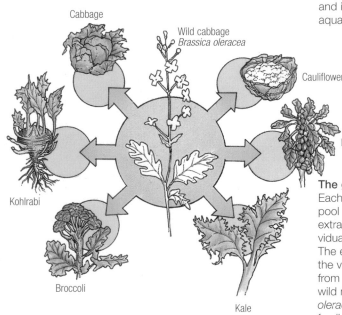

Cabbage
Wild cabbage *Brassica oleracea*
Cauliflower
Brussels sprout
Kohlrabi
Broccoli
Kale

The gene pool
Each species has a gene pool from which an extraordinary array of individuals can be selected. The examples here show the variety that is enjoyed from the gene pools of wild mustard, *Brassica oleracea*, and the dog family. If all but pedigree greyhounds disappeared from the Earth, we could say that "the dog" had been conserved – but imagine the loss of genetic variety.

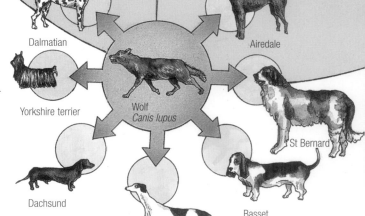

Dalmatian
Airedale
Yorkshire terrier
Wolf *Canis lupus*
St Bernard
Dachsund
Basset
Greyhound

Guayule
Guayule, a desert shrub, produces a natural rubber. The shrub's genetic diversity is exceptionally large.

Every day, and almost always unaware, we use products whose very availability and usefulness reflect that genetic wealth. Our staple food crops achieve marvels of productivity every year because of genetic improvements by the world's crop breeders in order to make crop plants more amenable to irrigation, fertilizers, and pesticides.

Similar advances are made every day in medicine. Every time we buy a drug or other pharmaceutical, there's a 50:50 chance that we can thank the genetic resources of a wild species. If you had leukaemia as a child in 1950, or if you had Hodgkin's disease or a related cancer, you had only a 1:20 chance of long-term survival. Today, thanks to two drugs developed from the rosy periwinkle, a tropical

forest plant, you would have an 8:10 chance. Plant-derived, anti-cancer drugs now save 30,000 lives in the US each year, with economic benefits of at least $370 billion (1990 $s). During the 1990s, the cumulative commercial value of plant-based medicines in developed nations was at least $500 billion.

Similarly, many forms of industry process this genetic wealth into useful products. Every time we polish the furniture, pull on our jogging shoes, hit a golf ball, or ride in a jet, we can thank genetic resources that in one way or another contribute to such products.

Today's benefits are astonishing enough, yet they represent the tip of an iceberg. So far, scientists have taken only a preliminary look at a mere 10 percent

Molluscs
Molluscs are first-rate pollution monitors. Other marine organisms have proved useful for viral research.

Sharks
Sharks are the only vertebrates that seem immune to cancer. Hence, they are vital models for research into human cancer.

Value of the wild

Every hour of every day, a growing number of plants and animals underpin the quality of our lives. A single gene from Ethiopia protects California's barley crop against yellow dwarf disease. Aspirin, probably the world's most widely used drug, has been developed from a chemical blueprint supplied by willow bark. The contraceptive pill stems from diosgenin in wild Mexican yams. Yet we are destroying this wealth as fast as it is being discovered. The overfishing of the Great Rift Lakes of eastern Africa, for example, which contain hundreds of endemic Cichlid fish species, could destroy this wild gene pool and reduce our chances of breeding superior fish. (Lake Victoria was once home to more than 500 different species of haplochromine Cichlids before Nile perch were introduced in the 1950s and subsequently wiped out half of them.) Similarly, despite its value to haemophilia research, the ungainly Florida manatee has been reduced to only 2,000 individuals. Perhaps worst of all is the certain knowledge that we are destroying species before their full value has been estimated.

Armadillos
The only animal known to contract leprosy, the armadillo helps to manufacture a vaccine.

Manatees
The Florida manatee has slow-clotting blood, a characteristic that has led to new insights into haemophilia.

Genetic engineering

By unlocking the potential of our genetic resources, genetic engineers could make exceptionally helpful advances. The new gene-manipulation techniques could accelerate breeding programmes, and thus achieve genetic combinations which would scarcely be possible in nature.

As the examples show (right), we still benefit from accelerated plant-breeding techniques. But the use of tissue culture and gene transfer promises to launch a new era. If we could, say, transfer the nitrogen-fixing ability of the bean to wheat, we could dispense with many costly fertilizers. The agricultural biotechnology industry could have been worth more than $100 billion a year in the late 1990s, but future advances could be restricted if the world's wild gene pools continue to be depleted.

Lycopersicon pimpinellifolium

Tomato
Many of today's commercial tomato varieties could not have remained viable without the resistance to Fusarium wilt provided by the wild Peruvian tomato.

Helianthus petiolaris

Sunflower
The symbol of a healthy diet, the sunflower ranks as one of the world's most important oil crops, thanks to inputs from the gene pool of its wild relatives.

Manihot glasiovii

Cassava
The yield of this front-rank food crop has been boosted experimentally by as much as 18 times since disease-resistance traits were transferred from its wild cousin, *Manihot glasiovii*.

of the 300,000 higher plant species, several dozen of which have already proved to be of major economic importance. And we have scarcely begun to investigate the potential of the animal kingdom.

Librarians of the rainforest

How are we to unlock the secrets of the wild? How can we best penetrate the ancient "library" that is the genetic resource?

The people of Suriname have a saying: "Na boesi, ingi sabe ala sani", which means "In the jungle, the Indian knows best". It is here, amongst the populations of traditional and vanishing cultures, that one important answer lies. Traditional cultures are the "librarians" of our "gene library" and each holds a stack of index cards carefully drawn up after hundreds of years of patient trial and error.

There are various other ways to "unlock the wild". Scientists can try random screening of plants. But this ultimately entails thousands of screening tests, much time, and a great deal of money. A better option is to search through the literature of traditional cultures. Or we can carry out studies of unpublished ethnobotanical data, which, combined with spot tests, often lead us to species worthy of further research.

But the best option of all is for ethnobotanists to concentrate on fieldwork. For example, one study of the Amazonian rainforests by two US scientists has resulted in the identification of more than a thousand plants which have potential economic benefits. The project was dedicated to examining traditional uses of forest plants by native dwellers of the rainforests. The research revealed that at east six plants were

Keys to the wild

As we become increasingly remote from natural environments, and from the resources they contain, so we become ever-more dependent on the knowledge and skills of those who live in close harmony with their immediate environment. Many of our foods and pharmaceuticals were first investigated because of their use by indigenous peoples. Instead of bulldozing aside these "human keys" to the wild, we should see them as a vital, intrinsic element of the ecosystems we are trying to conserve.

Even with the extraordinarily sophisticated equipment now available for extracting and analysing animal, microbial, and plant materials, our basic problem is simply knowing where to start. There are many examples of the ways in which traditional societies have helped focus our search for new medicines, new foods, and other products. By respecting and conserving human diversity, we will ensure that we can tap the hidden wealth in conserved areas.

Heart-stopping poison from Guyana

Indians in a Guyana rainforest have for centuries used a fish poison which, rather than leaving the fish prey to other fish eaters, such as piranhas, drastically changes their behaviour – causing them almost to fly out of the water. Dr Conrad Gorinsky has pointed to the possibilities of this drug in heart surgery, since it is able to stop the heart without killing the organ. The heart can be re-started after surgery. The plant species responsible for this poison was discovered in 1774 by Christophe Fusee Aublet, but was wrongly described as having the characteristics of a very close but inactive relative. This type of confusion is not uncommon. To the Indians of Guyana, Aublet's *Clibadium sylvestre* (Aubl.) is quite distinct and can be identified by its smell and the different bracts on its leaves.

being used as contraceptives by the forest's inhabitants. Other discoveries, to name but a few, included a cure for fungal skin infection, a high-protein coconut fruit that could be used for feed and fertilizer, and a seed that could be used to make soap.

Yet forest peoples, probably the only humans who successfully manage forests on a sustainable basis, are themselves in a state of crisis. These "librarians" look set for dismissal, their libraries threatened with closure. Experience shows that these cultures, which have evolved and developed over thousands of years, can disappear at virtually instant speed. In Amazonia alone, more than 90 tribes are thought to have died out during the last century. Many more forest peoples will shortly cease to exist as cultural entities.

One way out of this tragedy is to put the world of the "gene librarians" on a sound economic footing. Already, several African and Asian nations have begun to encourage the development of traditional medicine as an important component of their public health care programmes – the World Health Organization estimates that 80 percent of people in the world rely on traditional medicine. Indigenous medicines are relatively cheap, and readily accepted by the local populace.

Developing countries often cannot afford to spend millions of dollars on importing medicines. Some countries, such as Thailand and Nepal, have developed their medicinal plants into a means of earning foreign exchange. Even in Germany, a few forests are managed to encourage the growth of purple foxglove, the source of digitalis.

Indians, mayapple, and cancer

North American Indians have provided a key to an important wild resource – the mayapple. The vanishing tribes of North American Indians, centuries ago, unlocked the secrets of this remarkable plant species. Used by Penobscot Indians to treat warts and by Cherokees to treat deafness and kill parasitic worms, the secret properties of the mayapple were then passed on to the colonists. Today, they are under the microscopic eye of modern chemists. VePesid, a semi-synthetic derivative of podophyllotoxin – a natural extract of mayapple, is used to treat testicular cancer. In some instances, it has attained up to 47% recovery rate for treated patients.

The mayapple story is not yet over. Following the advice of North American Indians, it has also been successfully used to repel potato beetles. Moreover, the mayapple shows some interesting activity towards important viruses, such as Herpes 1, Herpes 2, Influenza A, and measles.

Medicine men and toothache trees

Local experts, like the medicine man shown above, are being consulted in their hundreds in an attempt to collect information on the uses of plants by traditional societies. In Tanzania, one scientist discovered a tree used by local people to cure toothache – not only was it a completely new species, but its genus had not been recorded in Africa. In Amazonia, an ethnobotanic team has catalogued more than 1,000 plants used by South American rainforest Indians which have economic potential as food, medicines, or industrial raw materials. Tubocurarine, for example, is used as a muscle relaxant. Derived from the pareira plant, it is found wild in the tropical forests of southern Brazil, Peru, Colombia, and Panama.

Evolution in Crisis

On the timescale of evolution, our species scarcely registers. But in terms of its impact on the resources of the planet, as on the genetic heritage which is the living foundation of the future, our brief history is all too significant. It is a story of destruction.

Habitat destruction

So far as we know, ours is the only green planet in the universe. Yet we, the latest inhabitants, are depleting this rich heritage at a rate that will grossly impoverish the Earth's green cover in a twinkling of geological time.

We have already seen that we are expanding deserts and eliminating tropical forests at a critical rate (see pp. 40–41, 44–45). We look set to destroy much of our inheritance of coral reefs, mangroves, estuaries, and wetlands. We shall plough up enormous areas of grassland. Still other areas will be paved over, chopped down, dug up, drained, and poisoned – or will be "developed" until their natural potential is homogenized out of existence. All this we shall do in the name of human welfare.

Unless we achieve a remarkable turn-around in the stewardship of our heritage, the century ahead will witness a speeding up of the destructive process as human numbers continue to surge and human appetites for raw materials grow keener. Yet who can blame the subsistence farmers who, in order to feed their starving families, degrade the natural resource base of tomorrow's livelihood? More culpable are the super-affluent citizens of the developed nations who, by demanding ever-greater flows of natural resources from all over the world, are even more destructive.

Our great-grandchildren may well look out on a planet that has suffered far greater depletion than during the course of a major glaciation. Were they, by then, to have learned how to live in ecological accord with the Earth's life-support systems, they will surely find that the damage of 200 years of human activity will take millennia to restore.

We are finding that some tropical forests, once removed, do not readily re-establish. When soil cover disappears, together with critical stocks of nutrients, the forest's comeback is pre-empted. Desertification is also irreversible except at massive cost. Moreover, certain sectors of the biosphere, notably tropical forests, coral reefs, and wetland ecosystems, serve, by virtue of their biotic richness and their ecological complexity, as "powerhouses" of evolution. By destroying these salient sectors of the biosphere, we are impoverishing the future for millions of years.

The irreplaceable heritage

Living organisms are the heirs of almost 4 billion years of evolution. Just as the complexities of their inheritance almost defy calculation, so the consequences of our disruption of their networks of biological interdependence cannot readily be analysed or predicted. Yet humanity often seems to regard this heritage with indifference at best. Mismanagement now threatens to destroy entire sectors of the biosphere, inflicting grievous injury on our very life-support systems.

Various pressures bring this about. Poverty in one part of the world is matched by excessive consumerism elsewhere, but the outcome tends to be the same – wholesale over-exploitation of humanity's environment. Entire ecosystems are undermined: over-grazing and brush clearance constantly extend the deserts; coastal wetlands, drained for agriculture, spill toxic chemicals instead of nutrients into the sea, while industrial wastes and sewage aggravate their impact; each minute around 30 ha of tropical forest are destroyed, diminishing the habitats of thousands of species; in Europe, intensive cultivation eliminates woodlands and hedgerows, together with their myriad organisms.

The balances and linkages that are the very process of life on Earth thus come under threat. What if they finally unravel?

Britain's vanishing countryside

Between 1984 and 1990, hedgerows were vanishing at a rate of 22,000 km per year, with all the plants and animals they supported. Lowland heath has declined by four-fifths since the 1800s. Mature grasslands with their wildflower meadows have also been ploughed up or built over.

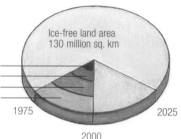

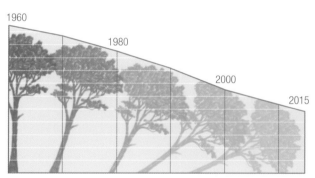

The shrinking forest
Brazil has already lost almost 600,000 sq. km of its Amazonian forests – an area the size of France – and deforestation continues at 24,000 sq. km a year. Indonesia has lost over 70% of its original forest. The graph (above) shows the decline in area of tropical forests (see also pp. 40–41).

The disappearing soil
20 million sq. km (15% of the Earth's land surface) have been degraded, while water and wind erosion combined have affected around 17 million sq. km (13% of the Earth's land surface). What of the next 25 years?

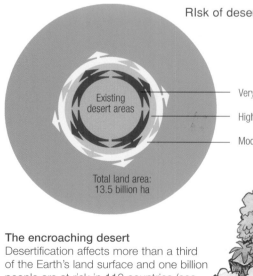

Risk of desertification

Very high

High

Moderate

Existing desert areas

Total land area: 13.5 billion ha

The encroaching desert
Desertification affects more than a third of the Earth's land surface and one billion people are at risk in 110 countries (see also pp. 44–45). Each year 150,000 sq. km – an area larger than Greece – becomes desertified.

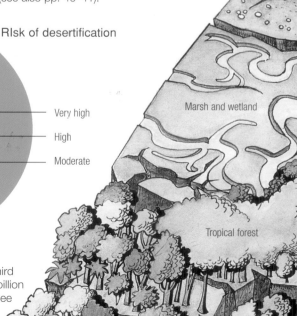

Marsh and wetland

Tropical forest

Threatened Cape flora

The Cape Floristic Province's biodiversity hotspot has already lost more than 75% of its original primary vegetation – just 18,000 sq. km remain. This hotspot harbours one of the most significant concentrations of flora on Earth, with 5,682 of its 8,200 plant species found nowhere else (see also p. 49).

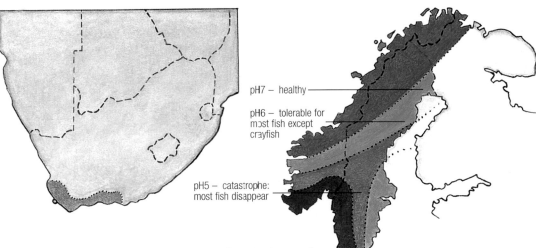

pH7 – healthy

pH6 – tolerable for most fish except crayfish

pH5 – catastrophe: most fish disappear

pH4 – eels are the only fish species able to survive

Acid rain in Scandinavia

In a lake with a pH of 5.5, most fish perish; with a pH of 4, the ecosystem can die. Lower figures on the pH scale indicate greater acidity. About 17,000 of Sweden's 90,000 lakes are acidified – 10,000 of them so severely that sensitive organisms cannot survive. Since 1977, a further 7,000 lakes have been kept alive with regular liming – the costs of which reached $270 million by 1998. Sweden has made great advances in reducing sources of acid rain within its own borders, but it receives large quantities of acidifying sulphur dioxide from other countries.

Deciduous woodland

Tundra

Mountain

Meadow

Savannah

River

Island

Lake

Coral reef

Estuary

Loss of species

Well over 90 percent all the species that have ever lived have disappeared. They have become extinct through natural processes, often giving way to "better" or "fitter" species. After humankind appeared on the scene and learned to hunt animals for food, commerce, and sport, often disrupting wildlife habitats in the process, the extinction rate started to soar until eventually it reached at least several species a year in the early 20th century.

Today, when natural environments are being degraded and destroyed on many a side, the effective extinction rate has surely reached 25–50 species a day. The extinction rate is "effective" as many species will become doomed to die – known to biologists as "the living dead" – because their habitats will have become too small and fragmented for long-term survival, even though they may take a century or more to finally disappear. Within the next few decades we stand to witness the effective extinction of several million species, conceivably as many as half of the Earth's total number – unless we make much greater efforts to save them.

In its sheer scale and compressed time span, this extinction spasm will represent a greater biological débâcle than anything experienced since life began. In terms of numbers alone, it could well exceed the "great dying" of the dinosaurs and associated species 65 million years ago, when half of Earth's species disappeared.

Scientists have documented approximately 52,000 species of vertebrate and 300,000 species of higher plant, together with, very roughly estimated, at least 100,000 species of lower plants. The great bulk of the 7 to 13 million species currently thought to exist are invertebrates, of which insects comprise 80–90 percent. It is the invertebrates, particularly the insects, that feature in the great bulk of extinctions underway.

When conservationists used to say that we were losing two or three species a year, they were referring almost exclusively to plants, mammals, and birds, the latter two groups accounting for less than 15,000 species. Botanists have compiled a fairly detailed account of the plants currently threatened with extinction, coming up with a total of 5,611 species (though some botanists would say several times as many, perhaps 30,000). Further, they believe that, as a rough rule of thumb, there are at least 20 animal species for every one plant species, often dependent on those plants for survival. So for every plant that disappears, many more animal species will eventually disappear.

Ironically, the reduced stock of species which survives this wave of extinctions is likely to include an unusually high number of opportunistic species, able to move into ecological niches vacated by recently extinct species or to thrive on humans' rubbish. Such opportunists include the housefly, the rabbit, the rat and "weedy" plants. We are creating a pest-dominated world.

The destruction of diversity

We are into the early phase of what looks set to become an unprecedented era of extinctions. True, extinction has always been a fact of life on Earth, but the present wave of extinctions is between 1,000 and 10,000 times the natural or "background" rate of prehistory. Indeed, the grand-scale biological impoverishment underway threatens to disrupt evolution itself.

The flame of life

From its first flickerings, almost 4 billion years ago, the flame of life has burned ever brighter, dying down during the major periods of extinction but leaping back to even greater heights thereafter. Today, the flame of life is threatened by intense human pressures: habitat destruction is gathering pace.

Millions of years ago

Cambrian 540–500	Ordovician 500–435	Silurian 435–395	Devonian 395–345	Carboniferous 345–280

NEWTON-LE-WILLOWS
LIBRARY
TEL: 01744 677886
01744 677887

Unravelling the tapestry of life

Like a child tugging threads from an enormous piece of tapestry, we continue to tear at the web of life with scant knowledge of possible impacts. Consider, for instance, the backlash of digging limestone out of caves near Kuala Lumpur in Malaysia. This resulted in destruction of the roosting sites and feeding grounds of a bat, *Eonycteris spelaea*. This bat species turned out to be the prime pollinator of one of Southeast Asia's most prized fruit crops, the durian tree, with a crop worth $120 million per year.

Today's dodos

Everybody has heard of the dodo, extinct 300 years ago, but few people are aware of other life-forms now under threat. When the dodo disappeared, at least one tree species, reliant on the dodo for its seed germination, started a long-term slide towards extinction.

The scale of destruction

We are effectively losing 25–50 species a day from the 7–13 million species thought to exist. By the time humans reach a degree of environmental equilibrium with their One Earth habitat, at least a quarter and possibly a half of all species could have disappeared. Habitat destruction is now the most important cause of species loss. If present trends continue, particularly the loss of tropical forests, we can expect far higher annual rates of species extinctions.

| ermian 30–230 | Triassic 230–195 | Jurassic 195–140 | Cretaceous 140–65 | Tertiary 65–1.8 | The future |

A crisis of uniformity

Each mammal, insect, or plant that is pushed into the abyss of extinction takes with it genes which could have proved valuable to humans. As species disappear, so do gene pools, and so does the prospect of exploiting those genes to improve our future welfare. Losses through extinction are irreversible, and our ignorance about the economic potential of many of our genetic resources means we are often unaware of what we have lost.

Worse, the erosion of genetic diversity is greater than the statistics on species loss alone would suggest. If a species with one million individuals is reduced to only 10,000 (which may still be enough to ensure the species' survival), it could well have lost at least 90 percent of its races, populations, and other genetic sub-units. The result could be a concomitant loss of at least half of its genetic diversity. This "concealed" erosion of genetic diversity is generally overlooked, although ultimately it could represent as grave a threat as the loss of the species itself.

More immediately, we are losing wild and semi-domesticated plants whose genes are essential if we are to maintain our major crop plants. Of the estimated 80,000 edible plants, only about 150 have been cultivated on a large scale, and a mere 30 plants provide 95 percent of our nutrition. The more we bend these 30 plants to fulfil our needs, the more vulnerable they become and the more they need infusions of genes from outside their own shrinking gene pools.

There has been a parallel decline in the number of strains of many farm animals. The livestock industry tends to concentrate on a limited number of breeds, with the result that we are heading towards emergency levels of "homogenized breeding". Half of all domestic animal breeds in Europe have become extinct since the beginning of last century. Less than 800 remain, and one-third of those could soon disappear.

The case of the Cornish chicken illustrates the error of allowing older strains to die out. This fast-growing subspecies of the domestic fowl was superseded by new breeds which laid more eggs or tasted better. As the Cornish chicken faded away, breeders decided they needed an infusion of its genes to boost the growth rate of the very chickens which had usurped its place on the farm.

Sometimes, too, a plant or animal can act as a signpost to hidden genetic riches. For example, the rosy periwinkle, a forest plant from Madagascar, has provided us with two potent anti-cancer drugs (see pp. 164–65). So rare are the critical alkaloidal chemicals in most forms of the plant, that pharmacologists had to process 500 tonnes of plant material to extract one kilogram of drug. Then a West Indian variant of the plant was found which contained 10 times more of the alkaloid, enhancing the production process.

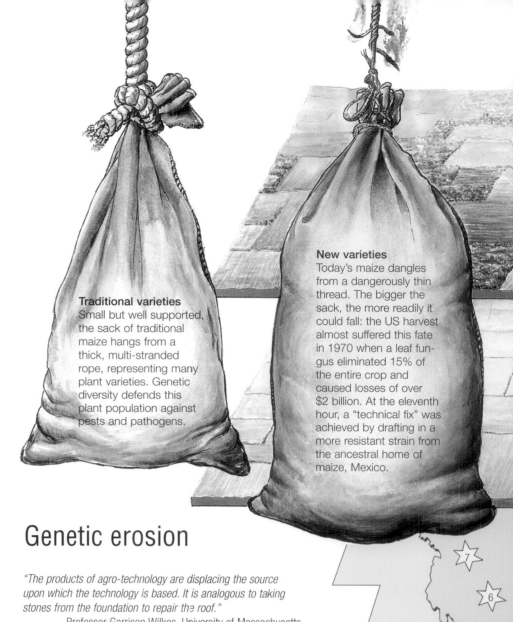

Traditional varieties
Small but well supported, the sack of traditional maize hangs from a thick, multi-stranded rope, representing many plant varieties. Genetic diversity defends this plant population against pests and pathogens.

New varieties
Today's maize dangles from a dangerously thin thread. The bigger the sack, the more readily it could fall: the US harvest almost suffered this fate in 1970 when a leaf fungus eliminated 15% of the entire crop and caused losses of over $2 billion. At the eleventh hour, a "technical fix" was achieved by drafting in a more resistant strain from the ancestral home of maize, Mexico.

Genetic erosion

"The products of agro-technology are displacing the source upon which the technology is based. It is analogous to taking stones from the foundation to repair the roof."
Professor Garrison Wilkes, University of Massachusetts

Habitat destruction is not the only threat to the process of evolution. Genetic erosion is depleting the gene base of many crop plants and farm animals. Productive diversity is replaced by dangerous homogeneity, and future avenues of agricultural development are cut off.

The scale of the potential loss is indicated by the history of *Zea diploperennis*, a rare perennial maize. Discovered in 1978 in a few hectares of farmland in the Sierra de Manantlan, Mexico, this hitherto unknown variety was down to some 2,000 individual plants. Yet its genes could open up the prospect of perennial maize production and increased resistance to at least four of the seven most important maize diseases, all of which could lead to billion dollar savings.

There are many more examples, such as the Rio Palenque Research Station in Ecuador. It amounts to as little as 100 ha, yet it supports 1,216 plant species – the highest recorded concentration of plant diversity on Earth. Regrettably, this last patch of wet forest of coastal Ecuador is being undermined by local people who cut wood for fuel and construction.

1 1840s Irish potato blight, 2 million died.

2 1860s Vine diseases crippled Europe's wine industry.

3 1870–90 Coffee rust robbed Ceylon of a valuable export.

4 1942 Rice crop destroyed, millions of Bengalis died.

5 1946 US oat crop devastated by fungus epidemic

6 1950s Wheat stem rust devastated US harvest.

7 1970 Maize fungus threatened 80% of US corn hectarage.

Counting human cost
The potential impacts of monoculture collapse have become ever greater as increasing numbers of people come to depend on a shrinking number of crop varieties. If the world maize crop failed tomorrow, it would do a great deal more than cut our supplies of food and feed. It would also impinge on many other products to which maize makes a contribution, such as aspirin, penicillin, tyres, and plastics.

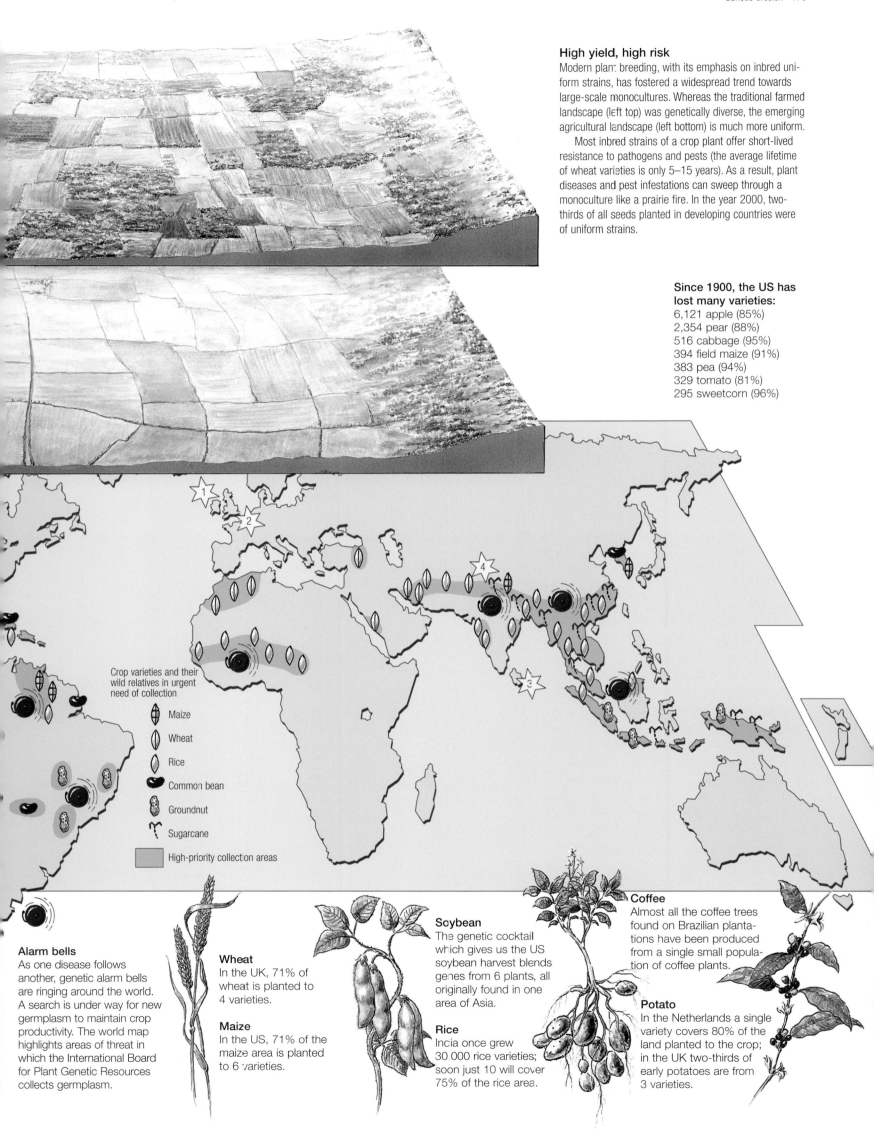

High yield, high risk

Modern plant breeding, with its emphasis on inbred uniform strains, has fostered a widespread trend towards large-scale monocultures. Whereas the traditional farmed landscape (left top) was genetically diverse, the emerging agricultural landscape (left bottom) is much more uniform.

Most inbred strains of a crop plant offer short-lived resistance to pathogens and pests (the average lifetime of wheat varieties is only 5–15 years). As a result, plant diseases and pest infestations can sweep through a monoculture like a prairie fire. In the year 2000, two-thirds of all seeds planted in developing countries were of uniform strains.

Since 1900, the US has lost many varieties:
6,121 apple (85%)
2,354 pear (88%)
516 cabbage (95%)
394 field maize (91%)
383 pea (94%)
329 tomato (81%)
295 sweetcorn (96%)

Crop varieties and their wild relatives in urgent need of collection

⊕ Maize

◊ Wheat

◊ Rice

● Common bean

Groundnut

Sugarcane

High-priority collection areas

Alarm bells

As one disease follows another, genetic alarm bells are ringing around the world. A search is under way for new germplasm to maintain crop productivity. The world map highlights areas of threat in which the International Board for Plant Genetic Resources collects germplasm.

Wheat
In the UK, 71% of wheat is planted to 4 varieties.

Maize
In the US, 71% of the maize area is planted to 6 varieties.

Soybean
The genetic cocktail which gives us the US soybean harvest blends genes from 6 plants, all originally found in one area of Asia.

Rice
India once grew 30,000 rice varieties; soon just 10 will cover 75% of the rice area.

Coffee
Almost all the coffee trees found on Brazilian plantations have been produced from a single small population of coffee plants.

Potato
In the Netherlands a single variety covers 80% of the land planted to the crop; in the UK two-thirds of early potatoes are from 3 varieties.

A world distinctly poorer

"Death is one thing, an end to birth is something else."

Michael Soule, US scientist

The biotic crisis underway will not only cause the loss of large numbers of species. It will reduce the capacity of evolution to generate replacement species within the next five million years, that being the "bounce-back" time following mass extinctions in the prehistoric past. Indeed, the recovery phase this time could prove to be a good deal longer than five million years. Such a profoundly impoverishing impact will derive from the current destruction of tropical forests and wetlands, which have served as the main source of new species following past mass extinctions. We have already lost half of tropical forests and wetlands, and we look set, in the absence of conservation measures of much expanded scope, to lose most of the rest within the foreseeable future.

By what we do, or don't do, within the next few decades, we shall determine the vitality of the planet for a period of time that, if it is "only" five million years, will be 20 times longer than humans have been humans. How many future people will be affected? Suppose the global population will not be 6.4 billion as today, but a more sustainable 2.5 billion. The total in question will be 500 trillion, or 10,000 more people than have existed to date. (Just one trillion is a large number; to put it in perspective, figure out how long a period of time is represented by one trillion seconds.)

We have noted (see p. 170) that a near-term result of today's mass extinction will likely be an outburst of new pests, weeds, and diseases. There will be many more environmental upheavals which levy severe costs on our descendants. Beyond these utilitarian consequences there are questions of morality: what right do we have to pass on a grossly degraded planet to future generations? This is a question that lies way beyond all the musings of philosophers on justice to future generations. Our best experts on intergenerational equity do not probe the future beyond half century or so, yet here we are talking about millions of years. Philosophers have not examined longer-term futures because they assume, based on much positive experience, that if we pass on a few problems to our descendants, they will be so much richer than we are that they will be able to handle the problems. This time around, however, our descendants may find themselves with a world distinctly poorer than today's.

If we fail – well, that does not bear thinking about. But if we triumph in face of this supersize challenge, won't the experience make us feel giants of human history? And won't our descendants say "Ah, those people of the early 21st century: when they realized what hung in the balance, they proved equal to the task and saved the planet and its species at a time of peril unprecedented since we came out of our caves". To cite Charles Dickens in this different context, "It is the worst of times, it is the best of times".

The future of evolution

Human beings, uniquely intelligent, have achieved a self-awareness that both gives them power over and separates them from the life around them. The natural world is seen as theirs to exploit and despoil. The biological and mineral storehouses of the Earth, once thought inexhaustible, are plundered. In the process, the web of interdependence from which humanity itself is derived begins to fall apart. Yet in this rage to prosper lie the seeds of despair. As the human species creates around it a constantly growing desolation, it is in danger of finding itself isolated on a desecrated planet. Its only companions will be the cowed species it has domesticated and the rodent survivors that have resisted its assault. Racing along our current path of development, we ignore at our peril the warnings sounded by those whose eyes are not blinkered by short-term priorities.

There are two certainties about biological evolution. Firstly, it never stops. Secondly, it is a slow process requiring many generations to produce significant changes in a species.

Historically, natural selection pressures acting on species came from the surrounding natural environment, but that natural world is long gone for most of the world's biotas. Only a minority of the world's species – for example, in terms of the world's last great wilderness areas – still evolve in a world that is not changing rapidly due to human influence.

The long-term fate of many of the world's species over the next millennium will be determined primarily by whether they can adapt to the rapidly changing environments of a world dominated by a single species – *Homo sapiens*. For many species, especially those from isolated islands, the historic pace of evolution has been slow, and recent human-induced changes are so large and fast that no evolutionary adaptation will be possible before they are swept to extinction. For example, unless we can control alien invasive species, all of the flightless birds in New Zealand and other islands are likely to be driven to extinction by introduced mammalian predators (weasels, cats, dogs) before they can adapt.

In general, the larger and longer-lived a species is, the slower the rate of evolution. It will be extremely difficult for any large vertebrate species to adapt genetically to the changing world around them. As habitats alter through climate change, for example, these species will be able to adapt only if they can relocate to environments (niches) similar to the current one. For many species, this will be impossible due to habitat fragmentation and isolation. For smaller species with shorter generation times, there is some evidence that they are capable of evolving to adapt to human influences. The peppered moth, *Biston betularia*, has adapted to the soot-darkened trees of industrial England, thus enhancing its camouflage from predatory birds. Hundreds of insect species, including mosquitoes, have evolved resistance to DDT and other pesticide chemicals.

But these examples of species adaptation to humanity are exceptions rather than the rule. Unless we can dramatically change the scale of the impact we are having on the natural environment, and start to use our ingenuity to find ways to maintain or recreate the ecological niches of species – what evolutionary biologist Michael Rosenzweig has termed "reconciliation ecology" – there will be scant future for the evolution of most species.

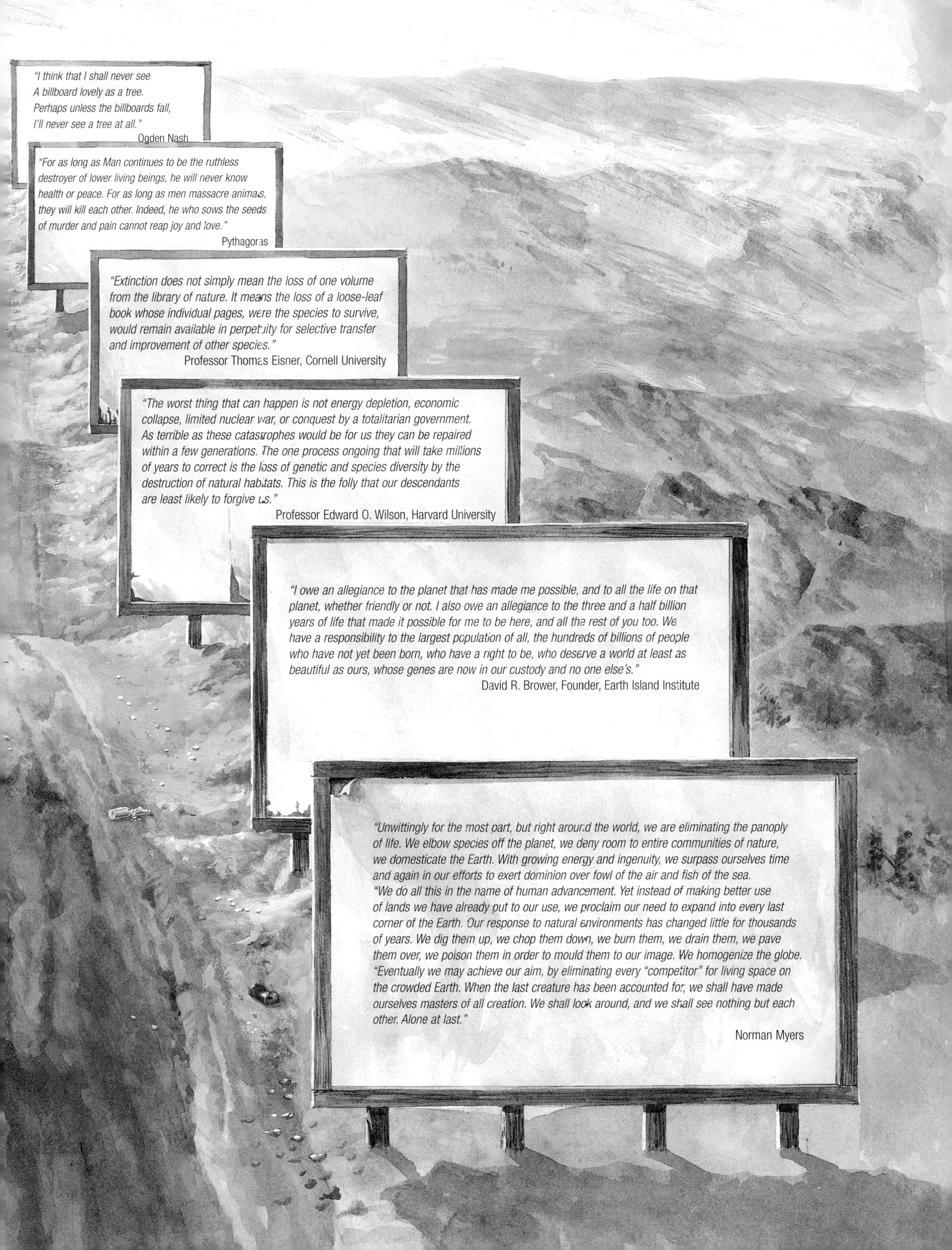

"I think that I shall never see
A billboard lovely as a tree.
Perhaps unless the billboards fall,
I'll never see a tree at all."

Ogden Nash

"For as long as Man continues to be the ruthless
destroyer of lower living beings, he will never know
health or peace. For as long as men massacre animals,
they will kill each other. Indeed, he who sows the seeds
of murder and pain cannot reap joy and love."

Pythagoras

"Extinction does not simply mean the loss of one volume
from the library of nature. It means the loss of a loose-leaf
book whose individual pages, were the species to survive,
would remain available in perpetuity for selective transfer
and improvement of other species."

Professor Thomas Eisner, Cornell University

"The worst thing that can happen is not energy depletion, economic
collapse, limited nuclear war, or conquest by a totalitarian government.
As terrible as these catastrophes would be for us they can be repaired
within a few generations. The one process ongoing that will take millions
of years to correct is the loss of genetic and species diversity by the
destruction of natural habitats. This is the folly that our descendants
are least likely to forgive us."

Professor Edward O. Wilson, Harvard University

"I owe an allegiance to the planet that has made me possible, and to all the life on that
planet, whether friendly or not. I also owe an allegiance to the three and a half billion
years of life that made it possible for me to be here, and all the rest of you too. We
have a responsibility to the largest population of all, the hundreds of billions of people
who have not yet been born, who have a right to be, who deserve a world at least as
beautiful as ours, whose genes are now in our custody and no one else's."

David R. Brower, Founder, Earth Island Institute

"Unwittingly for the most part, but right around the world, we are eliminating the panoply
of life. We elbow species off the planet, we deny room to entire communities of nature,
we domesticate the Earth. With growing energy and ingenuity, we surpass ourselves time
and again in our efforts to exert dominion over fowl of the air and fish of the sea.
"We do all this in the name of human advancement. Yet instead of making better use
of lands we have already put to our use, we proclaim our need to expand into every last
corner of the Earth. Our response to natural environments has changed little for thousands
of years. We dig them up, we chop them down, we burn them, we drain them, we pave
them over, we poison them in order to mould them to our image. We homogenize the globe.
"Eventually we may achieve our aim, by eliminating every "competitor" for living space on
the crowded Earth. When the last creature has been accounted for, we shall have made
ourselves masters of all creation. We shall look around, and we shall see nothing but each
other. Alone at last."

Norman Myers

Evolution in Management

We have demonstrated exceptional capacity to disrupt the planet in every last which way. Now we are challenged by a unique opportunity to turn that same capacity for planet-wide impacts to the task of large-scale management of Earth's living resources, to be achieved for the indefinite future.

Protecting our heritage

To safeguard the world's wildlife and wildlands, we have established a growing number of parks and reserves. Some, such as Tanzania's Serengeti and Australia's Great Barrier Reef, have been set up to protect wildlife and its habitats. Others, such as Yosemite in the US and Nepal's Mount Everest Park, protect spectacular scenery.

The protected-areas movement emerged 130 years ago with the establishment of the Yellowstone National Park in the US. It has really taken off only during the last 30 years, as country after country has recognized the need to safeguard pristine nature. Conversely, we still require many more protected areas, since our present network meets far less than half of overall needs.

Meanwhile, just as natural landscapes are being modified, so the protected-areas movement is adapting to growing pressures. The traditional purist approach has sought to establish parks and reserves from which all forms of human exploitation are banned. Increasingly, however, conservationists recognize that it will become ever-more difficult to declare large tracts of land "off limits" to human use and development. We know what we want to protect

Protecting marine biodiversity

Another "top ten" biodiversity hotspots are in the oceans, with 36% of coral reef species most vulnerable to extinction confined to 0.02% of the marine realm. The 2002 World Summit on Sustainable Development and the 2003 World Parks Congress called for a global network of marine protected areas to help restore the health of the oceans and sustain fishing industries. The estimated costs for 83 parks protecting 20–30% of the world's seas are $10–14 billion (far less than "perverse" subsidies in the fishery sector – see pp. 232–33). Today, just 0.5% of the seas lie within marine parks, by contrast with 12% of the land.

Conserving the wild

Only a small percentage of the world's land surface has been set aside to protect wild species and their ecosystems. Worse, parks and reserves are far from representative of major types of ecosystems. North America has 4 million sq. km, mostly the boreal forest and semi-frozen areas of Greenland and Arctic Canada. Whilst the number of protected areas topped 100,000 in 2003, we are still a long way from achieving an extensive and strategically sited network of protected areas. Some of the most important gaps are highlighted here. By providing maps like this, biogeographers help conservationists to identify priorities and achieve a representative spread in the ecosystems protected.

Wilderness areas

A few areas are wild enough still to safeguard large numbers of species in places little affected by humans: 37 such areas each cover at least 10,000 sq. km and retain 70% or more of their original vegetation. Most feature <5 people per sq. km outside cities. Five high-priority wilderness areas are large (>750,000 sq. km) and have high levels of endemism (>1,500 plants). They include the three tropical wilderness areas on the map (right), plus the Miombo-Mopane Woodlands and Grasslands of Southern Africa, and North American deserts in northern Mexico and adjacent parts of the southwestern US.

Megadiversity countries

Earth's species are not evenly distributed. Just a few countries, mainly those with tropical forests, feature huge numbers of species: 17 mega-diversity countries contain more than two-thirds of all species. The leader is Brazil, followed by Indonesia and Colombia.

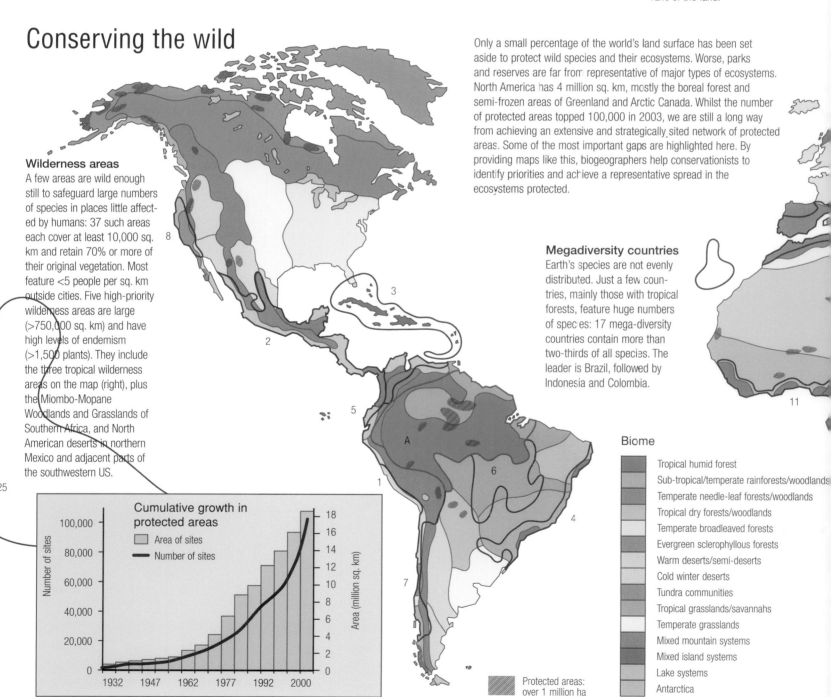

Biome
- Tropical humid forest
- Sub-tropical/temperate rainforests/woodlands
- Temperate needle-leaf forests/woodlands
- Tropical dry forests/woodlands
- Temperate broadleaved forests
- Evergreen sclerophyllous forests
- Warm deserts/semi-deserts
- Cold winter deserts
- Tundra communities
- Tropical grasslands/savannahs
- Temperate grasslands
- Mixed mountain systems
- Mixed island systems
- Lake systems
- Antarctica

Cumulative growth in protected areas
- Area of sites
- Number of sites

1932 1947 1962 1977 1992 2000

Number of sites: 0, 20,000, 40,000, 60,000, 80,000, 100,000
Area (million sq. km): 0, 2, 4, 6, 8, 10, 12, 14, 16, 18

Protected areas: over 1 million ha

parks from: now we must focus more on what we are protecting them for. If present parks are to survive, let alone be joined by new ones, they must be seen to meet the basic needs of all people, not just the interests of nature enthusiasts. This is all the more urgent in the developing world, where there is the greatest need to achieve a comprehensive parks system, and where there is the greatest pressure on protected areas from land-hungry farmers.

Fortunately, we can demonstrate that parks serve the cause of development. In northern Sulawesi, for example, a rainforest park was set up which meant that Indonesia would forfeit revenues from uncut timber, but the government backed the initiative on the grounds that it would protect a rainfall catchment zone critical for several million rice-paddy farmers in the valley bottomlands. In several African parks where dams have been built to supply water for wildlife, local people raise fish for market. In other areas, dry-season grazing for livestock may be permitted. In all the instances cited, local people do not clamour for the park to be abolished, rather they support its survival.

Biodiversity hotspots

Much conservation action has been a case of trying to be many things for many threatened species; for lack of sufficient funds, it has ended up being a few things to many species at best. A better way is to identify areas with two attributes: exceptional concentrations of endemic species (those found nowhere else), and facing exceptional threat of habitat destruction. A list of 25 areas (see map) covering 1.4% of Earth's land surface features the final habitats of 44% of Earth's plant species and 35% of non-fish vertebrates. In late 2004, the list was expanded to 34 hotspots covering little over 2% of Earth's land surface yet containing 52% of all plants and 36% of all terrestrial vertebrates. The hotspots strategy has already mobilized $850 million for conservation. If we can safeguard hotspots, we shall go a long way to reducing the mass extinction underway.

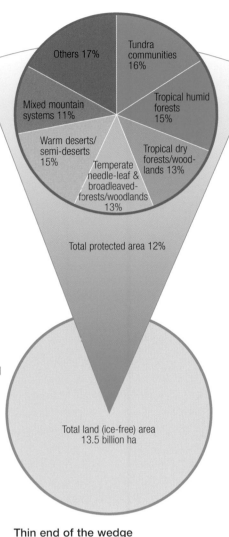

Thin end of the wedge

The precariously thin wedge of protected land (above) is dangerously short of such key biomes as tropical grasslands, evergreen forests, and mixed island systems.

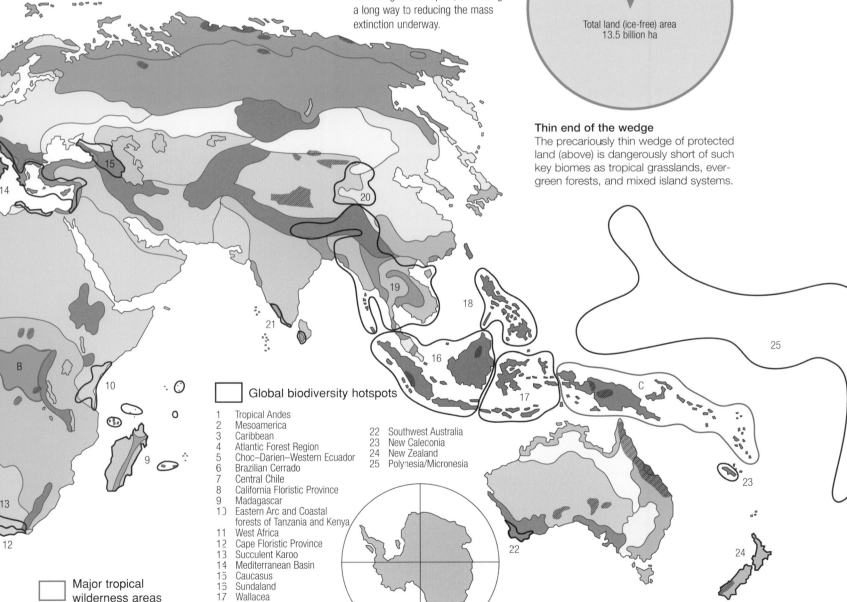

Global biodiversity hotspots

1 Tropical Andes
2 Mesoamerica
3 Caribbean
4 Atlantic Forest Region
5 Choc–Darien–Western Ecuador
6 Brazilian Cerrado
7 Central Chile
8 California Floristic Province
9 Madagascar
10 Eastern Arc and Coastal forests of Tanzania and Kenya
11 West Africa
12 Cape Floristic Province
13 Succulent Karoo
14 Mediterranean Basin
15 Caucasus
16 Sundaland
17 Wallacea
18 Philippines
19 Indo-Burma
20 Mountains of South Central China
21 Western Ghats and Sri Lanka
22 Southwest Australia
23 New Caledonia
24 New Zealand
25 Polynesia/Micronesia

Major tropical wilderness areas

A Upper Amazonian and Guyana shield
B Congo basin
C New Guinea and Melanesian islands

Conserving the unknown

The best way to preserve threatened gene pools is to protect their habitats by designating them as national parks or game reserves. A second option involves protecting the gene pools "off-site", whether in botanical gardens, herbaria, aquaria, zoos, or gene banks. This second approach offers many apparent advantages, but it also suffers from some critical drawbacks. Almost all our present gene banks are off-site, including seed and germplasm storage facilities, clonal plantations, seed orchards, and rare-breeds farms. Such facilities will play an increasingly important role, but their contribution will be limited by a number of key factors. First, there is the sheer size of the task. The diversity of wild genetic resources is so great that it seems highly unlikely that off site gene banks could ever save more than a fraction of the total stock.

More importantly, the seeds of some crop species and their wild relatives cannot be dried prior to storage, being killed in the process. Gene banks, for example, cannot preserve many seed plants. This applies especially to most vegetatively propagated plants, such as potato, cassava, members of the orchid family, and tree species, such as apples and pears, that do not breed true from seeds. Many tropical plant species, such as the cacao tree, can be conserved outside the wild only with the greatest difficulty. Some wild species also prove much more difficult to maintain and regenerate than their domesticated relatives, including a number of peanut and sunflower species. Other species, such as barley, beans, and maize, sustain genetic damage during long-term storage.

In addition, the entire stock of a gene bank can be destroyed by a prolonged power cut or by human negligence. Worst of all, a plant's evolution is effectively frozen while it enjoys the refrigerated safety of the gene bank. Outside, evolution goes on – and the protected plant may emerge to find that wild pathogens and pests have evolved new forms of attack to which it is now unduly vulnerable.

So off-site gene banks can provide only part of the answer to genetic erosion. Ultimately, the only viable long-term approach must involve safeguarding gene pools in the wild. But even today, very few on-site conservation areas coincide with the most valuable concentrations of genetic resources – the so-called "Vavilov centres". Even if we can get such "gene parks" set up in the right places, other solutions are needed to protect the traditional crop varieties which are still cultivated by small-scale farmers throughout the developing world.

How about taxing corporations selling genetically improved seed? Even a one percent tax on sales from the global seed industry would generate hundreds of millions of dollars every year. The revenues could be used to subsidize peasant farmers, enabling them to maintain some of their traditional varieties alongside higher-yield varieties.

Preserving the genetic resource

If conserving habitats and ecosystems is not possible, we can store part of an organism, such as its seed or semen, in some form of gene bank. Or we can keep whole organisms off-site – in an aquarium, botanical garden, culture collection, plantation, or zoo. Most progress has been made with off-site conservation of crop genetic resources, through an international network of "base collections" covering more than 20 of the world's most important crops.

Gene banks

The seeds of many plant species, especially those with small, dry seeds, can often be stored in a dormant state for long periods at a humidity level of 5% and at a temperature of –20°C. A small gene bank can protect many thousands of species. The US National Genetic Resource Program comprises a network of seed banks storing 450,000 samples from 8,000 species. The UK's Royal Botanic Gardens at Kew oversees the Millennium Seed Bank Project – an international plant conservation initiative aiming to safeguard 24,000 plant species from extinction by 2010. It has already successfully protected virtually all of the UK's native flowering plants.

Botanical gardens

The world's 1,600 botanical gardens and arboreta play a vital role, but they have a problem of storage capacity. They contain 4 million living plants from 80,000 species. The Royal Botanic Gardens (a World Heritage site) at Kew, UK, is the world's largest and contains 25,000 plant species, including 2,700 threatened species.

Zoos

Zoos have recorded a string of successes with their captive breeding of some threatened species. But there is a rule of thumb that a vertebrate stock of less than 50 individuals is liable to carry the seeds of its own destruction, with harmful genes accumulating rapidly in inbred populations. Moreover, many species refuse to breed at all in captivity.

Rare-breeds centres

At least 20 breeds of British farm animal became extinct during the 20th century – their genetic diversity lost. To counter this trend, rare-breeds survival centres have been set up, serving as living museums. They provide a chance for the general public to underwrite genetic conservation, by paying to see breeds on which their own future may well depend.

On-site protection

The focus of on-site protection programmes tends to be on species of popular appeal, and on species under threat; on unique ecosystems; on ecosystems which are representative of a particular type of habitat; or on some combination of all these approaches. The key objective is to protect as much genetic diversity as possible.

On-site gene banks score over off-site gene banks for a number of reasons, not least because the evolution of species in on-site reserves can continue uninterrupted, providing the breeder with a dynamic reservoir of genes that confer resistance to pests or pathogens.

On-site reserves also serve as living laboratories, allowing the breeder to study a species' ecology. This can throw up valuable information which might otherwise be overlooked; several crucial characteristics of wild tomatoes have surfaced in this way, including their tolerance of saline soils, high temperatures, and humidities, and their resistance to insects and disease

Land races and wild genes

Among the most threatened gene pools are those of "land races", a term covering primitive or traditional plant cultivars and animal breeds. With most wild species, extinction tends to be a fairly gradual process, but land races, developed by local farmers, often enjoy only very limited distribution and can be lost in a single episode of habitat destruction.

Wild gene pools are now increasingly recognized as vital resources for future plant and animal breeding. Variety, in genetic terms at least, is more than the spice of life – it is the key to future survival.

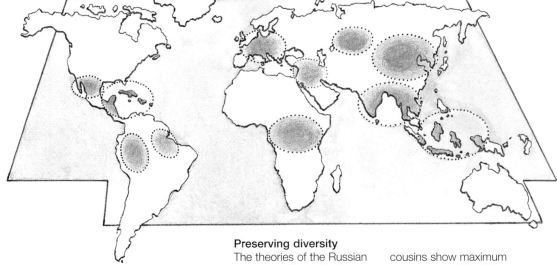

Preserving diversity

The theories of the Russian geneticist Nikolay Vavilov are at the heart of many conservation programmes. He suggested that the centre of origin of a cultivated plant is to be found in the region where its wild cousins show maximum adaptiveness. The "Vavilov centres" are prime targets for conservation (the map shows these centres in modified form).

The gene library

International seed companies can borrow and benefit from the gene libraries of the world (many in developing countries) at virtually no charge. As the wild resource becomes more valuable, a strong case develops for making the end-user pay a "lending fee" for "books borrowed". Putting a value on the wild resource in this way will give developing countries an economic incentive to preserve wild habitats.

Legislating for life

There are three notable ways to put wildlife conservation on a legal footing. The first is to establish laws for individual species, such as the vicuna, or for a small group of species, such as marine mammals. The second is to establish a treaty for a region, as in the case of the Convention on Conservation of European Wildlife and Natural Habitats. The third is to establish a treaty of worldwide scope, such as the Convention on Wetlands of International Importance. Of these three, the first is easiest to establish, while the third tends to have the most significant impact.

When more than one nation is involved, negotiations become complex and enforcement can be a problem. Since many species occur in several countries at once (the cheetah, for example, is found in more than 20 African countries) or they migrate from one country to another, it is often essential that several nations make common cause together.

Until a century ago, international law, based on treaties and conventions, was not used to protect wildlife. The first wildlife treaties were largely concerned with economically important species – and with eliminating species viewed as pests. Two years before the first European wildlife treaty was signed in 1902, a convention was concluded which aimed to protect African game for trophy hunters and ivory traders – and which called for the destruction of such "noxious" pests as crocodiles, lions, leopards, hyenas, poisonous snakes, and birds of prey. Since then, there has been a growing spate of treaties and conventions, the most important of which is CITES (right). The legitimate trade in wildlife products is worth at least $10 billion a year. While the illicit trade has been cut back by CITES, it remains big business at an estimated $6–10 billion a year.

Meanwhile, wildlife continues to disappear faster than ever. The problem is not so much the poacher or other law-breaker with rifle or trap in hand. Rather, it is the settler and the subsistence farmer, being persons without any malign intent towards wildlife. But they use tools, such as the axe or plough, which are ultimately far more destructive. We need a global treaty which builds on the undoubted successes of CITES, a treaty which protects critical habitats. How about a Convention on the Protection of Endangered Species, to be known as COPES? The idea would be that each nation should accept responsibility for all species within its borders. In return, a nation would be able to apply for support from the community of nations to enable it to do a better job. Many developing nations harbour enormous concentrations of species but they lack the financial and scientific resources to protect them properly.

Wherever species may be found, they are part of everyone's heritage, so we should all share the cost of their protection. To date, there is no adequate mechanism allowing the richer nations to help others on a suitable scale.

Laws and conventions

The Convention on Biological Diversity (CBD)

One of three international agreements opened at the 1992 Rio Earth Summit, the CBD has subsequently been signed and/or ratified by almost every country in the world, though the US has still to ratify and become a full party.

The CBD has 3 main objectives: the conservation of biodiversity, the sustainable use of its components, and the equitable sharing of benefits from the use of genetic resources. Developing countries (mostly in the South) possessing high biodiversity agreed to grant fair and equitable access to these biological resources (e.g. pharmaceutical chemicals and genes from wild plant/animal species), in return for funding and technical assistance for the conservation and sustainable use of wild areas in the South.

The Convention represents a landmark in international environmental law in view of its comprehensive, ecosystems approach – rather than focusing on single species – and linking conservation to issues of bio-safety, intellectual property rights, traditional knowledge, and indigenous peoples. While much has come out of the CBD since 1992, it is regrettable that the steady decline in biodiversity has still not been reversed – mainly because the CBD lacks strong implementation mechanisms to tackle the major forces driving this loss – loss of wild habitat to human expansion (agriculture and cities), and the spread of invasive alien species.

Success stories

Crocodiles – in 1969, all 23 species were threatened or in decline. In 2004, a third could sustain a regulated commercial harvest and 4 species are critically endangered.
Elephants – prior to the 1989 CITES-signatory ban on the ivory trade, 10,000 elephants a year were killed in Tanzania. After the ban this fell to fewer than 100; the average value of a tusk fell from almost $4,000 to $35.
Cats – the global trade in cat skins fell drastically as fashion trends altered in the US and Europe.
Parrots – trade in live parrots fell following a US ban on imports of wild species in 1992.
Pandas – in China, panda smugglers are sentenced to life in prison and poaching levels have plunged.

Traditional medicines (TMs)

The $20 billion global market for traditional medicines threatens many endangered species. Throughout Asia, nearly every part of a tiger is believed to benefit ailments ranging from epilepsy to laziness. A bear's gall bladder can sell for up to $15,000. The Chinese Taoist Association has urged its 40 million members to stop using endangered wildlife in traditional medicines.

Protecting wetlands and migratory species

The Ramsar Convention has 141 parties, and 1,387 wetland sites, covering more than 120 million ha, have been included in the convention's List of Wetlands of International Importance. This convention was one of four signed in the 1970s – it was not limited to a few species or to geographical regions. The other three were CITES, the World Heritage Convention, and the Convention on the Conservation of Migratory Species of Wild Animals (CMS).

The CMS (or Bonn Convention) aims to conserve terrestrial, marine, and avian migratory species throughout their range. As of mid-2004, its membership included 86 parties from Africa, Central and South America, Asia, Europe, and Oceania. Several agreements have been concluded under CMS covering European bats, cetaceans in the Mediterranean Sea, Black Sea, Baltic Sea, and North Sea, seals in the Wadden Sea, as well as African–Eurasian migratory waterbirds, albatrosses, and petrels.

The 1995 UN Agreement Relating to the Conservation and Management of Straddling Fish Stocks and High Migratory Fish Stocks entered into force in 2001 and "advocates a cooperative, precautionary approach to the management and conservation of relevant fish stocks".

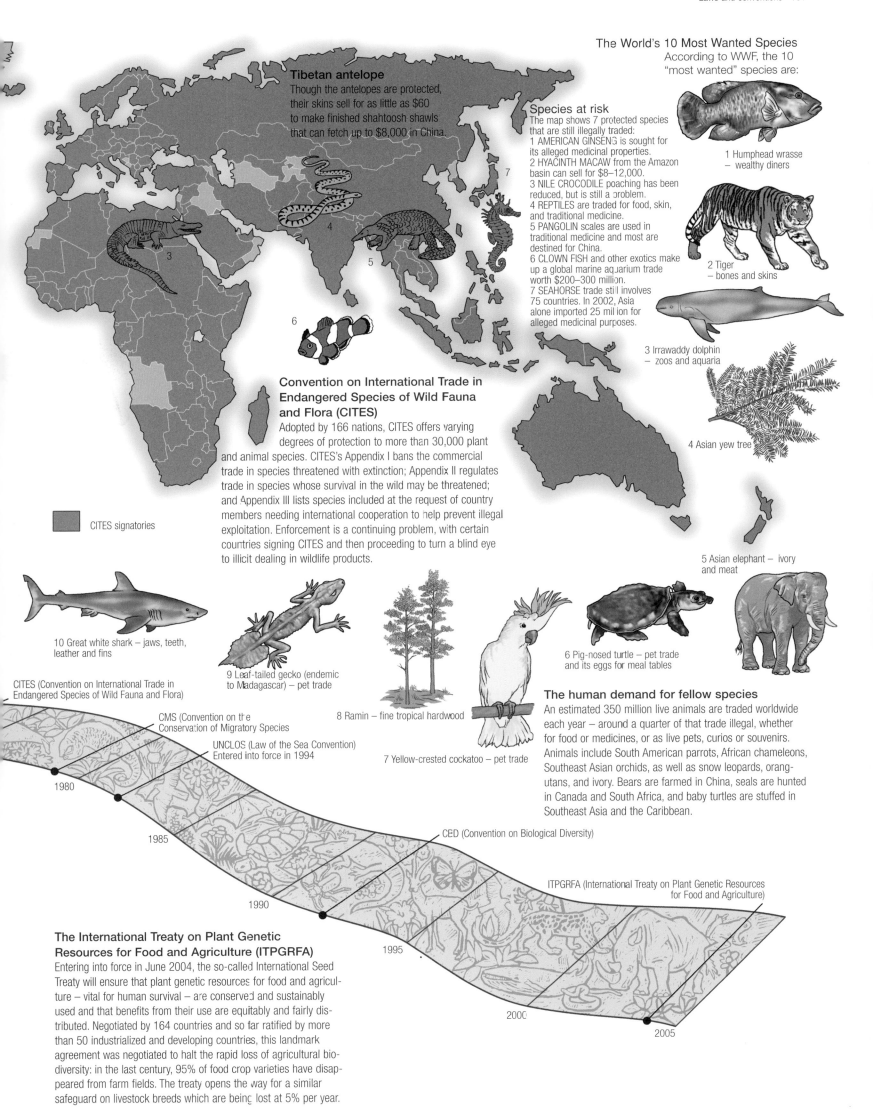

Tibetan antelope
Though the antelopes are protected, their skins sell for as little as $60 to make finished shahtoosh shawls that can fetch up to $8,000 in China.

The World's 10 Most Wanted Species
According to WWF, the 10 "most wanted" species are:

1 Humphead wrasse – wealthy diners

2 Tiger – bones and skins

3 Irrawaddy dolphin – zoos and aquaria

4 Asian yew tree

5 Asian elephant – ivory and meat

6 Pig-nosed turtle – pet trade and its eggs for meal tables

Species at risk
The map shows 7 protected species that are still illegally traded:
1 AMERICAN GINSENG is sought for its alleged medicinal properties.
2 HYACINTH MACAW from the Amazon basin can sell for $8–12,000.
3 NILE CROCODILE poaching has been reduced, but is still a problem.
4 REPTILES are traded for food, skin, and traditional medicine.
5 PANGOLIN scales are used in traditional medicine and most are destined for China.
6 CLOWN FISH and other exotics make up a global marine aquarium trade worth $200–300 million.
7 SEAHORSE trade still involves 75 countries. In 2002, Asia alone imported 25 million for alleged medicinal purposes.

Convention on International Trade in Endangered Species of Wild Fauna and Flora (CITES)
Adopted by 166 nations, CITES offers varying degrees of protection to more than 30,000 plant and animal species. CITES's Appendix I bans the commercial trade in species threatened with extinction; Appendix II regulates trade in species whose survival in the wild may be threatened; and Appendix III lists species included at the request of country members needing international cooperation to help prevent illegal exploitation. Enforcement is a continuing problem, with certain countries signing CITES and then proceeding to turn a blind eye to illicit dealing in wildlife products.

CITES signatories

10 Great white shark – jaws, teeth, leather and fins

9 Leaf-tailed gecko (endemic to Madagascar) – pet trade

8 Ramin – fine tropical hardwood

7 Yellow-crested cockatoo – pet trade

The human demand for fellow species
An estimated 350 million live animals are traded worldwide each year – around a quarter of that trade illegal, whether for food or medicines, or as live pets, curios or souvenirs. Animals include South American parrots, African chameleons, Southeast Asian orchids, as well as snow leopards, orangutans, and ivory. Bears are farmed in China, seals are hunted in Canada and South Africa, and baby turtles are stuffed in Southeast Asia and the Caribbean.

CITES (Convention on International Trade in Endangered Species of Wild Fauna and Flora)

CMS (Convention on the Conservation of Migratory Species)

UNCLOS (Law of the Sea Convention) Entered into force in 1994

1980

1985

CED (Convention on Biological Diversity)

ITPGRFA (International Treaty on Plant Genetic Resources for Food and Agriculture)

1990

1995

2000

2005

The International Treaty on Plant Genetic Resources for Food and Agriculture (ITPGRFA)
Entering into force in June 2004, the so-called International Seed Treaty will ensure that plant genetic resources for food and agriculture – vital for human survival – are conserved and sustainably used and that benefits from their use are equitably and fairly distributed. Negotiated by 164 countries and so far ratified by more than 50 industrialized and developing countries, this landmark agreement was negotiated to halt the rapid loss of agricultural biodiversity: in the last century, 95% of food crop varieties have disappeared from farm fields. The treaty opens the way for a similar safeguard on livestock breeds which are being lost at 5% per year.

Strategies for a sustainable future

We have a good idea of how to set about protecting our heritage of wildlife and genetic resources. The key will be to establish more parks and reserves – already covering 12 percent of land areas. But what, meanwhile, happens to the other 88 percent? If we let these areas be "developed out of existence" we shall undermine a sizeable proportion of our renewable resource base. At the same time, many protected areas will almost certainly be swamped by tides of humanity seeking new farmlands.

We need to expand our vision beyond traditional concerns of conservation and pay more attention to the entire biosphere and its life-support systems. In short, we need a strategy for a new conservation that embraces all life on Earth. We have some excellent ideas, summed up in the term eco-development, which takes into account the environmental underpinnings of all our societies. Two pioneering manifestos spelled out the basics: the World Conservation Strategy and its successor Caring for the Earth (right).

Conservation and development, the WCS suggested, are two sides of the one coin: conservation cannot succeed without sustainable development, and development cannot be sustained without conservation. Brave words – but how can we convert them into action? Since 1980, the WCS has been tried and tested as the basis for national conservation policies right around the world. Simultaneously, international agencies, such as the UN and the World Bank, have become more aware of conservation needs and opportunities. The UN set up the World Commission on Environment and Development and its "Brundtland Report" of 1987 contributed to the recognition of sustainable development.

Caring for the Earth was structured around principles upon which sustainable living can be built. It called for a new commitment from governments, organizations, and individuals to the ethic of sustainability, and listed the conservation of the Earth's biotic diversity as a core principle for sustainable living. It advocated that, by 2000, all countries adopt comprehensive strategies to safeguard their biological diversity, and a system of protected areas covering at least 10 percent of each of its main ecological regions. Parts of this fine purpose have been achieved, but many "holes" remain.

Since the clarion call of the Rio Earth Summit and "Agenda 21" in 1992, six major multilateral treaties have been adopted and several older agreements have been beefed up through protocols and amendments. To counter the reluctance of many governments to sign treaties that require sizeable changes in socio– economic practices, treaties often include incentives (economic, institutional) to induce collaboration and penalties to discourage foot dragging.

By 2000, there were 240 international environmental treaties of one sort or another, but overall we must consider that the situation today is a good deal worse than in 1991.

Towards a new conservation

When it was launched in 1980 by IUCN, UNEP, and WWF, the World Conservation Strategy was a revolutionary document, presenting a single, integrated approach to environmental problems. It rested on three important propositions. First, species and populations must retain their capacity for self-renewal. Second, the basic life-support systems of the planet – climate, water cycles, and soils – should be better conserved. Third, genetic diversity is a major key to the future. The world applauded the WCS when it first appeared, and it formed the basis for national conservation policies in dozens of countries. The contribution of national strategies to sustainability is considerable, as the case of Nepal (right) demonstrates.

In 1991, the same organizations launched a new conservation strategy, Caring for the Earth: A Strategy for Sustainable Living, extending and emphasizing their original message, setting targets, and suggesting methods for the implementation of the strategy. In 1992, at the Rio Earth Summit world leaders agreed on a comprehensive "sustainable development" strategy, i.e. one that meets the needs of both current and future generations. One of the key agreements adopted at Rio – the Convention on Biological Diversity – had three main goals: conservation of biological diversity, the sustainable use of its components, and the fair and equitable sharing of the benefits from the use of genetic resources. In 2002, at the Johannesburg World Summit on Sustainable Development, the complexity of the problems the world faces had become clearer, and the need to act even more pressing.

National Conservation Strategies (NCSs) in action

Conservation strategies are tailored to the needs of individual countries, e.g. in New Zealand priority is given to monitoring fish stocks and regulating levels of exploitation. In Zambia, the NCS looks to minimize the adverse effects of mining. In Nepal, fuelwood and soil erosion are high on the list. The 1988 NCS for Nepal aimed to put environmental planning on a permanent footing, which involved creating new governmental agendas (right).

Integrating conservation

Most attempts to assess the environmental impacts of development have focused on specific projects, whereas many critical decisions are taken higher up the decision chain (left). Conservation objectives must be integrated with other main objectives in formulating national policies before they crystallize into projects and programmes. When environmental factors are considered only at the bottom of the chain, their influence is limited at best. If integrated at the top level of decision making, they can have a highly positive influence.

Social objectives — Economic objectives — Objectives

Development policy — Policies

Energy — Agriculture — Housing — Sectoral plans/ programmes

Dam — Land clearance, irrigation — New settlements — Projects

Ecological factors — Conservation objectives

NCS in action: Nepal

Nepal is critically dependent on its natural resources and has given priority to conservation since the early 1970s, when its first national park was established. Today, almost a fifth of the country is under protection in 22 parks and protected areas. This is more than double the area of 1989. Nepal is a small country – less than 0.1% of the Earth's land surface – but has a vast richness of biodiversity: 844 bird species (9.3% of the global total), 181 mammal species (4.5%), 2,893 butterfly and moth species (2.6%) and 5,856 flowering plant species (2.7%). Nepal's Tenth Five Year Plan (2002–2007) strongly emphasizes livelihoods and poverty reduction (community forestry, buffer zone management around protected areas, and people's participation in conservation areas). More than 646,000 ha of forests have been handed over to almost 9,000 Forest Users' Groups through community forestry, mainly in the hills. In 1997, the Ministry of Forests and Soil Conservation formed a National Biodiversity Unit to facilitate and implement the Convention on Biological Diversity (CBD). The Annapurna Conservation Area Project – the largest conservation area in Nepal covering 7,600 sq. km – was launched as a pilot programme by the King Mahendra Trust for Nature Conservation to integrate nature conservation and community development. Nepal also took the lead to establish the International Center for Integrated Mountain Development (ICIMOD) – a significant achievement towards mountain biodiversity management.

Reforestation

Properly managed, Nepal's forests can supply fuelwood and soak up heavy rainfall, releasing it gradually to downstream lands in India and Bangladesh.

UNESCO's Man and the Biosphere (MAB) programme

Launched over 30 years ago, it began by promoting "in situ" long-term conservation of the world's representative ecosystems with their component plants, animals, and micro-organisms. The programme departed from traditional conservation concepts by emphasizing the need for scientific research and constant monitoring of the environment. Over the years, the programme has evolved to reflect the pervasive influence of humankind in the biosphere. It also aims to provide "ways and means to implement the Ecosystem Approach adopted in May 2000 by the Convention on Biological Diversity".

National Parks pay their way

Nepal's Royal Chitwan National Park hosts 570 flowering plant species, 40 mammal species, 486 bird species, 17 reptile species, and 68 fish species. It also protects rhinos, tigers, elephants, and gaur (bison). It became a World Heritage site in 1983. Once a year local people are permitted into the park to harvest grass which they dry and use for thatch or animal feed. The park is a very popular tourist destination, bringing in important foreign exchange. The Sagarmatha National Park (Everest) reinvests a share of revenues in community development activities – which are found to add to the success of conservation projects. Tourism overall contributes 4% to Nepal's GDP and 8% of employment.

HUMANKIND

Introduced by Sunita Narain
Director, Centre for Science and Environment, New Delhi

Many of us in India were introduced to environmental concerns by poor women living in remote Himalayan villages. These women were ecologists of a different variety. They hugged their trees, saying that the government could cut forests only over their dead bodies. Not because they believed that trees should not be cut, but because they believed that they should have the first right to decide. For them the environment was much more than beautiful forests and tigers. Their cause actually had very little to do with trees; rather it was that their own lives were so deeply intertwined with the existence of those trees that their very lifestyles, their culture, and even their survival were at stake. Their protest to hug trees, called the Chipko movement, has become like the conscience of the environmental movement in many parts of the world. Indeed, from this stems the vital message that the environment is so important for poor countries like India.

These women have taught us that environment and development are two sides of the same coin. This is because for hundreds of millions of people what matters is the Gross Natural Product, not the Gross National Product. The environment, literally, is their survival. They live on the basic subsistence needs that they can procure from forests and grazing areas, and from lakes, streams, and wells. The degradation of the environment impinges directly on their lives: it destroys their livelihoods, leaving them destitute.

It is no wonder then that paradigms of environmental management vary across the world. In many regions the paradigm is about "protectionist conservation" where the environment has to be safeguarded from development. In the world of the Chipko women, the environmental movement is built on the concept of "utilitarian conservation". At one and the same time, it is deeply humanist and deeply conservationist.

In this paradigm it is clear that cultural diversity in the world is no accident of history. It is the direct outcome of the biological diversity of the world. People living in different ecosystems – from cold deserts, mountain pastures, and hot deserts to tropical forests, riverine plains, and coastal regions – all have learned to live with their environments, making the best use of these environments by improving their productivity. In this discovery of the natural world, we begin to understand how these ecological formations are inhabited by a whole variety of people – nomadic people with sheep, goats, and cattle in desert lands, hundreds of millions of farmers living in vast fertile plains growing rice, wheat, maize, and millet, indigenous tribes living in the diverse forests of the world, and fisherfolk living on wetlands, rivers, and coastal waters.

Thus we begin to appreciate that it is in the wholeness, complexity, beauty, innovativeness, and intelligence of these varied human–nature interactions that we will begin to find roads towards a sustainable and equitable future.

The Human Potential

The Chinese proclaim that "Of all things, people are the most precious". And so they are. When one person is joined by a second, their joint capacity is not simply doubled: they can inspire one another, laugh together, and love each other. Considered together, all the peoples of the planet represent a capacity for labour, knowledge, creativity, conscious understanding, and happiness that cannot be measured. Yet however much the Chinese delight in people as the finest manifestations of life's forces on Earth, they certainly do not believe that more must be better.

In fact, no other community matches the Chinese in their efforts to limit their numbers on the grounds that more Chinese will result in poorer Chinese. In any country the quality of human life is quite distinct from its quantity. There are 5.4 million Danes and 1.1 billion Indians, yet it would be absurd to suppose that Indians are 200 times better off than Danes.

The size of a country's or region's population can increase its political influence. But this relationship is far from automatic; indeed the control of wealth is far more significant. In 1900, 17 percent of global population lived in Europe; by 2004, only 11 percent did so. The developing world, which today is home to 80 percent of global population, could account for 86 percent by 2050. The weight of numbers may well effect a shift in focus towards parts of the South, especially as concerns the emergence of semi-superpowers such as China, India, Brazil, and Mexico.

Moreover, the South's population is predominantly young, putting pressure on child health and education services. In the North, the size of the over-60s sector has social and economic implications. As longevity increases, nations will be affected by the "grey wave", and we will have to develop new ways to care for the world's senior citizens, who represent a valuable reservoir of skills and experience.

In light of social and economic advance, also technological change, the potential of young people should be even greater. The level of education, training, and creative enthusiasm in a population can powerfully influence the extent to which the potential of its human resource is harnessed. Some developing countries, notably China, have achieved near-miracles in improving the education, health, and life expectancy of their citizens, giving a powerful boost to their capacity to contribute to their societies. The real challenge is to enable all people, old and young alike, to realize more of their potential. Freeing our human resources from the difficulties that prevent their participation represents our best hope of making the transition in good order and in good time.

People potential

The greatest natural resource on the planet is the human race itself. And in a world in need of ever-increasing care and protection, the full potential of every individual has never been more in demand. Releasing such potential is rarely easy, but the scale of the challenge we now face makes it essential. There is no shortage of urgent tasks, all of which are well within our capacity – provided we can mobilize the political will and physical energies, both amplified through appropriate technologies. But lack of basic needs, such as food, water, fuel, and shelter, plus social neglect and sheer prejudice, continue to obscure many elements of the human resource. One of the most blatant examples has been the failure to capitalize on the abilities of women; another is the neglect of the young and unemployed.

Sustainable cities are adaptable cities: point apparent. They achieve this by building up their social capital that in turn provides the "institutional glue" binding communities together. These support networks can be specially helpful to new immigrants drawn to mega-cities, where they can readily feel isolated while struggling to adapt to new and severely strange lifestyles.

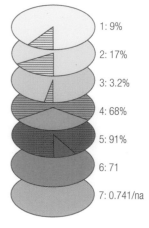

Religious communities
Religious communities oversee 80% of the world's people, thus they have vast scope to influence lifestyle change. According to the UK-based Alliance of Religions and Conservation, 200,000 religious communities worldwide are involved in environmental activities. Even the Pope and Ecumenical Patriarch Bartholomew have made pronouncements in favour of less environmentally harmful lifestyles.

China
China has made much progress in developing its people potential. Its population is 1.3 billion, and GNI PPP$4,500 per person (2004). Adult literacy is 91%, a comprehensive health service has boosted life expectancy to 71 years, and the fast-growing private sector is boosting employment. During the two decades 1980–2000 economic growth averaged almost 10% per year, enough to double per-capita income every 7 years. As a result, there are more than 300 million "new consumers" – likely to reach over 600 million as soon as 2010 (see pp. 236–37). By 2020, China could become the world's leading economic power.

China

1: 9%

2: 17%

3: 3.2%

4: 68%

5: 91%

6: 71

7: 0.741/na

Global provisions

Attempting to express in global terms the numbers of people, out of 6.4 billion (2004), whose basic needs are fulfilled is probably one of the ultimate exercises in statistical frustration. But however rough the measures, the revelations of recent global surveys are overwhelming – both in numbers of those who are literate and in good health, and in areas of massive neglect. On the sunlit face of life, there is an abundance of human energy; in the shadows, a lost resource of millions trapped in the struggle to survive.

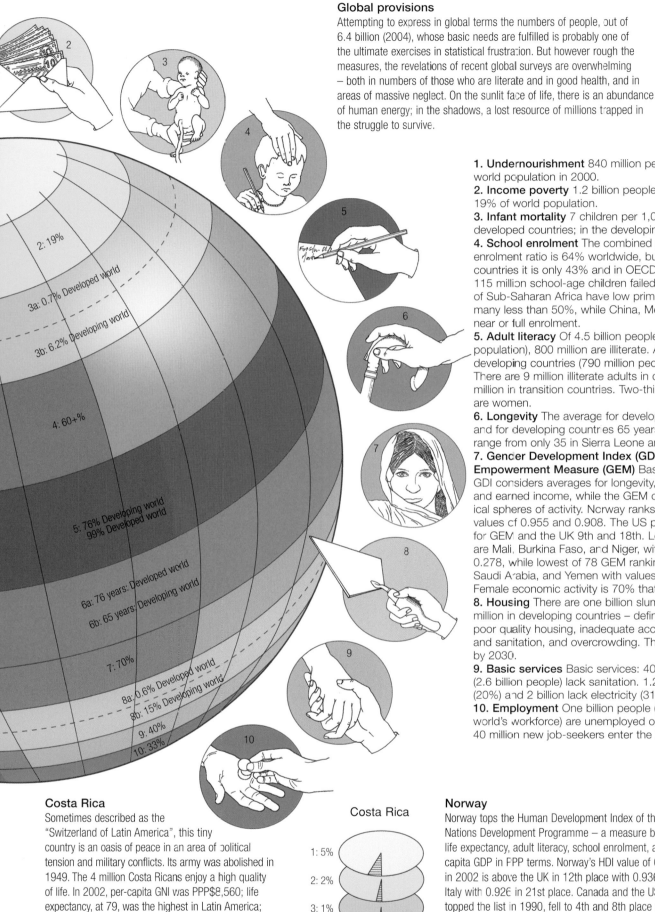

1. Undernourishment 840 million people undernourished, 13% of world population in 2000.

2. Income poverty 1.2 billion people live on less than $1 a day, 19% of world population.

3. Infant mortality 7 children per 1,000 die before age one in the developed countries; in the developing countries 62 per 1,000.

4. School enrolment The combined primary/secondary/tertiary enrolment ratio is 64% worldwide, but in the least developed countries it is only 43% and in OECD countries 93%. In 1999, 115 million school-age children failed to attend. Most countries of Sub-Saharan Africa have low primary school completion rates, many less than 50%, while China, Mexico, and Russia are at near or full enrolment.

5. Adult literacy Of 4.5 billion people aged 15+ (70% of world population), 800 million are illiterate. Almost one in four adults in developing countries (790 million people) cannot read or write. There are 9 million illiterate adults in developed countries and 1 million in transition countries. Two-thirds of the world's illiterates are women.

6. Longevity The average for developed countries is 76 years, and for developing countries 65 years, though national averages range from only 35 in Sierra Leone and Zambia to 82 in Japan.

7. Gender Development Index (GDI) and Gender Empowerment Measure (GEM) Based on gender inequality, the GDI considers averages for longevity, literacy, school enrolment, and earned income, while the GEM considers economic and political spheres of activity. Norway ranks first for both measures with values of 0.955 and 0.908. The US places 8th for GDI and 14th for GEM and the UK 9th and 18th. Lowest of 144 GDI rankings are Mali, Burkina Faso, and Niger, with values between 0.309 and 0.278, while lowest of 78 GEM rankings are Egypt, Bangladesh, Saudi Arabia, and Yemen with values between 0.266 and 0.123. Female economic activity is 70% that of the male rate.

8. Housing There are one billion slum-dwellers worldwide – 960 million in developing countries – defined by insecurity of tenure, poor quality housing, inadequate access to safe drinking water and sanitation, and overcrowding. The total could reach 2 billion by 2030.

9. Basic services Basic services: 40% of the world's population (2.6 billion people) lack sanitation. 1.2 billion lack clean water (20%) and 2 billion lack electricity (31%).

10. Employment One billion people (at least one-third of the world's workforce) are unemployed or underemployed, while 40 million new job-seekers enter the labour market each year.

Costa Rica

Sometimes described as the "Switzerland of Latin America", this tiny country is an oasis of peace in an area of political tension and military conflicts. Its army was abolished in 1949. The 4 million Costa Ricans enjoy a high quality of life. In 2002, per-capita GNI was PPP$8,560; life expectancy, at 79, was the highest in Latin America; and the adult literacy rate, 96%, second only to Argentina in the region. During the past two decades, poverty has been reduced from 40% of the population to less than 20%, and extreme poverty has been halved since 1990, meaning the country has already achieved the first Millennium Development Goal, and others are in sight. Protection of the environment has been a top priority, but foreign debt ($4.1 billion in 2003) threatens to undermine its economic stability.

Costa Rica

1: 5%
2: 2%
3: 1%
4: 69%
5: 96%
6: 79
7: 0.823/ 0.664

Norway

Norway tops the Human Development Index of the United Nations Development Programme – a measure based on life expectancy, adult literacy, school enrolment, and per-capita GDP in PPP terms. Norway's HDI value of 0.956 in 2002 is above the UK in 12th place with 0.936 and Italy with 0.926 in 21st place. Canada and the US, which topped the list in 1990, fell to 4th and 8th place respectively. Norway's HDI value is twice as high as the average for Sub-Saharan Africa. With a population of less than 5 million, it has achieved a 100% literacy rate, an average life expectancy of 80 years, and at PPP$36,690 in 2002 its per-capita GNI was the highest in Europe apart from Luxembourg. In aid to developing countries, Norway achieved the highest ODA/GNI ratio in 2003 with 0.92%, and was one of only five countries meeting or exceeding the target of 0.7% of GNI to foreign aid.

Norway

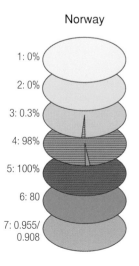

1: 0%
2: 0%
3: 0.3%
4: 98%
5: 100%
6: 80
7: 0.955/ 0.908

The working potential

In earlier days, "work" and "activity" meant much the same thing – learning or teaching, preparing food or hunting for it, growing up or growing old, were all of equal importance. But in "advanced" societies, there has long been a dominant popular equation linking work to jobs, jobs to money, and money to human worth. This is fast becoming questionable in the North and was never entirely relevant in the South. Two key factors are contributing to the shift of values: the growth of the workforce, and the changing nature of work.

We can already enumerate the workforce of the year 2015, because its numbers are now among us. The greatest increases will be in the developing countries of the South, adding almost 400 million to the 2005 global workforce of 2.9 billion. In the transition countries the workforce will stay more or less constant, and in developed countries it will add around 10 million for a total workforce in 2015 of 3.3 billion. The implication is that about 40 million new jobs will need to be created each year in developing countries.

As for the changing nature of work, the industrialized nations have already undergone a massive transformation. There are freely entered contracts and increasing employee protection. The welfare state cushions the workforce from the impact of recession and unemployment. The premium set on waged employment by citizens of developed countries stems from the legitimacy it bestows in society. A job not only provides money but psychological

The world at work

Human skill and energy represent a resource which is potentially renewable in perpetuity. But tremendous shifts are now taking place in the way these skills and energy are used. Some 300 years ago it took over 90% of the world's labour force working on farms to feed a much smaller population, whereas today the proportion of population working on the land in many developed countries has fallen to below 10%, in some cases considerably less, e.g. 2% in the US. Major changes in the structure and technological base of industries, fuelled partly by the information revolution and partly by market changes have created labour surpluses in many regions, coupled with shortages of many skills. Globalization and economic integration has expanded job opportunities for many but it has also exposed migrant workers to exploitation as cheap labour in countries of the North.

Labour force estimates
The histograms (below left and right) show male and female workforces, in millions, for seven regions of the world. This is the economically active population – that is, all those above a specific age (15 in most countries) who work for profit or who seek work.

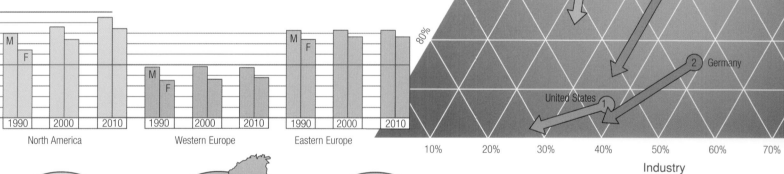

1 United States
The shift from traditional land-based employment is nowhere clearer than in the US. Agricultural work has shrunk dramatically. Fewer than 3 million people (2% of the 148 million labour force) are employed in agriculture – down from 12% in 1950, 7% in 1960 and 3% in 1990.

2 Germany
Europe's strongest industrial nation nonetheless has an unemployment rate of 10%. Like the US, the recent trends in employment have moved away from agriculture and industry towards the services.

3 Hungary
Hungary's workforce has shown a marked shift from agriculture towards industry and services. Some 45% of the workforce is female.

Labour distribution triangle 1960–1990
The seven countries whose labour distribution trends (1960–1990) are plotted in the diagram (above) mostly mirror world trends in the three main areas of work. Arrows pointing down show agricultural work waning, with employment in industry and services increasing. Many developing countries still have large agricultural workforces. Moving towards an environmentally sustainable economy has already generated 14 million jobs, with millions more to come in e.g. the recycling/remanufacturing of goods and the development of renewable energy.

rewards. In traditional rural societies, by contrast, whole families invest their labour in a great deal of unpaid work, which escapes definition by conventional statistics. Of the measured workforce, agriculture still claims 40 percent in the developing countries (70 percent in India and 60–80 percent in many countries of Sub-Saharan Africa) and contributes 20 percent of GDP. Agriculture also provides much employment to women.

Formal employment is supported by a massive informal sector averaging 40 percent of employment in developing countries – sometimes more, e.g. 50 percent in rural Ethiopia and 55 percent in rural India. Of the 1.3 billion men, women, and children who work in agriculture, only 450 million work for wages.

Work patterns are likely to change radically in the future. The key characteristic of many new technologies is that they amplify the productivity of workers, whether they work predominantly with their biceps or brains. Some believe that the result in developed economies will be widespread deskilling of workers, others that the future lies with retraining, job sharing, and self-employment. For the present, problems in the South are different. Here, the need is to ensure that people have not only jobs but adequate income. Recall that many newly independent countries have already come far, demonstrating that populations previously restricted to unskilled labour can produce, within a few decades, the professional and other skilled workers they need.

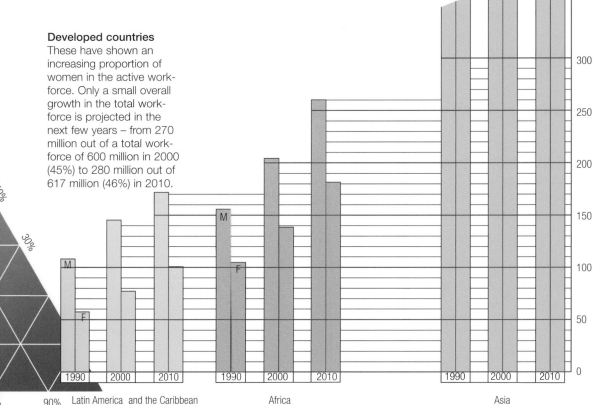

Developed countries
These have shown an increasing proportion of women in the active work-force. Only a small overall growth in the total work-force is projected in the next few years – from 270 million out of a total work-force of 600 million in 2000 (45%) to 280 million out of 617 million (46%) in 2010.

Developing countries
The burgeoning pool of labour represents both a daunting challenge for policy makers and an enormous potential resource. Few countries have made sustained efforts to draw the un- and underemployed into the economy, but there have been highly successful job-creation programmes in several countries including China. In South Korea, too, resource regeneration programmes have boosted employment.

Micro-enterprises (MEs)
In many countries these small, locally owned businesses account for a large share of production and jobs. In Latin America there are almost 60 million micro-entrepreneurs and MEs account for one-fifth of the region's GDP. In Ghana, women process oil from palm, coconut and groundnuts; and they practise dry-season vegetable farming, batik printing, basket and mat-making, soap making, fish smoking, cassava processing, and pottery.

Latin America and the Caribbean   Africa   Asia

Children at work
One in six children world-wide today is involved in labour for a total of 250 million children, more than 70 million of whom are less than 10 years old. Most work in agriculture while many work in factories or on the streets. All deserve an education and better lives. More than 80 countries are working to combat child labour.

4 Brazil
Brazil's economic transition has ridden on the back of rapid industrial growth. Less than one-quarter of workers are now employed in agriculture and a similar share in industry, while services account for more than half of the workforce.

5 Mali
Of Mali's workforce 86% are in agriculture, 12% in services, and only 2% in industry. Upgrading the farming economy could release resources for other developments. The government has funded sectoral and micro-level programmes targeting the unemployed, the underemployed and the poor.

6 China
Of the 1.3 billion population in 2004, 72% work in agriculture, but as China continues to industrialize the peasant force will shrink. China has become the world's factory and is 4th in terms of world exports (a 6% share). It could have the world's largest PPP economy before 2020 (see pp. 236–37).

7 India
With the second largest population, India ranks as the 4th largest PPP economy and the 8th largest industrial power. While two-thirds work in agriculture, the economy is thriving due to new sectors such as IT, biotechnology, and the media. By 2008, IT could account for more than one-third of exports.

Knowledge versus wisdom

The human race can be justly proud of its science and learning. In the few centuries since Galileo deduced our position in the heavens, the ingenuity, imagination, and perseverance of our species have led to the detailed exploration of our solar system. As one quantum leap in understanding has followed another, new technologies have emerged in their wake, enabling us to deal far more capably with our tasks. Like the proverbial lilypads multiplying on a pond, knowledge breeds knowledge at an exponential rate, carrying science forwards ever faster.

Recent times have witnessed an unprecedented spread of knowledge throughout our community. The advent of machine printing sparked the information revolution, creating a base for mass education. Press, radio, and TV have successively reached ever larger audiences. The worldwide web reached 10 billion pages in less than a decade and by 2004 a quarter of a billion host computers had an audience of almost one billion people. While one-third of sites were in English, many were in Chinese, Japanese, Spanish, German, French, Italian, Portugese, and Dutch, meaning that "online communities" can form no matter where people currently live. E-conferencing has allowed discussion and input from every corner of the globe. Mobile phones serve as an information medium, enabling call-up of e.g. the latest market reports, weather or football news. Annual book production includes almost one million new titles (China's readership gains another 100,000 new or established titles). In addition, there are 165,000 published journals and almost 9,000 electronic journals (e-journals). Thanks to ICT (see pp. 218–19), the world has the scope to learn and communicate like never before.

Although formal education systems and school enrolments are growing faster there remains a huge challenge in developing countries, where many children do not have a school or fail to attend (see p.198). But learning and knowledge is not necessarily wisdom. In acquiring new knowledge, traditional communities have been overwhelmed, losing some of the perceptions which previously sustained them. Some of our new skills run counter to all conventional wisdom: several nations now have the power to atomically sterilize whole regions of the planet.

While science is pre-eminent, it is increasingly remote from the humanities. Indeed, Western civilization has almost relinquished the holistic approach to learning, understanding, and acting. The "systems theories", which attempt a unified overview, also tend towards specialization. Yet the keys to reintegration are beginning to emerge. Many people seek guidance from traditional societies on re-establishing a balance between humankind and its environment, e.g. the Global Ecovillage Network (see p. 208). Our species is in the adolescent phase, learning more facts than it knows what to do with. But the global challenges we face are now provoking new levels of understanding.

Homo sapiens

Every species other than *Homo sapiens* adapts its form and behaviour to the pressures of its environment. *Homo sapiens*, on the contrary, has achieved the remarkable feat of being able to adapt the environment instead, overcoming many natural limitations through the development of technologies and cultures. While this has brought myriad benefits, the spiralling growth of knowledge has been possible only through a high degree of specialization (top right). We need to develop a new holism, appropriate for our advanced societies in the Gaian ecosystem.

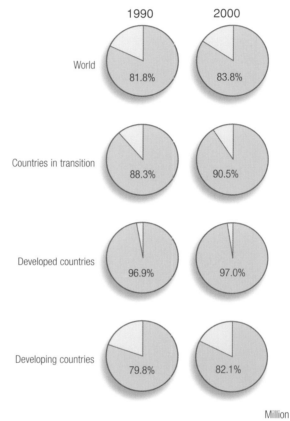

Primary school enrolment ratio (net)

1990 — 2000

World: 81.8% / 83.8%

Countries in transition: 88.3% / 90.5%

Developed countries: 96.9% / 97.0%

Developing countries: 79.8% / 82.1%

Internet host computers worldwide

The global school

The 1960s and early 1970s were the great boom years in education. By 1980, 70% of developing countries primary-age children were in school, and 32% of secondary-age children. Since the 1990 World Conference on Education for All, 10 million more children in developing countries have been enrolled in school, but 115 million children still do not attend, including 38 million (four out of ten children) in Sub-Saharan Africa. Almost three-fifths of the 115 million are girls, who often have to direct their time to carrying fuelwood and water.

Explosion of E-learning

E-conferencing, e-journals, e-newspapers, e-books – the rapid growth of the Internet and the web since the early 1990s has revolutionized the amount and the way we are able to access information. E-journals grew from 36 in 1994 to more than 6,000 in 1998 and 9,000 in 2003, many freely available through "open access" sites.

The information explosion

The output of new knowledge is growing side by side with economic and social development, if not with wisdom. Growth is funded by research and development (R&D) budgets totalling $800 billion/PPP$1.2 trillion, or 2.5% of global GDP, though with a major proportion going on military research and development. New technologies have been developed to store, index and analyse the explosion of data.

NEWTON-LE-WILLOWS
LIBRARY
TEL: 01744 677886
01744 677887

Life sciences

Physical sciences

Technology

Medicine

Social sciences

History

Philosophy and religion

Arts

Literature

World output of books

950,000
842,000
789,500
715,500

572,000
521,000
426,000

1965 1970 1975 1980 1985 1990 1995 2000 2003

Gods

History

Occult medicine

Stories

Arts and crafts

Folklore ritual

Social awareness

Knowledge of the natural world

Brought to book

World output reached almost one million in 2003. While e-books benefit many they are unlikely to replace traditional books – titles available worldwide could now total 100 million.

Western and traditional knowledge

The explosive proliferation of knowledge in the North has produced millions of highly trained people, though often ill informed of what is going on outside their own disciplines. In a highly complex, rapidly changing world, this fragmentation of knowledge has emerged as a major obstacle to understanding. A great deal of effort has gone into interdisciplinary projects designed to reintegrate knowledge and to develop multi-stranded solutions for multi-faceted problems. Building design, for example, increasingly involves team discussion between architects, other experts, and users. The new synthesizers of knowledge in the North have come to recognize the wisdom embodied in more unified, holistic cultures.

The Inability to Participate

Statistics on people excluded from the benefits of global society can be numbing: 115 million children out of school, 186 million adults unemployed, 840 million undernourished, 1 billion without adequate housing, 1.2 billion in absolute poverty (less than $1 a day, 1.2 billion without access to safe water, 2 billion with no electricity, and 2.6 billion without adequate sanitation.

Millions die each year from malnutrition and disease. The tragedy of this waste of human potential is that much of it could be avoided through minor adjustments to our budgets, and large ones to our "priorities". What cannot be avoided is the disastrous consequences for humanity of our runaway numbers, in some regions outstripping efforts to increase food and basic social services.

We have witnessed huge increases in global food output since the 1950s and until the mid-1980s the global grain harvest grew faster than global population, thus the plough kept ahead of the stork. Since 1984, however, per-capita grain production has fallen from a peak of 342 kilograms to less than 300 kilograms in 2003, though much less for the three billion people with incomes of less than $2 a day who cannot afford to buy grain. This scenario is likely to be repeated. Every year the world has to find the food to feed another 80 million mouths. The existing inequities of supply and the geographic mismatch between people and resources are seriously exacerbated by current population growth rates – generally highest in the poorer countries. Challenge: if we are to feed another 1.6 billion people by 2030, and feed everyone better, we need to produce twice as much food. But we are now trying to feed 6.4 billion people with less than half the per-capita grain-harvested area we had for 2.5 billion in 1950.

A key factor in the growth of human numbers is a population's age profile. A greater proportion of young people gives a greater potential for future growth in numbers. Some 42 percent of Africans, 32 percent of Latin Americans, and 30 percent of Asians are under 15 years old – a series of potential population time bombs.

The human species is unique in having developed artificial means to limit reproduction, yet many nations fail to use this capability. All too often, a combination of poverty, high child mortality, and a lack of social provision convinces parents that they need more children to ensure enough survive the rigours of childhood to help work for the household income and to care for their parents in old age. And so the cycle of deprivation and environmental degradation continues.

The numbers game

In a world with a finite capacity to support life, our near infinite capacity for reproduction remains a central problem. In the last century, world population increased from 1.5 billion to 6.1 billion. UN estimates project a world population of 7.9 billion by the year 2025 and 8.9 billion by 2050, peaking at 9.2 billion around 2075 – these being medium estimates. The low estimate indicates a peak of 7.4 billion in 2050, but the high estimate steadily increases, reaching 10.6 billion in 2050 and 12.5 billion in 2075.

How alarming are these figures? If all available land is used for agriculture, together with an increase in fertilizer use, and if food surpluses are shipped across frontiers, most regions could support more than their current populations. But a more realistic breakdown of the demand-and-supply picture, country by country, indicates a major crisis ahead. By the year 2000, there were 425 million people in countries with land scarcity (less than 0.07 ha per person), and 245 million people in countries with water scarcity (less than 1,000 cu. m per person per year). By 2025 these numbers could rise to 640 million and 852 million – possibly many more. If governments do not face the issue of curtailing population growth, their struggle against famine, disease, and high infant mortality will be even harder. Various of the Millennium Development Goals (see p. 251) would accelerate the shift to smaller families.

The population switchback

Many populations of wild animals explode and collapse regularly. Stability requires a finely tuned balance between numbers born and numbers dying (see below). The large "S" curve diagram (right) shows the maximum populations in several regions up to the year 2300 according to UN medium long-range estimates. North America continues a gradual increase up to 2300 while Europe does the opposite, declining by more than 100 million. Although an obvious route to stability is to reduce the birth rate, this does not achieve an immediate balance. A nation with a "youthful profile" to its population contains many potential parents. China's population policies led to the growth rate declining from 1.4% per year in the late 1980s to 0.6% in 2003, but because of the size of the population this still meant an addition of 8 million people in 2004. Similarly India's population growth rate has declined from 2.1% to 1.7%, but the country added another 18 million people in 2004. India is projected to add a further 515 million people to its population between 2000 and 2050, surpassing China as the world's most populous country by 2040.

Infant mortality rate, 2001
per 1,000 live births

- 100 or more
- 50–99
- 25–49
- 10–24
- Less than 10

Latin America
and the Caribbean
1.6% per annum
Maximum 779 million

North America
1.1% per annum

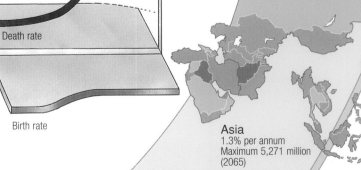

Death rate

Birth rate

Asia
1.3% per annum
Maximum 5,271 million
(2065)

6000 BC   5000 BC   4000 BC

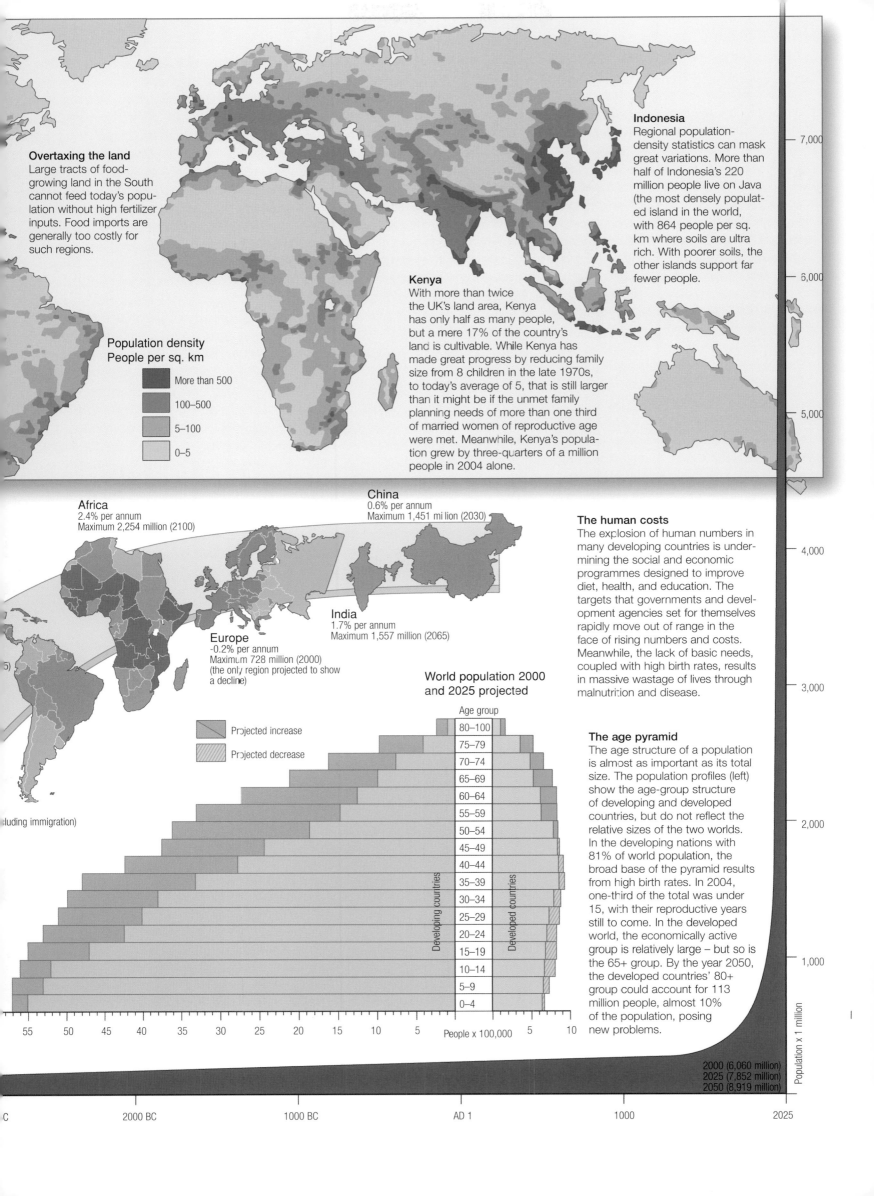

Overtaxing the land
Large tracts of food-growing land in the South cannot feed today's population without high fertilizer inputs. Food imports are generally too costly for such regions.

Indonesia
Regional population-density statistics can mask great variations. More than half of Indonesia's 220 million people live on Java (the most densely populated island in the world, with 864 people per sq. km where soils are ultra rich. With poorer soils, the other islands support far fewer people.

Kenya
With more than twice the UK's land area, Kenya has only half as many people, but a mere 17% of the country's land is cultivable. While Kenya has made great progress by reducing family size from 8 children in the late 1970s, to today's average of 5, that is still larger than it might be if the unmet family planning needs of more than one third of married women of reproductive age were met. Meanwhile, Kenya's population grew by three-quarters of a million people in 2004 alone.

Population density
People per sq. km
- More than 500
- 100–500
- 5–100
- 0–5

Africa
2.4% per annum
Maximum 2,254 million (2100)

China
0.6% per annum
Maximum 1,451 million (2030)

Europe
-0.2% per annum
Maximum 728 million (2000)
(the only region projected to show a decline)

India
1.7% per annum
Maximum 1,557 million (2065)

(including immigration)

The human costs
The explosion of human numbers in many developing countries is undermining the social and economic programmes designed to improve diet, health, and education. The targets that governments and development agencies set for themselves rapidly move out of range in the face of rising numbers and costs. Meanwhile, the lack of basic needs, coupled with high birth rates, results in massive wastage of lives through malnutrition and disease.

The age pyramid
The age structure of a population is almost as important as its total size. The population profiles (left) show the age-group structure of developing and developed countries, but do not reflect the relative sizes of the two worlds. In the developing nations with 81% of world population, the broad base of the pyramid results from high birth rates. In 2004, one-third of the total was under 15, with their reproductive years still to come. In the developed world, the economically active group is relatively large – but so is the 65+ group. By the year 2050, the developed countries' 80+ group could account for 113 million people, almost 10% of the population, posing new problems.

World population 2000 and 2025 projected

- Projected increase
- Projected decrease

Age group
80–100, 75–79, 70–74, 65–69, 60–64, 55–59, 50–54, 45–49, 40–44, 35–39, 30–34, 25–29, 20–24, 15–19, 10–14, 5–9, 0–4

Developing countries | Developed countries

55 50 45 40 35 30 25 20 15 10 5 People x 100,000 5 10

Population x 1 million

7,000
6,000
5,000
4,000
3,000
2,000
1,000

2000 (6,060 million)
2025 (7,852 million)
2050 (8,919 million)

2000 BC   1000 BC   AD 1   1000   2025

The employment crisis

In 2003, 186 million people were unemployed, representing six percent of the global labour force. This is the highest number ever recorded by the International Labour Office (ILO). Almost three-fifths were men. Hardest hit were the 15–24 age group, with 88 million affected, for a of 14.4 percent.

Sub-Saharan Africa struggles with official unemployment averaging as high as 11 percent (unofficial unemployment is twice or even three times higher). The region is home to 230 million of the so-called "working poor" – the 1.4 billion workers worldwide (almost half of the total workforce) who earn less than $2 a day – not enough to escape the poverty trap. A grossly inadequate supply of jobs in developing countries as a whole is being severely aggravated by rapid population growth. Between 2005 and 2015, these countries need to provide 40 million new jobs a year. The problem is not only lack of an effective waged employment sector, but extremely low incomes

generally – the agricultural sector employs over 40 percent of workers. Many of the world's absolute poor (on less than $1 a day) are small farmers or landless peasants searching for work. HIV/AIDS is having a marked impact on labour markets, together with the "brain drain" as people seek better economic opportunities overseas.

In developed countries of the North politicians wrestle with the social and economic implications of unemployment at a time when more pension funds are required because of the "greying/ageing" of the population. In OECD countries the total unemployed in 2003 was less than 40 million. One-quarter of these jobless were in the United States, a country not without its own class of "working poor" – an estimated one-quarter of working families are struggling financially. In Poland and Slovakia, almost one-fifth of the workforce is unemployed.

The decline of unions in the North made it somewhat easier for companies to lay off workers, though in the UK there are employment laws covering

The working poor

More than half a million people are classed as "$1-a-day working poor" and 1.4 billion as "$2-a-day working poor".

The work famine

In both North and South there are problems of un- and under-employment, the latter being unproductive work for little reward. In the developing countries those who will reach working age over the next decade threaten to overwhelm opportunities for adequate work. The labour force has been declining in the transition countries during the past decade and average unemployment rates have risen from 6.3% to 9.2%. Contrast the industrialized countries, where unemployment declined from 8% in 1993 to 6.8% in 2003. In OECD as a whole, 36 million people were unemployed in 2002, with 8.4 million in the US, 3.6 million in Japan, 3.4 million in Germany and Poland, and more than 2 million in each of France, Italy, and Spain.

Underemployment in developing countries

In the South, the most pressing crisis is one of huge underemployment as well as unemployment. Without unemployment benefits and social security, the poor must work if they are to survive at all. But survival often depends on a job with little substance to it apart from low pay and long hours, unprotected by work legislation of any sort. Many are self-employed. Government intervention and overseas aid often focus on inappropriate high-technology, capital-intensive projects. They also concentrate on boosting production of cash crops and goods, rather than providing the work which the poor need to buy food. Many leave the countryside for the cities, which often increases urban poverty and pressures on infrastructure.

Youth (15–24) unemployment rates 2001

- More than 40%
- 31–40%
- 21–30%
- 11–20%
- Less than 10%

Global unemployment, total and rate, 1993–2003

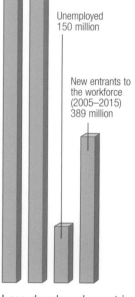

Population aged 15+ 3,269 million

Economically active population aged 15+ 2,279 million (70%)

Unemployed 150 million

New entrants to the workforce (2005–2015) 389 million

Less developed countries: Year 2000

A bleak prospect

Textiles, shipbuilding, and steel are among Northern industries which have been badly hit by lower wages and higher productivity in the South.

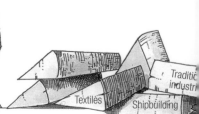

Population aged 15+
973 million

Economically active
population aged 15+
601 million (62%)

Unemployed
36 million

New entrants to
the workforce
(2005–2015)
10 million

**More developed countries:
Year 2000**

redundancy and worker rights – while the lack of them in many developing nations has produced lax labour laws fostering child labour, long hours, and little or no employee rights.

The 2005 labour force of 2.9 billion accounts for 45 percent of the global population and those of non-working age, viz. those in the under-15 and over-65 age groups, account for 37 percent. Then there are the "others", adults outside the workforce who may be unpaid family labourers, volunteers, or unregistered unemployed people.

Women, the young, and racial minorities are particularly disadvantaged, both in the North and the South. In the South, women suffer exploitation in the unpaid family-labour system, while those who have succeeded in finding a paid job tend to be the first to be hit by recession and upgrading of technology. But those who suffer most are often the migrants and minorities. The lure of jobs encourages migration from rural, undeveloped areas to urban, industrialized areas – where the streets are seldom paved with gold. In Western Europe, the post-war economic boom attracted more than 15 million immigrants and "guest workers", often treated as scapegoats during a recession.

By 2015, the workforce is projected to reach 3.3 million people, with 430 million still classified as $1-a-day working poor and 1.3 million as $2-a-day working poor. One way out of the work famine might be to recognize the need to adapt and embrace change. Our economies have already begun to make the transition and can gain greater output from less labour because of advancing skills and technologies.

We could also embrace that change by running our economies in such a way that (1) everybody who wants one has a job and (2) nobody need work ridiculously long hours for less than a fair amount of pay. It is no longer the case that the job one has at 20 will be the job one retires from at age 65. Job sharing and flexitime, too, could open up opportunity for new modes of employment.

Unemployment and the young

Youths aged 15–24 make up one-quarter of the 15–65 year working-age population. They account for 130 million of the world's 550 million $1-a-day working poor who struggle to survive. Almost 90 million of the world's youth are unemployed – equivalent to half the world's people without jobs. Youths are more than 3 times as likely to be unemployed as older adults, a problem that is particularly acute in developing countries. They often face major obstacles when competing for jobs, e.g. lack of work experience or lack of skill-specific training and education. In both industrialized and developing economies, they are more likely to work longer hours, under informal employment, intermittent (temporary, part-time, casual) work and insecure arrangements, which tend to be characterized by low productivity, low wages, and limited labour protection. The lack of work can create a sense of exclusion or uselessness which in turn can engage illegal activities.

"Halving the world youth unemployment rate would add at least $2.2 trillion to global GDP… Enlarging the chances of young people to find and keep decent work is absolutely critical to achieving the UN Millennium Development Goals."

ILO, 2004

The "invisible" workforce

The statistics on the male and female workforce in developing countries suggest that women are less than half the total. In fact, their work is officially invisible, like that of children. Women in the South suffer a "double burden" of duties, bearing domestic responsibilities and acting as unpaid family labourers in the fields. A 15-hour day is not uncommon. Of the 1.3 billion men, women, and children who work in agriculture, only 450 million work for wages. Where productivity is lowest, children are engaged in work and in conditions which may well retard their development. There are around 250 million child labourers, almost one-third of them less than 10 years old. While the majority are in developing countries, there are also 2.5 million in developed and transition countries. Most (127 million) are in the Asia–Pacific region, but Sub-Saharan Africa employs 48 million under-14s. The majority of child labour is involved in agriculture, but more than 8 million children worldwide are trapped in slavery, bondage, prostitution, or pornography. One million have been subjected to trafficking even though it is illegal under international law.

South hit by North

Employment in the South is hit both by accumulation of wealth by the few and by Northern protectionism. The European Union spends 3.3 Euros for every 1 Euro of exports of sugarbeet, a product better grown in developing countries. Similarly, US supports for its cotton farmers have driven the price of cotton so low that 10 million people in West Africa are no longer able to make a living from the crop (see pp. 232–33). Much Northern investment has gone into job-destroying technology.

Women

In 2003, there were 1.1 billion women in the world's workforce, an increase of 200 million women in employment over the previous decade. However, women still face higher unemployment rates and lower wages than men. They also make up 60% of the world's 550 million $1-a-day working poor. At least 400 million decent jobs are needed to lift the 78 million unemployed and 330 million working poor women out of poverty.

Crisis in health

Ill-health incapacitates an enormous proportion of the world's 6.4 billion people. Consider: 6 million people are partly blind with trachoma; 146 million are threatened by blindness; 300 million people are sweating and shivering with malaria (and one million mainly children die from the disease each year); 200 million people are urinating blood because of schistosomiasis; and 1.6 million die from TB.

These show only part of the grotesque extent of world sickness: AIDS affects almost 40 million people – equivalent to the population of Poland; 840 million people worldwide are undernourished, yet more than one-third of the world's grain goes to feed livestock to satisfy meat-centred diets of the affluent (see pp.

234–35). Those same meat-centred diets, including fatty and calorific foods such as steaks, hamburgers and hot dogs, contribute to the fast-growing pandemic of obesity in developed and developing countries alike, 1.1 billion affected worldwide, the health costs of which are enormous: $120 billion in the United States alone.

The microbe, meanwhile, continues to display extraordinary ingenuity in outwitting medical science, with new health threats constantly emerging. The last century saw epidemics resulting from lifestyles in the North: coronary heart disease; cancers; industrial disease; nervous and mental health problems; and the growing toll in road accidents, alcoholism, and drug-addiction deaths.

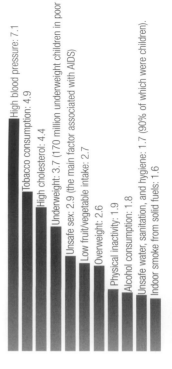

High blood pressure: 7.1
Tobacco consumption: 4.9
High cholesterol: 4.4
Underweight: 3.7 (170 million underweight children in poor countries)
Unsafe sex: 2.9 (the main factor associated with AIDS)
Low fruit/vegetable intake: 2.7
Overweight: 2.6
Physical inactivity: 1.9
Alcohol consumption: 1.8
Unsafe water, sanitation, and hygiene: 1.7 (90% of which were children)
Indoor smoke from solid fuels: 1.6

Burden of Disease:
The 10 leading risk factors in 2000
Deaths in millions

Sickness and stress

Worldwide, the bulk of health expenditure still goes on curing illnesses rather than on preventing them. High-technology medicine consumes vast budgets. By contrast, primary health care, community schemes, and preventive medicine are drastically underfunded (pp. 206–207). Despite major publicity campaigns, the public at large is often ignorant (or ignore-ant!) of the links between illness and diet or cigarettes or alcohol. (By 2030, smoking could be responsible for 10 million deaths a year.)

Death tolls
Between 1977 and 2000, there were 6 times as many deaths from hunger as all the deaths from war since 1945. Note world military expenditure in 2003, $880 billion; funding required to tackle AIDS in 2005, $12 billion.

Health problems in the North
In the industrialized North, most of the pressing health problems have sprung from the very conditions generally considered to be the hallmarks of progress. Many older people are suffering from neglect as well as ill-health. Most seriously, there are the "new deaths": AIDS, cancers, and cardiovascular disease promoted by modern environments and lifestyles. There is also a growing array of minor illnesses, many readily preventable.

The new deaths
Cardiovascular diseases account for almost a third of all deaths, and three-quarters of cardiovascular disease can be attributed to the majority risks: high cholesterol, high blood pressure, low fruit/vegetable intake, inactive lifestyle, and tobacco. One-quarter of deaths each year are due to cancer, one-fifth to diseases such as AIDS, TB, and malaria.

Minds under stress
According to the WHO, more than 120 million people suffer from depression – roughly 6% of men and 10% of women experience a depressive episode in any given year. Almost 40 million people live with dementia, Alzheimer's causing most cases.

Ivory tower medicine
In the North, emphasis on hospitals and high technology has often locked up resources which might otherwise have been used to prevent illness.

Health expenditure: North vs. South
There is a huge disparity in health care spending: from highs of $4,900 per capita in the US and $3,300 in Switzerland to lows of $12 in DR Congo and $14 in Ethiopia (all in PPP$s).

North   Age

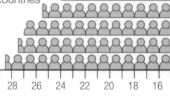

Male   Female

100,000s of people (2005 projection)

The new outcasts
One in ten people worldwide is aged 60+. By 2020, the share will be one in eight. Over 420 million older persons live in developing countries and 245 million in developed countries – many living alone or in nursing homes and hospitals. According to UNFPA, population ageing is increasingly a major development challenge, especially where there are limited institutional, human, and financial resources and where social safety nets do not exist.

HIV/AIDS
There have been 23 million deaths since 1981, and 15 million children have lost one or both parents to the disease. In 2004: 5 million new infections, 3 million deaths, 39 million sufferers. By 2010 life expectancy in several Southern African countries could fall to 30–40 years.

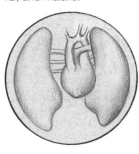

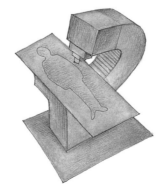

516

181

190

The developing countries have a double burden to bear. The central battleground for them remains infectious diseases, but they also have to provide the infrastructure for health care. Even simple, readily countered threats, such as the micro-organisms that cause diarrhoeal diseases, kill more than two million children in the South. Malnutrition is perhaps the cruellest affliction, with children, young girls, and pregnant and lactating women most at risk. Vitamin-A deficiency is the leading cause of preventable blindness in children (100–140 million children are vitamin A deficient), yet it can be tackled with supplements costing just a few cents a dose.

In developing countries a short period of ill-health can push a family into a deepening spiral of poverty, forcing it to sell land, animals, or other possessions which, with high interest rates, it will never be able to buy back. With all these existing problems, they can ill afford to import the lifestyle-related diseases of the North. By 2030, smoking could become the leading cause of death, with 7 million of the projected 10 million deaths worldwide a year occurring in low- and middle-income countries.

Around the world, too, there is the rising spectre of infirm old age. Even in the North, where the average age of populations is highest, far too little is being done to help the aged cope with such chronic health problems as rheumatism and arthritis, while growing numbers of old people try to cope alone or are sidelined into institutions.

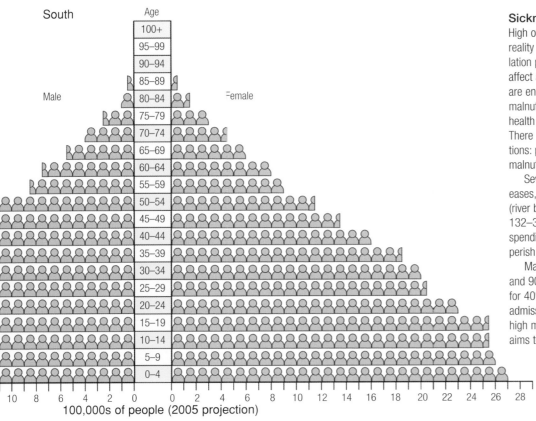

South — Age — Male — Female

100,000s of people (2005 projection)

Sickness in the South

High overall mortality and very high infant mortality are the bitter reality in many developing countries. In the first step on the population pyramid (left) 1 in 11 children dies; disability and illness affect a large share of the population. Poverty and malnutrition are endemic: two-thirds of people in Sub-Saharan Africa suffer malnutrition, 100 million people severely so. There is a lack of health workers and information about drugs, and poor sanitation. There is a complex interplay that frustrates single-minded solutions: poor sanitation causes diarrhoea, which aggravates malnutrition, sapping energy and earning capacity.

Several hundred million people suffer from waterborne diseases, notably schistosomiasis (bilharzia) and onchocerciasis (river blindness). Tackling water hazards (see pp. 116–17 and 132–33) has proved a Herculean task, due to mis- or underspending. Without urgent action 34–76 million people could perish from water-related diseases by 2020.

Malaria is the leading cause of under-5 mortality in Africa and 90% of all malaria deaths are in this region. It accounts for 40% of public health expenditure, 30–50% of inpatient admissions, and up to 50% of outpatient visits in areas with high malaria rates. The WHO's Roll Back Malaria Campaign aims to halve the burden of by 2010.

Number of physicians per 100,000 people

The child killers

Millions of child deaths in the developing world each year could be prevented through a combination of good care, nutrition, and medical treatment. Malnutrition is associated with more than half of all child deaths.

Diarrhoea

Diarrhoeal disease is associated with one-fifth of child deaths in developing countries. The best cure, Oral Rehydration Therapy (ORT), is cheap and simple, but fails without education for its use.

Imported drugs

Private spending on health in developing countries outstrips government spending by 3 to 4 times, and at least a third of this money goes on useless or harmful drugs. Companies are notoriously slow to remove "contra-indicated" drugs from the developing world markets.

"Education is development. It creates choices and opportunities for people, reduces the twin burdens of poverty and diseases, and gives a stronger voice in society. For nations, it creates a dynamic workforce and well-informed citizens able to compete and cooperate globally – opening doors to economic and social prosperity."

World Bank

Barriers against progress

The predicaments of ill-health and lack of education cannot be examined in isolation. A global map of ill-health would coincide with maps of malnutrition, poverty, and illiteracy. The illiterate person is not only unable to read or write, but he, or more usually she, is also poor, hungry, and highly vulnerable to disease and exploitation. Literacy in developing countries lags way behind that of developed countries, with women still further behind (in 2004, the male adult literacy rate was 83 percent, that of women 69 percent).

While many developing countries have made great progress in promoting literacy, a focus on sheer numbers helps us see the gap between the people and the provisions. There are still 800 million illiterate adults in the world, 515 million of them women – 115 million in Africa alone, where the female adult literacy rate is 53 percent (cf. 70 percent for men). Asia contains most illiterate adults (565 million) with 186 million in Africa, 42 million in the Americas, 6 million in Europe, and 1 million in Oceania. Developed and transition countries feature only 10 million.

Financial factors dictate priorities. Many developing countries find themselves having to stretch other social budgets, by e.g. the HIV/AIDS crisis, civil strife, or unforeseen upheavals such as the 2004 tsunami disaster, which wiped out much infrastructure and left many children orphaned. In 1999, spending on education as a percent of GDP averaged around 5 percent in OECD countries but in Indonesia little over one percent (compare the Philippines six percent and Chile seven percent).

Over 80 percent of primary-age children in developing countries were enrolled in school in 2000 (compare high-income countries' 97 percent), but at least 115 million children were not attending school at all. In addition, the school enrolment rate can be very different to the school completion rate. In Madagascar 80 percent of students do not complete primary education despite the country's 68 percent enrolment rate. Many countries in Sub-Saharan Africa have primary completion rates of less than 50 percent. If current trends persist, children in at least half of developing countries will not complete a full course of primary education in 2015. There has been some progress. In 1960, Chile's adult population had spent an average of only six years at school but by 2000 the average had climbed to ten years. Those who fail to learn basic skills by the end of normal school age have little chance of acquiring them as adults.

The literacy chasm

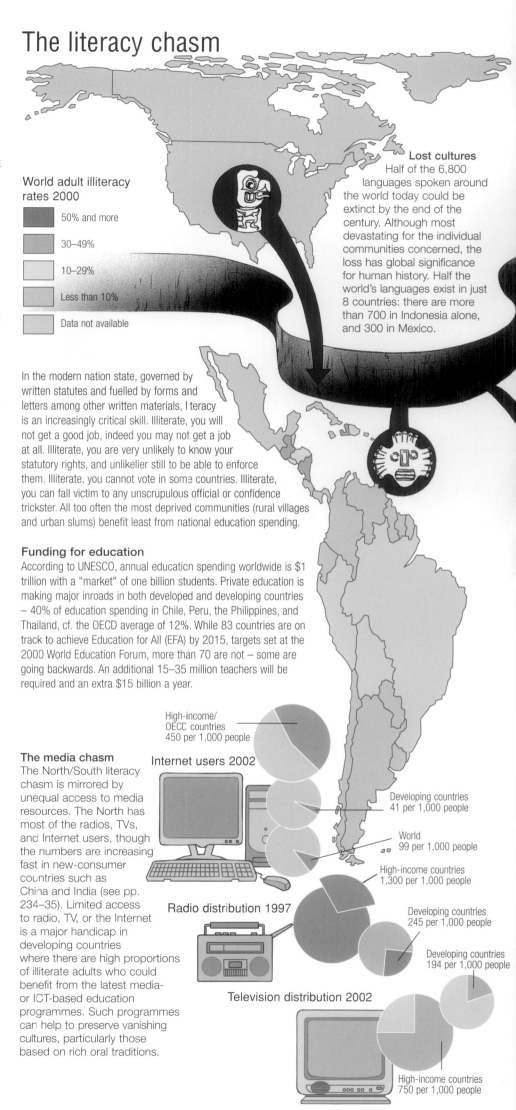

World adult illiteracy rates 2000

- 50% and more
- 30–49%
- 10–29%
- Less than 10%
- Data not available

Lost cultures
Half of the 6,800 languages spoken around the world today could be extinct by the end of the century. Although most devastating for the individual communities concerned, the loss has global significance for human history. Half the world's languages exist in just 8 countries: there are more than 700 in Indonesia alone, and 300 in Mexico.

In the modern nation state, governed by written statutes and fuelled by forms and letters among other written materials, literacy is an increasingly critical skill. Illiterate, you will not get a good job, indeed you may not get a job at all. Illiterate, you are very unlikely to know your statutory rights, and unlikelier still to be able to enforce them. Illiterate, you cannot vote in some countries. Illiterate, you can fall victim to any unscrupulous official or confidence trickster. All too often the most deprived communities (rural villages and urban slums) benefit least from national education spending.

Funding for education

According to UNESCO, annual education spending worldwide is $1 trillion with a "market" of one billion students. Private education is making major inroads in both developed and developing countries – 40% of education spending in Chile, Peru, the Philippines, and Thailand, cf. the OECD average of 12%. While 83 countries are on track to achieve Education for All (EFA) by 2015, targets set at the 2000 World Education Forum, more than 70 are not – some are going backwards. An additional 15–35 million teachers will be required and an extra $15 billion a year.

The media chasm

The North/South literacy chasm is mirrored by unequal access to media resources. The North has most of the radios, TVs, and Internet users, though the numbers are increasing fast in new-consumer countries such as China and India (see pp. 234–35). Limited access to radio, TV, or the Internet is a major handicap in developing countries where there are high proportions of illiterate adults who could benefit from the latest media- or ICT-based education programmes. Such programmes can help to preserve vanishing cultures, particularly those based on rich oral traditions.

Internet users 2002

High-income/OECD countries
450 per 1,000 people

Developing countries
41 per 1,000 people

World
99 per 1,000 people

Radio distribution 1997

High-income countries
1,300 per 1,000 people

Developing countries
245 per 1,000 people

Developing countries
194 per 1,000 people

Television distribution 2002

High-income countries
750 per 1,000 people

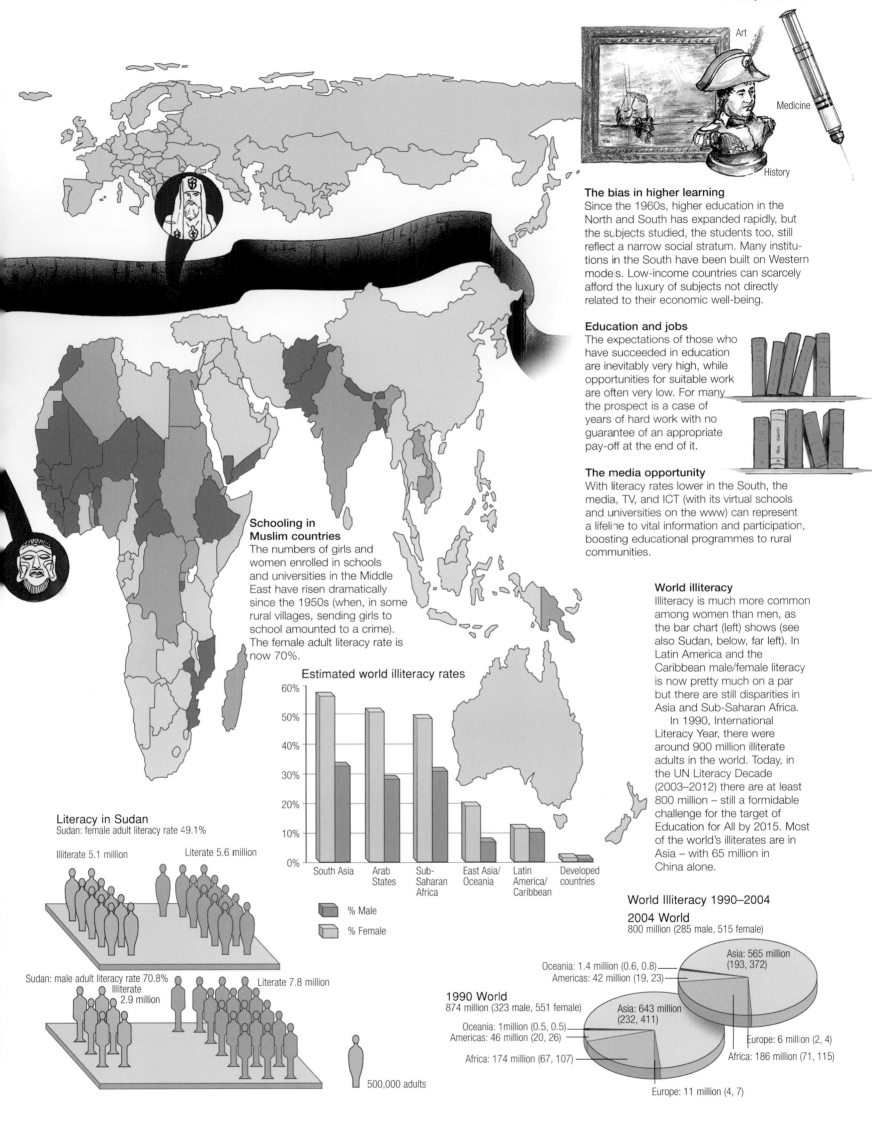

The bias in higher learning

Since the 1960s, higher education in the North and South has expanded rapidly, but the subjects studied, the students too, still reflect a narrow social stratum. Many institutions in the South have been built on Western models. Low-income countries can scarcely afford the luxury of subjects not directly related to their economic well-being.

Education and jobs

The expectations of those who have succeeded in education are inevitably very high, while opportunities for suitable work are often very low. For many the prospect is a case of years of hard work with no guarantee of an appropriate pay-off at the end of it.

The media opportunity

With literacy rates lower in the South, the media, TV, and ICT (with its virtual schools and universities on the www) can represent a lifeline to vital information and participation, boosting educational programmes to rural communities.

World illiteracy

Illiteracy is much more common among women than men, as the bar chart (left) shows (see also Sudan, below, far left). In Latin America and the Caribbean male/female literacy is now pretty much on a par but there are still disparities in Asia and Sub-Saharan Africa.

In 1990, International Literacy Year, there were around 900 million illiterate adults in the world. Today, in the UN Literacy Decade (2003–2012) there are at least 800 million – still a formidable challenge for the target of Education for All by 2015. Most of the world's illiterates are in Asia – with 65 million in China alone.

Schooling in Muslim countries

The numbers of girls and women enrolled in schools and universities in the Middle East have risen dramatically since the 1950s (when, in some rural villages, sending girls to school amounted to a crime). The female adult literacy rate is now 70%.

Estimated world illiteracy rates

% Male
% Female

South Asia | Arab States | Sub-Saharan Africa | East Asia/Oceania | Latin America/Caribbean | Developed countries

Literacy in Sudan
Sudan: female adult literacy rate 49.1%

Illiterate 5.1 million
Literate 5.6 million

Sudan: male adult literacy rate 70.8%
Illiterate 2.9 million
Literate 7.8 million

500,000 adults

World Illiteracy 1990–2004

2004 World
800 million (285 male, 515 female)

Oceania: 1.4 million (0.6, 0.8)
Americas: 42 million (19, 23)
Asia: 565 million (193, 372)
Europe: 6 million (2, 4)
Africa: 186 million (71, 115)

1990 World
874 million (323 male, 551 female)

Oceania: 1 million (0.5, 0.5)
Americas: 46 million (20, 26)
Asia: 643 million (232, 411)
Africa: 174 million (67, 107)
Europe: 11 million (4, 7)

Art
Medicine
History

Human migration

The world's population is increasingly mobile. This is because, thanks to television, films, magazines and other mass media, people are far more aware of how the grass is greener next door, even if that next door is around the back of the Earth. The have-nots want an entry into haves-land, and airplanes enable many to make the move with unprecedented ease. Many migrants travel illegally, finding they can skip across the Rio Grande from Mexico into the US by a simple overnight hike, or from North Africa to Spain and from Tunisia to Sicily by a quick boat trip.

Migrant totals are estimated to have increased from 84 million in 1975 to 175 million in 2000. Each year over two million people migrate from developing to developed countries, thus accounting for a large share of the population growth in the latter countries. By 2050, the 175 million could become 230 million – or even, driven by global warming, to twice as many.

Migrants are a mixed bunch. Some are driven by harsh conditions: religious persecution, political oppression, or ethnic conflicts. Others, the great majority so far, are drawn by economic opportunity. The former want to escape a dreadful existence, the latter are attracted by a more prosperous life.

The period 1850–1913 saw the first era of mass migration, mainly from Europe to North America and reaching a peak of about a million people per year. In the 1950s and 1960s, Germany introduced its Guest Worker programme with Turkey, taking in more than a million people per year. Workers from Southern and East Asia to the Middle East rose from 100,000 a year in 1975 to a million in 1991. During 1989–2000, a million Jewish people migrated from the former Soviet Union to Israel. In the late 1990s, some 200,000 migrants arrived in Canada each year, mainly from India and China. The upshot is that today a large proportion of the world's migrants is made up of Chinese, Indians, Pakistanis, Bangladeshis, Vietnamese, and Filipinos. The Indian Diaspora has topped 20 million people, and the Chinese 30 million people.

A quarter of a century ago only six percent of countries had policies to curb immigration, now they amount to 40 percent. Only five countries have official policies to encourage immigration, being the US, Canada, Australia, New Zealand, and Israel.

The big picture is that migration is a fast-growing fact of global life, and trying to prevent it leaves us looking like latter-day Canutes. In any case, should we in the rich world want to practise a pull-up-the-drawbridge response? Shouldn't we recognize the immense contributions, both quantitative and qualitative, of immigrants to our national well-being, notably on the part of doctors and nurses, business leaders and financiers, lawyers and writers, and sports stars? Developed countries would do well to regulate migration to their greater benefit rather than simply pretend it can be abolished through crude prohibition.

Our world on the move

Where are the migrants?

Given that 175 million people now live in a country other than where they were born (roughly every 36th person in the world, for a total twice as large as in 1970), 60% of them are in developed countries and the rest in developing countries. More migrants live in Europe than any other continent, fully 56 million of them; another 50 million are in Asia. In North America, 41 million migrants (mostly in the US) make up 12% of the population, and in Australasia 4.7 million make up 25%. By contrast, Africa has only 2% and Asia and Latin America 1%. During the 1990s, migrants in North America increased by almost half. Almost one in every ten persons in developed countries is a migrant, by contrast with only one in every 70 persons in developing countries.

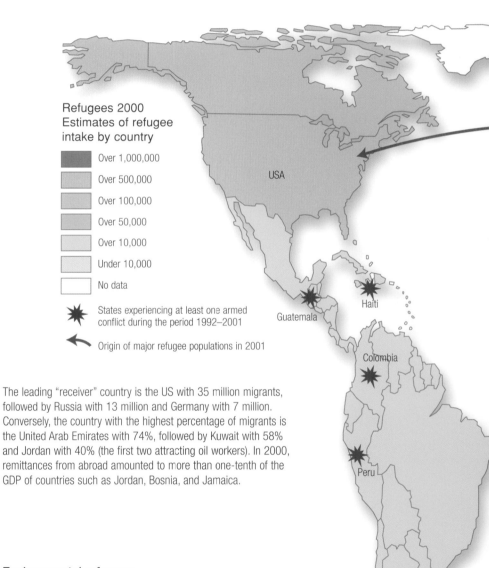

Refugees 2000
Estimates of refugee
intake by country

- Over 1,000,000
- Over 500,000
- Over 100,000
- Over 50,000
- Over 10,000
- Under 10,000
- No data

✳ States experiencing at least one armed conflict during the period 1992–2001

← Origin of major refugee populations in 2001

The leading "receiver" country is the US with 35 million migrants, followed by Russia with 13 million and Germany with 7 million. Conversely, the country with the highest percentage of migrants is the United Arab Emirates with 74%, followed by Kuwait with 58% and Jordan with 40% (the first two attracting oil workers). In 2000, remittances from abroad amounted to more than one-tenth of the GDP of countries such as Jordan, Bosnia, and Jamaica.

Environmental refugees

Environmental refugees are people who feel driven from their homelands for environmental reasons, such as soil erosion, water shortages, desertification, deforestation and fuelwood deficits, plus associated factors, such as population pressures and widespread poverty. They can no longer gain a secure livelihood in their homelands. In their desperation, they feel they have no alternative but to seek sanctuary elsewhere, however hazardous the attempt (pp. 50–51). Not all of them have fled their countries, many being internally displaced. But all have abandoned their homelands on a semi-permanent if not permanent basis, with little hope of a foreseeable return. In the mid-1990s, environmental refugees totalled 25 million. In a globally warmed world their numbers could soar tenfold – possibly even more. Sadly, there is a lack of official recognition, whether on the part of governments or international agencies, that there is an environmental refugee problem at all.

Exile and persecution

A refugee, in the blunt definition of the UN Convention of 1951 and the Protocol of 1967, is a person who cannot return to his or her own country because of a "well-founded fear of persecution for reasons of race, religion, nationality, political association or social grouping". Thus many refugees have been created not by natural disasters but by political instabilities, including the 160 or so undeclared wars waged since 1945. The very word refugee rings alarm bells; it evokes a sense of immediate crisis.

In early 2003, the refugees total was just short of 21 million people, equivalent to Greater New York. Of these, half were official refugees and the rest were returned refugees, asylum seekers, internally displaced persons and others "of concern". During the past decade, developing countries produced 86% of the world's refugees. Some of the countries now hosting considerable numbers of refugees are among those least able to afford such an increased burden.

Pandemic diseases

The 1919 Spanish Flu pandemic killed 20–40 million people worldwide. An event of this sort today could cause more than 100 million deaths. A possible pandemic was averted in 1997 when avian flu posed a significant threat to humans. At the source – Hong Kong – the entire poultry population was destroyed in order to reduce further human infection. Severe Acute Respiratory Syndrome (SARS) first appeared in southern China in 2002 and quickly spread thanks to international travel. In 2003, the WHO identified the cause as a coronavirus never before seen in humans.

Afghan refugees

In 2001, 700,000 people were internally displaced in Afghanistan; 200,000 escaped to Pakistan and another 200,000 to Iran.

Bangladesh inundated

Bangladesh is a huge delta of the rivers Ganges, Brahmaputra and Meghna, hence it is low lying and very vulnerable to sea level rise (see pp. 50–51). An effective rise of 1.5 metres, entirely on the cards by 2050, would flood one-fifth of the country and one-third of its ricelands. Other deltas at risk include those of the Nile, the Niger, and the Mississippi. Global warming would force huge numbers of people to flee.

Extreme rainfall and floods

In June 2004 1.5m of rain fell in south-eastern Haiti in 36 hours (just 5cm is considered "extreme"). The December 2004 tidal wave in Southern and Southeast Asia caused at least 300,000 deaths. Floods impact more than half a billion people worldwide each year. By 2050, that number could rise to two billion. Floods and other weather-related disasters already cost the global economy $50–60 billion per year, much of it in developing countries – roughly equal to total development aid (pp. 126–127). The 2002 floods in Europe caused $20 billion in damages.

Sudanese on the move

By the end of 2001, 4 million Sudanese were internally displaced and almost half a million were living outside the country either as refugees or asylum seekers.

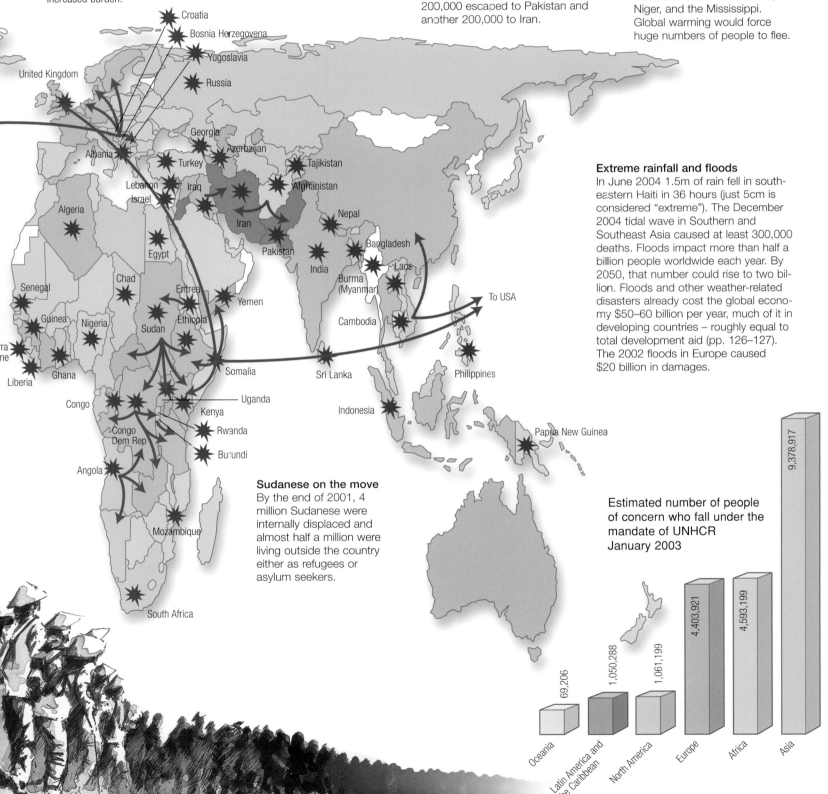

Estimated number of people of concern who fall under the mandate of UNHCR January 2003

Oceania	Latin America and the Caribbean	North America	Europe	Africa	Asia
69,206	1,050,288	1,061,199	4,403,921	4,593,199	9,378,917

Managing Ourselves

"'Well, in our country,' said Alice, 'you'd generally get to somewhere else if you ran very fast for a long time, as we've been doing.' 'A slow sort of country!' said the Queen. 'Now, here, you see, it takes all the running you can do to keep in the same place. If you want to get somewhere else, you must run at least twice as fast as that!'" These words by Lewis Carroll aptly express the plight of many countries in the development race – they have to "run twice as

fast" to make any headway because they are handicapped by rising numbers, wars, sickness, and inequity. Removing the handicaps is an urgent task for each nation and for the global community. Fortunately, development is showing signs of reaching entire communities, to help the women, the poor, the illiterate, the workless, and the rejected minorities.

Population management

Population trends are not easy to influence. In a sense, governments face a "chicken and egg" situation. Birth control is most effective in a context of improved health care and rising employment and incomes, but it is often the lack of birth control that makes these factors hard to achieve. Best results are obtained when improved status and education for women runs in tandem with family planning.

Human Development Index (HDI) (see scale on p. 203, far right)
This measure of human progress averages achievement in three basic dimensions: long and healthy life (life expectancy at birth); knowledge (two-thirds based on adult literacy, one-third on combined primary/secondary/tertiary gross enrolment); and reasonable standard of living (GDP per capita in PPP$). Norway heads the list with an HDI of 0.956 and last is Sierra Leone, with 0.273. The United States ranks 8th with 0.939, then Japan 0.938, followed by Ireland, Switzerland and the UK with 0.936.

Managing numbers

The forces working against the lowering of fertility rates are deeply rooted in cultural, social, and economic conditions that have prevailed for generations. It is no coincidence that fertility rates are highest in least developed countries, where economic deprivation is endemic, and lowest in affluent educated societies with good social provision. The desire for large families is the result of many factors, among them high infant mortality (African infants are 13 times more likely to die than European or North American infants), labour-intensive means of subsistence, and the need for support in old age. Average fertility rates (the number of children born to a woman during her lifetime) are still high in many countries, e.g. 4.7 in Haiti, 5.0 in Kenya, almost 5.7 in Nigeria, 6.8 in Afghanistan, and 8.0 in Niger. Some aspects of the developmental process, such as improved health, better education, and increased employment opportunities for women, work together with family planning to cut fertility rates.

Ethiopia
Growth rate 2.4%

Ethiopia
Less than 10% of all Ethiopian couples use any form of contraception, and government support for birth control is very recent. Ethiopia's population could reach more than 170 million by 2050, for an increase of 139% over 2004.

World population target: 7.7 billion
The aim should be to bring down population growth so that the UN's medium projection figure for the year 2050 is reduced from 9.1 billion to the UN's low projection figure of 7.7 billion.

Family planning and US AID cuts
When US Congress slashed funding by $191 million (35 percent) in late 1995, 7 million developing-world couples lost protection. Result: an estimated additional 4 million unwanted pregnancies, 1.9 million unwanted births, and 1.6 million abortions.

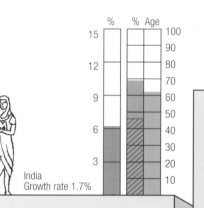

India
Growth rate 1.7%

India
India's population has exploded to reach almost 1.1 billion in 2004. By 2040 the country will likely have the largest population in the world. Infant mortality and illiteracy are still high, but the state of Kerala has succeeded in lowering child deaths by improving health services and working conditions (more than one-third of state expenditure goes to health and education). Average family size is half that of the Indian average, and more than 90% of girls attend high school.

Supersize challenges (2004–2050 projected population growth)

China	1,301–1,437 million
India	1,087–1,628 million
Other Asia/Oceania	1,520–2,367 million
Africa	885–1,941 million
Latin America	549–778 million
North America	326–457 million
Europe	728–668 million
World	6,396–9,276 million

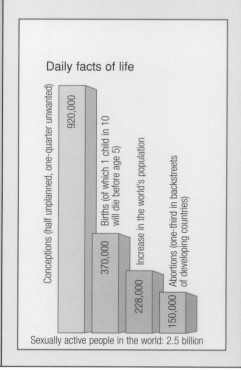

Sri Lanka
Growth rate: 1.3%

Sri Lanka
Government policies encouraging smaller families have enabled Sri Lanka's TFR to fall from 5.0 in the early 1960s to 2.1 at the end of the 1990s, despite more than a doubling of the number of women in the reproductive age group during the same period. A range of policy measures has included incentives for voluntary sterilization.

Daily facts of life

Conceptions (half unplanned, one-quarter unwanted) 920,000

Births (of which 1 child in 10 will die before age 5) 370,000

Increase in the world's population 228,000

Abortions (one-third in backstreets of developing countries) 150,000

Sexually active people in the world: 2.5 billion

In many developing countries family planning has been spreading strongly over the past two decades, with some countries making major cuts in their population growth rates. In Brazil, 76 percent of women use some form of contraception and the annual population growth rate is only 1.3 percent. Contrast Madagascar, 19 percent and 3 percent.

In Kerala, India, family planning has been assisted by good health services, the strong economic status of women, high literacy, and excellent communications. Indonesia introduced family planning to the poor of East Java and Bali, thanks to government support for village services. Other successes have been achieved in Cuba, Costa Rica, Hong Kong, South Korea, Mauritius, and Taiwan. Family planning has been less successful in Muslim countries such as Pakistan (growth rate of 2.4% in 2004), underscoring the impact of cultural traditions regarding women. Sub-Saharan Africa has been least successful because of cultural factors and very weak health care.

Despite much progress as a result of family planning over the past 50 years (half of all couples in developing countries now use modern contraception), there is much more that could be done: the needs of 120 million women in developing countries for ready access to safe contraception are not being met. Almost two-fifths of all pregnancies around the world every year are unintended, and three-fifths of unplanned pregnancies result in abortion.

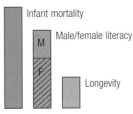

Infant mortality

Male/female literacy

Longevity

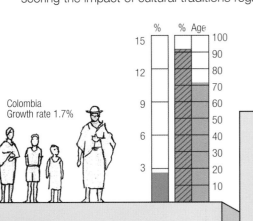

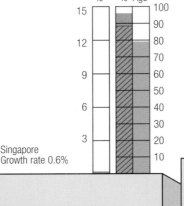

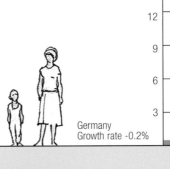

Colombia
Growth rate 1.7%

Singapore
Growth rate 0.6%

Germany
Growth rate -0.2%

Colombia
Colombia has achieved a dramatic demographic transition – from an annual rate of population growth of 3% in 1970 to 1.7% in 2004. The government's multi-faceted social policy has increased life expectancy, while infant deaths have dropped to 26 per 1,000 live births (cf. India's 64).

Singapore
While population pressure had been a critical concern in Singapore – by 2004 its 4.2 million people were living at a density of 45,400 per sq. km – a dramatic fall in the birth rate has led to a change in family planning policy with various financial and tax incentives being offered to encourage people to have more children, including tax rebates for third children and subsidies for day care.

Germany
With one of the lowest population growth rates in the world, Germany has a problem. Following reunification, the German population was 77.6 million, but this is projected to fall to 75 million by 2050, when there will be one retired person for every two people in work. As in Europe as a whole, 28% of Germany's population will be over 65 by 2050. The implications for social services are momentous.

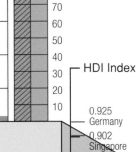

HDI Index

0.925 Germany
0.902 Singapore

0.773 Colombia
0.740 Sri Lanka

0.595 India

0.359 Ethiopia

Percentage of women with unmet needs for family planning

0–20%

21–40%

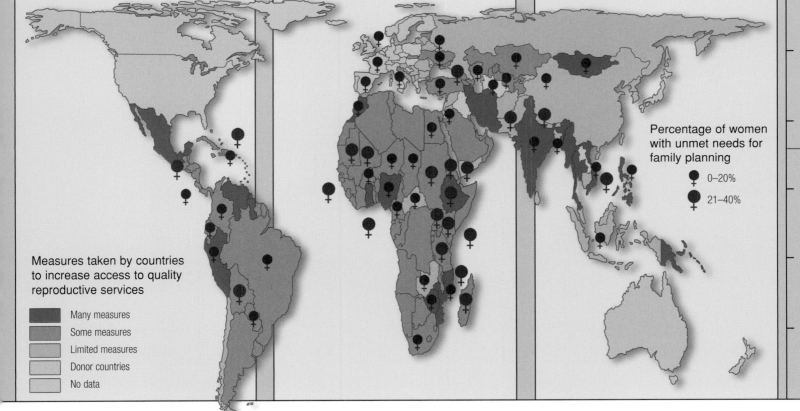

Measures taken by countries to increase access to quality reproductive services

Many measures
Some measures
Limited measures
Donor countries
No data

"Women have an enormous impact on the well-being of their families and societies – yet their potential is not realized because of discriminatory social norms, incentives, and legal institutions. And while their status has improved in recent decades, gender inequalities remain pervasive."

World Bank and Millennium Development Goal 3: Promote Gender Equality and Empower Women

Equality for women?

Think about women today, especially in developing countries, and it is difficult to avoid thinking about oppression. Yet their contribution is remarkable. In many countries rural women endure heavy workloads with responsibility for both farm and household production. This work is often made all the harder and time-consuming due to changing agricultural technologies and practices and to ecological degradation (e.g. long hours spent in search of fuelwood for cooking food). Just think: women are deeply involved in crops, livestock, forestry, and fisheries.

In developed countries, one of the most significant socioeconomic trends in the last half-century has been the entry of women into the ranks of official workers, counting 60 percent of women in Norway, Sweden, Australia, Denmark, the US, and Canada (OECD average, 52 percent). In certain of the rapidly expanding developing countries it is even higher, with 73 percent in China and Thailand (developing country average 56 percent).

The unpaid or "invisible" work done by women at home is still substantial. In Canada in 2001, one-fifth of women devoted 30 hours or more a week to unpaid housework, compared with less than 10 percent for men. Canadian women perform two-thirds of unpaid work, worth up to $320 billion to the country's economy and the equivalent of millions of full-time jobs. In waged work, discrimination hits women in both the North and the South, with a strong tendency for them to be regarded as "cheap labour". So the problem is twin headed. Women often end up in the worst-paid jobs, or, where they break out of stereotypical female work, they are paid less for comparable work. In the UK in 2002, female earned income averaged PPP$19,800 compared to the male average of almost PPP$33,000.

A few countries like Sweden and Cuba have encouraged equal sharing of home responsibilities to facilitate power sharing at the top. Getting men to share both political power and the breadwinner role can be a major hurdle in male-oriented cultures, but women are making inroads by taking the initiative both in the work sector and in political movements.

Educating girls is the key to empowering women to take control of their own lives by reducing fertility rates, improving maternal and child health, and eliminating poverty and malnutrition. Tackling gender inequality in developing countries – especially education, in that 515 million of the world's 800 million illiterate adults are women – is a priority.

Voice of women

While only a small fraction of women are actively engaged in politics today, more and more women are making their voice heard. More and more too it is a voice in defence of peace, conservation, and humanitarian values. The contemporary women's movement comprises hundreds of international organizations and thousands of pressure groups. It can be described as one of the most global social movements of recent times. Self-help groups are legion. Peace campaigners such as the Greenham Common Women in the UK and the tree huggers of the Chipko Andolan movement in India have been part of an upsurge of activity which first found international expression in the UN Decade for Women 1975–1985.

Despite the growing impact of women's movements, women are still under-represented at all levels of decision-making. Fortunately, there have been major advances since 1945. In India one-third of all seats in local elections are reserved for women and in Brazil at least 20 percent of each party's candidates must be women. Quotas also exist in Argentina, Finland, Germany, Mexico, South Africa, and Spain. Organizations such as Sisterhood is Global span 70 countries and educate people on women's rights. Similar groups exist even in Islamic countries. The 1995 fourth World Conference on Women held in Beijing attracted 189 governments and 2,600 NGOs.

The UN Development Programme's Gender-Related Development Index (see p. 187) ranks Norway first with a GDI of 0.955, but there are more than 50 countries (almost all in Africa) with a GDI of less than 0.60 – Niger's is only 0.278.

Time allocation in developing countries:
Men spend more time on market-oriented production activities than women.

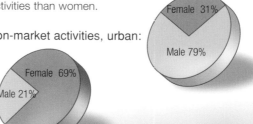

Market activities, urban:
Female 31%
Male 79%

Non-market activities, urban:
Female 69%
Male 21%

Female education
The number of girls in primary education still lags behind that of boys in many developing countries. In 2003, at least 115 million children were not in school at all, 66 million of them girls. Yet female education is a strategy that will positively impact on many other development goals, e.g. poverty, malnutrition, maternal and child health generally, plus HIV/AIDS and other diseases. The UN's 10-year Girls' Education Initiative 2001–2010 has five objectives: building political and resource commitments, ending the gender gap, ending gender bias and discrimination within education, helping girls' education in crisis, conflict and post-conflict situations, and eliminating ingrained gender bias that limits demand for girls' education.

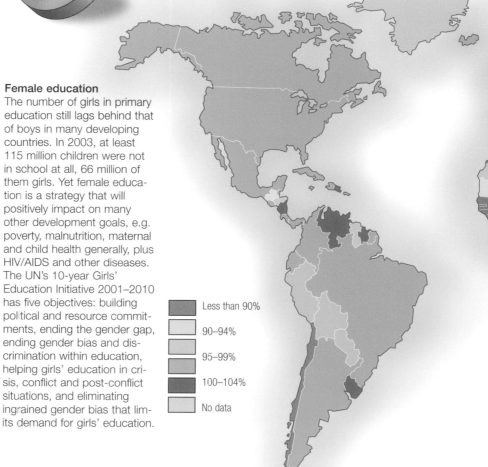

Less than 90%
90–94%
95–99%
100–104%
No data

Equal work, equal pay?
Women account for 40% of the economically active population in developing countries and 45% in developed countries. In 2003, there were more than 1 billion women in the world's workforce. While this was 200 million more over the previous decade, the growth was not accompanied by true socio-economic empowerment. There are still imbalances between female work-hours, income, and ownership. Equal-pay laws need to be enforced rigorously and extended. On top of all this, a key target must be the sharing of household work.

Women's work in Zambia
During the planting season, Zambian women combine strenuous agricultural activity with child care and housework. This intense workload begins at an early age. Family nutrition deteriorates during the heavy working season because women are too tired to cook. Although they produce much of the food, they are more likely to be undernourished than are men.

Women in the legislature

In 1945, only 31 countries let women vote. Today, most countries grant women the right to vote and be elected, yet women still find difficulty in exercising this right. In 2003, women held only 15% of seats in national parliaments, a mere 6% higher than in 1987. Regionally, the voice of women is strongest in the Nordic countries where women make up almost 40% of national legislatures. Some developing countries reserve seats for women. In Rwanda, women have 39 of 80 seats in the single/lower house (cf. Iran 9 of 290) and there are still countries where women are barred from full political participation, e.g. Bahrain, Kuwait, and the United Arab Emirates.

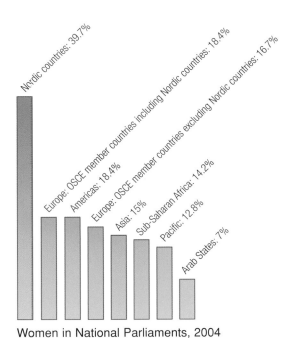

Women in National Parliaments, 2004

Nordic countries: 39.7%
Europe: OSCE member countries including Nordic countries: 18.4%
Americas: 18.4%
Europe: OSCE member countries excluding Nordic countries: 16.7%
Asia: 15%
Sub-Saharan Africa: 14.2%
Pacific: 12.8%
Arab States: 7%

The Self-Employed Women's Association (SEWA)
Founded in 1972 in Gujarat, India, SEWA provides new horizons for some of the country's poorest women. At least 25,000 women have benefited from special credit schemes, training programmes, welfare facilities, and minimum earnings. Members range from weavers to vegetable sellers, and their aims are the same: economic and social uplift. SEWA has helped its members to form 70 cooperatives, the most successful being the SEWA Bank, owned by the self-employed women as shareholders with policies made by their own elected board. The bank offers credit to its mainly illiterate women members – services they could not otherwise find. Today, the bank has nearly 50,000 depositors. Other cooperatives include health care, child care, training and literacy, and legal aid. Other "kickstarts" for women are the "tontines" and "pari" in West Africa and the Grameen Bank in Bangladesh (see p. 267).

Women in the Muslim world
While the number of girls and women enrolled in schools and universities in the Middle East has risen dramatically since the 1950s (when, in some villages, sending girls to school amounted to a crime), some orthodox Muslim states still bar women from voting. There are only 40 women per 100 men in the workforce but rising numbers, particularly in non-oil states, have begun to modify 1,000-year-old customs. Certain countries, e.g. Jordan, Iraq, and Egypt, have forged ahead with government-backed programmes designed to attract more women into the workforce.

... and in the non-Muslim world
A few of the world's 1.4 billion Muslims live in traditionally non-Muslim countries. Occasionally this has caused sizeable social problems. In France, for instance, with just 5 million Muslims among its 60 million population, Muslim schoolgirls have wanted to wear a headdress to school, even though this sometimes conflicts with rules about school uniforms.

Women and the environment
In the mid-1970s, the women of Reni in northern India took simple but effective action to stop tree felling by hugging trees that lumberjacks wanted to fell. Kenya's Green Belt Movement, founded by Nobel Prize winner Wangari Maathai, has assisted women in planting 20 million trees.

Women's protest movements
At Greenham Common in the UK (below), women kept a non-violent permanent vigil to demonstrate their opposition to the installation of Cruise missiles. They did this despite continual official harassment. Peace has become a unifying theme in women's movements worldwide.

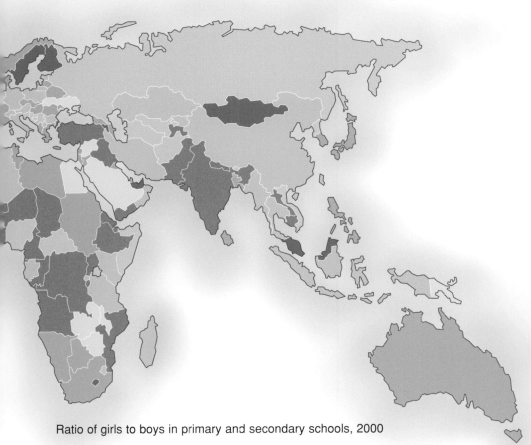

Ratio of girls to boys in primary and secondary schools, 2000

"The growing disparity between the haves and the have-nots in terms of access to basic services is killing around 4,000 children every day and underlies many more of the 10 million child deaths each year. We have to act now to close this gap or the death toll will certainly rise."

WHO and UNICEF 2004

Global health care

Health problems do not hinge only on primary health, vaccines, clean drinking water, and sanitation. They include political decisions on the relative priorities of health and defence, employment and decent low-cost housing, and the status of women and the underprivileged. A critical element in ending global inequality is primary health care, based on a close alliance between local communities and health workers. Strengthening this sector alleviates the distress of isolation and ignorance, and promotes prevention through early recognition of problems – an approach which makes good financial sense. The North could well learn from those nations of the South which, like China and Cuba, have pioneered networks of paramedics or "barefoot doctors".

The battle to achieve health in developing nations is being pursued across a large field. There is an acute need for much more safe drinking water and sanitation. Family planning services are not available

Community care

Primary health care

Self-help groups

Health for all

Health care for the North

Community programmes are a recent phenomenon in the North. In the US, Neighbourhood Health Centers reduce infant deaths in particular and hospital admissions in general. In Karelia, Finland, a voluntary campaign promoting healthy lifestyles has lowered the incidence of heart disease. Self-help groups like Alcoholics Anonymous can also play a vital role. In most countries, healthy lifestyle programmes, e.g. those aimed at stopping smoking and adopting regular exercise, are based on public education.

Prevention is the key

Provided there is a safe environment, balanced diets, clean water, and access to housing, work and education, the ultimate success of preventive medicine lies in people's own hands. There has been enormous media support for health-promoting lifestyles in the US and Europe. Information on the risks involved in eating fatty foods, sugar, and salt has influenced diets. Cigarette smoking is declining in the North, reducing the incidence of illnesses, but it is rising in Russia where per-capita consumption reached almost 2,000 cigarettes in 2002, more than twice the global average. Smoking kills 5 million people a year. In the US the health care costs of smoking are $80 billion a year, plus a similar sum in lost worker productivity.

AIDS: treatment or prevention?

In 2004, 39 million people were infected. UNAIDS estimates that 12 billion condoms are needed for HIV prevention each year. Of 7 billion condoms used in 2003, less than half were for disease prevention. In Africa alone, there is a shortage of 2 billion condoms each year – donation programmes provide just 3 per year for every adult male in Sub-Saharan Africa. In Thailand, a decade-long campaign promoting condom use in red-light districts reduced new HIV infections from 143,000 to 20,000 a year. In Uganda, 30% of the population was infected in the early 1990s, but a huge public education campaign based on the 'ABC' strategy reduced the infection rate to 6% and condom use rose 28-fold. In Sub-Saharan Africa half of school children receive AIDS education. On the downside, less than 10% of the 5-6 million developing country people in the advanced stages of the disease receive anti-retrovirals (cf. 95% in rich countries) – and only 5% of pregnant women, even though these drugs can sharply reduce transmission of HIV to newborns. Funding needs to increase from $5 billion in 2004 to $12 billion in 2005 and $20 billion in 2007 to effectively fight AIDS in developing countries. Comprehensive prevention could avert 29 million of the 45 million new infections projected by 2010. HIV/AIDS increases a person's vulnerability to diseases such as tuberculosis and malaria. In 2003, the combined deaths from all three was 6 million, yet TB can be prevented, treated, and – unlike HIV – be cured. The economic, social, and political impacts of these diseases highlights the urgent need for global commitment and action: The "Global Fund to Fight AIDS Tuberculosis and Malaria" had made a fine start, but much more help is needed.

Complementary/Alternative Medicine (CAM)

Doctors in the North have mostly lost the art of treating the whole person, although many are now rediscovering the benefits of a comprehensive approach to health and sickness. Acupuncture is recommended by half of doctors in the UK, and it is available in three-quarters of Germany's pain clinics. In the US, spending on CAM has reached almost $3 billion a year. Homeopathy, acupuncture, and Eastern exercises such as yoga are gaining widespread recognition. Clinical studies have shown that many traditional medicines and therapies can be highly effective.

Healthier diets

WHO identifies low fruit and vegetable intake as one of the top 10 risk factors contributing to mortality, and attributes almost 3 million deaths globally each year. Experts indicate that a daily intake of fruit and vegetables could help prevent major micro-nutrient (vitamin and mineral) deficiencies, cardiovascular diseases, and certain cancers.

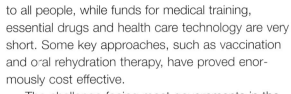

to all people, while funds for medical training, essential drugs and health care technology are very short. Some key approaches, such as vaccination and oral rehydration therapy, have proved enormously cost effective.

The challenge facing most governments in the South demands new priorities, with city-centred, doctor-oriented administrations converted into extensive networks for community care. Primary health care can cost little. Many resources are often already available, and traditional healers and midwives can be trained in basic hygiene and primary medicine. Ultimately, the drive for health comes from people, not from governments.

The central objectives of health promotion and health care programmes should be to improve health, eliminate poverty and inequality, spread education, and enable the poor and underprivileged groups to assert themselves. In both North and South, there is a new awareness of the far-reaching advantages of primary health care.

Let us bear in mind, too, that health is not just the absence of disease. It includes emotional and psychological well-being.

Regional hospitals
The decentralization of health care and hospital services is essential in the developing countries. Regional hospitals help to bridge the gap between rural and urban health.

Immunization success
Since 1980, the proportion of the world's children protected against the major immunizable diseases has increased massively. 70% of developing-country babies are immunized against measles and almost 80% against TB.

Family planning
Experience in many countries confirms that family planning services can improve the health of mothers and children. Better spacing between births cuts infant deaths and allows for longer breast-feeding. Growth monitoring is effective in preventive child care.

Adequate diet
The world can easily afford to feed its 840 million undernourished people, but for many it's a case of not enough in the right place and at the right time. Just 5% (34 million tonnes) of the world's grain that goes to feed livestock would be enough to make up the diets of these 840 million people. And vitamins and protein supplements, which combat serious illness, cost less than $1 per child per year.

Traditional medicine
Official health services in the South have begun to exploit the skills of traditional healers and midwives. In China, 95% of hospitals have traditional medicine units. In Japan, 72% of Western-style doctors use kampo. In Tanzania, Uganda, and Zambia there is one traditional healer for every 200–400 people, compared to one doctor for every 20,000.

Health for all in the South
Several developing countries have made enormous strides in community health, life expectancy, endemic diseases, and child mortality. Oral rehydration therapy (ORT), or a simple mixture of sugar and salts in water, is a major cure for diarrhoea. The benefits of primary health schemes have included improvements in educational performance and worker productivity. China spends PPP$225 per person per year on health and has achieved major successes by giving priority to primary health care and to birth control measures. Key targets include breast-feeding, immunization programmes and safe water. Kerala State in India has health indicators similar to those of the US, yet spends less than $30 per person on health. Cuba's infant mortality rate is 7 per 1,000 live births – the same as the US – and the country has also managed to control HIV/AIDS. These and other success story countries focus spending on basic health services and primary education. Better education leads to more demand for health services, plus improved child care.

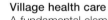

Sanitation

Safe water

Paramedic

Village health care
A fundamental element in any Primary Health Care (PHC) strategy is the involvement of the community. This is vital to mobilize human, material and financial resources. WHO research shows that a trained local health worker, equipped with only 15–20 drugs, can treat the majority of common illnesses. Community PHC depends on a multi-stranded approach, from drugs to sanitation and decent housing.

Costs and benefits of action
In 2003, more than 2.6 billion people lacked access to basic sanitation, and more than a billion had to use unsafe sources of drinking water. To halve these numbers by 2015 will require additional funding of only $13 billion a year, yet the benefits would be enormous: an estimated $63 billion for the sanitation target alone

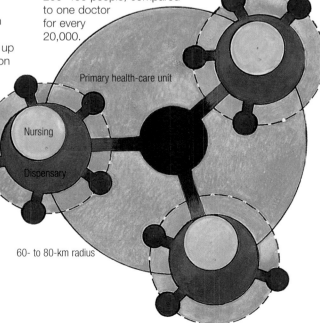

Primary health-care unit

Nursing

Dispensary

16-km radius

60- to 80-km radius

Community tools and access to ideas

A growing number of communities watch angrily as their economic life-blood flows away. In the North, structural change is ripping the economic heart out of entire regions which depend for their livelihood on "sundown" industries. In the South, the powerful undertow exerted by exploding cities is undermining rural communities by attracting their young people.

What can be done? Are these "community deaths" as inevitable as they seem? Sometimes they are, especially when communities have established themselves on a single, precarious resource or on a narrow economic base peculiar to a particular location, e.g. the cotton mill towns of northern England. They are then left out on a limb when their economic monoculture collapses. But as often as not, communities find that there are other ways of making a living, of rebuilding a viable community.

When dealing with outright disaster, such as a flood or a major factory accident, it is often easier for a community to cope than with a long drawn-out process of decline. Yet there are many examples of communities which have gone against the flow of economic decay, refusing to give way to despair. With inadequate resources, they have managed to pull themselves by up communal will. Policy makers and planners need to support all these regenerative activities.

In the North, old industrial buildings have been converted into thriving community workshops. Urban "greening" projects have harnessed the enthusiasm, energy, and skills of local residents, which are the true "tools for community". In the UK, many towns and cities have started to upgrade derelict areas to attract new employment such as Cardiff's Bay area, one of the UK's most successful regeneration projects, revitalising 1,100 hectares of decaying and derelict land in the former dockland area with residential, retail, commercial, and leisure developments.

In the South, the provision of local employment, often based on cooperatives and various forms of appropriate technologies, has helped build local economies to counter the call of the big city. In Sri Lanka, Sarvodaya Shramadana draws on a "strong organizational network of volunteers and paid workers, active at the grassroots level and from the village up, who can be mobilized for development activities" taking a "holistic perspective of human development which can be passed on from individual to individual, community to community".

The Global Ecovillage Network (GEN) supports sustainable settlements worldwide, such as Sarvodaya Shramadana and the Los Angeles ecovillage, through communications and facilitating the flow of information (see p. 267). GEN comprises people and communities that "meet and share ideas, exchange technologies, develop cultural and educational exchanges … and are dedicated to restoring the land and living 'sustainable plus' lives by putting more back into the environment than [they] take out".

Tools and ideas

Unemployment and underemployment are undermining the economic base of an alarming number of communities in both North and South. Technological change, the fluctuating world economy, and the exploding world population are all contributing factors. To turn the tide of people surging into the cities in search of work and better facilities, it is essential that rural and small-town economies should be stimulated and educational and health services decentralized. Community participation has proved to be a vital ingredient in the planning and implementation of public and private-sector development programmes. Given the tools and other resources, communities have pushed through their own programmes. The Naam movement in Burkina Faso is "an example of development adapted to local needs, created by the people themselves, which instead of destroying traditional structures from the outside … transforms them from the inside … It starts with what people are (appreciation of their African identity), what they know (respect for traditional knowledge and values), their know-how (rediscovery of traditional techniques), and what they wish to achieve (which implies meaningful grassroots participation in defining the very objectives of development processes)'. There are thousands of communities now pulling together.

The International Cooperative Alliance (ICA)

An independent, non-governmental association uniting cooperatives worldwide. Founded in London in 1895 and one of the first NGOs to be given UN Consultative Status, its members derive from all sectors of activity – agriculture, banking, energy, industry, insurance, fisheries, housing, tourism, and consumer societies. ICA has 230 member organizations from 100 countries, representing 760 million people worldwide.

Communities in schools

Education has to keep pace with changes in work and technology. Schools and colleges are vital tools for communities adapting to new needs, and are major employers. In both North and South, good rural schools, used as a resource by all the community, can help stem the flow of people to overcrowded cities.

Cooperative membership 2002

- Communications/internet (7.8%)
- Workers (6.1%)
- Housing (7.8%)
- Health (2.6%)
- Agriculture (17.8%)
- Insurance (23%)
- Banking and credit unions (19.6%)
- Consumer societies (8.7%)
- Tourism (2.6%)
- Fisheries (0.4%)
- Energy (3.5%)

Working ideas

Improved methods and low-cost technologies can revitalize existing work and help create new industries. The Intermediate Technology Development Group (ITDG) promotes systems and appropriate tools for use where expensive technologies are often irrelevant. In Bangladesh, women "grow" fish in local ponds using specially designed cages and feed the fish on scraps and waste. In Sudan, farmers are trained to use ploughs, enabling them to cultivate larger areas, whereupon simple donkey carts allow them to transport produce to market in a single trip. In the Kajiado region of Kenya, ITDG has helped women develop simple smoke hoods which reduce indoor smoke levels (a major cause of death) by up to 80%.

TV education networks

Special TV channels in China have led to the largest education network in the world with 100 million students. In 1997, Hunan University became the country's first on-line university. By 2000, there were 30 such universities with 200,000 students. The UK has the Open University International Centre for Distance Learning.

Distance learning

Millions of people in distant localities can now be reached thanks to the power of ICT, with students learning at home through correspondence, TV/radio, telephone, or Internet and CD-ROM.

Community cooperatives

Worker participation and profit-sharing schemes can both boost productivity and encourage innovation. There have been many ventures throughout Asia, including the Self-Employed Women's Association (SEWA) of Gujurat, India (see p. 205), and Sarvodaya Shramadana, Sri Lanka, which has mobilized as many as 11,000 villages (see p. 266). The ICA membership (left) covers multitudinous schemes.

Children's learning via TV and the Internet

Mass communication has done much to build up the "global village". Programmes such as "Sesame Street" can help children understand their polycultural world. The UN's "Cyberschoolbus" is part of its Global Teaching and Learning Project for students aged 5-18, as well as teachers.

Rural regeneration

Most developing countries that are committed to tackling rural poverty have implemented land reforms, notably China, Cuba, South Korea, and Taiwan. Such land distribution promotes employment and rural development. Where there is surplus labour, large-scale regeneration schemes prove highly productive. Examples include reforestation schemes in both India and South Korea.

The "social economy"

Made up of non-profit organizations including community businesses, cooperatives, local self-help/interest groups, housing/property management, cultural activities, sport, manufacturing, care services, and arts. The social economy includes the work of citizen groups, youth clubs, parent associations supporting local schools and voluntary groups assisting the elderly or disabled. It often includes many local initiatives, such as supervised play space, sport and recreational opportunities for children and youth, or care of green space/community gardens.

CIVILIZATION

Introduced by Sir Crispin Tickell
Chairman of the Earth Systems Science: Gaia Special Interest Group at the Geological Society of London.

Civilization as we know it is fragile. Even the most cheerful of us tend to forget its ephemeral, chancy, precarious, contingent character, not unlike evolution itself.

Since the last ice age, there have been some thirty urban civilizations. There is a kind of pattern in them which goes back to the time of hunter-gatherers and the first settled communities. If the environment is favourable, human numbers will rise. Resources of plants and animals will be increasingly exploited, sometimes to extinction. Communities will expand, almost like rings of spinifex, beyond their resource base. Towns will become cities. Division of labour and creation of hierarchies will follow. With greater complexity will come greater vulnerability. Societies of this kind can cope well enough with minor disasters. But big changes can cause catastrophes with food shortages, loss of confidence in the system, and eventual collapse.

During the last 250 years our society has become the only global civilization. It has greatly increased the human impact on the earth and its resources. By also increasing material production, it has also vastly improved living conditions for most people in terms of their material wealth and longevity. Successive technological changes, particularly in the field of communications, have brought the world together. But all this has created problems which are unprecedented in history. This was well brought out in a remarkable declaration published by some 1,500 scientists from the four great global research programmes at Amsterdam in July 2001. The key conclusion was that "the accelerating human transformation of the earth's environment is not sustainable. Therefore the business as usual of dealing with the earth's system is not an option". These thoughts were carried forwards in a statement by the European Commissioner for the Environment and three eminent scientists in January 2004 when they said that "the earth's life-support system is in peril".

Together, our environmental problems are so intimidating that most people, including politicians and leaders of all kinds, simply do not want to confront them. Many have entered into a state of denial. Each of us has his own priorities for action, but my own are simply stated. First we need to operate within an international framework, and develop approaches that take account of the diversity of national circumstances and interests, based on a shared political will for action. In spite of much rhetoric and many conferences, this is still far away.

Next we need to look at economics, and the way we measure wealth, welfare, and the human condition. Neither state-directed economics nor market economics can alone supply the right framework. Governments have a particular responsibility to determine what is in the public interest, and to use the right instruments to promote it. Nowhere is this more true than in the field of technology.

Then there are such specific issues as climate change. This means action on energy policy in all its aspects. Better conservation of biodiversity requires new thinking. We need to do far more to educate public opinion, not least in the financial and investment communities; and we also need to focus on the needs and attitudes of coming generations.

In short, we need to work with accelerating change, learn to think differently, and drastically modify our behaviour. No previous generations have had to respond to such an alarming challenge.

The Power of Civilization

For more than 5,000 years this planet has witnessed the rise and fall of successive civilizations. Each has spread its technology, culture, and beliefs widely. Each has declined when its resource base, or its administration, or both, became overstretched, and thus vulnerable to external attack or internal disintegration. The powerhouse behind all these cultures has been the phenomenon of the city – the centre of civilization, reflecting the best and worst of human aspirations.

We've been building cities ever since we learned to drain and effectively use the fertile valleys of Egypt, Mesopotamia, and China. The resultant agricultural surplus allowed a division of labour, and the leisure to think and organize, which underpin urban civilization. Over the ages, our towns and cities, often sited strategically on trading junctions, have served as cultural and racial melting pots. At their best, they have poured forth the wealth of art, literature, architecture, scientific discovery, and social, political, and ethical concepts which are humankind's legacy to the future.

But the sheer pressure of human numbers in cities has always created problems. Poverty, as well as wealth, is concentrated; crime as well as justice; disease as well as medicine. Today, many developing-country cities are ringed by vast shantytowns encompassing much human wretchedness. Some, like Delhi, where more than one-third of the residents live in slums and squatter settlements, have become administrative nightmares; everywhere space is at a premium.

The burgeoning cities demonstrate another high cost of urban civilization. Cities are in essence parasitical with an insatiable appetite for food, energy, raw materials, and human labour. The economy of early cities was linked directly to the productivity of the surrounding countryside; later, colonialism and trade links helped to support their growing populations. Modern cities, by contrast, are nodes on a web of long-range communications, dependent on local, regional, and global markets for their supplies.

Until the Industrial Revolution, only one person in five lived in a settlement of over 10,000 people. In the past 100 years, however, there has been a massive influx to the cities, first in the North, latterly in the developing nations. What potential will the mega-cities of the South have as centres of the newly emerging 21st-century civilization? Will they retain their central role? The upsurge of communications and new information technologies makes it increasingly possible for city functions to be decentralized. It also opens the door to integration of urban and rural sectors in a one-world economic network.

The world city

When people congregate in cities, they can specialize to a much greater extent than in rural areas. This specialization becomes more diverse as cities grow until, as with the modern city, the functions of its inhabitants are almost as different, yet as interdependent, as those of individual cells in the human body.

When cities were relatively isolated, each developed a distinct culture. Some became famous for their religious sites, others for their universities, public buildings, textiles, glass, or other artefacts. But today, worldwide cultural diversity is being eroded by mass markets and media. The middle classes in the big cities around the world often wear the same clothes, listen to the same pop music and watch the same television programmes. We are seeing the emergence of a global "city culture".

The major conurbations are increasingly linked by transport and telecommunications, creating a single 'world city' with increasing functional specialization of its individual members. Although separated geographically, they are combined in action: London, New York, Zurich, and Tokyo operate as linked financial centres, and the UN, based in New York, has specialized agencies in Paris, Rome, and Nairobi.

Literature
It is impossible to imagine world literature without Joyce's Dublin, Dickens' London, or Sartre's Paris. Most social, intellectual, and spiritual currents which fuel literature still concentrate in the cities.

Financial control
While economic and political power once coincided, telecommunications have relaxed the link: New York, Rio de Janeiro, and Frankfurt are financial, but not political capitals.

Sustainable cities
We need both environmentally and financially sustainable solutions to solve urban problems. The UN-HABITAT Sustainable Cities Programme (SCP) assists with "broad-based stakeholder involvement rather than master planning; bottom-up problem solving rather than top-down decision-making; mobilization of local resources; a framework for coordination of external support; environmental concerns in urban planning and management; and an instrument for ocalising Agenda 21". The SCP is undertaking demonstration projects in 20 cities worldwide.

The changing city
Cities first developed 4,000–5,000 years ago when agricultural and technological developments boosted productivity to the point where urban economies could support a range of specialist workers. Early cities were walled for defence, and within these walls craft industry flourished, sustained by the peasantry of the hinterland. As cities outgrew the productive diversity of the surrounding areas, trade developed in importance, remaining the principal engine of city growth until the Industrial Revolution. It brought the need for banking and other commercial services, and with them a wealthy and powerful merchant class. With the fall of the Roman Empire, urban life dwindled until the resurgence of European trade in the 11th and 12th centuries. In the 18th century, the mechanization of agriculture and industry released labour from the land and created a growing demand for it in factory cities. Railways and later the internal combustion engine helped reshape cities, the spreading suburbs and expanding new towns draining population from inner city areas. Now another wave of change, based on new technologies, is beginning to shift the world's cities into the "post-industrial society".

Architecture
Many cities still bear the imprint of Rome's 1,000-year domination of European civilization. The 20th-century counterpart is New York with its trendsetting skyscrapers.

3000 BC

200 BC

The "chained" cities
The circles (above) represent stages of development of an idealized city, the chains their growing dependence on trade. Key factors are the financial, industrial and defence sectors.

Principal world air routes

Energy
No city could survive without massive energy inputs to drive machines and power transport systems. The harnessing of fossil fuels allowed the increases in agricultural productivity to sustain urban growth.

Religion
Our cities have always been centres of worship; their temples, mosques, and cathedrals are among our most precious buildings. Rome, Mecca, and Jerusalem are religious capitals for three of the world's foremost faiths.

Law
The major trading centres inevitably became legal centres. Cities like Rome, London, Amsterdam, and Paris exported both goods and legal codes.

Food
Today's cities have come to rely on ever-increasing trade with remote regions, having mostly long outstripped the productive capacity of their original hinterlands, and they are more vulnerable to interruptions of supply.

Art
Throughout their history, cities have made unique artistic contributions, many exerting a powerful influence on subsequent and distant cultures, including the Athens of Pericles, Michelangelo's Florence, and Nigeria's Benin.

State power
Cities are great centres of power – economic, military, and political. As commerce grows, however, the military function usually disperses and state power, with its bureaucracy, is often transferred to new capitals.

Mega-city 2015
World population is increasing by 225,000 people a day. In little more than a decade we will add 1 billion people to the global population – and we would need to build an equivalent to London every month to house them. Instead, we expand existing cities, creating the mega-cities of the future. Northern cities are already merging, while in the South, centres such as Mexico City dwarf even sprawling Chicago.

1870

2000

An urbanized world
By the year 2000, almost 50% of the world's population was urbanized, compared with 14% in 1900. By 2030, 60% could be urbanized.

Industry	Defence	Housing, wealthy
Food	Policing	Housing, poor
Transport	Finance	Housing, wealthy and poor
Administration	Culture	

60%
50%
40%
30%
20%
10%

1800 1825 1850 1875 1900 1925 1950 1975 2000 2030

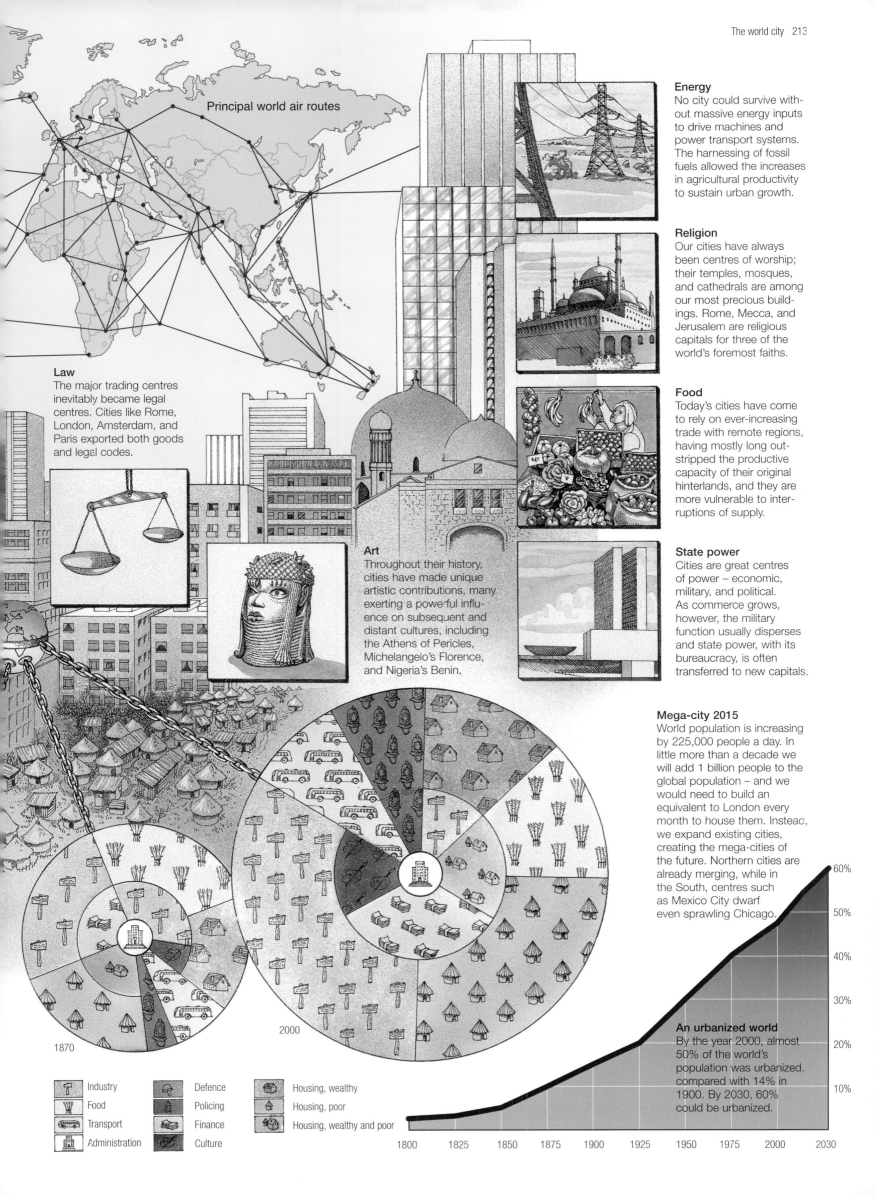

A sense of global citizenry

We are on the cusp of breaking into a new world order. The old order has become outdated, hopelessly unable to cope with the challenges of a world that has changed as much in the past half century as in the previous four centuries. Even more to the point, our 2005 world will be scarcely recognizable in the eyes of our descendants of 2050.

Consider, for instance, the nation state. Potent as it has been for centuries, it is simply being left behind. It has been leaking power and legitimacy upwards towards international if not global institutions (United Nations, mega-corporations, global communications), and it has been leaking authority and executive capacity downwards to civil society (numerous NGOs). The nation state is no longer sovereign and independent, whatever certain political leaders might assert. This represents as seismic a shift as any since the first emergence of the nation-state system four centuries ago.

In a world with one predominant political system, democracy, and with one predominant economic system, marketplace capitalism, there is a need for "one world-ism" to take over from the splintered system of nation states. What is lacking and what could serve as a kind of glue to hold together the disparate elements of one world – its numerous cultures, customs, perceptions, hopes, fears, visions, etc. – is a sense of global citizenry. Into this vacuum may leap groups of people with simplistic views of what makes the world tick, and how to make it tick to the dictates of their ideology. Enter the demagogues of religion, or rather the pseudo-religion of absolutism ("I know ultimate truth, and I'll knock your head in to persuade you"). These would-be leaders of a new global order include the fundamentalists of perverted Islam, the extremists of China with its Middle Kingdom tradition ("We are so right that non-Chinese cannot understand how right we are"), visionaries of the Moral Majority (which is neither), and deep-denial purveyors of Christianity (or rather Christendom, an altogether different affair).

In face of these ideological threats, we need to build a new world order that delights in differences, that thrives on diversity, and that welcomes what is not established wisdom. Certainly, our 2005 world is radically altered from the world that most readers will recall from their youthful times. The Soviet Union is gone together with its hegemonic outlook, and thus the Cold War has become history, too. We now have a single superpower, which in theory could foster stability and security for the global community, but in practice seems to breed discord and even divisiveness. We are also witnessing an end to the old-style "developed" and "developing" worlds. In the latter there are now one billion people who have attained enough affluence to rank as distinctly middle class (see pp. 234–35). Conversely, many developed world people feel they live in mis-developed or over-developed societies.

New world orders

Is the United Nations a spent force?

The United Nations often presents itself as a singularly disunited body, and many "realpolitik" people scorn its apparent lack of clout. But its many development agencies – FAO, WHO, etc. – have achieved wonders off overall budgets no larger than that of a medium-sized American city.

New powers emerging?

The old order is fragmenting in many ways. What if China maintains its extraordinary economic growth of the last two decades and becomes number one in the world by 2020 if not before? What if other semi-superpowers emerge, such as India and Brazil? What additional shifts should we anticipate for the new world order? It is difficult to discern the shapes and forms of a radically different future, or futures. What is clear is that we are entering an entirely new phase of the human enterprise.

Europe as a new superpower

The European Union already has 25 members, with a population of 454 million (the US 295 million) and an economy of $7.4 trillion (the US $10.4 trillion) (2002 totals). Thus far it lacks the political cohesion to rank as a true superpower. But recall that the US' original 13 states showed scant promise of ever dominating the world of 1800.

Other potential powers

Could fundamentalist and militant Islam ever develop into a body – not simply a faith-driven movement but a distinctive community reaching across national borders and asserting common values – with enough political clout to impose its outlook on others? The prospect is unlikely, given Islam's numerous factions spread across countries as diverse as Iran and Indonesia, the first being a "loose cannon" and the second one of the more peaceful of nations. Other potential powers could include China, a Slavic confederation, and conceivably a form of Hispanic hegemony.

World government?

Perish the thought. Whatever its apparent attractions and however difficult it might be to devise such an organization, it could carry huge threats for humankind. Were such a government ever to be established, it could quickly declare itself a permanent body and thus morph into a *de facto* dictatorship. How could an opposition body emerge to vote it out of power? Let us rather rejoice in democracy with all its muddle and inefficiency, and devise a mode of global governance (altogether different from government) that reflects diversity and hence resilience.

The big players

In 2003, the top ten nations accounted for more than two-thirds of global GDP in PPP terms, led by the US with PPP$10.9 trillion. Among the top 20 are 10 of the 20 "new order" nations (see pp. 240–41), including China (PPP$6.4 trillion), India (PPP$3.1 trillion), and Russia (PPP$1.3 trillion). A large proportion is in the hands of the transnational corporations (see pp. 220–21) and more than 95% of the world's R & D funds are spent in the North (see pp. 216–17).

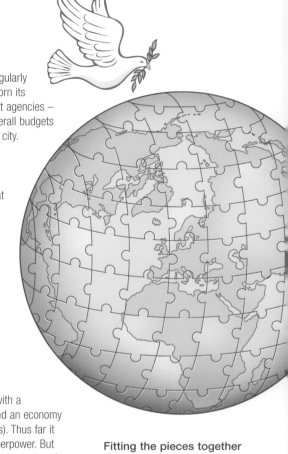

Fitting the pieces together
The jigsaw of the old world order (above) has become outdated, unable to cope with the proliferant challenges of a world that has changed as much since 1950 as the 1950's world had changed from that of the 1500s. We are faced with an extremely difficult puzzle (right) – how to fit the new pieces together in a new global and post-industrial society?

Religions worldwide

One of the most hopeful portents for a new world order should lie with the world's religions, provided they could make peace with each other. In nominal senses there are 2 billion Christians, 1.4 billion Muslims, around 750 million Hindus, and almost as many Buddhists. In other words, the great majority of people belong to one religion or another, though far from everyone practises.

In many developed countries, religious communities are exercising leadership in all manner of non-traditional ways, especially as concerns the environment. For instance, they urge their congregations to support "green" products such as Fair Traded coffee. The Ecumenical Patriarch Bartholomew assembles leading scientists and journalists together with religious leaders for extended conferences on environmental concerns. As for developing countries, the Worldwatch Institute has documented how environmentalist monks in Thailand have employed their moral authority to protect their country's forests; in India, environmental supporters have tried to prevent abuse of the Ganges River by invoking Hindu worldviews; in Sri Lanka, a Buddhist-inspired vision of development includes an ethic of restricted consumption; and in Pakistan, the government has been learning about the environment from Muslim clergy.

Religion and environment in the US

In the United States hundreds of congregations are listed in "A Directory of Environmental Activities and Resources in the North American Religious Community", published by the National Religious Partnership for the Environment. The Partnership has documented activities in 2,000 model congregational projects, and it has undertaken leadership training sessions for 2,000 clergy and lay readers on how to integrate religious and environmental issues. The Directory has sent out over 100,000 education and action manuals to congregations, advising individuals how to conserve energy, set recycling targets, arrange car pooling, change consumption patterns, form coalitions with local environmental groups, and become active in public policy advocacy. There is much leverage here insofar as 100 million Americans go to church, synagogue, or other religious services every week. In a larger context, as many as 3.5 billion people, more than half the world's population, are (moderately) active members of organized religions. What a captive audience to be given the environmental message each week!

"For humans to cause species to become extinct and to destroy the biological diversity of God's creation; for humans to degrade the integrity of Earth by causing changes in its climate, by stripping the Earth of its natural forests, or destroying its wetlands; for humans to contaminate the Earth's land, its air, and its life with poisonous substances; all these are sins."
His All Holiness Ecumenical Patriarch Bartholomew
of the Eastern Orthodox Church, 1997

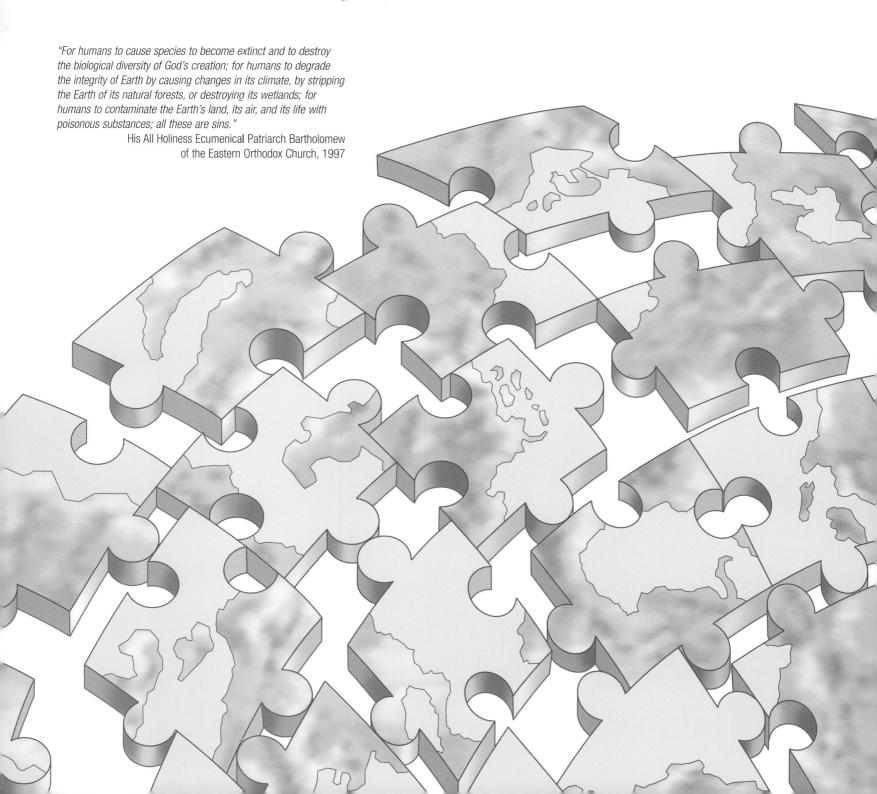

Our productive world

No civilization in history has held such technological power in its grasp as does our present generation. And none has allocated to science such a commanding, almost mystical role as the provider of health, wealth, power, freedom, and happiness. But while technology and mass production have brought enormous rewards, the global factory has proved a double-edged weapon.

The world production system has undergone a rapid, increasingly radical change since the optimistic post-war era. The key technologies of the 1950s and 1960s were based on steel, chemicals, and oil. The bulldozer, tractor, and chainsaw, together with fertilizers and pesticides, revolutionized agriculture. New drugs and surgical techniques transformed medicine. Wave after wave of durable goods, from refrigerators to radios, poured off faster, automated production lines. And then, during the early 1970s, a series of convulsions ran through the global economic system. Soaring oil prices, depleted natural resources, widespread pollution and health hazards, an escalating and ever-more sophisticated arms race, and worsening world poverty and hunger, dealt hammer blows to our faith in technology. In the 1980s and 1990s, the privatization of state assets and the deregulation of global markets led to increased globalization, especially in trade, finance, and the movement of people. As a result, wealth inequality has increased at both the national and international levels, tensions have grown over access to natural resources, and the use of fossil fuel with its resultant pollutants, has increased significantly.

Today, the global population has topped 6.4 billion and hundreds of millions of new, middle-class consumers have started to appear in rapidly developing countries, such as China and India. Evidence of human-induced climate change has led to calls for more effective global governance and for the inclusion of indirect environmental costs into prices and markets. However, the collapse of Communism and convergence of Western political parties have encouraged an increased reliance on free-market solutions, greater market liquidity, and more rapid stock market crashes.

These trends, combined with the loss of manufacturing and high-value financial service jobs to cheaper developing countries, and the ageing and shrinking of workforces in the developed world are likely to put great pressure on the post-war social contracts of many developed nations.

New technologies have emerged which, while they trigger some deep anxieties, may offer new hope for the developing nations. Micro-electronics, information technology, new materials, and biotechnology are just some of the locally adaptable, low-energy, and low-pollution technologies which may provide the means for many parts of the South to boost their productivity.

The world factory

The outpourings of the world factory spawned the affluent, throwaway society, much of it being wasteful, pressurized, dominating the global imagination with its seductive imagery of gleaming automobiles, beautiful people and shining cities. But it also produced cures for major epidemic diseases, doubled food production, and provided mass mobility, communications, and mass media, which effectively shrank the planet into a "global village". The engine that drives the global factory is commerce, fuelled by research, energy, and innovative ideas. Riding on successive waves of social and technological change, the factory is constantly adjusting to fluctuations in demand, partly created by advertising, and to changes in labour productivity and market upheavals sparked by new technologies. If it seems to promise happiness to many, it also provides power to the few. Both research and production are concentrated in the North; much in the hands of international megacorporations. This concentration of power often makes it almost impossible to develop equitable alternatives to the approaches and technologies promoted by the major industrial nations. But the present order is beginning to alter in the face of profound social and technological changes: we are seeing the birth of a radically different form of global factory

Technology – for whose benefit?

Fears of mass unemployment and an emerging technocracy beyond the control of citizens and governments may simply express natural hostility to change. The new technologies provide the possibility of greater diversity and freedom of work and more consumer control. Global R & D spending on the new nanotechnology is around $4 billion, with public investment increasing 500% between 1997 and 2002 across the "lead" countries. Total R & D expenditures in 2002 amounted to 2.6% of GDP in rich nations ($685 billion) and 0.6% in developing countries ($37 billion). Much of the former feeds the research and development needs of the military "albatross", an investment which contributes little to economic and social advancement.

The manufacturing base

A major impetus for technological innovation is humanity's constant desire for a greater variety of goods. Growth of the service sector depends on a strong manufacturing base to provide a large range of machines and equipment. Manufacturing operations are a key constituent of the world's technological resource. They consist of continuous-flow goods, such as chemicals and steel; and batch items, which make up the great mass of consumer goods, such as cars and clothes.

The importance of the financial services sector

The financial services sector makes up a large proportion of the economy and has become tightly enmeshed in a global 24-hour market which operates in an increasingly borderless world. Costs, profits, and interest rates are compared at the global scale and investment decisions are increasingly made outside the countries they affect most. This has altered the balance of power between governments and financial institutions and started to threaten some of the best paid jobs in the West.

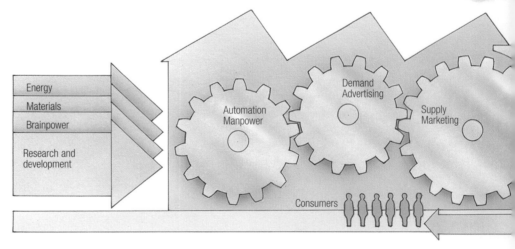

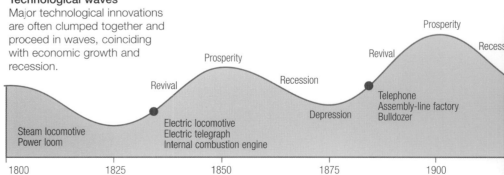

Technological waves
Major technological innovations are often clumped together and proceed in waves, coinciding with economic growth and recession.

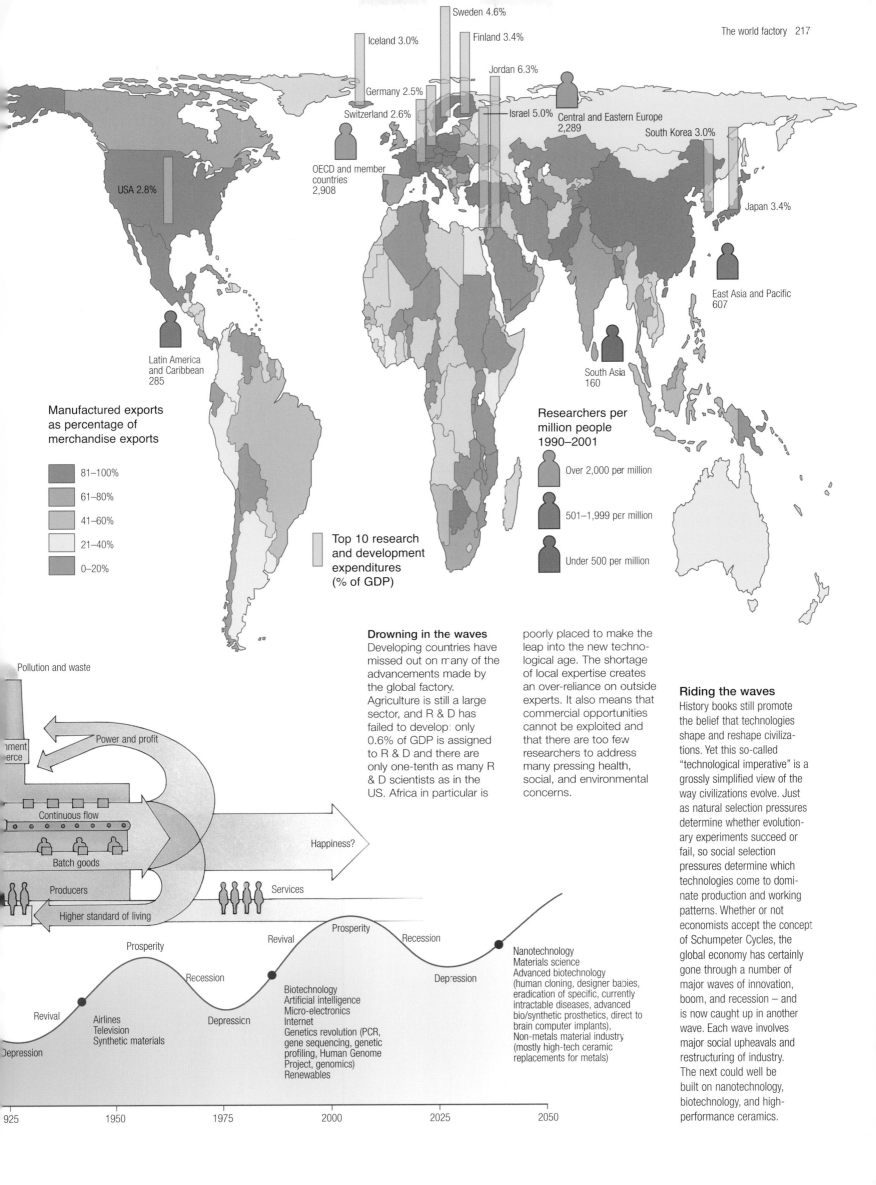

Sweden 4.6%

Iceland 3.0%

Finland 3.4%

Germany 2.5%

Jordan 6.3%

Switzerland 2.6%

Israel 5.0%

Central and Eastern Europe
2,289

OECD and member
countries
2,908

South Korea 3.0%

USA 2.8%

Japan 3.4%

East Asia and Pacific
607

Latin America
and Caribbean
285

South Asia
160

Manufactured exports as percentage of merchandise exports

- 81–100%
- 61–80%
- 41–60%
- 21–40%
- 0–20%

Researchers per million people 1990–2001

Over 2,000 per million

501–1,999 per million

Under 500 per million

Top 10 research
and development
expenditures
(% of GDP)

Pollution and waste

Power and profit

Continuous flow

Batch goods

Producers

Higher standard of living

Happiness?

Services

Drowning in the waves

Developing countries have missed out on many of the advancements made by the global factory. Agriculture is still a large sector, and R & D has failed to develop: only 0.6% of GDP is assigned to R & D and there are only one-tenth as many R & D scientists as in the US. Africa in particular is poorly placed to make the leap into the new technological age. The shortage of local expertise creates an over-reliance on outside experts. It also means that commercial opportunities cannot be exploited and that there are too few researchers to address many pressing health, social, and environmental concerns.

Riding the waves

History books still promote the belief that technologies shape and reshape civilizations. Yet this so-called "technological imperative" is a grossly simplified view of the way civilizations evolve. Just as natural selection pressures determine whether evolutionary experiments succeed or fail, so social selection pressures determine which technologies come to dominate production and working patterns. Whether or not economists accept the concept of Schumpeter Cycles, the global economy has certainly gone through a number of major waves of innovation, boom, and recession — and is now caught up in another wave. Each wave involves major social upheavals and restructuring of industry. The next could well be built on nanotechnology, biotechnology, and high-performance ceramics.

Prosperity

Revival

Prosperity

Recession

Prosperity

Recession

Depression

Revival

Airlines
Television
Synthetic materials

Depression

Biotechnology
Artificial intelligence
Micro-electronics
Internet
Genetics revolution (PCR,
gene sequencing, genetic
profiling, Human Genome
Project, genomics)
Renewables

Depression

Nanotechnology
Materials science
Advanced biotechnology
(human cloning, designer babies,
eradication of specific, currently
intractable diseases, advanced
bio/synthetic prosthetics, direct to
brain computer implants),
Non-metals material industry
(mostly high-tech ceramic
replacements for metals)

Depression

925   1950   1975   2000   2025   2050

The power of communications

In 2004, within 12 years of their launch, Global Systems for Mobile Communications (GSMs) were being used by more than one billion people in over 200 countries – nearly one in six of the world's population. Today you can visit a village cybercafé or tele-centre in India, Nigeria, or Brazil and instantly hook up with someone on the other side of the world via the internet. With the latest technology and wireless connection you can do it anywhere – in the car, in the bath, in bed. If you want a vital statistic, news about the latest war or the score in a football game, you can have it at the end of your fingers.

Information and Communications Technology (ICT) is an increasingly powerful tool that helps people to participate in global markets. It improves the delivery of basic services, and it enhances development at levels from local to international. It has the potential to rapidly change the whole structure of society and reshape the way we organize our economies, in much the same manner as did the internal combustion engine in the last century. It is having a major impact on how we live and work, even how we think.

Thus far, however, ICT applies primarily to the rich countries. The 930 million Internet users of 2004 were mostly in developed countries of the North: there are more Internet servers in New York than in the whole of Africa. But there is a big role for ICT in developing countries, too: without its many innovations, developing countries, especially the poorest ones, will be left behind. Already it can link rural farmers to market information, craftwork to customers, patients to doctors, and students to teachers. The rise of cellphones used to access the Internet and worldwide web will open up access to information even further. China's mobile phone subscribers reached 335 million by 2004, adding 65 million in 2003 alone (cf. the total of fixed line subscribers 315 million). Wireless technologies connecting developing country communities to the Internet can help to promote education and health and reduce poverty. An international NGO, World Links, has given e-learning training to thousands of teachers and students from 25 African, Asian, Latin American, and Middle Eastern countries.

Still more important, ICT overall will drive innovation, launch industries, reorganize social relationships, and challenge our traditional notions about how our world works – or should work better. Indeed, the emergence of ICT can be compared with the onset of electricity and power-driven machinery that spurred the Industrial Revolution. It could even match the invention of the plough in the Agricultural Revolution that made large-scale agriculture possible.

There are other benefits. ICT underpins the "Internet economy" which increases efficiency in every economic sector, especially energy efficiency. In fact, the Internet economy can fundamentally alter the economy/energy relationship, enabling far faster economic growth while slowing energy use.

Chips, nets, and cells

In terms of communications, the world has shrunk rapidly. Today, the contents of a dozen volumes of Encyclopaedia Britannica can be transmitted across the world in seconds. Cable TV networks offer people a choice of a hundred or more channels catering to every possible taste and viewpoint; interactive facilities permit viewers to communicate directly with service providers. In 2001, more information could be sent over a single cable in just one second than was sent in 1997 over the entire Internet in a month. The cost of transmitting one trillion bits of information from Boston to Los Angeles fell from $150,000 in 1970 to 12 cents in 2001. There are now over 8,000 electronic journals, up from a handful in the mid 1990s, allowing rapid on-line publication and global access to the latest information. E-conferencing allows globalization of ideas and solutions.

The Internet economy

ICT is driving a boom in home-based work. US "home offices" grew from 12 million in 1997 to 30 million in 2002, though in the EU less than 5% of people engage in telework so far. When employees work several days a week at home, they sense greater job satisfaction and productivity. At AT&T, for example, one extra hour's worth of productivity per day for all at-home workers translates into $65 million per year for the company. There are energy benefits, too. Suppose that from 1997 to 2007, the Internet leads to an additional one million US home offices each year. Suppose, too, that half of these people are Internet telecommuters and half are Internet entrepreneurs, and that they avoid an average 14 sq. m and 28 sq. m of office space respectively. That will avoid the need for more than 186 million sq. m of office space by 2007 – plus the need for all the energy that space would consume for lighting, heating, and cooling.

Growth of the Internet

Internet servers grew from less than one million in 1991 to 280 million in 2004, when more than 930 million people (every seventh person on the planet) were regularly online. 185 million (20%) of users are in the US, 100 million (11%) in China, and 78 million (8% in Japan). The UK has 33 million. Much of the future growth is expected to be in China, India, Brazil, Russia, Indonesia, and other "new consumer" countries (see pp.188–89) – with many accessing the Internet via mobile/cellphones. By 2007, the number of users worldwide is projected to reach 1.35 billion. In India, literate and numerate university graduates are able to work for Western businesses and governments who are utilizing ICT to outsource large quantities of work to cheaper staff in developing countries. One-fifth of Fortune 1,000 companies outsource to India. While outsourcing creates job losses it can also create employment: in 2003, Delta Airlines outsourced 1,000 call-centre jobs to India, generating $25 million of savings which enabled 1,200 new jobs in the US. The McKinsey Global Institute calculates that the costs of outsourcing can actually be outweighed by the benefits.

Microcredit: bridging the communications gap

Bangladesh's Grameen Bank provides loans to "telephone ladies" who run phone-service businesses earning an average of $300 per year. The eventual aim is for 40,000 such telephone ladies and a service which will play an important role in the entire telecommunication sector of the country. Grameen Bank is closing the digital divide: Grameen CyberNet is the largest Internet company in Bangladesh with cyber kiosks bringing the Internet to rural villages; Grameen Communications aims to create an e-health care, e-banking, and e-education system reaching rural villages. Grameen Software Limited (GSL) is working to provide access to employment opportunities and will develop the Grameen Star Education programme to offer training for the unemployed with poor IT skills.

Mobile phones

The 1.5 billion subscribers of 2004 are expected to top 2 billion by the end of 2005. Mobiles in Africa outnumber fixed lines at a higher ratio than on any other continent. China is the world's largest market, with 335 million there already, though still only one for every four people whereas the UK has 50 million mobile phones and 60 million people. In 1992, only 1 in 237 people worldwide used a mobile and only 1 in 778 used the Internet, but by 2004 the numbers had soared to 1 in 5 and 1 in 7 respectively. The latest camera phones make up a large share of the market with users exchanging digital photos via the Multimedia Messaging Service (MMS). The Short Message Service (SMS) will facilitate sending of an estimated 1.2 trillion text messages in 2005. Sales of ring-tone downloads are estimated at $4 billion worldwide. Big business indeed!

Wireless networks

Mobile computing technologies eliminate the need for cable connections. Bluetooth, WiFi, WiMAX, and other wireless networks using radio or microwave signals to connect computers to the Internet have revolutionized the ways in which people can work and communicate. Many coffee shops and universities offer free wireless access, allowing home workers and students to collaborate in new ways and to study almost anything from almost anywhere in the world. Some Pacific islands have used wireless networks to connect to each other, and the world, in ways that would never have happened using telephone cables. Tuvalu even licensed the use of its national domain suffix .tv, raising funds for development projects. These new technologies can be utilized to enable poor countries to leapfrog from the stone age into the telecommunications age.

Blogging and surfing

Weblog ("blog" for short) is an online diary which can be updated and read from anywhere on the Internet. Updating ("blogging") the blog is undertaken by the "blogger" (user) who needs little or no technical know-how. Google is one of many search engines designed to dramatically increase the efficiency of collecting new and relevant information.

Semiconductors and chips

Sales of semiconductors, being the brains behind modern electronics, totalled $140 billion in 2002. During the 1990s, the industry grew almost three times faster than the global economy. The weight of fossil fuels and chemicals used to produce a 2-gram memory chip is 630 times the weight of the chip itself.

Early warning systems

ICT allows us to pre-empt adverse weather conditions to warn of e.g. flooding or drought and famine crises. In addition, because the December 26th 2004 tsunami took several hours to cross the Indian Ocean, its arrival in Sri Lanka and India could have been anticipated with safeguard measures to reduce the impact.

The "intelligent" house

This is where most electricity components, from the heating system to the refrigerator, can communicate with each other and with the outside world. It can optimize energy use and thus help the inhabitants to live in a more sustainable fashion. Refrigerators can be programmed not only to keep track of what food they contain, but to recommend a menu based on seasonal organic food grown locally, thus reducing CO_2 emissions.

Changing trade flows

The huge stepping-up of activity on the global "trading floor" since World War II has profoundly influenced the world economy. By 2003, global output of goods and services exceeded $36 trillion (PPP$54 trillion), of which more than two-thirds occurred in just seven countries (the US, UK, Germany, Japan, France, Italy, and China). In 1960, world merchandised exports as a proportion of GDP were only 10 percent – in 2003, they were more than 20 percent. Nations exchanging goods and services are ever-more interdependent, as suppliers in one region rely on buyers in another, and consumers enjoy a growing choice of foreign products.

As markets have expanded, the production of goods has increasingly split up around the world – components and raw materials from one country are shipped overseas for assembly or processing, then returned to their origin, or re-exported to a third nation. It is mainly technology-based and labour-intensive processes that are shifting Southwards, while more profitable and emerging (sunrise) service industries remain in the North. This "assembly line" approach has been fuelled by the emergence of multi- or transnational corporations (MNCs/TNCs), and of newly industrialized countries (NICs) like South Korea or Brazil, where low wage rates have attracted Western investment. These "new tigers" are elbowing their way on to the trading floor, and increasingly challenging older industrial countries at their own game.

MNCs/TNCs have long been involved in the production of primary commodities in developing countries, from minerals and rubber to tea, coffee, palm oil, and bananas. But the growth of their role in manufacturing, with subsidiaries around the world taking a sizeable share of global production and trade, is a more recent phenomenon. Of the 100 biggest economic entities on Earth, only 49 are countries – the other 51 being mega-corporations.

These trends are a matter of controversy. Some argue that rapid expansion of trade has been the engine of economic growth, and that market specialization encourages efficiency so that all prosper. Others are more hostile to the whole trend toward interdependence. They hold that the benefits have gone overwhelmingly to rich nations, and that specialization simply means developing countries stay locked into low-wage, low-technology functions.

This debate has influenced decisions by the developing countries on whether or not to link their economies to the world market. To follow the process of export orientation means gearing production to satisfying overseas demand, while importing goods needed at home. The alternative, import substitution, means self-sufficiency through gearing production to domestic needs. Of the countries trying self-sufficiency, a few manage above-average economic growth, despite the attendant problems. Some export-oriented nations

The world market

The traders in the world market do not bargain on an equal footing. There are huge disparities in their share of trade and the value of goods they export. A large part of the trade flows are directed by mega-corporations, mainly based in the rich North, which dominates the market. Snapping at the North's heels, however, are newly industrialized developing nations such as South Korea. The OPEC group exploits its finite high-earning commodity, oil, but the majority of developing nations still export only low-value primary products. Developing nations are often unable to buy the North's manufacturing exports: Africa's share of global merchandised imports is only 2%. If the rapid growth of the world market is to provide prosperity for all, much depends on restructuring the trading flow to make room for the "new tigers" and to increase the earnings of the poor majority.

The manufacturing boom

The volume of world exports of manufactured goods averaged 8% growth per year between 1995 and 2000. As a share of total merchandised exports, manufactures grew from 61% in 1990 to 73% in 2002 in developing countries, and 78% to 81% in rich countries. Manufactures form 75% of world merchandised exports, but in Sub-Saharan Africa only 35% and in Central/Eastern Europe and former USSR 55%. High-tech exports average one-fifth of manufactured exports from developing countries and as much as 60% or more in Malaysia and Philippines.

Transnationals (TNCs)

Many large corporations have expanded and diversified their activities abroad, out-sourcing their manufacturing to developing countries like China, where labour is cheap and flexible, and markets have scope for massive growth. The change in global production by these huge businesses with mega supplies of scientists, advertisers, and marketeers has allowed corporations to greatly increase their profits and their competitiveness. Regrettably, their influence is not always benign and may involve the exploitation of workers and the environment.

Transition economies

Value of exports 2003: $0.4 trillion

The value of merchandized exports has grown from $156 billion in 1994 to $401 billion in 2003, a rise of 157% in less than 10 years. Russia accounted for $134 billion of world exports (one-third of the transition total) and $74 billion of imports (one-fifth).

Developed economies

Value of exports 2003: $4.9 trillion

The world's leading industrial power is the US but in terms of trade the US' $724 billion (10% of the total) of world merchandised exports is below that of Germany with $748 billion. Fourth-placed China had a $135-billion trade surplus with the US (and other countries a further $447 billion). Asia is the country's largest importing region, taking $202 billion of exports compared with Latin America $149 billion, Canada $169 billion, and Western Europe $165 billion.

Most oil-rich nations have little industry. OPEC is an international organization of 11 oil-exporting developing nations with 525 million people: Algeria, Indonesia, Iran, Iraq, Kuwait, Libya, Nigeria, Qatar, Saudi Arabia, United Arab Emirates, and Venezuela. After the 1973 Arab–Israeli war, OPEC's share of world oil production rose to 76% by 1978, and overall prices rose tenfold. In 2003, oil prices reached their highest level (in nominal terms) for 20 years, then declined after the war in Iraq before climbing again, reaching almost $50 a barrel in 2005. OPEC's share of global oil production was 40% and its oil exports represented around half of the oil traded internationally. Oil exports totalled $374 billion in 2003, almost $8 billion from Iraq.

Oil Producing and Exporting Countries (OPEC)

Value of exports, 2003: $380 billion
Share of world oil production: 40%

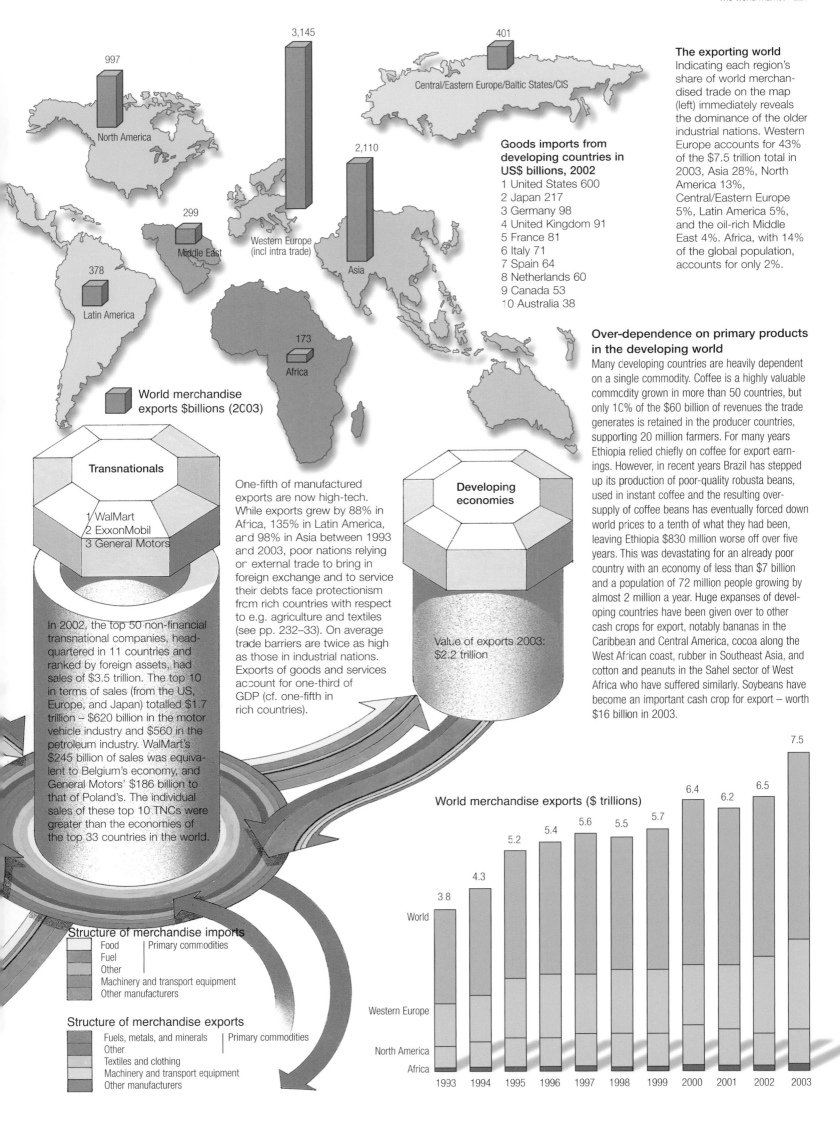

3,145 Western Europe (incl intra trade)

997 North America

401 Central/Eastern Europe/Baltic States/CIS

2,110 Asia

299 Middle East

378 Latin America

173 Africa

World merchandise exports $billions (2003)

Goods imports from developing countries in US$ billions, 2002
1 United States 600
2 Japan 217
3 Germany 98
4 United Kingdom 91
5 France 81
6 Italy 71
7 Spain 64
8 Netherlands 60
9 Canada 53
10 Australia 38

The exporting world
Indicating each region's share of world merchandised trade on the map (left) immediately reveals the dominance of the older industrial nations. Western Europe accounts for 43% of the $7.5 trillion total in 2003, Asia 28%, North America 13%, Central/Eastern Europe 5%, Latin America 5%, and the oil-rich Middle East 4%. Africa, with 14% of the global population, accounts for only 2%.

Over-dependence on primary products in the developing world
Many developing countries are heavily dependent on a single commodity. Coffee is a highly valuable commodity grown in more than 50 countries, but only 10% of the $60 billion of revenues the trade generates is retained in the producer countries, supporting 20 million farmers. For many years Ethiopia relied chiefly on coffee for export earnings. However, in recent years Brazil has stepped up its production of poor-quality robusta beans, used in instant coffee and the resulting over-supply of coffee beans has eventually forced down world prices to a tenth of what they had been, leaving Ethiopia $830 million worse off over five years. This was devastating for an already poor country with an economy of less than $7 billion and a population of 72 million people growing by almost 2 million a year. Huge expanses of developing countries have been given over to other cash crops for export, notably bananas in the Caribbean and Central America, cocoa along the West African coast, rubber in Southeast Asia, and cotton and peanuts in the Sahel sector of West Africa who have suffered similarly. Soybeans have become an important cash crop for export – worth $16 billion in 2003.

Transnationals
1 WalMart
2 ExxonMobil
3 General Motors

In 2002, the top 50 non-financial transnational companies, headquartered in 11 countries and ranked by foreign assets, had sales of $3.5 trillion. The top 10 in terms of sales (from the US, Europe, and Japan) totalled $1.7 trillion – $620 billion in the motor vehicle industry and $560 in the petroleum industry. WalMart's $245 billion of sales was equivalent to Belgium's economy, and General Motors' $186 billion to that of Poland's. The individual sales of these top 10 TNCs were greater than the economies of the top 33 countries in the world.

One-fifth of manufactured exports are now high-tech. While exports grew by 88% in Africa, 135% in Latin America, and 98% in Asia between 1993 and 2003, poor nations relying or external trade to bring in foreign exchange and to service their debts face protectionism from rich countries with respect to e.g. agriculture and textiles (see pp. 232–33). On average trade barriers are twice as high as those in industrial nations. Exports of goods and services account for one-third of GDP (cf. one-fifth in rich countries).

Developing economies
Value of exports 2003: $2.2 trillion

Structure of merchandise imports
Food | Primary commodities
Fuel
Other
Machinery and transport equipment
Other manufacturers

Structure of merchandise exports
Fuels, metals, and minerals | Primary commodities
Other
Textiles and clothing
Machinery and transport equipment
Other manufacturers

World merchandise exports ($ trillions)

Year	1993	1994	1995	1996	1997	1998	1999	2000	2001	2002	2003
World	3.8	4.3	5.2	5.4	5.6	5.5	5.7	6.4	6.2	6.5	7.5

Western Europe
North America
Africa

prosper but their dependence on fluctuating markets and prices, especially of raw commodities, makes their long-term prospects uncertain.

Assets and earning power

The wealth of the planet is enormous. Even our human share of it, including the monumental assets of civilization, is considerable. What we have "made" of this resource is a different matter.

In 2003, per-capita Gross National Income (GNI, formerly GNP) was more than 60 times greater in the high-income countries than in the low-income countries, even though the latter accounted for little over one-third of the global population. These stark indicators of world inequality do not tell us all about relative affluence and poverty, or about future potential. GNI is the conventional yardstick for assessing a nation's prosperity. We need to know, too, about national wealth, whether in the form of unexploited natural resources, railways, factories, or workforce skills and the health and education of a nation's children. This kind of wealth is, like the proverbial talents, a stock of assets that can be increased or depleted, and from which income can be derived. In this sense, a poor country in the South, such as Zaire, with vast but unexploited natural resources, is potentially very rich. By contrast, high-income Japan is rich through the ingenuity of its people, plus their capacity for hard work.

A high GNI tends to bring power and influence. GNI determines a nation's shareholdings in the International Monetary Fund (IMF)and the size of its shareholdings in turn determines its votes and borrowing rights. The rich countries may not borrow much, but they decide policy and so ensure that the international economic system functions in ways that they prescribe.

Exploitable natural wealth can provide counter-bargaining power, as witness the disruption of the global economic patterns caused by OPEC's oil bonanza or the emerging value of genetic resources in the South.

The problem for poorer countries is that, whatever their resources, their development costs investment. They must either save the little income they earn, or they must borrow. During the 1970s, banks were the major source of capital, largely because of vast, virtually unspendable sums of petrodollars that were deposited in banks – which then went looking for creditworthy customers in the South. Today, bank lending has almost dried up as high interest rates have turned the resulting debts into almost unsupportable burdens.

By 2003, international debt on the part of developing countries had risen to $2.3 trillion. Despite decades of growth and development planning, the numbers of absolute poor remain at a massive level, almost 1.1 billion (see pp. 240–41). The gap between rich and poor threatens the very roots of our global civilization.

The world's wealth

No nation's wealth is independent of world power structures and priorities. Income is increasingly dependent on market factors, and development values on world rankings for aid, creditworthiness and investment. Since the 1944 Bretton Woods agreement on the World Bank and the IMF, the flow of wealth across the world and the ground rules for who gets what and on what terms have been controlled by a group of largely North-based institutions comprising the financial community. Properly managed, international wealth flows can help poorer nations realize their potential, yet wealth tends to flow towards wealth rather than where it is better needed.

Global shares of GDP

In 2003, the world's GDP totalled $36 trillion. The high-income countries accounted for $29 trillion, including $11 trillion on the part of the US alone, while Sub-Saharan Africa accounted for only $417 billion. All the low-income countries (home to 2.3 billion people and many of the world's poor) accounted for $1.1 trillion and an average GNI of just $450. However, if we take account of Purchasing Power Parity (PPP), the world's GDP totalled PPP$54 trillion, of which the high-income countries accounted for PPP$28.6 trillion (for the US, conventional and PPP dollar values are the same), Sub-Saharan Africa PPP$1.3 trillion and all low-income countries $5.1 trillion. China is the world's sixth largest economy in conventional $ exchange terms but in PPP terms it is second only to the US. Before 2020, China could become the world's leading economy

Credit and investment

A nation's ability to raise credit or attract multinational investment is more often a measure of its strength than its need. The sources of credit are private banks, plus two major sister institutions: the World Bank, which provides investment capital, and the IMF, which concentrates on short-term balance-of-payments assistance for countries in difficulty. Creditworthiness hinges not only on performance indicators (some countries have brought good returns through their rapid economic growth). It also reflects political stability and "preferred" economic policies. A handful of rich industrialized nations control the voting rights at the IMF (see pp. 250–51).

Wealth vs. income

For individuals, as for nations, income and wealth do not necessarily go together (see map).

Technology and aid

Access to technology and skills for development costs money. Increasingly, developing countries rely on commercial enterprise or aid – multilateral funds from agencies like UNICEF or bilateral agreements between countries. Official Development Assistance (ODA) was $70 billion in 2003, but at 0.25% of donors' GDP this was far short of the target of 0.7% agreed upon as far back as 1970. There are 64,000 transnational corporations, whose foreign affiliates have generated 53 million jobs. Foreign Direct Investment is a large source of external finance for developing countries.

IMF, credit agencies, and commercial banks

Terms of credit

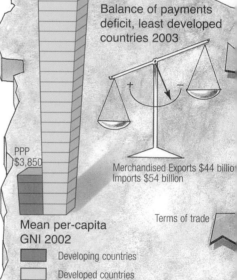

PPP$23,700

Balance of payments deficit, least developed countries 2003

PPP $3,850

Merchandised Exports $44 billion Imports $54 billion

Terms of trade

Mean per-capita GNI 2002

- Developing countries
- Developed countries

Share of technology

Technology

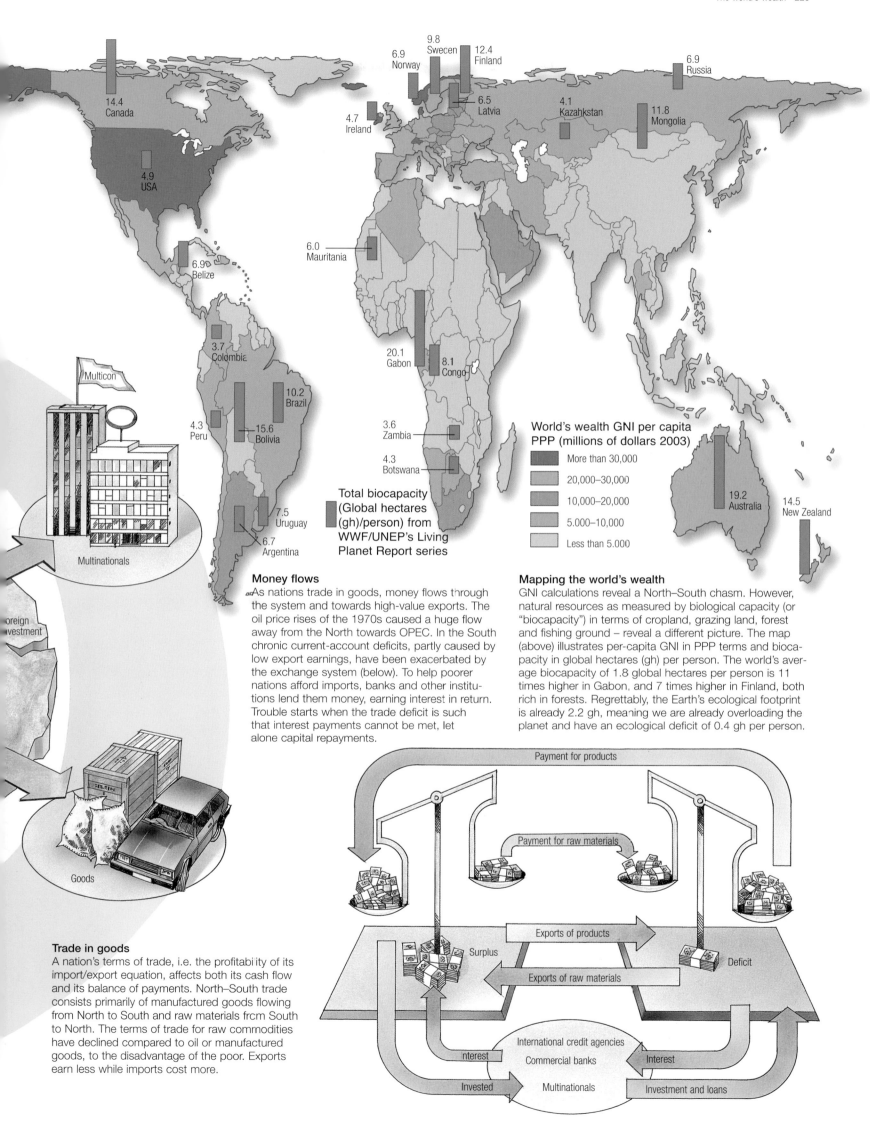

Map labels (Total biocapacity – Global hectares (gh)/person):

14.4 Canada
4.9 USA
6.9 Belize
3.7 Colombia
4.3 Peru
15.6 Bolivia
10.2 Brazil
7.5 Uruguay
6.7 Argentina
4.7 Ireland
6.9 Norway
9.8 Sweden
12.4 Finland
6.5 Latvia
6.9 Russia
4.1 Kazahkstan
11.8 Mongolia
6.0 Mauritania
20.1 Gabon
8.1 Congo
3.6 Zambia
4.3 Botswana
19.2 Australia
14.5 New Zealand

World's wealth GNI per capita PPP (millions of dollars 2003)

- More than 30,000
- 20,000–30,000
- 10,000–20,000
- 5,000–10,000
- Less than 5,000

Total biocapacity (Global hectares (gh)/person) from WWF/UNEP's Living Planet Report series

Money flows

As nations trade in goods, money flows through the system and towards high-value exports. The oil price rises of the 1970s caused a huge flow away from the North towards OPEC. In the South chronic current-account deficits, partly caused by low export earnings, have been exacerbated by the exchange system (below). To help poorer nations afford imports, banks and other institutions lend them money, earning interest in return. Trouble starts when the trade deficit is such that interest payments cannot be met, let alone capital repayments.

Mapping the world's wealth

GNI calculations reveal a North–South chasm. However, natural resources as measured by biological capacity (or "biocapacity") in terms of cropland, grazing land, forest and fishing ground – reveal a different picture. The map (above) illustrates per-capita GNI in PPP terms and biocapacity in global hectares (gh) per person. The world's average biocapacity of 1.8 global hectares per person is 11 times higher in Gabon, and 7 times higher in Finland, both rich in forests. Regrettably, the Earth's ecological footprint is already 2.2 gh, meaning we are already overloading the planet and have an ecological deficit of 0.4 gh per person.

Trade in goods

A nation's terms of trade, i.e. the profitability of its import/export equation, affects both its cash flow and its balance of payments. North–South trade consists primarily of manufactured goods flowing from North to South and raw materials from South to North. The terms of trade for raw commodities have declined compared to oil or manufactured goods, to the disadvantage of the poor. Exports earn less while imports cost more.

Diagram labels:
Multicon
Multinationals
Foreign investment
Goods

Payment for products
Payment for raw materials
Exports of products
Exports of raw materials
Surplus
Deficit
International credit agencies
Commercial banks
Multinationals
Interest
Interest
Invested
Investment and loans

Crisis: The Divided World

In 1952, Winston Churchill declared that he had lived all his life without bothering with obscure distant countries like Cambodia. How different today when every citizen is involved, whether aware of it or not, with citizens around the back of the world. We affect them and they affect us in myriad ways every day. If a British person boils a kettle with more water than needed, he or she is wasting electricity that has probably been derived from fossil fuels with their greenhouse gases, and thus he or she is contributing to the time when entire sectors of Bangladesh disappear beneath a rising sea level. When the Chinese decide that the finest manifestation of development is to put several million more cars on their roads each year, they are likewise contributing to global warming which may one day dislocate Britain's agriculture to an extent that will undercut Britain's very capacity to feed itself.

When I, Norman Myers, go the airport, I reflect that the bit of cardboard in my hand, known as a passport, is a hangover from a former age. Although I have lived and worked in a world of 200 management packages that we call nations, it is increasingly one indivisible world – a continuum of economies, environments, politics, cultures, and security. We are no longer just Americans or Britishers, we are also card-carrying citizens of a single global community. The fossil-fuel pollution of the aeroplane I fly in and the global warming it generates mean I am much more than a Britisher.

Consider globalizing processes of an economic sort. Thanks to the one global stock exchange that never stops trading, at least $1.5 trillion is transferred across international frontiers every day. I'm sure that some of my own funds join the stream, but I'm totally unsure what activities they support beyond the horizon – perhaps destroying natural resources such as tropical forests. My funds generate globalized impacts, and I think about it all too little. I do not look beyond the old-time horizons of my mind.

Consider, too, that of the world's 100 biggest economic entities, only 49 are governments, the rest being multinational corporations. The world is no longer governed by governments alone. Then there are the intergovernmental bodies of global scope: the UN system and the World Bank for starters. Plus the non-governmental bodies such as the World Wildlife Fund, Christian Aid and Save the Children.

Globalization means that for the first time in history, we are often acting as the single entity of humankind (human for sure, kind maybe). From here on our common futures are globalized, and for ever.

Globalization

Globalized living

We live in a world where everybody is involved in everybody's affairs, whether they want it or not. Most of us, and this writer includes himself, are not as aware as we should be of that profound fact of life. This Atlas describes a plethora of problems we have not foreseen, e.g. ozone layer depletion, AIDS, terrorism, etc. What problems ahead do we not see because we do not expect to see them? Similarly, how shall we find what we are looking for unless we know where to look? What messages are we failing to hear, and how shall we grow bigger ears? What, let us ask ourselves, is the full scope of globalization, and how far do we all contribute (albeit unwittingly for the most part)?

The many forms of globalization

Apart from the items listed in the running text, there are:
- Fast growing markets in services, such as banking, insurance, and transport.
- New financial markets that are deregulated, globally linked, and working right around the clock. While there are separate stock exchanges in New York, London, Zurich, Tokyo, etc., they operate as one global stock exchange that never closes. Each day the stock exchanges of the world transmit $1.5 trillion, 10 times more than in 1975.
- Proliferation of mergers and acquisitions in the wake of deregulation of antitrust laws.
- Global consumer markets with global brands, especially reflecting the emergence of "new consumer" countries with aggregate spending power of PPP$6.3 trillion in 2000 (see pp. 240–41).
- The establishment of the World Trade Organization as the first multilateral body with power to require governments to comply with its rules.
- The arrival of regional blocs with some supranational clout, notably the European Union, the Association of Southeast Asian Nations, and the North American Free Trade Association.
- Human rights conventions that reflect growing awareness in much of the world.
- Conventions on certain aspects of the global environment, notably desertification, climate, the ozone layer, hazardous wastes, and biodiversity.
- The Millennium Development Goals with their action agendas (see p. 251).

The price of globalization

"The collapse of space, time and borders may be creating a global village, but not everyone can be a citizen. The global elite faces low borders, but billions of others find borders as high as ever."
The 10th annual UN Development Programme's Human Development Report.

The Internet

One of the most facilitating factors of globalization is the Internet. During just 2000–2001 its users grew by a whopping 23% and by 2004 they totalled around 930 million. This last figure amounted to almost 1 in 7 of all humankind, up from 1 in 14 in 2000.

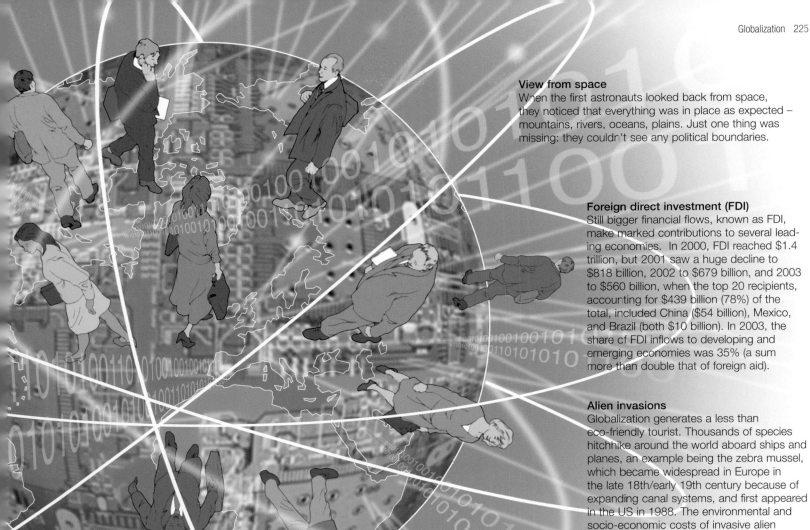

View from space
When the first astronauts looked back from space, they noticed that everything was in place as expected – mountains, rivers, oceans, plains. Just one thing was missing: they couldn't see any political boundaries.

Foreign direct investment (FDI)
Still bigger financial flows, known as FDI, make marked contributions to several leading economies. In 2000, FDI reached $1.4 trillion, but 2001 saw a huge decline to $818 billion, 2002 to $679 billion, and 2003 to $560 billion, when the top 20 recipients, accounting for $439 billion (78%) of the total, included China ($54 billion), Mexico, and Brazil (both $10 billion). In 2003, the share of FDI inflows to developing and emerging economies was 35% (a sum more than double that of foreign aid).

Alien invasions
Globalization generates a less than eco-friendly tourist. Thousands of species hitchhike around the world aboard ships and planes, an example being the zebra mussel, which became widespread in Europe in the late 18th/early 19th century because of expanding canal systems, and first appeared in the US in 1988. The environmental and socio-economic costs of invasive alien plant/animal species in the US alone is estimated at $137 billion a year. Controlling water weeds such as hyacinth costs African nations $60 million a year. The Global Invasive Species Programme (GISP) addresses the problem. Globalization spawns another traveller with worldwide impacts – one that benefits from the ease of international networking: the terrorist.

Indigenous peoples
Globalization can go far to improving the lot of those 350 million indigenous people who are still in poverty. It can supply jobs, medicines, and cheaper goods all round. But it can also disrupt their cultures, even their basic wellbeing.

The power of mega-corporations
In 2002, the US corporation General Motors achieved sales of $186 billion, on a par with the economy of Poland. Japan's Mitsubishi achieved $109 billion, on a par with Iran. Royal Dutch/Shell $180 billion, on a par with Denmark. WalMart $245 billion, on par with Belgium. In terms of foreign assets, General Electric was the leader with $230 billion, followed by Vodafone $208 billion, Ford Motor Co. $165 billion, BP $126 billion, and General Motors $108 billion.

Global trade
Globalization is expressed through trade. In 2003, Asia and the transition economies recorded the most dynamic trade performances. Germany and the US both accounted for roughly 10% of the $7.5 trillion worth of world merchandised exports in 2003, followed by Japan and China, each 6%. China's merchandised imports jumped 40% in 2003 and the country entered the top 3 with $413 billion of imports (cf. $438 billion of exports).

International tourism
Thanks to air travel and other high-speed links, international tourism numbers increased from 25 million in 1950 to 715 million in 2002. France topped the destination list, followed by Spain, the US, Italy, and China, which in 2001 overtook the UK for fifth place. By 2020, China could be in first place, attracting 130 million visitors a year. Tourism-related spending reached $4.2 trillion in 2002.

American power
Americans are members of a country that possesses power – whether economic, technological, military – to affect the entire world to a degree undreamed of by Alexander the Great, Julius Caesar, Napoleon, or Stalin. Yet four out of five Americans have never held a passport. Do they realize that yesterday's world is made to look truly ancient by today's globalization?

Overseas remittances
A further form of globalization lies with the huge numbers of people, 200 million of them (over every 30th person in the world), who have chosen to make their futures in lands outside their own countries. Many of them send home sizeable shares of their earnings to support those relatives and others whom they have left behind. In 2000, migrants from India remitted $11.6 billion, 73% of the flows into South Asia and equivalent to 15% of exports of goods and services, or almost five times as much as foreign direct investment. Mexico's $6.6 billion accounted for almost 40% of the flows into Latin America. Other top recipients in 2000 were China and the Philippines $6 billion, Turkey $5 billion, Egypt $4 billion, Spain and Portugal $3 billion, Morocco, Bangladesh, Jordan, El Salvador, Dominican Republic, and Greece all around $2 billion.

Cities in crisis

Cities in the developing world are exploding under the pressure of their populations. Their surging growth is similar to that of the l9th-century industrializing North, but on a more massive scale. Every day tens of thousands of poor people, hoping for work, stream in from rural areas to overwhelm city services and administrations. The majority of the newcomers head for the barrios, favelas, and shantytowns, made from corrugated iron, plastic sheets, and packing cases located on the outskirts of many cities, such as Cape Town in South Africa (see opposite).

Many millions of people live in the most degrading and menacing environments. In 2000, almost 200 million people in developing-world cities did not have safe drinking water and 400 million were without adequate sanitation. Widespread diarrhoea (see p. 133), dysentery, and typhoid are inevitable. With high unemployment the urban poor are trapped in a vicious circle. Those lucky enough to have a job suffer long hours, low wages, exposure to chemicals and dust, excessive noise, and dangerous machinery.

Administrations stretched beyond capacity by the swelling slum-lands have developed harsh policies, the most draconian of which are the eviction of those living on illegally occupied land, and the bulldozing of settlements. Many city governments refuse to extend basic services and infrastructure, fearing that such improvements will attract more newcomers.

The world's urban population is projected to grow by 2.1 billion people between 2000 and 2030, almost all in the developing nations. Added to this is the fact that the developing world's labour force is growing rapidly, requiring 40 million new jobs a year. All this will place added pressure on urban infrastructure and transport systems as people head for better economic opportunity in the cities. Many of these economic opportunists will head for the shantytowns and slums surrounding many major cities in developing countries. Most slum-dwellers depend on the informal sector for income but in parts of India and Nigeria the slum-dwelling population can include university students and lecturers, civil servants and workers from the private sector. More than two-fifths of Calcutta's slum-dwellers have lived in slums for more than 30 years.

In the least developed countries three-quarters of the urban population live in slums. At the global level, the proportion is almost one-third, around one billion people. There are approximately 550 million slum-dwellers in Asia, 187 million in Africa, and 128 million in Latin America and the Caribbean. And it is not just a developing country problem: 54 million urban dwellers in high-income countries still live in slum-like conditions. Unless the problem is tackled swiftly, the one billion could become two billion in the next 30 years.

Chaos in the cities

Most major cities in the developing world are really two cities: the inner city of the rich elite, which mimics the forms and lifestyles of the affluent North, and the largely self-built outer city of the poor. Urban incomes in the South often average several times rural incomes, and modern services such as doctors, teachers, sanitation, clean water, and electricity are at least within reach. Thus the city acts as a "honeypot" for the rural poor; appalling though conditions are, they can be much better than in the countryside. Unable to afford ready-built housing, immigrants have no choice but to swell the shantytowns, where populations grow much faster than the overall city growth rate. Many are already unmanageable. Many are in areas susceptible to environmental problems such as flooding.

Populations of cities

Projected change 2015
2005
1980

38

Urbanized world population 2030: 61%

Urbanized world population 2003: 48%

Proportion of urban population
By 2003, almost half of the world population was urban – more than 3 billion people – including 30 cities with populations over 7 million (only 8 in the developed world).

Mega-cities
In 1920, the world's urban population amounted to 360 million. Urban conglomerations of 5 million or more were once considered "mega-cities". In 1950, there were nine such cities: New York, Chicago, London, Paris, Moscow, Rhein-Ruhr, Buenos Aires, Tokyo, and Shanghai. By 1980, the number had risen to 26, 19 of which exceeded 7 million (see map). By 2005, the 20 became 30 and by 2015 the 30 will likely become 39. London was the third largest city in 1950: by 2015, it will not even make the top 30. Mumbai (Bombay) has grown from almost 9 million in 1980 to 18 million in 2005 and is projected to reach almost 23 million by 2015 – second placed behind Tokyo with 36 million. Lagos in Nigeria is projected to grow from fewer than 3 million in 1980 to 17 million by 2015.

Trends in Urbanization

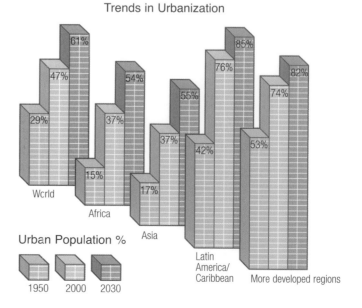

61%
47%
29%
World

54%
37%
15%
Africa

55%
37%
17%
Asia

85%
76%
42%
Latin America/ Caribbean

82%
74%
53%
More developed regions

Urban Population %

1950   2000   2030

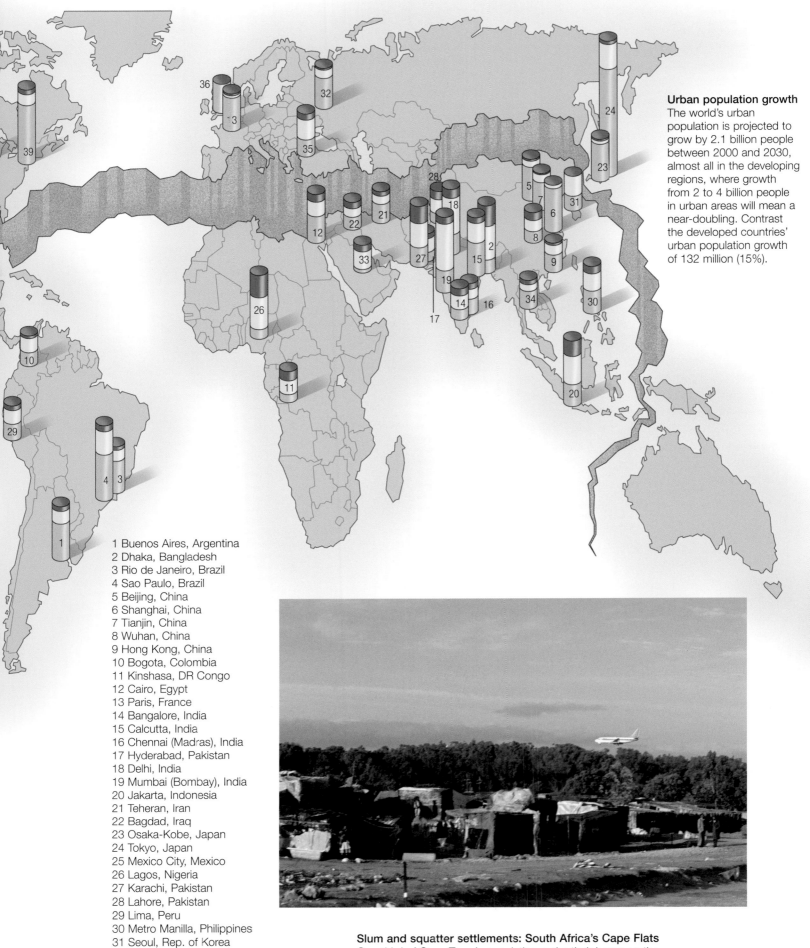

Urban population growth
The world's urban population is projected to grow by 2.1 billion people between 2000 and 2030, almost all in the developing regions, where growth from 2 to 4 billion people in urban areas will mean a near-doubling. Contrast the developed countries' urban population growth of 132 million (15%).

1 Buenos Aires, Argentina
2 Dhaka, Bangladesh
3 Rio de Janeiro, Brazil
4 Sao Paulo, Brazil
5 Beijing, China
6 Shanghai, China
7 Tianjin, China
8 Wuhan, China
9 Hong Kong, China
10 Bogota, Colombia
11 Kinshasa, DR Congo
12 Cairo, Egypt
13 Paris, France
14 Bangalore, India
15 Calcutta, India
16 Chennai (Madras), India
17 Hyderabad, Pakistan
18 Delhi, India
19 Mumbai (Bombay), India
20 Jakarta, Indonesia
21 Teheran, Iran
22 Bagdad, Iraq
23 Osaka-Kobe, Japan
24 Tokyo, Japan
25 Mexico City, Mexico
26 Lagos, Nigeria
27 Karachi, Pakistan
28 Lahore, Pakistan
29 Lima, Peru
30 Metro Manila, Philippines
31 Seoul, Rep. of Korea
32 Moscow, Russian Fed.
33 Riyadh, Saudi Arabia
34 Bangkok, Thailand
35 Istanbul, Turkey
36 London, UK
37 Chicago, USA
38 Los Angeles, USA
39 New York, USA

Slum and squatter settlements: South Africa's Cape Flats
One-third of Cape Town's population make their home on the "Cape Flats". Many live in tin shacks which are not connected to electricity or running water and offer little protection from the elements. Many cook with paraffin stoves. Over the past six years, the South African government has attempted to address the problem using a combination of the private sector and the poor themselves. In Kenya, three-fifths of Nairobi's population live in slums and in informal settlements.

The surveillance revolution

The ICT era means that we are forever being watched. A shopping mall, a high street, a railway station, an airport is likely to have dozens of CCTV cameras beaming at us. Our mobile phones can be tracked, and many of us can be traced through the Internet. Our credit card transactions are kept on numerous files, as are lots of other items of our personal details. At myriad points of our daily lives, we go on a record somewhere. This multi-form surveillance is undertaken for our safety and protection, and certainly it does a good job in helping the police and others who have a valid interest in our doings.

All this is fine if it serves our needs. But it opens up a Pandora's box of opportunities for people to keep a prying eye on us, whether we want it or not. Digital cameras are commonplace, and so are other types of surveillance at every turn. Already the average citizen is caught on camera no fewer than 300 times a day. Worldwide there are 25 million CCTV cameras, and the next five years could see a tenfold increase until we find them in every last public space.

This opens up a debate about whether so many of the cameras should be widely available. Cameras in every shop will curb shoplifting, but even wall-to-wall public surveillance may do little to counter drug dealing which can simply shift indoors. There is a huge difference between cameras on the streets and having them intrude into our homes in ultimate Orwellian style.

The surveillance revolution has been accelerated by the war on terrorism. If individual identity cards help to keep track of suicide bombers, who could object to being fingerprinted and offering up their retina data, even their DNA material? Many criminals have been convicted on DNA evidence through a single hair left on the body of a murder victim. But should we take the momentous step of requiring all major criminals to yield up a DNA sample for centralized computerization, in order that police investigations can zero in on "possible suspects"? Isn't that part way to asserting that criminal X may be considered semi-guilty of some putative crime until he is proved innocent? That would strike at the very foundations of civilized law and its supposed protection of the individual citizen. Or should the citizen be ready to forgo some of his individual liberty in the greater interest of society? Or again, is that not a step on the primrose path to democracy's demise?

The rise of constructive surveillance will trigger a backlash – valid in many respects – from the civil liberties coterie, and eventually to a polarising of public opinion on certain essentials of democracy. Where to draw the dividing line? This writer once saw a demonstration of satellite imagery. Thrown up on the screen was a shot of Indonesia, followed by a shot of the country's capital, then a suburb, then a patch of scrubland, then a patch of that patch, and finally a clump of bushes. Squatting in the bushes was a man relieving himself, thinking he was unobserved.

Technological invasion of personal rights

Smart labelling

Little chips as small as pinheads could soon become part of our everyday lives. With over 500 bits of memory and an antenna that reacts to radio waves, they store data that can be read remotely. They do not require batteries, direct current or the optical scanners currently used to read bar codes. Such "smart labels" will allow "contactless" communication with objects. The basic technology, known as Radio Frequency Identification (RFID), is a traceability technology that could threaten citizens' liberties as well as supply many benefits. True, smart labels can help stock management, they can reduce costs, and they can help prevent theft by tracing products all the way from the warehouse to the cash desk. In addition, electronic labels will mean an end to queueing at checkout counters: the contents of a supermarket trolley will be remotely identified by a simple radio scan. They could also support recycling by facilitating robot waste sorting. The giant American supermarket chain WalMart and Germany's retailer Metro plan to introduce electronic labels in their warehouses in 2005, before introducing them into their retail stores. Similarly the Central European Bank is considering this type of marker for its bank notes. But – and this is a truly big "but" – these smart labels will be able to record all manner of personal data several times a day, without our suspecting that some of our most individual information is being stored for retrieval by multitudes of unseen "watchers".

Biometric information

The arrival of this technology breakthrough, by courtesy of radio-frequency chips, enables governments to check on the whereabouts of all people within their borders – and thus it aims to better monitor the immigration issue. On February 18th 2004 – a landmark day – the European Commission adopted a proposal for the introduction of radio-frequency chips containing biometric information – digital photo and fingerprint – in visas and residence permits for nationals of non-EU countries, before their extension to all European passports. The procedure was approved by the French Senate in 2003, as part of the bill related to the "control of immigration and visits by foreign nationals".

"Loyalty cards"

Chain store cards allow all sorts of consumer choice and hence personal information to be circulated.

Cybercrime

Phishing, started by criminals in Eastern Europe, refers to fraudulent online activity designed to fool victims into revealing personal information, such as passwords and credit card or account user names and numbers, for criminal gain. Phishers send out millions of emails that appear to come from established companies or they initiate pop-up messages on respectable web sites inviting readers to "verify personal details". There are 14 million people banking online in the UK alone and auction-selling sites, such as e-Bay (which facilitates 2 million auctions every day and logged 2 billion sales by 2004), present other valuable targets.

Global positioning systems (GPS)

Originally designed for military purposes, GPS are increasingly utilized in diverse ways, e.g. vehicle tracking (car crime), route planning (worker productivity), roadside assistance and human/animal positioning. The Eurotunnel used GSM technology to ensure that the English and French excavators met in the middle. GPS-equipped balloons monitor the ozone layer over the polar regions.

The Internet's pros and cons

The Internet provides many advantages, but it also causes problems for personal privacy. It was originally established as an "open" research tool, and was never designed to enable privacy or security. Conversely, Net users suppose the technology offers them total anonymity; as an Internet expert has put it, "Who hasn't said or done something online which we wouldn't do in the "real world"? Unfortunately, the question of Internet privacy now features conflicting interests, misinformation, and technology snafus. Whereas customers generally want to share as little information about themselves as possible, websites want to know all they can about you. Internet chat rooms allow identities to be bought and sold, even traded like options on a stock exchange. The Net is a paradise for computer hackers. However inadvertently, we encourage further loss of privacy each time we allow ourselves to be contacted by mobile phone – just as we foster misuse of our data by criminals each time we allow access to our financial information, even our medical and other personal records. Credit card numbers can be sold online for $1 a piece. The Net even allows women and children to be stalked by predatory males.

Potential economic crisis

Can we learn from past experience? However buoyant the world market may now be for many countries, it could readily slip into trouble. Consider unexpected turbulence in the past. During the early 1980s and as the world economy began to deteriorate, the outlook for international trade became steadily worse. Economic growth declined as unemployment and inflation in developed countries took hold. Overproduction in some industries contrasted with idle factories in others. The price of money rose steadily, thrusting developing countries further into debt, and the exchange rates of key currencies became badly misaligned.

Alongside these malfunctions, a fresh trade protectionism has emerged in the North. The transfer of some production processes to low-cost developing countries and the rise of the "new Japans" begin to pose a threat to well-paid and skilled jobs in Europe and North America. Workers and employers have started to demand protection and the rationing of imports, often by artificial "agreements" imposed on exporters in the South.

Protectionism and unstable pricing make trade and production less efficient, with additional adverse consequence for the North. If the developing world's earnings are restricted, so too is its spending, and a deflationary bias enters the world economy. The developing countries themselves practise protectionism. Barriers are erected around infant industries (especially those involved in advanced technologies) which would otherwise decline in the wake of powerful competition from the North.

Debt has exacerbated the problem, with many developing countries forced to slash their imports in order to fund debt repayments to the rich North. During the period between 1996 and 2005, while world output averaged 3.8 percent per year, external debt in the emerging-market and developing economies grew from $2.2 trillion to $2.8 trillion and debt service payments from $312 billion to $454 billion per year.

Roughly one-quarter of the $2.8 trillion was accounted for by each of Central/Eastern Europe and the former Soviet Union, Western hemisphere nations (such as Brazil and Mexico), and developing Asia, while the Middle East accounted for 11.5 percent and Africa 10 percent. Only 27 countries have so far qualified for debt relief under the 1996 Heavily Indebted Poor Countries Initiative. In 2005, the G7 (made up of the world's seven richest countries) were being urged to offer poor countries considerably more debt relief, sometimes as much as 100 per cent.

As the newly industrializing countries of the South clash with the dominant North, major market shifts could lead to a rash of protectionist barriers which are unlikely to help anyone in the long term. World trade slows down, economic distortions grow, and the North/South gap widens.

Market tremors

In 2003, both the UK and the US bought more goods than they sold. If these outflows of currency are not compensated for by foreign investors it could lead to poor investment returns, which in a global market may eventually drive away investors who had previously helped balance economies. Such a market tremor occurred in both countries following the burst of the high-tech bubble and subsequently put downward pressure on the values of both the Dollar and Sterling relative to the Euro. This affects not only US- and UK-priced goods but the cost of imports, the value of overseas sales, and profit margins at home. Weakening of the US dollar caused by trade imbalances could finally push the American economy to a "tipping point" from which it might not recover. When is difficult to estimate but the greater the trade imbalance the greater the possibility of the US dollar losing its role as a provider of hard currency to the world and a profitable sink for the rest of the world's surpluses and investment capital. The dollar fell 26% against six major currencies in the three years 2002–2004 and the US trade deficit in 2003 was almost $600 billion. In addition, the country is $7.6 trillion in debt (cf. the national economy, almost $11 trillion).

Newly industrializing countries (NICs)

The NICs sell all manner of goods from textiles to computers. To the first wave of NICs such as South Korea and Taiwan is added a second wave: what will happen as their manufacturing muscle grows and they challenge the established high-technology markets of the North? In 2002 65% of the Philippines' merchandised exports were high-tech, 58% of Malaysia's and 31% of Thailand's. China, which joined the WTO in 2001, has exported so many goods to the US in recent years that in 2003 it enjoyed a trade surplus of $135 billion. This whopping total lends China an exceptional amount of economic and hence political muscle. The same could soon be said, collectively at least, of other emergent economic giants such as India, Brazil, Mexico, and Russia. They will have the power to rewrite the geopolitical rules of the world. The transition economies of Central and Eastern Europe account for only 5% of merchandised exports as yet.

Development distortion

Export-led growth does not benefit all equally. Lured by the North's import appetites, many developing nations have neglected fundamental development issues such as agricultural reform, rural development, and health care, in favour of prestige projects from airports and hospitals to dams and motorways, and concentrated on cash exports to pay for them. As the market fails them, they reap a bitter reward. They have not been helped by bilateral aid deals (aid flowing directly between donor and recipient countries) tied to purchasing expensive Northern manufactured goods in return for aid. Burdened with debt, or locked in the commodity trap with rising poverty, many developing nations face a radical rethink of their development policies.

Developed countries

Percentage share of merchandised exports in 2003: 64.5%

Average annual growth 1960–2002: 10.7%.

Developed countries

Older industrial nations face competition from many developing and transition countries whose economies have fared well in the past decade and whose workforces are eager to earn. Worst hit are the sundown industries, such as textiles, cars, and steel. The North will have to plan for adjustments on an unprecedented scale such as new working practices and industries.

Least developed countries

Percentage share of merchandised exports in 2003: 0.6%

Average annual growth 1960–2002: 6%.

Least developed countries

Globalization benefits have not yet reached the LDCs. Their small share of merchandised exports was due mainly to deteriorating physical and social infrastructures, a lack of technical and institutional capacity, and the harmful consequences of Northern protectionism. The trade in goods as a share of GDP is 45%. In 2003, this group of 49 countries accounted for $44 billion of merchandised exports compared to $54 billion of imports.

Developing countries

Percentage share of merchandised exports in 2003: 30%. Average annual growth 1990–2000: 9%. Shifts away from dependence on commodity exports have mostly been hampered by restrictive trade rules, though countries with robust internal economies such as China and India have successfully diversified towards manufactured goods and services. In the 1960s, primary commodities, excluding fuels, accounted for almost two-thirds of the value of exports in developing countries; by 2001, they had declined to only a fraction as much. During the same period the share of manufactured goods in exports increased more than fivefold.

Japan

Third in the rankings of the world's merchandised exports, with $472 billion (6%) of the total in 2003, Japan is behind the US with $724 billion and Germany $748 billion (both around 10%). Its neighbour China comes a close fourth, with $438 billion. Between 1990 and 2000, export growth averaged 5% a year and the country was a net exporter in 2003.

OPEC: oil power

In 1973 and again in 1979, OPEC sharply raised oil prices in a bid to boost its purchasing power. Worst hit were the poorest nations who could not afford the oil, nor the dearer Northern goods, as costs were passed on. More recently terrorism, the war in Iraq, and increased energy demands in countries such as China have threatened the security of oil supplies and forced up prices. This trend will only be corrected when extra oil producing capacity is slowly brought onstream. Meanwhile, OPEC has agreed to supply sufficient oil to keep prices within a profitable but stable range. This is partly to avoid another global economic slowdown, and partly to delay any fresh impetus to develop alternative energy sources such as renewables.

Barriers to trade

The "new protectionism" against goods manufactured in developing countries has employed many invisible barriers: import quotas, licensing regulations, health restrictions, customs procedures and petty requirements. Then there are "orderly marketing agreements" and "voluntary" export deals which are usually far from voluntary for the exporters. Subsidies are increasingly used by the rich countries to protect their products: in 2003, their agricultural subsidies totalled $350 billion, supplied by taxpayers and by consumers. They distort the world's food economy. Note that $350 billion is roughly the same as the collective gross national incomes (GNI) of Sub-Saharan Africa. In the developed world, cartels (producer associations) have multiplied. By comparison, equivalent groups in developing countries such as those for bananas and coffee have achieved little. Agricultural protectionism in rich countries imposes long-term costs on South and North alike. Northerners can pay several times world prices for certain foodstuffs and commodities while dumping their own surpluses on the South. Large agri-businesses become rich at the expense of impoverished small-scale farmers. Food items represented only 7% of world trade in 2003.

Japan
Old industrialized countries
Newly industrializing countries
Those left out
Non-market economies and emerging market economies

The commodities trap

Julius Nyerere, former President of Tanzania, once remarked "In 1965 I could buy a tractor by selling 17.25 tonnes of sisal. By 1974, I needed 57% more. Now the sisal price has fallen again but the tractor price has risen still further."

The top trillions

The global economy is dominated in part by a series of sectors with undue leverage. They include developing/transition country debt totalling $2.8 trillion; international finance flows of $1.5 trillion per day; the insurance industry worth $1.4 trillion per year; and military spending almost $1 trillion per year. The GDP of the top 7 countries accounted for more than two-thirds of the world's $36.3 trillion in 2003. In 2002, sales of the top 10 non-financial transnational corporations combined was $1.3 trillion.

Economic upheavals ahead

A number of countries in Sub-Saharan Africa face collapse unless they bring their AIDS epidemics under control. Only Uganda is doing so. India's emergence as an economic power could be stymied by AIDS, with 4 million HIV cases already. In China unless infection rates slow quickly, at least 10 million Chinese could suffer from AIDS within 6 years. Tackling AIDS needs funding of at least $12 billion in 2005, rising to $50 billion by 2007.

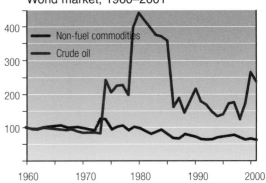

Commodity price index
World market, 1960–2001

- Non-fuel commodities
- Crude oil

400
300
200
100

1960   1970   1980   1990   2000

Economic cankers

There is a canker at work in our economies, in the form of "perverse" subsidies. Germany's coal mines, for instance, are so heavily subsidized that it would be economically efficient for the government to close down all the mines and send the workers home on full pay for the rest of their lives. That would also reduce coal pollution such as acid rain, urban smog, and global warming. The subsidies are perverse in that they harm both the economy and the environment.

So, too, with marine fisheries. The annual catch, well above sustainable yield, is worth around $100 billion at dockside, where it is sold for some $80 billion, the shortfall plus profits being made up by government subsidies. Result, more and more fish-ermen chase after fewer and fewer fish until stocks collapse and fishing businesses go bankrupt. In 1992, one of the richest fisheries in the world, that of cod along the Grand Bank in northeastern US and Newfoundland, had to be closed because of sheer shortage of fish. Dozens of businesses went bankrupt and 42,000 workers lost their jobs. Many other US fisheries are heading towards commercial extinction, yet if all these fisheries were allowed to recover, sustainable exploitation would boost the nation's economy by $8 billion per year and supply 300,000 jobs.

Perverse subsidies total at least $2 trillion world-wide per year, or more than all but the world's three largest national economies. On both economic and environmental grounds, they defer the time when we can achieve the holy grail of sustainable develop-ment. Ironically, the total of $2 trillion is three and a half times as large as the Rio Earth Summit's pro-posed budget for sustainable development – a sum that governments dismissed as simply not available.

The rich industrialized countries account for two-thirds of perverse subsidies, and the US over one-fifth. A typical American taxpayer pays at least $2,500 a year to fund perverse subsidies, then pays another $1,000 through increased prices for con-sumer goods or through environmental degradation. Yet the subsidies persist virtually untouched. This is because subsidies tend to create special interest groups and political lobbies, leaving the subsidies hard to remove even though they persist long after their sell-by date. In Washington DC there are 14,000 lobbyists, or 25 for each member of Congress. They are bent on advancing narrow sec-toral interests such as perverse subsidies, and they ply their trade at a cost of $100 million per month.

Were just half of these perverse subsidies to be phased out, just half of the funds released would enable many governments to abolish their budget deficits at a stroke. They would be able to reorder their fiscal priorities in fundamental fashion, to restore their environments more vigorously than through any other single measure – and to throw a week-long party for the whole country.

Perverse subsidies

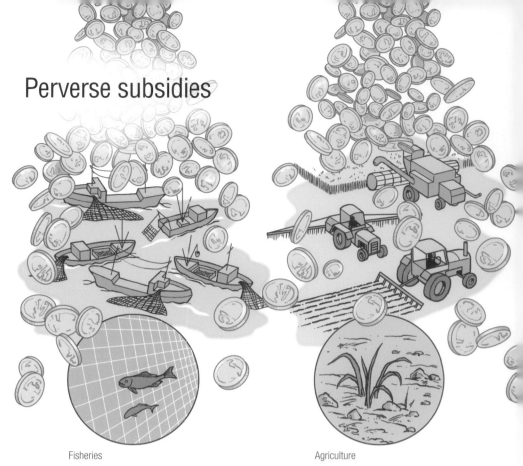

Fisheries   Agriculture

"Poor Mexico: close to God but closer to the US"

The Mexican corn sector is in acute crisis because of the influx of cheap subsidized corn imports from the US. 15 million poor Mexican farmers cannot compete against American producers who have received $10 billion a year in subsidies or ten times more than Mexico's total agricultural budget. Since the early 1990s, US corn exports to Mexico have expanded threefold, until they now account for one-third of Mexico's needs. Since 1994 these surging imports have contributed to a price decline of more than 70%. Mexican farmers' incomes have plunged and malnutrition has soared. Millions of Mexicans are migrating to escape rural poverty, many of them to the US. The crisis is a microcosm of the larger crisis facing vulnerable rural communities across the developing world as "agricultural dumping" of huge amounts of rich-world crops causes mass poverty.

The World Trade Organization (WTO)

The WTO urges its members, mostly developing nations, to practise free trade on the grounds that this will expand economies everywhere. "I'm good at making cars, you're good at growing coffee, so let's trade and we'll both prosper." Alas for fine intentions. The rich nations trade like crazy among themselves while shutting the door on goods from developing nations. Or they subsidize their own businesses which then undercut developing-nation "competitors."

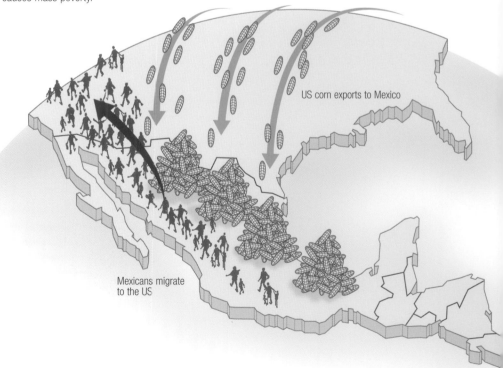

US corn exports to Mexico

Mexicans migrate to the US

Forestry   Water   Fossil fuels   Transportation

Subsidies to six main sectors

Absurd subsidies are prominent in six main sectors: fossil fuels, road transportation, fisheries, agriculture, water, and forestry. In all cases, the subsidies promote economic boondoggles and otherwise undermine national economies. At the same time, subsidies for fossil fuels generate grandscale pollution. Subsidies for road transportation also promote pollution, plus other ills such as road congestion. Subsidies for fisheries foster over-exploitation of depleted fish stocks. Subsidies for agriculture foster overloading of croplands, leading to erosion of topsoil, pollution from synthetic fertilizers and pesticides, and release of greenhouse gases. Subsidies for water encourage misuse and overuse of supplies that are increasingly scarce in many lands. Subsidies for forestry encourage overlogging and other forms of deforestation.

Agriculture subsidies gone crazy

In the US, one government agency subsidizes irrigation for crops that another agency has paid farmers not to grow. To cite the economist Paul Hawken: *"The government subsidizes energy costs so that farmers can deplete aquifers to grow alfalfa to feed cows that make milk that is stored in warehouses as surplus cheese that does not feed the hungry."*

OECD subsidies totalled $311 billion in 2001 (cf. foreign aid, $52 billion, and Sub-Saharan Africa's GDP, $315 billion). Despite criticism of many of these subsidies, they totalled $350 billion in 2003. The US has subsidized its cotton farmers to such an extent that they captured 40% of the world market and drove the price so low that 10 million people in West Africa were no longer able to make a living from the crop. The EU has spent 3.3 Euros for every 1 Euro of exports of sugar beet, another product better grown in developing countries. On local markets in Ghana, EU-subsidized Italian tinned tomatoes are cheaper than home-grown. Japan, exceptionally short of farmland, imposes import tariffs on rice of almost 500%. Pressure from the newly formed G20 Group of developing countries has caused the US and Europe to take a serious look at their subsidies, particularly export-distorting ones. The WTO's upheld its preliminary ruling against US cotton subsidies following a strong complaint by Brazil about "unfair export subsidies". Soybean subsidies next?

Success stories

It is often said that it is impossible to get rid of perverse subsidies because of the special interests that support them. But note that New Zealand has eliminated virtually all its agricultural subsidies, even though – or perhaps because – its economy is more dependent on agriculture than almost any other developed country. In similar style, Russia, China, and India have greatly reduced their fossil fuel subsidies. Australia, Mexico, and South Africa are moving toward "full cost pricing" of their water supplies.

German coal mines

In 2002, Germany had three-fifths of the EU's 86,000 coal miners, so the coal sector exerts vast political leverage. While subsidy support fell from €4.7 billion in 1998 to €3.7 billion in 2002, the amount per person employed in the sector was still €77,000. Projections for 2005 are €2.7 billion subsidies for 36,000 employees, or €75,000 per employee. Were the subsidies to be redirected to renewables such as solar, thermal, and biomass, 9,000 new jobs would be created by 2010; and if some of the funding included energy efficiency in buildings, then a further 30,000 jobs would be created.

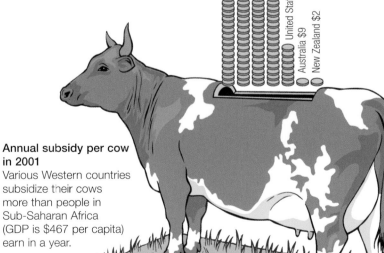

Switzerland $1,560
Norway $1,313
Japan $1,297
European Union $436
United States $152
Australia $9
New Zealand $2

Annual subsidy per cow in 2001

Various Western countries subsidize their cows more than people in Sub-Saharan Africa (GDP is $467 per capita) earn in a year.

The new economic elite

There is a remarkable phenomenon emergent in the world, in the form of the new consumers, being people who already total 950 million in 17 developing countries and 115 million in three transition countries. They enjoy sufficient income to buy household appliances of many sorts, notably fridges and freezers, washing machines and air conditioners, television sets and videos – all the usual items that mark the "newly arrived". They are also shifting to a diet strongly based on meat, which they enjoy every day at least instead of once a week at most. Still more importantly, they are buying cars in large numbers.

Of course, they are to be applauded for lifting themselves out of the poverty that still oppresses four billion of their fellow citizens. Already they account for a sizeable share of consumption worldwide, around one-quarter in 2000. The 15 percent of global population in high-income countries accounted for almost 80 percent of personal (as opposed to public) consumption; the 11 percent in Sub-Saharan Africa accounted for just one percent.

Notwithstanding their good fortune, the new consumers should bear in mind that certain of their consumption activities have significant environmental impacts. Household appliances use much electricity, which, mostly generated from fossil fuels, means widespread pollution. Secondly, much meat is raised in part on grain, thus putting pressure on limited irrigation water and international grain supplies. Several countries import large amounts of grain for the primary purpose of feeding livestock rather than people. Thirdly, the 1.1 billion new consumers possess 125 million cars or one-fifth of the global total, a proportion that is rising rapidly. CO_2 emissions, which cause half of global warming, are rising more swiftly from cars than from any other source. To this extent, the entire world community has an interest in all those new cars in new consumer countries – just as the new consumer countries have an interest in the far larger numbers of cars in developed countries.

In 2000, the new consumers enjoyed a collective purchasing power of PPP $6.3 trillion, almost on a par with that of the US. They are likely to increase their numbers by half and to almost double their purchasing power as soon as 2010, making for the biggest consumption boom in history.

How the new consumers be persuaded to enjoy their high-flying lifestyles in sustainable fashion? A first step is for us all to recognize that consumption patterns will inevitably change in the future, if only by force of environmental circumstance which is becoming ever more forceful. Secondly, we must try to change consumption patterns right around the world. Many observers believe that consumption patterns are set in concrete, but they may prove to be rather more adaptable. For example, during a recent 20-year period, some 55 million Americans gave up smoking – a social earthquake, virtually overnight.

Consumption: the rise of the new consumers

The new imperative: sustainable consumption

We need to establish sustainable consumption as a norm. It will be not only about quantitative reductions in our use of materials and energy, but about ways in which we can achieve an acceptable quality of life for all in perpetuity, and exemplify it throughout our lifestyles. How, for instance, can we attain a better balance between work, income, and consumption? How can we prevent yesterday's luxuries from becoming today's necessities and tomorrow's relicts? How can we make fashion sustainable and sustainability fashionable? However hard it will be to live with the profound changes required, it will not be nearly so hard as to live in a world profoundly impoverished by the environmental injuries of current consumption.

The new consumer countries

	New consumers 2000 (millions)	Purchasing power 2000 (PPP$ billions)
China	303	1,267
India	132	609
South Korea	45	502
Philippines	33	150
Indonesia	63	288
Malaysia	12	79
Thailand	32	179
Pakistan	17	62
Iran	27	136
Saudi Arabia	13	78
South Africa	17	202
Brazil	75	641
Argentina	31	314
Venezuela	13	87
Colombia	19	136
Mexico	68	624
Turkey	45	265
Poland	34	206
Ukraine	12	44
Russia	68	436
TOTAL	1,059	6,305

$s and PPP$s

Economies have long been measured in "international" dollars, or dollar values used for inter-nation exchange rates. But whereas a dollar in a New York supermarket might buy you only 3 or 4 bananas, on a New Delhi street it would buy you at least 20, thus reflecting the very different costs of living in terms of basic staples. The world's economies are now measured in Purchasing Power Parity dollars as well as conventional dollars, which gives a radical rejigging of rankings in the global arena (see table below).

The Top 12 Economies in 2002

Measured in $ billions		Measured in $PPP billions	
1 USA	10,138	1 USA	10,138
2 Japan	3,979	2 China	5,732
3 Germany	1,976	3 Japan	3,261
4 UK	1,552	4 India	2,695
5 France	1,410	5 Germany	2,172
6 China	1,237	6 France	1,554
7 Italy	1,181	7 UK	1,511
8 Canada	716	8 Italy	1,481
9 Spain	650	9 Brazil	1,312
10 Mexico	637	10 Russia	1,142
11 India	515	11 Canada	902
12 South Korea	477	12 Mexico	879
World	32,000		47,000

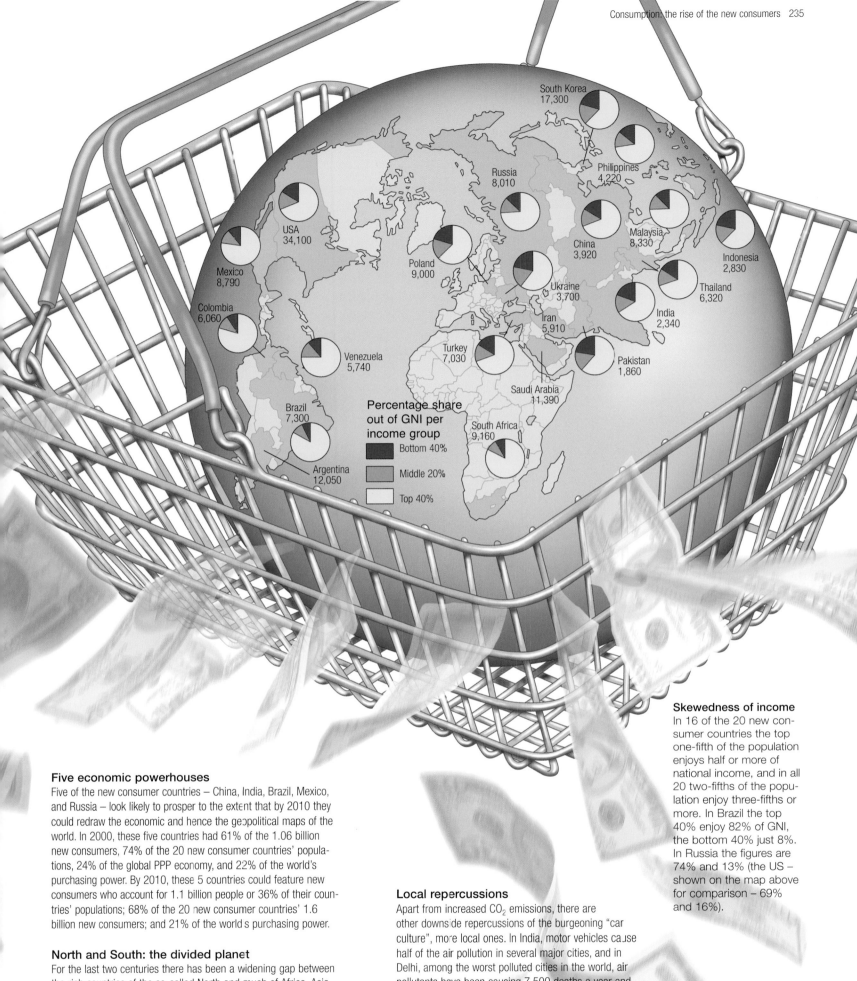

Percentage share
out of GNI per
income group

Bottom 40%

Middle 20%

Top 40%

South Korea
17,300

Philippines
4,220

Russia
8,010

Malaysia
8,330

China
3,920

Indonesia
2,830

USA
34,100

Poland
9,000

Thailand
6,320

Mexico
8,790

Ukraine
3,700

India
2,340

Colombia
6,060

Iran
5,910

Venezuela
5,740

Turkey
7,030

Pakistan
1,860

Saudi Arabia
11,390

Brazil
7,300

South Africa
9,160

Argentina
12,050

Five economic powerhouses

Five of the new consumer countries – China, India, Brazil, Mexico, and Russia – look likely to prosper to the extent that by 2010 they could redraw the economic and hence the geopolitical maps of the world. In 2000, these five countries had 61% of the 1.06 billion new consumers, 74% of the 20 new consumer countries' populations, 24% of the global PPP economy, and 22% of the world's purchasing power. By 2010, these 5 countries could feature new consumers who account for 1.1 billion people or 36% of their countries' populations; 68% of the 20 new consumer countries' 1.6 billion new consumers; and 21% of the world's purchasing power.

North and South: the divided planet

For the last two centuries there has been a widening gap between the rich countries of the so-called North and much of Africa, Asia, and Latin America. By the middle of the 180Cs, the difference in per-capita income was about two to one. In the last century, the divergence increased, particularly since the 1950s. Today, per-capita Gross National Income (in $PPP) in high-income countries is 13 times higher than in the low-income countries, and 3 times greater than in even the fast-developing countries such as Mexico and Malaysia. And this evidence of a divided world conceals ever deeper divisions at levels other than those of national economies.

Local repercussions

Apart from increased CO_2 emissions, there are other downside repercussions of the burgeoning "car culture", more local ones. In India, motor vehicles cause half of the air pollution in several major cities, and in Delhi, among the worst polluted cities in the world, air pollutants have been causing 7,500 deaths a year and 1.2 million people receive medical treatment. Fortunately, the new consumers can, if they feel inclined, purchase those cars that are more sparing in their CO_2 emissions, notably the Toyota Prius and the Honda Insight.

Skewedness of income

In 16 of the 20 new consumer countries the top one-fifth of the population enjoys half or more of national income, and in all 20 two-fifths of the population enjoy three-fifths or more. In Brazil the top 40% enjoy 82% of GNI, the bottom 40% just 8%. In Russia the figures are 74% and 13% (the US – shown on the map above for comparison – 69% and 16%).

A giant awakening

China is not only the leading country in the world in terms of population. It has the second largest PPP economy, and if it can maintain its economic surge of the last two decades it will become the number one economy by 2020. Here is a new superpower in the making, and with a scale and speed without equal in all of human history. Not surprisingly, it features more new consumers than any other country, 300 million of them in 2000. That was well over twice as many as the second country, India, and by 2010 China's total could at least double. Imagine: about as many new consumers as the old consumers in North America and Western Europe.

So prominent is China's economy already that the country is the world's foremost producer of meat, grain, coal, steel, cement, cotton cloth, textiles, and TVs. It is the world's leading consumer of such basics as grain, meat, coal, steel and fertilizers. Much of its success stems from its being one of the largest industrial powers along with the US, Japan, and Germany. It has overtaken Japan to become the leading industrial exporter to the US. It produces 10 percent of the world's computer monitors, 20 percent of its refrigerators, 25 percent of its washing machines, 30 percent of its air conditioners and TV sets, and 50 percent of its cameras. Truly it qualifies as factory to the world. Even more to the point, high-tech products, likely to remain in surging demand for the foreseeable future, make up over a fifth of China's manufactured exports, an increase of two-thirds during just the half-decade 1997–2002.

China has at least 500 million TVs and 140 million refrigerators. Mobile phones topped 330 million in 2004 and China has the world's largest mobile phone market. The country has also become the third largest personal computer market after the US and Japan.

But there are environmental costs to this headlong advance. For instance, there are growing shortages of water for all those grain crops to feed 1.3 billion people, plus water for household use and for the factories that fuel China's economy. China is the world's leading producer of both wheat and rice, and the second producer of corn; it grows over one-fifth of the world's grain on one-fourteenth of the world's croplands.

This is a giant awakening, even though the outside world does not seem to be listening as closely as it might. What geopolitical shifts might stem from the arrival of this superpower on the global stage? China has the potential to call both the economic and environmental shots of the future. Already its CO_2 emissions have placed China second to the US, even though per capita they are only one-eighth as much. When more of China's multitudes achieve the prosperity that marks the 300 million middle classers of the coastal zone, CO_2 emissions could soar. Then people in North America and throughout Europe would pay attention to this giant of the Orient.

China – an emerging superpower

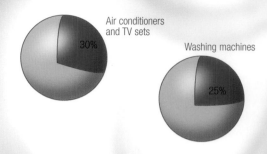

Chinese percentage global production

Air conditioners and TV sets 30%

Washing machines 25%

Cameras 50%

China's muscle in 2003

Population: 1.3 billion.
Economy: China PPP$6.4 trillion, second only to the US, PPP$10.9 trillion.
CO2 emissions: 3.3 billion tonnes, cf. the US 5.8 billion tonnes.
IT: 100 million internet users; 335 million mobile phones.
Grain consumption: 382 million tonnes, becoming the world's largest importer.
Meat consumption: 63 million tonnes, cf. the US 37 million tonnes.

Meat in China

During the 1990s, China nearly doubled its meat intake, to become the world's number one carnivore country, accounting for four-fifths more meat than the US. Already the country is the pig capital of the world, with one pig to every three Chinese (by contrast, only one in ten of the world's cattle is in China as yet, less than the US' one in eight). This is fine – except that much of China's meat is raised on grain, which aggravates pressure on limited stocks of irrigation water for grainlands as well as increased demand for grain supplies from international markets. If each Chinese were ever to consume as much beef as today's average American, and if the cattle were to be raised largely on grain, that would require more grain than the entire US harvest.

Because of increasing affluence plus population growth (the first more than the second), the country's grain demand rises by at least 3 million tonnes a year. During 2000–2002, however, China's grain harvests plunged, with over 30 million tonnes each year of shortfall between consumption and production (and accounting for a major part of the global grain harvest shortfall). In 2003, the global harvest again fell short of consumption by 93 million tonnes, with China accounting for a record 47 million tonnes. China's import needs mean that the 100-plus countries that import US grain have to compete with the new giant grain consumer.

China's cars

The government has declared the auto sector is to be the chief pillar of the future economy, making cars the primary form of transportation, whereas the main form of travel thus far, the bicycle, is to be hustled into history. China is already the fourth largest car market in the world. The 8 million cars of 2000 could become 23 million by 2010, or even 40 million if recent trends persist. If China's cars were ever to consume fuel at the US gas-guzzling rate, China would need more oil than the world now produces each year. To provide the required roads and parking lots, it would also need to pave at least 150,000 sq. km of land, most of which would be cropland with an expanse equal to half the country's ricelands. China's motor vehicles are responsible for at least half of the severe pollution problem in major cities. Until recent clean-up measures, Beijing's air was 5 times more polluted than that of Los Angeles.

Computer monitors

10%

Refrigerators

20%

The thirsty dragon
The North China Plain features two-fifths of the country's population and two-thirds of its croplands but only one-fifth of its surface water. Over-pumping of the region's aquifers has been causing water levels to decline by a whole metre or more per year.

Shanghai

Beijing

CHINA

Or more than 40,000,000 cars?

23,000,000 cars

China's car fleet

8,000,000 cars

2000

2010 (projected)

The car race
China is set on building up its car fleet from only 8 million in 2000, no more than Chicago's, to one of the biggest in the world. As early as 2010 the cars total could surpass 40 million, or one-quarter as many as in the US today.

59

26

Shanghai

New York

Number of computers per 100 households

3.8

4.5

Shanghai

New York

Number of doctors per 1,000 people

China's coastal provinces
The coastal provinces constitute the country's centre of gravity in not only economic and commercial senses but social and cultural senses too. While Shanghai citizens' food spending is merely one-thirteenth as much as New Yorkers' (food is much subsidized), they possess 26 computers per 100 households as against 59 in New York, and they enjoy 3.8 doctors per 1,000 people, not far behind New York's 4.5 doctors. Here are the bulk of China's televisions, video and DVD players, cellphones, upmarket cars and stylish clothes. In the Pudong district of Shanghai there is the new Super Brand Mall, the largest retail venue in developing Asia and with Chinese and Japanese chain stores interspersed with McDonald's and Starbucks. In many respects, affluent Shanghai has more in common with Detroit or Madrid than with cities of inland China.

Trade is an environmental issue

Many environmental problems are associated with the trade and debt crisis. The need for foreign exchange to service debts fuels efforts to expand exports, and these add to the many other pressures on natural resources. As people are pushed into poverty, in part by government measures to deal with debt, and as prices rise faster than incomes, the daily struggle for survival forces the poor to exploit ecologically fragile environments.

The central tenet of today's economics is that developing countries can export their way into prosperity. Lending institutions have devoted much of their efforts to promoting export-led growth. Freer trade could give poor nations better access to world markets, thus raising incomes to alleviate poverty and protect the environment. This, at any rate, is the view of the World Trade Organization (WTO), the international organization that lays down rules for almost all world trade and aims to smooth the path of free trade and remove import and export controls. Of some 210 countries in the world, 148 are now members of the WTO and a further 31 are observer nations (which must start accession negotiations within five years of becoming observers). These are Western market economies, newly industrialized economies, emerging market economies, and even relatively low-income, developing economies (over three-quarters of the 148 are developing or least-developed countries) which are fit to do business on the world market on equal terms among all. In this sense, the WTO is more than the World Trade Organization, it is the assembly of the world market economy, the framework of the global market.

Environmental trade-off?

International trade has long been a front-rank engine of economic growth. Much of the benefit depends on what is known as "comparative advantage". Generally speaking, the more international trade we have, the more the world prospers. This has been especially the case in the past few decades while there has been some, but only some, easing of the rules governing trade. The downside is that nations often compete through unacceptable modes of production. Developing nations in particular have been pressurized by multinationals into tolerating adverse employment practices, trade union restrictions and other social dis-benefits. Environmentally, too, enhanced trade often means overloading of croplands, overlogging of forests, and excessive levels of pollution. If governments of the North bite the bullet and legislate against polluters, the industries will be more inclined to relocate to countries with poorer legislation, mostly in the South. It is therefore important that the laws protecting the global environment retain and strengthen supremacy over those governing trade.

Trade liberalization

It has been estimated that trade liberalization would lead to gains of $140 billion for developing countries. However, liberalization needs to be carefully monitored as market failures can lead to increased poverty. The DOHA trade negotiations were launched with the goal of producing measures focused on the needs of developing countries and ways to help the least developed countries to trade their way out of poverty rather than relying on aid.

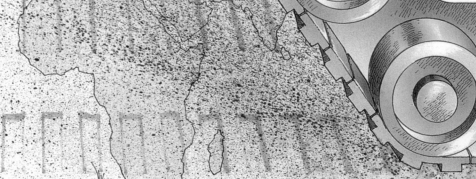

Major international accords are intended to achieve trade liberalization by reducing or eliminating regulations that interfere with the free flow of goods and resources between nations. Yet this may be a double-edged weapon. It may promise developing nations better access to world markets, but it also has the potential to increase the rate of environmental destruction, especially if it caused the prices of commodities to fall. Developing world governments are aware of a new form of "green protectionism" as a threat to their development efforts. Any concern for the global environment necessitates the tackling of North/South inequality. If free trade is to be of environmental benefit, it must first be fair trade. Easing debt burdens and improving commodity prices (adjusted to reflect the real value of natural resources), would reduce pressure to over-exploit the environment. Tackling poverty in the South would benefit both the global environment and world trade.

Thus trade rules and agreements are a major determinant of how natural resources are used, what pressures are put on the environment, and who ultimately benefits from the $7.5 trillion that crosses borders annually with the exchange of goods. Note that growth of trade has usually been twice as high as growth of the global economy. The interactions between trade and the environment are increasingly recognized. Energy-intensive and trade-based growth in the North has caused most of the global pollution in terms of ozone-depleting and greenhouse gas emissions, along with hazardous waste. In the South, debt-fuelled export expansion continues to play its part in the destruction of the natural resource base.

Trade protectionism

As an example of trade protectionism consider the case of agriculture in rich countries – subsidized to absurd degree so that these countries can sell their products to poorer countries for less than the poorer countries can grow them. In South Africa, one tonne of wheat cost $325 to produce in early 2005 but the farmer could sell that same tonne for only $160. While South Africa could charge import tariffs of up to 72% on wheat (50% on corn) under WTO rules, its current levy was only 2% (13%). Poorer countries cannot compete with richer countries whose farmers receive a large share of their income from the state.

The trend in trade

Multilateral trade negotiations have, in the past, focused on trade barriers for goods. The trend now is to include trade in services, foreign investment, and intellectual property – areas where the North has a "comparative advantage" and seeks to protect its service industries, expand investment opportunities, and guard its technologies from imitation.

Maquiladoras and free trade

There has been an economic boom on the Mexican border with the US. Between 1990 and 1999, foreign-owned companies soared from 2,000 to 4,000 and the number of employees reached more than one million. These "maquiladoras" primarily produce electronic goods, clothing, plastics and automotive parts, or they assemble imported components into finished products. Special trade agreements exempted these companies from US tariffs and other restrictions, meaning they could supply markets with goods produced at a fraction of the cost elsewhere, using workers earning barely enough to survive and facing exposure to toxic pollutants. Such relocation also avoids expensive anti-pollution equipment needed to meet US health, safety, and environmental standards. In 2001, changes to North American Free Trade Agreement (NAFTA) trade policy made maquiladora operations more difficult and costly by banning tariff rebates for non-NAFTA imports. Thus firms importing from Asia, assembling in Mexico and exporting to the US – particularly electronics – found their costs soared overnight and some began taking their operations elsewhere. Competition from China has also caused many plants to move on. These maquiladoras in Mexico have accounted for a large share of the country's exports.

The world's poor

Absolute poverty with an income of less than $1 per day afflicts 1.1 billion people – every sixth person in the world. South and East Asia and Sub-Saharan Africa constitute "the epicentre of the world's development crisis". Welcome to a phenomenon that should shock anyone's sense of fair play, and is all the more shocking in that it could readily be remedied – but isn't.

Eradicating absolute poverty is one of the UN's Millennium Development Goals (MDGs) proclaimed in 2000 and endorsed by all UN heads of state. There are another seven MDGs for tackling health, education, employment, and the like (see p. 251). To meet these Goals rich nations must urgently double their foreign aid, with more spent on training and infrastructure in education, nutrition, health, and public sector management. Even an extra $100 billion would be no big deal, amounting to $1 every two to three days for every rich world taxpayer, or less than one month of military spending. Which will buy us greater security – more lasting security, better all-round security?

Of these absolute poor most are landless labourers, marginal farmers, and unskilled labourers in cities. There is rarely any system of state benefits to ease their plight. They are most likely to be with-out the medical facilities to cope with sickness and disability, without schools to raise their levels of literacy, and without a hope of better employment. On top of physical isolation, they suffer the social isolation of being unwanted. Women, in particular, find it impossible to escape their burdens. Furthermore, the poor household may belong to a socially inferior class, forced by custom to accept the lowest paid and most menial tasks, and physically segregated. Their children are condemned to the same lowly status.

Developing-world poverty is self-generating. The poor in the North can at least survive through a safety net of social services, and their poverty can be seen as "extreme social deprivation". In the South, the term "absolute poverty" is the only one applicable. Even if they survive a malnourished childhood, hundreds of millions will never have the opportunity to realize their human potential. All the routes out of the trap are firmly shut because of lack of education, technical aid or credit, employment, sanitation and safe water, and access to health services, transport, and communications.

The increasing division of wealth and power is inimical to all our interests. Interdependence applies not only to the global systems existing between North and South, but also within nations, and between countryside and cities. Lopsided rural and urban development, with cities monopolizing the attention of government, has already proved a disastrous recipe. Reliant on each other, our management objectives and resources should be shared universally between nations, and between peoples and their governments.

The poverty bomb

Haves and have-nots

The source of the North's affluence is much disputed, being variously attributed to industrialization, climatic factors and cultural values, as well as colonialism which transferred resources from the South to Europe and the US. In recent decades a form of neo-colonialism has become prominent. When Western banks found themselves in the 1970s with billions of petrodollars to invest, the developing world seemed to offer a good prospect. But no sooner had the loans been spent than commodity prices fell and interest rates rose. In 2001, developing countries owed more than $2.3 trillion in international debt. To pay interest on the loans, there has been a massive transfer of funds from the South to the North. The debt problem is akin to a blood transfusion from the sick to the healthy.

The working poor

More than half a billion people are classed as "$1-a-day working poor" and 1.4 billion as "$2-a-day working poor". Many endure long hours in difficult conditions, without basic rights or representation, and doing jobs that do not enable them to escape poverty for themselves and their families. It is "decent and productive" employment, not employment alone, that counts in reducing poverty. To achieve the Millennium Development Goal of cutting $1- and $2-a-day working poverty to half the 1990 levels by 2015, GDP growth would need to average 4.7% and 10.4 % respectively per year. The first target is possible, the second is not.

The mechanics of famine

While 800 million developing-world people are undernourished, there is not necessarily a link between severe malnutrition and food shortages. In Ethiopia and Bangladesh, for example, it has not so much been famine that has caused the poor to starve, but rather the inability of poor people to purchase what food was available. Most at risk have been the landless, plus the unskilled.

The plight of Africa

Particularly acute is the problem in Sub-Saharan Africa, where at least half of all people live in absolute poverty. Most are poorer and hungrier than forty years ago, making this a region of despair – and a region containing most of the world's least developed countries, i.e. those with per-capita GNI of $300 a year. During 1980–1990, the region's economy increased by an annual average of 1.6% and during 1990–2002 by 2.6%, though the surging increase in human numbers meant that per-capita growth of GNI was low in many countries. Today, the region has more than 11% of the global population but less than 1% of the global economy. If it is to achieve the UN target of halving the proportion of people in absolute poverty by 2015, its economic growth must rise from today's annual 3% to at least 7% throughout the period. This exceptional target will demand exceptional efforts, though given the experience of a number of "success story" countries such as Uganda it might just be within sight. The G8 "Africa Action Plan" includes developing a peacekeeping force, eradication of polio by 2005, improving global market access for African exports by tackling trade barriers and farm subsidies by 2005, and working towards more development aid on nations governing justly.

Power

Democratic franchise is generally denied to the homeless. The poor are simply powerless to represent themselves.

Credit

A few credit schemes have been set up for the urban poor. There is still little hope for those in remote rural regions.

Fuel

Almost 3 billion people worldwide rely on wood, charcoal, or other biomass (such as dung, crop residues) for energy. In many developing countries the search for fuelwood dominates daily life. Two billion people are without electricity.

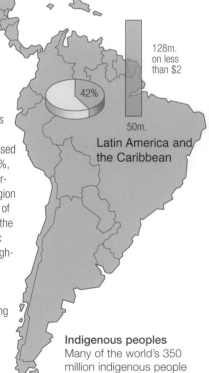

128m. on less than $2

50m.

42%

Latin America and the Caribbean

Indigenous peoples

Many of the world's 350 million indigenous people face increasing poverty.

93m. on less than $2
17m.

Eastern Europe and Central Asia
53%

The lighted fuse
The poverty bomb (left) has a multi-stranded fuse made up of population growth, political inequity, and environmental misuse.

Illiteracy
There are 800 million illiterate adults, almost all in the South with the majority being women (see p. 198).

The pattern of subsistence
A typical poor family lives in a hut or rudimentary house with little furniture, no electricity, and no sanitation or safe water. These people are generally subsistence farmers or lowly paid workers. Household chores, such as fetching water and fuelwood, often take hours every day. Poverty means that such people have little ability to dispute wage levels, crop prices, or interest rates.

Rich and Poor
The rich world's share of world population, 19%; share of CO_2, CFCs and other global pollutants, 70-87%. During the 1990s the 43 million additional Northerners polluted the world more than the 760 million additional Southerners.

Increasing debt
Brazil is the biggest debtor in the world. By 1990, it already owed $111 billion and by 2002 this had more than doubled to $228 billion. For millions of poverty-stricken Brazilians looking for jobs, in rural areas or crowded into the notorious shantytowns, the nation's economic crisis is a harsh, daily experience.

Needing shelter
One billion people are without adequate housing (see p. 187).

865m. on less than $2
271m.
East Asia 80%

7m.
70m. on less than $2
Middle East and North Africa 63%

1,064m. on less than $2
431m.

77%
South Asia

Millions of people living below $1-a-day poverty line in 2001, and equivalent figures for those living on less than $2 a day in 2001

Share of poor people living in rural areas

Income poverty
While a few newly industrialized countries have managed to make substantial progress, a sizeable sector of humanity enjoys little advance. Some are even going backwards, and many Africans are poorer today than in the 1960s. The world's total of $2-a-day poor has continued to rise from 2.6 billion in 1990 to 2.7 billion in 2001, while the number of $1-a-day poor has fallen little since 1990.

Some measures of poverty in developing countries
• One child in 11 dies before its fifth birthday.
• 115 million school-age children are not in school.
• Around 800 million people are undernourished – many are semi-starving.

516m. on less than $2
313m.
73%
Sub-Saharan Africa

Managing our Civilization

Coping with city chaos

The management of city problems cannot be separated from wider issues – of income distribution (both between social groups and between nations), the international economy, sustainable development, and human values. There may well be many innovative schemes to improve life in cities, but they nearly all hinge on economic strength, on cities having the resources, and the will, to pay for their infrastructure and services.

Developing countries are experiencing the 150-year-old rural exodus experienced in the North. This has brought people flooding into the cities in search of better opportunities, creating mega-cities with wealth and poverty living alongside one another. What the poor of developing world shantytowns lack most is a voice in city management, plus security of tenure for inhabitants who live in perpetual fear of eviction. Even the poorest settlement is bursting with human energy: the provision of cheap materials and tools would enable families to build and improve houses. Above all, safe water and sanitation are critical, plus the environmental controls needed to prevent pollution and uncontrolled dumping of waste. What is needed includes new affordable housing, more secure land tenure, and urban planning that is sensitive to the needs of the poorest and most vulnerable sections of society.

Much of this can be done only with government backing, and within the framework of national development, since plans must strike a balance between the interests of the city and the countryside. Holding down food prices in towns, for example, may upset the rural economy; then even greater numbers of rural poor flock to the cities, swelling the shantytowns. Improving city health care, schools, transport, and other services should not be achieved at the expense of the countryside. In some developing countries, rural land reform and agricultural development have helped slow down the stampede to cities, as well as improved food supply.

Ultimately, much depends on national priorities. The question applies just as much in the North, where financial constraints are far less acute. Northern cities, too, require investment for development, plus grants, loan-credit schemes and enterprise zones to attract new business.

Encouraging a dialogue between city officials and shantytown dwellers can produce better initiatives than top-down planning. Redirected, local skills and organization can carry out low-cost schemes on a large scale. Establishing local administrative

Urban regeneration

Towards sustainability in the South

The city of Curitiba has been referred to as the "ecological capital of Brazil." Three decades ago the city launched a plan to address urban issues, focusing on environmentally friendly public transport and social programmes. There was then less than one sq. m of green space per person but today a network of parks and wooded areas, and more than one million trees planted along city streets, mean there is 50 times as much. Incentives encourage green space in new building projects. Most important of all, an all-bus transit network with allocated lanes encourages people to leave their cars in the garage (despite the city having one car for every three people). More than 2 million passengers a day travel by these buses, encouraged by cheap "one-rate" fares covering up to 70 km and helping poor people commute from the outskirts. A "green exchange" programme turns garbage into bus tickets or food, and children can exchange recyclable garbage for school supplies. Almost three-quarters of the city's trash is recycled. Paper recycling alone saves the equivalent of 1,200 trees a day. Not only does the environment benefit, so do the residents with funds going to social programmes as well as employment schemes for the homeless in garbage separation plants. The city's Open University runs low-cost courses for would-be mechanics, hairstylists, and conservationists. Curitiba is an inspiration for urban regeneration everywhere.

Towards sustainability in the North

The slum clearance and building boom of the 1960s and 1970s are over. All too evident are the human costs of uprooting communities to rehouse them in socially and constructionally inappropriate high-rise blocks. Gradual renewal of our decaying city centres has since taken place through re-use of existing structures plus more sensitive architecture. We now have much experience of urban regeneration in various guises, some of which have worked well. One Planet Living Communities highlight principles such as zero waste, zero carbon (from fossil fuels), energy efficiency, eco-agriculture, wildlife habitats, fair trade products, and sustainability all round. Find out more from WWF-UK.

Urban employment

The huge informal economy of many of the South's largest cities (between 40% and 60% of the total economy) is a major provider of jobs and at present receives negligible support through government credit. There is much demand for loans and sites for small businesses, for the establishment of credit union savings, and vocational training for the urban poor. Microcredit schemes are being supported by e.g. Bangladesh's Grameen Bank (see pp. 250–51).

Targeting the inner city

Bringing the decaying areas of older cities back to life typically requires a multi-pronged approach, with inputs of private, voluntary, and official effort. The rehabilitation of usable existing housing is matched by small "in-fill" schemes of new homes which are harmonized with the existing street architecture. The conversion and re-use of obsolete industrial buildings provide space for small workshops and businesses, or for commercial or community centres from markets to sports halls. Local employment projects and light-industry units help to revitalize the community, which also needs new open spaces, communal facilities and environmental improvements, from pedestrian or limited car access schemes to tree planting and gardens. Based on these approaches, the "village in the city" is emerging all over Europe, and the US.

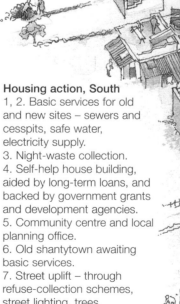

Housing action, South

1, 2. Basic services for old and new sites – sewers and cesspits, safe water, electricity supply.
3. Night-waste collection.
4. Self-help house building, aided by long-term loans, and backed by government grants and development agencies.
5. Community centre and local planning office.
6. Old shantytown awaiting basic services.
7. Street uplift – through refuse-collection schemes, street lighting, trees.
8. Improved market area with new well.

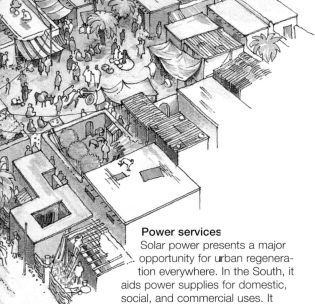

Renewing a community in the North

The "gradual renewal" strategy was applied to a Victorian area of a UK city (left). The city government worked with housing agencies and cooperatives to repair the most damaged properties. Improvement grants help upgrade the area, while community employment and environmental schemes inject new life. Home improvement packages for housing focus on structural repair, economical use of energy, better insulation and more efficient washing/hygiene facilities.

Housing action, North

1. Newly built community centre and day nursery run by local people.
2. Modern infill housing for sale, supported by low-cost home ownership scheme.
3, 4, 5. Renovation – through improvement grants for private owners, or undertaken by non-profit agency, or city government.
6. New extensions for bathrooms and kitchens.
7. Street uplift – speed humps, controlled parking, landscaping.
8. Community art – murals decorating blank walls; painted by community artist and local children.
9. Corner shops retained for local shopping – also for use as Neighbourhood Office of city government.
10. New neighbourhood park with children's playground.
11. Unimproved terrace awaiting action.
12. Small workshop development for locally based employment.
13. Local bus transport.
14. Waste recycling points.

Urban transportation

Some cities have more people than entire countries. One of the challenges facing our rapidly expanding cities is how to solve the problem of urban transportation and all its harmful externalities such as air pollution and congestion – both of which are a major drag on urban economies both North and South. Until recently Bangkok's drivers faced 44 days a year stuck in traffic. Fortunately, new congestion-relieving measures are being introduced such as flyovers, underpasses, expressways, and mass transit routes. London's £5 "congestion charge", covering a 21-sq. km central-city area, was introduced in 2003 because traffic often moved no faster than during horse-drawn carriage times. One year later traffic had been cut by 18% and delays by 30%.

Community participation

A Kenyan community group, Abalimi Bezekhaya, promotes and facilitates urban food gardens for slum residents. Non-profit garden centers provide low-cost resources such as seed, tools and pest control, while partnerships with schools, youth clubs and community gardens have helped to improve open spaces and support urban farming.

Renewing a community in the South

In 1987, Bob Munro, a Canadian environmentalist, created the Mathare Youth Sports Association (MYSA), which uses sport to empower more than 16,000 youths from the Mathare Valley. the valley is Nairobi's biggest shantytown with at least half a million people, where people often queue at 3 a.m. to get water from public standpipes and to use the public lavatories. Most young men are unemployed. 70% of the population are working mothers and their children. MYSA links sports participation to community services ranging from cleaning up the streets to helping children. It has become the largest youth sports organization in Africa with 25 football teams for boys and girls. Such is its success that MYSA has been nominated for the Nobel Peace Prize.

Southern city regeneration

Whenever cityward migrations have reached unusual proportions, conventional housing and infrastructure services have been hard-pressed to cope. The one billion people worldwide now crowding into slums and squatter settlements cannot afford even the simplest permanent housing schemes. Authorities are forced to tackle only the most basic provision themselves, letting the settlers do the rest, with minimal aid. Just one of their intractable problems is that of water supply which is often privately owned – and very scarce. The most urgent need is for greater rural investment, to slow the flood to the cities.

South Africa's government has attempted to address the slum problem by using a combination of the private sector and the poor themselves. Income-earners contribute towards the cost of improvements, and the unemployed contribute "sweat equity" building new housing and services with their own hands. There is much to be done. As in the North, community involvement and leadership are critical. But all these efforts must go hand-in-hand with better employment opportunities to generate income.

Power services

Solar power presents a major opportunity for urban regeneration everywhere. In the South, it aids power supplies for domestic, social, and commercial uses. It brings power and the Internet to schoolchildren. In the North, it is often built into new housing and commercial developments.

centres helps to focus community spirit and allows a measure of self-management.

UN-HABITAT's Sustainable Cities Programmes lists projects underway in a number of countries – China, Chile, Ecuador, Egypt, Ghana, India, Malawi, Nigeria, the Philippines, Poland, Russia, Senegal, Sri Lanka, Tanzania, Tunisia, and Zambia. In the North, over 2,000 local and regional authorities from 42 countries have signed up to the Charter of European Cities and Towns Towards Sustainability, the 1994 Aalborg Charter.

Strategies for communication

The ability to communicate and share a huge reservoir of human knowledge has never been greater. The new information and communications technologies (ICT) have revolutionized the way we learn, speak, and think. Advanced ICT offers immense power to assist the development process. It has been used to control locust damage in Africa; to exploit rangelands in Kenya; and to understand the humid tropical forests of Peru. It helps in the conservation of wildlife, the design of road and rail networks, mineral prospecting, weather forecasting, and in warning of famine. In addition, satellite technology fosters education and transmits medical, nutritional, and agricultural advice to isolated communities.

If the communications revolution is to benefit everyone, we must make the technology more widely available. We need to aim for universal access to information by establishing a diversity of information sources and achieve far greater partici-pation in the transmission of ideas. Huge libraries of information via the Internet and worldwide web can now be made available at the touch of a few keys and can go far to reduce the information gap between South and North. Best of all, the communications revolution can break the informa-tion monopolies. Many government departments now make data freely available via the Internet, though many others still practise censorship. ICT has created a far greater diversity in the media as cable television, video/DVD, home PCs and soft-ware programs provide an immense choice, like books on a library shelf.

As for the longer-term future, the entire role of communications needs to move to a full dialogue between North and South in order that the current information advantage of the rich countries can be somewhat shared with the rest of the world. Better communication of ideas and information is a vital key to the management of our global crises. At present, there are many voices – of minorities and of other communities outside the communications network – that go unheard. Getting access to the medium as well as the message is particularly important in the South, which also needs to benefit from the abundance of information collected about Southern resources from Northern satellites.

The will to communicate

Thanks to the power of communications (see pp. 218–19), this is a time when everybody can be somebody and nobody need be nobody. Given the technology, we can now operate as fully fledged citizens of one great global community and make common cause with people round the back of the world – especially the cause of humankind's future. We can voice our opinions, we can share our views and we can plan action together. The Internet has created "virtual nations" with no limitations of space and time, no political boundaries, no territorial frontiers, no social differences – in fact none of the traditional divisions that separate old-style nations. The Internet makes the nation-state system seem so last century. As has been graphically stated in an article on virtual nations (The Futurist, 2002) "Posing a direct challenge to the world's existing nations, v-nations will be both the cause and effect of a monumental shift in global economic, political, and social structures. These new nations will at once threaten and stimulate hope for worldwide cooperation, security and use of resources."

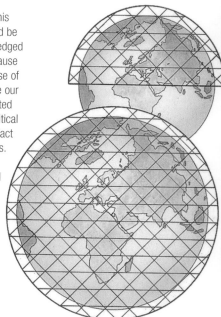

Extending the network

Access to information technology

Sharing technology regionally offers independence while reducing costs. If developing countries are to make full use of information gathered by satellites or collected in data banks, they need the capacity to process and analyse the information. Multinational corporations could assist by setting up local data-processing industries in the South to share their skills, technology, and data with the host community.

Reversing the flow

From a global viewpoint, news coverage and analysis of events in the South are as important to the North as vice versa. The Panos Institute, with centres worldwide, has established regional partner-ships to strengthen the skills of media and private groups in the South. The Inter Press Service was started in 1964 by a group of journalists writing about problems in Latin America and now covers 120 countries. This global news agency produces news and analysis of global processes "affecting the economic, social and political development of peoples and nations, especially in the South."

Early satellites for education in India

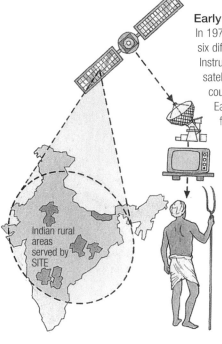

In 1975, satellite broadcasts reached 24,000 villages in six different states. The joint Indian–American Satellite Instructional Television Experiment (SITE) used the ATS-6 satellite provided by NASA and demonstrated that India could manufacture and maintain both the required Earth stations and the community receiving sets in far-off villages. The communities, many of whom had never seen TV, showed large gains in knowl-edge about health and hygiene, family planning and political awareness. The experiment also gave experience in designing programmes for widely spread areas with different languages and prob-lems. Satellite TV broadcasts became immensely valuable to developing countries where they could reach rural communities with information and education.

Indian rural areas served by SITE

Breaking the monopolies

The information pool once held chiefly by governments and multinational corporations gave them massive power. They decided what data the satellites should collect and they maintained control of the media. Properly managed, communications can prevent abuse and encourage public participation in government processes. Opening the sluice-gates of the monopolies' dam (inset below) through the ICT revolution has released a vast reservoir of information. Government and corporate accountability is now becoming the norm in many nations.

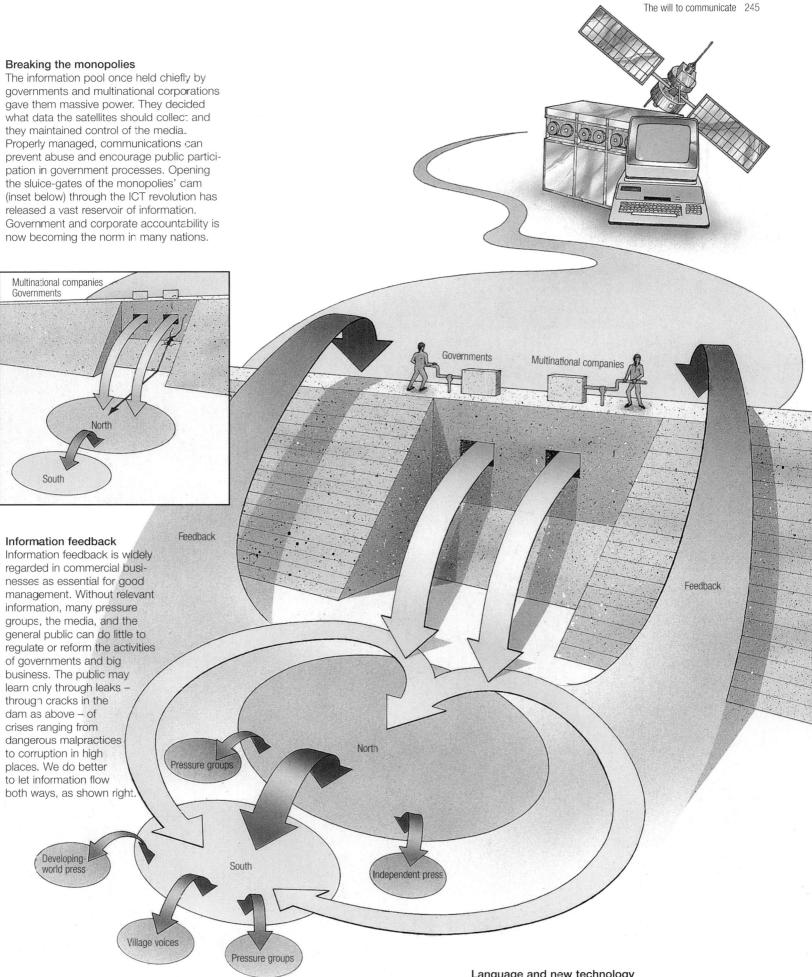

Information feedback

Information feedback is widely regarded in commercial businesses as essential for good management. Without relevant information, many pressure groups, the media, and the general public can do little to regulate or reform the activities of governments and big business. The public may learn only through leaks – through cracks in the dam as above – of crises ranging from dangerous malpractices to corruption in high places. We do better to let information flow both ways, as shown right.

Independent media

Today's media promotes, in Alvin Toffler's phrase, the "demassification of society", discouraging tight control while broadcasting minority views.

Village access

At grassroots level, communications need not demand advanced technologies. A small 500-watt transmitter powered by two heavy-duty car batteries can broadcast over a range of 20 km. Local newspapers can be launched cheaply too. Such services not only provide information of all kinds, they stimulate communications skills.

Language and new technology

For most of human history, languages have diverged and multiplied as human groups have dispersed and developed different identities. The mass media have tended to standardize and to strengthen official languages. We can now support language diversity through cable TV and the Internet. While English-speakers comprised more than one-third of the online population in 2004, Chinese comprised 14%, Spanish 9%, Japanese 8%, German 7%, and Korean, Italian, and French each around 4%.

Towards new technologies

The technologies developed by the North since the Industrial Revolution can sometimes seem like a Pandora's box of mischief and sorrow, accompanied by forlorn hope. Many of the latest fruits of our supposed civilization fly in the face of conventional wisdom and humanitarian concern. For instance, the latest refinements in missiles of destruction, nuclear experiments, and the debate over the scientific use of human embryos, all raise questions about science and human needs. On occasion, modern technology can even be seen as a means of magnifying the chasm between the world's elite and the poor majority, enabling Northern governments and businesses to exercise undue control.

Of course no technology is intrinsically wrong. Like information, it often depends on who pulls the strings. Scientific research and development have produced stunning solutions to disease and food shortages. The benefits of satellites have been applied to communications in both the North and the South. The immediate issue is not only the nature of some of our "advances", but the sharing of technological control. As the Brandt Commission concluded way back in 1970, "It can even be argued that their [the developing countries'] principal weakness is the lack of access to technology."

This imbalance is reflected through many of the technologies transferred, including those for nuclear power and weaponry. Some technologies have

The technology circuit

Technology no longer flows in one direction insofar as the "current" can be reversed. Technology transfer is becoming a dialogue. As developing-world governments and tribal communities discover the value of their knowledge, it becomes a potent commodity. The knowledge held in shamens' huts and in traditional farming communities may often prove as vital to planetary well-being as that held in Northern laboratories.

Technology transfer

Technology is transmitted through e.g. publications, personal exchanges, development aid, and outright piracy. Mostly it is transferred commercially. More attention needs to be paid to the usefulness of the technologies transferred to the South, to ensure that they are not, unwittingly, a Trojan Horse, bringing unsuspected political, social and environmental problems in their wake. At present the rate of transfer from the North is lamentably slow. We need to accelerate transfer, build up Southern R & D, nurture new skills, and lift those information controls that impede the sharing process.

Southern technology impetus

Targeting the South's "technofamine" requires inputs from both North and South. A small fraction of current Northern R & D spending is focused on problems in the South (much more is devoted to defence and space research). In order to build up R & D capacity by the South and for the South, governments and Southern businesses should persuade multinational corporations and academia to play a more supportive role in North–South relations. When university curricula are enabled to reflect specifically Southern needs, they can expand existing schemes for bringing technology right down to the village level, as in the case of India's Peoples' Science movements.

Technology and (mis)development

Not only is technology globalizing communications, but globalization itself, together with its new rules, is shaping the path of new technologies. These twin processes have fostered increasing privatization of R & D, plus ever-more liberalization of markets and a general tightening of intellectual property rights. These three factors have triggered a contest to "privatize knowledge", and as a downside result the South's interests are being systematically discounted. These regrettable trends are far from inevitable. To cite the United Nations Development Programme, "The technology divide does not have to follow the income divide". Throughout history, technology has been a powerful tool for human development and poverty relief.

Accelerating technology

Today's technological advances are rapid indeed. The power of a computer chip doubles every 18 months. The cost of one megabit of storage fell from over $5,000 in 1970 to $0.17 in 1999. In like manner, the Internet is breaking centuries-old barriers of geography by opening up more markets, by creating scope for widespread income generation, and by enabling increased local participation.

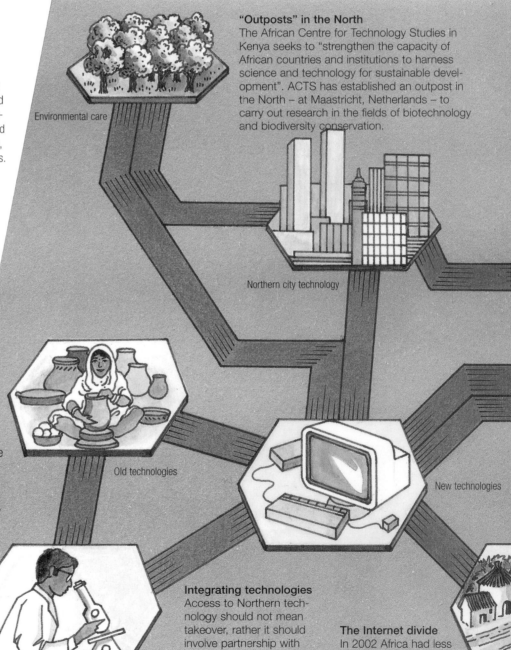

"Outposts" in the North
The African Centre for Technology Studies in Kenya seeks to "strengthen the capacity of African countries and institutions to harness science and technology for sustainable development". ACTS has established an outpost in the North – at Maastricht, Netherlands – to carry out research in the fields of biotechnology and biodiversity conservation.

Environmental care

Northern city technology

Old technologies

New technologies

Research and Development

Integrating technologies
Access to Northern technology should not mean takeover, rather it should involve partnership with traditional techniques. The World Health Organization has promoted a marriage of traditional and Western medicine in China and Vietnam.

The Internet divide
In 2002 Africa had less than 2% of the world's 815 million Internet users and Latin America/the Caribbean 7%, while Europe and North America both had 28%.

Advances in the North

Having experienced some of the worst ill effects of industrialization, Northerners are leading the way in environmental protection, pollution control, decentralizing information, and exploration of renewable energy sources. Opportunities abound under the Kyoto Protocol's "Clean Development Mechanism" (see pp. 144–45) for development of high-tech renewables in developing countries, many of which are richly endowed with sunlight, wind, or ocean currents/flows, but lack the investment funds required.

proved expensive, and almost useless or even harmful in the South, despite the myriad efforts of organizations which develop "appropriate" technologies, a concept envisaged by the late E. F. Schumacher (see below).

Fortunately, a number of international agencies are taking a growing interest in the social, economic and environmental implications of technology transfer. The International Labour Organization, for example, has conducted a worldwide programme of research on the blending of emerging technologies (notably solar energy, micro-electronics, biotechnology, and new materials) with the traditional technologies of the South. A range of pioneer projects explore technological fusions that could boost

productivity and competitiveness, without causing unemployment or other dislocations.

We should be en route to a polytechnical world, with space-age know-how partnering traditional technologies, with high and low technologies operating together, and with labour-intensive techniques taking their appropriate places. But these developments should be conditioned by a planet-wide perception of our technologies as double-edged swords. We need to concentrate on resource efficiency, pollution control and environmental safeguards. In short, we need a Gaian technology that is sustainable, energy efficient, diverse, non-toxic, peaceful, and people centred. Yes, all of that!

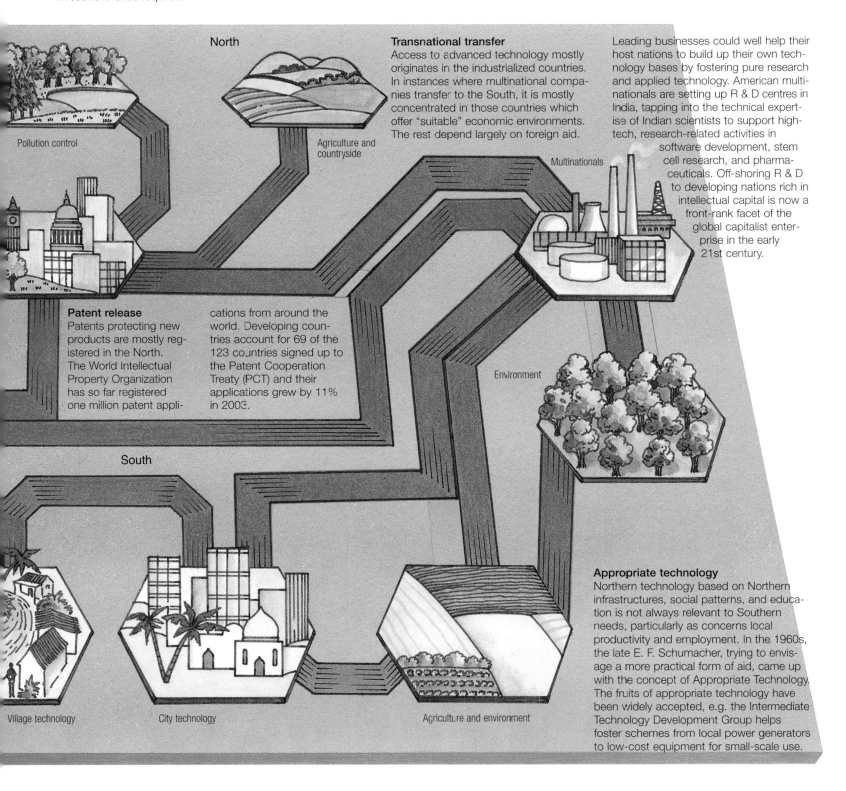

North

Transnational transfer
Access to advanced technology mostly originates in the industrialized countries. In instances where multinational companies transfer to the South, it is mostly concentrated in those countries which offer "suitable" economic environments. The rest depend largely on foreign aid.

Leading businesses could well help their host nations to build up their own technology bases by fostering pure research and applied technology. American multinationals are setting up R & D centres in India, tapping into the technical expertise of Indian scientists to support high-tech, research-related activities in software development, stem cell research, and pharmaceuticals. Off-shoring R & D to developing nations rich in intellectual capital is now a front-rank facet of the global capitalist enterprise in the early 21st century.

Pollution control

Agriculture and countryside

Multinationals

Patent release
Patents protecting new products are mostly registered in the North. The World Intellectual Property Organization has so far registered one million patent applications from around the world. Developing countries account for 69 of the 123 countries signed up to the Patent Cooperation Treaty (PCT) and their applications grew by 11% in 2003.

Environment

South

Village technology

City technology

Agriculture and environment

Appropriate technology
Northern technology based on Northern infrastructures, social patterns, and education is not always relevant to Southern needs, particularly as concerns local productivity and employment. In the 1960s, the late E. F. Schumacher, trying to envisage a more practical form of aid, came up with the concept of Appropriate Technology. The fruits of appropriate technology have been widely accepted, e.g. the Intermediate Technology Development Group helps foster schemes from local power generators to low-cost equipment for small-scale use.

Trade and development

Most attempts to redress the world's many inter-locking crises are threatened by the current market crisis. Any solution to the growing global economic malaise generally involve a recognition of the interdependence of North and South, both in establishing demand and in sharing the means of supplying it. A range of possible approaches to this end is being proposed, three of which merit discussion. They can be summarized as "the market knows best", "the market should change", and "the South must delink its markets from those of the North".

The "marketeers" view the basic problem as excessive government interference which has prevented the proper functioning of the market. Price controls, protectionism, and subsidies have given the wrong signals to entrepreneurs, leading to misallocation of resources. Marketeers think in terms of a development "continuum" running from the poorest to the wealthiest countries, with the implication that the poorest can pull themselves up by their bootstraps.

In contrast, the "reformers", whose views have been convincingly stated in the Brandt Commission Report, argue that nations do not compete as equals, and that global measures are needed to mobilize the weaker nations. Even if the free market could bring benefits to the poor, this would take too long.

The "delinkers" are essentially a coalition of those who have been disillusioned by failures to win reforms and those who believe that the internatio-nal capitalist system, whether reformed or not, is inimical to the interests of the developing countries. Some delinkers would go for a total delinking of the South from the rich economies of the North, while others would prefer to see a greater stimulation of South–South trade and cooperation. Some also believe that this approach would ultimately benefit the North too. While the Northern share of trade would be proportionately smaller, the global economic "cake" would be bigger.

Until the early 1980s the reformers represented the biggest constituency, whereas the centre of gravity has recently shifted towards market-oriented solutions. The prospect of continuing economic problems, with erratic growth rates in the North and protracted debt problems in the South, suggests that the plight of the South could well deteriorate further.

There is a growing consensus that any attempt to manage the global market in its present state must take a somewhat pragmatic approach by combining market solutions, with Brandt-style reforms and greater cooperation between developing countries. Success will increasingly depend on a willingness to dispense with economic dogma and to experiment with alternative management approaches.

Growing interdependence

Some Northerners believe that they can get along without the South. They are mistaken. The North needs the fuel, minerals, and foodstuffs it imports from the South, as well as the cash it earns from exporting goods and skills. Some 40% of all North American exports of manufactured goods go to developing countries, 60% of Japan's. If demand falls in the South, the effects are soon felt in the North. North and South often like to imagine that they are separate, but while self-sufficiency may be appropriate in some cases, at the global level it's interdependence that counts.

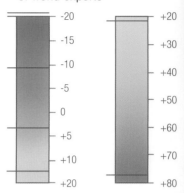

Scales showing percentage change in regions' shares of world exports

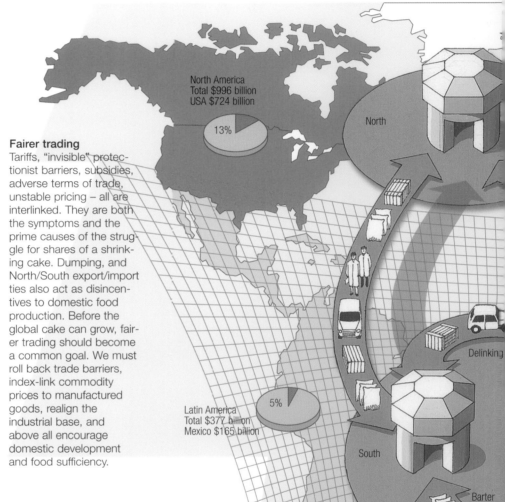

Fairer trading
Tariffs, "invisible" protec-tionist barriers, subsidies, adverse terms of trade, unstable pricing – all are interlinked. They are both the symptoms and the prime causes of the strug-gle for shares of a shrink-ing cake. Dumping, and North/South export/import ties also act as disincen-tives to domestic food production. Before the global cake can grow, fair-er trading should become a common goal. We must roll back trade barriers, index-link commodity prices to manufactured goods, realign the industrial base, and above all encourage domestic development and food sufficiency.

Sharing the bigger cake
Present world trade includes a little known sector – barter, which, broadly defined, may account for a growing share of world trade. "Pure barter" is when a commodity, e.g. rubber, is exchanged for cocoa beans, timber for transport equipment, and just about anything for oil. Most of this trade takes place between develop-ing countries, who lack the foreign exchange to employ conventional trade methods. "Counter-trade" commits the seller to take goods from the purchaser in return. "Buyback" commits the seller of a production facility to purchase some of the output of that facility.

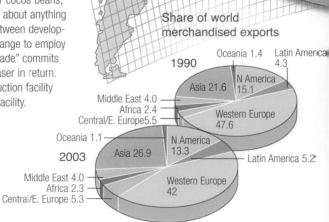

Share of world merchandised exports

1990
Oceania 1.4   Latin America 4.3
Asia 21.6   N America 15.1
Middle East 4.0
Africa 2.4
Central/E. Europe 5.5
Western Europe 47.6

2003
Oceania 1.1
Asia 26.9   N America 13.3
Middle East 4.0
Africa 2.3
Central/E. Europe 5.3
Western Europe 42
Latin America 5.2

Trade 1990–2003

The developing countries' share of world merchandised exports has increased steadily, and stood at 29% in 2003. Remarkable growth has occurred in China, with exports increasing from $62 billion to $440 billion. In the developed world, North America's share declined slightly to 13%. Of the top exporters in 2003, Germany and the US were in the lead with 10% each, followed by Japan and China with 6%. Russia, the only East European country in the top 30, had less than 2%. Manufactures comprise almost three-quarters of world merchandised trade, agricultural products, 9%, and mining products, 13%.

Delinking the South from the North

The traditional market structure established during the colonial period is changing fast – hence the rash of "new protectionism". Some economists, however, argue that the North, in order to maintain its position, must keep the poorer South in a state of "economic servitude" – and will never voluntarily reform the biased market. The only hope for the South, some believe, is a complete "delinking" of its economy from that of the North, and freedom from the stranglehold of international capitalism.

The benefits of trade

Over the past two decades world trade has averaged 6% growth per year, twice as fast as world output. Intra-developing world trade has grown most rapidly, with almost 40% of their exports now going to other developing countries, up from just 28% in 1990. Opening up their economies has been essential in enabling many countries to develop comparative advantages in the manufacture of certain products. In these "new globalizer" countries (as the World Bank calls them) absolute poverty declined by over 120 million people between 1993 and 1998. The benefits of trade liberalization can exceed the costs by more than a factor of 10. Estimates of the gains from eliminating all barriers to merchandise trade range between $250 billion and $680 billion per year. Two-thirds of these gains would likely accrue to industrial countries.

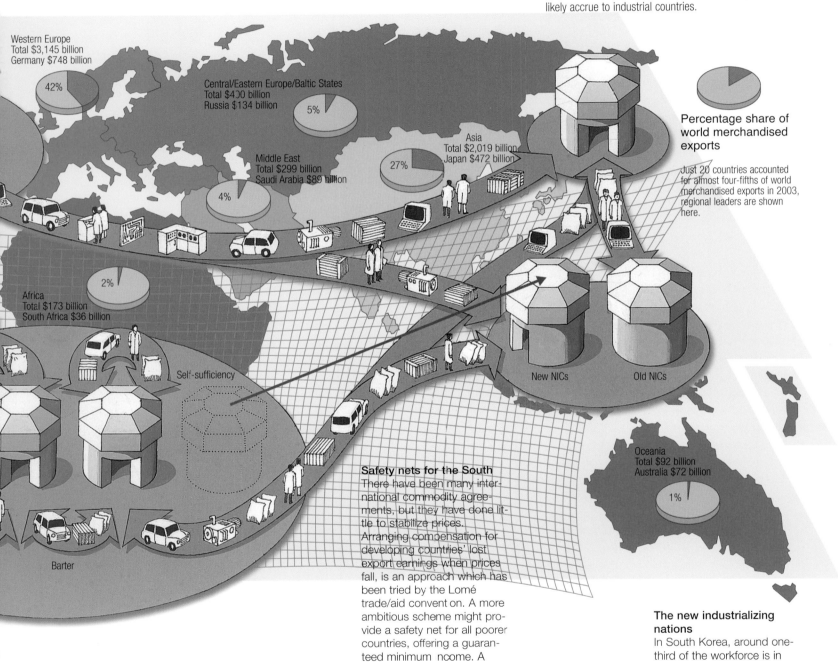

Western Europe
Total $3,145 billion
Germany $748 billion
42%

Central/Eastern Europe/Baltic States
Total $400 billion
Russia $134 billion
5%

Middle East
Total $299 billion
Saudi Arabia $89 billion
4%

Asia
Total $2,019 billion
Japan $472 billion
27%

Africa
Total $173 billion
South Africa $36 billion
2%

Self-sufficiency

Barter

New NICs

Old NICs

Oceania
Total $92 billion
Australia $72 billion
1%

Percentage share of world merchandised exports

Just 20 countries accounted for almost four-fifths of world merchandised exports in 2003, regional leaders are shown here.

Self-reliance and South–South trade

Despite recent increases, South–South trade remains at a lower level than common sense would dictate. In 1990, it accounted for 28% of developing countries' total merchandised exports. By 2001, it reached 37%. Among the reasons: prejudice against so-called "second best" products made by other developing countries; and poor transport and communications links. Worse, many developing nations tend to produce competing rather than complementary products, while the rich markets of the North offer a better return. A system of generalized tariff preferences would help compensate for Northern trade barriers.

Safety nets for the South

There have been many international commodity agreements, but they have done little to stabilize prices. Arranging compensation for developing countries' lost export earnings when prices fall, is an approach which has been tried by the Lomé trade/aid convention. A more ambitious scheme might provide a safety net for all poorer countries, offering a guaranteed minimum income. A Common Fund for the South is also mooted. Producers and consumers of the top commodities exported by low-income countries could contribute to a central financing facility, buying up surpluses and so maintaining prices at an agreed stable level.

The new industrializing nations

In South Korea, around one-third of the workforce is in manufacturing, wage rates are rising, and the service sector is growing. A second wave of low-wage nations is taking over the labour-intensive products, among them India and China. Asia exported 29% of world manufactures in 2003, cf. Western Europe, 47%.

Managing the world's wealth

For the last two centuries there has been a widening gap between the rich countries of the so-called North and much of Africa, Asia, and Latin America. By the middle of the 1800s, the difference in per-capita income was about two to one. During the last century the divergence increased, particularly since the 1950s. In the 1960s, the emphasis of economic experts was on rapid economic growth for those above poverty in the belief that the benefits would "trickle down" to the poor at the bottom of the pile. By the early 1970s, however, it was clear that this would achieve too little, too late. A seminal speech in 1973 by Robert McNamara, then President of the World Bank, signalled a switch to "growth with redistribution", aiming to ensure that the poor shared directly in the benefits of development through measures such as land reform, improved access to credit facilities, and projects providing jobs and adequate incomes to the landless and unskilled.

A key element in this new approach was focusing aid on education, health care, and training programmes for the poor, plus the "basic needs" strategy together with integrated rural development. These fine ambitions were all overtaken, however, by the early 1980s global recession. As one poor country after another ran into debt and balance-of-payments problems, so they were forced to cut social services, wages and imports and switch finances instead to fund their exports.

While a few newly industrializing countries have managed to make substantial progress, a sizeable sector of humanity enjoys little progress. Some are even going backwards; most would take hundreds of years to close the gap with the North. One in six of humankind falls below the income threshold necessary for the most meagre existence.

If there is to be any hope of reducing poverty, a massive effort is required across a broad front. It will involve reforms in trade and financial systems, with far-reaching policies promoting income redistribution at the most localized level. We need to redesign the international economic system to provide poor nations with a fair return on their exports and the means to invest in the sustainable development of their natural resources. All this should be backed by aid programmes geared to equitable development and reduced poverty. Voting power within the IMF needs to reflect more fairly the interests of both North and South, and to foster reform of loan conditions.

The most far-reaching proposals to the gap crisis include measures such as a tax on arms spending which totalled $880 billion in 2003 – nearly 13 times more than foreign aid. A 5 percent tax would yield $44 billion. If diverted to ODA it would still be short of the 0.7 percent of donor GDP target first agreed in 1970. Third World poverty is a luxury we can no longer afford.

Closing the gap

GDP per-capita growth, 1990-2001

- Less than 0.0%
- 0.09%
- 1.0–1.9%
- 2.0–2.9%
- 3.0 or more
- No data

Net foreign aid received
(US$ billions 2002)

Net foreign aid given
by rich countries
(US$ millions 2002)

Foreign direct investment

FDI can assist in technology transfer, job creation, and increased productivity, thus boosting exports and GDP. Foreign affiliates of the world's 64,000 transnational corporations generated 54 million jobs by 2003 – double that of 1990.

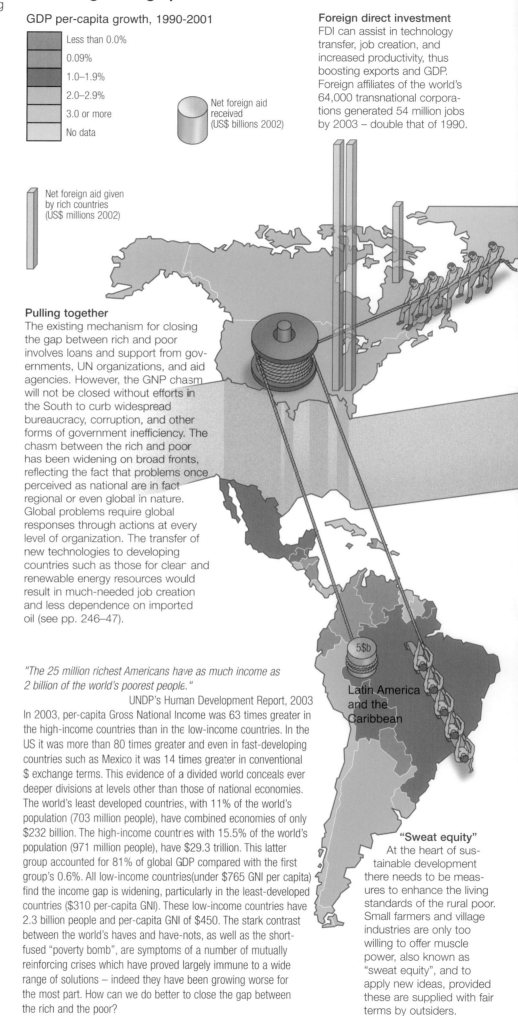

Pulling together

The existing mechanism for closing the gap between rich and poor involves loans and support from governments, UN organizations, and aid agencies. However, the GNP chasm will not be closed without efforts in the South to curb widespread bureaucracy, corruption, and other forms of government inefficiency. The chasm between the rich and poor has been widening on broad fronts, reflecting the fact that problems once perceived as national are in fact regional or even global in nature. Global problems require global responses through actions at every level of organization. The transfer of new technologies to developing countries such as those for clean and renewable energy resources would result in much-needed job creation and less dependence on imported oil (see pp. 246–47).

5$b

Latin America and the Caribbean

"The 25 million richest Americans have as much income as 2 billion of the world's poorest people."
UNDP's Human Development Report, 2003

In 2003, per-capita Gross National Income was 63 times greater in the high-income countries than in the low-income countries. In the US it was more than 80 times greater and even in fast-developing countries such as Mexico it was 14 times greater in conventional $ exchange terms. This evidence of a divided world conceals ever deeper divisions at levels other than those of national economies. The world's least developed countries, with 11% of the world's population (703 million people), have combined economies of only $232 billion. The high-income countries with 15.5% of the world's population (971 million people), have $29.3 trillion. This latter group accounted for 81% of global GDP compared with the first group's 0.6%. All low-income countries(under $765 GNI per capita) find the income gap is widening, particularly in the least-developed countries ($310 per-capita GNI). These low-income countries have 2.3 billion people and per-capita GNI of $450. The stark contrast between the world's haves and have-nots, as well as the short-fused "poverty bomb", are symptoms of a number of mutually reinforcing crises which have proved largely immune to a wide range of solutions – indeed they have been growing worse for the most part. How can we do better to close the gap between the rich and the poor?

"Sweat equity"

At the heart of sustainable development there needs to be measures to enhance the living standards of the rural poor. Small farmers and village industries are only too willing to offer muscle power, also known as "sweat equity", and to apply new ideas, provided these are supplied with fair terms by outsiders.

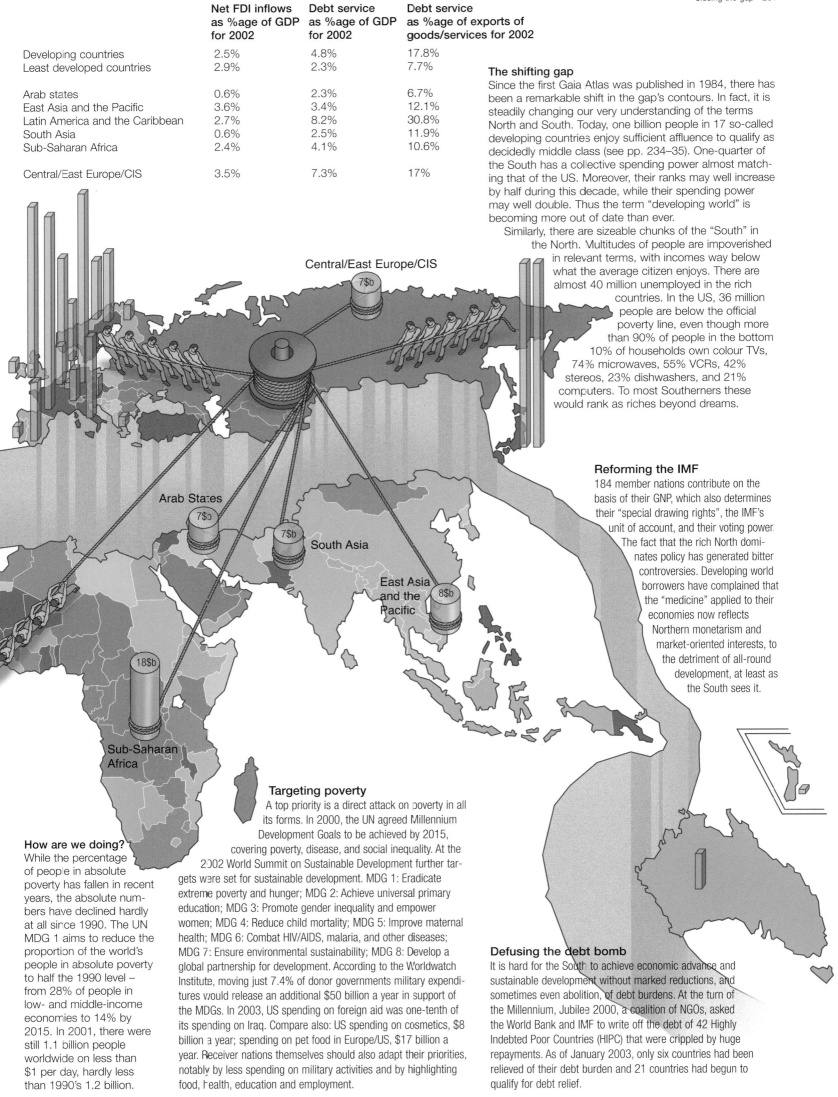

	Net FDI inflows as %age of GDP for 2002	Debt service as %age of GDP for 2002	Debt service as %age of exports of goods/services for 2002
Developing countries	2.5%	4.8%	17.8%
Least developed countries	2.9%	2.3%	7.7%
Arab states	0.6%	2.3%	6.7%
East Asia and the Pacific	3.6%	3.4%	12.1%
Latin America and the Caribbean	2.7%	8.2%	30.8%
South Asia	0.6%	2.5%	11.9%
Sub-Saharan Africa	2.4%	4.1%	10.6%
Central/East Europe/CIS	3.5%	7.3%	17%

The shifting gap

Since the first Gaia Atlas was published in 1984, there has been a remarkable shift in the gap's contours. In fact, it is steadily changing our very understanding of the terms North and South. Today, one billion people in 17 so-called developing countries enjoy sufficient affluence to qualify as decidedly middle class (see pp. 234–35). One-quarter of the South has a collective spending power almost matching that of the US. Moreover, their ranks may well increase by half during this decade, while their spending power may well double. Thus the term "developing world" is becoming more out of date than ever.

Similarly, there are sizeable chunks of the "South" in the North. Multitudes of people are impoverished in relevant terms, with incomes way below what the average citizen enjoys. There are almost 40 million unemployed in the rich countries. In the US, 36 million people are below the official poverty line, even though more than 90% of people in the bottom 10% of households own colour TVs, 74% microwaves, 55% VCRs, 42% stereos, 23% dishwashers, and 21% computers. To most Southerners these would rank as riches beyond dreams.

Reforming the IMF

184 member nations contribute on the basis of their GNP, which also determines their "special drawing rights", the IMF's unit of account, and their voting power. The fact that the rich North dominates policy has generated bitter controversies. Developing world borrowers have complained that the "medicine" applied to their economies now reflects Northern monetarism and market-oriented interests, to the detriment of all-round development, at least as the South sees it.

How are we doing?

While the percentage of people in absolute poverty has fallen in recent years, the absolute numbers have declined hardly at all since 1990. The UN MDG 1 aims to reduce the proportion of the world's people in absolute poverty to half the 1990 level – from 28% of people in low- and middle-income economies to 14% by 2015. In 2001, there were still 1.1 billion people worldwide on less than $1 per day, hardly less than 1990's 1.2 billion.

Targeting poverty

A top priority is a direct attack on poverty in all its forms. In 2000, the UN agreed Millennium Development Goals to be achieved by 2015, covering poverty, disease, and social inequality. At the 2002 World Summit on Sustainable Development further targets were set for sustainable development. MDG 1: Eradicate extreme poverty and hunger; MDG 2: Achieve universal primary education; MDG 3: Promote gender inequality and empower women; MDG 4: Reduce child mortality; MDG 5: Improve maternal health; MDG 6: Combat HIV/AIDS, malaria, and other diseases; MDG 7: Ensure environmental sustainability; MDG 8: Develop a global partnership for development. According to the Worldwatch Institute, moving just 7.4% of donor governments military expenditures would release an additional $50 billion a year in support of the MDGs. In 2003, US spending on foreign aid was one-tenth of its spending on Iraq. Compare also: US spending on cosmetics, $8 billion a year; spending on pet food in Europe/US, $17 billion a year. Receiver nations themselves should also adapt their priorities, notably by less spending on military activities and by highlighting food, health, education and employment.

Defusing the debt bomb

It is hard for the South to achieve economic advance and sustainable development without marked reductions, and sometimes even abolition, of debt burdens. At the turn of the Millennium, Jubilee 2000, a coalition of NGOs, asked the World Bank and IMF to write off the debt of 42 Highly Indebted Poor Countries (HIPC) that were crippled by huge repayments. As of January 2003, only six countries had been relieved of their debt burden and 21 countries had begun to qualify for debt relief.

The problem with GNP

The usual label for the economy, Gross National Product (GNP), is a term much beloved by politicians, economists, stock markets, the media, and others who wish to show the citizenry that the economy is growing endlessly, hence we shall all enjoy ever-greater affluence. Trouble is, there are problems with the very concept of GNP. Not only is it hopelessly inaccurate, it is downright misleading.

For a start, GNP does not reflect the many externalities, both environmental and social, that reduce the value of the economy in significant senses. These externalities – pollution, crime, etc. – are viewed by GNP accounting methods as contributing just as much to human well-being as growing a field of wheat or educating a child. The established mode of calculating GNP does not differentiate between constructive and adverse economic activities. In the US, waste alone may account for one-tenth of the official economy, while all externalities may account for one-third. The externalities of certain US business enterprises may be greater than business profits, e.g. the obesity costs of the fast-food industry cause the industry to act as a net drag on the economy. A citizen would be an exceptional contributor to GNP if he/she has been involved in a horrific car crash, has been fearfully burgled, is enduring a drag-out divorce, and is suffering long-term cancer – all of which problems generate much economic activity. Rising levels of depression, as witnessed in many Northern societies, count towards the output figures because of the huge sums spent on anti-depressants and psychotherapy.

At the same time, GNP does not reflect the many positive economic activities and values that are unregistered in the marketplace. It says much about quantity of livelihood but little about quality of life such as health, leisure, security, environment, and general amenity. Nor does it register underground and hence non-market activities such as tax evasion, trade in stolen goods, narcotics, and other drugs, covert gambling, fraud, prostitution, and a host of other illicit activities. In many countries these amount to 10 percent of GNP; in India the unofficial economy may be 30 percent as large as the official one, and in Russia it may be as much as half as large, with many citizens earning their living through black markets. Could Russia be a poor country full of rich people? All in all, then, GNP should be replaced by a more realistic indicator such as Net National Income, an Index of Sustainable Economic Welfare, or a Genuine Progress Indicator (see pp. 254–55).

Bottom line: the above implies that we'll never attain the imperative of Sustainable Development without radical reform of the GNP concept. Insights of mainstream economics can go far to fine-tune the system, but we need to redesign much of the economic engine. No matter how hard we struggle to establish Sustainable Development, let alone human well-being, our economic models mean we effectively push an ever-bigger rock up an ever-steeper hill.

The true economy

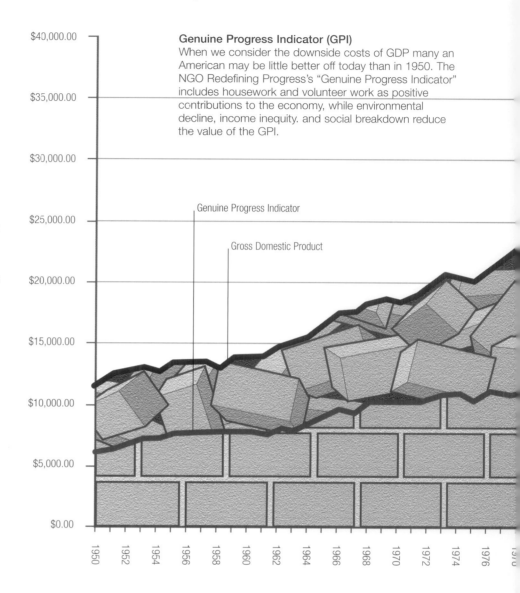

Genuine Progress Indicator (GPI)
When we consider the downside costs of GDP many an American may be little better off today than in 1950. The NGO Redefining Progress's "Genuine Progress Indicator" includes housework and volunteer work as positive contributions to the economy, while environmental decline, income inequity. and social breakdown reduce the value of the GPI.

Genuine Progress Indicator

Gross Domestic Product

The growth economy

Political leaders proclaim that we must, absolutely must, aim to keep our economies growing ad infinitum. Well, we cannot keep the quantity of growth growing indefinitely; there just isn't enough planet to accommodate it. But we can keep the quality of growth expanding, courtesy of eco-technologies that enable us to do more and more off less and less. Or: we don't need to expand our economies in order to develop our societies, just as we don't need to expand the Earth in order to develop the Earth.

Economic growth and human development

Key question: does economic growth necessarily promote human well-being? For much of the past, as for the present in the case of developing countries, it is valid to say that advances in the economy lead to advances in human well-being. But in the so-called developed countries – better termed, in some respects, mis- or over-developed countries – this is questionable. Could it be that in certain countries an advance in the economy may be purchased at an outright cost in human well-being, due to overwork, stress, rush-rush, decline in community values, impoverished relationships, grandscale pollution, waste, and overuse of raw materials and key natural resources? An average American household now earns half as much again as in 1980, but does it enjoy a similar increase in lifestyle fulfilment?

The British underworld

Organized crime is costing Britain up to £40 billion a year as gangsters cream off profits from drug trafficking, people smuggling, and fraud. This sum is as large as the British defence budget. The estimate is based on the profits generated from organized crime, revenues lost from VAT and excise fraud, and costs to industry.

Adverse externalities

Many externalities, such as pollution, waste, and crime, are not reflected by GNI.

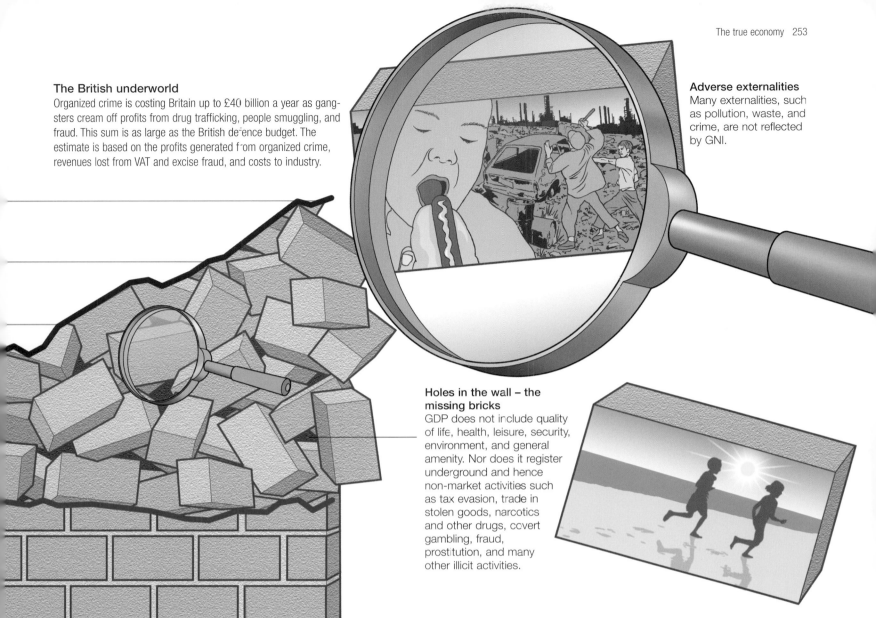

Holes in the wall – the missing bricks

GDP does not include quality of life, health, leisure, security, environment, and general amenity. Nor does it register underground and hence non-market activities such as tax evasion, trade in stolen goods, narcotics and other drugs, covert gambling, fraud, prostitution, and many other illicit activities.

1982 1984 1986 1988 1990 1992 1994 1996 1998 2000 2002

"GNP does not include the beauty of our poetry or the strength of our relationships, the intelligence of our public debate or the integrity of our public officials. It allows neither for the justice in our courts, nor for the justness of our dealings with each other. It counts air pollution, cigarette advertising and medical costs, yet it does not allow for the health of our children, the quality of their education, or the joy of their play."
Robert F. Kennedy, former U.S. Senator

Economics of happiness

Many countries are finding that they are shifting from problems of scarcity to problems of surfeit. We have so many cars on the road that we are running out of space to drive them. We have so much food to eat that we are suffering from a pandemic of obesity. We have so many things to buy, see, and do that we cannot find time to enjoy them all. As a result, there has been a recent outburst of studies in a field that may sound esoteric but is actually pressing: how to ensure that economic advancement delivers a corresponding improvement in people's sense of well-being?

Problem: during the past several decades, people's levels of reported happiness have at best stayed much the same, and in some cases have actually declined. While people on low incomes become happier when their earnings rise, they find that once they reach $10,000 a year, extra earnings bring little extra happiness. So should governments still seek to keep their economies moving ever onwards and upwards?

Suppose we extrapolate GNP growth for 100 years ahead. Thanks to compound growth, an annual economic increase of 3.0%, the aim of many governments, would make us 19 times richer. Would we then want 19 times as many cars, 19 times as many houses, 19 times as many holidays? Or would we end up 19 times more "time starved", 19 times more stressed and 19 times more unhappy?

The value of the environment

It has long been supposed that since environmental goods and services (water supplies, soil stocks, genetic resources, the atmosphere, climate itself, etc.) are not marketed and hence carry no price tag, they must be valueless. That is a main reason why they are so widely and severely over-exploited. Fortunately, an international team of economists has come up with a "shadow pricing" calculation: $33 trillion a year worldwide (1998 values), pretty much the same as the marketed items comprising GNP. Hence, global natural product is on a par with Global National Product.

The growing economy and the growing human being

The economy can be likened to a human being. A newborn has a tremendous appetite for raw materials, which cause it to grow – and then to demand still more raw materials. This physical growth continues unbroken until the late teens, when it suddenly halts, for ever. But this does not mean that the human being enjoys no further growth. On the contrary, its richest and longest phase of growth lies ahead – mental, emotional, and even spiritual growth. Challenge: how can we get our economies off their adolescent trip and embark on more adult growth?

New economics

The Greek root of the word "economics" essentially means "household management". That is an appropriate meaning given our new awareness of the need to preserve the integrity of our One Earth home. Yet our North-dominated economic structures seem to be destroying, rather than managing, our "home", not only laying waste to the environmental resource base that ultimately sustains our economies but grossly disrupting whole communities.

Yet Homo economicus still hankers after traditionally defined forms of economic growth, reinforcing the supposed link between economic advance and human well-being. The same economic animal still measures development in terms of GNP and other material indices, overlooking the notion that the best things in life are not things.

Conventional economic indicators, however, can't assess the value of endless economic growth, nor do they ask who is benefiting most. There is scant recognition of democratic freedoms in society, nor of basic amenities such as access to media, nor of the impacts of income (mal)distribution. Nor do they take account of desertification, acid rain, the ozone layer hole, or the dislocation of climate itself. A country that has cut down all its trees and gambled away the revenues would appear from its national accounts to have grown richer in terms of per-capita GNP, but in many other respects it would have mortgaged its future to the hilt.

A key premise of the new economics is to set economic growth at a level that is environmentally sustainable (see pp. 252–53). In such a system, the cost of goods and services will bear a direct relationship to their environmental impacts in both production and disposal. Also crucial is the aim of eliminating the poverty trap.

The new economics further seeks to create a system which allows the poor to satisfy their needs, and to reduce the gap between the haves and have-nots, both within societies and between societies. Under the new economics model, money will reflect wealth that is of true benefit to human well-being, and act as a stimulator of sustainable economic activity. What money most certainly is not, is wealth itself.

We need a new economics that enables people to enlarge their ability to support themselves sustainably. Its prime concern should be the well-being, not of the business bottom line, but of the human and environmental bottom lines. While brushing your teeth each evening, ask yourself if you have paid anywhere near the full price – covering all costs of production, etc., plus environmental, social and other "hidden" costs – of a banana, a gallon of petrol, a cup of coffee. You can vote for your political leader only once every several years, but you can use your dollar votes many times a day to register your support for "the good guys".

New rules of the game

"Trying to run a complex society on narrow indicators like GNP is like trying to fly a Boeing 747 aircraft with nothing on the instrument panel but a single oil pressure gauge!"

Hazel Henderson

If the world economy and its impact on people and planet can be considered a game, then a new set of rules for playing is long overdue. Indeed, even the concept of "winning" and "losing" requires a radical rethink. One of the main methods of scoring economic performance has been Gross National Product (GNP), a measure reflecting the prices for which goods and services are sold in the marketplace. An increase in GNP is regarded as a "good" thing since it indicates economic growth. What it generally fails to account for is the environmental implications of that growth: the $3 billion clean-up costs from the Exxon Valdez oil spill counted, perversely, as an increase in GNP, whereas a rational system of accounting would score this event down heavily.

Fortunately, we now have some preliminary indicators that take a larger look such as Redefining Progress's Genuine Progress Indicator, and Friends of the Earth/the New Economics Foundation's Index of Sustainable Economic Welfare (ISEW). UNDP's Human Development Index measures both economic growth and human well-being, based on such factors as life expectancy, literacy, and purchasing power.

The "new economics" aims to balance the present accounting system by attaching economic value to the many non-market needs of people and planet. As the Brundtland Commission put it, "No business can survive without a capital account – and neither can the planet."

FINISH
Learning the rules of the new economics is essential. Fundamental to its success is acceptance that we are a single, global community; that inequality not only affects the poor but also eventually rebounds on the rich; and that all of us are dependent on the continuing health of Gaia. New economics is not the finish, it is a new start.

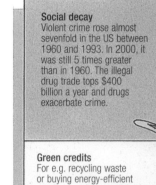

Social decay
Violent crime rose almost sevenfold in the US between 1960 and 1993. In 2000, it was still 5 times greater than in 1960. The illegal drug trade tops $400 billion a year and drugs exacerbate crime.

Green credits
For e.g. recycling waste or buying energy-efficient goods – could be collected as points for supermarket discounts.

START
In the context of new economics, our game of Snakes and Ladders is played for high stakes – the sustainable existence of humankind. Landing on the tail of a snake leads us down the route of environmental and human degradation, while landing at the foot of a ladder points in the direction of new accounting strategies that to replace the true costs of our activities.

Health and education
These allow everybody to contribute to society by nurturing spiritual, creative, and physical needs.

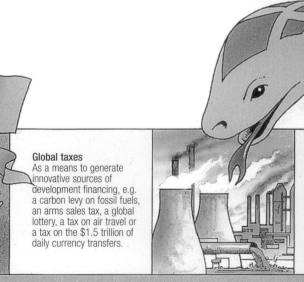

Global taxes
As a means to generate innovative sources of development financing, e.g. a carbon levy on fossil fuels, an arms sales tax, a global lottery, a tax on air travel or a tax on the $1.5 trillion of daily currency transfers.

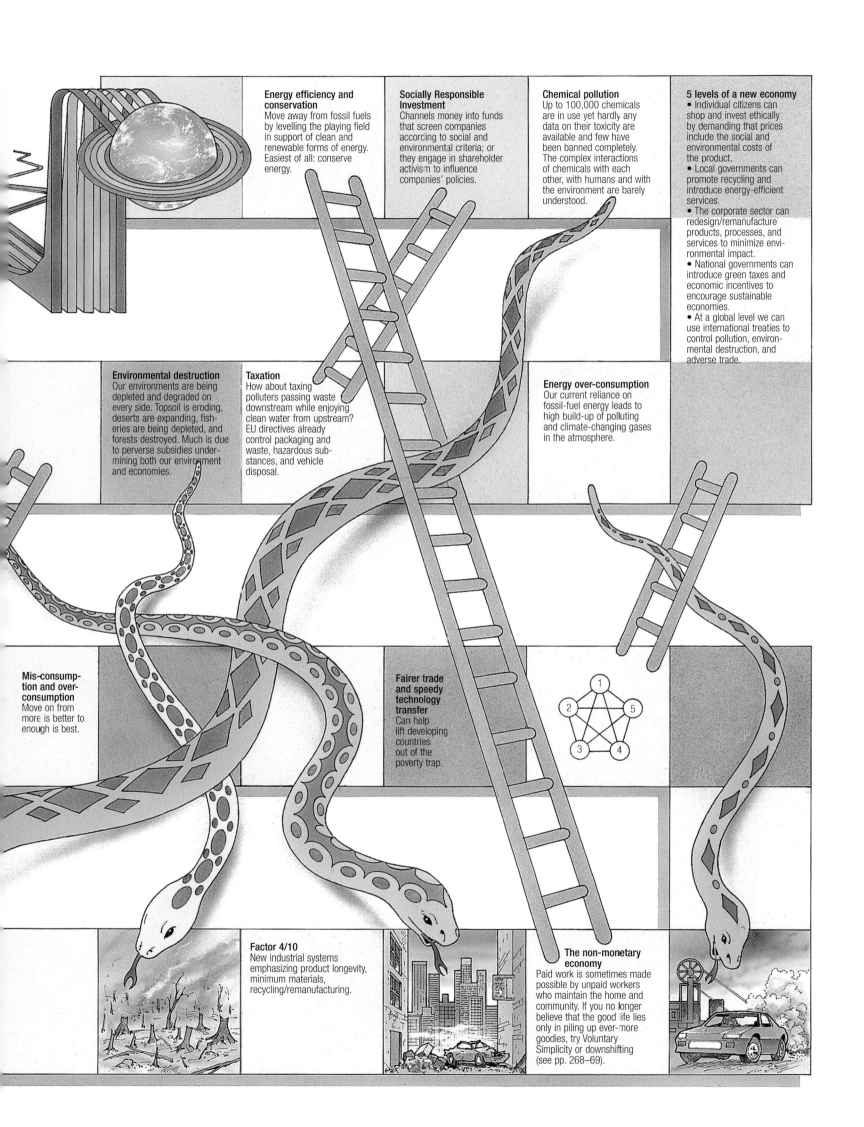

Energy efficiency and conservation
Move away from fossil fuels by levelling the playing field in support of clean and renewable forms of energy. Easiest of all: conserve energy.

Socially Responsible Investment
Channels money into funds that screen companies accorcing to social and environmental criteria; or they engage in shareholder activism to influence companies' policies.

Chemical pollution
Up to 100,000 chemicals are in use yet hardly any data on their toxicity are available and few have been banned completely. The complex interactions of chemicals with each other, with humans and with the environment are barely understood.

5 levels of a new economy
• Individual citizens can shop and invest ethically by demanding that prices include the social and environmental costs of the product.
• Local governments can promote recycling and introduce energy-efficient services.
• The corporate sector can redesign/remanufacture products, processes, and services to minimize environmental impact.
• National governments can introduce green taxes and economic incentives to encourage sustainable economies.
• At a global level we can use international treaties to control pollution, environmental destruction, and adverse trade.

Environmental destruction
Our environments are being depleted and degraded on every side. Topsoil is eroding, deserts are expanding, fisheries are being depleted, and forests destroyed. Much is due to perverse subsidies undermining both our environment and economies.

Taxation
How about taxing polluters passing waste downstream while enjoying clean water from upstream? EU directives already control packaging and waste, hazardous substances, and vehicle disposal.

Energy over-consumption
Our current reliance on fossil-fuel energy leads to high build-up of polluting and climate-changing gases in the atmosphere.

Mis-consumption and over-consumption
Move on from more is better to enough is best.

Fairer trade and speedy technology transfer
Can help lift developing countries out of the poverty trap.

Factor 4/10
New industrial systems emphasizing product longevity, minimum materials, recycling/remanufacturing.

The non-monetary economy
Paid work is sometimes made possible by unpaid workers who maintain the home and community. If you no longer believe that the good life lies only in piling up ever-more goodies, try Voluntary Simplicity or downshifting (see pp. 268–69).

MANAGEMENT

Introduced by James Gustave Speth
Dean, School of Forestry and Environmental Studies, Yale University

What is environmental management? In the deepest sense, it is the new business of bringing our human enterprise into harmony with the natural world. The good news is that we are in the midst of a necessary and timely paradigm shift in our thinking about environmental management. In 1970, when the modern era of environmental concern was born, the style was confrontational; business was the enemy; "sue" the motto. Today, we know we must try to put collaboration ahead of confrontation. Business must be on board, not overboard. We must all be environmentalists.

In 1970, we were against; today, we must be for. Then, we defined problems; today, we must design solutions. Then, we responded; today, we must anticipate.

In 1970, technology was the devil that got us into this mess. Today, we know that technology must get us out of this mess. Then, we saw market forces as taking us over the cliff. Now, we know that the market can and must be guided for environmental as well as economic goals.

In 1970, it was "put the polluters in a straitjacket". Today, it is let them out of the regulatory tangle if they can show they have a better solution.

In 1970, it was environmental protection; today, it is sustainable development – sustainable development in the poorer countries, for we will never sustain the biosphere unless the poorer countries are achieving their anti-poverty objectives; and sustainable development for the rich, for it is a much more profound goal than achieving another three percent growth in GDP.

In 1970, it was national; today, it is "global". Pollution has gone global, species have gone global, and so must we. Global governance must come to the environment. We need a World Environment Organization to match the World Trade Organization. But in the end, we know that all action is local.

In 1970, we created a separate environmental sector; today, we must make every economic sector an environmental sector. Every government agency must be an environmental protection agency. The problem-by-problem approach must be replaced by a holistic approach that perceives the challenge of sustaining the biosphere in all its complexity and responds accordingly.

In 1970, we took a top-down approach; now, we must encourage innovative bottom-up, grassroots approaches – green jazz that is improvisational, creative, and unscripted.

In 1970, we were too elitist. Now, we must stress equity: equity both among and within nations, and equity between the sexes – all in addition to equity for future generations. Too often we have neglected the poor, the minorities, the indigenous peoples. Let their environmental rights now be asserted.

In 1970, we looked for government leadership. Today, we must generally do it ourselves, with or without government. Business is often ahead of government; scientists are often ahead of government; consumers and environmentalists are often ahead of government.

In 1970, we were from Mars; today, we must be from Venus. Then, we broke things down into their component parts and laid out rational plans of attack for tackling isolated problems. Now, we know the most important resource is human motivation – hope, caring, our feelings about nature and our fellow humans. We need the preachers, the philosophers, the psychologists, even the poets! W.S. Merwin said: "On the last day of the world I would want to plant a tree".

The old paradigm of environmental management was necessary and appropriate in its day. Now, we must reach for something better.

The Management Potential

We live in a world dominated by nations, over 230 of them, from micro-states to superpowers. And whether we like it or not, the nation state remains the principal actor in international relations, and could remain so for some time to come. A few nations are old: Egypt has been a continuous nation for 5,000 years. Most are new: 150 are only 50 years old.

A nation is typically a large group of people inhabiting a defined territory, and united mainly by common history, culture, language, or religion. In many nations, however, unity is still superficial. Large minority groups, often ethnic, effectively form nations within nations, but without adequate representation at government level.

Just how thin the veneer of unity within nations can be is shown by events in what was Communist Eastern Europe and the former Soviet Union, where communism effectively kept the lid on nationalism. The collapse of authoritarian regimes and the Soviet Union's disintegration into independent republics released a tide of nationalist fervour that has taken us into a highly volatile period of history. Nonetheless, at the international level the nation state has proved a tolerable vehicle for trade, commerce, and communications. No other available management structure rivals it as a basis for collective living.

Like any other family, it suffers from squabbles, rifts, and outright conflict. In the wrong hands, the nation state can be a deadly instrument of divisiveness. But however much national leaders may proclaim their rights of sovereign independence, their rhetoric is often overtaken by their day-to-day dealings with one another. By virtue of trade flows, monetary patterns, inflation linkages, and myriad other relationships, nations are becoming ever-more involved in each other's affairs.

Modern nations face many predicaments that can be tackled only through collaborative effort and swapping independence for interdependence. These problems range from threats of war and terrorism, through energy and food-supply issues, to environmental problems such as carbon dioxide build-up.

The formation of new nations is not yet over. Ethnic conflicts fracture existing nations into smaller nation states. At the same time, governments are ceding some sovereignty to supranational bodies. Both internal fracturing and external agglomerating are growing pains in the transition towards a new global order.

Phoenix nation states

We live in a time of revolutionary change, a time of much hope and opportunity. We are witnessing the rebirth of the nation state, like a phoenix, from the ashes of the Cold War. Old ideologies are swept away in a heady rush for freedom. Across the world people are demanding a fairer, more equitable future, and seeking this through self-determination, individual liberty, and the development of democratic institutions. Even totalitarian governments can no longer ignore popular uprisings. Yet the opportunity may be transitory. In many areas, persistent turmoil works against moves to democracy and encourages intervention by outsiders. Building a more stable family of nations will be difficult. Governments seldom generate innovation, they tend only to react to pressure from democratic process or revolution. The sudden implosion of an empire as huge as the former Soviet Union is unprecedented. When this is accompanied by the chaos produced by the rapid transformation of a massive non-market economy to a free-market one, the resulting privation, internal economic crises, ethnic conflicts, and large-scale disorders may well lead to the emergence of xenophobic and aggressive governments.

National time bombs
Ethnic conflict is the greatest source of tension in a number of regions and is hampering the growth of democracy. All of the countries in Eastern Europe have significant populations of minorities. Yugoslavia, with no clearly dominant ethnic group, has fractured bloodily into a morass of independent states. In addition, there are Hungarian minorities in the Czech and Slovak republics and Romania; there is a large Turkish minority in Bulgaria, and there are over one million ethnic Poles scattered throughout the former Soviet Union. Ethnic violence has marred the birth of independent republics out of the former Soviet Union – as, for example, in Nagorny Karabakh and Kurdistan. Domestic ethnic conflicts in Eastern Europe and the former USSR states are likely to lead to disputes between nations, some of which could flare up into armed conflict.

Local, regional, global

The nation state plays a central role as a conduit between local, regional, and global levels of interest and power. We need to ensure a system of debate and decision-making with close involvement of those who will be affected. Global problems need global forums whereas local matters call for town or community meetings rather than edicts from a remote central bureaucracy. The Swiss, for example, have 23 cantons, each with its own constitution, and central government acts largely as an administration consulting the population by popular referendum.

Emerging democracies

Authoritarian control is declining. Across the world, people are demanding peace, democracy, human rights, and effective economic systems. A generation ago the great majority of Latin America lived under authoritarian governments. Now almost all live under democratically elected governments. Communism in Eastern Europe and the former USSR has collapsed. Germany has been peacefully reunified, while communist regimes in China, Cuba, North Korea, and Vietnam are under pressure to change.

International and regional organizations

Despite the upsurge in the number of nations, in nationalist sentiment too, during the past few decades, there has been a simultaneous growth in internationalism. We now have a multitude of organizations whose sole purpose is to take care of our international needs.

Indeed, we can take heart from this growing web of international bodies, reflecting the increasing interdependence of nations. No nation can afford to go totally its own way, not even a superpower. Disputes between and within nations often depend for their outcome on world opinion – a fact of which most national governments are all too well aware. Good public relations may win more battles than firepower. The fast-growing interdependence of the community of nations is one of the most striking revolutions of our time. Far from feeling daunted by the increasing complexity of the global community, we should view it as a remarkably diverse resource to meet our ever-more complex needs.

True, the two major attempts to establish an international order have stemmed from periods of acute crisis: World War I produced the League of Nations, World War II the United Nations. The 1991 Gulf War generated major coalitions. Today we face an even greater challenge: we need to produce a dramatically more capable system for collective endeavour ahead of any future crisis.

The omens are by no means all poor. Despite outbursts of hostility, the community of nations displays sizeable capacity for cooperation. Virtually every nation willingly operates within a network of international relationships. Already we have an array of regional bodies and broader-scale consultative bodies (see right). We have more cohesive groupings which begin to override national sovereignty, like NATO and North–South organizations like the Commonwealth. And at the global level, we have the United Nations, with a wide array of programmes, bodies and specialized agencies – a system of near-universal membership for near-universal concerns.

Note, moreover, that the basic block of international relations, the nation state, is "leaking" much of its authority and autonomy upwards to international agencies. It is also leaking power downwards to "civil society" or the plethora of citizen bodies that parallel governments with their versions of governance. This reduction of the nation state's role is shaping up to be the biggest change in the nation-state system since its emergence 500 years ago.

After decades of efforts by governments and despite many success stories, we are losing ground faster than ever. Problems proliferate, leaving us trying to push ever-larger rocks up ever-steeper hills. How can we get ahead of the game and prevent problems from becoming problems in the first place?

Some of the elements of the One-Earth society are here. How can we expand the array and put together the parts of the jigsaw in a way which

Reluctant internationalists

The world is walking a tightrope and it needs a safety net. We risk not just war but environmental collapse so long as we continue to view the major "organs" of the biosphere in terms of national self-interest. We have established safety nets before: the League of Nations, for example, emerged from World War I and the United Nations from World War II. But we cannot afford to wait for the nuclear convulsions of a possible World War III to put an improved safety net in place.

We already have many strands of cooperation from which this net can be woven. A central strand must be the UN, together with its myriad specialized agencies. Another strand is made up of the many geopolitical organizations which have emerged since 1950, including the EU, the African Union (formerly the OAU), Comecon, and the Association of Southeast Asian Nations. We have broader-scale consultative bodies such as OECD and more cohesive groupings like NATO. All these need to be set into the new planetary pattern, just as all help to supply building blocks for the new international order. Reluctant internationalists as we may sometimes appear, the freshly arrived organizations of the past half century represent as great a revolution as any in half a millennium.

Every day, fine threads of global activity help pull us together, from international collaboration in space and posting an airmail letter, to sending an email or expanding knowledge and commerce through the worldwide web. Our new safety net is far from complete and in many areas it already looks frayed. New strands must be added soon: we are a long way out on the tightrope.

Fragile nets

Safety nets of the past have relied too heavily on fragile strands of political and diplomatic accords. The Congress system, fashioned by diplomats in Vienna in the wake of the Napoleonic Wars, held together an unsteady peace until 1914, when it was torn asunder. The League of Nations introduced some harder-wearing strands based on functional relationships, but the central strands were still predominantly political and diplomatic – a safety net that was shredded by World War II. The third major attempt has focused much more on functional relationships, such as those tied together within UN agencies, notably FAO, UNEP, UNESCO, WHO, and the World Bank Group. These strands help hold the half-completed net in place.

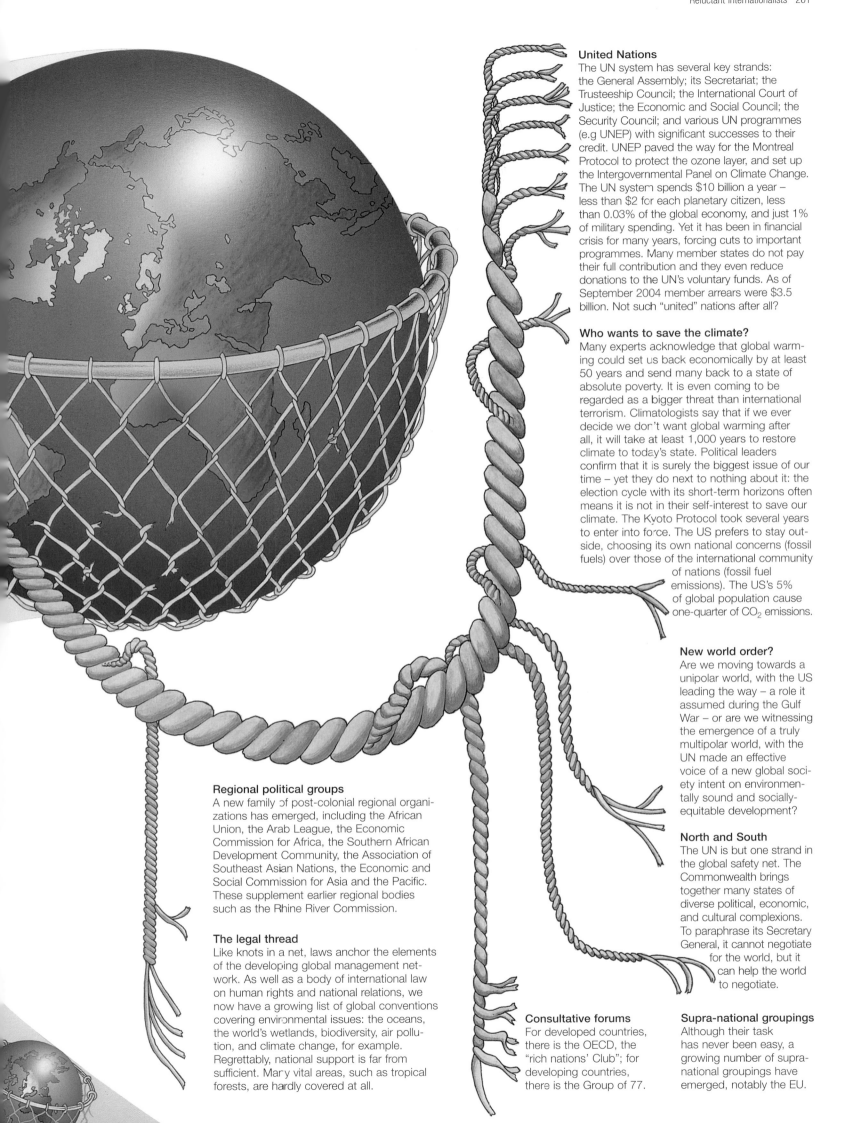

United Nations

The UN system has several key strands: the General Assembly; its Secretariat; the Trusteeship Council; the International Court of Justice; the Economic and Social Council; the Security Council; and various UN programmes (e.g UNEP) with significant successes to their credit. UNEP paved the way for the Montreal Protocol to protect the ozone layer, and set up the Intergovernmental Panel on Climate Change. The UN system spends $10 billion a year – less than $2 for each planetary citizen, less than 0.03% of the global economy, and just 1% of military spending. Yet it has been in financial crisis for many years, forcing cuts to important programmes. Many member states do not pay their full contribution and they even reduce donations to the UN's voluntary funds. As of September 2004 member arrears were $3.5 billion. Not such "united" nations after all?

Who wants to save the climate?

Many experts acknowledge that global warming could set us back economically by at least 50 years and send many back to a state of absolute poverty. It is even coming to be regarded as a bigger threat than international terrorism. Climatologists say that if we ever decide we don't want global warming after all, it will take at least 1,000 years to restore climate to today's state. Political leaders confirm that it is surely the biggest issue of our time – yet they do next to nothing about it: the election cycle with its short-term horizons often means it is not in their self-interest to save our climate. The Kyoto Protocol took several years to enter into force. The US prefers to stay outside, choosing its own national concerns (fossil fuels) over those of the international community of nations (fossil fuel emissions). The US's 5% of global population cause one-quarter of CO_2 emissions.

New world order?

Are we moving towards a unipolar world, with the US leading the way – a role it assumed during the Gulf War – or are we witnessing the emergence of a truly multipolar world, with the UN made an effective voice of a new global society intent on environmentally sound and socially-equitable development?

North and South

The UN is but one strand in the global safety net. The Commonwealth brings together many states of diverse political, economic, and cultural complexions. To paraphrase its Secretary General, it cannot negotiate for the world, but it can help the world to negotiate.

Regional political groups

A new family of post-colonial regional organizations has emerged, including the African Union, the Arab League, the Economic Commission for Africa, the Southern African Development Community, the Association of Southeast Asian Nations, the Economic and Social Commission for Asia and the Pacific. These supplement earlier regional bodies such as the Rhine River Commission.

The legal thread

Like knots in a net, laws anchor the elements of the developing global management network. As well as a body of international law on human rights and national relations, we now have a growing list of global conventions covering environmental issues: the oceans, the world's wetlands, biodiversity, air pollution, and climate change, for example. Regrettably, national support is far from sufficient. Many vital areas, such as tropical forests, are hardly covered at all.

Consultative forums

For developed countries, there is the OECD, the "rich nations' Club"; for developing countries, there is the Group of 77.

Supra-national groupings

Although their task has never been easy, a growing number of supra-national groupings have emerged, notably the EU.

makes sense in both economic and environmental terms? A key answer is to tackle the inertia and myopia of institutional roadblocks.

Integration: the imperative

Institutional roadblocks are profound and pervasive, and growing worse in many sectors of government. This applies especially to environmental problems, stemming as they often do from lack of integration – whether economic, political, or otherwise – among our principal institutions of government and other forms of governance.

The guts of the problem are that we are blighted by a historic division of government into rigorously defined sectors, a division that is antithetical to the types of changes required to integrate environment into policy throughout governmental systems. The fiefdoms of Energy, Transport, and Agriculture have their own interests and agendas, which often induce them to subvert each other's activities. Energy policy amounts to a fragmented approach to energy supply, instead of offering a coherent framework with emphasis on reductions in both supply and demand. Transport policy encourages the car culture to the detriment of alternatives. Agriculture policy promotes unsustainable forms of farming based on high-energy inputs, plus over-intensive use of fertilizers and pesticides.

Key question: why are environmental concerns not better translated into public policy in light of their blazing common sense? This raises an even more basic question: why are proper policy initiatives not a more frequent feature of government systems? These questions have exercised policy analysts and political leaders for thousands of years, yet it is rare for leading politicos and policy makers to confront the challenges head on.

One way to make government work better is to know who works therein. Who are the main movers and shakers, and how can one best influence them? Where are the prime pressure points in the nerve ganglia of bureaucracies? How to counter the super-preoccupation of governments with the short term ("A week in politics is a long time")? Related topic: how to institutionalize the rights of future generations extending for centuries if not millennia?

How to ensure that government operates as an organic whole, with policies that are consistent throughout the entire system? Translation: how to persuade individual sectors and departments to coordinate rather than compete? How to counter turf rivalries and empire building? How to tackle the tendency of governments to react rather than act (the squeaking door syndrome of special interest groups and potent lobbyists)? With particular reference to environmental issues, shall we need a catastrophe or three before it becomes clear to governments that they cannot continue with business as usual – even though that option is increasingly foreclosed by force of circumstance (becoming ever-more forceful)?

Institutional roadblocks

Two major roadblocks

The first concerns the lack of economic integration in government. Transportation policy, for instance, is often pursued with indifference to energy policy; agriculture policy with indifference to land conservation policy; and both sets with indifference to climate factors. In addition, national policies are often formulated with scant concern for their international repercussions. Linkages are all – as is demonstrated by the objective world of the environment, whether at national or global levels. The British government continues to subsidize fossil fuels many times more than it supports non-polluting energy sources.

Second major roadblock

"Institutional inertia" reflects officialdom's attitudes and perceptions, deeply entrenched as they are in myriad ways. It is an exceptionally powerful force, and changes will demand an even more powerful countervailing force. Recall the problem of perverse subsidies (see p.232), which constitute a major roadblock. These subsidies remain alive and well because they typically benefit the politically influential. Recall, too, that at the World Summit on Sustainable Development, political leaders engaged in rousing rhetoric in support of the issue but studiously avoided commitments to actual action in the form of specific policy measures backed by concrete programmes and time targets. Result, there have been hardly any solid initiatives to counter excessive consumption in developed nations, and inadequate action to slow excessive population growth in developing nations; little action to stem deforestation and species loss in much of the world, and meagre efforts to cut back greenhouse gases everywhere – even to expand energy efficiency anywhere.

Since WSSD, moreover, there has been scant mention of the environmental cause in the councils of power, in the media, or in most other sectors of the public arena. If the road to WSSD was difficult, how much more so is the road from WSSD in face of gross indifference and an implicit readiness to maintain institutional inertia. The longer we delay with measures to counter the inertia that infects the body politic, the more deeply the present patterns of departmentalized government will become institutionalized.

Levers of power

The ultimate locus for environmental responsibility in the US government does not lie with a special institution such as the US Environmental Protection Agency. Even if the Agency's head were to be accorded Cabinet status, true authority for environmental concerns would still rest with those charged with running the economy, viz. the Chairman of the President's Council of Economic Advisors, the Director of the Office of Management and Budget, and the Secretary of the Treasury – also the Secretaries for Trade, Energy, Transportation, Agriculture. All the EPA chief can do is to contain environmental damage after the fact – rather than to change those economic practices that cause the damage in the first place. The basic governmental system remains the same, and it thus serves to defer the day when reforms will be introduced with a scale and scope to match the system-wide problem. Policy power rests with institutional inertia.

Institutional handicaps

Government leaders and departments are isolated on their pedestals of expertise, blocked off from one another by barbed-wire divisions. They are also restrained by a variety of institutional handicaps, as depicted here: a limited view of the world (globe on head); no long-term vision (bag over head); limited freedom (hands tied together); deaf to progress (ears blocked); snowed under by bureaucracy (mountains of paper out of control).

Short-sighted thinking

"X-rays are a hoax." Lord Kelvin, 1900; "The radio craze will die out." Thomas Edison, 1922;

"There is a world market for about five computers." Thomas Watson, Chairman of IBM, 1943;

"Space travel is impossible." Richard Wooley, British Astronomer Royal, 1956;

"No individual needs a computer in his own home." Ken Olson, President, Digital Corp., 1977;

"640k of memory is enough for anybody." Bill Gates, CEO of Microsoft, 1981.

New paradigms

"There is nothing more difficult to carry out, more doubtful of success, nor more dangerous to handle, than to initiate a new order of things. For those who would institute change have enemies in all those who profit by the old order, and they have only lukewarm defenders in all those who would profit by the new order."
Niccolo dei Machiavelli, 1490

"Any population-economy-environment system that has feedback delays and slow physical responses, and that has thresholds and erosive mechanisms, is literally unmanageable. In our computer analyses, the world system does not run out of land or food or resources or pollution absorption capability. It runs out of the ability to cope."
Donella Meadows et al, 1992

"The essence of inertia is that there can be increasing returns to scale. When an idea becomes successful, it easily becomes even more successful: it becomes entrenched in social and political systems, which assist in its further spread. It then prevails even beyond the times and places where it is advantageous to its followers ... a case of "ideological lock-in". Big ideas often become orthodoxies, enmeshed in social and political systems, and difficult to dislodge even if they become costly."
J.R. McNeill, 2000, "Something New Under The Sun"

The better news

Fortunately, there can be productive inertia triggered by a turn-around in our institutional systems, generating multiple benefits of progressive size and inducing a constructive form of momentum. The more a government engages in policy measures to promote the environment, the more the benefits will become plain, percolating through every sector of government and segment of society. When once the disruptive change in direction is achieved, traditionalist resistance can quickly give way to organic support.

How to persuade governments that to do nothing is to do a great deal in a fast changing world? And how to educate governments on the new nature of change, which often arrives in non-linear character, i.e. in jumps rather than curves?

Global constituency

Civil society is a many-bodied phenomenon. It includes religious groups, consumer organizations, shareholder groups, labour associations, sports clubs, scientific networks, service groups, research centres, philanthropic foundations, as well as a vast variety of informal bodies that address more specialized concerns. They operate at every level: local, national, international, and worldwide. Environmental NGOs range from grassroots outfits with just a few members, to global organizations such as the World Wide Fund for Nature, with five million members and offices in 50 countries. NGOs used to be confined to rich countries, but in Central and Eastern Europe there are now 3,000 environmental NGOs, led by Hungary with only 10 million people and yet 726 NGOs.

Whereas most NGOs are local in nature and impact (see pp. 266–69), there are tens of thousands of NGOs of international scope, known as INGOs, some of them with global reach. They are adept at the vital task of tugging forwards the elephantine agencies and bureacracies that are ponderous at best. (The United Nations Committee on Trade and Development sports the acronym UNCTAD – which in some eyes stands for Under No Circumstances Take Any Decision.) Given their vast numbers and their abundant skills, the INGOs can spur the most turgid of government bodies into action.

The number of INGOs soared from fewer than 5,000 in 1983 to almost 50,000 in 2001. They first made a strong impact when they mobilized the public concern that lead to the 1972 Stockholm Conference on the Human Environment. In turn, this spawned the United Nations Environment Programme which has mounted many highly successful campaigns. At the Stockholm Conference all the NGOs could have fitted into one room, but by the time of the 1992 Rio Earth Summit they would have filled several halls, and at the 2002 World Summit on Sustainable Development almost 3,000 were accredited to participate.

Although NGOs lack political power, they exert a moral authority which cannot be ignored. More importantly, they can transcend national boundaries, politics, and prejudices by engendering a spirit of "global constituency". Indeed, the spread of INGOs around the world represents one of the most hopeful portents for the future. They not only act as a conscience and stimulus for the growing array of official agencies that claim to act on behalf of the world community, but they are the most visible expression of a growing global citizenry.

Voice of the world

The giant bodies of the state and transnational industries are powerful but often slow moving and cumbersome like an elephant. But the world is beginning to find its global voice. Citizens talk to each other across political boundaries and ally themselves together to lobby in the corridors of power. A striking symptom of this global "clearing of the throat" is the proliferation of INGOs in the last few decades, ranging from the Red Cross to anti-Vietnam War protest groups, and more recent leaders like Amnesty International, Oxfam, Greenpeace, Friends of the Earth, and the World Wide Fund for Nature. All of these organizations can reach out to both the individual and the community in a way that expresses the ultimate good in health and property of both our Earth and our world.

Voice of the corporates

The transnational corporations (TNCs) are enormous in both size and influence; just 100 non-finacial TNCs had assets of $7 trillion in 2002 and employed 14 million people. They control whole industrial processes from shaping demand to resource extraction, from production to end use, and wield so much control through trade that they markedly influence governmental decisions. Their actions will dictate much of our future course to a sustainable society. Industry's response to the challenge has been to create the World Business Council for Sustainable Development (WBCSD), which seeks to reconcile commercial objectives with environmental and social needs.

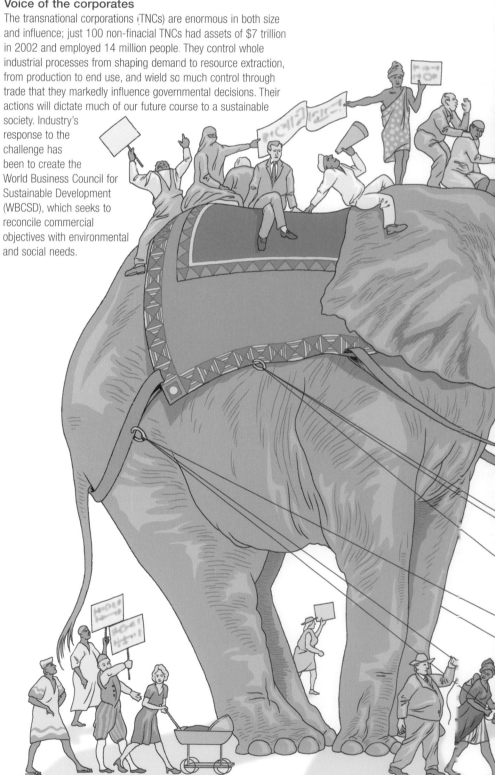

The rise of the INGOs

In 2001, there were almost 50,000 international NGOs, an embryonic nervous system for our global society, affording a degree of sensitivity unmatched by the nation states and their thousands of intergovernmental agencies which are often tongue-tied by diplomatic niceties.

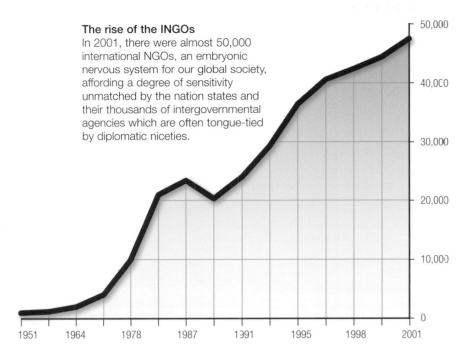

50,000

40,000

30,000

20,000

10,000

0

1951 1964 1978 1987 1991 1995 1998 2001

Planned parenthood

Fifty years ago, the dissemination of information about birth control was illegal in many countries, and only 50 years ago the global population explosion was not considered a problem. Today, birth control facilities are available in almost every country, and the majority of the world's governments have population programmes. Blazing the trail through this dramatic historical about-face has been the International Planned Parenthood Federation (IPPF), formed in 1952. After clashes with government officials, the medical profession, and the Catholic Church, IPPF eventually gained consultative status with the UN. The real turning point came with the 1974 World Population Conference, the first to focus on birth control. Today, IPPF member associations in 166 countries aim to increase support for, and access to, sexual and reproductive health services.

Environment-friendly business

Consumers are becoming aware of the impact of their purchasing decisions and they are starting to avoid products with adverse effects. Faced with lost markets and increased competitiveness between corporations, industry is re-evaluating its processes and standards. A US-based company, 3M, that produces a range of office goods (notably Scotch tape), has taken a lead in reducing the impact of its operations. In 1975, the company introduced its Pollution Prevention Pays (3P) programme, based on the concept that the best way to prevent pollution is not so much to control it, rather to avoid generating it in the first place. Between 1975 and and 2001, 3M prevented more than 820,000 tonnes of pollutants contaminating the environment and saved itself $850 million. By 2005, 3M aims to have reduced its GHG emissions by 50% over 1990 levels.

The Body Shop

A company which has tried from its start-up to protect the environment is The Body Shop. Its founder, Anita Roddick, opened her first shop in Brighton, UK, in 1976, and, through a network of almost 2,000 outlets in 50 countries, reportedly sells two products every second. It sells cosmetics not tested on animals, it uses recycled packaging, and it sources natural products from developing-world communities, thus helping to set up small businesses and supporting rainforest peoples.

INGOs and ICT

The emergence of civil society at the global level has been helped by an emergence of a different sort, the Internet and cell phones. These devices help individuals and groups to get, share, and act on information, and to do it speedily. They facilitate INGO efforts of diverse kinds: international collaboration; regular monitoring of environmental changes; holding institutions accountable, especially TNCs; and circumventing government controls. Because INGOs, like all NGOs, are not prone to bureaucratic inertia, several European governments have chosen to channel up to one-third of their foreign aid through such organizations.

Forest Stewardship Council (FSC) and Marine Stewardship Council

Through product labelling these two initiatives enable people to make informed consumer choices. The FSC network reaches 30 countries and the MSC 20.

Sustainable societies and public opinion – hopeful signs:

50 million "cultural creatives" in the US alone; Socially Responsible Investment (SRI) from 1% of managed assets to 15% in a single decade. The Voluntary Simplicity movement (see pp. 268–69); cutting-edge technologies like clean/renewable energy and hybrid cars (see pp. 140–41).

Broadening the power base

As described elsewhere (see pp. 212–23), the world is run principally by governments and mega-corporations. But a third force, civil society, is changing the power balance. A multitude of citizen groups routinely participate in decisions about all aspects of development and environment. Indeed, they enjoy an increasingly strong voice in global councils of governance.

It's not before time. When Churchill and Roosevelt together drafted the Preamble to the United Nations Charter, they began with "We the people of the United Nations ..."– which became, in practice, "We the governments of the United Nations", with all the problems that entrained. For decades, the citizen groups, technically known as non-governmental organizations or NGOs, were barely allowed any say in international discussions. Now they enjoy a place at the negotiating table as of right.

In this spread we shall look at NGOs that oper-ate within a national framework, by contrast with those that are more international or even global in scope (see Voice of the world, pp. 264–65). Not all "Voice of the Community" NGOs are nationwide in their activities, many being limited to local groupings of people who find they can make their individual voices heard with greater impact when they unite to speak together.

NGOs are expert at mobilizing democratic liber-ties and press freedoms, both in conjunction with cheap communications technologies. They supply information, they shape public opinion, they sway markets, they mobilize political action, and they

Voice of the community

"Never doubt that a small group of thoughtful, committed citizens can change the world. Indeed it's the only thing that ever has."
Margaret Mead

NGO successes

Kenya's Green Belt Movement has enabled citizens to plant trees at their own initiative. In its first year of activity, the Movement planted more trees than the government had managed in the previous 10 years.

The Chipko movement

When commercial loggers began large-scale felling of trees in northern India, their chainsaws were slicing through the livelihoods of local communities. The villagers wrapped their arms around the trees to protect them from being felled, thus sparking off the Chipko movement or the "movement to hug". In face of this protest, the government declared 12,000 sq. km of the local watershed to be off limits to loggers (see pp. 58–59). Today, the Chipko movement runs reforestation programmes in the many other villages where livelihoods are threatened.

provide many other citizen services. In particular, they have made environmental decision-making far more inclusive and representative.

The new-found citizen power manifests itself through abundant instances. In many developing countries, church bodies have aided coffee farmers to link up with Western consumer markets and thereby earn a decent living through the Fair Trade and Equal Exchange Movements.

In India, a nationwide movement by traditional fishermen forced the government to stop issuing licences to environmentally destructive trawlers. In other parts of Asia and despite powerful financial interests, NGOs have blocked plans for huge dams. Still other environmental groups have effectively purchased tracts of tropical forests to protect them from heavy-handed development.

These instances show the impact of "bottom up" efforts, by contrast with the "top down" approach of many governments and international agencies. Nor are these efforts confined to the developing world. In Poland, a critical role in establishing democracy was played by the labour unions, which eventually expanded into environmental activism. In the US and the European Community, local citizens sometimes take matters into their own hands. Faced with the decay of inner cities and especially of localities and buildings in which they live, communities have set up tenants' associations and small-scale cooperatives. Local communities have also scored remarkable successes in protecting wildlife habitats and opposing pollution from local factories and waste incinerators. In the US alone, thousands of grassroots groups have united in their call for "environmental justice".

Bangladesh's Grameen Bank

This NGO makes loans at very favourable rates to assist the rural poor, almost all to impoverished women. The repayment rate is a whopping 99%, a level to turn the World Bank green. A typical loan enables borrowers to plant a new crop, to buy an extra cow, or to set up a small business such as a grain mill. The Bank now has more than 1,260 branches in 46,000 villages. It has helped more than 4 million borrowers pull themselves up above the poverty line.

The role of religion

Around 200,000 church communities in the world are involved in various forms of environmental activity. Pope John Paul II has urged Catholics to reduce their resource consumption, not only as part of his campaign for them to become less materialistic but also because excessive consumption imperils the planet's life-support systems. The Ecumenical Patriarch Bartholemew has declared that pollution and other environmental assaults are "a sin against creation". The Chinese Taoist Association has called on its 40 million members to stop using products of endangered species (such as the panda, the tiger, and the rhinoceros) in their traditional medicines. In Japan, the Shinto community has agreed to use only sustainably grown timber for its 80,000 shrines. There are hundreds of similar examples among the world's 2 billion Christians, 1.4 billion Muslims, 750 million Hindus, 700 million Buddhists, and 13 million Jews.

Ecovillages

These are communities of people who strive to integrate a supportive social environment with a low-impact way of life. They integrate various aspects of ecological design, permaculture, ecological building, green production, alternative energy, community building practices, and much more. Members of the Global Ecovillage Network include Sarvodaya (11,000 sustainable villages in Sri Lanka); EcoYoff and Colufifa (350 villages in Senegal); the Ladakh project on the Tibetian plateau; ecotowns like Auroville in South India, the Federation of Damanhur in Italy, and Nimbin in Australia; small rural ecovillages like Gaia Asociación in Argentina and Huehuecoyotl, Mexico; urban rejuvenation projects like Los Angeles EcoVillage and Christiania in Copenhagen; permaculture design sites such as Crystal Waters, Australia, Cochabamba, Bolivia and Barus, Brazil; and educational centres such as Findhorn in Scotland, the Centre for Alternative Technology in Wales, and Earthlands in Massachusetts.

Society's basic building block

The most basic unit of society is the individual citizen and he is thus at the centre of a network of change. He expresses his opinion through two main forms of "voice": as a member of the citizenry and as a consumer of goods and services. Each of these roles has become enmeshed in numerous spheres of influence, notably economic, environmental, social, and political spheres. The result is that the last decade has seen the voice of the individual grow in power. In particular, our new environmental understanding has led to a surging pressure for change on the part of governments, international agencies, and businesses.

We can look at it from a further standpoint. What do a community, a city, a nation consist of? What makes them function at the basic level? Answer: individuals. The nation state and businesses may shape our economies and our societies, but it is individuals who drive the shaping.

Over the last two decades, the number of people living in liberal, multi-party democracies has increased greatly. More citizens than ever before have the chance to vote, to support political parties, even to stand for election – and they have thus gained a huge number of options to express their viewpoint. Moreover many emerging democracies have found that environmental concerns have become a strong factor in people's desire for change of many sorts. Expressed through the ballot box, these concerns gain prominence. There are now "green" parties in over 80 countries.

The individual voice is also expressed through their consumer choices. Whereas they can express a political opinion only occasionally, they can "vote" with their dollars, Euros, etc., several times every day. A good many citizens expect products which are environmentally friendly in both content and production. The "green consumer" movement has long exercised influence on businesses, and certain investment companies now offer ethical trusts which direct funds towards businesses with distinctive environmental orientation.

In addition, individual consumers can make changes in their lives as they learn that excessive consumption places pressures on planetary resources. Consumer demand for bottle banks, paper skips, and can bins is even starting to outstrip supply of facilities. Consumer boycotts of companies such as Shell petrol in the wake of Brentspar are powerful measures.

For countries that engage in the profligate consumption of energy, a reduction in demand is vital. Many citizens respond by selecting energy-efficient products, just as they also choose to travel by public transport or even by bicycle as they realize the full environmental impacts of travelling by car. In addition, shared car ownership schemes are popping up in countries across Europe, North America, even Asia.

Voice of the Individual

Ethical investment

Many individuals are favouring "green" trust funds that avoid companies with links to e.g. the arms trade and repressive regimes, and instead invest in companies with positive policies towards e.g. the developing world and workers' rights. This Socially Responsible Investment (SRI) strategy dates back to the 19th century when religious movements in Britain mobilized their investments to support their campaign to abolish slavery. The movement gathered momentum in the 1920s when many US churches chose not to invest in alcohol or tobacco products. Then in 1971, the US Pax World Fund was set up in order to avoid investments associated with the Vietnam War. This was followed in the early 1980s by ethical investments that countered apartheid in South Africa. In a more recent initiative, a group of churches and charities has set up the Ethical Investment Research Service (EIRS), being an umbrella organization to undertake research on putting principles into practice via investment decisions. EIRS now carries out independent investigations covering 40-plus fields, including the ones listed above. The Service researches over 2,500 companies from North America, Britain, continental Europe, Australia, and Japan. While most SRIs feature environmental criteria among others, strictly environmental funds total at least 40 in Europe and 25 in North America.

Cultural creatives

In the US there are 50 million people, every fourth adult, known as "cultural creatives". There are even more in Europe. They espouse strong environmental viewpoints, they highlight relationships, they are generally committed to psycho-development and even spirituality, they are turned off by large institutions (including both the extreme left and right in politics), and above all they reject conspicuous consumption. They focus on renewable energy and resource-efficient products, alternative transportation, nature protection, organic goods, alternative health care, socially responsible investments, eco-tourism and lifelong education. They watch only half as much television but listen to twice as much radio as does the general public; they read as many books as magazines; and they are Internet addicts. They include the 30 million Americans who practise yoga, up from four million in 1990. Two-thirds of the cultural creatives are women.

The Four Rs

Each individual could consider applying the Four Rs. Refuse products if they are inefficient or will not last. Re-use products thoroughly before disposing of them. Repair products so that they last longer. Recycle items so as to complete the resource loop.

Education

Literacy empowers the individual, who then has the basis for informed choice. Through education we can assess the claims of politicians, indeed the quality of our democracies overall, plus the impact of new technologies and the role of the media.

Volunteerism

In the Netherlands, volunteer work equates to 445,000 full-time jobs worth $13.6 billion. In South Korea, 4 million people volunteer 450 million hours per year worth $2 billion. In Brazil, one-sixth of adults volunteer some part of their free time. The number of volunteers with environmental NGOs worldwide has risen by half in 10 years.

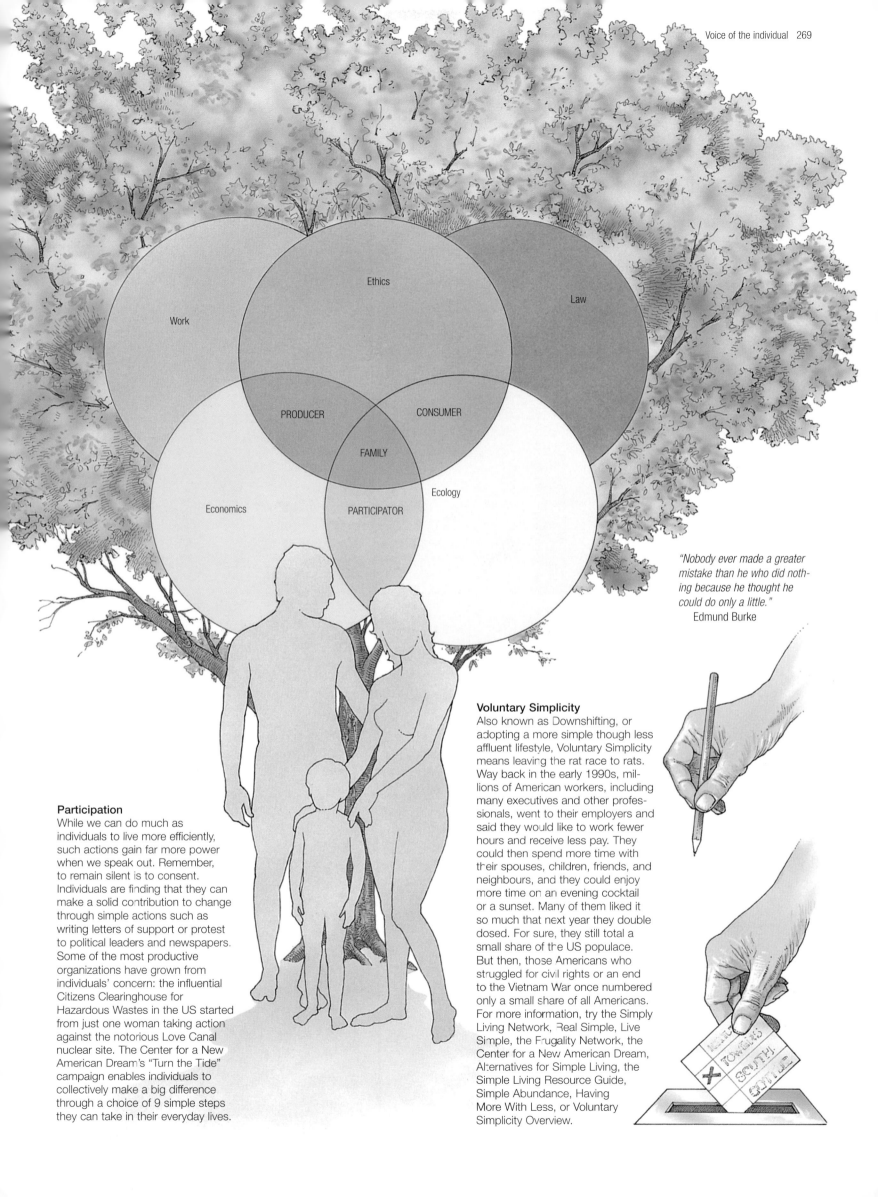

Ethics

Law

Work

PRODUCER

CONSUMER

FAMILY

Economics

PARTICIPATOR

Ecology

"Nobody ever made a greater mistake than he who did nothing because he thought he could do only a little."
Edmund Burke

Participation

While we can do much as individuals to live more efficiently, such actions gain far more power when we speak out. Remember, to remain silent is to consent. Individuals are finding that they can make a solid contribution to change through simple actions such as writing letters of support or protest to political leaders and newspapers. Some of the most productive organizations have grown from individuals' concern: the influential Citizens Clearinghouse for Hazardous Wastes in the US started from just one woman taking action against the notorious Love Canal nuclear site. The Center for a New American Dream's "Turn the Tide" campaign enables individuals to collectively make a big difference through a choice of 9 simple steps they can take in their everyday lives.

Voluntary Simplicity

Also known as Downshifting, or adopting a more simple though less affluent lifestyle, Voluntary Simplicity means leaving the rat race to rats. Way back in the early 1990s, millions of American workers, including many executives and other professionals, went to their employers and said they would like to work fewer hours and receive less pay. They could then spend more time with their spouses, children, friends, and neighbours, and they could enjoy more time on an evening cocktail or a sunset. Many of them liked it so much that next year they double dosed. For sure, they still total a small share of the US populace. But then, those Americans who struggled for civil rights or an end to the Vietnam War once numbered only a small share of all Americans. For more information, try the Simply Living Network, Real Simple, Live Simple, the Frugality Network, the Center for a New American Dream, Alternatives for Simple Living, the Simple Living Resource Guide, Simple Abundance, Having More With Less, or Voluntary Simplicity Overview.

Crisis: The Threat of War

The nation state has become too big for the small problems and too small for the big problem. We are reaching the ultimate breaking point. If we do not get our act together fast, we shall suffer the consequences of management breakdown – confrontation rather than cooperation, conflict rather than harmony, and, in the end, war of an intensity that we have not hitherto envisaged. What greater incentive could we possibly have to accomplish planet management?

The crisis of perception

As we over-stress the natural resource base of our planet, we set up strains and tensions that lead to fractures in our societies. Often these environmental "breaking points" trigger conflicts, both within nations and between nations.

Human communities depend for their livelihood on a range of basic resources, on living resources such as grasslands, forests, and soils, and on non-living resources such as water, fossil fuels, and minerals. If a community depletes its endowment of resources, or is denied fair access to resources elsewhere, its economy is undermined, its political structure becomes destabilized, and its social fabric starts to fray.

Such problems are greatly compounded by the nation-state system which has dangerous limitations when it comes to managing the emerging threats to our planetary life-support systems. National leaders, with honourable exceptions, have been slow to recognize the new sources of conflict. There is, in short, a crisis of perception which could prove the most critical of all. Without the political capacity to adapt to new threats, we face a continuous slide into chronic anarchy and endemic violence. Manageable problems will deteriorate into unmanageable conflicts.

Consider Central America. Whatever the ostensibly political nature of the upheavals that have afflicted the region, the central problems can often be traced back to the maldistribution of resources, e.g. the grossly inequitable distribution of farmland, applicable to most of the region's countries. This tragic story of misperception has been replicated in several other regions of the world, such as Southeast Asia, the Horn of Africa, and the Middle East. Israel's reluctance to share water supplies on the West Bank, water which it regards as vital to the development of its agriculture, constitutes a leading factor in determining the future security of the whole Middle East region. Competition for limited resources will spark many more such confrontations, unless we act promptly and imaginatively to defuse these issues before they finally explode (see pp. 138–39).

Breaking points

"In the global context, true security cannot be achieved by a mounting build-up of weapons (defense in a narrow sense) but only by providing basic conditions for solving non-military problems which threaten them. Our survival depends not only on military balance, but on global cooperation to ensure a sustainable biological environment."

Report of the Brandt Commission

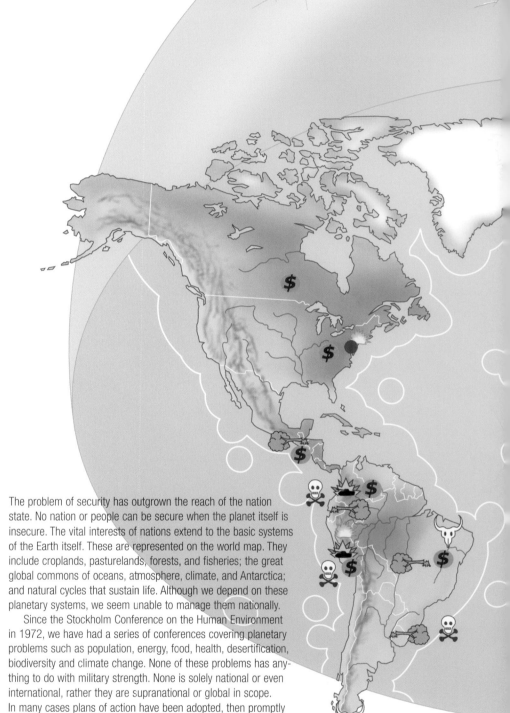

The problem of security has outgrown the reach of the nation state. No nation or people can be secure when the planet itself is insecure. The vital interests of nations extend to the basic systems of the Earth itself. These are represented on the world map. They include croplands, pasturelands, forests, and fisheries; the great global commons of oceans, atmosphere, climate, and Antarctica; and natural cycles that sustain life. Although we depend on these planetary systems, we seem unable to manage them nationally.

Since the Stockholm Conference on the Human Environment in 1972, we have had a series of conferences covering planetary problems such as population, energy, food, health, desertification, biodiversity and climate change. None of these problems has anything to do with military strength. None is solely national or even international, rather they are supranational or global in scope. In many cases plans of action have been adopted, then promptly sidelined by governments immersed in geopolitical traditions. Problems of such dimensions, which are everybody's concern, tend to be nobody's business. The US, for instance, has continued to turn its back on the Kyoto Protocol.

US vs. "rogue" states

The 2003 US military budget was $417 billion. Compare Iran $19 billion, North Korea $1.8 billion, and Syria $5.9 billion.

Environmental backlash
In the developing world, population pressures on non-renewable resources force more and more people out of rural areas into cities. Greater urbanization generates increasing violence, terrorism, and political unrest. Dangerous cracks in our mismanaged system are appearing in the war zones, shown above. Obvious symptoms of stress include drought, pollution, deforestation, and the glaring divergence between the life expectancies of people living in the North and South.

Nuclear confrontation in Southern Asia
Hindus in India and Muslims in Pakistan have both spoken about using nuclear weapons to "resolve" their differences. There is a chance greater than zero that one day, or rather one minute, the subcontinent will be reduced to a smoking pile of radioactive debris.

Future shocks
Nuclear proliferation, world economic instability, overpopulation, and pollution of air and water threaten the most predictable parts of all our daily lives. There is worse to come. The projected increase of carbon dioxide in the global atmosphere will grossly disrupt agriculture and the global economy. Increased pressure for migration could swell the cities of the South, and lead to South to North population movements. North/South conflict will produce other future shocks. These two halves of the world are already locking horns in the battle over genetic resources which could represent a powerful weapon for developing nations. Mexico and Ethiopia, two major germplasm suppliers, are finding ways to exploit the dependence of the North on the genetic diversity of the South. If we make no attempt to manage these existing crises, we risk a slide into far deeper conflict.

Ocean conflict
Nations conflict over common resources of the oceans. Already national lines cut across Antarctica (below), while the EEZs place 40% of the ocean under national control. The UK and Iceland came to the edge of hostilities over cod fisheries. Many other such conflicts can be documented around the world. The North has clashed with the South over the Law of the Sea as developing countries attempt to secure their share of deep-sea minerals. There has been an alarming growth in piracy of ships on the world's oceans.

Breaking point: Ethiopia
Gross degradation of the natural resource base of countries in the Horn of Africa precipitated the downfall of Haile Selassie in 1974 followed by conflict in the Ogaden desert in the late 1970s. Super-powers were alerted in response to the threatened security of the near-by oil-tanker route from the Persian Gulf to the West.

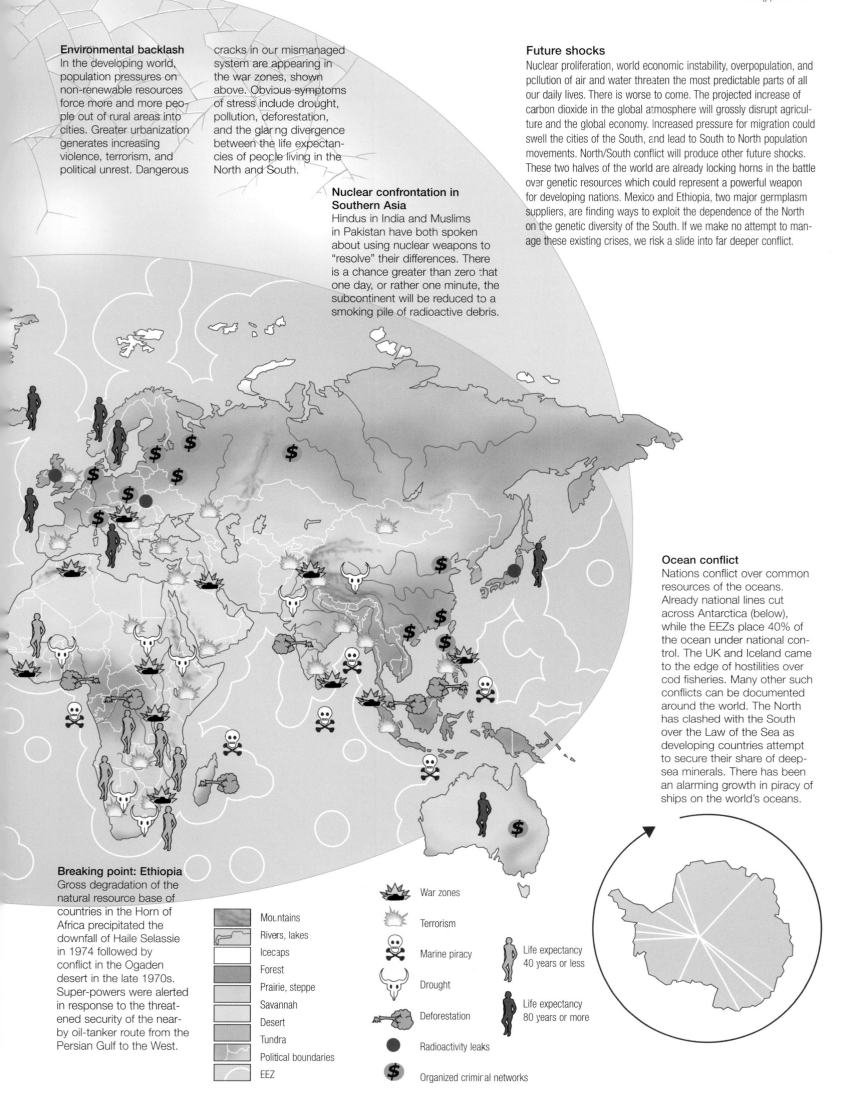

Mountains
Rivers, lakes
Icecaps
Forest
Prairie, steppe
Savannah
Desert
Tundra
Political boundaries
EEZ

War zones
Terrorism
Marine piracy
Drought
Deforestation
Radioactivity leaks
Organized criminal networks

Life expectancy 40 years or less
Life expectancy 80 years or more

Discontinuities

Many people will respond "What are those? Never heard of them". And rightly so. They have been an infrequent phenomenon thus far. But we should start to wrap our minds around the concept since they are likely to become ever-more frequent within the lives of most readers of this book.

A discontinuity arises when something suddenly occurs to mark a profound change from the way things have been. For instance, when water cools it turns from a liquid to a solid – all in a moment. The same when it warms up and turns into a gas. Its change is not evolutionary, following a regular path, rather it is revolutionary and moving in jerks – hence the alternative name of non-linearity. If you, the reader, are still puzzled, consider that we all have had first-hand experience of an absolute discontinuity, and of a profoundly personal sort: when we were born (a related discontinuity awaits us).

We are acquainted with all kinds of other discontinuities, particularly in the fields of economics (for example, the emergence of OPEC, politics (for example, the fall of the apartheid regime in South Africa), and the environment (for example, the collapse of the Peruvian anchovy fishery).

All these events (see right) have been unpredictable – or rather, they have exceeded our present capacity to predict them. Entirely predictable is our readiness to be caught unawares, time after absurd time. We profess to have been surprised by the eruption of AIDS, yet the truly surprising thing is that we were surprised. It was surely inevitable that as huge numbers of people pressed deeper and deeper into tropical forests with their huge reservoirs of new pathogens, one would eventually make the leap from wild animals into humans – whereupon the pathogen would find itself in a bacterium's paradise, with human hosts travelling far and wide across landscapes local and global. As humans invade one "foreign" ecosystem after another, should we not anticipate a whole series of disease disasters ahead?

All this raises a key question that should be at the top of any research agenda for environmentalists, economists, and political analysts. What discontinuities should we anticipate for the foreseeable future and hence what can we do to head them off at the pass? What if China were to break up into half a dozen "Chinas", a not impossible prospect? Or consider Saudi Arabia, only semi-stable at best and now a net debtor with its lavish, untaxed and oil-subsidized lifestyles becoming unaffordable; what if its autocratic regime were to be undermined by educated princes returning from Harvard and Oxford, plus equally educated princesses told they must wear the veil, not drive a car, and submit to numerous other restrictions? Were the Saudi regime to collapse or be despatched by a coup, there would be a swift and sharp rise in oil prices, the spot market leaping to at least $60 per barrel, conceivably $75, not impossibly $100.

Discontinuities and other non-linearities

Discontinuities in nature

Sometimes designated by ecologists as "jump effects", environmental discontinuities occur when ecosystems absorb stress over long periods without much outward sign of damage, but eventually are pushed to the limits of their coping. They reach a disruption level at which the cumulative consequences of stress finally reveal themselves with critical impact. In the case of acid-rain damage, a forest ecosystem can successfully buffer stress for long periods and its ecosystem changes are hardly visible; yet even while the ecosystem remains apparently unchanged and healthy, it moves ever-closer to the limits of its resilience – and thereafter towards an abrupt collapse.

Other examples include the bleaching of coral reefs, the mass mortality episodes among dolphins and seals, the widespread decline of sea urchins, the increase in phytoplankton blooms, cancer epizootics in fish, and sudden population declines in e.g. the anchoveta fishery off the coast of Peru, songbirds in North America, saguaro cactuses in the southwestern US and northern Mexico, and amphibians worldwide.

Economic discontinuities

In the economic field, there has been the abrupt end of Japan's "bubble economy" in 1989, the sudden arrival of OPEC, the dire "Black Wednesday" on the US Stock Exchange, and the late 1990s upheavals in Asian financial markets. Indeed, economists have predicted six of the last three recessions. These crashes constantly take economists by surprise, as if crashes, however often repeated, lie entirely outside the established order of things.

Political discontinuities

Recall the fall of the Berlin Wall and the end of South Africa's apartheid seemingly overnight, plus the peaceful breakup of Czechoslovakia and the democratization of the Philippines, South Korea, Argentina, and Brazil, also the peaceful demise of the Suharto regime in Indonesia.

Environmental discontinuities

Environmental instances include the abrupt emergence of acid rain and the ozone hole, likewise the collapse of the Peruvian anchovy fishery in the 1970s and of the New England cod fishery in the early 1990s. Broadly viewed as environmental issues too are population surprises, notably the sudden soaring of population growth rates in over one hundred countries during the 1960s, followed by steep plunges in a few countries in recent times (Thailand, Iran, Kenya). Who would have supposed that Iran, a fundamentalist Islamic state and as chauvinistic as they come, would need only 14 years to bring down its population growth rate from 3% to 1% per year?

Sea temperatures and hurricanes

In the tropical Atlantic, water can grow warmer and warmer without causing any severe storms, but once it passes 28°C it starts to generate hurricanes. Even though the increase is marginal at most, it is enough to trigger a discontinuity, and one of exceptional impact. What if, as is all too possible, Caribbean hurricanes no longer bypass Miami but one of them were to land on top of the city? The damages could easily exceed $100 billion – whereupon the discontinuity would immediately become economic as much as environmental.

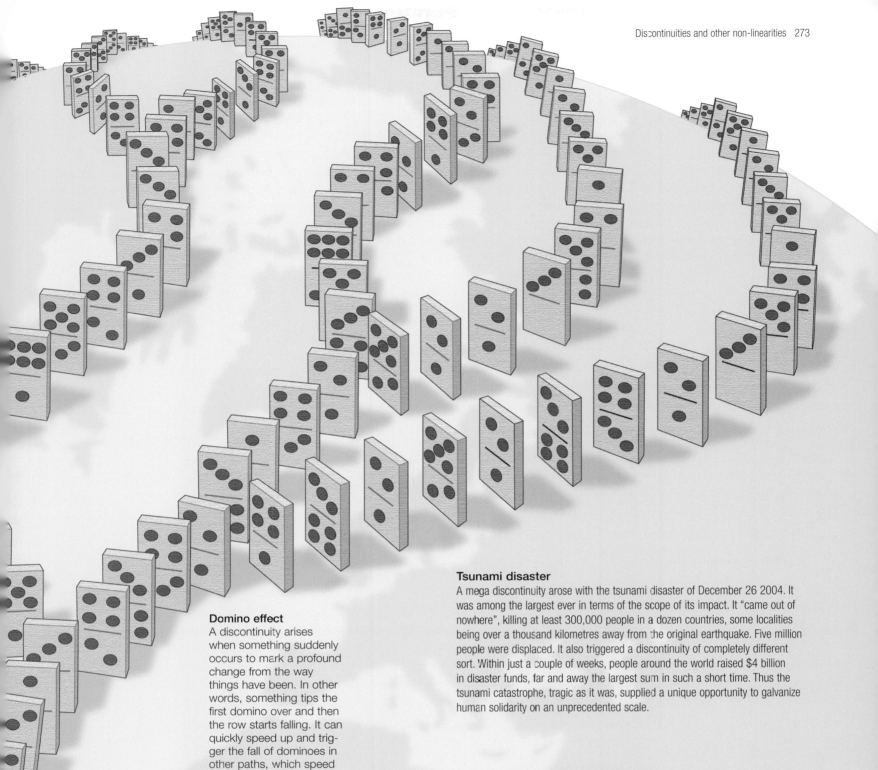

Domino effect

A discontinuity arises when something suddenly occurs to mark a profound change from the way things have been. In other words, something tips the first domino over and then the row starts falling. It can quickly speed up and trigger the fall of dominoes in other paths, which speed off in another direction. For example, the knock-on effects of the ozone hole.

Tsunami disaster

A mega discontinuity arose with the tsunami disaster of December 26 2004. It was among the largest ever in terms of the scope of its impact. It "came out of nowhere", killing at least 300,000 people in a dozen countries, some localities being over a thousand kilometres away from the original earthquake. Five million people were displaced. It also triggered a discontinuity of completely different sort. Within just a couple of weeks, people around the world raised $4 billion in disaster funds, far and away the largest sum in such a short time. Thus the tsunami catastrophe, tragic as it was, supplied a unique opportunity to galvanize human solidarity on an unprecedented scale.

Discontinuities ahead

Given the many future global upheavals likely in a world with pressures from unprecedented growth in human numbers and human activities, we can surely expect that environmental changes will emerge faster, larger, and more intense. In turn, these will entrain abundant discontinuities of both economic and political kinds, also social and cultural kinds, all arriving at once and making for super discontinuities. As has been well observed by John McNeill in his 2000 book "Something New Under The Sun", there could well be one discontinuity series after another, or rather side by side with each other, overtaking us at accelerating pace and producing fundamental shifts in global systems of every sort from grand-scale ecosystems to nation states, in fact the entire human enterprise.

Whether it will precipitate a shift in their understanding is debatable. Thus far we have scant idea of what discontinuities lie ahead, nor are we likely to know until they start to happen (even if then). The expert in greatest demand will be the specialist in surprises. The secret is to spot those trends that are headed for terminal decline after long build-up of forces bubbling away beneath the surface. Reader, why not take a moment to try your hand at becoming such an expert – by looking beyond the headlines to seek out the true news of our world that advances in zigzags as much as in straight lines. Attempt, in other words, a discontinuity in your own manner of thinking.

"Sudden" landlessness

In Philippines, Costa Rica, and a number of other tropical forest countries, it has recently happened that no more lands remain readily available for opening up to conventional agriculture. There has occurred a "break point" in conventional patterns of settlement on the part of small-scale farmers, the result being a greatly and suddenly increased pressure on forests.

The "Third World" war

Since World War II there have been more than 200 wars, almost all in developing countries. In 1950, the number of outbreaks was 13, reaching 31 by 1970 and 50 by 1990, and peaking by 1992 with 55. But by 2002, there were still 28 wars raging, together with 17 lesser armed conflicts. Many wars in developing countries have been civil wars of one form or another, often fought over tribal or religious differences. But their real roots can also lie in basic resource problems, reflecting the inequities in resource distribution both within and between countries (see pp. 138–39).

Tragically, it is safer to be a soldier in battle than a civilian on the so-called sidelines. Of the 50 million killed in war or violent conflict since 1945, most have been civilians. War now involves and consumes entire communities: it has become total in a way we have not known before. Modern wars may be ostensibly local affairs, but there tends to be a great deal of involvement by rich nations. In fact, a large number of developing-country wars have been "proxy wars", fought by locals on behalf of big power blocs, and heavily supplied with arms and advisors from outside. Without this support, most of these conflicts would have been shorter and less destructive.

Although the end of the Cold War brought a thaw in relations between East and West, it also brought ethnic and territorial rivalry between newly independent states. The old East–West axis of confrontation is itself shifting to the North versus the South. Defence planners in the North increasingly see a very unstable world, with bitter divisions of

Landmines

Landmines constitute one of those huge problems that could be readily fixed but aren't. At least 100 countries have stockpiled almost a quarter of a billion mines, the great bulk of them in countries that have not signed the Mine Ban Treaty ratified in 1999. China is the leader with more than 100 million, followed by Russia (60 million), and the US (11 million). As many as 50 million mines are buried in nearly 60 countries, poised to do their damage. In 2000, over 10,000 people, possibly twice as many, were hurt or killed by landmines. More than $1 billion has been spent on de-mining activities during the past decade.

Towards a violent planet

Our world has become an increasingly violent place. Wars are shockingly more destructive and deadly than ever before. In the 20th century, there were 130–140 million war-related deaths – almost ten times as many as in the 400 years preceding. Since 1945, some 50 million lives have been lost in war and other violent conflicts, many of them civilian lives.

War deaths tell only part of the story. Millions more have been injured and maimed. In the last 20 years refugees have increased from 10 million to 20 million (peaking at 27 million in the mid-1990s), mostly living miserable lives in refugee camps, unable to return to their homes. Not all have been displaced by war but all are considered "of concern" to the UNHCR, with 12 million officially recognized as refugees who "owing to well-found fear of being persecuted for reasons of race, religion, nationality, membership of a particular social group or political opinion, is outside the country of his nationality". In 2001, 200,000 Afghans fled to Pakistan and another 200,000 to Iran; 340,000 Columbians were forced to flee from political violence and 26,000 Palestinians fled to Jordan from the Gaza Strip/West Bank.

During the past decade, developing countries have produced 86% of the world's refugees, some of them heading for countries among the least able to afford such an increased burden. Many of the world's governments have turned on their own citizens. A number of others have resorted to defiance of the law, even terrorism. Despite the end of the Cold War, the world is still ridden with weaponry.

The killing continues
During the 1990s, there were 107 armed conflicts in 63 states. Millions were killed in battles over resources wars.

The toll of war and conflict
0–1900: 38 million war-related deaths;
1900–1995: 110 million
(World War 1, 26 million,
World War II, 54 million).

1968–1998 Northern Ireland: 3,250;

1976–1993 Argentina: 9,000–30,000;

1960–1996 Guatemala: 200,000;

1983–1999 Sri Lanka: 57,000

1983–1999 Sudan: 1.5 million;

1998–1999: tens of thousands of Ethiopians and Eritreans during fierce border war;

1992–1998 Algeria: 75,000;

1984–1999 Turkey: 37,000

1989–1997 Liberia: 150,000;

1991 Persian Gulf war: 4,500–45,000 (civilian death toll from allied bombing as low as 2,500 recorded by US and as high as 35,000 by Iraq);

1992–1999 Sierra Leone: 14,000 (civil war fuelled by valuable natural resources, e.g. diamonds);

1993–1999 Burundi: 200,000–250,000;

1990s D.R. Congo: 2.5 million

April–July 1994: 800,000 Rwandans murdered in the ethnic Hutu–Tutsi war;

1979–1992 Afghanistan: 2 million

1991–1995 Bosnia: 250,000;

1994–1996 Chechnya: 18,000–100,000;

1948–1997 Israel 125,000 from 2000: 3,400 Palestinians, 990 Israelis

wealth and poverty coupled with the proliferation of advanced weapons producing a dangerous world disorder. While the global nuclear arsenal peaked at 65,000 warheads in 1986, there were still 30,000 in 2002, including 10,640 in the US and 18,000 in Russia but excluding an estimated 50–100 in Israel, 60+ in India, 24–48 in Pakistan, and an unknown quantity in North Korea. Since September 11 2001, terrorism has reared its ugly head around the world (see pp. 270–71), bringing about huge increases in US military spending (though the recent Iraq War is said to be about oil supplies. Terrorism could be tackled in other ways according to energy expert Amory Lovins, who says that by 2015 the US could save more oil through energy efficiency than it gets today from the Persian Gulf.

Ironically, wars consume resources which, used more wisely, could have addressed the root causes of conflict more cost effectively. It is almost always more expensive to go to war than to choose an alternative course, if political leaders were to consider the needs of their people rather than the dictates of national and individual prestige.

The 1991 Gulf War cost the US and its allies around $84 billion (2004$s) – way more than all foreign aid worldwide. The 2003 Iraq War will likely cost over three times as much. By contrast, Brazil is taking steps to look at an altogether different form of security. In 2003, it froze its purchase of $760 million worth of jet fighters, planning instead to tackle hunger among the 17 million Brazilians who are undernourished.

Legend:
- Disputed borders
- ★ International conflicts
- ☆ Civil war
- ◉ Serious civil/interior conflicts
- ○ Negotiations complete or ongoing
- ■ Independence movements
- Terrorism
- Countries with nuclear weapons

Fuelling the flames
Conflict still rides the world. From the 1991 Gulf War, when a coalition of 37 countries repelled one aggressor, to the civil wars affecting several nations in the 1990s, to the 2003 war and final capture of Sadam Hussain in Iraq. The emergence of post-communist, independent states has not been without bloodshed, particularly the violent fracturing of Yugoslavia. Almost all wars since 1945 have taken place in the South, and most of these have been internal conflicts. Their flames are fuelled by arms bought on the open market. The number of political conflicts (only a quarter of which are violent) rose from 108 in 1992 to 173 in 2002.

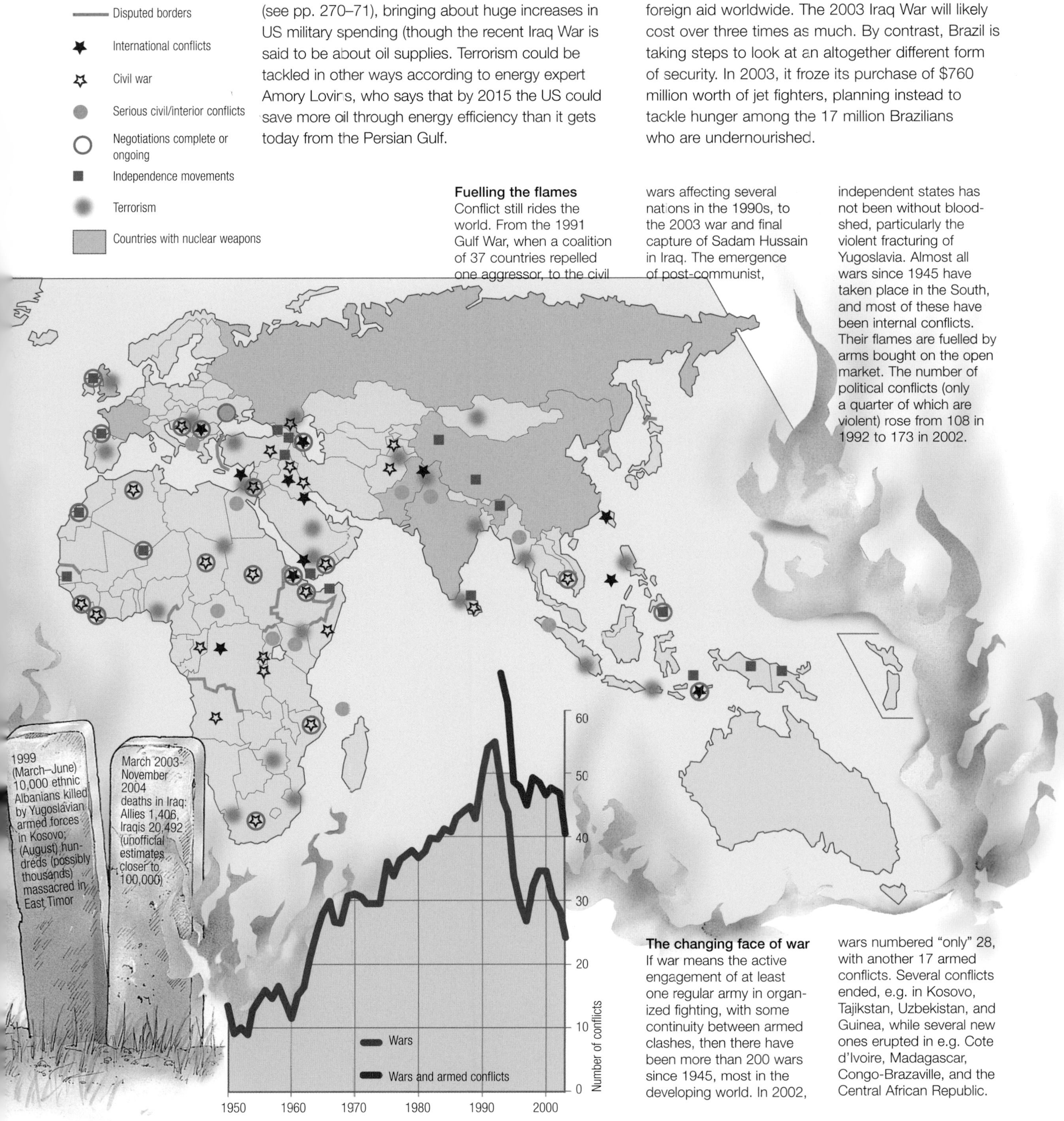

1999 (March–June) 10,000 ethnic Albanians killed by Yugoslavian armed forces in Kosovo; (August) hundreds (possibly thousands) massacred in East Timor

March 2003-November 2004 deaths in Iraq: Allies 1,406, Iraqis 20,492 (unofficial estimates closer to 100,000)

The changing face of war
If war means the active engagement of at least one regular army in organized fighting, with some continuity between armed clashes, then there have been more than 200 wars since 1945, most in the developing world. In 2002, wars numbered "only" 28, with another 17 armed conflicts. Several conflicts ended, e.g. in Kosovo, Tajikistan, Uzbekistan, and Guinea, while several new ones erupted in e.g. Cote d'Ivoire, Madagascar, Congo-Brazzaville, and the Central African Republic.

Number of conflicts

—— Wars

▬▬ Wars and armed conflicts

1950   1960   1970   1980   1990   2000

The global spread of terror

Terrorism is becoming internationalized at the same time that it becomes more proficient in its global reach. It is no longer restricted to Israel/Palestine, India/Pakistan, Colombia, or Chechnya. Despite their fearful local impacts, these have all been sideshow efforts with limited significance for the wider world. In the post 9/11 world, international terrorism embraces communities in Kenya, Spain, Indonesia, and Turkey, with massive repercussions far beyond these countries. The list of targets is surely set to grow ever longer and the death tolls to climb ever higher as the terrorists' fanaticism becomes ever fiercer and their weapons ever stronger. Recall those thousands of nuclear warheads that were left lying around in Central Asia following the breakup of the Soviet Union.

The ranks of the terrorist armies are growing more numerous even as they remain anonymous. In certain instances they seem to be made up of religious fanatics, supported by "rogue" states such as Afghanistan and Iran. In other instances, they seem to be detached from any country. In both cases, the operative word is "seem" because it has proved hard for the best intelligence services to figure out who these terrorists are, where they are located, and who supplies them with funds and weapons. Much of their set-up remains largely untraceable. Their most frequent common attribute is allegiance to Islam, or their version of it – they are oblivious to the peaceful injunctions of the Koran. Indeed, the more moderate forms of Islam reject terrorism and all it stands for. We are certainly not witnessing the start of an indefinite war between Islam and Western civilization.

So what ideology drives the terrorists? In as much as anyone knows, the answer is: none, except a distorted form of Islam. Perpetrators of terror outrages are hard to capture since no-one generally rushes to claim responsibility. Terrorists do not lodge protests against poverty, and the individual perpetrators usually appear to be middle-class people. They make no demands except the victory of Islam (a goal that is not proclaimed by genuine Islam). They support no government nor system of governance, even though they are effectively dictating the terms of e.g. major types of public transportation in target countries. They precipitate economic crises if not disasters, though this seems to be largely a means to an unproclaimed end. They oblige governments to make security practices trend towards the draconian, thus shifting the balance between public order and individual freedom. Their prime *modus operandi* is terror pure and simple.

This all means that we shall respond to terrorism in one of two ways. We shall either work together to overcome it, or we shall all suffer the consequences – again, together.

The price of "security"

Within the few minutes that it takes the reader to read this portion of text, governments will devote several million dollars to military activities. In 2003,

International terrorism

Relative deaths

As the Worldwatch Institute points out, the 9/11 attacks killed more than 3,000 people, yet 10 times as many people are killed in the US per year through non-military gunfire. The probability that an American who flies once a month in a commercial airplane will die in 2005 through a crash, supposing that terrorists crash one plane every month, is 1 in 540,000. While we deplore the 9/11 deaths of the four planes' passengers, let us remember that the equivalent of a jumbo jet full of children crashes every thirty minutes, the children killed by hunger or diseases that could be cured or prevented at a cost for a rich-world taxpayer of a Coke every two months.

Globalized terrorism

The 9/11 atrocities killed not only Americans but people from 41 other countries. The attackers came from a part of the world with different economies, different politics, different values. Yet in planning their attack they exploited the same technologies that we all use: e-mail, the Internet, computer networks, financial systems, and easy around-the-world travel. Terrorism is nothing if not globalized.

Terrorism and the global economy

Terrorism may damage the world economy in ways we do not suspect. If the US' extra spending on military responses to terrorism is eventually big enough to push up interest rates, that will add tens of billions of dollars to Third World debt. In turn, that will reduce the capacity of Third Worlders to buy US exports. Every third job in US manufacturing is linked to trade with developing countries. More than ever, Third World debt is a luxury we cannot afford.

Our blinkered outlooks

9/11 was, as many people said, a day that left our world different. True enough. Did it also change the world we carry around in our heads? Did it alter the way our inner world sees our outer world? Or are we still stuck with outmoded eyes? It was partly because we had seen the world in terms of a world gone by, rather than as a world that is changing at breakneck pace, that 9/11 took place. For instance, who would have thought that an aeroplane could be converted into a missile, one with power to match all but the biggest military missiles? If we had looked at a plane with the insight of a terrorist, we would have made sure he could never hijack the plane. And which American leader would have supposed in the 1980s that by supporting Bin Laden in his fight against the Russian invaders of Afghanistan, he might be funding a future enemy of the US?

Cyber terrorism

Could terrorists eventually use viruses and zombie computers to bring down the Internet? Such an army, helped by a few bombs, could disable route servers and render the Internet unworkable. A single computer virus could knock out routers or attack the Border Gateway Protocol (a language that routers use to talk to each other). In addition, the big exchange points could be attacked physically.

Anti-terrorism

More than 180 nations, 80% of the world's total, have joined an international coalition to fight terrorism. A few offer military support, while most make other contributions such as humanitarian aid and air space.

The arms trade

Much as we deplore mass killings by "rogue" governments and by rebel groups in numerous countries, we should bear in mind that the combatants would be unable to wreak such fearful injury to life and limb if they were denied the support of those many arms dealers in Europe and North America who supply weapons of every sort. In 2001, as part of its "war on terror" the US supplied $100 million of military equipment to the Philippines to fight militias and other rebel groups. Revolvers could be bought on the streets of Mindanao for $15 and machine guns for $375. In Africa, Asia, the Middle East, and Latin America, $22 billion a year is spent on weaponry. This sum would readily achieve the Millennium Development Goals of primary education for all children, $10 billion per year, and reduced infant/maternal mortality, $12 billion a year. In 1999, the arms trade was worth $52 billion, with developed countries accounting for 96% of exports.

Terrorist attacks in the 30 months after 9/11

1 United States Sept 11.01
New York, Washington, and Shanksville, over 3,000 people dead.

2 Tunisia April 11.02
Djerba, 21 dead.

3 Yemen Oct 6.02
Onboard an oil tanker, 1 dead.

4 Indonesia Oct 12.02
Bali, 202 dead.

5 Jordan October 28.02
Amman, 1 dead.

6 Kenya Nov 28.02
Mombasa, 15 dead.

7 Saudi Arabia May 12.03
Riyadh, 34 dead.

8 Morocco May 16.03
Casablanca, 41 dead.

9 Indonesia August 5.03
Jakarta, 13 dead,

10 Saudi Arabia Nov 8.03
Riyadh, 17 dead.

11 Turkey Nov 15. 03
Istanbul, 23 dead.

12 Turkey Nov 20. 03
Istanbul, 27 dead.

13 Spain March 11. 04
Madrid, 200 dead.

What makes a terrorist tick?

This is a fearful question since we have few worthwhile answers. We know for certain that many terrorists are driven by an overwhelming compulsion of some sort, otherwise they would not throw away their lives to support their cause. They occasionally tell us what they are against: Americans, Westerners in general, rich-world lifestyles, Christianity, irreligion, democracy, individualism, and women (except for men's pleasure). They rarely say anything about what they are for except random violence.

the world spent an average of PPP$150 per citizen on the arms race. Suppose that we could divert a mere 10 percent of the world's military budget into constructive activities, then we could eliminate many of the problems of our overburdened planet. The money spent in just 24 hours on the 1991 war over Kuwait could have funded a child immunization programme for five years, and prevented the deaths of one million children annually.

True, there was a decline in military expenditure following the end of the Cold War, and for several years thereafter expenditures remained more or less constant. But since 1999 – and especially since 9/11 – there has been a substantial increase. At the same time, resources devoted to military research and development (R&D) have increased, reflecting the continuing efforts to achieve military superiority. Armies absorb vast scientific and technological capabilities. Furthermore, decreasing military budgets in arms-producing countries have increased pressure to sell weapons abroad. With the end of the Cold War, the US overtook the former USSR as the number one arms exporter. The North often finds willing customers in the South: in 2001, the US exported $14 billion worth of arms to Latin America, Africa, Asia, and North Africa/Middle East (UK $4.6 billion, France and Russia $3.4 billion each).

The supreme irony is that, while political leaders around the world proclaim that they will not surrender one square metre of territory to a foreign invader, they allow huge areas of once-fertile lands to wash or blow away each year. They could purchase more real security, in the proper full sense of that term, if they used the funds to safeguard natural resources and enhance the human development on which their country's future depends.

Due to increased spending following the invasion of Iraq, world military expenditures reached $880 billion in 2003 (PPP$991 billion). Just 15 countries accounted for four-fifths of the world total, with the US share alone being 47 percent (cf. the developing world, 28 percent). In PPP$ terms and to show the economic muscle of these countries, China, India, and Russia make the top five (along with the US and France). In fact, nine of the top 15 in PPP$s are all new consumer countries (see pp. 234–35).

The United Nations, set up to help preserve peace through "international cooperation and collective security", enjoys funding equivalent to little over one percent of world military spending, with $2.6 billion spent on peacekeeping between 2002 and 2003, including $700 million in Sierra Leone, $608 million in Congo, $300 million in each of Kosovo and East Timor, and $200 million in Ethiopia/Eritrea. Yet that same year this "united" agency features "disunited" members leaving a peacekeeping fund with a $1.34 billion deficit. The US owed $536 million, Japan $312 million, Italy $41 million, China $39 million, Spain $32 million, and Brazil $28 million.

The cost of militarism

US spending in Afghanistan and Iraq
Most of the $84 billion (2004$s) cost of the 1991 Gulf War was covered by the allies, with US taxpayer costs of about $6.4 billion. By contrast, the 2003 Iraq War has already (late 2004) cost the US $150 billion, with long-term costs estimated at $3,400 for every US household. The same $150 billion could have provided health care for 82 million American children. At the global level the $150 billion could have halved world hunger as well as supplied HIV/AIDS vaccines, childhood immunization, and clean water/sanitation for the developing world for more than two years. A single Cruise Missile costs $800,000: 320 were launched at Baghdad. The US has also spent at least $50 billion on military activities in Afghanistan. Rebuilding Iraq could cost $50–75 billion – contrast US support for the Marshall Plan to rebuild Europe after World War II, around $90 billion in 2004 dollars.

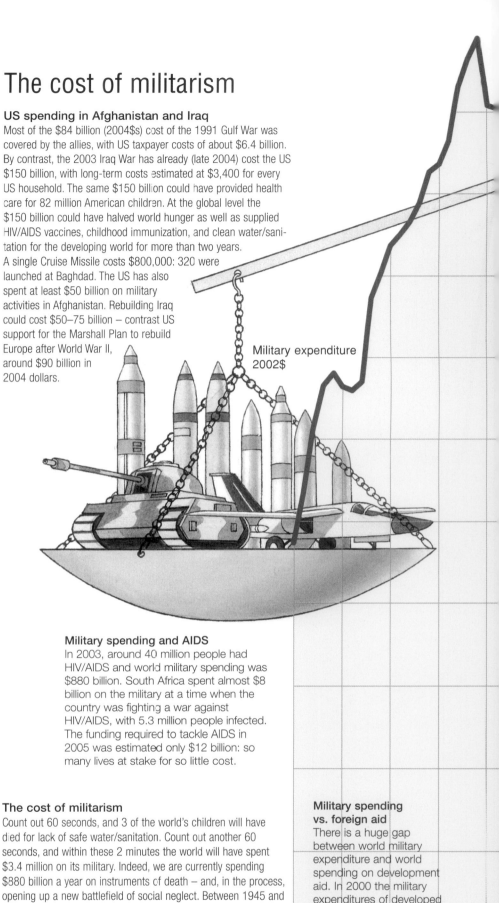

Military expenditure 2002$

Military spending and AIDS
In 2003, around 40 million people had HIV/AIDS and world military spending was $880 billion. South Africa spent almost $8 billion on the military at a time when the country was fighting a war against HIV/AIDS, with 5.3 million people infected. The funding required to tackle AIDS in 2005 was estimated only $12 billion: so many lives at stake for so little cost.

The cost of militarism
Count out 60 seconds, and 3 of the world's children will have died for lack of safe water/sanitation. Count out another 60 seconds, and within these 2 minutes the world will have spent $3.4 million on its military. Indeed, we are currently spending $880 billion a year on instruments of death – and, in the process, opening up a new battlefield of social neglect. Between 1945 and 2000, at least 50 million lives were lost in war and other forms of violent conflict. Contrast the number dying each year from social neglect: 3.7 million deaths among the underfed, 1.7 million due to unsafe water and sanitation, and 1.6 million from indoor smoke (cooking stoves).

The Romans were among the first to insist that the only way to secure peace was to prepare for war, regardless of the cost. But around the world the cost is mounting. Rehabilitation costs following the 1991 Gulf War – let alone the latest invasion of Iraq – totalled over $200 billion. In addition to the tens of thousands of civilian casualties, the allied bombing seriously damaged water supply, purification and sewerage systems. The death rate of children under 5 years old increased almost fourfold.

Military spending vs. foreign aid
There is a huge gap between world military expenditure and world spending on development aid. In 2000 the military expenditures of developed countries were 10 times larger than their aid outlays. In 2004, the US budgeted $1 in aid for every $19 in defence. Between 2000 and 2005, the US will have spent roughly $2.2 trillion on military activities. The tragedy is that sustainable economic development could remove many pre-war tensions.

1965   1970   1975   1980   1985

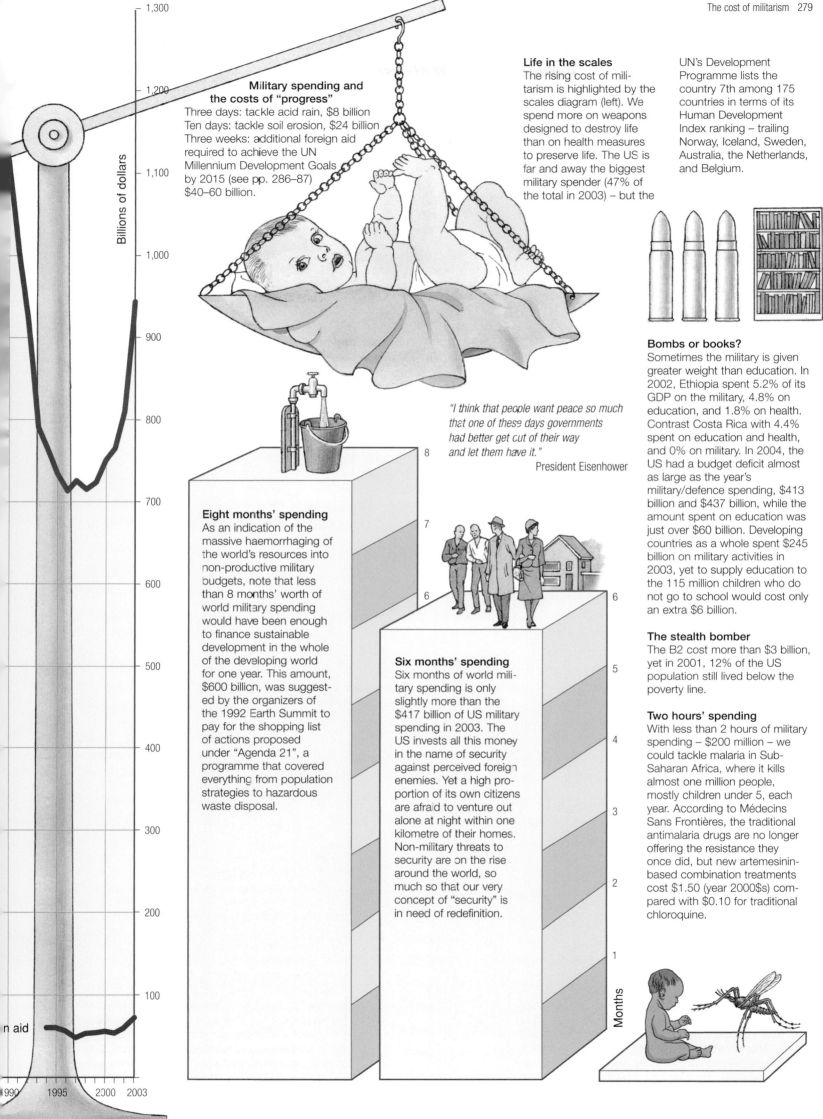

Military spending and the costs of "progress"

Three days: tackle acid rain, $8 billion
Ten days: tackle soil erosion, $24 billion
Three weeks: additional foreign aid required to achieve the UN Millennium Development Goals by 2015 (see pp. 286–87) $40–60 billion.

Life in the scales

The rising cost of militarism is highlighted by the scales diagram (left). We spend more on weapons designed to destroy life than on health measures to preserve life. The US is far and away the biggest military spender (47% of the total in 2003) – but the UN's Development Programme lists the country 7th among 175 countries in terms of its Human Development Index ranking – trailing Norway, Iceland, Sweden, Australia, the Netherlands, and Belgium.

Bombs or books?

Sometimes the military is given greater weight than education. In 2002, Ethiopia spent 5.2% of its GDP on the military, 4.8% on education, and 1.8% on health. Contrast Costa Rica with 4.4% spent on education and health, and 0% on military. In 2004, the US had a budget deficit almost as large as the year's military/defence spending, $413 billion and $437 billion, while the amount spent on education was just over $60 billion. Developing countries as a whole spent $245 billion on military activities in 2003, yet to supply education to the 115 million children who do not go to school would cost only an extra $6 billion.

The stealth bomber

The B2 cost more than $3 billion, yet in 2001, 12% of the US population still lived below the poverty line.

Two hours' spending

With less than 2 hours of military spending – $200 million – we could tackle malaria in Sub-Saharan Africa, where it kills almost one million people, mostly children under 5, each year. According to Médecins Sans Frontières, the traditional antimalaria drugs are no longer offering the resistance they once did, but new artemesinin-based combination treatments cost $1.50 (year 2000$s) compared with $0.10 for traditional chloroquine.

Eight months' spending

As an indication of the massive haemorrhaging of the world's resources into non-productive military budgets, note that less than 8 months' worth of world military spending would have been enough to finance sustainable development in the whole of the developing world for one year. This amount, $600 billion, was suggested by the organizers of the 1992 Earth Summit to pay for the shopping list of actions proposed under "Agenda 21", a programme that covered everything from population strategies to hazardous waste disposal.

Six months' spending

Six months of world military spending is only slightly more than the $417 billion of US military spending in 2003. The US invests all this money in the name of security against perceived foreign enemies. Yet a high proportion of its own citizens are afraid to venture out alone at night within one kilometre of their homes. Non-military threats to security are on the rise around the world, so much so that our very concept of "security" is in need of redefinition.

"I think that people want peace so much that one of these days governments had better get out of their way and let them have it."

President Eisenhower

Mass slaughter

We can now be poisoned, burned, or simply vaporized by courtesy of weapons that can kill thousands or even millions of people in an instant, and do it all over again within another instant if need be. Weapons of Mass Destruction (WMDs) have featured in the Vietnam War and the two Gulf wars, though not nearly on a scale to match their potential. The principal WMDs are nuclear bombs, and the ultimate horror is a nuclear exchange. It would not be a war as generally understood, since the conflict would all be over within minutes at most as both combatants wiped each other out – and entire non-combatant nations would qualify as "collateral damage".

Apart from the grave disputes between the nuclear haves and have-nots, there is a further threat in nuclear armouries. Only a fraction of such weapons needs to be detonated to lift so much smoke, soot, dust, and other debris into the atmosphere that the sun would be blotted out over not only the combatant nations but much of the rest of the planet, thus precipitating a "nuclear winter" of sub-zero temperatures and darkness halting all plant growth. The ecological consequences would be devastating, with massive destruction of agriculture, forests, and other major ecosystems. Our civilization could go out with a multi-megaton bang.

Plus we are living with a new warfare spectre: the deliberate use of diseases. Recall the anthrax letters in the US in 2001 which killed several people and infected many more. Throughout history, diseases have caused as many deaths during wars as weapons, and military strategy has often encouraged their spread among the enemy. Biological warfare embraces disease-causing micro-organisms, notably viruses and bacteria. It can also involve the deployment of toxins or poisonous substances such as ricin. Their destructive potential is enormous. One-quarter of all deaths worldwide are due to infectious diseases, many of which could be readily released by terrorists. Many nations have signed the Biological and Toxin Weapons Convention, but it is very difficult to monitor and to enforce.

There is still more bad news, this time in the form of chemical weapons such as nerve gases, poisons, and defoliants. These weapons are becoming popular choices for developing countries because they are cheaper and easier to acquire than nuclear weapons. Although they are not as destructive as nuclear bombs, chemical weapons can serve as an affordable deterrent. Iraq is the only developing country to admit to possessing a few minor chemical weapons, but around a dozen more are suspected to have undeclared stocks. There are substantial stocks too in developed countries, some left over from World War II. The US and some of the former Soviet Union countries have tens of thousands of tonnes each.

Weapons of mass destruction

Nuclear powers

There are five fully-fledged nuclear powers with 30,000 nuclear warheads in 2002, fewer than half as many as in the 1986 peak. But the US still has 10,640 warheads and Russia 18,000, while the other three – UK, France, and China – together have roughly 1,000. India, Pakistan, and Israel possess a much smaller number (see pp. 275–76). Since 1945, at least 128,000 warheads have been built (the US 70,000, the former Soviet Union 55,000). There is enough weapons-grade plutonium worldwide to supply 85,000 warheads. As many as 4,600 US and Russian warheads are still on the "hair trigger" alert status that allows immediate launch on warning – and that also carries a high risk of accidental war. The ultimate aim should be to reduce US and Russian arsenals of strategic warheads down to 2,500 or fewer, by contrast with the 3,500 established by recent negotiations.

As many as 44 countries possess nuclear power reactors or research reactors. All nations that have signed the Nuclear Non-Proliferation Treaty are committed to the "unequivocal elimination of nuclear weapons", yet none of the "Big 5" has done anything to suggest they will eventually abolish their arsenals – a failure that guarantees grave disputes between the nuclear haves and have-nots.

Detection of WMDs

As the 2003 Iraq War demonstrated, it is virtually impossible to comb an enemy country with weapons inspectors and find WMDs Consider the challenge of searching an area the size of Vermont or Wales, relatively small expanses, and needing to check every last patch of territory the size of a tennis court.

Miniaturization of WMDs

Innovative science has come up with a nuclear weapon that could be hidden in a car boot. Maxi-miniaturization can be achieved by a few grains of anthrax, still more by a handful of lethal bacteria or viruses. A whole city could be held in thrall to mere specks of bugs.

The Nuclear Non-Proliferation Treaty (NPT)

This had only a few dozen signatories in 1970; by 2004, there were 188. All but three – India, Pakistan, and Israel – have now formally joined or have pledged. The Treaty's objective is to "prevent the spread of nuclear weapons and weapons technology, to promote cooperation in the peaceful uses of nuclear energy and to further the goal of achieving nuclear disarmament and general and complete disarmament".

World Nuclear Arsenal 1945–2000

Year	Number of nuclear warheads
1945	2
1950	303
1955	2,490
1960	20,368
1965	39,047
1970	39,691
1971	41,365
1972	44,020
1973	47,741
1974	50,840
1975	52,323
1976	53,252
1977	54,978
1978	56,805
1979	59,120
1980	61,480
1981	63,054
1982	64,769
1983	66,979
1984	67,585
1986	69,478
1987	68,835
1988	67,041
1989	63,645
1990	60,236
1991	55,772
1992	52,972
1993	50,008
1994	46,542
1995	43,200
1996	40,100
1997	37,535
1998	34,535
1999	31,960
2000	31,535

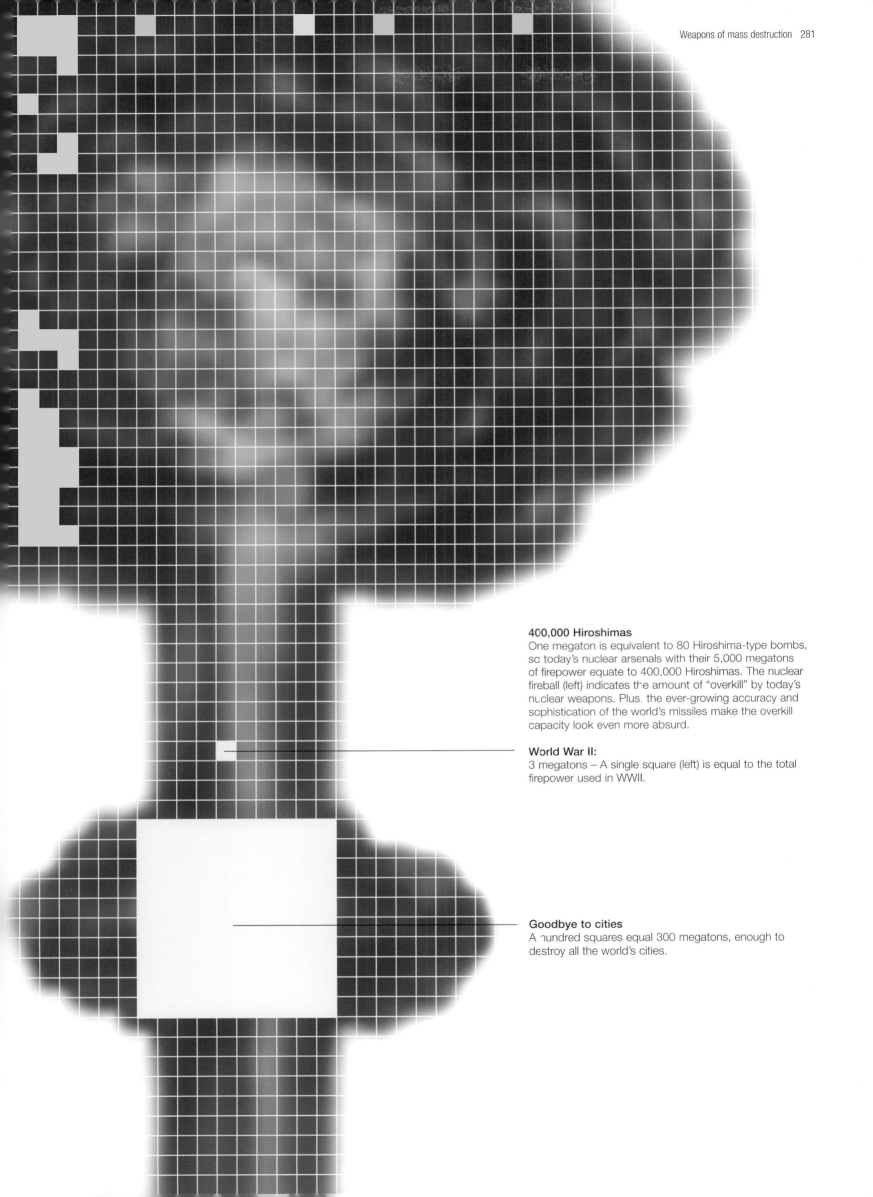

400,000 Hiroshimas
One megaton is equivalent to 80 Hiroshima-type bombs, so today's nuclear arsenals with their 5,000 megatons of firepower equate to 400,000 Hiroshimas. The nuclear fireball (left) indicates the amount of "overkill" by today's nuclear weapons. Plus, the ever-growing accuracy and sophistication of the world's missiles make the overkill capacity look even more absurd.

World War II:
3 megatons – A single square (left) is equal to the total firepower used in WWII.

Goodbye to cities
A hundred squares equal 300 megatons, enough to destroy all the world's cities.

Under New Management

We are a privileged generation, to be living at a great turning point in the story of Gaia and humanity. Faced by multiplying crises, we are challenged to a creative endeavour surpassing that required of any earlier society. To survive and prosper, *Homo sapiens* must now advance from a pioneer species, which is aggressive, prolific, and greedy for resources, into a climax species, which recognizes ecological limits, swaps assertiveness for cooperation, and makes a golden rule of self-regulation. After setting ourselves apart from nature, we must become a part of nature again: truce, treaty, and reconciliation – and so become, truly, humankind. This is a challenge indeed, one that requires a sweeping revolution in how we act, think, and feel; in how we use our technology; and above all, in how we manage ourselves.

Today's international institutions and laws are compacts between governments, not peoples, and have failed to evolve in step with economic, political, and environmental pressures. In order to steer our way through coming crises we need to reshape these institutions to foster better "governance".

Better governance does not mean more government or improved government. It means cooperative self-management by everyone. It means creating a global "network" of participatory mechanisms that involve people from all sectors of society and at all levels, from local to global. Whereas government involves states, governance involves us all.

The key organ of governance is the UN. After a chequered history, it plays a growing role in environment and security issues. Democratization of the UN is thus very important in broadening the global decision-making process. Its aim is to foster international governance for self-reliant societies. A new Non-Governmental Assembly could be added with delegates from NGOs, including trade unions, the professions, cities, women's groups, corporations, financial bodies, etc. As a UN "upper house" with voting powers, such an Assembly would be pioneering and better able to take a global view. The General Assembly would still decide much of UN policy, but the smallest city would also be able to influence world affairs.

Sustainable development should become the cen-tral thrust of UN reform. We need a UN system of collective security which can prevent conflicts and avert environmental threats. The UN Commission on Sustainable Development (CSD), established by the 1992 Earth Summit, is one example and the 2002 World Summit on Sustainable Development in Johannesburg put sustainable development on international agendas and led to various commitments.

Global governance

The world community is ever-more interdependent with a growing commitment to internationalism, as witness the transnational links between NGOs and professional bodies. But we need a political transformation too, to meet the challenge of building global self-governance, with institutions assuring environmentally sound and socially equitable development. This new global governance will have its sovereignty rooted in empowered communities, manifested in national and regional governments. It will feature the legitimacy to govern responsibly, expressed through international institutions with the strength to hold their members accountable. Bottom line: we live in an unusually dynamic era with a historic opportunity for global governance.

Programmes and funds
UNCTAD
United Nations conference on Trade and Development
> **ITC**
> International Trade Centre
> UNCTAD/WTO

UNDCP
United Nations Drug Control Programme

UNEP
United Nations Environment Programme

UNHSP
United Nations Human Settlements Programme

UNDP
United Nations Development Programme

UNIFEM
United Nations Development Fund for Women

UNIV
United Nations Volunteers

UNPFA
United Nations Population Fund

UNHCR
Office of the United Nations High Commissioner for Refugees

UNICEF
United Nations Children's Fund

WFP
World Food Programme

UNRWA
United Nations Relief and Works Agency for Palestine Refugees in the Near East

Phoenix of the new nations
Although political leaders pay lip service to the need to protect the sovereignty of the nation state, it is being steadily eroded as nations become ever-more interdependent. Sovereignty has already been reduced by: regional laws (such as those controlling the European Union) and supranational laws on human rights, the environment, and disarmament. Although the nation state will not "wither away" in the foreseeable future, its main role will often reflect policies devised by global bodies.

World citizens
An alert citizenry is the ultimate check on the activities of politicians and corporations. Governance depends on individuals exerting their rights and responsibilities, so as to monitor the activities of governments and apply pressure to ensure that the rule of international law is not violated. Good "world citizens" will refuse to be influenced by the propaganda of governments or the media. They will be sensitive to the need to match consumerism with sustainable development, and to use their voting power to ensure that economic policies reflect proper care of the world's resources.

A new UN net

The UN's structure has not been adequate to solve security, political, or ideological problems, although its record on humanitarian issues is quite good. Now that the East–West ideological conflict is over, the time is ripe for UN reform. Under the auspices of the international Conferences on a More Democratic United Nations, there have been many reform proposals, from changing the patterns cf voting power in the Security Council to the establishment of a people's cr parliamentary assembly as another UN organ – a counterbalance to the General Assembly.

The village voice

A main aim of international governance will be to establish the means of sustainable development in the global, as well as the national, interest. This will require the maximum involvement of local human knowledge. Problems should be initially addressed and solutions devised at local levels. Such grassroots involvement and community action will stimulate citizens' movements to influence a UN Second Assembly.

NGOs and the voice of the world

The growth of NGOs was one of the main political features of the 20th century. While only 41 NGOs enjoyed "consultative" status with the UN system in 1948, almost 3,000 were accredited at the 2002 World Summit on Sustainable Development. NGOs are strengthening their case by acting internationally – almost 50,000 INGOs in 2001 (see pp. 264–65).

A prime phenomenon: synergisms

Synergisms are an increasingly frequent phenomenon of our world, little though we may be aware of them. Meaning, literally, the uniting of energies, they are exceptionally significant. For instance, a plant's tolerance of one stress tends to be lower when other stresses are at work. If it experiences reduced sunlight and hence less photosynthesis, it suffers more in the cold than would a plant enjoying normal growth and full vigour. A similarly amplified effect operates the other way round as well. It's not a case of 4 + 4 = 8. It's 4 x 4 = 16. In certain circumstances, a synergisms-induced outcome can be ten times greater than the simple sum of the component mechanisms. Put one problem together with another and you don't get a double problem, you get a super problem.

Yet many scientists – who should be more aware of synergisms than anyone else – seem disinclined to comprehend the phenomenon in its full scope. While they are well aware of the main mechanisms of, for example, species extinction – notably reduced numbers, reduced gene pool, shrunken habitat, polluted environment, and threat from competitor species (especially "alien invaders") – these mechanisms tend to be studied in isolation from each other. We know much less and understand less still about the dynamic interplay between individual mechanisms.

Synergisms are unusually prominent in the biodiversity sphere, to the extent that they will surely lead to an extinction episode of greater scale than generally envisaged. They may also cause the episode to be telescoped in time, meaning that the full biotic crisis could arrive even sooner than we anticipate. To the extent that we can discern some possible synergistic interactions, the better we shall start to understand some potential patterns and processes as the species extinction spasm works itself out – and we'll be better able to anticipate and even prevent some of them.

Let us look at a specific instance. The decline of many amphibian species in several parts of the world is thought to be due to synergized interactions between pollution (acid rain, mercury toxification, etc.), fragmentation if not destruction of habitats (notably aquatic eutrophication), altered soil chemistry (moisture, pH, silt, and organic matter), vegetation loss (especially deforestation), and shifts in atmospheric temperatures. Also involved could be enhanced UVB radiation through depletion of the ozone layer, and desiccation of ecosystems through incipient global warming. The general decline of amphibians could have sizeable repercussions for their ecosystems and associated communities.

In short, it will increasingly be the case for several environmental factors to interact with multiplicative impacts. They include deforestation, desertification, acid rain, freak weather phenomena, global warming, ozone-layer depletion, alterations in wildlife habitats, and chemical pollutants. The result could be pronouncedly adverse repercussions for biodiversity.

Synergisms

Linkages to global warming

Climate change makes things warmer at the surface of the Earth, by contrast with what happens in the stratosphere, with its marked cooling. This cooling further depletes the ozone layer, meaning in turn that more UVB radiation reaches the Earth's surface. In turn again, the UVB causes greater damage to phytoplankton in the topmost layer of the ocean – and in turn yet again, this means a decline in the phytoplankton's capacity to absorb carbon dioxide from the atmosphere, thus adding to global warming processes including cooling of the stratosphere. These feedback-loop processes could one day lead to an emphatic tightening of the multiple linkages at work, ending up with a global warming outcome that finally overtakes us with ever-increasing speed. Were we to then decide that we don't like global warming, we could find ourselves far too late to do anything much about slowing it, let alone reversing it.

Acid rain in the moist tropics

This is already a problem in the forests of southern China, and it appears set to shortly affect several other sectors of tropical forests, including central Indonesia, central-southern Thailand, southwestern India, West Africa, southern Brazil and northern Colombia. Present stresses on tropical forests, such as over-logging and agricultural settlement, are grossly increasing the forests' susceptibility to injury from acid rain – and the depletive process works the other way round as well.

Genetic depletion and crop plants

The changed temperatures and rainfall regimes expected in a greenhouse-affected world will not prove appropriate for many crops insofar as these are finely attuned to current climatic patterns. There will be a premium on expanding the genetic underpinnings of crops in order to increase their resistance to too much or too little rainfall, or new diseases and pathogens, among other problems arising from global warming. Yet the gene reservoirs of many crop plants are being more rapidly depleted than ever due to virtual wipe-out of wild relatives of crop plants.

Saving the Fynbos

The fynbos plant community in the southern tip of Africa is so rich in plant species that it ranks as one of six plant kingdoms in the world. The biggest threat to this exceptional biodiversity comes from invasive alien plants, such as pines and wattles. The invasives are also a curse in terms of water security, the productive potential of land, and the ecological integrity of natural systems. They also exacerbate wild fires and erosion. The government's "Working for Water" programme – Africa's biggest conservation programme that in 2004 employed 33,000 people with a budget of US$80 million – combats these invaders. The outcome is a win-win affair.

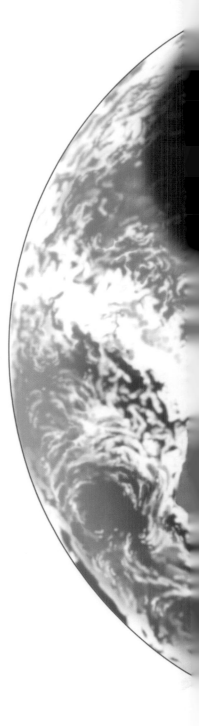

Positive synergisms

Of course there can be positive synergisms, too. For instance, the rise to ultimate power of Gorbachev coincided with a build-up of citizen anger at widespread environmental decay in the former Soviet Union. The two together gave Gorbachev an opportunity to exercise his exceptional power by approving the destruction of the Berlin Wall. Without both factors operating at once and with mutually reinforcing effect, it is doubtful whether there would have been enough political momentum to precipitate such a cataclysmic event as the Wall's destruction. Moreover, the end of the Wall then linked up with other political and economic phenomena to warrant the collapse of the Soviet Union and its Communism, plus an end to the Cold War.

A similar synergism arose much earlier, and this time in the US. The civil rights movement mobilized millions of followers who struggled for years before their energies were finally galvanized by the emergent leadership of Martin Luther King. There have been lots of occasions when a citizenry movement has not achieved its ultimate potential until it has been fired up by the vital spark from a charismatic leader. For instance, Churchill – and Hitler.

Citizens in every country should mark these examples of how grassroots activism can be made much more productive when allied to a parallel source of action.

Linkages

Linkages have become a pervasive feature of everyday life. They seem set to become still more numerous and significant as more people engage in more activities of more sorts. Far from being isolated and occasional aspects of everyday life, linkages are now a built-in feature that impinges upon many if not most aspects of the human enterprise. There are, for instance, the hamburger connection, the cassava connection, and the tropical timber trade. Each of these illustrates how marketplace mechanisms in developed nations of the temperate zones cause excessive use of natural resources in developing countries of the tropics.

One example of linkages is the variation of the "songbird connection" in North America. Each autumn more than 150 species of North American songbirds, or about two-thirds of all woodland and forest bird species, leave North America for winter habitats in Central and South America. As these several billion birds arrive in their wintering grounds, they find their forest habitats declining, largely because of the hamburger connection. As a result, each spring in North America sees fewer birds returning to their breeding grounds. It is precisely at the time of the songbirds' return that a number of insect species emerge after the winter. Many of them are at a critical stage of their life cycles, in the form of e.g. larvae that leave them unusually vulnerable to insect-eating birds, notably songbirds.

This linkage applies notably to the boreal forests of eastern Canada, where 35 insectivorous bird species serve as a natural control of the spruce budworm and thus of forest renewal patterns. Already certain of these bird species have lost 50% of their numbers, and if they were to decline by 75%, the loss of functional diversity would flip the boreal forest renewal pattern into a wholly different state.

The international sugar trade

The US protects its sugar producers with subsidies that effectively create prices several times above world market levels. This has resulted in the decline of a major export market for the Philippines, in turn eliminating the jobs of numerous sugarcane workers. In turn again, this has forced large numbers of unemployed Filipinos to migrate into the country's uplands, where they cause much deforestation and hence depletion of habitats for some of the 3,700 plant species, plus associated animal species, confined to the country and concentrated in the upland forests. Thus Washington's sugar subsidies play a prime part in the loss of species in a country thousands of miles away.

Sustainability – too expensive?

We hear much about sustainability, whether of the economy, the environment, or of development overall. Plainly we need sustainability in the long run, otherwise we shall simply run out of planet. So why haven't governments, businesses, and other major players got on with the job? Answer, it is considered too expensive. But as so often, political leaders, corporate chiefs, and others highlight the costs of action while ignoring the concealed costs of inaction. Here are a few illustrative costs of unsustainability.

Burning a gallon of gasoline costs much more than the $2 that Americans pay at the pump. The pollution, road congestion, and other "externalities" it causes cost the US economy almost $700 billion per year, or a whopping $2,500 per citizen. Burning fossil fuels other than gasoline causes environmental problems that cost roughly $200 billion worldwide. While the total costs of global warming remain largely unknown, there is broad agreement that they could well exceed $1 trillion per year, possibly many times more. Other environmental problems, such as soil erosion, desertification, agricultural pests, and mass extinction of species, total at least $850 billion a year. This, like the other estimates, is very cautious, with actual costs likely to be a good deal higher.

Many of these problems could be overcome in a highly cost-effective manner. For instance, in the early 1990s desertification was estimated to cause annual food losses of $42 billion worldwide, whereas rehabilitation of those lands suitable (about 50 percent) would cost only $11 billion. Soil erosion in the US costs $44 billion per year, whereas soil conservation would take only $8 billion.

Consider an alternative calculation, this one centring not on particular problems but reckoning the total benefits received from all our environments, including grasslands, forests, oceans, the atmosphere, and wild species (insects pollinate our crops with benefits of $200 billion per year). According to a worldwide team of economists, total benefits, supplied free, were worth $33 trillion per year in the late 1990s. Hence the world's "gross natural product" was roughly the same as the world's gross economic product.

The Rio Earth Summit in 1992 proposed a budget for sustainable development of $600 billion per year, whereupon the 163 governments assembled protested they could not possibly afford anything so costly. Yet they could have found funds aplenty if they had looked in the right place. "Perverse" subsides amount to at least $2 trillion a year worldwide (see p. 232).

Our present mode of exploiting the Earth and its environmental resources suggests that we view our planet as a business liquidating its capital, even though the "interest" available could increase indefinitely. Or, to put it another way: should we not live on our planet as if we intend to stay, rather than as if we are visiting it for a weekend? Bottom line: we should view the world's economy as a wholly owned subsidiary of the world's environments.

The great transition

Although we live in the finite environment of Earth, we continue to exploit its resources as if they were infinite, or as if we had another planet parked out there in space for us to use when Earth runs out. We cannot continue this way for long. We will soon have to bring under control the dangerous trends of overpopulation, energy depletion, environmental abuse, and wasteful military spending, as shown by the exponential curves of the graphs (right). This unsustainable growth is setting our civilization on a course for eventual collapse. Before we can make the transition to sustainable and equitable global living in balance with Gaia and ourselves, we have to turn these growth rates into stable, "steady state" cycles of consumption and renewal. Any economic growth we achieve thereafter will have to come from more efficient use of our resources.

Millennium development goals to be achieved by 2015:
• Halve extreme poverty and hunger.

• Achieve universal primary education (India should have 95% of its children in school by 2005).

• Empower women and promote gender equality (two-thirds of the world's illiterates are women, and 80% of its refugees are women and children).

• Cut under-five mortality by two-thirds (11 million children die every year, albeit a total down from 15 million in 1980).

• Reduce maternal mortality by three-quarters.

• Reverse the spread of diseases, especially HIV/AIDS and malaria (Brazil, Senegal, Uganda, and Thailand show that we can stop HIV in its tracks).

• Supply safe water and sanitation (more than one billion people still have no safe water, even though during the 1990s nearly one billion people achieved access).

• Cut malnutrition by half (equates to a cut of 28 million per year; achieved thus far, 3 million).

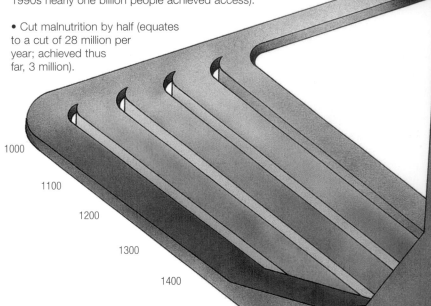

1000
1100
1200
1300
1400
1500
1600
1700
1800
1900
2000

Population growth

We already have a range of prophecies and prescriptions which encourage us to make the transition to sustainable planet management, such as:

"In the end, sustainable development is not a fixed state of harmony, but rather a process of change in which the exploitation of resources, the direction of investments, the orientation of technological development, and institutional change are made consistent with future as well as present needs."
Our Common Future (World Commission on Environment and Development, 1987)

The new security

Our transition to a sustainable society will encompass a new definition of "security", one based on "the four Es" of Energy, Environment, Economics, and Equity. Attaining energy security means abandoning the supply-side addiction of exploiting ever-more oil and gas fields, in favour of increased energy efficiency and use of renewable sources. This will reduce our dependency on oil-rich regions as well as cutting emissions of greenhouse gases, thus contributing to environmental security. Improving economic security requires the transfer of capital and human talent from the military to the civilian sectors. Building and maintaining the infrastructure for a sustainable, energy efficient and socially equitable society would create far more jobs globally. In the early 1990s, spending $1 billion on guided-missile production created only 12,000 jobs, whereas the same money spent on pollution control created 22,000 jobs and on educational services 85,000 jobs.

The world's priorities?

Additional expenditure required per year to supply:

Universal primary education	$15 billion
Basic health and nutrition for all	$21 billion
Water and sanitation for all	$23 billion
Reproductive health for all women	$11 billion
Adult literacy campaign	$4 billion
Upgraded agriculture in Third World	$40 billion
To slow desertification	$11 billion
To prevent soil erosion	$18 billion
To safeguard 25 biodiversity hotspots	$1 billion

Total $140 billion

Roughly 60 days of military spending.

Compare:

Military annual spending worldwide	$880 billion
Alcoholic drinks in Europe	$105 billion
Cigarettes in Europe	$50 billion
Ice cream in Europe	$11 billion
Pet foods in Europe & US	$17 billion
Perfumes in Europe & US	$12 billion
Cosmetics in the US	$8 billion

Total $1,083 billion, say $1 trillion per annum

Energy
consumption

Environmental
abuse

Military
spending

Primary-resource
consumption

Tools for transition

The transition to a sustainable society is eminently possible. We have the tools but we lack the will. First and foremost, we need to stabilize both population and consumption. Media predictions show population increasing by almost half before it levels out. If we want to avoid having nature do the job for us, and in distinctly unpleasant fashion, we can achieve it earlier ourselves by redoubling our efforts to provide family planning and lifestyle security for all.

The greatest sign of hope is the slow shift in world opinion towards more responsible care of Earth's resources. The principles of Sustainable Development, formulated in the 1987 report "Our Common Future" by the World Commission on Environment and Development, have been accepted by a majority of governments, key NGOs, and all major international agencies. Since 1987, the twin issues of environment and development have risen higher on our political

agendas, be they international, national, community, or individual. This surge of concern has been further articulated by the 1992 Earth Summit and the 2002 World Summit on Sustainable Development.

Management or medicine

Many civilizations in the past have foundered through failure of their natural environments, leaving ruined landscapes to remind us of their fates. Where ancient Sumer once flourished with gardens and irrigated fields, now is desert. Parts of the Sahara itself were fertile and wooded before the Romans arrived. Environmental science today sees such past events in a new light, revealing that these cultures exploited their environments beyond their powers of regeneration and so brought about their own society's demise. The history of humanity looks like a similar tale of growing injury and impoverishment, precipitated by an opportunist species which over-exploits its environments.

Signs of hope

The rise of human numbers and activities has cast a long shadow across the Earth. Fortunately we now possess the tools to make a transition to a sustainable society – one not of shadows but of light. A society where human civilization is integrated within Gaia, and both the managed lands and the wild lands are synchronized in harmony, as this illustration suggests. Many signs of hope stem from new ways of thinking about our common future. There are numerous paths towards sustainable development, and many groups and individuals have already started along them.

Is Sumer's fate now to be ours but on a global scale? Or can we, by prudent management, prevent it? "Planet management" is now an established term, even adopted by large governmental and corporate programmes for satellite communications and long-term environmental monitoring. There is a risk that these powerful bodies may begin to use the term to imply control or rule of the planet by humans, thus setting humans "above" nature. We are a part of nature, a single member of Gaia or the "very democratic entity" described by James Lovelock. Of course we cannot rule the biosphere – rather we are ourselves ruled by the biosphere. Thus planet management must imply management of ourselves.

The art of planet management is to regulate our human affairs so that the well-being of Gaia – including all peoples, both present and future – comes first on the grounds that we depend on the whole for our survival. Such self-management cannot be imposed from above by governments. To be effective it needs to draw on all the diversity of human cultures, just as evolution draws on the biological diversity of Gaia.

There is a sharpening debate over what should be the role of humans in relationship to planet Earth. Rather than "managers", how about "stewards" or "caretakers"? Lovelock himself, noting that on past performance humans make poor managers, suggests the designation "shop stewards", i.e. active representatives of all life forms. He has also proposed "planetary medicine" with respect to the health of Gaia, akin to the role of the family doctor who, after cleaning up cuts and bruises, prescribes fresh air and good food in order to allow nature to do its healing. As planetary doctors we need to repair the injuries we have inflicted: stop polluting the air and water and depleting the nutrients of the soil; and allow forests and other ecosystems of the Earth some respite from our assaults. Then Gaia's systems can recover their naturally robust good health.

The Auroville experiment

A community in southern India shows a specially sustainable path into our future. Auroville, meaning "city of the dawn", has 1,500 residents, 500 of them Indians and the rest from 40 countries around the world. Their eventual aim is to build up to 50,000 members. When the first pioneers arrived, they were armed with little more than their ideals for a new model of life on Earth, centred on simplified living, self-reliance, and environmental know-how. They could hardly have been assigned a more unpromising place. They were allotted 10 sq. km of land so degraded that it was officially declared "unfit for human habitation". There were only a few dozen trees, there were scant streams and no rivers, and there was next to no topsoil. Today, the soil cover has been restored, rivers flourish, and there are 2 million trees. The community's agriculture supplies half of its food while depending on organic fertilizers and pesticides. Energy is supplied mainly by solar and wind power. Members use photovoltaics to supply electricity to light their buildings, to pump and heat water, and to cook food. In still more striking ways, Auroville's lifestyles epitomize the goal of "living lightly on the face of the planet" Members agree to a cash income of only $100 per month, together with subsidized food, housing, water, clothing, and other basic needs, plus permanent employment, worth $250 per month.

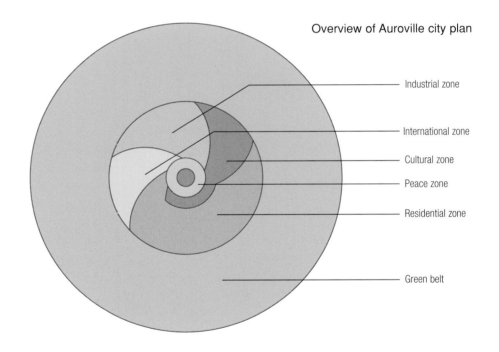

Overview of Auroville city plan

- Industrial zone
- International zone
- Cultural zone
- Peace zone
- Residential zone
- Green belt

"The unleashed power of the atom has changed everything except our way of thinking ... we need an essentially new way of thinking if mankind is to survive."

Albert Einstein

"I have a high regard for our species, for all its newness and immaturity as a member of the biosphere. As evolutionary time is measured, we arrived here only a few moments ago and we have a lot of growing up to do. If we succeed, we could become a sort of collective mind for all the Earth. At the moment, for all our juvenility as a species, we are surely the brightest and brainiest of the Earth's working parts. I trust us to have the will to keep going, and to maintain as best we can the life of the planet."

Lewis Thomas

A new ethic

Alone among species, humankind has been able to leave the biosphere and study it from the outside. We are now able to look in on the fragile miracle of Gaia, and on our own behaviour towards it with a sharpened perception.

As our vision clears and our danger becomes more apparent, we should question our role in an otherwise harmonious world. We have already acquired considerable power, that much is obvious. We are witnessing the consequences of our economic and technological penetration of the planetary cycles of energy and materials – cycles that have co-evolved with life for almost the past four billion years.

The challenge we face is to bring our activities within the carrying capacity of the Earth's supporting ecosystems, while still improving the quality of life for people today and without reducing the prospects for future generations. This is the challenge of sustainability. Meeting it will require changes in how we all evaluate our needs, how we want to live, and how we perceive other life and each other.

Pre-industrial peoples have often expanded their populations beyond the available resource base until they starved or were forced to migrate. Eventually a growing urban population demanded intensive agriculture yielding a surplus, and then an expansion of production to be met by conquest, colonization, or improved technology. The Earth and its creatures were increasingly considered the property of human-kind: for domination, control, and manipulation, until ultimately the whole of nature was seen like some giant machine designed solely for human benefit.

The belief that we are "apart from" nature, instead of a part of nature, has become an intrinsic aspect of the dominant world view – a human-centred or anthropocentric philosophy.

Fortunately, we can create a new ethic, one that cares for all species and all humanity. It will be a new world view, a new planetary concern. Creation of such an ethic is recognized as an imperative by certain world institutions. It features prominently, for example, in "Caring for the Earth: a Strategy for Sustainable Living", launched by IUCN, UNEP, and WWF in 1991, which proposed "a world ethic for living sustainably" as a foundation for its principles. No longer apart from nature, "Every human being is a part of the community of life, made up of living creatures. This community links all human societies, present and future generations, and with the rest of nature. It embraces both cultural and natural diversity."

Many analysts go further and stress that because of the interdependence of all living things, the natural world has certain rights, including the right to future existence, which are quite independent of its utilitarian value to humankind.

A major contribution to the debate over anthropocentrism has been generated by James Lovelock's Gaia hypothesis, viz. the concept of the Earth as a "super-organism" where life and the environment have co-evolved in a way to promote the maintenance of life. This "organic" concept of the Earth has great force. It signals the awakening of a new and more mature vision: a culture and a technology that seek not to control the world but to participate with it, not to operate upon nature but to cooperate with nature. Some scientists have even taken the concept further, to an ethic of healing our troubled relationship with Gaia.

We now have the skills to derive benefit from natural systems without destroying their ability to renew themselves. We can live off the biosphere's income rather than depleting its capital. We can cause forests to spring up on barren lands, safeguard species from extinction, renew the soil, reverse the pollution of oceans and atmosphere, harness the renewable power of the sun, and minimize the consumption of resources.

Paul Hawken and Amory and Hunter Lovins in their book "Natural Capitalism":

"Imagine for a moment a world where cities have become peaceful and serene because cars and buses are whisper quiet, vehicles exhaust only water vapor, and parks and greenways have replaced unneeded urban freeways. OPEC has ceased to function because the price of oil has fallen to five dollars a barrel, but there are few buyers for it because cheaper and better ways now exist to get the services people once turned to oil to provide. Living standards for all people have dramatically improved, particularly for the poor and those in developing countries. Involuntary unemployment no longer exists, and income taxes have largely been eliminated. Houses, even low-income housing units, can pay part of their mortgage costs by the energy they produce; there are few if any active landfills; worldwide forest cover is increasing; dams are being dismantled; atmospheric CO_2 levels are decreasing for the first time in two hundred years; and effluent water leaving factories is cleaner than the water coming into them. Industrialized countries have reduced resource use by 80% while improving the quality of life.

Among these technological changes, there are important social changes. The frayed social nets of Western countries have been repaired. With the explosion of family-wage jobs, welfare demand has fallen. A progressive and active union movement has taken the lead to work with business, environmentalists, and governments to create "just transitions" for workers as society phases out coal, oil and nuclear energy. In communities and towns, churches, corporations, and labor groups promote a new living-wage social contract as the least expensive way to ensure the growth and preservation of valuable social capital. Is this the vision of a utopia? In fact, the changes described here could come about in the decades to come as the result of economic and technological trends already in place."

Epilogue

We hardly know our planet. There are countless gaps in our understanding and in our ability to compute both the cost of environmental damage and the cost of inaction. The world's environmental database is incomplete and of variable quality. For instance, scientists do not even agree on how much vegetation there is on Earth, critically important as that is to our understanding of where we can grow crops, support livestock and harvest wood. And scientists know even less about the vegetation of wildlands, though we know that we are extinguishing numerous species not yet even discovered. Indeed, we have only meagre estimates of the Earth's total complement of life forms. As for knowledge of the effects of human actions, very few nations establish the true rates of soil loss, deforestation or pollution; and some nations cannot accurately count their hungry, poverty-stricken or workless populations. In the oceans, we do not know the size of the fish stocks we are depleting, nor the rate of spread of the toxins we pour into them. Our ignorance is so vast, in fact, that we are not even aware of it.

True, we have grown familiar with spacecraft photos of that lonely-looking globe hanging in the void, covered with a life-sustaining biosphere that makes our planet both uniquely beautiful and uniquely fragile. Yet while we are unlocking the secrets of DNA and life's molecules, we have only begun to grasp the nature of planetary life as an organic whole. Scientists are only just refining questions such as "To what extent does the network of all living things actively control the make-up and temperature of the atmosphere, to maintain our biosphere as a single life-support system?" What, in short, is the nature of the Gaian functioning of our planet? Far from supplying essential answers, we are not even sure of the right questions to ask. And despite our rudimentary understanding, we pursue unwitting experiments of global scope, altering the Earth's climate with results that will affect every citizen now and for hundreds of years to come.

It is difficult to conceive of the speed at which we are overloading the Earth's ecosystems. We should remind ourselves of the image of lily pads extending across a pond. If the pads double in area each day, and if the pond is to be entirely covered in 30 days, on which day is the pond half covered? Answer: the 29th day.

Still more worrying, the degradative processes underway have built up so much momentum that they cannot be halted overnight. Our situation is like that of the captain of a supertanker. If he decides he wants to turn around, he will need half an hour to slow the ship, let alone to head in a different direction.

Against this backdrop of accelerating global deterioration, there are, however, signs of hope. The environmental agenda has undergone remarkable progress and built up ever-greater momentum over recent years, thanks largely to the lead taken by "ordinary people", notably NGOs working in conservation, recycling and clean-up schemes, or raising public awareness and lobbying policy makers. Both Environment and Development have moved from the periphery into the forefront of numerous concerns: political, economic and security issues, from local to global. Many governments have begun to enact tougher environmental standards, and are building ecological considerations into their policies. Underlying this activity is the growing realization by many governments that no nation can successfully quarantine itself from environmental destruction. As the contours of our economic activity have assumed global dimensions, so we had better understand that the environment knows no boundaries: the winds carry no passports.

The world now faces convulsive change. The task of building a sustainable future entails across-the-board reshaping: of our economies, politics, lifestyles and values. Time is not on our side for such a "revolution", comparable in scale only to the two other great revolutions which have transformed human civilization. The Agricultural Revolution began 10,000 years ago and the Industrial Revolution 300 years ago. Both required centuries to fully develop. By contrast, the revolution we now need, the Environmental Revolution, must be compressed into decades at most.

Our thinking itself will be much modified by the full flowering of the Environmental Revolution. The prospect of change may be daunting at first, but the promise – of living in accord with our planet Gaia, as with each other – is more compelling than anything we have envisaged since we came out of our caves.

Norman Myers and Jennifer Kent

Appendices

For this new edition of *The Gaia Atlas of Planet Management* all existing text was fully revised and updated by Norman Myers and Jennifer Kent, and all new text was provided by them.

Dr Norman Myers is a best-selling author and Norman Myers is an Honorary Visiting Fellow at Green College, Oxford University, an External Fellow at the Said Business School, Oxford University, and an Adjunct Professor at Duke University. He is a foreign associate of the U.S. National Academy of Sciences and an Ambassador for WWF/UK. He has received the Volvo Environment Prize, the UNEP/Sasakawa Environment Prize, the Blue Planet Prize and a Queen's honour for "services to the global environment." His 18 books span a wide range of issues and disciplines. Jennifer Kent is an environmental researcher and analyst specializing in interdisciplinary studies. Norman Myers and Jennifer Kent have co-authored *Environmental Exodus: An Emergent Crisis in the Global Arena* (1995), *Perverse Subsidies: How Tax Dollars Can Undercut the Environment and Economy* (2001), and *New Consumers: The Influence of Affluence on the Environment* (2004).

Acknowledgements
Our thanks to the many people who have provided very helpful insights to previous editions of this book. Special thanks now to our colleagues Ed Wilson, David Pimentel, Carl Safina, James Lovelock, Paul Ehrlich, Sunita Narain, Crispin Tickell, and Gus Speth, whose writings we esteem, and whose pages in this book will surely illuminate the reader; to our production team of Lucy Guenot, Philip Morgan and Bill Donohoe, for helping us to present complex issues in un-complex style; to David Duthie and Matthew Prescott, who helped us crucially when the finishing line seemed elusive; and, finally, to Patrick Nugent, who was there for the first edition and without whom this latest edition would have remained a dream.

Consultants and Contributors for previous editions:
Peter Adamson, Stewart Ainsworth, Raul Hernan Ampuero, Brian Anson, David Baldock, Barry Barclay, Frank Barnaby, Pamela Berry, Patricia Birnie, John Bowers, Tom Burke, Julian Caldecott, William Clarke, Trevor Davies, Erik Eckholm, Paul Ehrlich, John Elkington, Scarlett Epstein, Peter Evans, Graham Farmer, Lois Marie Gibbs, John Groom, David Hall, Jeremy Harrison, Paul Harrison, Tony Hill, Colin Hines, Sidney Holt, Mick Kelly, Gillian Kerby, Derrick Knight, Ken Laidlaw, Roy Laishley, Jean Lambert, Alan Leather, Stephanie Leland, James Lovelock, Simon Lyster, Donald Macintosh, Peter Marsh, Simon Maxwell, Hugh Miall, Stephen Mills, Barbara Mitchell, Dorothy Myers, Uma Ram Nath, Adrian Norman, David Oliver, Peter O'Neill, Timothy O'Riordan, Philip Parker, David Pearson, Joss Pearson, David Pimentel, Brian Price, John Rowley, Peter Russell, Nafis Sadik, David Satterthwaite, Steve Sawyer, Viktor Sebek, Paul Shears, Jonathan Simnett, Robin Stainer, Kaye Stearman, Hugh Synge, Jorge Terena, Harford Thomas, Jane Thornback, John Valentine, Karl Van Orsdol, Janos Vargha, Melvin Westlake, Peter Willets, Thomas Wilson.

The following websites have proved invaluable sources of statistics and information:

American Cetacean Society Fact Sheets (www.acsonline.org)

Center for a New American Dream (www.newdream.org)

Central Intelligence Agency (CIA) World Fact Book (www.cia.gov/cia/publications/factbook/geos/xx.html)

Centre for Science and Environment, India (www.cseindia.org)

CITES Secretariat (www.unep.ch/cites)

Clean Development Mechanism (CDM) (www.cdm.unfccc.int)

Commission for the Conservation of Antarctic Marine Living Resources (CCAMLR) (www.ccamlr.org)

Commission on Sustainable Development (CSD) (www.un.org/esa/sustdev/csd/csd13/csd13.htm)

Conservation International (CI) (www.conservation.org)

Convention on Biological Diversity (CBD) (www.biodiv.org)

Convention on Migratory Species (www.cms.int/about/intro.htm)

Coral Health and Monitoring Program (NOAA) (www.coral.noaa.gov)

Development Goals (www.developmentgoals.org/tmaps.htm)

Earth Policy Institute (www.earth-policy.org)

European Conservation Agriculture Federation (ECAF) (www.ecaf.org)

European Environment Agency (EEA) (www.eea.eu.int)

Fair Trade (www.fairtrade.org.uk)

Food and Agriculture Organization (FAOSTAT) (www.fao.org)

Forest Stewardship Council (FSC) (www.fsc.org)

Friends of the Earth (FOE) (www.foe.org)

Global Environment Facility (GEF) (www.gefweb.org)

Global Forest Watch (GFW) www.globalforestwatch.org

Global Resource Information Database (GRID) (www.grid.unep.ch)

Global Terrestrial Observing System (GTOS) (www.fao.org.gtos)

Greenpeace (www.greenpeace.org)

Intergovernmental Panel on Climate Change (IPCC)

(www.ipcc.ch)

International Energy Agency (IEA) (www.iea.org)

International Food Policy Research Institute (IFPRI) (www.ifpri.org)

International Institute for Applied Systems Analysis (IIASA) (www.iiasa.ac.at)

International Institute for Environment and Development (IIED) (www.iied.org)

International Institute for Sustainable Development (IISD) (www.iisd.ca)

International Labour Organization (ILO) (www.ilo.org)

International Maritime Organization (IMO) (www.imo.org)

International Monetary Fund (IMF) (www.imf.org)

International Organization for Migration (IOM) (www.iom.int)

International Tropical Timber Organization (ITTO) (www.itto.or.jp/live/index.jsp)

International Whaling Commission (IWC) (www.iwcoffice.org)

IWC. Whale Population Estimates. (www.iwcoffice.org)

Man and the Biosphere (MAB) (www.unesco.org/mab)

Marine Stewardship Council (MSC) (www.msc.org)

National Association of Farmers Markets. (www.farmersmarkets.net/newsviews/news/default.htm)

National Geographic (www.nationalgeographic.com)

National Oceanographic Data Center (www.nodc.noaa.gov)

Natural Environment Research Council (NERC) (www.nerc.ac.uk)

New Economics Foundation (NEF) (www.neweconomics.org)

New Roadmap Foundation (www.newroadmap.org)

Organization of Petroleum Exporting Countries (OPEC) (www.opec.org)

Organic Trade Association (www.ota.com)

Organization for Economic Co-operation and Development (OECD) (www.oecd.org)

Oxfam (www.oxfam.org.uk)

Pesticides Action network (www.pan-uk.org)

Panos (www.panos.org.uk)

Population Action International (PAI) (www.populationaction.org)

Population Coalition (www.popco.org)

Population Reference Bureau (www.prb.org)

Ramsar Convention on Wetlands (www.ramsar.org)

Redefining Progress (www.rprogress.org)

Rocky Mountain Institute (www.rmi.org)

Sarvodaya Network. (www.sarvodaya.org)

Species 2000 (www.sp2000.org)

Stockholm Environment Institute (SEI) (www.sei.se)

Stockholm International Peace Research Institute (www.sipri.org)

SustainAbility (www.sustainability.co.uk)

TATA Energy Research Institute (TERI) (www.teriin.org)

TRAFFIC (www.traffic.org)

UNEP/GRID-Arendal (www.grida.no)

United Nations (UN) (www.un.org)

United Nations Centre for Human Settlements (www.unchs.org)

United Nations Children's Fund (UNICEF) (www.unicef.org)

United Nations Conference on Trade and Development (UNCTAD) (www.unctad.org)

United Nations Convention on the Law of the Sea (UNCLOS) (www.unclos.cm)

United Nations Development Programme (UNDP) (www.undp.org)

United Nations Economic Commission for Europe (UNECE) (www.unece.org)

United Nations Educational, Scientific and Cultural Organization (UNESCO) (www.unesco.org)

United Nations Environment Programme (UNEP) (www.unep.org)

United Nations Fund for Population Activities (UNFPA) (www.unfpa.org)

United Nations Human Settlements Programme (UN-Habitat) (www.unchs.org)

United Nations High Commissioner for Refugees (UNHCR) (www.unhcr.ch)

United Nations Industrial Development Organization (UNIDO) (www.unido.org)

United Nations Population Information Network (POPIN) (www.un.org/popin)

United Nations Statistics Division http://unstats.un.org/unsd/default.htm

U.S. Department of Energy (Energy Information Administration-EIA) (www.eia.doe.gov)

U.S. Geological Survey (www.usgc.org)

World Bank (www.world-bank.org)

World Bank Data and Statistics (www.worldbank.org/data/maps/maps.htm)

The World Conservation Union (IUCN) (www.iucn.org)

World Conservation Monitoring Centre (www.wcmc.org)

World Energy Agency (www.worldenergy.org)

World Health Organization (www.who.ch)

World Meteorological Organization (WMO) (www.wmo.ch)

World Resources Institute (www.wri.org/earthtrends.wri.org)

World Trade Organization (www.wto.org)

Worldwatch Institute (www.worldwatch.org)

World Wide Fund for Nature (www.panda.org)

World Wildlife Fund (WWF) (www.wwf.org)

Wuppertal Institute (www.wupperinst.org)

References and reading:

Abramowitz, J. and A. Mattoon. Paper Cuts: Recovering The Paper Landscape. Worldwatch Institute (1999).

ActionAid. Farmgate: The Developmental Impact of Farm Subsidies. www.actionaid.org.

American Association for the Advancement of Science. AAAS Atlas of Population and Environment. University of California Press (2000).

American Friends Service Committee. Human Costs in Wars of the 1990s. www.afsc.org/pwork/0599/0509.htm

American Wind Energy Association. Windpower Outlook 2004. American Wind Energy Association, Washington DC.

Annamraju A. et al.

Financing Water and Sanitation, WaterAid, London (2001).

Atomicarchive.com Nuclear Accidents. www.atomicarchive.com/Reports/Japan/Accidents.html

Ausubel, J.H. The Great Reversal: Nature's Chance to Restore Land and Sea (2000). http://phe.rockefeller.edu/great_reversal

AVERT.Org. World HIV and AIDS Statistics: The Impact of HIV and Aids on Africa. www.avert.org.

Balmford, A. et al. Why Conserving Wild Nature Makes Economic Sense. Science 297: pp.950–953 (2002); The Worldwide Costs of Marine Protected Areas. PNAS 101 (26): pp.9694–9697 (2004).

Barber, C.V. et al. (eds.) Securing Protected Areas in the Face of Global Change: Issues and Strategies. World Conservation Union/IUCN (2004).

Bartolomeo, M. and G. Familiari. Green, Social and Ethical Funds in Europe. (2004). www.avanzi-sri.org/pdf/Complete_report_2004_final.pdf

Baxter, J. Cotton Subsidies Squeeze Mali. www.double-standards.org/baxter1.html

Benedick, R. Ozone Diplomacy. Harvard University Press (1991).

Better World for All. Poverty. www.paris21.org/betterworld/poverty.htm

Beyond Pesticides. What's Your Poison? (2003) www.beyondpesticides.org.

Bigg, T. The World Summit on Sustainable Development: Was it Worthwhile? IIED, London (2003).

Blacker, J. Kenya's Fertility: How Low Will it Go? www.un.org/esa/population/publications/completingfertility/RevisedBlackerpaper.PDF

Bland, J. The Water Decade. People and Planet. www.peopleandplanet.net/doc.php?id=679 (2001).

Bot, A.J. et al. Land Resource Potential and Constraints at Regional and Country Levels. FAO (2000).

Botkin, D. and E. Keller. Environmental Science: Earth as a Living Planet. Wiley (1998).

BP Statistical Review of World Energy. BP/AMOCO, London (2003 and 2004).

Bright, C. Life Out of Bounds: Bio Invasion in a Borderless World. Norton (1998); Why Poison Ourselves: A Precautionary Approach to Synthetic Chemicals. Worldwatch Institute (2000).

Brown, L.R. Record Temperatures Shrinking World Grain Harvest. Earth Policy Institute, Washington DC (2003); Plan B: Rescuing a Planet Under Stress and a Civilization in Trouble. Norton (2003); Outgrowing the Earth: The Food Security Challenge in an Age of Falling Water Tables and Rising Temperatures. Norton (2004); World's Rangelands Deteriorating Under Mounting Pressure (2002); Record Temperatures Shrinking World Grain Harvest (2003); Glaciers and Sea Ice Endangered by Rising Temperatures (2003); Troubling New Flows of Environmental Refugees (2004); Europe Leading World Into Age of Wind Energy (2004); Earth's Ice Melting Faster Than Projected (2004); China Replacing the United States as World's Leading Consumer (2005) – all at www.earth-policy.org.

Brown, L.R. et al. Vital Signs 1995–2000 (annual publication); State of the World 2000. Norton (2000).

Brown, P., ed. Sustainable Agriculture and Common Assets: Stewardship Success Stories. Redefining Progress, San Francisco (2002).

Bryant, D. et al. The Last Frontier Forests: Ecosystems and Economies on the Edge. WRI, Washington DC (1997).

Bryant, D. et al. Reefs At Risk: A Map-Based Indicator of Threats to the World's Coral Reefs. WRI, Washington DC (1998).

Carson, R. Silent Spring. Penguin (1965).

Carstens, A. Twenty Years Without a Crisis in Costa Rica: The IMF's View. www.imf.org (2004)

Center for a New American Dream. Turn The Tide: Nine Actions for the Planet. www.newdream.org/tttoffline/actions.html

Certified-forests.org. Global

FSC (18 June 2004). www.certified-forests.org

Chape, S. et al (compilers). 2003 United Nations List of Protected Areas. IUCN/UNEP-WCMC (2003).

CIDA Forestry Advisers Network (CFAN). Deforestation: Tropical Forests in Decline. www.rcfa-cfan.org/english/issues.12-3.html

Cincotta, R. and R. Engelman. Nature's Place: Human Population and the Future of Biological Diversity. Population Action International (2000).

Cincotta, R., R. Engelman and D. Anastasion. The Security Demographic: Population and Civil Conflict After the Cold War. Population Action International (2003).

Climateark.org. Carbon Dioxide Emissions from Land Use Change. www.climateark.org/vital/10.htm

Colborn, T. et al. Our Stolen Future. www.ourstolenfuture.org

Compassion in World Farming Trust. The Global Benefits of Eating Less Meat. CIWFT (2004).

Conservation International. Top 10 Coral Reef Hotspots Fact Sheet; High-Biodiversity Wilderness Areas; Biodiversity Hotspots. www.conservation.org.

Conservation Technology Information Center. Conservation Tillage and Plant Biotechnology. http://www.ctic.purdue.edu/CTIC/Biotech.html

Convention on Biological Diversity Secretariat. The Value of Forest Ecosystems (2001); Global Biodiversity Outlook (2001); Invasive Alien Species: Introduction; Sustaining Life on Earth: How the Convention on Biological Diversity Promotes Nature and Human Well-being. www.biodiv.org.

Costanza, R. et al. The Value of the World's Ecosystem Services and Natural Capital. Nature 387: pp.253-260 (1997)

Daily, G.C. ed. Nature's Services: Societal Dependence on Natural Ecosystems. Island Press (2000).

Deen, T. UN to Put Global

Taxes Centre Stage. www.un.org/esa/ffd/media-ipsnews-0704.htm (2004).

Delgado, C.L. et al. Livestock to 2020: The Next Food Revolution (2001); Outlook for Fish to 2020 (2003); and Outlook for Food to 2020: Meeting Global Demand (2003). IFPRI.

Devarajan, S., M. Miller and R.E. Swanson. Development Goals: History, Prospects and Costs. World Bank (2002)

Diao, X., E. Diaz-bonilla and S. Robinson. How Much Does It Hurt?: The Impact of Agricultural Trade Policies On Developing Countries. IFPRI (2003).

Dillard, M. et al. The Approaching Age of Virtual Nations. The Futurist, July 1st (2002).

Dixon, R.K. et al. Carbon Pools of Global Forest Ecosystems. Science 263: pp.185-190 (1994).

EEA. State and Pressures of the Marine and Coastal Mediterranean Environment (1999); Indicator Fact Sheet Signals 2001 – Chapter Households (2001); Oil Spills from Tankers.

Ehrlich, P.R. Human Natures: Genes, Cultures and the Human Prospect. Island Press (2000).

Ehrlich, P. and A. Ehrlich. One with Nineveh: Politics, Consumption, and the Human Future. Island Press (2004).

Emerson, C. Aquaculture Impacts on the Environment. www.csa.com/hottopics/aquacult/oview.html (1999).

Engelman, T. et al. People in the Balance: Population and Natural Resources at the Turn of the Millennium. Population Action International (2000).

Ethical Investment Research Service. The Ethical Investor. www.eiris.u-net.com.

European Commission. On the Monitoring of Illicit Vessel Discharges: A Reconnaissance Study in the Mediterranean Sea. European Commission (2001).

EWG. Farm Subsidy Database: Farms Getting Government Payments by State. www.ewg.org/farm/subsidies/farms_by_state.php

FAO. Agriculture: Towards

2015 (1995); Dimensions of Need: An Atlas of Food and Agriculture (1995); Human Induced Soil Degradation (1996); Forests, Fuels and Food (1996); Global Climate Change and Agricultural Production: An Assessment of Current Knowledge and Critical Gaps (1996) www.fao.org/docrep/W5183 E/w5183e0f.htm; Direct and Indirect Effects of Changing Hydrological, Pedological and Plant Physiological Processes (1996); Mapping Nutrition and Malnutrition (1998); Global Forest Products Consumption, Production, Trade and Prices (1998); Cleaning up the Pesticides Nobody Wants (1999); Analysis of the Vessels Over 100 Tons in the Global Fishing Fleet (1999); World Soil Report (2000); The State of Food and Agriculture (2001); Forest Resources Assessment 2000 (2002); The State of World Fisheries and Aquaculture (2002); The State of Food Insecurity in the World 2002 (2003); The State of Food and Agriculture 2002 (2003); The State of the World's Forests (2003); World Agriculture: Towards 2015–2030 An FAO Perspective (2003); Kenya: Geography, Population and Water Resources (2003); Gender and agricultural support systems (2003); Regional Fishery Bodies: World Oceans Coverage (2003); Aquaculture: Not Just an Export Industry (2003); Shutting the Door on Illegal Fishing (2004).

Fisher, S. et al. Climate Change and Agricultural Vulnerability. IIASA (2002).

Francis, D.R. Has Global Oil Production Peaked? Christian Science Monitor. Jan 29 (2004).

Friends of the Earth. Main EU Directives on Waste. FOE, London (2001).

Gardner-Outlaw, T. and R. Engelman. Forest Futures: Population, Consumption and Wood Resources. Population Action International (1999).

German, T. and J. Randel. Global Pledges Sacrificed to National Interests. In The Reality of Aid (2004). www.realityofaid.org/content/RoA.htm

German Federal Environmental Agency. Reduction of Coal Subsidies. Federal Environmental Agency (2003).

Gleick, P. The World's Water 2000–2001, 2002–2003, 2004–2005. Island Press; Soft Water Paths. Nature 418: 373 (2002); Dirty Water: Estimated Deaths from Water-Related Diseases 2000–2020 (2002); Water Fact Sheet Looks at Threats, Trends, Solutions. www.pacinst.org.

Gleick, P.H. et al. Threats to the World's Freshwater Resources. www.pacinst.org

Global AIDS Alliance. Taking Stock of the Global Fight Against AIDS. www.global-aidsalliance.org/bangkok_background.cfm

Global Desertification Dimensions and Costs – in H.E. Dregne, ed., Degradation and Restoration of Arid Lands. Texas Tech. University Press (1992).

Global Ecovillage Network. www:gen.ecovillage.org/about/index.html.

Global Forest Watch. Indonesia's Forests in Brief and Brazil's Forests in Brief. www.globalforestwatch.org

Global Fund to Fight AIDS, Tuberculosis and Malaria. www.theglobalfund.org/en/.

Global Policy Forum. UN Financial Crisis (2003). www.globalpolicy.org/finance/tables/core/un-us-04.htm

Global Reach. Global Internet Statistics by Language www.glreach.com/globstats

Goddard Space Flight Center. Ozone 'Hole' Approaches, But Falls Short of Record (2003); Arctic and Antarctic Sea Ice Marching to Different Drivers (2003). www.gsfc.nasa.gov/

Goddard Institute for Space Studies. Soot's Effect on Glaciers. www.giss.nasa.gov/research/stories/20031222

Goreau, T.J. and R.L. Hayes. Coral Bleaching and Ocean 'Hot Spots'. New Scientist (April 12th 2002).

Grameen Bank Bangladesh: Bridging the Digital Divide. www.microcreditsummit.org/press/grameen.htm

Gray. D.D. Asia's Wildlife Hunted for China's Appetite. www.forests org/articles/reader.asp?linkid=30716 (2004).

Greenpeace. Whales. www.whales.greenpeace.org

/whales/fin_whale.html; Dumping and Discharging Radioactive Waste into the Ocean: What's the Difference? www.greenpeace.org (2000).

Groombridge, B. and M.D. Jenkins, eds. Global Biodiversity: Earth's Living Resources in the 21st Century. UNEP-WCMC (2000).

Halweil, B. Organic Gold Rush. World Watch May–June (2001); Home Grown: The Case for Local Food in a Global Market. Worldwatch Institute (2002); Eat Here: Homegrown Pleasures in a Global Supermarket. Norton (2004).

Hansen, J. Defusing the Global Warming Time Bomb. Scientific American March: pp.3–11 (2004).

Hansen, K. A Plague's Bottom Line. Foreign Policy, July/August (2003).

Hawken, P. et al. Natural Capitalism. Little/Brown (1999).

Heap, R. and J. Kent, eds. Towards Sustainable Consumption: A European Perspective. The Royal Society, London (2001).

Hermida, A. Smart Homes on Trial (2002). www.bbc.co.uk/2/hi/science/nature/1776047.htm

Hinrichsen, D. The Oceans are Coming Ashore. World Watch (Nov/Dec 2000). pp.26–35; Down to the Last Drop: The Fate of Wildlife is Linked to Water, But too Many People are Sucking it up. International Wildlife (Nov–Dec 2001).

Hughes, P.P. et al. Biodiversity Hotspots, Centers of Endemicity and the Conservation of Coral reefs. Ecology Letters 2002 (Issue 5) pp.775–784.

ICLEI. Orienting Urban Planning to Sustainability in Brazil. www.iclei.org (2002).

ICSU/SCOPE. The Global Carbon Cycle. ICSU (1979).

ID21 Insights. Cost of US Military Operations in Afghanistan and Iraq (2004). www.id21.org

IEA. Key World Energy Statistics (2003); Renewables in the Global Energy Supply (2002); Renewables Information (2002). www.iea.org

IFPRI. Agriculture and Trade Facts. www.ifpri.org/media/

trade/tradefacts.htm; Global Water Outlook to 2025: Averting an Impending Crisis, Factsheets (2004). www.ifpri.oprg/media/water_facts.htm

IIED. Breaking New Ground. Mining, Minerals and Sustainable Development (2003). www.iied.org/mmsd/

ILO. Global Employment Trends (2003); Key Facts on Child Labour (2003); HIV/AIDS and Work: Global Estimates, Impact and Response (2004); World Employment Report 2004–2005 (2004); Economic Security for a Better World (2004); Employment in the Informal Economy (2004); More Women are Entering the Global Labour Force than Ever Before, But Job Equality & Poverty Reduction Remain Elusive (2004); Youth Unemployment at All Time High (2004); Key Indicators of the Labour Market (2004). www.ilo.org

IMF. Global Trade Liberalization and the Developing Countries (2001); Primary Commodity Prices (2005); World Economic Outlook (2004); Globalization: Threat or Opportunity? (2000). www.imf.org

IMO. Prevention of Pollution by Garbage from Ships. www.imo.org/Environment/mainframe.asp?topic_id=297

INFORM. Strategies for a Better Environment. Community Waste Prevention Toolkit: Carpet Fact Sheet. www.informinc.org

Institute for International Mediation and Conflict Resolution. World Conflict and Human Rights Map 2001–2002. www.iimcr.org/info/conflictmap.asp

Institute for Policy Studies and Foreign Policy in Focus. A Failed 'Transition': The Mounting Costs of the Iraq War. www.ips-dc.org/iraq/failedtransition/

Interamerican Development Bank. IDB Celebrates 25 years of Support for Microenterprise in Latin America and the Caribbean (2004). www.iadb.org

Intergovernmental Panel on Climate Change (IPCC). The Regional Impacts of Climate Change: An Assessment of Vulnerability (2001); Climate

Change 2001. The Scientific Basis, Summary for Policymakers (2001); A Report of the Working Group I of the IPCC, Geneva. www.ippc.ch

International Forum on Globalization. Globalization: Effects on Indigenous Peoples. www.ifg.org/programs/indig/IFGmap.pdf

International Fund for Agricultural Development (IFAD). Ghana – Rural Women's Micro and Small Enterprises (2000); Desertification as a Global Problem. www.ifad.org/pub/desert/scheda1.pdf

International AIDS Vaccine Initiative. The State of Global Research. www.iavi.org/viewpage.cfm?aid=13

International Atomic Energy Authority. Number of Reactors in Operation Worldwide as of 15 February 2003; Nuclear Power Reactors in the World (1990). www.iaea.org

International Fund for Animal Welfare. Conservationists Stunned: Iceland to Hunt 250 Whales in the Name of Science (2003); Think Twice Before Buying Souvenirs: The Exotic Pet Trade. www.ifaw.org

International Publishers Association. Annual Book Title Production (2003). www.ipa-uie.org.

Internet World Stats. Internet Usage Statistics: The Big Picture. www.internetworldstats.com/stats.htm

IOM. World Migration Report (2003). www.iom.int

ITTO. For Services Rendered: The Current Status and Future Potential of Markets for the Ecosystem Services Provided by Tropical Forests (2004). www.itto.org

IUCN-UNEP-WWF; Caring for the Earth: A Strategy for Sustainable Living. Earthscan (1991).

IWMI/CGIAR. Pesticide Use and Abuse in Irrigated Areas (2003) www.iwmi.cgiar.org/health/pesticide/

James, C. Global Status of Commercial Transgenic Crops (2003). International Service for the Acquisition of Agri-Biotech Applications (ISAAA).

Kaimowitz, D. Hamburger Connection Fuels Amazon Destruction. CIFOR (2004).

Kane, H. Microenterprise: The Other Half of the World's Economy. World Watch Magazine (March/April 1996).

Kapsos, S. Estimating Growth Requirements for Reducing Working Poverty: Can the World Halve Working Poverty by 2015? ILO (2004).

Khan, S. Arsenic: Bangladesh Remains Worst Affected Region. OneWorld South Asia (11 March 2004).

Kidd. S. Uranium: Resources, Sustainability and Environment. The World Energy Council. www.worldenergy.org

Klare, M. Resource Wars: The New Landscape of Global Conflict. Metropolitan Books/Henry Holt (2001).

Krebs, J.R. et al. The Second Silent Spring? Nature 400: pp.611-612 (1999).

Lammers, G. A Third Way for the Electricity Industry. Environmental Defense Fund, Washington DC. www.un.org/esa/sustdev/sdi ssues/energy/op/nepadlam-mers-ppt.pdf

Langrock, T. et al. 2003. Environmentally Friendly ICT Products – in D. Pamlin (ed.). Sustainability at the Speed of Light: Opportunity and Challenges for Tomorrow's Society. WWF (2002).

Laporte, A. Water Wars: Conflict and Cooperation Along the Nile. (2003). www.interaction.org/library/d etail.php?id=1982

LaRovere, E. The Brazilian Ethanol Program: Biofuels for Transport (2004) www.renewables2004.de/pp t/Presentation4-SessionIVB (11–12.30h)-LaRovere.pdf

Larsen, J. Forest Cover Shrinking (2002); Record Heatwave in Europe Takes 35,000 Lives (2003); Glaciers and Sea Ice Endangered by Rising Temperatures (2004). www.earth-policy.org.

Laurance, W.F. et al. Deforestation in Amazonia. Science 304: 1109 (2004).

Layard, R. Happiness: Has Social Science a Clue? London School of Economics (2003).

Leitenberg, M. Deaths in Wars and Conflicts Between 1945-2000 (2001).

www.pcr.uu.se/conferens-es/Euroconference/Leitenber g_paper.pdf

Lerner, J. What are Sustainable Communities? Case Study of Curitiba, Brazil. National Council for Science and the Environment, Washington DC (2001).

Levy, E. and M. Fischetti. The New Killer Diseases: How the Alarming Evolution of Mutant Germs Threatened Us All. Crown (2003).

Lineback N.G. U.S. Coasts Vulnerable to Sea Level Rise (2001). www.geo.appstate. edu/536_090800tidec.pdf; Chernobyl: World's Worst Nuclear Accident. www.geo. appstate.edu/553_010501n uclearc.pdf

Lloyds Register of Shipping. World Fleet Statistics. www.coltoncompany.com/s hipping/statistics/wldflt-growth.htm

Lovelock, J. Gaia: A New Look at Life on Earth. Oxford University Press (1979); The Ages of Gaia. Norton (1988).

Lovins, A.B. US Energy Security Facts for a Typical Year (2000); US Security Linked to Efficiency (2003). www.rmi.org.

Makower, J. et al. Clean Energy Trends. Clean Edge, San Francisco (2004).

Maps of world.com World Map of Major Air Routes. www.mapsofworld.com.

Mastny, L. Status of Coral Reefs Around the World. World Watch May/June 20-21 (2001); Coming to Terms with the Arctic. World Watch Jan/Feb (2000).

Mastny, L. and H. French. Crimes of (a) Global Nature. World Watch pp.12–23 (Sep/Oct 2002).

Matthews, E. Understanding the Forest Resources Assessment 2000. WRI (2001).

McGinn, A.P. Why Poison Ourselves: A Precautionary Approach to Synthetic Chemicals. Worldwatch Institute (2000); From Rio to Johannesburg: Reducing the Use of Toxic Chemicals Advances Health and Sustainable Development. Worldwatch Institute (2002); Malaria, Mosquitoes, and DDT: The Global War Against a Global Disease. World Watch May/June

(2002).

McNeely, J.A. Costs and Benefits of Alien Species. IUCN/World Conservation Union (2001).

Meadows, D. The Global Citizen, Island Press (1991);

Meadows, D. et al. Beyond the Limits, Earthscan (1992).

Midgeley, G., M. Rutherford and W. Bond. Impacts of Climate Change on Plant Diversity in Southern Africa. SANBI (2001).

Millennium Development Goals: Promote Gender Equality and Empower Women (map); People Living on Less than $1 and $2 a Day (map); Freshwater Resources Per Capita (map); Deaths Among Children Under 5, Global. www.devel-opmentgoals.org.

Mittermeier, R. et al. Setting Priorities for Saving Life on Earth: Megadiversity, Countries, Hotspots and Wilderness Areas. Asahi Glass Foundation, Tokyo (2001).

Mittermeier, R. et al. Wilderness and Biodiversity Conservation. PNAS 1073 (2003).

Mongaybay.com. Deforestation in the Amazon 2004. www.mongabay.com/ brazil.html

Mulongoy, K. and S. Chape. Protected Areas and Biodiversity: An Overview of Key Issues. UNEP/WCMC (2003).

Multilateral Environmental Agreements Repository: Deforestation and the Unsustainable Use of Forests. www.gdrc.org/ ngo/mea/factsheets/fs6.html

Murray, R. Creating Wealth from Waste (1999). www.grrn.org/zerowaste/de moschap14.html

Myers, N. The Gaia Atlas of Future Worlds: Challenge and Opportunity in an Age of Change. Doubleday/ Robertson McCarta (1990); The Primary Source, Norton (1992); Ultimate Security: The Environmental Basis of Political Stability. Island Press (1996); Biodiversity's Genetic Library – in G.C. Daily, ed., Nature's Services: Societal Dependence on Natural Ecosystems: 255–273. Island Press (1997); Population Dynamics and Food Security. – in A.E. el Obeid, S.R. Johnson, H.H. Jensen and L.C. Smith,

eds., Food Security: New Solutions for the 21st Century: 176–208. Iowa State University Press (1999); The Management and Repercussions of Nuclear Power. Ditchley Conference Report (1999); Environmental Refugees: Our Latest Understanding. Philosophical Transactions of the Royal Society B: 356: 16.1-16.5 (2001); Institutional Roadblocks – in G. Tyler Miller, ed. 'Living in the Environment', 13th edition (2005).

Myers, N. and J. Kent. Environmental Exodus: An Emergent Crisis in the Global Arena. Climate Institute (1995); Food and Hunger in Sub-Saharan Africa. The Environmentalist 21: 41–69 (2001); Perverse Subsidies: How Tax Dollars Can Undercut the Environment and the Economy. Island Press, Washington DC (2001); The New Consumers: The Influence of Affluence on the Environment. Island Press (2004).

Myers. N. and J. Kent et al. Biodiversity Hotspots for Conservation Priorities. Nature 403: pp.853–858 (2000).

Myers, N. and A. Knoll. The Biotic Crisis and the Future of Evolution. PNAS 98: pp.5389–5392 (2001).

Myers, N. and S. Pimm. Mass Extinction of Species. Foreign Policy March/April: pp.28–29 (2003).

Nadir A.L. Mohamed. Civil Wars and Military Expenditures: a note (1999). www.worldbank.org/researc h/conflict/papers/civil.pdf

NASA Goddard Space Flight Center. Mt. Kilimanjaro (2000). www.svs.gsfc.nasa.gov/vis/a 000000/a002700/a002701/

National Botanical Institute and the Global Invasive Species Programme. Invasive Alien Species: A Challenge to NEPAD. SANBI, Cape Town (2004).

Natural Resources Defense Council (NRDC). Nuclear Weapons and Waste. www.nrdc.org/nuclear/nudb/ datab19.asp

NEF. The Price of Power: Poverty, Climate Change, The Coming Energy Crisis and the Renewable Revolution. New Economics Foundation (2004).

Nepal Ministry of Population and Environment. State of the Environment (Eco-Tourism Sector) (2004). www.mope.gov.np/environ-ment/state2004.php

Newscientist.com. The World's Disappearing Forests (map). www.newsci-entist.com/hottopics/cli-mate/img/spread-2-4.jpg

Norris, R.S. and W.M. Arkin. Nuclear Notebook: Known Nuclear Tests Worldwide 1945–1998. Bulletin of the Atomic Scientists Nov–Dec (1998).

Ocampo, J.A. United Nations Asia-Pacific Leadership Forum: Sustainable Development of Cities (2004). www.un.org/esa/20040402 HongKong.html

OECD. Modest Increase in Development Aid in 2003; Total Net Flows of DAC ODA; Economic Outlook; Statistics on the Member Countries (2004); The World Economy: Historical Statistics (2003). www.oecd.org.

Offshore-Environment.com. Global Conventions on Protection of Marine Environment. www.offshore-environment.com/conven-tions.html

OPEC Annual Statistics Bulletin (2003). www.opec.org

Orozco, M. Worker Remittances: The Human Face of Globalization (2002). www.thedialogue.org/publi-cations/country_studies/remi ttances/worker_remit.pdf

Orr, D.W; Ecological Literacy. State University of New York Press (1992).

Owen, J. Antarctic Wildlife at Risk from Overfishing (2003). news.nationalgeographic.co m/news/2003/08/0805_030 805_antarctic.html

Oxfam. Mugged: Poverty in Your Coffee Cup (2002); Shattered Lives: The Case for Tough International Arms Control (2003); Stop the Dumping: How EU Agricultural Subsidies are Damaging Livelihoods in the Developing World (2004); Trading Away Our Rights (2004); Poor are Paying the Price of Rich Countries Failure (2004); The Cost of Childbirth: How Women are Paying the Price for Broken Promises on Aid (2004); The Asian Tsunami: Three Weeks On (2005); Do the Deal: The

G7 Must Act Now to Cancel Poor Country Debt (2005). www.oxfam.co.uk

Pamlin, D. (Ed.). Sustainability at the Speed of Light: Opportunity and Challenges for Tomorrow's Society. WWF (2004).

PAN-UK and FOE. Breaking the Pesticide Chain. PAN UK/FOE (2003).

Patz, J.A. et al. The Effects of Changing Weather on Public Health. Annual Review of Public Health 21 pp.271–307 (2000).

Pauly, D. and R. Watson. Counting the Last Fish. Scientific American 289 (1): pp.42–47 (2003).

PeopleandPlanetnet. Cape Flats are Going Green (2002); Nairobi's Silent Majority Fights Back (2004). www.peopleandplanet.net.

People's Daily Online. Acid Rain Costs China Annual Loss of 110 billion yuan. (2003) www.english. people.com.cn/200310/11/e ng20031011_125803.shtml

Persson, R. Fuelwood: Crisis or Balance. www.handels.gu.se/econ/ EEU/chapter1.pdf

Pew Center on Global Climate Change. Climate Change Activities in the United States: Update (2004); The Main Greenhouse Gases; Sources of Anthropogenic GHG emissions. (2004). www.pewclimate.org.

Pimentel, D. Genetically Modified Crops and the Agroecosystem. Conservation Ecology (2000). www.consecol.org /vol4/iss1/art10; Renewable Energy: Current and Potential Issues. BioScience 52 (12): pp.1111–1120 (2002); Land Degradation and Environmental Resources – in G. Tyler-Miller, ed., Living in the Environment: pp.232–233. Thomson/Brooks Cole (2002); World Population, Food, Natural Resources, and Survival. World Futures 59: pp.145–167 (2003).

Pimentel, D. and M. Pimentel, eds. Food, Energy, and Society. University Press of Colorado (1996).

Pimentel, D. et al. Environmental and Economic Costs of Soil Erosion and Conservation Benefits. Science 267: pp.1117–1123 (1995);

Economic and Environmental Benefits of Biodiversity. BioScience 47: pp.747–757 (1997); Water Resources: Agricultural and Environmental Issues. BioScience 54 (10) pp.909–918 (2004).

Planet Ark. EU Ministers Clear German Coal subsidies. www.planetark. com/dailynewsstory.cfm/ newsid/6354/story.htm

Ploughshares. World Hunger and Armed Conflict (map). www.ploughshares.ca/image sarticles/ ACR02/hunger map.02.pdf

Population Action International. Why Population Growth Matters to the Future of Forests (2003). www.populationac-tion.org.

Population Reference Bureau. World Population Data Sheet 2002 and 2004. Population Reference Bureau, Washington DC.

Postel, S. Dividing the Waters: Food Security, Ecosystem Health, and the New Politics of Scarcity. Worldwatch Institute (1996).

Pretty, J.N. 1995. Regenerating Agriculture: Policies and Practice for Sustainability and Self Reliance. Joseph Henry Press (1995); Agri-Culture: Reconnecting People, Land and Nature. Earthscan (2002); The Real Costs of Modern Farming (2001) www.resurgence. org/resurgence/issues/pret-ty205.htm; The Rapid Emergence of Genetic Modification in World Agriculture: Contested Risks and Benefits. Environmental Conservation 28 (3), pp.248–262 (2001).

Prindle, B. How Energy Efficiency Can Turn 1300 Power Plants into 170. The Alliance to Save Energy, Washington DC (2001). www.ase.org/media/fact-sheets/facts1300.htm

Project Ploughshares. Armed Conflicts Report 2004. www.plough shares.ca/imagesarticles/ ACR04/ACRPoster2004.pdf

Rabalais, N. Oil in the Sea. Issues in Science and Technology (Fall) pp.74–78 (2003).

Raloff, J. Dead Waters: Massive Oxygen-Starved Zones are Developing along the World's Coasts. Science News (June 5, 2004).

Ramirez-Vallejo, J. A Break for Coffee. Prime Numbers. Foreign Policy (13 August, 2002).

Ray, P.H. and S.R. Anderson. The Cultural Creatives: How 50 Million People are Changing the World. Three Rivers Press (2000).

Reality of Aid. World Aid Trends. www.realityofaid. org/content/RoA.htm

Redefining Progress. Genuine Progress Indicator (2004 update); Ecological Footprint of Nations. www.rprogress.org

Reeves, R. et al (compilers). Dolphins, Whales and Porpoises: 2002–2010 Conservation Action Plan for the World's Cetaceans. World Conservation Union/IUCN. Gland, Switzerland (2003).

Regmi, A. and M. Gehlhar. Consumer Preferences and Concerns Shape Global Food Trade. Food review 24(3): pp.2–8 (2001).

Rehydration Project. What is Diarrhoea and How to Prevent It. www.rehydrate. org/diarrhoea/

Renner, M. Swords Into Plowshares: Converting to a Peace Economy. Worldwatch Institute (1990).

Riggs, P. and M. Watles. Accountability in the Pesticide Industry. Rockefeller Brothers Fund (2002).

Roberts, C.M. et al. Marine Biodiversity Hotspots and Conservation Priorities for Tropical Reefs. Science 295: pp.1280–1284 (2002).

Romm, J. The Hype About Hydrogen: A Realistic Primer on the Promise of Hydrogen. Island Press (2004).

Rosegrant, M. et al. Global Food Projections to 2020: Emerging Trends and Alternative Futures (2001); World Water and Food to 2025: Dealing with Scarcity. IFPRI and International Water Management Institute (2002).

Rosemann, N. Financing the Human Right to Water. www.choike.org/cgi-bin/choike/nuevo_eng/jump_ inf.cgi?ID=1767.

Rosenberg, M. Maquiladoras in Mexico. www.geography.about.com/ od/urbaneeconomicgeogra-phy/a/maquiladoras_p.htm

Royal Botanic Gardens (Kew). The Millennium Seed Bank Project. www.kew.org/msbp/

Royal Society (London). Nuclear Energy: The Future Climate. The Royal Society (1999).

Safina, C. The World's Imperiled Fish. Scientific American 273(5): pp.46–53 (1995). Song for the Blue Ocean: Encounters Along the World's Coasts and Beneath the Seas. Blue Ocean Institute (1999).

Sampat, P. and G. Gardner. From Grassroots to Boardrooms: Slashing Raw Materials' Use to Increase Profits and Protect the Environment. Worldwatch Institute (1998).

Sawin, J.L. Mainstreaming Renewable Energy in the 21st Century. Worldwatch Institute (2004).

Scherr, S. Soil Degradation: A Threat to Developing-Country Food Security by 2020? IFPRI (1999).

Schneider, F. Size and Measurement of the Informal Economy in 110 Countries Around the World (2002). www.economics.uni-lnz.ac.at.

Schneider, S.H. and P. Boston. Scientists on Gaia, MIT (1991).

Schorr, D.K. Healthy Fisheries, Sustainable Trade: Crafting New Rules on Fishing Subsidies in the World Trade Organization. WWF (2004).

SeaWorld/Busch Gardens Animal Information Data-base. Balleen Whale Popu-lation Estimates. www.sea-world.org/infobooks/Baleen/ estimatesbw.html

Seedquest. 2025: A European Vision for Plant Genomics and Biotech-nology. www.seedquest. com/News/releases/2004/ june/9089.htm

Sehrt, M. Digital Divide into Digital Opportunities. UN Chronicle. www.un.org/ Pubs/chronicle/2003/issue4/ 04C3p45.asp.

SEI. Comprehensive Assessment of the Freshwater Resources of the World. SEI (1997).

Sheehan, M.O. Gaining Perspective. World Watch (March/April 2000) pp.14–21.

Silvarolla, M.B. et al. A

Naturally Decaffeinated Arabica Coffee Nature 429: p.826 (2004).

SIPRI. SIPRI Yearbook 2003 (Major Armed Conflicts; The Nuclear Confrontation in South Asia); World Military Expenditure 1993–2002; Biotechnology and the Future of the Biological and Toxic Weapons Convention (2001). www.sipri.org.

Smith, C. Pesticide Exports from US Ports 1997–2000. International Journal of Occupational Environmental Health 7(4) pp.266–268 (2001).

Soel. The World of Organic Agriculture (map). www.soel. de/oekolandbau/weltweit_gr afiken.html (2005).

Speth, G. Red Sky at Morning: America and the Crisis of the Global Environment. Yale University Press (2004).

Statistics Canada. Unpaid Work. www.statcan.ca/eng-lish/research/71F0023XIE/71 F0023XIE.pdf

Sullivan, B. Online Privacy Fears are Real: More People are Tracking Than You Think (2004). www.msnbc.msn. com.id/3078835/.

SustainAbility Ltd. A Responsible Investment? SustainAbility (2001).

Swedish EPA. Facts About Swedish Policy: Acid Rain; Acidification. www.internat.naturvardsver-ket.se.

Thinley, L.J.Y. Gross National Happiness and Human Development: Searching for Common Ground. Centre for Bhutan Studies, Thimphy, Bhutan (1999).

Third World Academy of Sciences. Safe Drinking Water: The Need, the Problem, Solutions and an Action Plan. Third World Academy of Science (2002).

Thompson, J. et al. Drawers of Water: 30 Years of Change in Domestic Water Use and Environmental Health. IIED (2002).

Tickell, C. Sustainability and Conservation: Prospects for Johannesburg. Speech to Society for Conservation Biology at Canterbury, Kent (2002).

Tilton, J.E. Depletion and the Long-Run Availability of Mineral Commodities. Colorado School of Mines

(2001).

TRAFFIC. Recent Study Shows Ivory Use and Trade Shift Underground in India (2003); Growing Passion for Exotic Pets in France. Dispatches 21 (2003); Far from a Cure: The Tiger Trade Revisited. Bulletin 20 (1) (2004). www.traffic.org.

Twentieth Century Atlas. Deaths by Mass Unpleasantness: Estimated Totals for the Entire 20th Century. www.users.erols.com/mwhite28/warstat8.htm#Total;

Tyler-Miller, G., ed. Living in the Environment, 12th edition. Thomson/Brooks Cole (2002)

UK Government. Developing Countries and WTO (www.dti.gov.uk); Environment. Habitat Loss (www.environment-agency.gov.uk); Climate (www.environment-agency.gov.uk); Climate Change and Agriculture (2000) (www.maff.gov.uk); North Sea Fish Stocks (www.statistics.gov.uk); Safety (www.statistics.gov.uk); Measuring Foodborne Illness Levels (www.food.gov.uk); GM Food (www.food.gov.uk); DEFRA. Key Facts about: Global Atmosphere & Key Facts about: Coastal and Marine Waters (www.defra.gov.uk); The Costs and Benefits of Genetically Modified (GM) Crops (2002) (www.strategy.gov.uk); H.M. Treasury Spending Review (July 2004) (www.hm-treasury.gov.uk).

UNAIDS. Global Summary of the AIDS Epidemic (December 2004); The 2004 Report on the Global AIDS Epidemic. www.unaids.org

UNCCD. Financing Action to Combat Desertification. www.unccd.int/piblicinfo/factsheets/showFS.pho?number=8; 2002.

UNCHS. The Sustainable Cities Programme. www.unchs.org.

UNCTAD. World Investment Report 2004: The Shift Towards Services; Foreign Direct Investment: A Rebound In the Offing. www.unctad.org.

UNDP. Human Development Report 1999–2004 (annual Publication). www.undp.org

UNEP. Introduction to Climate Change: Carbon Dioxide Emissions from Land Use Change. www.grida.no/climate/vital/10.

htm; Global Environment Outlook 2 (GEO2); Global Environment Outlook 3 (GEO3). Earthscan, London; Status of Ratification/Accession/Acceptance/Approval of the Agreements on the Protection of the Stratospheric Ozone Layer; Multilateral Environmental Agreements; An Assessment of the Status of the World's Remaining Closed Forests (2001); Potential Impact of Sea-Level Rise on Bangladesh (map); Protecting Our Planet, Securing Our Future (1997); Caribbean Environment Programme: Land-Based Sources of Marine Pollution. www.cep.unep.org/issues/lbsp.html#Sewage.

UNEP/WCMC. Global Maps and Statistics (Forest, Dryland and Freshwater Programme). www.unep-wcmc.org/forest/world.htm; World Atlas of Coral Reefs www.enn.com/new/enn-stories/2001/10/10032001/s_45158.asp

UNESCO. Regional Youth and Adult Literacy Rates and Illiterate Population by Gender for 2000–2004; Adult Literacy by Gender and Region, 2000–2004; Illiteracy Rates Worldwide, 2000 (map); Education For All Global Monitoring Report: Is the World on Track? (2002); Youth (15–24) and Adult (15+) Literacy Rates by Country and by Gender for 2000–2004; Expenditure on education as a percentage of GDP (1999). www.unesco.org

UNFCCC. Framework Convention on Climate Change. Sea Levels, Oceans and Coastal Areas. www.unfccc.int/2860.php

UNFPA. Measures Taken by Countries to Increase Access to Quality Reproductive Health Services (map). www.unfpa.org/icpd/10/survey/map.htm; Water: A Critical Resource (2002); State of World Population (2003). www.unfpa.org

UN-Habitat. Slum Population Projection 1990–2020; Water and Sanitation in the World's Cities; City Level Statistics About Water and Sanitation; The Challenge of Slums: Global Report on Human Settlements 2003. www.unhabitat.org

UNHCR. Refugees by Numbers (2003); Estimated Number of Persons of

Concern Who Fall Under the Mandate of UNHCR 1 (2003); Map: Major Refugee Populations Worldwide 1999.

UNICEF. End Decade Databases. www.childinfo.org/eddb/water/current.ht; Water Coverage 2000 (map) www.childinfo.org/eddb/water/printmap.htm; State of the World's Children (annual publication). www.unicef.org.

Union of Concerned Scientists/USA. A Rogue's Gallery of Foodborne Illness. See also Monarch Butterflies and Toxic Pollen. www.ucsusa.org

United Nations. Atlas of the Oceans; World at 6 Billion (2000); Millennium Indicators. http://millenniumindicators.un.org/unsd/mi/mi_goals.asp; Kyoto Protocol: Status of Ratification (25 November 2004); System-Wide Earthwatch. Forests; System-Wide Earthwatch: Desertification. www.earthwatch.unep.net; Convention on the Law of the Sea. Facts and Figures About the Oceans; Oceans: The Source of Life/UN Convention on the Law of the Sea. www.un.org.

United Nations Economic Commission for Europe (UNECE). Convention on Long-Range Transboundary Air Pollution: Protocol on heavy Metals. www.unece.org

United Nations Economic Commission for Europe and FAO. Trade, Environment and Forests: Working Together for Sustainable Development. FAO (2003).

United Nations Population Division. World Population Prospects Database; World Urbanization Prospects: The 2003 Revision; World Population to 2300 (2004); International Migration Report (wall chart) (2002); World Contraceptive Use, 2003 (wall chart) (2003).

UN Volunteers. Volunteerism and the Millennium Development Goals. www.worldvolunteerweb.org/development/mdg/volunteerism/UNV_mdg.htm

Uranium Information Centre (UIC). World Nuclear Power Reactors 2003–2004. Plans for New Reactors Worldwide (2004). www.uic.com

U.S. Center for Disease Control. About Childhood Lead Poisoning. www.cdc.

gov/nceh/lead/about/about.htm; Health Care Spending is on the Rise. www.cdc.gov/nccdphp/power_prevention/pop_spending.htm

U.S. Department of Agriculture. Agriculture Fact Book 2001–2002; Census of Agriculture: United States Data. Market Value of Agricultural Products Sold (2002); Natural Resources Conservation Service. Natural Resources Inventory (2001); Land Degradation. www.nrcs.usda.gov; Economic Research Service. Global Resources and Productivity: Questions and Answers (2000). www.ers.usda.gov

U.S. Department of Energy (EIA). Energy and Emission Forecasts Database, reference case; Commercial Nuclear Power 1990: Prospects for the United States and the World; Maps of Nuclear Power Reactors; Nuclear Timeline; International Energy Database; International Energy Outlook 2002 and 2004; Annual Energy Outlook with Projections to 2025. www.eia.doe.gov

U.S. Dept of State. Military Expenditures and Arms Transfers 1999–2000. Department of State (2003).

U.S. Environmental Protection Agency. The Effects of Ozone Depletion. www.epa.gov/ozone/science/effects.html; Eutrophication. www.epa.gov/maia/html/eutroph.html

U.S. Geological Survey. Uranium-Fuel for Nuclear Energy (2002); Minerals; Obsolete Computers, 'Gold Mine' or High-Tech Trash? (2001); Mineral Commodities Summaries (annual). www.minerals.usgs.gov.

Water Year 2003: International Year Aims to Galvanize Action on Critical Water Problems; Facts and Figures: Desertification and Drought. Freshwater. Water Resources During Armed Conflicts. www.wateryear2003.org

Vannuccini, S. Overview of Fish Production, Utilization, Consumption and Trade, Based on 2001 Data (2003). FAO, Rome.

Von Braun, J., A. Gualti and D. Orden. Making Agricultural Trade Liberalization Work for the Poor. IFPRI (2004).

Von Weizsacker, E. et al. Factor Four: Doubling Wealth, Halving Resource Use. Earthscan (1998).

Wackernagel, M. et al. Tracking the Ecological Overshoot of the Human Economy. PNAS (USA) 99: pp.9266–9271 (2002).

Wakefield, J. Watching Your Every Move. BBC News Online (7 February 2002). www.news./bbc.co.uk/1/hi/sci/tech/1789157.stm

WasteOnline: Plastics recycling Information Sheet; Glass Recycling Information Sheet. www.wasteonline.org.uk.

Wateraid.org. Mega Cities and Mega Slums in the 21st Century. www.itt.com/waterbook/mega_cities.asp

Waterandhealth.org. What are the Costs/Benefits of Global Water and Sanitation Improvements? www.waterandhealth.org/newsletter/new/winter_2005/cost_benefits.html

Water Resources e-Atlas. Watersheds of the World: Annual Renewable Water Supply Per Person By Basin, 1995–2025. WRI.

WEHAB. A Framework for Action on Water and Sanitation. UN, New York (2002).

Whale and Dolphin Conservation Society. Managing Antarctica, CCAMLR and the Antarctic Treaty System. www.wdcs.org

WHO. Schistosomiaisis (1996); Reducing Mortality from Major Killers of Children. Fact Sheet 178 (1998); What is Malaria? Fact Sheet 95 (2000); World Health Report (2002); Risk Factors (2002); Climate Change and Human Health: Risks and Responses (2003); Global Atlas of Infectious Diseases (2004); World Health Report (2004); Water, Sanitation and Hygiene Links to Health Fact Sheet; Mental and Neurological Disorders (2001); Disease Portfolio (2004); Childhood Pesticide Poisoning: Information for Advocacy and Action; Roll Back Malaria: 2001–2010 UN Decade to Roll Back Malaria (2002); World Facing "Silent Emergency" as Billions Struggle Without Clean Water or Basic

Sanitation (2002); Water-Related Diseases (2005). www.who.int.

WHO and UNICEF. Global Water Supply and Sanitation Assessment. WHO and UNICEF (2000).

Willer, H. and M. Yussefi, eds. The World of Organic Agriculture: Statistics and Emerging Trends (2004). www.fibl.org

Wilson, E.O. (ed). Biophilia. Harvard University Press (1984); Biodiversity. National Academy Press (1988); The Diversity of Life. Belknapp/Harvard University Press (1992); The Future of Life. Knopf (2002).

Wolfe, T.J. Waste Not. Environmental Law Institute (2002). www.capanalysis. com/docs/200201wastenot. pdf

Women in Parliaments: World Classification. www.ipu.org/wmn-e/clas-sif.htm

Woodward, C. A Run on the Banks: How 'Factory Fishing' Decimated Newfoundland Cod (2001). www.emagazine.com/march-april_2001/0301feat2.html.

World-Aluminium.org. Aluminium Recycling (2000). www.world-aluminium.org/production/recycling/

World Bank. World Development Indicators 2004; China-Yangtze Flood Emergency Rehabilitation Project (1998). www.world-bank.org.

World Cities Alliance. Cardiff. www.worldcitiesalliance.com/index.cfm/5924

World Commission on Environment and Develop-ment; Our Common Future, OUP (1987).

World Commission on Forests and Sustainable Development. Our Forests Our Future (1999). www. whrc.org/policy/world_forests.htm.

WCMC. Certified Forest Sites Endorsed by FSC (August 2002). www.wcmc.org.uk/forest/ffl/f is/fsc_small.htm

World Conservation Union (IUCN). Nepal. www.iucn-nepal.org/context/Default.htm

World Food Summit. Forests, Fuels and Food. World Food Summit (1996).

World Nuclear Association. Nuclear Share Figures 1995–2003. www.world-nuclear.org/info/printable_inf ormation_papers/nshareprint .htm (2002); World Nuclear Power Reactors 2002–2004 and Uranium Requirements. www.world-nuclear.org/info/printable_information_papers /reactorsprint.htm (2004).

World Organization for Animal Health. Geographical Distribution of Countries that Reported BSE: Confirmed Cases from 1989 to 2002. www.oie.nt/Cartes/BSE/a_ Monde_BSE.htm

Worldwatch Institute. State of the World. Norton (2000–2004, annual publica-tion); Vital Signs. Norton (1995–2005, annual publica-tion); Melting of Earth's Ice Cover Reaches New High (2000); Map in World Watch (Nov/Dec 2000); Signposts 2003: Envisioning a Sustainable Future (2003); International Environmental Treaties 1921–1999; Death Tolls of Selected Wars 1500–1945; War-Related Deaths by 5 Year Period 1951-1995. Chesapeake Bay Oyster Catch 1880–2001; World Oil Production and Estimated Resources 1900–2100; The Impacts of Weather and Climate Change (2003); Good Stuff? A Behind-The-Scenes Guide to the Things We Buy (2004); Worldwatch University: Internet Host Computers Worldwide, 1981–2003; State of the World Trends and Facts: Purchasing for People and the Planet (2004). Watching What We Eat (2004). www.worldwatch.org

WRI. World Resources Report 1998–1999: Environmental Change and Human Health. OUP (1998); World Resources Report 2000–2001: People and Ecosystems: The Fraying Web of Life. OUP (2000); World Resources Report 2002–2004: Decisions for the Earth: Balance, Voice, and Power. OUP (2003); Biodiversity and Protected Areas: Nepal (2003); Mining and Critical Ecosystems: Mapping the Risks (2003); Earth Trends: Public Health: Physicians per 100,000; Global Livestock Density; Global Population Density;

Armed Conflict, Refugees and the Environment; Global Extent of Grassland; Undying Flame: The Continuing Demand for Wood as Fuel; Per-Capita Total health Expenditure; Laden with lead; Acid Rain Downpour in Asia?; Numbers of Adults and Children Infected; Endanger-ed Species: Traded to Death; Dirty Water: Pollution Problems Persist; Stratos-pheric Ozone Depletion: Celebrating Too Soon; Frag-menting Forests: The Loss of Large Frontier Forests; Bioinvasions: Stemming the Tide of Exotic Species; No End to Paperwork; Wasting the Material World: The Impact of Industrial Econ-omies; More Democracy: Better Environment; Sustainable Cities, Sustainable Transportation. www.earthtrends.wri.org

WTO. The WTO in Brief, Part 4 Developing Countries (2004); World Trade Report (2004). www.wto.org.

WWF. Living Planet Report 2002 (2002 and 2004); Flagship Species: The Great Whales (2001); Forests for Life: Working to Protect, Manage and Restore the World's Forests; Wildlife Trade. CITES. The 10 Most Wanted Species; Souvenir Alert Highlights Deadly Trade in Endangered Species. (19 Sept 2001); Working to Protect, Manage and Restore the World's Forests; Food for Thought: The Use of Marine Resources in Fish Feed (2003); Spain Oil Spill: Potential Impacts (2002); Spain Oil Spill: Single v Double Hulls (2000); PASSAs Particularly Sensitive Sea Areas; The Prestige: One Year On, a Continuing Disaster (2003); Marine Pollution; Global Warming and Terrestrial Biodiversity Decline (2000); WWF/ Bioregional. One Planet Living www.oneplanetliving. org; Death by Drowning (2003); A Whale of a Tragedy (2003); Marine Turtles: Global Voyagers Threatened with Extinction (2003).

WWF-Norway. 2004. The Barents Sea Cod: Last of the Large Cod Stock. www.wwf.no/core/pdf/wwf_ codreport_2004.opdf

WWF South Pacific Whale Campaign. Flow-on Benefits

of Sanctuaries. www.wv/fpa-cific.org.fj/whales_cam-paign_benefits.htm

Yearbook of International Cooperation on Environment and Development. Agree-ments on Environment and Development; Areas Covered by the UNEP Regional Seas Programme. www.greenyearbook.org

Yudelman, M. et al. Pest Management and Food Production: Looking to the Future. IFPRI (1998).

Yunus, M. The Grameen Bank. Scientific American November 1999: pp.114–119 (1999).

Note: Because of space constraints the editors are unable to include a compre-hensive reading list and weblinks. Readers are wel-come to contact Jennifer Kent (jenniekent@aol.com) for further information.

Index

Picture Credits

pp.4–5 Getty
Images/Richard Elliot

pp.6–7 Oxford Scientific
Films/Seiden Allan

p.9 Corbis UK Ltd/George
H.H. Huey

pp.22–23 Getty
Images/Yann Layma

pp.74–75 Oxford Scientific
Films/Thomas Haider

pp.108–109 Corbis UK
Ltd/Gary Braasch

p.129 bottom right Science
Photo Library/NASA

pp.154–155 Science Photo
Library/Georgette Douwma

pp.184–185 The Hutchison
Library/Julia Waterlow

pp.210–211 CNES, 1994
distribution spot
image/Science Photo Library

p.227 bottom right Corbis
UK Ltd/Tony Aruza

pp.256–257 Getty Images/
Lonely Planet Images